Business in Context

Business in Context

An introduction to business and its environment

Fourth edition

David Needle

THOMSON

™

Australia • Canada • Mexico • Singapore • Spain • United Kingdom • United States

THOMSON

Business in Context, 4th edition

Copyright © Thomson Learning 2004

The Thomson logo is a registered trademark used herein under licence.

For more information, contact Thomson Learning, High Holborn House, 50-51 Bedford Row, London WC1R 4LR or visit us on the World Wide Web at: http://www.thomsonlearning.co.uk

British Library Cataloguing-in-Publication Data
A catalogue record for this book is available from the British Library

ISBN-13: 978-1-86152-992-3
ISBN-10: 1-86152-992-9

First edition published 1989
Second edition published 1994 by Chapman & Hall
Third edition published 2000 by Thomson Learning
Reprinted 2001 and 2003 by Thomson Learning
Fourth edition published 2004 by Thomson Learning
Reprinted 2005 and 2006 by Thomson Learning

Typeset by Photoprint, Torquay

Printed in China by C&C Offset Printing Co., Ltd.

Contents

3 The environment and business: economy, state, technology and labour

4   Cultural influences and business   143

6 Management and leadership 251

7 Management strategy 281

8 Business ethics and corporate social responsibility

List of cases

Preface to the fourth edition

The origins for this book lie in a course I developed and taught at the University of East London and at Queen Mary, University of London. An important theme of the course was the inter-related nature both of business activities themselves and their relationships with the strategic, organizational and environmental contexts in which they operated. A second important theme was the identification of what were considered at the time to be key issues in business. These two themes remain the basis of *Business in Context* as it goes into its fourth edition.

The book was aimed originally at first- and second-year undergraduates studying business and management, to give them a multidisciplinary approach to their studies and an insight into the real world of business and management. The book has been found to be useful wherever there is a need for an overview of business or a treatment of business and the environment. As a result, previous editions of this text have been adopted on MBA and specialist masters programmes and on some professional courses.

A number of key themes appear throughout the book.

- Businesses are perceived as operating through a complex network of inter-relationships and our model is a simplification of this complexity.

- While business activities are undoubtedly influenced by their strategic, organizational and environmental contexts, those same business activities help shape those very same contexts.

- In all aspects of business life we need to remind ourselves that decisions are made by people. An understanding of behavioural and political issues is therefore important, as is the need to view issues from a number of different perspectives to gain a more complete understanding.

- Very rarely can we view business activities in isolation, as decisions made in one area inevitably have significant consequences, not only for other parts of the same business but for other businesses and even the wider community.

- Many of the new ideas, issues and techniques that have emerged over the years are undoubtedly products of influences that were operating at the time. While some have stood the test of time, others have become passing fashions and fads.

The business world is as dynamic as ever. In 2003, Japan and Germany were still in recession and major firms, such as Grundig, were threatened with extinction. In Japan, Nissan has been saved by the French company Renault, which is typical of the rapid increase in cross-border acquisitions and alliances. Many businesses were affected by the terrible events of September 2001 in New York, not least the global airline business and most major economies have experienced economic difficulties in the early years of the millennium. There have been spectacular falls, as with Enron and WorldCom, underscoring the fragility of most businesses. There are signs that parts of Asia are recovering from the crash of 1997 and the economies of most East European countries are in various stages of dynamic transition. This edition will reflect these changes and the dynamic nature of business.

One development that is both permanent (insofar as anything in business can be permanent) and far-reaching is globalization and this edition acknowledges its impact on aspects of business by devoting an entire chapter to the phenomenon. Related to the topic of globalization is the growing awareness of cultural diversity and this is recognized in its own chapter. Two further chapters have been added, reflecting important current concerns. These are on management and leadership and on ethics and the social responsibility of business. The new chapters in this edition are therefore:

Chapter 2   Globalization
Chapter 4   Cultural influences and business
Chapter 6   Management and leadership
Chapter 8   Business ethics and corporate social responsibility.

All the other chapters have been modified in some way.

Some cases have disappeared and new ones have been added, including Beijing Jeep, Sleek, Railtrack, two cases on the football industry dealing with merchandising and finances, Enron and Sogo, and on management pay. Almost all the retained cases have been brought up to date. In the first edition of this book, in 1989, I introduced a case on Orlake Records, as a firm in the declining industry of making vinyl records. I am delighted to report that the firm still thrives with many of the same staff.

The first chapter offers an explanation of the Business in Context model and illustrates this with reference to the European car industry and the UK-based News International. Chapters 2–4 examine the environment of business, starting with globalization and ending with culture. In between we examine economic, political, technological and labour market influences. Chapter 5 examines the organizational context and reviews issues relating to goals, ownership, size, structure and organizational culture. Chapters 6–8 focus on management issues. Chapter 6 examines the nature of management and leadership, followed in Chapter 7 by a review of strategy. Chapter 8 deals with the topical subject of business ethics and corporate social responsibility. Chapters 9–13 each focus on a specific business activity and cover innovation, operations, marketing, human resource management, and finance and accounting. Aspects of all these activities are clearly defined and, in addition, they are placed within their environmental, organizational and strategic contexts. The book therefore offers both general and specific views of business.

The core elements of previous editions are retained:

● Each chapter highlights key concepts and provides a separate explanation of these.

● Each chapter illustrates key issues by using cases, all written by the author, to support the information in the chapter.

● Each chapter is supported by a summary, a list of discussion questions and suggestions for further reading.

● This edition will be supported by a website, accessed through http://www.thomsonlearning.co.uk. The website will contain links to general business sites and links to the homepages of each of the case study companies. To assist those lecturers who adopt the text, there will be general advice on how the book may be used as part of a planned series of lectures, PowerPoint presentations will be available to accompany each chapter, and there will be suggested answers to the discussion questions

In addition some new features have been added:

- Each chapter starts with a set of learning objectives.
- Case questions have been provided at the end of each case.
- Wherever possible the text has been broken up by the inclusion of new headings and the use of bullet points to make the text easier to follow.
- Each chapter is provided with a bullet-point summary.

In my preface to the first edition in 1989, I stated that with any book that takes as broad a sweep as this one does there is bound to be a great deal of selectivity. This is as true today as it was then. The main criteria for the inclusion of material was that it interested me. Many of the ideas are attributed to their rightful source, but many are the product of years discussing business issues with students, friends and colleagues. I thank all of them for their contribution, with the rider that the misinterpretations are all my own.

David Needle, January 2004

Acknowledgements

There are many who deserve my thanks for helping me write this book. The students and staff at the University of East London assisted me in developing many of the ideas, which resulted in the first and subsequent editions. In particular I must thank my students on the MBA courses in Beijing, Cologne and Lisbon for broadening my horizons about contemporary international business. I am grateful for the time given to me by Bill Coulson of Orlake Records and Brendan McParland of Sleek in the development of case studies on those two companies.

This book and those that preceded it could not have been completed without the help and support of my wife Jacquie. She has an excellent knowledge of business herself and has helped in many other practical ways.

Visual tour of the book

Learning objectives at the start of each chapter highlight what you should have achieved at the end of each chapter to help you focus your learning and evaluate your progress.

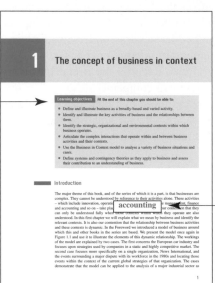

Terms defined in the Glossary at the end of the book are **highlighted** throughout the text.

Key concept boxes throughout the text provide substantial in-situ explanations of each chapter's core concepts to emphasize these important terms.

Cases throughout the text show how each chapter's main issues are applied in real-life business situations in different types of organizations. Each case is accompanied by questions to help you test your understanding of the issues.

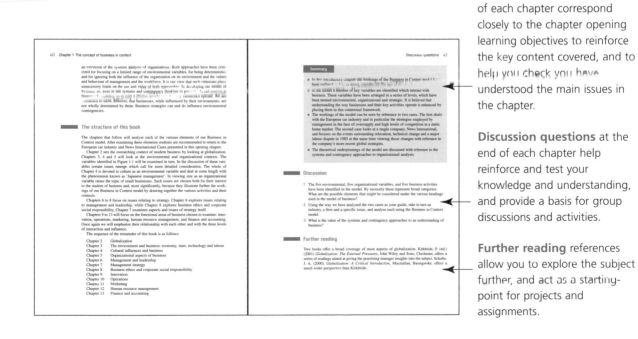

Summary bullet lists at the end of each chapter correspond closely to the chapter opening learning objectives to reinforce the key content covered, and to help you check you have understood the main issues in the chapter.

Discussion questions at the end of each chapter help reinforce and test your knowledge and understanding, and provide a basis for group discussions and activities.

Further reading references allow you to explore the subject further, and act as a starting-point for projects and assignments.

Accompanying Web Site

Visit the companion website for *Business in Context 4th edition* at:
www.thomsonlearning.co.uk/businessandmanagement/needle4/
to find valuable teaching and learning material including:

For Students

- Multiple choice questions designed to test your understanding and improve your results
- Weblinks to relevant sites mentioned in the text to enable you to read around the subject and further your knowledge
- Online glossary to explain key terms

For Lecturers

- A secure, password-protected site with teaching material
- Tutor notes giving an overview of each chapter's content
- Additional PowerPoint slides of key material in the book
- Extra case material to use with your students in the classroom or as part of their home study

The concept of business in context

- Define and illustrate business as a broadly-based and varied activity.
- Identify and illustrate the key activities of business and the relationships between them.
- Identify the strategic, organizational and environmental contexts within which business operates.
- Articulate the complex interactions that operate within and between business activities and their contexts.
- Use the Business in Context model to analyse a variety of business situations and cases.
- Define systems and contingency theories as they apply to business and assess their contribution to an understanding of business.

Introduction

The major theme of this book, and of the series of which it is a part, is that businesses are complex. They cannot be understood by reference to their activities alone. These activities – which include innovation, operations, marketing, human resource management, finance and accounting and so on – take place in a series of contexts. It is our contention that they can only be understood fully when those contexts within which they operate are also understood. In this first chapter we will explain what we mean by business and identify the relevant contexts. It is also our contention that the relationship between business activities and these contexts is dynamic. In the Preface we introduced a model of business. We present the model in Figure 1.1 and use it to illustrate the elements of this dynamic relationship. The workings of the model are explained by two cases. The first concerns the European car industry and focuses upon strategies used by companies in a static and highly competitive market. The second focuses more specifically on a single organization, News International, and the events surrounding a major dispute with its workforce in the 1980s and locating those events within the context of the current global strategies of that organization. The cases demonstrate that the model can be applied to the analysis of a major industrial sector as well as to events at a single firm. We introduce briefly two theoretical approaches to the analysis of business organizations: the systems and contingency approaches. These are often used as the starting point for our analysis throughout this book and reference will be made to them in other chapters. We will conclude this first chapter by outlining the layout of this book.

Businesses and their contexts

The popular image of a typical business firm is invariably that of a manufacturing industry, and probably large-scale mass production at that. Such an image is somewhat misleading as the service industries, and particularly financial services, assume the greater part of a nation's economic activities in many countries. In this text we hope to present a broad view of business. Businesses operate in all kinds of areas, including manufacturing industry, but are to be found also in such activities as retailing, banking and other financial services, transport, media and entertainments and so on. The publishers of this book are engaged in a business activity, involving the production, marketing and selling of books to generate income both to make profits and to finance future operations. Businesses also vary considerably in terms of size. Indeed, in recent years, the focus has shifted away from large-scale operations and small businesses have become popular with governments and academics alike and, accordingly, will be acknowledged in this text.

Key concept 1.1 Business

A business is the organized effort of individuals to produce and provide goods and services to meet the needs of society. We view business as a broad concept, incorporating profit-making concerns such as manufacturing firms and banks, and non-profit-making or not-for-profit concerns such as schools, hospitals and charities.

The image that businesses are exclusively profit oriented will also be challenged. Business systems and methods operate in all kinds of organizations. Many institutions of higher education operate with budgets in excess of £80 million, and represent fairly complex organizations in which all the activities normally associated with business may be identified. For example, there are few colleges that do not market their courses, or have to operate in highly dynamic and competitive markets both at home and overseas. Hospitals, too, are large complex organizations experiencing the type of management problems found in businesses anywhere. In recent years this has been acknowledged by the creation of new hospital top-management posts, many of which have been filled by candidates from the private sector business world. In any case, the distinction between profit and non-profit organizations has become increasingly blurred. All universities and colleges must rely increasingly on generating their own income owing to changes that have taken place in public funding. The growth of medical provision outside the National Health Service (NHS) has seen the growth of profit-oriented private hospitals which compete in the market place for customers and advertise their services internationally as well as nationally.

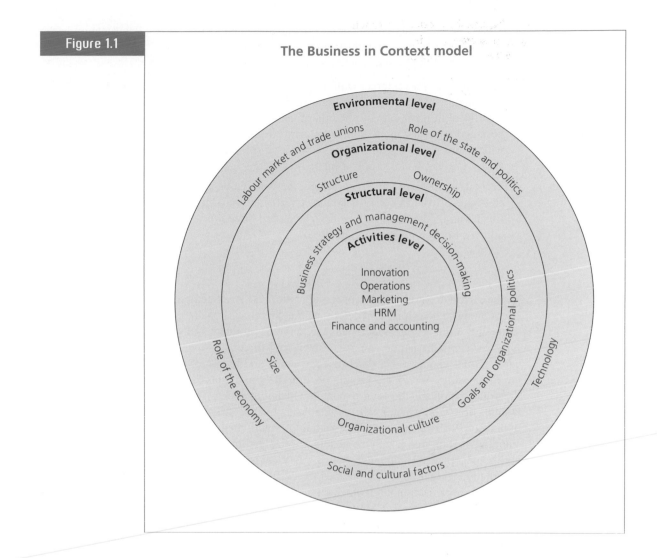

Figure 1.1

The Business in Context model

Environmental level

Labour market and trade unions

Role of the state and politics

Organizational level

Structure   Ownership

Structural level

Business strategy and management decision-making

Activities level

Innovation
Operations
Marketing
HRM
Finance and accounting

Role of the economy

Size

Goals and organizational politics

Technology

Organizational culture

Social and cultural factors

Business activities

As can be seen from Figure 1.1, a number of business activities have been identified. In this book we deal with them as five main groups:

- innovation
- operations
- marketing
- human resource management
- finance and accounting.

Each of these groups is sufficiently broad to cover a number of related functions. For instance, it is acknowledged that **supply chain** management is an important business activity, but it is dealt with under the heading of operations for the purposes of this text. The operations function itself is present in all forms of business organization and not confined to the production function of manufacturing. Operations is a key function in the service sector, as it is in manufacturing.

When examining business activities there are two points to consider.

● First, the activities interact with one another, so that operations decisions influencing the quantity and quality of the goods produced and the services provided will have significant implications for the other functional areas. Can products and services be designed to differentiate them from competitors' offerings? Is there a market and where does it exist? Can staff be recruited in sufficient numbers and with sufficient skills? Can the planned operation be financed?

● Second, as we have already indicated, these activities do not exist in a vacuum, but are shaped by and in turn shape the contexts within which they operate. In our Business in Context model we have identified three types of context: strategic, organizational and environmental.

Business contexts

At the **strategic level** we are concerned with those management decisions, and the influences on those decisions, that determine the direction of business activities. Strategic decisions will influence such factors as the range of products and services, the amount spent on advertising, the nature and use of the labour force and so on. Strategic decisions in the case of joint ventures will determine the shape and nature of the organization. Strategies are often a question of reconciling opportunities and constraints which exist within both the organization and the environment in which it operates. The managing director (MD) of a small firm with a potentially profitable innovation often faces a strategic dilemma. Its organizational size means that expanding production capacity is impossible and its credit standing is such that it may be unable to raise sufficient development capital. The availability of finance is, in any case, a function of the economic and political climate. Alternatives might be to sell the idea for development by a larger firm or simply sell out to a larger organization, both of which may be personally unacceptable to the owner of the small business. In this way, strategic issues are inseparable from the organization and environment in which they operate and can, in fact, alter those two other contexts. It is widely accepted that the structure of a firm is often a product of its strategy (Chandler, 1962 offers a particularly forceful argument for this). Economic, cultural and political globalization have changed the nature of business and created globally complex business structures. The overseas investment strategies of large **multinational corporations (MNCs)** have been seen to have considerable influence on the economic and political affairs of other nations, especially those in the Third World.

Key concept 1.2 Strategy

A strategy comprises a set of objectives and methods of achieving those objectives. A strategy is usually formulated by top management and is based on a mixture of careful analysis of the environment and the organization, the personal preferences of the managers involved, and a process of negotiation with various other stakeholders.

Strategies are invariably the product of managers and in this edition we explore the concept of **management** and **leadership** in Chapter 6, which sets the immediate context for strategic decisions. A current theme in **business strategy** and a currently popular rhetoric of business leaders and annual reports is that of corporate social responsibility. In this edition we explore both the rhetoric and reality in Chapter 8 on **business ethics** and **corporate social responsibility** (CSR).

At the **organizational** level we are concerned with a number of issues grouped under the following headings:

- goals
- structure
- ownership
- size
- organizational or corporate culture.

Many such issues are interrelated. The public ownership of business firms may well mean the pursuit of social as well as business goals, and publicly owned firms invariably have bureaucratic structures. This is partly a function of organizational culture, and partly a function of the large scale of most **public sector** operations. All firms as they increase in size tend to adopt more formalized structures. Such organizational factors can place limitations on the nature of business activities. Formalized structures can inhibit certain types of product and process development and the existing size can be a restriction on expansion, as we saw in our illustration of strategic issues. In more general terms these organizational factors combine with management strategy to create distinctive organizational cultures.

Key concept 1.3 Organization

An organization refers to the way in which people are grouped and the way in which they operate to carry out the activities of the business. We define the key elements of the organization as the goals of the business and the way they are formulated, ownership and control, size, structure and organizational culture (Chapter 4).

We have identified five factors that operate at the **environmental** level as follows.

- the economy
- the state
- technology
- labour
- culture.

Some of these factors are deliberately broad. The state includes discussion of government, legal and political issues; labour takes into account both the workings of the labour market and the activity of trade unions; culture includes social factors related to business as well as those issues that differentiate businesses in different countries. As with the other factors in our model, there is considerable interaction between these various environmental factors. The membership and power of trade unions are functions of the level of economic activity and the restrictions imposed by the law, which in turn reflect the policy of governments. The composition of the labour market reflects changes in technology, and the mobility of labour within and between different countries varies with the social and cultural traditions of those countries as well as with the laws on immigration and work permits. Technological innovations are often motivated both by declining economic fortunes and by direct state intervention. Similarly, we can cite illustrations of the interaction between the environment and our other contexts. The technological complexity of the product market in which the firm operates will largely determine the extent of its **research and development** (R&D) activity, and hence its strategies and structure. In traditional manufacturing industry, a strong trade union presence has determined the size, shape, policies and activities of the HR (human resource) department. In the 21st century such characteristics of HR departments are as likely to be determined by cost considerations in an increasingly competitive global business environment. The increasing need to view all businesses in a global context is dealt with in Chapter 2 about **globalization**.

The interplay that typifies the relationship between business activities and the contexts in which they operate will be a constant theme in this book. We will attempt to show that many of the relationships are two-way. The economic environment referred to above not only shapes businesses but is, in turn, a product of business activity. Changes in technology are products of innovation activity at the level of the firm. We are thus able to build up a model of business as a constant interplay of interactions and influences.

We are able to illustrate the workings of the model by reference to two cases, the first concerning the European car industry and the second focusing on a single, albeit large firm in the newspaper industry. In both cases we will explain the events and central issues following with an analysis of each case using our Business in Context model as a framework.

Case 1.1	**The European car industry**

This case examines aspects of the European car industry. It focuses upon the major problems facing the industry and examines some of the strategies management have used to tackle those problems.

For many years now the car market in Europe has been cyclical. In more recent years it has been relatively static as revealed in Tables 1.1, 1.2 and 1.3. Table 1.1 shows total passenger car use in the major markets from 1990–5. Tables 1.2 and 1.3 show production and sales respectively in a number of selected car producing countries with some comparisons drawn from Eastern Europe. The figures show fluctuating demand and production across the time period, and for Eastern Europe there are some encouraging signs of market and job growth. However, the figures reveal a market that has essentially reached its limits, at least in Western Europe.

The industry was hit by the oil shocks of the 1970s and was plunged into deep recession in the early 1980s. The growth in the late 1980s was short-lived and recession hit the industry once again in the early 1990s. Although sales in the UK rose to record levels in 1997, an 8.3 per cent increase on the previous year, output fell by 6 per cent. Growth in sales was maintained for 1998 before a slight fall over the next two years. This growth of sales in the UK was in stark contrast to France where falls in sales were a major cause of concern, although there was some recovery by the end of the decade. Despite the optimism of periodic surges in sales, the inescapable fact remains that the European car market is essentially stagnant. It is an industry that relies mainly on replacement purchases and, as such, is referred to as a mature cyclical market. In times of recession, when money is tight and jobs become less secure, the replacement purchase is delayed. Market opportunities have arisen in the emerging economies of Eastern Europe but these have attracted players from out-side Europe; although the Korean manufacturers initially made great inroads, their influence has declined.

Comparisons of production and sales are revealing. In Spain, Belgium, France and Germany there is more production than sales demonstrating both strong export orientation and the role of car production in these countries as part of a globally integrated strategy. This is discussed in more detail in Chapter 2. The UK, on the other hand, is a net importer of cars as sales always outstrip production. It also demonstrates that the UK is not a favoured location in terms of globally organized production. The production and sales figures for the Czech Republic and Poland reveal both rising sales and production in both countries, although sales have risen

Table 1.1   Passenger cars in use in Europe 1991–5 (in millions)

	1990	1991	1992	1993	1994	1995
France	23.5	23.8	24.0	24.8	24.9	24.9
Germany	34.6	35.3	38.4	39.3	40.2	41.4
Italy	27.4	28.5	29.5	30.1	31.3	32.3
UK	19.7	20.1	19.9	20.1	20.0	19.9
Europe total	145.5	149.2	154.3	158.0	160.7	164.0

Source: Consumer Europe 1996

Table 1.2   Car production in Europe 1990–2000 (in million units)

	1990	1991	1992	1993	1994	1995	1996	1997	1998	1999	2000
Belgium	1.16	1.05	1.08	1.09	1.20	1.17	1.14	1.00	0.95	0.92	0.93
France	3.29	3.19	3.33	2.84	3.18	3.05	3.15	3.35	3.80	4.16	2.88
Germany	4.66	4.68	4.86	3.75	4.09	4.36	4.54	4.68	5.35	5.31	4.69
Italy	1.87	1.63	1.48	1.12	1.34	1.42	1.32	1.56	1.38	1.41	1.38
Spain	1.68	1.73	1.79	1.51	1.82	1.96	1.93	2.00	2.22	2.21	2.32
Sweden	0.34	0.27	0.29	0.28	0.35	.39	0.37	0.38	0.37	0.39	0.29
UK	1.30	1.24	1.29	1.38	1.47	1.52	1.69	1.70	1.75	1.79	1.63
Czech Rep.	0.19	0.17	0.20	0.20	0.15	0.19	0.24	0.32	0.37	0.33	0.45
Poland	0.28	0.17	0.22	0.34	0.34	0.36	0.44	0.52	0.56	0.64	0.54
Russia	1.10	1.03	0.96	0.96	0.80	0.83	0.87	0.98	0.84	0.90	0.98

Source: www.autoindustry.co.uk/statistics/production/europe

Table 1.3	Car sales in Europe 1990–2000 (in million units)										
	1990	*1991*	*1992*	*1993*	*1994*	*1995*	*1996*	*1997*	*1998*	*1999*	*2000*
Belgium	0.47	0.46	0.47	0.38	0.39	0.36	0.40	0.40	0.45	0.49	0.52
France	2.31	2.03	2.11	1.72	1.97	1.93	2.13	1.71	1.94	2.15	2.13
Germany	3.04	4.16	3.93	3.19	3.21	3.31	3.50	3.53	3.74	3.79	3.38
Italy	2.35	2.34	2.37	1.70	1.67	1.73	1.73	2.41	2.36	2.35	2.42
Spain	0.96	0.89	0.98	0.74	0.91	0.83	0.91	1.01	1.19	1.41	1.38
Sweden	0.23	0.19	0.15	0.12	0.16	0.17	0.18	0.23	0.25	0.30	0.29
UK	2.01	1.59	1.59	1.78	1.91	1.95	2.03	2.17	2.25	2.20	2.22
Czech Rep.	0.11	0.10	0.17	0.08	0.09	0.11	0.16	0.17	0.14	0.15	n/a
Poland	n/a	n/a	0.20	0.24	0.25	0.27	0.37	0.48	0.52	0.64	n/a
Russia	n/a	n/a	n/a	n/a	n/a	n/a	n/a	n/a	n/a	n/a	n/a

Source: www.autoindustry.co.uk/statistics/sales/europe

much faster in Poland. The Czech Republic is establishing itself as a major car producer, due mainly to the investment by Volkswagen (VW) in Skoda and the launch
of a new range of models.

The European car industry faces problems of over-capacity and oversupply. The
market is both fragmented and highly competitive. There are a large number of
national players many of whom, in the past, have been supported directly and indirectly by their national governments. As a result, many of these firms are small,
almost certainly too small to be effective on a global scale in an industry where size
matters. The smaller European manufacturers face the highly organized competition
of much larger firms operating with much larger economies of scale. In addition, the
cost of relatively high wages and related social benefits places much of the industry
at a disadvantage in comparison to the emerging economies of Korea and Malaysia.
The currency crisis in South-East Asia in 1997–8 has made such imports even more
competitive and the relative weakness of the yen has increased Japanese competitiveness as well. The first part of the new millennium has seen a considerable
Japanese recovery in Europe with Honda and Toyota back in profit and Mitsubishi
announcing a planned 50 per cent increase in sales over a 5-year period.

Across Europe, car manufacturers are engaged in a series of strategies to remain
in business. It is important that such strategies are successful, not just for the firms
themselves but also for their national economy. The car industry is the world's
largest single manufacturing industry and embraces not only car production, but
also a vast parts industry, retail network and used car market. It does not end there.
Many car firms now earn as much from selling finance to enable customers to buy
their product as they do from manufacture. In addition, large financial services,
insurance and repair industries depend on the car industry, as does an entire fuel
supply industry.

We will examine some of the major strategies employed by firms in Europe to
search for new products and new markets, to seek economies of scale through joint
ventures and acquisitions and to cut costs through a variety of measures. Such
strategies have extended beyond the production companies themselves, to embrace

the supply industry as well. There have been significant job losses and inevitable closures. As in the past, household names such as Riley, Hillman and Austin have disappeared; many more are expected to follow in the next few years.

Before dealing with the strategies in more detail, we will first take a closer look at the extent of over-capacity and competition.

Over-capacity and competition

Over-capacity exists when a firm has more than it requires to fulfil its market demand. It may have more space, more machines and even more labour. Over-capacity is therefore a waste of resources and costs money. At the beginning of 1998, Alex Trotman, the then Chief Executive Officer (CEO) of Ford Motor Company, estimated world over-capacity at 40 per cent. The cheaper products available from Japan, Korea and Malaysia, as a result of the Asian currency crisis, added to over-capacity by oversupply. The analysts, Charterhouse Tilney, measured European capacity at 16.3 million vehicles, while European output was measured at 12.8 million. On this basis, Europe could easily lose a capacity of around 3.5 million vehicles and still meet market demand for local vehicles. A 1998 survey by PricewaterhouseCoopers was even more pessimistic, putting European over-capacity at 7 million vehicles. If one takes the optimistic prediction of a 3.5 million gap, this is about the size of production in the French car industry (see Table 1.2). The pessimistic prediction of a 7 million gap is the size of the German and UK industries combined. At the end of 2001, Ford closed its Dagenham assembly plant in East London with a loss of 3000 jobs.

Over-capacity is undoubtedly the product of an industry that is ever optimistic, fed by the belief among senior management that the next cyclical upturn is just around the corner and that their new model will take market share from their competitors. In the past this has been encouraged by governments wishing their national company to be a world player in an economically important industry. Given the size of most car plants and their contribution to local economies, most governments are reluctant to sanction plant closures, thereby adding to the problems of over-capacity.

Such optimism is faced by the reality of a largely static market with too many competitors. In terms of market share, local manufacturers still come out on top in national markets, but the position is less clear cut than before. European manufacturers still face considerable competition from the Japanese. The slow growth of Japanese imports in the early 1990s was a product of the high value of the yen, European Union (EU) import restrictions and voluntary restraint on behalf of the Japanese themselves. The high yen against the US dollar meant that European producers enjoyed considerable export success in the US market. By the late 1990s that position had changed; the yen had weakened significantly and import restrictions were due to end in 1999. The issue of quotas is still one of fierce debate. Without them, European manufacturers fear that the Japanese may swamp the market, yet the Japanese argue that quotas have been always been much higher than actual imports. The key issue here is the role played by Japanese transplants (Japanese manufacturing plants operating overseas) which have grown during the decade with plans for considerable expansion into the 21st century.

Competition also comes from the Koreans. Daewoo began selling in the UK in 1995 and achieved the fastest-growing car sales of any manufacturer. By the end of the 1990s the future competitiveness of Korean manufacturers was difficult to predict. The industry grew rapidly on the strength of relatively low wages, long working hours and considerable investment in plant. That same investment led to every major company over-stretching itself and the inevitable economic crisis, with the near collapse of Daewoo at the end of the decade. This has led to a slowing down of production, which is partly offset by a cheap product, owing to rapid devaluation of the currency, and an expansion in Eastern Europe tapping a relatively new market.

The case of Fiat illustrates the problems of over-capacity and competition. For many years the Italian market, Fiat in particular, was protected against Japanese and Korean competition. Italian cars were traditionally strong on design and engine power but overall there had been a lack of investment in product development and customer service. With a liberalization of the Italian market, Fiat's market share fell from 45 per cent in 1995 to 28 per cent in 2002. By contrast, Toyota doubled its market share in Italy between 2000–2. As a consequence, Fiat announced an annual loss for 2002–3 of 2 billion euros. The Agnelli family, who have owned and controlled Fiat for many years sold 20 per cent of the company to General Motors (GM) with an option on the remaining 80 per cent. With a GM takeover of Fiat, it is predicted that plants will close across Italy; although some jobs may be saved by switching production from GM plants in Germany, where labour costs are higher.

Problems of over-capacity and competition have been tackled by the various European producers utilizing a number of different strategies. It is to these we now turn.

Product strategies

Among the European producers there has been a tendency for the consolidation of components across a wide range of models, utilizing just-in-time (JIT) methods based on closer ties with a smaller number of suppliers. In 1994, VW announced a radical **restructuring** of its vehicle manufacture, reducing the number of chassis types from 16 to 4 across its entire range of VW, Audi, Skoda and Seat cars. The process had already begun with the VW Passat and the Audi 4 through shared engines and tracking systems. Other companies, like Ford, saw the ultimate consolidation for a global company in the form of a world car and launched the Mondeo, which shares 20 per cent of its internal parts with the Jaguar X type. However, there are undoubted cultural barriers to the world car concept, with car buyers expressing different national preferences. The stereotypical British buyer opts for performance, in France it is styling, in Sweden safety, in Germany engineering sophistication and so on.

Some manufacturers, such as Mercedes, decided to extend their product range launching a competitively priced small sports coupé in 1996, which proved so successful that demand outstripped supply with a resulting two-year waiting list. This was followed by the Smart car, a 2-seater micro city car, in an unusual joint venture with SMH, the company that launched the Swatch watch. Such developments have given Mercedes a high profile. Not all their ventures were initially successful. The launch of the A Class, a small family saloon, achieved notoriety when it overturned in manoeuvres for its Swedish press launch. The subsequent correction cost amounted to DM50 million, the resulting bad publicity caused many orders to be cancelled and the company share price fell. However the market for the A Class recovered and it became the brand image of Easycar, the car hire firm launched by easyJet, the cut-price airline.

The attempt by Mercedes to broaden its product range was a strategy pursued by other manufacturers, the majority preferring the acquisition route. Ford moved out of the mass market and into the luxury market to acquire Jaguar and Aston Martin, while BMW, in acquiring Rover, entered the small family car sector as well as the four-wheel drive market via Land Rover. VW purchased the Rolls Royce factory, but obtained the right to manufacture only the Bentley car. The right to manufacture the Rolls Royce was held, not by the factory, but by another company – Rolls Royce Aero-engines – who opted to sell this right to BMW. This illustrates the rather complex nature of acquisitions.

Despite the consolidation and the development of new models, the Europeans still spend less on research and development (R&D) than their USA or Japanese counterparts. However, there is considerable investment in engine technology and manufacture, particularly diesel and liquefied petroleum gas (LPG) engines. Both are considered to be more environmentally friendly than petrol engines and diesel engines are shaking off the image of being dirty and noisy as they become the preferred option in larger luxury cars. Despite the closure of the Ford Dagenham assembly plant there was considerable investment in the neighbouring engine plant to lead the development diesel engines for Ford Europe. In 2003, London introduced congestion charges for its central area, but exempting LPG engine cars. This resulted in an increase in sales of such cars in the London area. It is predicted that other major cities with traffic problems will follow London's lead.

The slow-down of car sales in the major European markets has led car producers to seek new sources of revenue from other products. Most companies have found that there are greater margins to be made from selling finance, insurance and parts. This, in turn, has led to other product developments such as mortgages and credit. Ford Credit is now a major company in its own right and Daimler-Chrysler have established an in-house bank.

New market opportunities

In 1994, 80 per cent of the world's population lived outside the three major car producing areas of the USA, Europe and Japan, yet accounted for only 8 per cent of the total market. The attention of the car manufacturers turned to such emerging markets as a solution to the problems of stagnant home markets. Opportunities clearly exist and two areas have been singled out as strategically important: these are Eastern Europe and Asia, in particular China.

The major European players see Eastern Europe as a natural extension of their current market, but in the early 1990s they faced strong competition from the Koreans and, more especially, Daewoo with plants either opened or planned in the Czech Republic, Poland, Romania and Uzbekistan. The prospect of an already cheap Korean product being manufactured in great numbers by cheap East European labour was seen as a huge threat, and there were fears of over-capacity in

▶

the emerging market of Eastern Europe. However, problems in the South Korean economy and considerable internal problems within Daewoo contributed to their rapid fall. The strongest presence in Eastern Europe is undoubtedly VW, followed by Fiat. VW were strong before the acquisition of Skoda and its rebranding as a major European product. As can be seen by Tables 1.2 and 1.3, the Czech Republic may be an emerging producer but the strongest market remains Poland, which has moved ahead of the Netherlands and Belgium as the sixth largest market in Europe.

Generally, in the Asian market GM has used its European company, Opel, to gain advantage in India, Indonesia and Thailand, while its USA counterpart has led the initiatives in China. Among the Japanese, Toyota has established strongholds in Thailand, Indonesia and the Philippines, while Mitsubishi dominates in Vietnam, as does Suzuki in India.

The prize of the Asian market is undoubtedly China. In 1990 car sales were 78 000 rising to 430 000 in 1993. Since then there has been rapid growth, and 2002 saw the fourth consecutive year of over 1 million sales. In 2002 the sales of cars was 62 per cent up on the previous year. During 2002, VW alone increased its sales by 40 per cent and lost market share. By 2003, China had become the seventh largest market in the world for cars. VW remains the market leader and has five joint ventures to manufacture cars in China. For VW, China represents its largest market after Germany. The other major players in China are PSA (Peugeot–Citroën), GM and Honda. More recent arrivals include Ford, Toyota and Nissan, and by the end of 2003 every major car manufacturer was represented in China. Alongside the joint venture with foreign companies' activity there has been the rapid growth of China's own car manufacturers, such as SAIC and Geely, concentrating on smaller, cheaper cars.

Growing competition will clearly be a problem facing firms entering emerging markets. A few years ago, such markets, especially China, were seen as highly problematic for a number of reasons, including the following:

- Weak infrastructures, with poor road systems creating major problems of congestion.
- While prospects of higher income levels are good in parts of Eastern Europe, along with a growing credit industry, countries such as China and Indonesia had very low levels of income.
- In many emerging markets there is a shortage of hard currency.
- In China, as with other emerging markets, entry is a highly political process at both local and national levels.
- Entry costs in setting up production plants have been historically high, and where, as in China, strict emphasis is placed on the localization of parts, there have been problems of supply, both in quantity and quality, resulting from skills shortages in the local population.

Many of the above issues can be seen in the Beijing Jeep case, Case 2.1, in the next chapter. However, while many of the above problems are only too real in many emerging markets the growth of sales in China in particular is seen as indicative of a number of changes. These can be summarized as follows:

- a stronger Chinese economy
- rising income levels
- lower prices both as a result of lower costs through improved efficiencies and through price cutting as part of the competitive process
- the introduction of new models
- road improvement programmes
- government support for private car ownership
- the introduction of international joint ventures with finance companies
- China's membership of the World Trade Organization (WTO).

Restructuring strategies

All the European firms have made significant attempts to cut costs. Some of that cost cutting has been associated with investment in **new technology** and new methods of manufacture both to achieve economies of scale through automation and in an attempt to achieve the efficiencies of some of their Japanese rivals. The attempts by the USA and European firms to copy Japanese methods, especially those associated with Toyota, have been dubbed lean production. (A fuller debate of this can be found in Chapter 10.) However, there are limits to productivity and efficiency gains through automation and methods alone. Some commentators believe that, for the better plants in Europe, those limits are about to be reached. If this is the case then further cost cutting can only be made by plant closure and by shedding labour.

Ford Motor Company made losses on its European operation of some US$3 billion during the 1990s and lost £400 million on its UK operations alone in 2000. As a result, plants were closed in the UK at Dagenham and in Portugal and Poland, at Azambuja and Plonsk respectively. The company reduced capacity at its plants in Germany, Belgium and Spain. In the UK, the focus shifted away from car assembly to the specialist manufacture of engines and gearboxes. These cuts follow a massive worldwide restructuring exercise to create a global matrix organization based on five vehicle centres; four in the USA and one in Europe. The aim was to break down barriers in the organization and bring together functional expertise wherever it is located. This was accompanied by a significant delayering exercise with many job losses, and the creation of cross-national teams.

In both Sweden and France plants were closed following the failure of Volvo and Renault to agree to a merger. In Germany the workforce was reduced from 788 000 in 1991 to 588 000 in 1994, together with an increase in outsourcing and the introduction of short-term contracts and flexible working. In 1993 the unions at VW agreed to a cut in pay and a reduced working week in an attempt to preserve 30 000 jobs. However, in 1996 further attempts at cuts were resisted by the same union, which was supported by the State Government of Lower Saxony (a 20 per cent shareholder in VW). The state's involvement was motivated by the fear of rising unemployment as a result of increased outsourcing, particularly to the cheaper labour markets of the former East Germany. The Lower Saxony government also attempted to block European grants to the East for the same reason.

▶

There is some evidence that companies have threatened a shift in production to Eastern Europe to gain increased efficiencies in their Western European plants and to gain the compliance of trade unions. Not only is pay lower in Eastern Europe but labour operates more flexibly. There are the added advantages that cars can be made where markets are expanding, thus cutting down on the costs of supply and distribution. Furthermore, East European governments have offered attractive packages to entice car manufacturers. The governments undoubtedly see a successful car industry as enhancing their credentials for EU entry.

Much of the above illustrates the highly political nature of the industry, hardly surprising given its contribution to **gross domestic product (GDP)** and employment. Lower Saxony has not been alone in attempting to protect the local car industry.

Almost all European governments have, at one time or another, given support to their national car industry, either through part ownership in the case of British Leyland (UK), Renault (France) and VW (Germany), or through **trade barriers** and general assistance programmes. The Italians and the French have at one time or another erected significant trade barriers to protect local industry.

Such measures have been notably absent in the UK, owing largely to the free market policies pursued by successive governments since 1979. Opinions are divided on the impact of this on the UK car industry. Critics have claimed that it has hastened the demise of UK companies both through acquisition by foreign competitors and through the encouragement of Japanese transplants. Supporters have claimed that it actually protected local industry by aligning it with more powerful companies and that the growth of transplants has been a boost to the local supply industry. Certainly, there is no evidence to suggest that job losses in the UK are any greater than under the more protectionist regimes of France and Italy.

Mergers and acquisitions

In 1960 there were 47 major car companies in Europe. By 1998 there were just 17, with predictions of further consolidation. Many of the reasons for such rationalization have already been mentioned and include the need to achieve economies of scale, to share the high costs of research and development and to confront the problems of over-capacity, stagnant prices and severe competition. In general, car firms have merged to survive in a global industry requiring global companies. Table 1.4 gives an indication of who owned whom in the world car industry at the beginning of 2003. In addition to acquisitions and shared ownership there has been a growth in the number of joint ventures as between Ford and Peugeot for the development of diesel engines or between Ford and VW in the development of a people carrier. Issues relating to joint ventures are presented in Chapter 2. This section will examine two mergers: the acquisition of Rover (UK) by BMW (Germany), which was ultimately dissolved, and the failed merger of Volvo (Sweden) and Renault (France).

In 1994 BMW paid £800 million for 80 per cent of Rover and took over debts of some £1 billion. Some years earlier Rover had been privatized and sold to British Aerospace for £150 million and the company had benefited from a joint venture with Honda. The complexities of the relationship with Honda, not least Honda's supply of engines, meant that ties with the Japanese company could not be cut entirely despite their displeasure at the BMW takeover. The attraction of Rover to

Table 1.4	Who owns whom in the European car industry in 2003

General Motors (USA)	General Motors, Vauxhall, Opel, Saab, Isuzu (49%), Suzuki (10%), Fiat (20%)
Ford (USA)	Ford, Jaguar, Aston Martin, Volvo Cars, Mazda (50%), Land Rover
Toyota (Japan)	Toyota, Lexus, Daihatsu
Volkswagen (Germany)	Volkswagen, Audi, Seat, Skoda, Bentley, Bugatti, Lamborghini
Fiat (Italy)	Fiat, Ferrari, Alfa Romeo, Lancia, Maserati, Iveco
PSA (France)	Peugeot, Citröen
Daimler Benz (Germany)	Mercedes, Chrysler, Jeep, Smart, Mitsubishi (34%)
BMW (Germany)	BMW, Rolls Royce
Proton (Malaysia)	Proton, Lotus
Renault (France)	Nissan (37%), Samsung (70%)

BMW was undoubtedly access to the smaller family saloon market and the acquisition of Land Rover, still a prestigious marque. Rover's gain was the link with a highly popular, luxury car manufacturer and access to a much wider market. In 1998 Rover announced 1500 redundancies from its 39 000 workforce and proposals for much greater labour flexibility incorporating the move to a 4-day working week. The reason for the cutbacks, as cited by BMW, was strong sterling, which contributed to operating losses of £98 million in 1997, despite investments totalling £2.5 billion since the acquisition in 1994. Those investments included rebuilding the Cowley plant at Oxford and the Land Rover plant at Solihull.

By 1999 there was considerable uncertainty surrounding BMW's UK operations. Losses at Rover were announced at around £650 million for 1998. The losses were attributed to rising costs, model changes, an over-strong pound, falling sales and the cost of restructuring the company. A further factor involved Rover's policy of using predominantly UK suppliers, when, owing to the strong pound, parts could have been sourced more cheaply overseas. The damaging impact of the losses on the overall profits of the parent company led the German press to refer to Rover as the 'English Patient' (using the title of a successful book and film). At the same time, BMW had plans for a rebuild of the Longbridge plant at a cost of £1.5 billion. They had expected the UK government to provide at least £300 million in grant aid, but viewed their original offer as 'derisory'. In any case, such government support met with fierce opposition from other European manufacturers. BMW announced that further cost cuts were inevitable and at least a further 1000 job losses were predicted. The failure of the UK government to dance to the BMW tune was accompanied by suggestions that Rover production could be moved to Hungary. The problems facing Rover led to resignations at board level and a rapid turnover of senior management, all moved into Rover from Germany, but none able to stem the tide. Rumours were rife that the Quandt family, who own 46 per cent of BMW, were disturbed by the events at Rover and that the problems made the company vulnerable to acquisition. BMW sold Land Rover to Ford and Rover itself was sold in 2000 to a consortium headed by ex-Rover boss, John Towers.

The proposed merger between Renault and Volvo in 1993 seemed a natural extension of existing joint ventures and partial ownership arrangements – both companies holding a proportion of shares in the other. The merger was seen as the means to turn around the fortunes of two established but ailing companies by achieving economies of scale, by reducing R&D costs and forming a stronger alliance to face Japanese competition. After a protracted negotiation, plans for the merger came to naught. There would appear to have been several reasons. Renault, through management statements and reports in the French media, clearly saw the merger as a takeover, with the French as the dominant partner, reinforced by a proposed 65–35 stakeholding favouring the French, and the appointment of a French CEO for the new company. The French government had a major stake in Renault, but with plans for privatization. The fear among Swedish shareholders was that the shares would be floated below market value to ensure that the privatization was a success, thereby forcing down the share price of the merged company. Middle management in Volvo were concerned that the merger would, at worst, lead to job losses, with the Swedes bearing the brunt. At best it was feared that there would be a conflict of managerial styles, the Swedes being more open, with greater delegation, while the French were more hierarchical. Culturally the Swedes are more international and outward-looking than the French. The merger was supported by the Swedish government, but consistently opposed by the workforce and Swedish public opinion. There were clear cultural and political reasons for their unease. There were also economic factors. The cost of employing workers in Sweden was much higher than that in France. Sweden has both higher rates of taxation and health and social security payments. It was feared that a combined Renault–Volvo company would mean significant job losses in Sweden. Volvo Cars was eventually acquired by Ford in 1999 and, in the same year, Volvo Trucks was bought by Mitsubishi. Renault turned its attention to Japan and acquired a 37 per cent stake in Nissan and managerial control through the secondment of Carlos Ghosn as the CEO of the Japanese company.

Restructuring in the supply industry

A number of major changes have been occurring in the supply industry. These may be summarized as follows.

- An increasing proportion of car parts are outsourced to the supply industry.
- Intense competition in car manufacture has had an impact on the supply chain resulting in pressure on prices and costs, the elimination of smaller firms and consolidation amongst the rest.
- Car manufacturers are now using the same basic components across the whole range of their products. In addition, several car manufacturers have collaborated with competitors in the development of parts. For example, Ford is working with Peugeot on diesel engine technology.

- There has been a shift in the supply industry to lower cost countries, mirroring changes in car manufacture. In part this is due to cost pressures and in part to the emergence of longer-lasting products, as with tyres. The latter has led to a slow-down in the industry and the need to cut costs still further.

- There is a closer relationship between many manufacturers and their suppliers. In some cases, manufacturers have moved into the supply chain themselves. In 1999, Ford acquired Kwikfit, the UK tyre and service operation, to extend their influence throughout the life of a vehicle and to access the Kwikfit customer database as a potential source of new sales to existing owners of non-Ford brands.

In 1995–6 there were 157 mergers of car components firms in Europe: 79 involving cross-border deals and 39 involving non-European companies. The largest consolidation has taken place in brakes and seating. Seating is now dominated by two USA companies, Johnson Controls and Lear Seating. Between them they control 50 per cent of the total market and 70 per cent of the outsourcing market.

For car manufacturers themselves, outsourcing is yet another means of cutting costs. Components suppliers, feeding a number of firms, can achieve economies of scale and, through specialization, are able to maintain product innovation. Wages are lower in the components industry than in the car firms themselves, so it is hardly surprising that outsourcing has increased dramatically. In recent years, the trend for the major manufacturers has been to focus on a small number of dedicated suppliers with whom they forge a special relationship, as between Mercedes and the tyre manufacturer, Continental. Such close relationships invariably include joint development of new products, joint training of staff and, in some instances, part ownership. Hand in hand with this development is the increasing use of components supplies from low-cost countries, including some in Europe such as Poland and the Czech Republic.

Merger and acquisition activity in the global car industry has had its impact on the supply chain. For example, the part acquisition by Renault of Nissan and the poor financial performance of the Japanese company led to a more focused strategy as far as suppliers were concerned. Plans were drawn up to reduce the number of suppliers from 1145 to 600, and suppliers wishing to win contracts must operate globally, cut costs and work together with Nissan/Renault engineers. Such policy changes will have an impact on those UK firms supplying the Nissan factory in Sunderland.

The increasing use of outsourcing has not met with universal approval. There have been industrial relations problems in plants where jobs have been lost as a result of outsourcing strategies and, as we have seen with Lower Saxony, there can be political pressures to resist the shift to lower-cost areas.

Marketing strategies

Changes in the supply industry have not been matched at the distribution end of the supply chain. There has been some move towards rationalization among dealerships but, compared with the USA, European dealerships are small, fragmented and have limited turnovers. Fragmentation is particularly a feature of distribution in Germany.

The car industry in Europe has been protective of dealerships that specialize in one brand and has been granted exemption from EU competition policy. However, changes are occurring.

The exemption from EU policy, known as the block exemption dealer agreement, allowed manufacturers to sell only to franchised dealers in a strictly defined sales area. The EU viewed this as anti-competitive and the system was opposed by UK consumer groups, accusing the manufacturers of operating a price cartel that disadvantaged UK consumers. For example, the pre-tax price of a Mazda 323 in July 2002 was:

UK	£10 525
Greece	£7404
Denmark	£6266

New rules were agreed by the EU in 2002 to come into force in 2005. In essence the new rules:

- Allow dealers to open showrooms wherever they like in the EU.
- Allow independent garages to service new vehicles through greater access to parts and manufacturer's information.
- Allow dealers to sell different brands in the same showroom, provided they use different sales areas.

The predicted outcomes of such changes are as follows:

- Dealerships are likely to be consolidated and there will be a rationalized network of large regional dealerships. There are fears that existing dealerships in less populated locations will disappear.
- Dealers will do all they can to hold on to servicing custom. At the time of writing, across Europe sales represent 80 per cent of turnover, yet servicing brings in 50 per cent of profits. New strategies have already emerged to tie customers to dealers for as long as possible. A 3-year warranty on new cars is now common and is likely to be extended with the increased durability of many parts. In 2003, Hyundai extended their warranty period to 5 years. Car manufacturers are paying increased attention to the concept of customer relationship management. Ford, in a publicity statement in 2002, set itself the target of becoming 'the world's leading consumer company for automotive products and services'.
- Contrary to predictions in the 1990s, the Internet has not emerged as a powerful tool in selling cars. This is partly a function of EU exemption policy, whereby web sites could only put customers in contact with dealers with stock. However, even with the removal of the restrictions, predictions are that consumers prefer to 'touch and experience' a major purchase such as a car rather than purchase online.

Concluding remarks

The pattern that emerged at the beginning of 2003 is complex. It is clear that there are too many manufacturers chasing a limited number of European customers.

Hopes that a rapidly expanding East European market would benefit home producers have receded in the face of intense competition and cheap imports. As a result, many have turned their attentions to the huge potential of the Chinese market. Of the big five producers, GM, Ford, VW, Daimler–Chrysler and Toyota, Ford would appear to be in most financial difficulties. Daimler–Chrysler appears much more like a German take-over, VW continues to flourish in emerging markets and Toyota, along with other Japanese firms, has had a resurgence in fortunes with the weak yen. Of the others, Renault has strengthened its hand and, at the same time, revived the fortunes of Nissan. Fiat appears to be in the most vulnerable position and may become part of the GM empire in the next few years. Some of these companies have been kept alive only through government support based on its perception of their contribution to the national economy and to national identity.

We see an end of nationalism in car manufacture, as global operations can mean that a USA company, such as Ford, can produce cars in Spain for the UK market, using Japanese parts made in the Philippines. There has been an increase in cross-border acquisitions involving producers outside Europe. The major acquisition has been that of Chrysler by Daimler, but we should not forget the purchase of Lotus, the specialist UK company, by Proton from Malaysia. Consolidations in chassis type, body shells, engines and a whole range of parts means that the era of the world car is upon us. Despite the trend to conformity, the picture is still very mixed. Acquisitions have resulted in much greater product variety within the same company: such as Fiat having a product range that embraces both the Fiat Cinquecento and the Ferrari Testarossa.

There are predictions of yet more plant closures and consolidation of suppliers and dealers across Europe as costs become the main driver. The attempts by the EU parliament to liberalize the market may lead to a restructuring of existing dealership arrangements and may result in cheaper cars, at least as far as the UK is concerned.

Questions

1 Before reading further, analyse this case using the Business in Context model.

2 Examine Tables 1.1, 1.2 and 1.3. What trends and issues emerge?

3 What opportunities and threats are presented to a single firm in the current situation of over-capacity and oversupply in the European car industry?

4 What do you forecast to be the main product developments in the industry from now until 2010?

5 Assess the relative strengths and weaknesses of Eastern Europe and China as markets for new cars.

6 Examine Table 1.4. What conclusions do you draw? Give reasons for them. What changes do you foresee in the next 25 years?

7 Examine the changing nature of the relationship between car manufacturers, their suppliers and dealers. What key trends do you expect to emerge in the future?

The European car industry in a business context

Environmental factors

The case demonstrates the important role of the car industry in the **economy** of the major European producers.

- It is the region's largest single manufacturing industry with a large number of related industries and jobs.

- However, it is also an industry where supply is greater than demand, which makes it vulnerable to recession and external forces, such as dramatic increases in the price of oil (as occurred in the 1970s).

- The market is essentially static, cyclical and highly competitive. Competition occurs not just among European firms, but from Japan and, more recently, South Korea. However, the threat posed by the South Koreans itself receded with severe economic problems in that country.

- The global nature of the industry has meant that many firms have taken advantage of economic differences and moved or outsourced some of their operations to low-wage areas. Some of those areas with growing economies, including parts of Eastern Europe, are seen as important emerging markets. Here, as at home, there is intense competition and the economic problems of the less prosperous emerging markets such as India and Indonesia present **barriers to entry**. Problems continue to exist in China but are seen as less restrictive than before.

- The industry is especially sensitive to economic changes, including currency movements, in other parts of the world. For many years, the strength of the Japanese yen against European currencies was a constraint on Japanese imports. The problems of the Japanese and many other South-East Asian economies in the late 1990s, with the subsequent weakening of their currencies, have meant that imports are more competitively priced.

- The industry demonstrates more than most the growth of global networks of manufacturers and suppliers. Most cars are now the product of parts made in a number of different countries and assembled in different locations as part of a global operations strategy.

The economic importance of the industry has led to the involvement of the **state**.

- Over-capacity within the industry is viewed by some as a direct result of government protection of uneconomic plants.

- In a number of the countries for many years, the state has been a whole or part owner of such firms as Renault, VW and British Leyland. In general, national firms are still supported by national governments although much of the industry has undergone privatization.

- Variations in government intervention exist between countries such as the UK, where a free market ideology has resulted in less protective policies, and those such as France, with more directive, protectionist policies. Such policies have included investment, trade barriers and incentives to the public to buy new cars.

- The political importance of the industry can be seen, as in Lower Saxony, by attempts to prevent closure, downsizing or movement of jobs to other areas. Politics also plays a part in gaining entry to emerging markets, most notably in China.
- Supranational bodies such as the EU and WTO have influenced the direction of the industry. The removal by the EU of its exemption for the car industry to its own competition policy may change the way that cars are sold. Undoubtedly, China's acceptance as a member of the WTO has led to increased liberalization of the market.

The oversupply and over-capacity in the industry has had a significant impact on **labour** and employment.

- Plants have closed down and throughout firms in Europe there have been major reductions in the workforce.
- The response of governments and unions has been mixed. As we have seen, state protectionism does exist and in a strongly unionized industry, unions have fought hard to prevent the growth in outsourcing. In other cases, they have agreed to reductions in pay and the working week and to greater flexibility in order to save jobs.

In terms of **technology**,

- The industry has made significant investment to improve both products and processes. While not in the same league as the pharmaceutical firms, the industry is still a major investor in R&D.
- The changes in process technology have been exclusively focused on cost reduction with the widespread introduction of automation and methods associated with lean production, such as JIT manufacture.
- Many of these technological changes have been carried out in close relationship with major suppliers and some as joint ventures with competitor manufacturing firms.

The case also demonstrates differences in **culture**.

- Despite the trend towards the concept of the world car we can still see variations in national preference.
- Cultural differences also played a part in the failure of Renault and Volvo to negotiate a successful merger, both in terms of management and organizational style and in arrangements for aspects of pensions and insurance.

Organizational aspects

Size is a significant issue in the car industry. We have seen that several of the European firms are too small to be effective on a global scale and more mergers are predicted as a route to survival. The investment needed for firms to be successful calls for economies of scale and access to global markets and global suppliers.

In terms of **structure**, there have been significant changes in the past decade.

- Mergers between firms like Daimler and Chrysler have had inevitable implications for the management and structures, particularly where Chrysler is seen as the weaker partner.

- The closer links between some manufacturers and major suppliers, with the creation of dedicated supply systems, have had implications for structural arrangements in both manufacturer and supplier.

- We have seen that in order to face global challenges some firms, such as Ford, have undergone major restructuring, creating a global **matrix organization**.

As far as ownership is concerned, acquisitions and mergers have been rife in an industry that must grow to stay in business.

- There are examples of both majority and minority ownership as a result of merger, acquisition and joint venture (see Table 1.4). However, as in the case of Nissan and Renault, Renault's 37 per cent stake belies its real influence.

- The growing trend is for ownership patterns to cross not just national borders but continental boundaries as well, as in the case of Nissan–Renault and Daimler–Chrysler.

- The picture is highly complex, none more so than the case of VW, who purchased the Rolls Royce car factory, but not the right to manufacture Rolls Royce cars. That right was sold separately to BMW.

- In BMW itself, board decisions are influenced considerably by a single family owning 46 per cent of shares.

- Changes in ownership patterns have affected the supply industry as well, with an even greater extent of consolidation through merger and acquisition but with an increasing share of ownership in the supply chain by the major manufacturers.

Whatever the patterns of ownership, the expressed **goals** of the manufacturers invariably reflect an optimism for expansion, either through new markets or new models, that is not always matched by the realities of the market place.

Issues of **organizational culture** come to the forefront with **mergers and acquisitions** as new alliances struggle to adapt to different cultures at the level of the firm. When these are compounded by national differences, as in the case of Renault and Volvo, they can threaten the success of the alliance.

Strategic aspects

The case illustrates a number of key generic strategies.

- Product strategies are exemplified by the regularity of model renewal by the manufacturers, although the frequency of that renewal is tempered by economic conditions.

- A favoured route to new products is through acquisition. Through its purchase of Rover, BMW gained an entirely new range of cars, including the specialist Land Rover models, although the company was soon sold to Ford. Rather than develop its own range, Ford entered the luxury car market by acquiring both Jaguar and Aston Martin and strengthened its position in the big car market through its acquisition of Volvo.

- Other companies, such as Mercedes, chose to develop their own products, in their case to enter the non-luxury market through the A Class and the Smart car.

- The static nature of home markets has led producers to go further afield and the emerging markets of Asia, Latin America and Eastern Europe have been pursued vigorously.
- All companies have engaged in a series of strategies focusing on cost reduction, including automation, plant closure, introducing more efficient production methods, reducing the labour force and seeking economies of scale through merger and other forms of consolidation.

Functional aspects

Innovation   The case contains several examples of **innovation** in terms of new product and process development. Other forms of innovation are present in terms of new global structures, as with Ford, or new forms of relationship with suppliers, as with Mercedes. New products have been developed in financial services as car makers seek profits from non-traditional businesses.

Operations   A major production issue in European industry **operations** is **over-capacity**, with the inevitability of future plant closures unless new markets can be found. Changes in production methods have resulted in considerable efficiency gains, although further gains are unlikely in some of the better plants. A major trend has been the consolidation of production through the sharing of parts across model ranges, including body shells, chassis and engines, as well as a whole range of smaller components. The Japanese have extended their influence in Europe through the expansion of transplants. The Europeans for their part have relocated some of their production, particularly the supply industry, where labour is cheaper, including parts of Eastern Europe.

Marketing   Most of the companies have been active in **marketing** – in the search for new markets – either by development or acquisition. While competition in the emerging markets is fierce, the real potential of some, like China, is beginning to be realized. Through mergers and acquisitions there has been a growth in differentiated markets within the same company. Luxury producers have moved down-market, while mass producers have acquired luxury and specialist marques. Despite this, and despite the sharing of body shells by different model ranges, marketing specialists within the companies have made considerable investments to ensure **brand** differentiation. This is reinforced by systems of dealership across Europe that protect brand specialization, irrespective of patterns of ownership. The future liberalization in dealership arrangements across Europe will have an impact on how cars are sold.

Human resource management   Twenty years ago the key issues in **human resource management** were undoubtedly dealing with unions to negotiate wages and conditions and to resolve conflict. With a changing economic climate and the weakening of trade unions, in countries such as the UK, the focus has shifted. The key issues are undoubtedly the creation of more flexible patterns of work, in terms of time and function, the holding down of wages and the shedding of labour through schemes for early retirement and redundancy.

Accounting and finance   Cost management has been a major consideration for all manufacturers and has occurred across the whole range of their activities, including the manufacturing process, component supply and labour. Cost reduction has been at the heart of most strategies. The producers themselves have expanded their activities to establish finance companies, which adds to their range of products. Customers are now sold not just a car but a financial package as well. For some producers this has been their major source of profit and has part-subsidized less profitable manufacturing operations.

| Case 1.2 | **News International and Wapping** |

For almost a year, every Saturday evening the residents of a fashionable warehouse conversion on the edges of London's docklands were denied free access to their property. The residents' access was blocked by mass picketing resulting from an industrial dispute between News International and its former Fleet Street employees over the printing of newspapers at the company's newly commissioned Wapping plant. In this case we will examine the background to the dispute and focus on events from December 1985 to February 1987. A postscript has been added to deal briefly with events after 1987 and places them in the context of the global strategy of News International's parent company, the global information and communications giant, News Corporation, with its headquarters in the USA.

Although what has become known as the Wapping dispute focuses on the events of the 1980s, the seeds of that dispute were laid much earlier and the implications had a significant impact on the size and structure of the newspaper industry. As with the car industry, we will see how this case illustrates our model of business.

News International is a company controlled by Rupert Murdoch, Australian by birth but with American citizenship. The company was founded by his father in Australia in 1923 and is still essentially family owned and controlled. News International now forms part of a large global business empire controlled by the parent company, News Corporation. The empire has considerable business interests in the UK, USA, Canada, Australia, most of Asia, the Middle East, Central and South America and parts of the former Soviet Union. It is a diversified information and communications business operating by the end of the 1990s in the following broad areas:

● the production and distribution of motion pictures and television programmes

● satellite, cable and terrestrial television channels

● newspapers, books and magazines

● computer-based information services.

The British company controls two daily newspapers, *The Times* and the *Sun*, and two Sunday newspapers, the *Sunday Times* and the *News of the World*. The *Sun*, the *Sunday Times* and the *News of the World* are the best-selling newspapers of their type in Britain and *The Times* is arguably the nation's most famous daily paper. A third daily paper, *Today*, was held briefly by News International until its demise.

In 1978 land was purchased in Wapping with a view to building a large printing works using the latest technology in newspaper production, and construction began within 2 years. At that time, News International owned only the *Sun* and the *News of the World* and the plant was part of a plan to increase both the output and the size of both newspapers. In 1981, the company purchased both *The Times* and the *Sunday Times* in the face of accusations that News International would be operating a monopoly against the public interest. Once again, there was a desire to increase both the production runs and the size of both newly acquired newspapers. In all cases, the size of the newspapers and the quantity of production were restricted by the size of the existing plants around the Fleet Street area of central London and what management saw as uneconomic manning levels imposed by the trade unions. The issues of new technology and trade union control over work practices lay at the heart of most major national newspaper disputes. No national paper was immune and in 1985 alone 95.6 million copies were lost to industrial disputes of one type or another.

A little background

The major technological innovations were direct input and photocomposition. This meant that the typesetting operation could in effect be carried out by journalists or typists, eliminating the need for traditional print working through a method referred to as 'cold-type' printing. Computer keyboards and VDUs are used to input material to be stored on a central computer which also contains programs for page composition. The computer prints the stories and advertisements onto photographic paper, which is then pasted up to form the eventual pages of the newspaper. These are photographed and a negative produced. The negative is converted into a flexible polymer plate to be clipped to the presses for the printing to commence.

Under this method around 3000 lines a minute could be typeset compared with seven lines per minute using the conventional technique, with the added advantage that stories and whole pages could be changed and mistakes corrected quickly and cheaply. Such methods had been used by American newspapers since the early 1960s. In Britain, however, the introduction of new technology had been slow. There was a strong adherence to the traditional process of using linotype, a method involving the creation of the type from molten lead, sometimes known as the 'hot metal' process. This method is labour intensive and is often performed by compositors using equipment some 50 years old. The new generation of printing presses are much cheaper and can therefore be replaced when further technical improvements are made. Even where photocomposition had been introduced the process was not used to its full potential as, under management–union agreements, keyboard operations were still being performed by print workers and not journalists or typists.

Murdoch saw the new technology as central to reducing costs and enabling greater productivity across his newspaper empire in Australia and the USA, as well as the UK. The only major dispute was in the UK. In Australia, the introduction proceeded at a much slower rate, since the Australian Labour Government was more sympathetic to the needs of the trade unions concerned. In the USA the existing contracts of print workers were bought out at considerable cost. In the UK the situation was different; traditional practices of the print unions were more entrenched, there was a need to expand away from the cramped conditions of Fleet Street in Central London, Murdoch wanted complete management control and the Conservative

▶

Government of the day assisted through legal changes to weaken the powers of trades unions.

The printing industry in the UK was one of the most traditional of the craft industries with a long history. The print unions were vigilant in maintaining control over the apprenticeship system, entry to the profession, and over the way the job was done. These traditional craft controls were aided by the rigid enforcement of a union closed shop, where union membership was a necessary condition of employment. Such controls were greatest in Fleet Street where job entry was reserved only for existing members of a recognized trade union (a pre-entry closed shop). The two major unions were the National Graphical Association (NGA), covering the printers themselves, and the Society of Graphical and Allied Trades (SOGAT, 1982), covering dispatch, distribution and clerical workers.

In this way the union controlled work allocation and, above all, manning levels for each job. Frequent management complaints concerned overmanning and the inability to implement changes that would invariably be accompanied by uneconomic staffing requirements. There was considerable resistance to the introduction of new technology, as this would effectively reduce the craft control of the job and make it accessible to those not trained as printers.

Despite management's frequent complaints, the situation was largely of their own making. Concessions to trade union control of manning levels had been made owing to the highly competitive nature of the national newspaper industry, the highly perishable nature of the product, and the need for maximum flexibility, especially when dealing with late changes in news items. Competition was not just for readers but for advertisers. Lost production could never be regained and lost distribution could not be sold at a later date. These factors also gave the trade unions considerable strength in wage negotiation and Fleet Street workers were able to achieve higher rates than those earned by other print workers.

It was partly competition that led to Fleet Street management adopting a new approach to the introduction of new technology. The relative cheapness of cold type over hot metal reduced one of the major barriers to entry to newspaper production. The initial challenges came in the provinces with the growth of the 'free newspaper' industry. These are, essentially, cheaply produced local papers where advertising takes precedence over news items. The income from advertising is such that the newspapers can be distributed free to all householders in a given area. This sharpened competition in the local paper market. The response among some existing local papers was to force through the introduction of new technology. The *Nottingham Evening Post* in the face of union opposition from the NGA simply replaced the print workers.

The real focus was in 1983 with the case of the Messenger group of free local newspapers in south Lancashire and its proprietor Eddie Shah. In expanding his distribution and introducing direct input printing he overcame bitter opposition from the NGA. He was backed in his quest by new laws redefining industrial disputes and imposing greater restrictions on picketing, drawn up by a government intent on curbing the power of the unions. The NGA were fined by the courts and Shah achieved all his objectives. He built upon his success with the local newspaper industry and launched a new national daily paper, *Today*, using new technology and non-traditional workers in a labour force one-tenth the normal size for such a news-paper. At the same time plans were announced for the launch of other new daily and Sunday national papers. Although Shah's ownership of *Today* was brief and unprofitable (he sold the paper to Lonrho who, in turn, sold it to News Inter-national), the relationship between Fleet Street management and the print unions had changed irrevocably. At the same time Express newspapers announced plans to reduce its workforce by 30 per cent.

Competition came not just from within the industry but through the coverage and expansion of the television news services. The advent of breakfast television posed an even greater threat to an already declining total newspaper readership. The newspaper industry needed new technology to provide a better quality product with clearer newsprint and sharper pictures and an ability to respond quickly to changing news stories.

Events at Wapping

Before Murdoch's acquisition, *The Times* had attempted to force the new technology issue, but an 11-month shutdown in 1978 altered very little and the NGA retained exclusive control over typesetting operations. The completion of the plant at Wapping and the expense involved in interest payments alone gave new urgency to some form of agreement with the print unions. Bill O'Neill, an ex-senior trade unionist in Australia and now part of Murdoch's management team was brought in from the USA to lead negotiations. News International wanted:

- legally binding contracts with the unions
- no strike agreement during the period of the contract
- no union closed shop
- acceptance of management's right to manage.

The unions refused to consider the demands of News International. Furthermore, negotiations to move the production of the *Sun* and *News of the World* to Wapping broke down in early 1984. The unions had refused to give way on the issue of staffing levels and demarcation. Murdoch was clearly frustrated by the failure to reach agreement and, undoubtedly spurred on by Shah's action against the NGA, ensured that Wapping was protected against the action of pickets. During the dispute the building was popularly known as 'Fortress Wapping'. Plans were laid to treat Wapping as a greenfield site for the production of a new London evening paper staffed with non-Fleet Street people. At the time the unions saw this as a diversion to mask the true intention of transferring production of all four newspapers to Wapping.

Whatever the intention, Murdoch was determined to introduce total management control over staffing levels and to achieve total labour flexibility. News International terminated all its existing collective agreements with the unions with the aim of replacing them with a legally binding contract and a no-strike clause, the elimina-tion of the closed shop, and binding arbitration in the case of a dispute. The penalty for breaking the agreement would be instant dismissal for individuals and the right to sue the union for unlimited amounts. Such a strategy was calculated to confront

▶

the unions on the issue of job control and, not surprisingly, was rejected by NGA and SOGAT '82. The two unions insisted that any move to Wapping should be accompanied by no redundancies and the maintenance of existing work practices. As a result Murdoch declared that negotiations were over and gave his print workers six months' notice and no option of jobs at Wapping.

One union, the Electrical, Electronic, Telecommunication and Plumbing Union (EETPU), was prepared to negotiate on the basis of the new proposals, much against the advice of the trade union movement's central body, the TUC. For some time the electricians' union had been keen to expand its membership in new areas and viewed its members as key workers in all workplaces increasingly operating under the demands of new technology. One of those areas was printing, and the union had even gone so far as to provide training for its members in newspaper production.

Electricians were recruited by News International initially to commission the new presses. However, by the end of January 1986 the Wapping plant was producing the four newspaper titles amid much secrecy, using electricians recruited from outside London and transported daily by an organized bus network. This led to considerable recriminations within the trade union movement and calls to expel EETPU from the TUC. They were eventually expelled at the 1988 TUC Conference; not for activities at News International but for 'poaching' members from other unions in South Wales.

The move had also affected the journalists on all papers. Many moved to Wapping for increased salaries but several refused to work under the new arrangements. For their part, the print unions held a secret ballot which showed that most were in favour of strike action. Picket lines were set up outside Wapping and SOGAT attempted to prevent the distribution of the newspapers with the help of the Transport and General Workers' Union (TGWU). Both unions were countered by the law. In the case of the TGWU the threat was sufficient, but SOGAT was fined £25 000 and had its assets sequestrated by the High Court for persistent attempts to prevent newspaper distribution.

By the following month, News International agreed to the involvement of ACAS (the Government's arbitration and conciliation service). The main issue that emerged was that of redundancy payments for those on strike. The company had always maintained that those choosing this course of action forfeited their right to severance pay and had effectively dismissed themselves. The company did offer the unions the old *Sunday Times* printing plant so that they could set up their own newspaper staffed by the displaced workforce. The offer was rejected by the unions, who insisted on the maximum number of workers being taken on at Wapping and generous redundancy payments for the rest. Increasingly, however, the union position was being undermined by events elsewhere. New technology agreements were being reached with unions at the Express and Mirror newspapers and several national newspapers announced their own plans to move to Docklands. In all cases, the owners saw the move as an opportunity both to expand and negotiate fresh deals with the trade unions.

By May 1986 the company made what they claimed was a final offer in a bid to end the picketing at Wapping. This comprised a redundancy payment deal totalling £50 million, an opportunity for all workers to apply for vacancies at Wapping as and when they arose, a withdrawal of all legal actions against the unions, and a promise to review the issue of union recognition after a year. The offer was rejected. Picketing was intensified, accompanied by a significant involvement of the police and further legal proceedings to prevent the picketing taking place. As a result of these proceedings SOGAT estimated its losses at £1.5 million. The estimated costs of policing the dispute up to June 1986 were £1 million.

In September, News International made a revised offer of redundancy payments to the dismissed workers, again rejected by the NGA and SOGAT '82. The mounting costs of the dispute forced SOGAT to appeal for funds among its membership nationwide. The appeal was rejected.

The first anniversary of the strike in January 1987 was accompanied by the largest mass picket to date and extremely violent clashes between the police and the pickets. Part of the violence was undoubtedly attributed to a growing frustration among the workers and a realization that the unions could no longer afford to continue. The cost of legal proceedings, the general cost of running the dispute and an impending contempt of court action was too much for the NGA and SOGAT to bear and would have resulted in the elimination of all their assets. By February 1987 both unions, along with the journalists' union, accepted a redundancy package for the dismissed employees and the dispute ended. In all some 4000 staff lost their jobs.

Postscript

At the time of the Wapping dispute, the UK newspaper industry employed over 30 000 people. By 1990, that number had fallen to less than 15 000. At the same time, newspapers had considerably increased the size of each edition and had introduced colour printing as a standard feature in almost all newspapers. Colour printing had a significant impact on advertising. In 1990 the Wapping plant benefited from a £500 million investment in state-of-the-art printing presses.

By the mid-1990s News International at Wapping was part of a large global network of companies. The network embraced around 50 national newspapers in six countries, 80 regional papers in Australia, over 30 magazines around the world and the major book publisher, HarperCollins. A large number of acquisitions were made in broadcasting. News International had a controlling interest in major cable and satellite companies in the UK, USA, Germany, Latin America, Australia and Asia. It owned 20th Century Fox Films and the television company, Fox Broadcasting, as well as control of 12 USA television stations. In Australia it owned Network 7. Amongst the company's many other interests during the 1990s could be numbered the transport firm TNT and the Australian airline, Ansett. The global network of companies comprises a highly complex organizational structure making full use of variations in national tax laws through a system of effective financial management. In 1995 the company made profits of £793 million, yet had to pay less than 10 per cent in tax, when the average for most firms is 20–40 per cent.

By 2000, newspapers were seen by News Corporation as less strategically significant than developments in film and television. Nonetheless, newspapers still held considerable symbolic importance in the UK, where they have been viewed by successive governments as being able to influence the electorate through their editorial position. A key feature of modern strategic thinking in News Corporation are the various moves to dominate pay-for-view television around the world. In 2003 the company bought a controlling interest in Hughes Electronics, taking control from General Motors. The acquisition gave News Corporation control of DirecTV and access to an American market, not formerly enjoyed. The global domination of News Corporation in the satellite and cable subscription television industry can be viewed in Table 1.5. The company is especially dominant across a large Indian sub-continent and Asian market, both with considerable growth potential. Moreover, StarTV is 100 per cent Murdoch owned.

Fears that Murdoch's dominance of the satellite TV market would extend to terrestrial channels was in part behind the UK government's introduction of the 1996 Broadcasting Act. This attempted to prevent control of the media by a single company. In 2003, proposals were made to liberalize the industry. While these are not a radical reform to the 1996 Act, they may be sufficient to allow News Corporation to buy one of the smaller UK channels, such as Channel 5. There is much speculation that such changes are related to the political support of the Government in the Murdoch press. That press supported the Labour Party in its election victory of 1997, but has since campaigned against the introduction of the euro as UK currency. Some commentators believe that a pro-euro stance by the Murdoch press in support of the Government would allow News Corporation to obtain control of a terrestrial television channel. This reinforces the notion of UK newspapers as important opinion leaders.

Table 1.6 shows three snapshots of daily newspaper sales for the best-selling titles in four categories. News International claimed top spot in three out of the four with the *Sun*, *News of the World* and *Sunday Times*, while *The Times* was second behind the *Daily Telegraph*. The mid-1990s was notable for a number of price wars among the daily titles, inevitably involving News International and its major rival in each category. *The Times* and the *Daily Telegraph* competed on price and special

Table 1.5   News Corporation control of satellite and cable pay television

Satellite and cable companies where News Corporation has a controlling interest	Number of subscribers (millions) in 2003
StarTV (India, Israel, Asia)	95.4
DirecTV (USA)	11.3
BskyB (UK, Ireland)	6.6
Sky PerfecTV (Japan)	3.4
SkyItalia	2.2
DirecTV (Latin America)	1.6
Foxtel (Australia)	0.83
Sky Brasil (Brazil)	0.72
Sky Mexico (Mexico)	0.69
Sky Multi Country (Chile, Argentina, Colombia)	0.15

Source: adapted from the Guardian, 11 April, 2003

Table 1.6	Average daily sales during March of best selling newspaper titles by category, 1999–2003		

Newspaper	Average daily sales		
	1999	*2002*	*2003*
Tabloid daily			
Sun	3 813 381	3 379 508	3 521 144
Daily Mail	2 362 184	2 318 023	2 341 999
Daily Mirror	2 303 510	2 089 539	1 997 846
Broadsheet daily			
Daily Telegraph	1 045 336	952 622	910 725
The Times	746 403	657 113	622 592
Guardian	402 494	382 057	396 849
Tabloid Sunday			
News of the World	4 301 502	3 970 726	3 849 013
Mail on Sunday	2 319 272	2 277 898	2 312 905
Sunday Mirror	1 993 074	1 762 500	1 603 578
Broadsheet Sunday			
Sunday Times	1 336 464	1 368 608	1 365 988
Sunday Telegraph	808 826	753 255	704 964
Observer	401 403	422 470	430 791

Source: http://media.guardian.co.uk, accessed 14 April 2003

offers, as did the *Sun* and the *Mirror*. In all cases profits were sacrificed for market share. However, the biggest gains during the 1990s were made by the Daily Mail Group. The price wars continued into the new millennium, with a particularly fierce battle between the *Sun* and the *Daily Mirror*, which is reckoned to have lost News International £7 million in July 2002 alone and contributed greatly to a fall in operating income of around 50 per cent over a 3-month period to September 2002, when price cuts were ended. The tactic of price cuts was also extended to the satellite TV business with the offer of free set top boxes for subscribers to the new digital satellite system.

The loss of revenue from the price wars was compounded by a general, albeit small, decline in sales overall and, more significantly, a worldwide fall in advertising revenue of around 20 per cent in 2001. Senior management in News Corporation announced that 10 per cent cuts were to be made across the board in its newspaper businesses.

In terms of trade union activity, the EETPU soon lost its favoured status and was de-recognized by the company. Despite the decline in trade union membership and influence in the UK, News International would still appear to be sensitive to the events of the 1980s. Proposals by the New Labour government in 1999 to give employees the right to join trade unions led News International to discuss plans to establish an Employee Consultative Council as a non-traditional company union in an attempt to avoid having to deal with an independent trade union.

There has been speculation that the Wapping operation may be reaching the end of its usefulness to News International. The original concept brought printers and journalists together on one site. Developments in computerized photocomposition make this no longer necessary and the printing equipment at Wapping is in need of updating. In 2002 there was considerable speculation that production of the news-paper titles would be split on a number of smaller sites in South-East England away from the congestion of London. Moreover the 14-acre Wapping site, bought for £10 million in 1978, was worth £200 million in 2002. One prediction is that News International at Wapping would retain its links with the media by becoming a multiplex cinema.

Questions

1   Before reading further, analyse this case using the Business in Context model.

2   Identify and assess the relative importance of the factors that led News International to move to Wapping.

3   What does the case tell us about the introduction of new technology in a traditional industry? To what extent is this case typical?

4   Many who lost their jobs at Wapping remain resentful at their treatment at the hands of News International. Have they a case? Do you believe that the management of News International behaved ethically?

5   What conclusions do you draw from the case about industrial relations in the UK in the 1980s and beyond?

6   Examine Tables 1.5 and 1.6. What conclusions do you draw?

7   What role do you believe newspapers will play in the future strategies of News International and News Corporation?

The News International case in a business context

The case illustrates all aspects of our Business in Context model.

Environmental aspects

Economic factors are represented by the highly competitive nature of the newspaper industry.

● The high potential profit from a national title led to fierce competition for circulation and advertising. Traditionally this resulted in a fierce rivalry and lack of cooperation between the owners.

● The availability of new technology combined with external competition from television and radio meant that technological changes were sought to reduce costs and maintain profit levels.

● Furthermore, the relative cheapness of the new technology lowered a significant barrier to entry, thereby increasing competition. This has broken the **oligopoly** of

Fleet Street and led to new national titles as well as major changes in regional newspapers resulting from the growth of the free newspaper industry.

- In a much broader sense, a high level of unemployment in the 1980s may have increased the resolve of the electricians' union to expand its field of activity and influenced the lack of wider support for the print workers in their dispute.

The **state** had a considerable influence on events at Wapping both directly and indirectly.

- There was a direct involvement through the policing of the dispute with extensive costs over a period of a year.

- The Employment Acts of 1980 and 1982 and the Trade Union Act of 1984 brought about changes in the legal definition of a dispute, and placed restrictions on both **picketing** and the formation of a **closed shop**. The unions were challenged on the legality of their dispute and were found wanting.

- The subsequent clashes between the unions and the courts led to substantial fines being imposed, which eventually brought an end to the dispute.

- Prior to the events at Wapping, the government of the day had, in 1981, become embroiled in a monopolies issue when News International negotiated to buy *The Times* and the *Sunday Times* when it already owned the biggest-selling national and Sunday papers. The deal was allowed to go through on the undertaking of editorial freedom for the newly acquired titles. More sceptical observers, like Harold Evans (successively the editor of the *Sunday Times* and *The Times*), saw the acquisition as a reward for News International's editorial support for the government in the previous general election (Evans, 1983). Whatever the situation, this aspect of the case raises the important issue of the relationship between politics and the press.

- The relationship between politics and the press was further in evidence when the News International titles switched their allegiance from the Conservative to the Labour Party for the 1997 election and, for some, were influential in the election of a Labour government with a particularly large majority.

- Politics was also in evidence during attempts to introduce changes in News International's Australian newspapers. Here management were non-confrontational. Unlike the UK, where legislation assisted the company's objectives, the Australian government in the 1980s was more favourably disposed towards trades unions.

- Fear of new legislation in 1999 to give employees rights of trade union membership brought a swift reaction from the company in the proposal of alternative structures.

Technology, or more specifically the introduction of new technology, was a central issue in this case.

- Changes in the technology of newspaper production brought about the possibility of changes in work allocation. The elimination of traditional printing work through the substitution of direct input and photocomposition challenged the job control of the print workers and ultimately the bargaining position of their trade union. Certain printing operations could now be performed by journalists and typists, considerably reducing operating costs and presenting much greater scope for editorial changes, allowing newspapers to be much more responsive to changes in the news and hence the needs of the market place.

- Traditional craft unions, like the NGA, do not yield their historical controls willingly hence the intensity and, at times, bitterness of the dispute.

- New technology also gave management a new strategic weapon in dealing with the trade unions and was doubtless seen by some as a means of gaining greater control over costs and workplace practices, especially manning levels.

- After the dispute continuing technological change made possible the introduction of colour printing and even further reduced staffing levels. Further developments in computerized photocomposition enabled journalists to have remote access to the process and removed the need for journalism and printing to be housed in the same location.

- By 2002 the 'new' printing technology at Wapping was in need of updating fuelling speculation that News International would move out of Wapping.

Labour issues, as we can see, are inseparable from those relating to technology.

- New methods not only mean changes in work allocation, but also an ultimate reduction in the number of jobs.

- The bargaining position of the trade unions was being challenged on the issue of job control at a time when their response was further weakened by high levels of unemployment.

- The case is not simply a matter of management versus the unions, but illustrates the complexity of the dispute on the union side. The Fleet Street workers had, for a very long time, considered themselves to be the 'aristocrats of labour', positioned at the very top of the printing hierarchy (Bassett, 1986). This had often rankled with print workers outside London, and may have explained their reluctance in giving full support to their Fleet Street colleagues. The *Independent* newspaper, launched in 1986, was printed at regional sites away from London, and its management had little difficulty in gaining the agreement of NGA and SOGAT '82 on the use of the new technology.

- Quite apart from the differences among the print workers themselves, their position was further challenged by the willingness of the electricians to be trained in newspaper operations. This forms part of a much broader debate within the trade union movement, as individual unions, mindful of a declining membership, seek to insure their own future by offering the kind of stoppage-free deals sought by management. In the case of Wapping, the EETPU were more than happy to replace the print workers and, on a broader front, to see themselves ideally placed to become the key trade union of the future in workplaces increasingly controlled by computers. Changes in the trade union movement are thus reflecting wider occupational changes. However, we should note that Wapping became a non-union operation within a relatively short period of time, although the electricians retained their importance as an occupational group.

- Weakened print industry unions may have been forced to widen their appeal to attract new members. This would further dilute the traditional power base of the craft union in printing.

- Job cuts associated with new technology in the 1980s gave way in 2000 to job cuts resulting from falling sales revenue due to price wars and to falling revenue from advertising.

The aspect of **culture** is relevant to this case in at least two ways.

- First, we have the issue of the distinctive culture of Fleet Street, brought about by the competitive nature of the industry and the job control of the craft unions. Work practices, manning levels and wage rates have marked off Fleet Street from the rest of the British newspaper industry. The distinctive Fleet Street culture has been especially resistant to change and thus a major factor in the dispute.

- Second, comparative studies of the newspaper industry reveal marked differences between Britain and other countries, notably the USA. The newspaper industry in the USA has embraced new technology with little union opposition, albeit at the high cost of buying out existing employee contracts. Moreover, in Britain there is much greater evidence of cooperation and solidarity between print workers, ancillary staff and journalists than exist in most other countries.

Organizational aspects

While the case clearly shows the interaction and influence of the environmental aspects of our model, there are significant organizational influences at work too.

In terms of **size:**

- News International's British operation was already large, yet part of the motivation behind the move to Wapping lay in the desire to expand. At its previous locations around Fleet Street the opportunities for expansion were denied both by available space, limiting production capacity and distribution, and by manning agreements limiting the size of each edition.

- Size and dominance became an issue, not just for newspapers, but was particularly evident in News Corporation's growth activity in the pay-television business.

The change to Wapping and the adoption of new printing technology had clear implications for **organizational structure.**

- A much more flexible structure has emerged for the newspaper industry. The role of the journalist has potentially broadened to assume responsibility for typesetting as well as content.

- The electricians have emerged as a fast-growing occupational group within the industry. Such changes in work allocation also have implications for management control.

Changes in the newspaper industry have been related to major changes in the **ownership** of national titles.

- The acquisition strategies of News International led to the grouping of five major titles under a single ownership. More significantly, the ownership style was one that had developed in Australia and the USA, where some aspects of the new technology in the newspaper industry were better established.

- Ownership changes away from Fleet Street were also having an impact. We have already made reference to the catalytic effect of Eddie Shah, but ownership changes in some local newspapers such as the *Nottingham Evening Post* led to a much more aggressive style by management, especially towards trade unions and the introduction of new technology.

Changes in ownership often went hand-in-hand with changes in **goals**.

● Historically, newspapers have often been regarded as a special kind of product under the control of individual press barons, such as Lord Beaverbrook at the *Daily Express*. As such, profit goals have co-existed with the less common business goals of political, social or moral reform. Increasingly, major titles have come under the control of business groups in which newspapers represent just one of a highly diversified stable of products. An extreme case here would be the holding company Lonrho's acquisition of the *Observer* Sunday newspaper. It is unlikely that such changes have taken place without a corresponding elevation of purely business goals.

● The case illustrates goal conflict in various ways. At its most obvious this is represented by the unions' need to retain job control in the face of a management desire to reap the cost savings of new technology. The NGA's and SOGAT's goal of union solidarity is sharply contrasted with the EETPU's goal of expansion.

● From an industrial relations perspective the case is interesting in revealing how goals shift as disputes develop; in this case from issues of job control to the negotiation of an acceptable redundancy package.

Strategic aspects

We have seen that changes at News International and in Fleet Street generally have been part of a pattern of interrelated environmental and organizational factors. These changes have resulted in changed culture within national newspaper organizations. A significant contribution to that changing culture has been the changes that have taken place in management strategy.

● In general terms, Fleet Street management appears to have shifted from a reactive, crisis-induced strategy to one typified by long-term, planned technological and organizational change. A combination of a technological imperative and market and economic conditions has led management to adopt a more confident and, as some would term it, aggressive approach in dealing with the trade unions. A widely voiced speculation concerning the strategic implications of News International's move to Wapping was that it represented a deliberate confrontation with the trade unions as a prelude to changing work practices once and for all. The unions certainly believed that Wapping was never intended for a new evening paper and that all along it was designed as the operating centre for the company's major titles. Certainly the initial management proposals, effectively removing the union's traditional control of work practices, were ones to which the union were never likely to agree.

● Aside from management, the case is an interesting illustration of strategy from a trade union perspective. Trade unions are faced with the problem of declining membership in an unfavourable economic and political climate. Like businesses in a declining market they have to be very careful about their choice of strategic option. In such a situation, the case of new technology presents an interesting dilemma; its acceptance by unions would inevitably entail job losses, yet a refusal to negotiate may have far more serious consequences for the future bargaining position of the union. Just as some businesses find declining markets favourable for growth, some trade unions can take advantage of seemingly disadvantageous conditions by proposing deals acceptable to management. In this way the EETPU has embarked upon a fairly vigorous growth strategy, not only securing recognition rights but, in doing so, creating work for electricians.

- On a broader front, the case illustrates the increasingly global nature of business strategies. Wapping has only ever been a small part of News International's operations. However, since the dispute, News International has grown into a vast complex global network of companies with more recent acquisitions focusing on film and television, and most growth taking place in the USA. The complexity of this global structure and the variations in national tax laws have been used by the company to its advantage. By 2000, the key strategic focus of News International and its parent company, News Corporation, had shifted to the pay-television business.

Functional aspects

At the heart of management strategy in this case are the implications for the functional operations of business. All our functional areas are implicated by News International's move to Wapping.

- **Innovation.** Changes in News International's operations have obviously been made possible through process innovations in the newspaper industry. Other types of innovation are illustrated by this case, especially the entrepreneurial activity of industry newcomers, like Shah, attempting to break the traditional Fleet Street monopoly on national newspaper titles.

- **Operations.** The new site operating under the latest technology offers management speedier and more flexible operations with a capability of increased capacity. The new location offers all the benefits of a **greenfield site**, with particular improvements in the supply of raw materials and the distribution of the finished product.

- **Marketing**. In marketing terms, the case illustrates how the need for change has arisen through increased competition and reduced barriers to entry for would-be competitors. The new printing processes offer the reader and the advertiser the potential for a much improved product. In the 1990s, major newspapers used product size and price as major competitive weapons. During one period of intense competition, profits were secondary to increased market share. Price cutting as a competitive weapon extended into the new millennium until falling revenues brought a halt.

- **Accounting.** Major motivations behind changes in the newspaper industry have been declining readership and reduced profits. The cost of setting up a new operating plant and its commissioning with state-of-the-art technology represents a considerable short-term investment with a potential for long-term cost saving. It is, however, important from a management perspective that operations commence at the new plant as soon as possible. The globalization of News International's operations meant that opportunities for enhanced profit were available through the management and movement of finances across national boundaries. However falling sales revenue through price wars and reduced advertising revenue led to cost-cutting in 2002.

● **Human resource**s. The case focuses around the industrial relations aspects of the transfer to Wapping and the introduction of new technology. The marketing and accounting factors identified above put pressure on the need for a speedy agreement with the unions. On the other hand, the setting up of a greenfield site has presented management with an ideal opportunity to introduce a completely new set of personnel and industrial relations policies. Strategies were also employed for reducing staffing levels driven by technological change in the 1980s and costcutting in 2000–3.

The systems and contingency approaches

It has been stressed elsewhere in this introductory chapter that the various elements of the Business in Context model interact with one another and influences go backwards and forwards across the various levels (see Figure 1.1). We are presenting an **interaction–influence model**. The idea of such a model for businesses is not new but forms the basis of the systems and contingency approaches that have been developed as part of organization theory. It is not our intention to present either a comprehensive review or a critique of these two approaches. Instead, we present a brief summary of their main ideas. Their importance as far as we are concerned is that they offer the student of business an important framework for analysis.

The systems approach

The **systems approach** assumes that all organizations are made up of interdependent parts which can only be understood by reference to the whole. As such, organizations may be analysed in terms of inputs, processes and outputs, as illustrated in Figure 1.2. It may be seen from this that there are many similarities with the Business in Context model.

The development of systems thinking from an organizational perspective starts with the analogy of the firm as a living organism. To be effective, the firm, like the organism, must adapt to its environment in order to survive. The inputs, processes and outputs must be balanced so that the firm can obtain equilibrium, especially with its environment. The application of the systems approach in organizational analysis first gained prominence through the utilization of a socio-technical systems perspective. This is based on the assumption

Figure 1.2   The systems approach

Inputs	Process	Outputs
Materials	Strategy formulation	Goods
Labour	Innovation	Services
Methods	Operations	Profit
Finance	Marketing	Information
Technology	Human resource management	Waste
Information	Accounting processes	Job (dis)satisfaction
		Economic growth

that the social system of the firm and its technical system interact in a complex way. The approach was popularized in the work of the Tavistock Institute and its associated researchers throughout the world using the same framework of analysis in different cultural settings (see, for example, Trist and Bamforth, 1951; Rice, 1958; Emery and Thorsrud, 1976). Unless the social system and the technical system work in harmony, a firm will be inefficient.

Key concept 1.4   The systems approach

The systems approach is a view of business involving two related concepts. First, businesses are made up of a series of interactions, involving the various business activities, the various aspects of the organization, and aspects of the environment. What we identify as a business is the sum total of all these influences and interactions. Second, the systems approach views business as a series of inputs from the environment, internal processes and eventual outputs.

The contingency approach

The contingency approach starts with an analysis of the key environmental variables, which shape the organization It then proceeds with the assumption that the successful firms are those that adapt to the key influences and achieve some kind of best fit with their environment. This approach has been very influential in the area of corporate strategy. The strategist attempts to match the environmental opportunities and threats with the organization's own strengths and weaknesses to develop an optimum strategy for the firm in question.

Key concept 1.5   The contingency approach

The contingency approach focuses on the relationship between the organization and its environment. It embraces the notion that business activities and the way they are organized are products of the environment in which they operate. The most successful businesses are therefore those that are organized to take advantage of the prevailing environmental influences.The contingency approach can be traced through the work of Woodward (1965) and Burns and Stalker (1966), although the term itself was popularized in the work of Lawrence and Lorsch who wrote,

> Organizational variables are in a complex interrelationship with one another and with conditions in the environment. If an organization's internal states and processes are consistent with external demands . . . it will be effective in dealing with the environment.

> (*Lawrence and Lorsch, 1967, p. 157*)

Both the systems and contingency approaches are based on the concept of an organization interacting with several key elements in its environment and adapting to them. Some writers (e.g. Burrell and Morgan, 1979, pp. 164–81) regard the contingency approach as an extension of the systems analysis of organizations. Both approaches have been criticized for focusing on a limited range of environmental variables, for being deterministic, and for ignoring both the influence of the organization on its environment and the values and behaviour of management and the workforce. It is our view that such criticisms place unnecessary limits on the use and value of both approaches. In developing our model of business we wish to use systems and contingency thinking to present a broad analytical framework, enabling us to gain a greater insight into the way businesses operate. We are concerned to show, however, that businesses, while influenced by their environments, are not wholly determined by them. Business strategies can and do influence environmental contingencies.

The structure of this book

The chapters that follow will analyse each of the various elements of our Business in Context model. After examining these elements students are recommended to return to the European car industry and News International cases presented in this opening chapter.

Chapter 2 sets the overarching context of modern business by looking at globalization. Chapters 3, 4 and 5 will look at the environmental and organizational contexts. The variables identified in Figure 1.1 will be examined in turn. In the discussion of these variables certain issues emerge which call for more detailed consideration. The whole of Chapter 4 is devoted to culture as an environmental variable and deals at some length with the phenomenon known as 'Japanese management'. Viewing size as an organizational variable raises the topic of small businesses. Such issues are chosen both for their interest to the student of business and, more significantly, because they illustrate further the workings of our Business in Context model by drawing together the various activities and their contexts.

Chapters 6 to 8 focus on issues relating to strategy. Chapter 6 explores issues relating to management and leadership, while Chapter 8 explores business ethics and corporate social responsibility. Chapter 7 examines aspects and issues of strategy itself.

Chapters 9 to 13 will focus on the functional areas of business chosen: innovation, operations, marketing, human resource management, and finance and accounting. Once again we will emphasize their relationship with each other and with the three levels of interaction and influence.

The sequence of the remainder of this book is as follows:

Chapter 2	Globalization
Chapter 3	The environment and business: economy, state, technology and labour
Chapter 4	Cultural influences and business
Chapter 5	Organizational aspects of business
Chapter 6	Management and leadership
Chapter 7	Management strategy
Chapter 8	Business ethics and corporate social responsibility
Chapter 9	Innovation
Chapter 10	Operations
Chapter 11	Marketing
Chapter 12	Human resource management
Chapter 13	Finance and accounting

Summary

- In this introductory chapter the workings of the Business in Context model have been outlined and in so doing mapped out the rest of this book.
- In the model a number of key variables are identified which interact with business. These variables have been arranged in a series of levels, which have been termed environmental, organizational and strategic. It is believed that understanding the way businesses and their key activities operate is enhanced by placing them in this contextual framework.
- The workings of the model can be seen by reference to two cases. The first deals with the European car industry and in particular the strategies employed by management in the face of oversupply and high levels of competition in a static home market. The second case looks at a single company, News International, and focuses on the events surrounding relocation, technical change and a major labour dispute in 1985 at the same time viewing those changes with reference to the company's more recent global strategies.
- The theoretical underpinnings of the model are discussed with reference to the systems and contingency approaches to organizational analysis.

Discussion questions

1 The five environmental, five organizational variables, and five business activities have been identified in the model. By necessity these represent broad categories. What are the possible elements that might be considered under the various headings used in the model of business?

2 Using the way we have analysed the two cases as your guide, take in turn an industry, a firm and a specific issue, and analyse each using the Business in Context model.

3 What is the value of the systems and contingency approaches to an understanding of business?

2 Globalization

Learning objectives   At the end of this chapter you should be able to:

- Define globalization and the key issues and debates associated with it.
- Describe and assess the different perspectives on globalization.
- Assess the main causes and drivers of globalization in an historic perspective.
- Articulate the links between globalization and the development of the multinational and transnational corporations.
- Articulate the links between globalization and the emergence of strategic alliances and joint ventures as a dominant business form.
- Identify key success criteria for strategic alliances and joint ventures.
- Assess the impact of globalization on the economy and on the production of goods and services.
- Assess the relationship between globalization and political change, particularly the creation of political alliances.
- Assess the relationship between globalization and culture change.
- Identify the limitations to globalization.

Introduction

Globalization is seen by many to be the dominant force in business today. The term globalization appears frequently in the popular press and academic literature alike. The impact of globalization is closely linked to the behaviour of multinational or transnational companies and is often linked to new forms of flexible and decentralized organization and with references to the 'virtual organization'. A major problem with all these terms, concepts and linkages is the imprecise and variable nature of the definitions used.

In this chapter we will examine some definitions of globalization and the different perspectives that have been taken. There will be a brief look at the history of globalization and an analysis of the key drivers. We will examine the role played by multinational companies and, in particular, the growth of strategic alliances and joint ventures. We will then turn to examine three specific aspects, reviewing globalization economically, politically and culturally. Finally we will examine a number of issues surrounding the concept including the limitations on the spread of globalization.

Key concept 2.1 Globalization

Globalization is a process in which the world appears to be converging economically, politically and culturally. Globalization is seen by many as a fundamental change where national borders become irrelevant, a process accelerated by developments in information and communications technology. It is considered by many to be the dominant force in modern business. In economic terms, many firms are producing goods and services for global markets, using labour in various locations in the world and using global sources for raw materials and components. In the past 20 years there has been an acceleration of cultural exchange across the globe, helped, in part, by advances in travel and communications. Business and cultural globalization have been accompanied by political globalization through the activities of supranational bodies such as the United Nations (UN), World Trade Organization (WTO) and the European Union (EU). There are strong links between globalization and the multinational corporation (Key concept 2.2).

Globalization and the Business in Context model

We have already noted in the Preface to this edition and in Chapter 1 that globalization does not appear in our model of business. We have also noted that the main reason lies in the pervasive nature of globalization and its alleged impact on all areas of business activity and the context within which those activities operate.

In terms of the **environmental context**, we shall see in this chapter how globalization has affected all aspects of our model.

- The world economy is now more closely interlinked through global markets and the global organization of the production of goods and services.
- Nation states have been brought together to form alliances for trade and defence.
- A key feature of a global economy is the speed and coverage of technology transfer.
- There is evidence to suggest that labour markets have become more fluid with many more people crossing borders for work.
- There is also evidence to suggest that cultures around the world are moving more closely together both in terms of lifestyle and certain core values.

In terms of the **organizational context** the following aspects can be observed:

- Ownership patterns of organizations around the world have become more complex as a result of cross-border acquisitions and joint ventures and the creation of transnational corporations.
- We shall see that the impact of globalization is not confined to large organizations and that many changes have occurred in the small business sector.
- In many organizations new structures and cultures have emerged to respond to global changes.

In terms of **strategy**, there has been a shift in emphasis from a national competitive focus to a global focus. Global strategies have emerged in product development, the production of goods and services, distribution and the management of labour. These in turn have had a significant impact on **business activities.** For example:

- The ease of technology transfer and the increase in collaborative ventures have changed the nature of innovation.
- Operations now involve the coordinated efforts of a number of organizations across the globe.
- For most organizations marketing is by definition an international activity, with the complexities that that entails.
- Firms must devise policies for attracting, retaining and relocating staff operating internationally.
- Finance has become a global resource and accounting procedures have had to adapt to this.

However, as we shall see as this chapter unfolds, not everyone is convinced of the all-embracing impact of globalization and some are critical of its impact. Students should be aware that many issues related to globalization are contentious.

What is globalization?

Essentially, globalization is about the increased interlinking of the world's societies and their economies. Discussions about development of globalization tend to focus on two key issues.

- First there has been an increased internationalization of trade, money and ideas. This has been helped in part by the removal of historic barriers. We are now supposedly living in an increasingly 'borderless world'.
- Second the world appears to be converging culturally. At the superficial level, we watch the same television programmes and movies, and we buy the same branded goods. At a more fundamental level, there is a convergence of values, including the **liberalization** of markets, the adherence to international regulations and a global shift from collectivism to individualism (see Chapter 4 for a full explanation of these terms).

As we will see from our brief analysis of the history of globalization, the processes of internationalization, and the liberalization and convergence of markets have been around for quite a while. For several commentators, globalization represents a fundamental change in international relations at all levels. The key issue is one of geography or territory. Through telephone calls, the Internet and the electronic transfer of finance we can undertake instant transactions across many countries. Satellite television is now commonplace and is taken for granted, so that, in almost all parts of the world, we had access to live broadcasts of every game in the 2002 soccer World Cup in Japan and South Korea. What is happening is that, through developments in electronic communications and travel, the world of many people has expanded beyond their national territory. We interact with others and gain access to information across borders with relatively few barriers and state controls. Unfortunately, this widening of our horizons also means that the lack of environmental care in one country can lead to a depletion of the ozone layer and have an impact on the lives of people in a totally different country. These aspects can be the downside of global-ization.

It is these cross-border developments of all types, that have led Scholte (2000) to coin the phrase **supraterritoriality** to indicate this fundamental change in international relations and the impact of globalization on the modern world.

Some other definitions

A social process in which the constraints of geography on social and cultural arrangements recede and in which people become increasingly aware that they are receding. (*Waters, 1995, p. 3*)

A process or set of processes which embodies a transformation in the spatial organization of social relations and transactions. (*Held* et al., *1999, p. 16*)

Both the above definitions reinforce Scholte's view of supraterritoriality. The next two definitions focus on the changes that have taken place in the economy and in markets, stressing the key role played by developments in electronic communications and travel. The quotes from Castells come from his influential book, *The Rise of the Network Society*. He considers that significant changes have taken place and are attributed to information and communications technology. This has enabled people and organizations to interact and work together as never before. For example, in both manufacturing and finance, activities in different firms across the globe are linked. Dealers in the stock exchanges and finance houses of Tokyo, Hong Kong, Frankfurt, London and New York are in continuous 24-hour communication. Changes in one country have an immediate impact on others. Designers of a new car at Daimler–Chrysler can work together as a team at the same time on the same project using the same computer software, although one team is working in Germany and the other in the USA.

A global economy is something different: it is an economy with the capacity to work as a unit in real time on a planetary scale. (*Castells, 1996, p. 92*).

The globalization of markets has only been made possible in the late twentieth century by dramatic changes in transportation and communications technologies, for information, people, goods and services. (*Castells,1996, p. 96*).

Perspectives on globalization

A number of perspectives have emerged on globalization. In this section we identify three; the globalist perspective, the anti-globalization perspective and the sceptical perspective. This classification is similar to the one used by Kirkbride *et al.* (2001). They offer interesting sub-titles to the classification listed below. They are 'Globalization is here to stay' (the globalist perspective), 'It's here and we don't like it' (the anti-globalist perspective) and 'Oh no it's not it doesn't exist' (the sceptical perspective).

- **The globalist perspective.** This recognizes that **convergence** has taken place through the creation of global products, services and markets. It recognizes cultural conversion in that many people around the world share the same tastes. Global products, services and markets are served by a global integration of production, distribution and marketing. Great economies of scale are achievable and the system favours large organizations in oligopolistic markets (a few big firms dominating an industry as in automobiles, pharmaceuticals, banking and the media). The globalist perspective believes we are living in an increasingly borderless world with ever-increasing flows of goods, services, money, people and ideas. As a result, firms become global and links with their country of origin are weakened. These ideas are to be found in seminal works by such as Yip (1995). Variations within the globalist thesis exist as to the extent and rate of change and about its impact. For example, Albrow (1996) believes there is a distinct break from the past, whereas people like Giddens (1991) see the changes having strong links with the past. However, all globalists believe that a significant change has taken place, that such changes have resulted in economic growth, for many if not for all, and that the process is irreversible. The idea that we are living and working in a new age is also supported by management gurus such as Tom Peters, providing, perhaps, yet more opportunities for new book titles.

- **The anti-globalization perspective.** This perspective accepts that the above changes have occurred but that the net result is exploitative and has resulted in a widening of the gap between rich and poor nations. Large multinationals are singled out as the key exploiters. International agencies such as the **World Bank**, **World Trade Organization (WTO)** and **International Monetary Fund (IMF)** are accused of being influenced too much by the rich and powerful nations and, in making loans to Third World countries, simply saddle those countries with debts they can never repay.

- **The sceptical perspective.** A number of writers, typified by Hirst and Thompson (1999), have argued that globalization represents nothing new and is part of a trend in world economics that can be traced back several centuries. They argue that the globalists have failed to come up with a convincing model of the global economy. The sceptics question whether the changes that can be seen are really global, citing the concentration of production and investment within the advanced economies of Europe, America and Japan. They also question the concept of the borderless world, seeing large multinationals such as Mitsubishi retaining strong links with its home country (Japan). In fact, they argue that most multinationals are still identified by their country of origin and that the concept of the truly global, stateless company is rare if not non-existent.

The above perspectives may be summarized in Table 2.1.

A brief history of globalization

Michael Porter traces globalization back to the 19th century (Porter, 1990). Others go back much further, whilst most recognize that the greatest changes, if not the most significant trends, have occurred since the 1960s. We present below a brief history of influences and key developments.

- **Pre 14th century.** During this period there were great movements for political and military reasons and certain groups, such as the Romans, wielded far-reaching influence. This period was also notable for the spread of key religious ideas such as Islam, Christianity and Judaism. There were some beginnings of trade.

- **The Renaissance – 15th and 16th centuries.** This period was typified, particularly in Europe, by considerable growth in trade and the exchange of ideas.

Table 2.1	Perspectives on globalization		
	Globalist	*Anti-globalization*	*Sceptical*
	• Growth of global products, services and markets	• Agree with globalists on changes but not impact	• Globalization not new but a continuation of existing trend
	• Convergence of cultures	• Widening gap between rich and poor nations and people	• No plausible model exists of the global economy
	• Global integration of production, marketing and distribution	• International agencies serve needs of rich nations	• Changes are not global but focus on major industrial nations
	• Dominance of oligopolies	• Exploitation by big businesses	• Firms still identify with country of origin
	• Borderless world		
	• Firms no longer represent nation states		
	• Increased flows of goods, services, money and ideas		
	• All results in economic growth		

- **17th to 19th centuries.** During this period trade expanded as did the flow of people, particularly to America. Many countries, such as Britain, expanded their colonial interests to create empires. The industrialization of Europe, America and, towards the end of the 19th century, Japan, encouraged technology transfer and led to new kinds of social arrangements in terms of urban living, skills and new values. Some convergence was visible among the leading countries of the new industrial world.

- **Late 19th to mid 20th century.** The impact of industrialization spread. There was a rapid growth in tourism and nations were brought together by industrial exhibitions, the World's Fair and sporting events such as the Olympic Games and World Cup in soccer.

- **1960s to the present day.** To many this represents the key change period that has shaped the modern world and created the globalization of the globalist perspective. This is the era of the post-industrial revolution as depicted by the American sociologist, Daniel Bell of the 'Third Wave' of futurologists like Alvin Toffler. We list below a sample of the key changes, many of which are identified in Scholte (2000).

  - We take it for granted that we can make direct calls to family, friends and colleagues living and working in other continents, yet the first International Direct Dialling systems did not appear, and then only between London and Paris, until 1963.

- We can watch live sporting events from around the world almost every night, yet the first satellite television broadcast did not occur until 1967.
- Developments in fibre optics means ever increasing amounts of information can now be sent transnationally.
- We now buy global products and shop with global retailers like Benetton and Ikea.
- We can buy textbooks such as this text via the Internet.
- The Internet was used by 0 people in 1985 and by 180 million in 1998.
- It is now commonplace to produce manufactured goods through collaborative processes over several countries.
- Similar developments have been made in service industries with the establishment of international **call centres**. In both manufacturing and service industries there has been an increase in cross-border collaborations and location has become less important.
- We pay our bills across the world using credit cards and can move money across the world by electronic transfer.
- In the 1950s share trading was largely domestic. Global trading of shares is now commonplace.
- In 1968 the total investment of companies in other countries (foreign direct investment or FDI) was US$68 billion. In 1996 the figure was US$3200 billion.
- International air travel was made by 25 million people in 1950 and by 400 million in 1998.
- Receipts by airlines for international travel rose from US$19 billion in 1970 to US$389 billion in 1996.

The causes and drivers of globalization

Linked to the historical development of globalization, we can identify a number of causal factors and driving forces. These are identified below.

- **The importance of rational knowledge.** In the 19th century the primacy of **rational knowledge** emerged and influenced most cultures. Rational knowledge emphasizes knowledge derived from scientific, objective methods and sees the importance of knowledge to solving problems and controlling our lives and environment. Knowledge related to science and technology became especially important.
- **Capitalism.** The developments in capitalism that have had the greatest impact on globalization were charted by Marx. Capitalism is concerned with **accumulation.** In a competitive capitalist system firms must increase the scale of production in order to continue to accumulate profit. This leads inevitably to them seeking new markets as national markets become too small to fulfil their needs. Capitalism is also concerned with **commodification**; this involves broadening the scale of consumption. New products and services must be developed to contribute to the process of accumulation. This often results in the opportunity to make money in ways previously not considered, as in selling information via WAP (wireless application protocol) mobile phones or from telephone chat lines. As a result of these processes, firms have sought to develop new products and services and to increase sales volume by seeking global markets. Through global production and

global markets, firms are able to achieve economies of scale and move costs to where they are cheapest, e.g. manufacture or establish call centres in low-wage countries.

- **Costs.** In the need to accumulate and to remain in business in an increasingly competitive world economy, attention to costs has become paramount. Global sales mean that economies of scale in production can be achieved. Global sourcing means that raw materials, components, labour and finance can be accessed from anywhere in the world and, often, price is the key driver. The ever-present need to develop new products increases the cost. Particularly in scientifically and technologically complex industries such as cars and pharmaceuticals the cost of R&D (research and development) has risen disproportionally to other costs. Competition has driven firms to bring out new products at more frequent intervals as product life-cycles are shortened. The net result of these developments is that most national markets are too small to achieve a return on investment and global markets and operations become a necessity.

- **Technological innovations.** A world economy that is networked electronically is only possible through developments in transport, particularly air travel, communications and data processing. The developments in computer technology and the falling costs of information storage, transmission and processing are particularly significant here. Such innovations in transport and communications have facilitated the easier movement and increased flows of people, goods, money and ideas.

- **Regulations.** A networked world economy has been made that much easier to achieve by the agreement on global standards. Standardization can be seen in such fields as computer systems, civil aviation and intellectual property rights. The **role of governments** has been crucial in the promotion of standardization and integration. Global and regional organizations such as the UN, WTO, EU, North American Free Trade Association (NAFTA) and the Association of South East Asian Nations (ASEAN) have contributed to the standardization process as well as being products of globalization and integration.

- **Multinational corporations.** Multinational companies are like regional and global organizations, both products and drivers of globalization. **Multinational corporations (MNCs)** are the product of global expansion. They have also contributed towards the diffusion of technology and ideas and the convergence of processes and management practices. A key feature of MNCs in the last 20 years has been the increase in the number of joint ventures and strategic alliances, which have resulted in yet greater integration. We examine the role of multinationals and alliances in more detail in the next two sections. In particular we will focus on the changing role of the **multinational enterprise (MNE)** and the emergence of the concept of the transnational corporation.

The multinational and transnational corporation

We have already noted that an important aspect of globalization has been the market dominance of the multinational corporation. In this section we will explore the characteristics and activities of MNCs. We also examine what some commentators see as the transformation of the traditional MNC into the **transnational corporation (TNC)**, a key organizational form in the development of globalization. However, we use the generic term MNC, despite the fact that this term has different meanings to different writers. We shall attempt to clarify those differences within this section.

Trade and finance have always been international and there are many interesting examples of early multinationals. Kikkoman, the Japanese company manufacturing soy sauce, established a factory in Denver, USA in the 1890s to supply the Chinese who were working on the expanding USA rail network. The British American Tobacco Corporation had established itself in China by 1914 and employed 25 000 Chinese workers by 1920. The company invested in cinemas and the film industry in China in the 1920s, not only to sell cigarettes and tobacco at cinema outlets but also to feature cigarette smoking in all their films to promote sales (Jones, 1996). It was not until the post-war period that the large American conglomerate with its divisionalized structure was attracted to expanding European markets. While Europe initially provided an open door to American investment, later protectionist policies, set up by the then European Economic Community (EEC), accelerated the growth of American subsidiaries in Europe. Japanese firms have also invested in both Europe and the USA for the same reasons.

Key concept 2.2 The multinational corporation

A multinational firm is one that operates and is managed from bases in a number of different countries. While small firms can and do operate multinationally, most multinationals are large corporations with diverse interests coordinated by a centrally planned global strategy. Many multinationals tend to compete in oligopolistic markets. Multinational growth was originally associated with firms from the USA and Europe, although there has been a significant growth in multinational activity from firms in Asia, notably from Japan.

Characteristics of the multinational corporation

A multinational may be identified by the following characteristics:

- MNCs have their headquarters and operations in one country and operations in one or more other countries. A true MNC has FDI, including overseas operations and a substantial management presence overseas.
- MNCs tend to draw upon a large pool of shared resources.
- Generally, the various operations tend to be linked by an overall strategic plan.
- Many MNCs tend to be large and operate in oligopolistic industry structures, e.g automobiles, banking, insurance, oil, pharmaceuticals, etc.

While they tend to be highly diversified, the multinational tends to concentrate in oligopolistic industries, those dominated by a few large companies, where the general pattern of competition is through expensive product development and expensive promotional strategies. The multinational corporation is able to draw upon a worldwide pool of skilled labour and exploit the advantages of centralized control and a centralized research and development function. Business empires are thus based around a centrally planned global strategy. As a result of the economic and political dominance of multinationals they have been viewed as a key device in the diffusion of management ideas and methods. Developments in transportation and electronic communications have greatly enhanced the MNCs capability for the control of global operations.

A number of changes have been charted in the development of multinationals. The USA is still dominant in terms of the number of firms but has been joined by the expansion of the Japanese and European multinational. Indeed, 86 per cent of the world's largest 500 MNCs originate from the USA, the EU or Japan. As Table 2.2 shows, the large Japanese conglomerates dominate in terms of value of sales.

MNCs and the global economy

The multinational has had a significant impact on national economies in a variety of ways. Many multinational companies are very large indeed, controlling much of global production, global resources and global money flows. Table 2.2 shows that if we equate GDP with sales, then 10 of the largest 40 economic entities are companies (indeed this becomes 20 of the largest 60 and 51 of the largest 100). If the list included measures of market capitalization, then Microsoft would feature at US$200 billion and would be the largest company in the world today. Such tables raise a number of issues about the relative power of corporations and nation states and the impact that the former can have on the latter. Some commentators have noted that whilst, in most cases, governments are accountable to their electorate, multinationals are accountable, if at all, to only their most powerful global shareholders.

Table 2.2	The world's top 40 economic entities in 1995	
	Country listed by GDP	Company listed by sales value US$ bn
1	USA	7100
2	Japan	4964
3	Germany	2252
4	France	1451
5	United Kingdom	1095
6	Italy	1088
7	China	745
8	Brazil	580
9	Canada	574
10	Spain	534
11	South Korea	435
12	Netherlands	371
13	Australia	338
14	Russia	332
15	India	320
16	Mexico	305

▶

17	Switzerland	286
18	Argentina	278
19	Taiwan	260
20	Belgium	251
21	Austria	217
22	Sweden	210
23	Indonesia	190
24	Mitsubishi (Japan)	184
25	Mitsui (Japan)	181
26	Itochu (Japan)	169
27	Turkey	169
28	General Motors (USA)	169
29	Sumitomo (Japan)	168
30	Marubeni (Japan)	161
31	Thailand	160
32	Denmark	156
33	Hong Kong	142
34	Ford Motor (USA)	137
35	Norway	136
36	Saudi Arabia	134
37	South Africa	131
38	Toyota (Japan)	111
39	Exxon (USA)	110
40	Royal Dutch /Shell (Netherlands/UK)	110

Source: *Observer*, 8 March, 1998

However, to some like Legrain (2002), such tables are highly misleading. He believes that a comparison of GDP and sales revenue is not comparing like with like and argues that a better representation of a firm's worth is its value added: the difference between the value of its sales and the cost of its inputs. Under this measure he calculates that only 2 companies would feature in the top 50 and only 37 in the top 100, with the USA company Wal-Mart heading the corporate list. Furthermore, he argues that nation states have far more power than individual companies, in that they can impose taxes, go to war, and make laws which affect the lives of every citizen. We examine the role of the state in more detail in the next chapter.

Rationale for the development of MNCs

A number of reasons can be given for the growth of the number of MNCs in the world economy. Many of these factors operate together. For example the growth of multinational activity in China, through joint ventures, is both a product of access to a potentially large market and to cheap labour. The following points identify the main reasons.

- Expansion overseas enables firms to protect themselves against the cyclical problems of national economies. The early expansion of USA firms, such as Esso and GM, overseas was a product of a home market that was both in recession and saturated.

- The traditional motivation for multinational growth was associated with accessing both the supply of raw materials and new markets. Through vertical integration and the acquisition of firms further down the supply chain, key supplies could be secured for both domestic and overseas operations. The growing investments in process and product technologies meant that home markets were too small and overseas expansion was imperative to exploit **economies of scale**. Large markets are particularly attractive, hence the amount of FDI in the USA and the EU.

- MNC expansion particularly through mergers, acquisitions and joint ventures was also seen as protection against competition. Such collaborations gave access to both expanded markets and economies of scale.

- Indeed, any expansion offers the potential for the exploitation of economies of scale.

- A major motivation was the need to reduce costs. Locations were favoured that gave access not only to low-cost materials, but also low-cost labour, rents and low rates of corporate taxation. The expansion of multinational manufacturers in Thailand and Indonesia has been to transfer labour-intensive activities to low-cost labour markets. Part of the attractiveness of Singapore to overseas firms was the availability of government-built factory shells, government rent subsidies and favourable tax rates.

- Overseas location is often motivated by the need to overcome import controls and tariff barriers. Under EU law, firms operating within an EU country, irrespective of their origin, are classed as an EU producer and therefore not subject to import restrictions. This resulted in large numbers of USA and Japanese firms locating operations within the EU.

- The expansion of multinationals has been facilitated by changes in organizational structure to assist control. These have included such structural developments as the creation of divisions and profit centres and by developments in transport and electronic communications.

From multinational to transnational

In the last 10 years or so, writers have used the term transnational corporation (TNC) rather than MNC to reflect the changes brought about by globalization.

Bartlett and Ghoshal (1995) see the transnational as part of a development involving a number of stages as indicated below:

- The **international** stage is typified by a focus on a home base and the growth of exports.

- In the **multinational** stage export markets continue to grow and the firm establishes operations outside the home country. According to Bartlett and Ghoshal (1995), at this stage the multinational is really a series of multi-domestic companies, with some variation in both product and operations from country to country.

- The **global** stage is typified by increased competition and the expansion of operations. The need arises for an integrative global strategy. Costs become the major consideration and operations are switched to locations offering cost advantages, e.g. low-cost labour markets or other advantages. At the global stage the whole world is treated as a single market as the size and control of markets becomes important. Companies such as Coca Cola, Sony and McDonald's typify this stage in development.

● When the **transnational corporation** stage is reached a number of factors emerge:

 – Firms are neither centralized nor decentralized but gain competitive advantage from both the integration of global resources to achieve economies of scale and from flexibility and the capability to respond to local market needs, i.e. operating both globally and locally.

 – Cross-border operation becomes a necessity for survival as high-volume sales become essential to recover investment costs, particularly those associated with shorter product life-cycles.

 – The strategies move away from the focus on a single issue of market, supply or cost to embrace a mixture of motives. Low-cost operation in cheap labour economies may be pursued for mass-market goods, whereas accessing skill and know-how may be more significant with more complex, high value-added products. LG, the Korean electronics firm, uses South-East Asian locations for its mass-market products, such as televisions and video recorders. The same firm uses its USA operations, and the experience of its subsidiaries, such as Zenith, to develop more advanced products. In another vein, high cost start-up operations in such countries as China can be offset by more profitable ventures elsewhere.

 – Diffusion of R&D across partner companies becomes important.

 – Transnational companies are associated with a corresponding growth in joint ventures and alliances. These enable the transnational corporation to share costs, access new markets, pool expertise and knowledge, and create synergies (more detail is provided in the section on joint ventures later in this chapter). In this way transnational companies create highly interdependent networks of resources.

 – Size, control and cost become less important and the key strategic and structural issues are flexibility, responsiveness, innovation, speed and integration. Different types of organization are created. Barriers are broken down vertically through the reduction in the layers of management and a reduction in the importance of hierarchies. Barriers are also broken down horizontally through the integration of suppliers and distributors.

 – A transnational mentality emerges based around a corporate rather than a national culture.

Key concept 2.3 The transnational corporation

The growth of the global economy has resulted in many multinationals becoming truly international businesses, having weakened ties with their country of origin. Some writers have referred to such firms as transnational corporations. A transnational integrates global resources to achieve economies of scale while having the capability of responding to local markets. Flexibility, responsiveness and innovation replace control and cost as primary strategic objectives.

Not everyone is happy with a distinction between a multinational and a transnational corporation. Bartlett and Ghoshal (1995) add to the confusion by using the term 'multinational' as a stage in the development of the transnational company. A better term for Stage 2 may be multi-domestic. Stages 2–4 of the model may then be reviewed as depicting different forms of multinational corporation. Figure 2.1 summarizes the differences between these organization types and identifies the differences as a function of efficiency, competition and responsiveness.

There are some who question whether the transnational has emerged as defined by Bartlett and Ghoshal (1995). In a study by Hu (1996), few examples were found of truly transnational companies. He argued that most so-called transnationals operate from a central base in their country of origin and they are, in most cases, owned, controlled and managed by home-country nationals. He further argues that only bi-national firms, such as Shell and Unilever, can be considered truly global. This represents a cautious view, which may be challenged by the changes that have taken place in the automotive industry in the last 10 years, as seen in the case presented in Chapter 1. Some European car companies, such as Renault and Daimler have major stakes in Japanese and USA firms and, in the case of Renault, have placed a CEO in charge of Nissan. However, the case of Daimler's merger with Chrysler may well illustrate Hu's point, in that there is increasing evidence that the USA operations of Chrysler are being controlled by Daimler in Germany.

MNCs and the Third World

Much has been written about the impact of the multinational corporation on the economy of Third-World countries (for example, Harrison, 1981). There has been a shift in operations to low-cost countries with the subsequent impact that non-multinational companies are finding it increasingly difficult to compete. While involvement in the Third World is

Figure 2.1

Differences between types of multinational operation

Increasing emphasis on responding to local needs

Multi-domestic company
- Production in a number of overseas operations
- Products geared towards local markets

Transnational company
- Mix of centralization and decentralization
- Mixed motives and strategies
- Diffusion of ideas via joint ventures and R&D
- Cross-border mentality built around corporate identity

International company
- Manufacture at a home base
- Growth of exports

Global company
- Cost reduction a priority
- Global strategy to achieve lower costs – use of low-cost locations
- Global products for global markets

Increasing emphasis on creating efficiencies on a global scale/increasing competition

Source: Adapted from Bartlett and Ghoshal (1995)

done with the cooperation of host governments, leads to an inflow of capital, provides local employment and improves the balance of payments, there are considerable problems involved. These include the exploitation of natural resources, allegations of bribery and corruption, the expatriation of profits, price speculation, the tendency of multinationals to move both capital and financial assets to gain the most favourable tax and exchange rate advantages and so on. In general, Third-World economies become dominated by companies whose primary aim is the maximization of profit, when those countries might benefit more from a planned, local approach to development. Such issues relate to the accountability of multinational firms and offer support to the anti-globalization perspective presented earlier in this chapter.

Strategic alliances and joint ventures

In all types of business, in most parts of the world, there is a long history of firms working together to achieve mutual advantages; however, the increase in alliances and joint ventures has been a major phenomenon of the business world in the last 10 years. The phenomenon is a product of globalization, increased competition, the attractiveness of emerging markets in developing nations and, for advanced economies, declining growth rates and the increasing cost of home operations, particularly in terms of labour and R&D.

Strategic alliances and joint ventures are essentially strategic options, where there is some advantage in working in collaboration with another partner rather than going it alone. Such collaborations may be a faster and more effective way for new market entry, a more cost-effective means of new product development or distribution, or simply a means of survival. Alliances and joint ventures represent less radical forms of collaboration than are found in mergers or acquisitions. A merger or an acquisition may not be wanted by any of the parties or they would be too costly. In some cases the kind of ownership patterns involved in a merger or acquisition would be politically difficult, as was the situation, until recently, in India and as currently operates in China.

The major difference between a strategic alliance and a joint venture is usually the depth of the contractual relationship. **Joint ventures** generally involve an element of shared ownership or involve fairly restrictive contractual obligations as with licensing and franchise agreements. In terms of ownership patterns a number of variations are possible as listed below:

- joint ownership with control by one party
- joint ownership with shared control
- majority/minority ownership with variations in control
- a third company owned and/or controlled by two or more other companies.

A **strategic alliance** occurs when two companies agree to cooperate on a specific venture or have an arrangement to share facilities. Contractual arrangements can and do exist but, generally, they are less restrictive than those found under licensing or franchise agreements. In the manufacturing industry, a pattern is emerging where major manufacturers such as Daimler Benz establish alliances with their major suppliers. At the main Mercedes factory, near Stuttgart, the supplier of exhaust systems (Eberspächer) and of tyres (Continental) have established operations next to the main assembly plant, and their production plans are tied in with those of Mercedes. The Eberspächer case in Chapter 10 illustrates this in more detail. In the airline industry a number of national carriers have joined together to form alliances. Two of the largest, the Star Alliance and the One World Alliance are identified in Table 2.3.

Such alliances between airlines, as those illustrated in Table 2.3, offer customers a number of advantages in the form of single booking, ticketing and baggage handling across different routes and airlines within the same alliance. For alliance partners there are potential cost savings via shared ticketing, check-in facilities, baggage handling and customer interaction, with further savings possible in such areas as maintenance.

The remainder of this section will focus on **joint ventures**, although many of the issues raised are also applicable to strategic alliances.

The main reasons for the growth of joint ventures

These can be identified as follows:

- **Survival and growth in the face of increased global competition.** This has been a major factor in the restructuring of the automobile industry in both Europe and the

---

Key concept 2.4   Joint ventures

Joint ventures are forms of collaboration between different firms to achieve specific strategic objectives such as technology transfer, new market entry or new product development. Joint ventures usually involve some element of shared ownership, as in the case of two firms collaborating to establish a new company. Many joint ventures involve firms from different countries and these are sometimes referred to as international joint ventures or IJVs.

Table 2.3

Example of alliances in the airline industry

Star Alliance	One World Alliance
Air Canada	Aer Lingus
Air New Zealand	American Airlines
ANA	British Airlines
Austrian Airlines	Cathay Pacific
British Midland	Finnair
Lauda Air	Iberia
Lufthansa	Lan Chile
Mexicana	Quantas
SAS	
Singapore Airlines	
Thai International	
Tyrolean	
United Airlines	
Varig	

USA, in which major firms have not only assimilated smaller companies, e.g. Ford has bought Jaguar and Volvo, but where competitors work together on joint projects, e.g. Ford and Volkswagen creating a new people carrier, built through a joint venture in Portugal. Sometimes the collaborations cross continental boundaries as between Ford and Mazda and Renault and Nissan. Across all types of industry, a joint venture may be the only effective way for some small firms to compete and survive.

- **Market growth and new market entry.** A joint venture can extend product distribution networks into new areas. All partners may gain access to a bigger market. This is especially true with IJVs. In some cases, a joint venture is a political necessity to gain entry into certain markets, such as China. In India, until relatively recently, foreign firms could only operate in a joint venture in the country where the Indian partner held the majority share. That restriction has now been lifted, reflecting the growing influence of globalization on joint venture activity and the need for more flexible arrangements. As a consequence there has been a corresponding growth in FDI in India.

- **Technology transfer** is a key motivator behind many joint ventures, particularly for firms in transitional and emerging economies. In China, the key exchange in many IJVs between Chinese firms and those from the West or Japan is the transfer of technology to the Chinese firm in return for market entry. This happened in the case of the joint venture between Chrysler and the Beijing Auto Works to manufacture the Jeep.

- **Access to specific core competencies**. An important strand in the development of the theory of strategic management in recent years is the belief that specific knowledge, skills and technology can be harnessed to differentiate a firm from its competitors and give it competitive advantage. This is referred to as a core competence and will be discussed further in Chapter 7 in our discussion of strategic issues. A core competence could reside in a specific area of knowledge and expertise, a specific technology or operating system or even an effective system of customer care. Through joint ventures, a firm may acquire core competencies or exchange complementary core competencies to benefit both parties. In this way a specialist credit insurer may work together on a project with a specialist surety firm, each contributing their knowledge and skills.

- **Synergy** is where an outcome is achieved by an activity that is greater than the sum of its constituent parts. In a joint venture the pooling of knowledge, skills and technology may achieve such synergy. This is particularly important as many projects and even industries (think of biotechnology) are interdisciplinary by nature. New solutions can also be created, for example to reduce the time taken to develop new products, vital in an increasingly competitive market.

- **Cost reduction** is the aim of many joint ventures. Through the pooling of both market demand and resource supply two or more firms can achieve economies of scale across global operations. In the case of some IJVs, high volume, low-tech work can be concentrated in low labour cost regions. Better deals can be struck through bulk purchasing from suppliers. Duplicated activities can be consolidated with a saving on labour, buildings costs and overheads.

- **Reduced risk** is achieved by sharing the risk between two or more partners. The development of the airbus is the result of a joint venture between the aerospace industries of the UK, France and Germany, while Concorde was the joint project of the French and British industries. In both these cases, the development of the project comprised high front-end expenditure and difficult market entry so that the industry of no one country alone was prepared to accept the risk.

- **Increased control of the supply chain** may be achieved by joint ventures between manufacturers of goods and services and their suppliers and distributors. In this way News Corporation around the world operates together with a part-owned partner, TNT, to distribute its newspapers.

- **Create tailored local situations.** A firm operating internationally may gain distinctive competence through partnership with a local firm to offer specific goods and services to meet the needs of local markets, to work more effectively with local labour or to increase market share through knowledge of the market.

In most joint ventures it is not one factor that predominates but a combination of the above. In the case of Airbus Industrie, a collaboration between the UK, France and Germany which started in 1970, a number of factors were at work. A joint venture reduced entry costs for the companies involved in a notoriously expensive business. The partners were supported by their respective governments, initially in a move to compete on a global scale with USA firms, Boeing and McDonnell Douglas. In addition, there was a clear demand from the major European Airlines for a new type of mid-range carrier (Lyons, 1991).

However, many commentators believe that the rationale for joint ventures has changed. In the 1970s and 1980s the key motivation was one of control – of markets, key resources, the supply chain and even forming alliances with competitors to discover and head off their initiatives. The classic model that developed in transitional and emerging markets was that where a multinational from an advanced economy would form a joint venture with a local firm and gain market entry in return for limited technology transfer. In this way, Chrysler formed a partnership with the Beijing auto works to create the Beijing Jeep Corporation. Through the joint venture, Chrysler gained entry to the Chinese market but carefully controlled the extent of the technology transfer. The type of Jeep built in China was an older model no longer made in the USA.

While this type of relationship continues to exist there emerged in the 1990s a new rationale. Control and competition were replaced by collaboration. This was sought with customers, suppliers, governments and even competitors as part of the development of global strategies.

Problems and issues with joint ventures

The Beijing Jeep case (Case 2.1) illustrates many of the key issues involved in a joint venture between an established western firm (in this case, Chrysler from the USA) and a firm from a less developed but changing economy. Such economies are often referred to as transitional, a concept we deal with in Chapter 3. In their study of international joint ventures in Eastern Europe, usually involving firms from an advanced industrial country, Rondinelli and Black (2000) found there to be both convergent and divergent interests at work. The incoming multinationals enjoyed the following advantages:

- increased profits

- low risks
- market access
- cheap labour costs
- extension of the product life-cycle.

The former state owned enterprise in Eastern Europe also enjoyed a number of advantages, including:

- increased profits
- raised productivity
- access to new technology and know-how
- new products
- access to export markets.

They also noted substantial gains for East European governments in the form of reduced subsidies, tax income and assistance in the restructuring of the economy. However, they also noted significant problems. These were:

- job cuts
- conflicting goals, especially over technology transfer
- problems over power and control
- limitations resulting from a less well-developed infrastructure.

Many of these problems are also apparent in the Beijing Jeep case.

A more generic approach to evaluating joint ventures has been developed by Medcof (1997). He uses the model of the '4 Cs' based on the concepts of capability, compatibility, commitment and control. These and other issues are dealt with below.

- Many joint ventures create **organizational complexities**, which can increase costs. Project teams and coordinating committees have to be set up. Staff have to be seconded from their regular roles and much time can be taken up in meetings and travelling. The chief executives of Renault and Volvo believed that a merger would be cheaper than a joint venture in the long term as it would cut out most of the joint committees and cut down on the number of meetings.

- The success of any joint venture is dependent upon a **strategic fit** between the parties concerned. Joint ventures are likely to be more successful where the partner firms offer complementary core competencies. For many years Renault and Volvo were engaged in a joint venture built on joint technical development and shared distribution. The joint venture was a success, largely because the strengths of each company were complementary. Volvo was strong in large cars, Renault in small ones, Volvo was strong in North America, while Renault had a larger market share in South America. However, attempts to turn the partnership into a full-scale merger failed due to issues of cultural compatibility and control (see below).

- **Capability** is concerned with what each of the parties brings to the joint venture and is about the expectations each has of the other. In the case of GM and Daewoo in South Korea, GM managers felt that the alliance was weakened by the Koreans' lack of quality capability. In the Beijing Jeep Corporation, there were numerous project delays due to the inability of local suppliers to produce on time and to the required quality. The service and spare parts industry was relatively undeveloped in China. Chrysler officials accused the Chinese of poor labour discipline and low productivity, while Chrysler management, with one exception, were unable to speak Mandarin Chinese.

- Problems of **compatibility** arise in working together and often do not emerge until the implementation phase. Such problems can arise as a result of differences in culture, management style and personality and in administrative and accounting procedures. Datta (1988) found that social and cultural issues are the ones most often overlooked by managers when establishing joint ventures. A major difficulty in establishing joint ventures between universities, involving the exchange of students, occurs around differences in teaching style, differences in the academic calendar and different requirements for assessment. With Beijing Jeep there were problems arising from differences between the USA and Chinese accounting systems and the large pay of the Americans compared to the local managers became a source of resentment for the locals. The biggest problem for Chrysler, however, lay in their frustrations arising from the highly political nature of doing business in China. The political problems involved dealing with a cumbersome bureaucracy, having to accept local suppliers recommended by local government and the increasing involvement of national government in the post-Tianamen Square period.

- **Commitment** is the extent to which the partners are willing to invest resources and effort on a continuing basis, more especially when problems arise either in fulfilling expected objectives or between the partners themselves. Many alliances fail through the lack of staying power.

- A number of problems can arise out of issues of **control**. Where one partner is dominant, then the weaker partner may have its core competences actually weakened. In a study of Japanese joint ventures with USA companies, Lei (1989) found that almost invariably the Japanese company was the dominant partner and there was a widespread fear (sometimes well-founded but sometimes not) that Japanese firms would take over the critical skills of the USA partner and give little in return. One of the reasons for failure in the Renault–Volvo case was the belief among the Swedes that French management and strategies would predominate in the new company. Control becomes even more of an issue when joint ventures involve more than two partners.

- There is also the problem of **measuring performance outcomes**. Brouthers *et al.* (1997) argue that this is far from simple, since it depends on the rationale behind the joint venture. For example, financial criteria alone would be inappropriate if the reason for the joint venture were either technology transfer or expanding market share. They cite the case of the alliance between the airlines KLM (Holland) and Northwest (USA). The alliance would appear to be successful on financial grounds, yet, initially, the senior managers encountered several difficulties in working together. Datta (1988) argues that too many joint ventures are assessed only from the perspective of the dominant partner. This is especially apparent in the entry of established firms into emerging markets. In most cases there will be trade-offs. Otis Elevators (USA) established a joint venture in Tianjin, China to access a large potential market. The Chinese, however, were more concerned with gaining access to elevator technologies and foreign currency. Although it is a broad generalization, several studies have commented that the primary motivation of Western companies in joint ventures is cost reduction, while that of Eastern companies lies in knowledge acquisition. The **evidence on performance** is very mixed. Successful alliances have been shown to outperform single businesses (Medcof, 1997), but against this there are a large number of failed joint ventures and alliances. Peters and Waterman (1982) advise strongly that managers should 'stick to the knitting' by focusing on core competencies rather than by trying to diversify into too many areas at the same time.

From the above points it can also be seen that attention to such issues as strategic fit, compatibility, capability, commitment and control will do much to ensure the success of a joint venture. It is for this reason that many writers focus on the importance of careful analysis in partner selection.

From the drivers and causal factors and our discussion of multinationals, joint ventures and alliances, we can identify three arenas of globalization: the economy, politics and culture. We deal with each one in turn.

| Case 2.1 | **Beijing Jeep** |

The Beijing Jeep Corporation is a joint venture between the Beijing Automotive Industry Company (BAIC), formerly the Beijing Auto Works, and Daimler–Chrysler. The joint venture was originally established between the then Beijing Auto Works and the American Motor Corporation (AMC) in 1983 and production of the jeep began in 1984. AMC was one of the smaller motor manufacturers in the USA and the company was bought by Chrysler in 1987. The jeep was the flagship product of AMC. In 1999, Chrysler merged with Daimler Benz to form Daimler–Chrysler. Responsibility for the joint venture in the West therefore passed from AMC to Chrysler to Daimler–Chrysler within a 12-year period. During that period the Chinese Government had taken significant steps to liberalize its economy and give more freedom for decision-making to individual managers.

In the 1980s, BAIC reported directly to the Beijing Municipal Government and was a typical state-owned Chinese company, whose production output was a function of targets set by a centrally planned economy. BAIC was established in the 1950s with backing from the former USSR and manufactured the first four-wheel drive vehicle in China based on a Soviet design, the BJ2020. However, this vehicle was far less sophisticated and less reliable than the jeep.

The joint venture between BAIC and AMC established a third, independent company, the Beijing Jeep Corporation (BJC). This company was to continue its manufacture of the Soviet-designed vehicle but would now focus on the jeep: a four-wheel vehicle with a global brand and reputation. Initially BAIC owned 69 per cent of BJC and AMC 31 per cent, although the intention was that AMC would be allowed to purchase more equity with profit from the operation. By 2003, BAIC held 57.6 per cent of the company and Daimler–Chrysler, 42.4 per cent (with 10 per cent of this owned by a special investment company set up by Daimler–Chrysler). The original agreement was for 20 years with the option to renew if both parties and the Chinese government were agreeable.

◀

The original benefits to AMC passed on to Chrysler were many. The financial risk involved was minimal. The initial investment was low and, in any case, the Beijing Municipal Government contracted to pay this back as share dividend. Moreover, the Americans would be allowed to increase their stake if the company was profitable. A further financial gain for AMC/Chrysler came through the sale of kit versions of the jeep and jeep parts. AMC/Chrysler sold these to the BJC for hard currency. AMC/Chrysler therefore benefited both from the sale of the jeep made by BJC and through the sale of the parts to BJC. Since a joint venture was the only route into the Chinese market, AMC/Chrysler gained entry to an emerging market with considerable potential, particularly for the sales of four-wheel drive vehicles. AMC/Chrysler were keen to control the extent of technology transfer to the new company. The model to be produced in China was an older version of that being produced in the USA. AMC/Chrysler were therefore doing what many had done before them, notably Fiat in the USSR. They were extending the product life-cycle of an older product and its parts through its manufacture in an emerging economy. BJC would therefore offer no competition in export markets and AMC/Chrysler were not 'handing over' state-of-the-art technology to the Chinese. An additional benefit to AMC/Chysler was learning more about the Chinese market and about joint ventures generally.

There were a number of benefits for BAIC and for the Chinese economy in general. They were gaining access to Western technology not just in terms of product but in terms of manufacturing processes as well. AMC/Chrysler was contracted to assist BAIC set up a local R&D centre. The knowledge gained from the west and from R&D could be disseminated to other industries. As well as technology transfer, the Chinese were also gaining knowledge of management practices and techniques. The jeep as a global brand would have export potential, with an initial focus on other emerging economies, and the promise of hard currency earnings for the Chinese. Although initially reliant on kits and parts from the USA, the intention was to shift the emphasis to local suppliers. The joint venture was therefore important in the development of the local supply chain, involving both suppliers and distributors, to the benefit of Chinese industry generally. In general the joint venture was part of the wider process in China of learning more about the West and its business methods. It also offered the promise of expansion and job creation.

From the early days of the joint venture in the 1980s there were a number of problems.

State bureaucracy   Although BJC was set up as an autonomous company it was soon clear to AMC/Chrysler that the hand of central planning by the Chinese was evident in everything the company did. In the early days, BJC was seen by the Chinese government more as a means of controlling the flow of foreign exchange than as the potential for a successful manufacturing company. AMC/Chrysler managers were frustrated by the politics and bureaucracy of doing business in China.

Accounting systems   BJC operated with Soviet-style accounting systems that provided vital information to a centrally planned economy. However, these were inadequate for the management of a joint venture with accountability needed in the USA. There were no cash-flow statements, budget forecasts or cost accounting information, all essential parts of a USA accounting system.

Localization   The initial plan was that 80 per cent of the jeep would be manufactured locally by the end of 1990. Only half of that was achieved, the key problems being delivery times and quality. For example, there was a high initial investment in new press shop machinery, which stamped out the body shapes. However this was dependent upon using high-quality steel, which none of the local suppliers were able to deliver. The machinery lay idle until Japanese imported steel was used.

After-sales   Income derived from servicing vehicles and parts sales make a greater contribution to the profit margins of most major vehicle manufacturers than the sales of new vehicles. This was not the case at BAIC and the tradition was passed on to BJC. Chinese companies were preoccupied with meeting production targets and after-sales customer care was not a consideration. Moreover, as a manufacturer of four-wheel drive vehicles, the majority of early sales were to the state. State employees traditionally had little interest in maintenance. If something needed to be fixed it was just as easy to order a replacement vehicle.

Personnel issues   The initial joint venture employed over 4000 Chinese and six expatriate workers from the USA. There were problems of labour discipline. Productivity at BJC was only 65 per cent of that at the Chrysler jeep plant in Ohio. As China had a full-employment policy, there was a reluctance to dismiss poor performers. Also, there were a number of problems involving the expatriate workers. They were paid significantly more than their Chinese counterparts, which caused considerable resentment. Of the first 24 expatriates sent by AMC/Chrysler, only one spoke Mandarin Chinese and only three completed their full tour of duty. Many expats complained about living conditions in China and all considered it a hard posting. There were differences of cultural perception based on the concept of age. The first group of USA workers were fairly young and China was seen as an important part of their management development. The fact that they were young disappointed the Chinese, who equate youth with inexperience. As a result, Chrysler changed its policy and sent older managers close to retirement age. The Chinese preferred this, assuming that as they were older they had more experience and status. The policy also served to revitalize the careers of some Chrysler managers.

Sales and profits   Between 1984 and 1996 over half a million vehicles were built by BJC. During that period sales increased annually by an average 29 per cent and profit by an average 7 per cent. In 1996, BJC was ranked third among the top 500 foreign-invested companies in China, and the company received several honours both locally and nationally. However, from a record production of 80 000 jeeps in 1995, only 30 000 were made in 1998.

When Daimler came on the scene a year later it inherited a company with an ageing plant that produced two outdated models. These were the Jeep Super Cherokee and the BJ2020, which was still essentially based around 40-year-old Soviet technology. BJC had significant problems competing with new entrants to the four-wheel drive market in China, notably VW and GM, with the Japanese not far behind. All offered newer models than the jeep, with more modern technology and comfort and added features at competitive prices. Profits at BJC had disappeared and the company was inefficient even by Chinese standards. For example, while BJC was building five vehicles per employee per year, the VW plant at Shanghai was building 24. The labour force at BJC, which had risen to 8000 when production was soaring, had been cut back to 4000. Daimler still considered BJC to be significantly over-staffed. Daimler–Chrysler was therefore faced with a dilemma. The contract was available for renewal in 2003. The company could be used as a platform for the introduction of the Mercedes range but massive investment would be required, and some commentators predicted that BJC would be sold off.

Daimler–Chrysler went for the investment route with significant capital injection in plant, the introduction of advanced technology and establishing a brand new management team. In 2001 the cooperation between Daimler–Chrysler and BAIC was extended for a further 30-year period. The company announced that the flagship model of the jeep range, the Grand Cherokee, was to be built in Beijing. By 2003, the company made three types of jeep, the Grand Cherokee, the Super Cherokee and the Jeep 250. In addition, the BJ2020 was re-branded as the City Cruiser. Daimler–Chrysler pledged to introduce a new model every year and planned to assist BJC extend its sales and service network from 11 provinces in 2001 to cover all 23 provinces in China.

Questions

1 What were the main reasons for the joint venture between AMC/Chrysler and BAIC, formerly the Beijing Auto Works?

2 Using Medcof's model of strategic fit, capability, compatibility, commitment and control, assess the problems and issues encountered by this joint venture.

3 Assess the dilemma facing Daimler–Chrysler in 1999. What opportunities and threats do you foresee for the current management of BJC?

Sources: Aiello, 1991; http://www.beijingjeep.com; *Wards Autoworld*, October 1999; http://fpeng.peopledaily.com.cn; *Automotive Intelligence*, September 2001; http://www.autointell-new.com

Economic and production aspects of globalization

The emergence of global competition, markets and globally organized production systems have had a radical effect upon management strategies and business behaviour.

Global markets have been created in consumer goods from CDs to tourism. The globalization of markets, referred to in a seminal article by Levitt (1983), has been supported by global branding and global advertising campaigns and the growth in global retailers such as Ikea. In addition to consumer goods, financial goods are also traded globally, including foreign exchange, shares and insurance. To meet the expansion of global trade in the financial sector, new stock exchanges have emerged around the world. Flows of capital now account for the majority of cross-border transactions. Financial markets around the world are linked and work together in real time. The availability of information across the world is instantaneous. Such networked financial markets have been held responsible for the crash that affected many Asian economies in 1997. The rapid economic growth of many Asian economies attracted considerable overseas investment of various kinds. At the first hint of trouble many of those investors withdrew. This was apparent to all in a networked information system and others followed. Most recently, we have seen global markets emerge for communication and information products such as mobile phones alongside new forms of product, where profit is derived from telephone calls, WAP systems and logging onto the Internet.

Globally organized production systems have been established to integrate production across many countries. This is now a common feature in many manufacturing industries. In the automobile industry, cars are now assembled using components from several countries. A UK citizen buying a Ford car is buying the product of an American multinational corporation, that could well have been made in Germany by a *Gastarbeiter* from Turkey and Italy, fitting spark plugs from the Nippondenso corporation in Japan – but spark plugs which were made in the Philippines. A company such as Nike manufactures trainers in South Korean firms located in Indonesia with components shipped from China, an operation financed by the Japanese. Even smaller firms operate on a global scale. The UK shoe manufacturer Loake obtains its leather from France, which it sends to Chennai in India for tanning and dyeing and where the uppers of the shoes are made. These products from India are transported back to the UK where they are assembled with the base of the shoe made in the UK. Such global production extends to the service industry. Globally interlinked firms operate in such areas as accounting (e.g. PricewaterhouseCoopers), and consulting (e.g. McKinsey). The ticketing for British Airways and Lufthansa is done in India. In many industries, call centres are located far from the company's country of origin. Many of these developments are a result of the need to access materials, skills and labour. The location of many manufacturing plants and service centres is based on the access of a cheap labour market. In this way **labour** has become a global resource, particularly in the textile, automobile and electronics industries.

Global production systems have created new forms of organization including offshore production centres, mergers and acquisitions, joint ventures and strategic alliances.

For some writers, notably Robert Reich (1993), there has been a change over the last 25 years in which multinationals have moved from being seen as representatives of their country of origin to being, in effect, independent global players. Under this system, exports are superseded by inward investment as measures of a nation's economic success. However, not all writers see a reduced role for the nation state. Michael Porter (1990), while acknowledging the general principles of globalization, argues that in the development of national economies, growth is a function of a set of competitive conditions which result in clusters of successful firms operating in the same industry and reinforced by the growth of associated industries as suppliers to the major firms. He cites the car industry in the USA, the chemical industry in Germany and the electronics industry in Japan as examples. It is undoubtedly true that economic development in a particular country is accompanied by a concentration of like firms in a particular area such as the computer industry around 'Silicon Valley' in California and financial services in Frankfurt and London.

Political aspects of globalization

Since the end of the Second World War a large number of **supranational** and regional organizations have been formed. Some, like the North Atlantic Treaty Organization (NATO), have defence as their primary concern. The EU was formed with the objective of uniting European countries in free-market trade thus avoiding the divisions that occurred as a result of the war. Other trading blocs were formed, such a NAFTA. At global level, the greatest activity is attributed to the UN and its many specialist arms and to the WTO (see the Case in Chapter 3) and the World Bank. Outside these structures, there are forums for politicians of the major economies of the world to come together (the G7 – Group of Seven – summits and meetings) and set agendas to control world economic policy.

The globalists argue that such changes have affected the way we are governed and that nation states have lost their sovereignty and are subsumed within regional and supra-national structures. People in the UK are subject to laws passed in Brussels by the EU and in many countries in Europe national currencies have been abolished in favour of the *euro*. The sceptics rebuff such views, maintaining that nation states still hold considerable power, and that some, such as the USA, extend that power outside their territorial borders. Whichever side of the debate is taken there have been observable changes in the way countries are governed. While the majority of decisions are still made by national governments, the influence of supranational bodies is present. However, some commentators have noted that in many countries in the world, there has been a decentralization of decision-making to more local levels.

Cultural aspects of globalization

Cultural convergence takes a number of different forms. English has maintained its position as a global language and is the working language in many global organizations. It is argued that a global consciousness has emerged through increased travel, television and identification with global causes such as feminism and response to disasters. The mass media is highly oligopolistic and controls what we read in newspapers and see on television across the world. By the mid-1990s Rupert Murdoch's News Corporation was a large global network of companies. The network embraced around 50 national newspapers in six countries, 80 regional papers in Australia, over 30 magazines around the world and a major book publisher, HarperCollins. A large number of acquisitions were made in broadcasting. News International had a controlling interest in major cable and satellite companies in the UK, USA, Latin America, Australia and Asia, including the 'Sky' and 'Star' networks (see Table 1.5). It owned 20th Century Fox Films and the TV company, Fox Broadcasting as well as control of 12 USA television stations. In Australia it owned Network 7.

With this global convergence has come a change in values. Individualism is replacing collectivism in many countries, as more traditional societies modernize. Societies built more around relationships than rules are changing to embrace universal rules (a fuller account of such changes in values is found in our discussion of culture in Chapter 4). Rules become more important in the coordination of complex global activities as doing business solely on the basis of relationships between individuals is no longer sufficient.

Issues and limitations of globalization

The supporters of globalization cite a number of **advantages**. These are:

- Increased prosperity with considerable gains made by the **newly industrialized countries (NICs)** such as the 'Asian Tigers'.

- Increased security through trade and international alliances resulting in an absence of global wars.
- A greater number of available products and services to a greater number of people.
- Global production has led to greater efficiencies.
- Access to greater information and knowledge.
- Global action on poverty and environmental problems.

The opponents claim a number of serious **disadvantages**.

- The beneficiaries are really in a minority and include those living in prosperous countries. The rest of the world has been marginalized, none more so than Africa.
- The gap between rich and poor nations has widened and globalization is accused of causing economic crashes of the sort experienced by Mexico, South-East Asia and Russia.
- There are still fierce local and regional wars.
- Globalization has brought with it new kinds of conflict. In particular global production occurs in criminal activities in such areas as money laundering and international drugs cartels (drugs is now one of the major global industries).
- Globalization is associated with ecological disasters such as the erosion of the ozone layer, the extinction of animal and plant species, global warming and specific problems such as HIV, BSE and GM (genetically modified) crops.

Whatever the perspective on the advantages and disadvantages, it is clear that currently there are a number of limitations to globalization. These may be summarized as follows:

- Many countries still limit the flow of goods and services in an attempt to protect their own markets.
- Most countries have currency and banking regulations, which limit the flow of capital.
- While we can cite the *Gastarbeiter* in Germany and, in the UK, the recruitment of Spanish and Filipino nurses, labour mobility does not occur on a great scale, restricted, in the main, by immigration laws. It is the movement of production to use labour as a global resource that is the key feature of globalization.
- Nation states still wield considerable power and most are concerned to preserve their own sovereignty.
- We can still see considerable cultural diversity among peoples of the world.
- The impact of globalization is highly uneven. Most advantages fall to Western Europe, USA and Japan. Even in the UK those advantages tend to be felt more by the young and the middle classes living in cities.

Case 2.2

Sleek International Ltd

Sleek International is a small company with its headquarters in Leyton, east London. The company was originally formed in 1989, selling beauty cosmetic products to the Afro-Caribbean community in the UK, but with an emphasis on the London market.

▶

The original company was joined by another, selling hair extension products, again with a focus on the Afro-Caribbean community. The two companies came together as one in 1998 and, although the product markets are related, the two arms of the business continued to be run separately. Stocks and packaging, although in the same building, are kept apart as is the sales function. However the company benefits from a shared management information and financial system.

The company is owned by two directors, each the original owner of the cosmetics and hair products company respectively. The directors share the same aims for the business which are:

- good quality products at a reasonable price
- wide product range
- focus on the Afro-Caribbean female market.

Sleek employs around 40 people in London, which serves as the headquarters for a growing international operation. Sleek now has offices and sales teams in France (Paris), Ghana (Accra) and South Africa (Johannesburg).

Sleek does not manufacture any of the products and operates as an intermediary in the distribution chain. It obtains its products from a number of suppliers and packages and brands them as its own. It offers a full range of cosmetic products, including lipsticks, eyeliners, creams, etc. In terms of hair products, Sleek focuses on hair extension pieces. These are made either from human or synthetic hair. Human hair is currently the preferred product, but this may change in the future. Much of the human hair comes from China. However, with a rapidly changing Chinese economy, many people have become more fashion conscious and opt for regular hairdressing rather than growing their hair for sale. In addition there are significant improvements in synthetic hair technology, making it more like the real thing. The hair extension pieces are attached to the purchaser's own hair by means of glue, weaving to braided hair or weaving to a cap. In the last case the hair is worn over the customer's own hair and can be removed like a wig.

Sleek sells its products through a variety of retailers, including high-street pharmacies and hairdressers as well as some supermarkets. The focus is on those locations where there is a large Afro-Caribbean population. Sleek's main supplier of both human and synthetic hair is a large Chinese manufacturer in Henan province in south-central China. The population of Henan have a history of selling their own hair. The company, Henan Rebecca Hair Products not only manufactures hair extensions and wigs but operates as a distributor itself and has sales operations in Nigeria.

The global market leader for Sleek's product range is Sensational. This is a USA company founded by South Koreans. Sensational dominates the large USA market and has made significant inroads into the European market as well. The current perceived advantages of Sensational are its keen pricing strategy, availability of product on demand and top-of-the-range packaging. In general, the market, especially for hair products, is highly price-sensitive as a large proportion of the market comes from lower income families. Sleek is a registered and established brand and its current share of the European market stands at around 10 per cent. The expansion of operations to France was to reach a large Afro-Caribbean population and act as a stepping point to widen coverage of the continental European market. It was also seen as a vehicle for entry into the markets of French Africa and the French Caribbean. The Ghana operation is a means of reaching a large West African population. Much is expected of the establishment of the South Africa operation. South Africa, with its emerging economy among the post-apartheid black and coloured population, offers an excellent potential for market growth. Although there is an expanding market of people concerned with their appearance, the market is still highly price sensitive. Sleek is firmly entrenched in products for the Afro-Caribbean market and, as yet, has not developed any inroads into the large Asian market, a community that dominates as an ethnic group in the east London region.

As can be seen from the table below, Sleek's sales value has risen over the last few years. The company has also enjoyed growth in profits and company value. Sales for 2001 represented a 73 per cent increase on the previous year and a massive 288 per cent rise in profits. A fall in profits for 2002 resulted from a large financial investment in a new computer-based management information system. This is part of the owner's determination to reinvest profit, which is seen as a major contributory factor in the dynamic growth of the company.

Table 2.4   Sleek International sales value (£ millions)

2000	2001	2002	2003
1.8	3.1	3.7	3.6

The owner's recognize two priorities for the future. A large drain on the current cash flow of the business is the large investment in stock, which they wish to reduce. Sleek's stock position is a function of its lack of control over the supply of products. Yet despite its large stockholding at any time, there are still occasions when Sleek is unable to fulfil market demand because of deficiencies in supply. The second priority is the improvement in packaging and presentation.

Questions

1 What aspects of globalization are illustrated by this case?

2 Do you consider Sleek to be a multinational company? How and why would you describe Sleek in terms of the classification presented in Figure 2.1?

3 What are the opportunities and threats, strengths and weaknesses of Sleek?

4 What is the contribution of small firms such as Sleek to a globally networked economy?

Summary

- Globalization is a key issue in modern business and involves the increased interlinking of the world's nations and their economies.

- It is a product of the tremendous growth in international trade and developments in information and communications technology that have broken down the barriers between nation states to create a 'borderless world'.

- Not everyone shares the same view of globalization. The globalists argue that the process is a key feature of modern life and is both advantageous and inevitable, while the anti-globalist lobby focuses on the disadvantages, particularly the undemocratic power of big business and the adverse effect on the environment. A more sceptical view sees globalization as nothing new but a continuation of an historic trend.

- Whichever perspective is taken, the impact of globalization can be seen economically, politically and culturally. We can see global markets developing and, in both manufacturing and the service industries, operations are often organized on a global basis. Nation states have combined in world organizations concerned with politics, defence and trade. There is also a view that the world is converging culturally.

- The forces behind globalization are many and varied and include developments in capitalism, the need to reduce costs and technological innovations, especially those concerned with information and electronic communications.

- A key feature of the modern global economy is the multinational enterprise and its modern form, the transnational. There would appear to be a shift in emphasis away from cost reduction and market exploitation towards more complex strategies combining global efficiencies with local responsiveness.

- Another key feature lies in the proliferation of joint venture activity. Such activity is not without its problems, which are viewed in terms of strategic fit, capability, compatibility, commitment and control.

Discussion questions

1   In what ways does globalization have an impact on either (a) your firm or a firm with which you are familiar, or (b) your college?

2   Outline the main arguments put forward by the globalists, the anti-globalization lobby and the sceptics. Which view do you support and why?

3   Examine the key drivers of globalization. Which are the most influential?

4   Assess the contribution of developments in information and communications technology to the growth of globalization.

5   To what extent can you argue the case that large corporations have become as powerful as nation states.

6   What are the main strategic objectives of multinational corporations and how have they changed over the years?

7   Contrast the main features of a transnational corporation with those of a multinational.

8   Why have joint ventures emerged as a major organizational form in a global economy? What are the main criteria for the success of a joint venture?

9   What are the main features and key strategic rationale for a global production system? Identify such a system in both manufacturing and the service industries.

10 Assess the advantages and disadvantages of globalization from the perspective of (a) a consumer and (b) a small firm.

Further reading

Two books offer a broad coverage of most aspects of globalization. Kirkbride, P. (ed.) (2001) *Globalization: The External Pressures*, John Wiley and Sons, Chichester, offers a series of readings aimed at giving the practising manager insights into the subject. Scholte, J. A. (2000), *Globalization: A Critical Introduction*, Macmillan, Basingstoke, offers a much wider perspective than Kirkbride. It deals much more with theoretical aspects but, at the same time, offers numerous excellent examples. More critical perspectives may be found in Held, D., McGrew, A., Goldblatt, D. and Perrator, J. (1999) *Global Transformations: Politics, Economics and Culture*, Polity Press, Cambridge and in Hirst, P. and Thompson, G. (1999) *Globalization in Question*, 2nd edn, Polity Press, Cambridge. A good summary of the transformation from multinational to transnational can be found in Bartlett, C. A. and Ghoshal, S. (1995) *Transnational Management; Text, Cases and Readings in Cross-border Management*, 2nd edn, Irwin, Chicago, IL, while Medcof, J. W. (1997) 'Why too many alliances end in divorce', *Long Range Planning*, **30**(5), 718–32 offers interesting insights into alliances and joint ventures. An idiosyncratic and occasionally entertaining view of globalization is found in Friedman, T. L. (2000) *The Lexus and the Olive Tree*, Anchor Books, New York.

The environment and business: economy, state, technology and labour

- Identify those aspects of the environment that most influence and are influenced by business and assess the relative importance of those influences over time.

- Illustrate and explain how the different aspects of the environment interact with each other and with business.

- Explain the main differences between Anglo-Saxon, social market, Asian and transitional models of capitalism and assess their impact on the economy and the role of the state.

- Explain the concepts of GDP, FDI and deindustrialization.

- Identify the types of state intervention and the problems associated with them

- Assess the role of the business community as a pressure group.

- Critically assess the significance of and issues related to economic and political integration in a modern global economy.

- Assess the impact of changing technology, more especially information and communications technology and e-commerce on business competitiveness and on the labour market.

- Identify changing trends in both the labour market and trade unions and assess the impact of globalization upon them.

Introduction

In Chapter 1 we introduced the model that forms the basis of our analysis of business. In this chapter and the next we focus on a major element of that model, namely the environment. We define the environment as comprising all factors that exist outside the business enterprise but that interact with it. As we pointed out in Chapter 1, all firms are, to a greater or lesser extent, constrained by the environment within which they operate but the activities of businesses themselves also change that same environment. This two-way process is an important theme throughout the book. In Chapter 2 the concept of globalization was examined and a number of different perspectives identified. Whichever perspective is taken, it is clear that changes, especially in **information and communications technology (ICT)**, have transformed business, and that all businesses, both large and small, operate in a global environment. The concept of globalization and its processes set the current scene for our discussion of the environment.

Apart from our discussion of globalization we have devoted two chapters to the business environment. Even so, the field is broad and the material is necessarily highly selective. Five key areas of the environment have been identified:

- the economy
- the role of the state
- technology
- labour
- culture.

A section is devoted to each of the first four of these topics and the whole of the next chapter to cultural issues and business. In both chapters we identify issues that illustrate the interaction between the firm and its environment. Each of the areas selected also interacts with the others, as the matrix presented in Figure 3.1 shows.

For the business manager, the environment comprises a number of key variables, which interact with the business either alone or jointly. The complexity does not end there. These interactions may occur at a number of different levels, as shown in Figure 3.2.

- At the immediate level a firm interacts with a local environment, in which plans to expand its buildings will need approval from the local council, and where its marketing and human resource strategies will be significantly influenced by firms operating in the same local market.

- A second type of interaction occurs in a national environment, influenced by such matters as law, bank interest rates, the rate of **inflation**, and national employment policies.

- Third, we have the international environment in which the firm may be affected by international money exchange rates, competition from cheap labour economies, and the regulations of supranational bodies such as the WTO and the EU. In recent years the international environment has become increasingly significant for businesses through the process of globalization as discussed in the previous chapter.

As a general rule, the ability of managers to influence their environment diminishes as they move further away from the local environment. As with all such rules, there are exceptions since the ability to influence the environment tends to increase with the size of the firm. The senior managers of the larger conglomerates can exert influences, that extend beyond national boundaries, to change international economics and politics with a significant impact on local economies and labour markets.

We will deal with each of our five variables in turn. As was stressed at the start of this chapter, each variable represents broad categories. For example, the role of the state will deal with issues pertaining to the general political environment. The next chapter includes a treatment of 'Japanese management', despite the relative decline of the Japanese economy in the 1990s. The issues of Japan and 'Japanese management' remain highly relevant for a number of reasons. Japanese methods have had a considerable influence in many areas of business, most notably in operations management. The issue of the rise of the

Figure 3.1	The interaction of environmental factors: some illustrations

			Economy	State
			The extent and direction of state intervention in the economy The power of the multinationals in influencing policy	
		State	The impact of innovation on economic growth	Technology
		State support of innovation and technical change and the specific impact on certain industries e.g. defence		
	Technology	Government policies to direct the supply of labour Legislation to regulate trade union activities	The impact of the economy on the type and levels of employment	Labour
	The impact of technical change on skills and trade union policy towards such changes			
Labour	The impact of changes in technology on society Cultural attitudes towards technology	Cultural explanations for the differences between nations regarding state intervention	The nature of the economy shaping family life e.g. agricultural vs industrial societies The influence of cultural values on the directions of economic development and specialization	Culture
Cultural influences on human resource strategies				

post-war Japanese economy provides us with insights into the relative significance of cultural, economic and political variables. Moreover, Japan represents a fascinating case study of a business community being shaped by and shaping its environment.

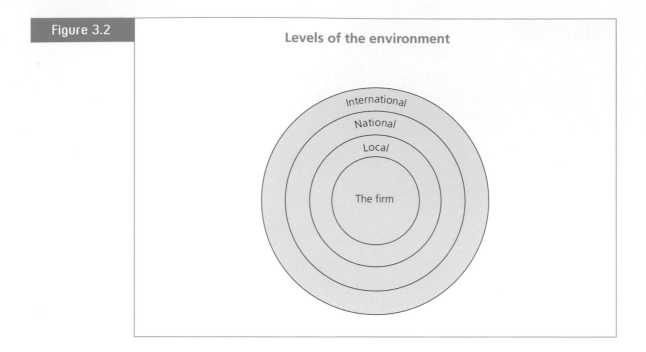

Figure 3.2

Levels of the environment

International
National
Local
The firm

The economy and business

With many aspects of our environment we are faced with the immediate problem of deciding where the environment ends and business begins and vice versa. In looking at the relationship between business and the economy this becomes particularly acute, since much of what we label as the economy is the product of business activity. By the same token, business enterprises are influenced significantly by economic developments. Figure 3.3 is an attempt to illustrate this relationship in the form of a simple model.

The economy interacts with businesses at all three levels depicted in Figure 3.2.

At the local level, immediate competitive issues related to firms operating in the same product market are the most significant. If the Virgin record store in London's Oxford Street reduces the price of all its best-selling CDs by £3.00, then the management of the large HMV store, just along the road, must determine their most appropriate strategic response. This may involve adopting the same price strategy or it may involve a more selective strategy offering larger discounts on multiple buys. In the 1960s labour shortages meant that firms actively competed for labour and often increased pay and bonus rates to attract labour from their competitors. Such conditions re-emerged in the market for IT specialists in the late 1990s. Competition can reach particularly fierce proportions and many firms prefer to cooperate rather than compete on issues like price or wage rates. In this way some businesses form themselves into cartels, which may be an effective way of controlling the immediate competitive environment and, perhaps, the wider environment too, as in influencing government policy. There are several examples of groups of local grocers being formed to buy in bulk from suppliers in an attempt to keep prices down and combat the threat posed by large supermarkets. The supermarkets themselves, while not behaving as a cartel, employ staff to keep a watch on the prices displayed by their competitors and respond accordingly.

Figure 3.3

We deal with the competitive environment in more detail in Chapter 7 and students are referred to Porter's model of competition (Figure 7.3) explained in that chapter.

In this section we will examine the model by looking at the impact of business on the economy and vice versa. This will be illustrated by examining the experience of Britain in the post-war period although, inevitably, comparisons will be drawn from other countries.

Britain, along with most capitalist countries, is an example of a mixed economy where free enterprise is entwined with state involvement through public ownership, legal regulation, and various forms of planning and direction. In the 1980s attempts were made, through government policy, to change the balance of that relationship to favour the workings of the **free market**. For this reason there is considerable overlap between the economy and the role of the state, dealt with in the next section.

The shift in emphasis towards a free market economy suggests that nations' leaders have a choice of economic model. The traditional division of capitalist versus socialist was crude 30 years ago and is even less appropriate today. In the section that follows we examine a range of economic models. It is generally accepted that we can identify three broad models of capitalism: Anglo-Saxon, social market and Asian. These will be contrasted with state-controlled economies of countries in Eastern Europe and China. However, most state-controlled economies have moved in varying degrees towards the capitalist models. Such economies in the process of change are often referred to as transitional economies.

The Anglo-Saxon model

The **Anglo-Saxon capitalism** model is sometimes called *laissez-faire* or competitive managerial capitalism. While all forms of capitalism see the market to be the ultimate arbiter and control of a well-regulated economy and certainly preferable to state control, this form of capitalism, above all others emphasizes the workings of the free market. Such a system can be seen best in the USA and the UK. We can identify its main features as follows:

- Markets are competitive and there is a belief that individuals should be encouraged to participate as entrepreneurs in an enterprise culture.

- The concept of private property is important and individuals are encouraged to own goods, capital and their own labour. Individualism is prized as a core value in society (our section on culture in the next chapter gives a fuller account).

- Shareholders are viewed as the most important stakeholder in business, and thus managers see an important part of their role is to deliver profit and dividend for shareholders.

- A key role in business ownership is played by institutional shareholders such as banks, insurance companies, pension funds and investment companies. These take an active interest in share price and dividend and seek returns on their investment.

- The system is typified by mergers and take-overs, many of them hostile, as share dealings result in rapid changes of ownership. As a result, dividends paid to shareholders are often higher in the UK than elsewhere.

- Managers are rewarded for maintaining share price and profits and part of that reward often includes shares. In the UK, senior managers have gained substantial pay rises as reward systems have tended to copy the USA.

- Trade unions are tolerated but their powers are often restricted by law.

- In a **recession**, costs, including labour costs, are cut to maintain profit levels.

Whilst the above has underpinned the capitalist systems of the UK and the USA for some time, there has been an even greater shift towards the free market in the last 20 or so years with even greater **deregulation** in most areas of the economy and, especially in the UK, wholesale privatization of publicly owned companies and utilities.

The social market model

The social market model is also known as the German model and the Rhineland model and is typified by the system found in Germany. The model is also prevalent in France, the Netherlands and in the Scandanavian countries. However, there is considerable variation in the way the model operates in these countries. For example, much greater emphasis is placed on high-cost social welfare, funded by taxation, in Sweden and some other Scandanavian countries. In Germany and the Netherlands more emphasis is placed on the legal regulation of business decisions and trade unions play a significant role. In France much more power lies in the hands of a centralist state. The main features of the social market model are as follows:

- The free market is seen to be important but needs to be carefully watched and in some cases regulated by the state.

- Private and state ownership operate side by side.

- There are comprehensive and well-funded social welfare systems controlled by the state.

- Both markets and individual firms are regulated by law and by state bureaucracy.

- Shareholders are viewed as one among several stakeholders in business. The stakeholders also include the employees. As a result, corporate governance focuses on responsibility to society and not on shareholder interest.

- Generally, share markets are stable with few mergers and takeovers which, in any case, are regulated by law.

- Major companies in each sector are seen as national champions and are protected by the state.

- Banks tend to be integrated into the system and have a close relationship both with individual firms and the state.

- Reinvestment in the business is favoured over high dividends to shareholders and managers tend to be less well rewarded than their counterparts in the USA and UK.

- Trade unions play an important role in decision-making and there is considerable employee involvement. Where the state, business and unions come together to determine policy as is often idealized in Germany, the system is referred to as corporatist.

- In a recession, there are job cuts but the trade unions are usually fully involved in the process.

In most social market systems, changes have been noted in the last 20 years. In many countries there has been a shift towards a freer market with deregulation and privatization. Some firms, particularly in Germany, have felt constrained by the system, leading them to acquire businesses overseas. In Germany several firms have acquired major USA companies as with Daimler and Chrysler, Siemens and Westinghouse, and Bertelsmann and Random House. In France, Renault, a former state-owned company, has taken a major share of Nissan in Japan. In an increasingly global labour market for top executives, managers were attracted to better paid jobs in the USA and UK. This has resulted in substantial pay rises for senior executives in Germany and France in particular.

The Asian model

The **Asian capitalism** model is also known as the Japanese model, alliance capitalism or community capitalism. It is found throughout Asia but its core characteristics are best illustrated in Japan and the Asian tigers' economies, especially South Korea. However, there are significant variations in the model across the various countries of Asia. Further insights into the model can be seen in Case 3.1 about the Asian tigers themselves and in Case 4.3 about Singapore. The key elements of the model can be expressed as follows:

- The dominant belief is that of the free market but with strong state intervention where necessary.

- Business practices and working life are dominated by Confucian values, including discipline, hard work, duty, harmony, perseverance and the importance attached to savings.

- The state operates in a fairly bureaucratic way, but for businesses rules tend to be applied pragmatically to smooth the way rather than hinder progress.

- Most states have weak social welfare systems and much is down to the individual and their family, hence the importance of savings.

- The firm and even its supply chain are viewed as a family.
- Stock markets tend to be stable. Even between competing firms there will be collaboration to prevent a takeover by a foreign company. Where mergers do occur, much attention is paid to the harmonization of the corporate cultures of the respective firms.
- Managers tend to pursue long-term strategies and goals. Individual reputation is often based on the success of the firm in general.
- Trade unions tend to be weak and are often controlled by management or the state. They are, however, seen to be important in the protection of weaker employees.
- In a recession every attempt is usually made to protect both employees and suppliers. As a consequence, firms have often been reluctant to restructure, and both managers and governments have been accused of reacting too slowly to economic problems.

The Asian system has been under threat in the last 10 years. Japan has suffered a recession since 1992 and the tiger economies suffered badly in the crash of 1997. Both these issues are dealt with in more detail in Cases 3.1 and 4.3 and in the section on Japan in Chapter 4. The limited industrial base of most Asian countries outside Japan was exposed in 1997 and continues to be exposed with each recession. Even stronger economies, such as Singapore, are not immune. Part of the problem has been the gradual move away from some of the core values that underpinned the Asian model. The slow growth of a strong manufacturing base was exchanged for the potentially richer and 'easier' returns from land and property speculation and international share trading. In tackling the recession in Japan, some firms have turned to Anglo-Saxon practices such as performance-related pay.

| Case 3.1 | **The Asian tigers** |

As we move towards the year 2000, Asia will become the dominant region of the world: economically, politically and culturally. We are on the threshold of an Asian renaissance. (*Naisbitt, 1996, p. viii*)

Two years later, commentators were reporting the collapse of the major Asian economies.

Tiger economies is the name given to the second wave of Asian economies, which emerged after the post-war rise of Japan. There is general agreement that the four main tigers are Hong Kong, Singapore, South Korea and Taiwan. These first-tier tigers have been followed by second- and even third-tier tigers in the form of Malaysia, Thailand, Indonesia, Philippines, China and Vietnam. This case will examine, in general terms, the rise and fall of the so-called tiger economies of Eastern Asia. A case in the next chapter will focus specifically on Singapore, perhaps the most successful tiger of all.

As Table 3.1 shows, the growth of the tiger economies has been significant.

Over the same period (1980–90) the average annual growth rate for all first- and second-tier tigers was 7.3 per cent. Such growth has rarely been seen anywhere else in the world, particularly in a region that had suffered years of disruption as a result

Table 3.1	Percentage increase 1980–90	
	GNP per capita	Earnings
South Korea	121.8	115.8
Taiwan	80.0	102.7
Singapore	77.5	79.8
Hong Kong	64.2	60.0

Source: World Bank, 1993

of wars and political change. The economic success of the region has had a significant impact on standards of living for the majority, and, as some commentators have noted, has been accompanied by a fall in income inequality. This is in marked contrast to the West, where economic growth has usually been accompanied by increases in such inequality.

Several explanations have been offered for this economic growth. These include culture, the operation of external forces, the impact of market forces and the role of the state.

- Cultural explanations have focused on the concept of Asian values, and, in particular, their link to Confucianism. Hofstede and Bond (1988) have labelled such Asian values as 'Confucian dynamism' and the key features include a future, long-term orientation, perseverance in the face of adversity, the role of savings, the importance of education and adaptability and dynamism. Hampden-Turner and Trompenaars (1997), based on a survey of 38 000 managers, argue that Eastern managers differ from those in the West in terms of their preference for collectivism over individualism, for consensus over conflict, for relationships over contracts and for their belief in virtue for its own sake. Eastern managers, they found, also differ in their attitude to time and the environment. It is such cultural values that have often been heralded as the source of competitive advantage, not just for the tigers, but for Japan as well. However, such explanations have their limitations. The exact nature of precisely how culture impacts upon economic performance is difficult to show and measurable links are notable by their absence. If Asian values are so significant in their explanation of economic growth then we must question why such growth has not occurred until comparatively recent times. Equally, if culture is accountable for the growth, can it also be used to explain the decline? If culture is part of the answer then other factors are at work as well. It is to these that we now turn.

- A popular explanation for the rise of new industrial economies is that of the late development effect. As we have seen elsewhere in this chapter, this is part of convergence theory and suggests that those countries industrializing later have an advantage in terms of being able to learn from the mistakes of the early industrializers, through technology transfer and by operating from greenfield sites. This was used to explain the rise of Japan at the end of the 19th century, a country that, in turn, has had a significant impact on the development of the tigers.

▶

- One factor that marks out Asian economies from the rest of the world is the proportion of the economy that is given over to savings. In East Asia savings account for 35 per cent of GDP, while the equivalent figures for the USA and Europe are 18 per cent and 12 per cent respectively. Although the inclination to save is Confucian in origin, its current manifestation has much to do with the role of the state. A combination of low taxes, low inflation, high interest rates and controls over the direction of saving and the saving institutions themselves have all contributed to high levels of saving. This, in turn, has led to a large pool of investable income being channelled into economic development. A further contributory factor is the relative lack of provision for social welfare and the historical reliance the people have placed on savings for family support during, for instance, sickness and old age.

- The labour forces of most tiger economies are relatively young and highly active. Furthermore, most East Asian countries have invested heavily in education, more especially at the primary and secondary levels. The nations are typified by intensive schooling regimes and high levels of literacy and numeracy. In the early stages of development in all countries people generally worked for long hours and low wages, factors which only changed in more recent times.

- The governments of tiger economies have clearly played a major role, although in their operation we can see a number of paradoxes. The governments tend to be more interventionist than those of the Western economies, yet spend less as a proportion of GDP. They are both more authoritarian and paternalist than those of the West, yet families are expected to be more self-sufficient. Their economic policies have tended to favour the operation of the free market, but with considerable assistance to the foreign multinationals, especially those representing export-led products. Governments are actively pro-business and there are many instances of intervention in labour markets to ensure their flexibility or to eliminate potential disruption.

The explanation of the rise of the tiger economies is almost certainly a combination of all or most of the above factors. However, it is misleading to regard all first- and second-tier tigers as the same. There are differences in economic structures, prosperity and cultures. There are significant differences in prosperity between first-tier countries, as with Singapore and South Korea, and cultural differences operate within as well as between countries, as illustrated by both Singapore and Malaysia. By the same token the economic crash that affected the region in 1997 did not affect all countries in the same way, as Table 3.2 illustrates.

While the impact of the economic downturn varied it was felt across the whole region, and even the established economy of Japan was not immune. A major factor in the collapse was that most of the local currencies were pegged to the USA dollar. Over the years the dollar had strengthened, while growth in the local economies had slowed down. For many economists this was a re-run of events in Mexico in 1994/5. Thailand was the first country to devalue its currency, followed by the Philippines, Malaysia, South Korea and Indonesia in that order. This led to a rapid worsening of the position in all these countries and the problems spread to other parts of the

Table 3.2	Economic collapse in 1997	
Country	*% fall in currency against US dollar*	*% fall in stock market value*
Indonesia	70	53
Thailand	55	59
South Korea	51	42
Malaysia	45	61
Singapore	20	53
Japan	13	29

Source: *Guardian*, December 1997

region, including the stronger economies of Hong Kong, Singapore and Japan. While the link to the US dollar was the catalyst, a number of contending theories have been put forward to explain the underlying causes. It is to these we now turn.

- Some consider that the fate of the tigers is a function of their rapid growth, in that growth was the goal, irrespective of the price to be paid at a later date. The weak underpinnings of the economy, injudicious lending and the workings of the stock market were of particular relevance here.

- Most of the tigers had opted for a relatively restricted manufacturing base in terms of product variety. This meant that they were especially vulnerable to global price changes. In South Korea, the three major electronics firms, Hyundai, LG and Samsung, had grown rich through their focus on the manufacture of the 16-megabit DRAM computer chip. South Korea had 30 per cent of the world market and these companies took most of the 30 per cent. The very success of the product led to over-investment, resulting in over-capacity. By the end of 1996, the price for the chip had dropped 80 per cent, resulting in a fall in profits in that year of 93 per cent for Samsung, 92 per cent for Hyundai and 88 per cent for LG.

- Considerable borrowing had been allowed to fund investment in firms such as those in South Korea. This left many companies with debts far in excess of their total assets. In 1997 the debt/equity ratios of the above electronics firms were 437 per cent for Hyundai, 347 per cent for LG and 267 per cent for Samsung. The growth of company debt was a feature throughout the region, particularly in the relatively weaker economies. Problems that have been identified include a lack of scrutiny of many investment projects, some attracting the additional criticisms of nepotism and corruption and too many prestige projects with little hope of pay-back. In some countries, especially Thailand, bad banking debts mounted as a consequence of poor lending strategies, mostly involving land and property speculators. The problem of bad debt was heightened by short-term borrowing from overseas banks and the ensuing difficulty of repayment, as the currencies destabilized.

- The fast growth of the tiger economies in the early 1990s attracted a large number of overseas stock market investors. At the same time there was a growing movement of investment away from manufacturing and into land and property. Many investors were interested only in short-term gains and tended to view the region as an entity. This meant that, at the first signs of trouble, investments were withdrawn across the whole region. Short-term speculation was not confined to the stock market. The artificially high currencies pegged to the dollar attracted considerable inward investment. While this operated as a virtuous circle when the economies were growing, it became a vicious circle as currencies were rapidly sold at the first signs of problems. Some politicians, such as the Malaysian Prime Minister, Dr Mahathir, attributed the economic collapse of 1997 to the activity of currency speculators. While this was a factor, it is only one among many, and other commentators have suggested that currency speculation was a symptom rather than an underlying cause.

In countries such as Thailand and South Korea, the economic problems of 1997 led to swift intervention by the International Monetary Fund (IMF), imposing severe restrictions on both borrowing and growth. In Indonesia, the economic problems were followed by political problems and social unrest. Without doubt, the economy of the East Asia region has been destabilized. The pessimists view this as an inevitable consequence of uncontrolled growth and forecast further problems ahead. Those of a more optimistic persuasion see the problems of 1997 as a warning and an opportunity for countries to place their economies on a sounder footing. Whichever view is taken, the impact on individual countries will vary substantially owing to the inherent differences contained in this far from homogeneous region.

Sources: Hofstede and Bond, 1988; World Bank Report, 1993; Naisbitt, 1996; Rohwer, 1995; Hampden-Turner and Trompenaars, 1997; Henderson, 1998; Jomo, 1998; *Financial Times* and *Guardian*, 1997–99

Questions

1   In what ways do the Asian tigers, as depicted in the case, conform to the model of Asian capitalism outlined earlier in this chapter?

2   Assess the factors behind the rise of the tiger economies. Which of these factors do you believe to have been most significant?

3   What reasons do you believe caused the crash of 1997? To what extent do the factors involved imply a shift away from the Asian capitalist model?

4   What do the tiger economies need to do to avoid a repeat of the events of 1997?

State controlled and transitional economies

In a **centrally planned (state controlled) economy**, such as ones that existed in the former Soviet Union and the former communist countries of Eastern Europe, the state has total ownership and control of the means of production. The activities of all firms in all sectors of the economy are under state ownership and control. Many of these economies underwent periodic reforms, but the key feature of the **transitional economy** is the radical nature of change, that is more far-reaching than any internal reform. Such economies present international firms, especially those from the advanced industrial nations, with opportunities for market expansion, business growth, foreign direct investment, and enable them to reap the benefits from many of the advantages associated with joint ventures. These issues were discussed in Chapter 2 and formed the basis of the Beijing Jeep case (Case 2.1).

Under a central planning system there are usually the following:

- Control of the supply and demand of goods and services.
- Individual enterprises are set targets and allocated resources to meet those targets.
- Control of prices, wages and employment levels.
- Control of the direction of consumer spending.

However, under most such economic regimes the reality never matched the expectations and several problems have been well documented. These include the failure to match targets and allocated resources, the failure to meet targets irrespective of resources, overproduction, inflexibility and inefficiencies in all sectors of the economy.

Processes and experiences of transition

Transitional economies are those economies that are in the process of change from a centrally planned or **command economy** to a **market economy**.

Two models have emerged: rapid or 'shock' change and gradualism. Rapid or shock change occurs when the former economic system and its institutions and processes are dismantled almost overnight. Such a change occurred in Poland with some resulting success but similar attempts in Russia resulted in near economic chaos. A more gradual change to a free market economy was favoured by Hungary, and this approach also defines China's economic changes over the last 20 years.

Most agree that the transition comprises four key-related processes as follows:

- **Liberalization**. This process involves the removal of state control on wages and prices. This process can result in inflation and increasing levels of unemployment. For this reason, some countries favour the retention of a number of state-owned enterprises in each sector to preserve jobs and keep a control of prices.
- **Stabilization**. This is primarily the control of inflation and unemployment, which usually follow the removal of state controls.
- **Internationalization**. This involves the opening up of the economy to international trade and the encouragement of inward foreign investment.
- **Privatization.** This is the selling of state-owned businesses. In former command economies, this usually takes two forms. State-owned enterprises may be sold to foreign investors, normally foreign companies. In some cases the enterprise is acquired by the foreign company, in others a joint venture is established between a foreign firm and either the state-owned enterprise or a newly created private company. The second form of privatization occurs when the state sells its enterprise, usually at very favourable rates, to its managers and employees. More general issues relating to **privatization** are discussed in Chapter 5.

The experience of most transitional economies have been mixed. In Eastern Europe, countries such as Poland, Hungary and the Czech Republic have made significant economic advances, while the experience of many of the countries of the former USSR have made the rapid decline into economic chaos (with the notable exceptions of the Baltic states; Latvia, Lithuania and Estonia). Such variations in performance may be attributed to both the extent and length of time of state control of the economy. In the former USSR, central planning had been a feature for 70 years whereas, for most Eastern European countries (including the Baltic states), state control was a feature from 1948 only. In the former USSR, central planning was an embedded feature of business processes and behaviour and many people had known no other system. The change, when it did arrive, was rapid and destabilizing. In countries such as Hungary and the Czech Republic, not only was the experience of state control for a shorter period, but a greater number of liberal reforms had taken place prior to the collapse of centralized communist control in the early 1990s.

In China, liberal reforms began to emerge at the end of the 1970s, introduced by the regime of Deng Xioaping. Such reforms accelerated rapidly during the 1990s with foreign direct investment pouring in and the establishment of joint ventures between former Chinese state-owned enterprises and major Western and Japanese firms such as IBM, Daimler Benz, Siemens, Hewlett Packard, VW and Mitsubishi. Such reforms culminated in 2001 with the acceptance of China as a member of the World Trade Association (see Case 3.4). The economy of China is still defined as centrally planned, although that planning incorporates liberal reforms. The transformation of major cities, especially those in the East and along the coast, has been dramatic. However, the GDP per capita for China, despite growth, still stands at a small fraction of its Western and Japanese counterparts and significant variations exist within China itself, particularly between the prosperous coastal area and the relatively undeveloped Western provinces. Moreover, as we saw in the section on joint ventures in the previous chapter, considerable tensions exist when centrally planned economies meet the free market. Nonetheless between 2000 and 2003 there were many signs of healthy growth in the Chinese economy.

The importance of joint ventures to the transition of the Chinese economy has led to a tendency for China to follow Western models of capitalism rather than the Asian model, with which it is much more closely related – both culturally and structurally – in terms of a strong state apparatus (Dore, 2000). While the three models of capitalism are necessarily idealized, they do present emerging and transitional economies with a choice of routes. However, we move from speculation to examine more closely the impact of business on the economy and of the economy on business.

The impact of business on the economy

All businesses produce goods and services and provide employment. In doing so they contribute to a nation's income, capital assets, and economic growth. Furthermore, contributions can be made to a nation's economy through the investment and outputs of foreign firms. This is referred to as **foreign direct investment (FDI)**.

In the previous chapter we explored the importance of the multinational and transnational company to the growth of the global economy. Both these types of company are also examples of FDI. Foreign direct investment is the full or partial ownership of a firm located in one country by investors in another country. The rationale behind FDI is similar to that for the existence of the multinational, although as a mode of entry it needs to have significant advantages over exporting and licensing to make the investment worthwhile. It goes without saying that significant FDI will have considerable impact upon a nation's economy. It was also noted in the previous chapter that FDI had replaced export volume and value as a measure of a nation's economic success.

Economies are often compared on the basis of their **gross national product (GNP)** and their gross domestic product (GDP). Gross national product is the sum total of the net outputs of each sector of the economy together with the earnings by its residents from overseas investments. **Gross domestic product** is the sum total of the same net outputs, including those of foreign firms but excluding earnings from overseas. In Table 3.3 we show actual levels of GDP and the GDP per head of population (**GDP per capita**), both expressed in US dollars. There are some omissions but nearly all the leading countries in their various regions are included. Tables 3.4 and 3.5 take the top ten countries by GDP per head and the total GDP respectively.

Table 3.3	GDP per head estimates for 2003 in rank order by region for selected countries		
Country		*Total GDP US$bn*	*GDP per head US$*
Europe			
Norway		222	48 710
Switzerland		306	41 880
Denmark		210	39 050
Sweden		292	32 800
Finland		163	31 090
United Kingdom		1 771	29 360
Austria		240	29 310
Germany		2 392	29 210
France		1 677	27 890
Italy		1 422	24 710
Spain		763	18 710
Greece		160	15 060
Portugal		142	14 070
Czech Republic		91	8 880
Hungary		77	7 690
Poland		198	5 120
Slovakia		27	4 900
Turkey		194	2 850
Russia		392	2 730
Bulgaria		19	2 560
Romania		53	2 380
Ukraine		47	979
Asia Pacific			
Japan		3 942	30 990
Australia		465	23 570

Country	Total GDP US$bn	GDP per head US$
Hong Kong	159	23 140
Singapore	97	22 180
New Zealand	64	16 340
Taiwan	249	12 940
South Korea	527	10 880
Thailand	131	5 770
China	1 388	1 070
Indonesia	217	1 010
Pakistan	72	476
India	538	507
Vietnam	35	428
The Americas		
USA	10 885	37 600
Canada	793	25 090
Mexico	641	6 210
Chile	69	4 500
Brazil	514	2 900
Argentina	99	2 580
Colombia	77	1 730
Middle East and Africa		
Israel	105	15 600
Saudi Arabia	196	8 740
Lebanon	19	5 120
South Africa	101	2 200
Algeria	59	1 880
Iran	125	1 880
Jordan	10	1 870
Egypt	78	1 140
Iraq	26	1 060
Nigeria	45	360
Kenya	10	326

Source: Economist Intelligence Unit, 2002, adapted from 'The World in 2003' *The Economist*, 2002

The data reveals a number of interesting points.

● There is an obvious gap between the rich and poor nations of the world. The gap is actually greater than shown, given that the poorest countries are not included in the tables. The relative gap is also shown between the countries of West and East Europe, and reveals the especially poor position of Russia given its large population. The large populations of China and India also account for the very low GDP per

Table 3.4

GDP per head estimates for 2003 for top ten countries

Country	Total GDP US$bn	GDP per head US$
Norway	222	48 710
Switzerland	306	41 880
Denmark	210	39 050
USA	10 885	37 600
Sweden	292	32 800
Finland	163	31 090
Japan	3 942	30 990
United Kingdom	1,771	29 360
Austria	240	29 310
Germany	2 392	29 210

Source: Economist Intelligence Unit, 2002, adapted from 'The World in 2003' *The Economist*, 2002

Table 3.5

Total GDP estimates for 2003 for top ten countries

Country	Total GDP US$bn	GDP per head US$
USA	10 885	37 600
Japan	3 942	30 990
Germany	2 392	29 210
United Kingdom	1 771	29 360
France	1 677	27 890
Italy	1 422	24 710
China	1 388	1 070
Canada	793	25 090
Spain	763	18 710
Mexico	641	6 210

Source: Economist Intelligence Unit, 2002, adapted from 'The World in 2003' *The Economist*, 2002

head compared with the total GDP. In total GDP terms, China appears as the seventh largest economy in the world, yet the GDP per head is only US$1070 per year. However the predictions are for a rapid growth in the Chinese economy.

- Although in terms of GDP per head the USA lags behind several countries in Europe, the figures reveal the sheer size of the USA economy. The GDP is nearly three times the size of the next largest economy, Japan.

- The figures for many of the Asian economies reflect the crash of 1997 and many Asian countries show their lowest GDP figures for some years. This is especially true for Singapore (see Case 4.3).

- Europe, in terms of GDP per head, is dominated by the Scandanavian countries. The strength of the UK economy in 2003 is reflected in its increase in GDP per head.

The UK has always featured in the world's top five economies but has jumped ahead of France in the overall size of the economy and both France and Germany in terms of GDP per capita.

Key issues for business managers are also key economic issues. These may be identified as products, productivity, markets, profits and the supply of labour. These themes re-emerge when we discuss the role of the economy in the chapters on the various business activities. For example, in Chapter 9 we examine the view that economic growth is dependent upon product and process innovation.

The impact of the economy on business

There are a variety of ways in which economic changes have affected businesses in a country such as the UK. These changes will be illustrated through the changing nature of world economies, including structural changes, the supply and price of raw materials, increased international competition, and the emergence of globalization as a dominant influence. Central to the development of globalization is the impact of multinational firms. These illustrate the difficulty of isolating business and environmental influences. Many businesses in the UK have undoubtedly been influenced by a world economy increasingly dominated by multinational corporations. These same multinationals are themselves businesses with the ability to influence national and international economies.

Changes in the world economy have, for a country like Britain, led to major structural changes involving the decline of the manufacturing sector (de-industrialization) and the growth of the service sector, especially the financial sector. In turn, these changes have had a significant impact on levels of employment, causing high levels of unemployment in those areas formerly dominated by traditional manufacturing industry, while creating many new jobs in the emerging **financial services** industry. We deal with these issues in more detail at the end of this section on the economy and in the sections on technology and labour elsewhere in this chapter.

The availability of key resources does not only have a significant influence on the fortunes of individual firms but can also lead to structural changes. In 1973 OPEC, representing the oil-producing countries, decided to restrict the supply of oil, with a subsequent dramatic increase in price. Similar price rises occurred in 1979. The impacts on businesses in the UK were several. Increased costs were passed on in the form of increased prices or resulted in reduced profits, with some firms unable to compete. Some industries sought substitute products with corresponding increases in demand for products of the coal and gas industries. Rising petrol prices meant increased costs of transport and led to major product changes in the car industry. These changes were even more significant in the USA, with a dramatic reduction in car size and the imposition of a national speed limit on all roads, the legacy of which remains today. When Britain became a major oil producer, changes in the price of oil had an effect upon the exchange value of sterling. An exchange rate strengthened by an oil economy meant that British exports became more expensive and particularly damaging for those businesses that depended for a large proportion of their revenue on exported goods.

As we noted in our two cases in Chapter 1 and through our discussion of globalization in Chapter 2, there has been a marked increase in the international dimension of most types of business. This has taken the form of a dramatic growth in international competition, initially from Japan but, more recently also from other South-East Asian economies. (Cases

3.1 and 4.3 examine the link between economics, politics and business in the Asian tigers.) The decline in competitiveness of many of Britain's industries, such as shipbuilding, motorcycles, domestic electrical products and cars, has been attributed to the rise of cheap labour economies, especially those in the Far East, or the product superiority of manufacturers in countries such as Japan and Germany. However, our perspective of international competition must be revised constantly, so dynamic are the forces at work. While de-industrialization in many 'advanced economies' was linked to a switch of manufacturing to those aforementioned cheap labour economies, such economies are becoming less cheap and, far from lagging behind, they began to take the lead in certain areas of manufacturing technology and product development. The dynamic forces continue to work, as we see in Case 3.1, leading to an economic downturn amongst the former rising stars of South-East Asia.

The impact of a changing economy on British business

If you want to buy a small business, buy a large one and wait. (*New English proverb*)

The major changes in the UK economy since 1970 have been the decline of manufacturing and the growth of the service sector, the growth in numbers of long-term unemployed, the weakening of trade unions, and the shift from public to private ownership. The last two aspects will be dealt with elsewhere and here the focus will be on the shift away from manufacturing to the service sector, and on rising unemployment. In the next section it will be argued that such changes are political and ideological as well as economic.

The decline of the manufacturing industry in the UK has been well documented. Since the 1950s, UK industry has lost market share to overseas competitors. In shipbuilding the UK was the world's leading exporter in 1950, yet in 6 years its market share fell from 38 per cent to 14 per cent. In 1955 the UK produced 70 per cent of the world's motorcycles, but was unable to meet the challenge first from the Italians and then from the Japanese. UK manufacturers retreated up-market only to be pursued and overtaken by the Japanese in every market segment. There is a potential link here between R&D and market share, an aspect explored in more detail in Chapter 9. In the late 1970s Norton-Villiers-Triumph employed 100 staff in R&D, while its Japanese competitors, Honda and Suzuki, employed 1000 each (Bowen, 1992).

While market share has declined, the domestic consumption of manufactured goods has increased. From 1973 to 1988 domestic expenditure on manufactured goods increased by 30 per cent while domestic output remained about the same (Wells, 1989). The impact of this has been a rise in imported goods and a worsening of the **balance of payments** deficit.

Apart from market share, the numbers employed in manufacturing are a good indication of the relative health of the manufacturing sector. Table 3.6 shows the decline of numbers employed in manufacturing 1971–91 relative to those employed in the USA, Germany and Japan. While other countries maintained their employment base in manufacturing, the UK lost 40 per cent of its manufacturing workforce. The decline in manufacturing employment was most severe during the recession of 1980–2. Optimistic commentators point to the impact such changes have had in clearing out ineffective and inefficient firms and how some firms and even entire industries are now more efficient and competitive. While this may be true, there is a real danger that manufacturing capacity has been lost to such an extent that it will be difficult to recover. As Wells (1989) states,

UK manufacturing production which remains at the end of the Thatcher decade may well be leaner, fitter, have a higher level of labour productivity and be more profitable than before – but it is totally inadequate in terms of the volume of its internationally competitive capacity. (*Wells, 1989, p. 58*)

The biggest decline has been in the more traditional industries. In 1948, 3 million people were employed in steel, dock and port work, agriculture, coalmining, the railways, ship-building and car manufacture. By 1998 the numbers employed in these industries was 0.5 million, with agriculture the largest employer amongst traditional industries with 250 000.

The decline in manufacturing has often been linked solely with the policies of the Thatcher administration in the 1980s. With hindsight, political policies were part of a process that saw the shift of much of manufacturing to lower-cost countries as a result of globalization. However, as Table 3.6 shows, the speed of the process, assisted by policies of **monetarism** and non-intervention, undoubtedly meant that more companies failed to survive into the 1990s than would otherwise have been the case. The growth of manufacturing in electrical and computer-related industry in the UK of some 60 per cent may be encouraging signs of manufacturing recovery but many of the new firms are for-eign owned. The UK ended the 20th century as the world's fifth largest economy, behind

Table 3.6

Employment in manufacturing 1971–91

	UK	USA	Germany	Japan
1971	100	100	100	100
1972	97	103	98	99
1973	98	108	98	100
1974	98	108	96	99
1975	93	98	89	94
1976	90	102	87	91
1977	91	106	86	90
1978	91	110	86	89
1979	90	113	86	88
1980	85	109	87	89
1981	78	108	85	90
1982	73	101	82	91
1983	69	99	78	91
1984	67	104	78	92
1985	67	103	79	94
1986	65	102	80	94
1987	64	102	80	93
1988	65	104	80	94
1989	65	104	82	96
1990	64	103	84	97
1991	60	99	85	100

Source: Datastream International 1992

the USA, Japan, Germany and France, and by 2003 had overtaken France. UK manufacturing firms are coping with the problems of a strong currency. With a strong currency, exports become more expensive, with the effect that selling prices must fall faster than costs for firms to compete globally. The 1997 fall of the Asian economies has made their products even cheaper and intensified that competition. Moreover, the growth of foreign ownership in UK manufacturing has threatened the UK supply industry with a switch from traditional sources to lower-cost alternatives elsewhere.

The impact on a single firm, Raleigh, is presented in Case 3.2.

The decline of manufacturing in the UK has been contrasted with the rise in the service sector of the economy. For example, while all employment fell by 6.2 per cent between 1979 and 1986, employment in the service sector rose by 6.6 per cent. In some sectors, such as financial services, the increase in employment has been quite dramatic accompanying the deregulation by the government of financial markets. The growth of the service sector of the economy undoubtedly has its roots in the historical development of the British economy. The City has always been a focus of attention owing to early British dominance in world trade and the international role played by sterling. Later in the chapter we also explore the view that the core cultural values of the British have favoured the development of the service economy at the expense of manufacturing.

High levels of unemployment are, however, a fairly recent phenomenon. Between 1948 and 1966 the average rate in Britain was 1.7 per cent with only 1.1 per cent in 1966. Along with other industrial countries, levels of unemployment have risen sharply since then, with an official figure of 3.25 million people being out of work in 1982, representing 13 per cent of the working population. Since 1982, the extent of unemployment has fluctuated. At the end of the 1990s, unemployment in the UK was lower than that in Italy and Germany and significantly lower than Spain and in 2003 fluctuated between 4 per cent and 5 per cent. This masks two social problems. There has been a steady increase in the numbers of long-term unemployed and levels of unemployment vary between regions. Highest levels inevitably occur in regions that were typified by traditional heavy manufacturing and extractive industries. Various policies have been initiated to deal with these problems, including government training schemes, regional aid, increasing public investment and direct state intervention to support ailing firms. Some of these aspects are dealt with in the next section.

A further problem relating to unemployment is the nature of the global economy. Cost cutting exercises by a USA, German or Dutch company have an impact on its operations in other countries. Thus the decision to close the Dagenham plant in the UK by Ford senior management in Detroit created job losses of around 3000. However, this is not solely a UK problem. The slow-down of the global economy in the early part of last century, created significant job cuts across Europe as Table 3.7 shows.

Over the past 25 years the impact of the above economic changes alongside globalization on a major UK employer, such as Ford Motor Company, has been considerable. No one single factor has dominated as most of the influences have operated interactively.

● Along with the rest of UK manufacturing, capacity at Ford Motor Company has been reduced including the closure of its main manufacturing plant at Dagenham, switching attention to the manufacture of engines.

● Before the closure there had been a reduction in the range of models produced and in the labour force.

Table 3.7	Number of job cuts announced in 2001 (a selected sample)	
	Company	*No. job cuts*
	UK	
	Marconi	10 000
	Unilever	8 000
	BT	6 000
	Sweden	
	Ericsson	22 000
	Netherlands	
	Philips	11 000
	Germany	
	Siemens	15 000
	Deutsche Post	7 000
	Dresdner Bank	7 000
	France	
	Alcatel	17 000
	Switzerland	
	ABB	11 000
	Swissair	9 000

Source: *Guardian*, 17 October 2001

- The decline of manufacturing throughout the UK means that the company has gone further afield for the sourcing of its components and hastened the trend towards the internationalization of manufacturing.

- The decline of the UK manufacturing base has also meant a reduction in the numbers being trained in up-to-date manufacturing skills. Despite the large pool of unemployed labour there is a reduced pool of labour in certain manufacturing skills.

- The growth in financial services has not gone unnoticed by manufacturing concerns themselves and Ford has joined the growing trend by expanding its activities in this area.

- Along with other employers, Ford has experienced fewer industrial relations problems. Weaker trade unions, unemployment and growing international competition have contributed towards a more cooperative industrial relations climate and management has been able to introduce changes in areas such as flexible labour practices that would hitherto have been impossible. Wage settlements too have been lower.

- As we shall see in the next chapter, the company has restructured along global dimensions. In functions such as logistics and buying, it is not unusual for UK employees to report to German and USA managers and vice versa with the creation of international teams operating in different locations, linked by regular meetings but dependent on electronic systems for daily communication.

Raleigh

Raleigh, the Nottingham-based cycle manufacturer, ceased production in Nottingham at the end of 2002 after 115 years. The company was founded in 1887 and became the market leader of bicycles in the UK, a position it retained until the early 1980s. The company was known for its product quality and reliability and as a paternalistic employer. Its reputation as a manufacturer was widespread amongst the general public and within cycle racing. The company sponsored individuals and teams for many years. It was a major employer in Nottingham and at the height of its success employed over 8000. When the factory closed it was employing just 280 people in manufacture.

For many years the company was owned by the Tube Investment Group (TI), a large holding company with diverse interests. However, during the 1980s the UK industry was under attack from foreign imports. Chinese-made bikes were entering the UK market at an increasing rate. Not only were these bikes cheaper, the build quality of the Chinese product had improved significantly and approached that of Raleigh bikes. The company's share of the UK market fell from 66 per cent in 1966 to under 40 per cent in 1981. Between 1982 and 1987 the Raleigh operation lost TI £40 million and the company was sold.

It was bought by Alan Finden-Crofts, an entrepreneur who owned the Derby Cycle Corporation. The Derby Cycle Corporation operated in the USA and manufactured the Gazelle, the best-selling bicycle in Holland. Raleigh was subsumed within this business and restored to profitability. Historically, Raleigh had prided itself on the manufacture of every part in-house. The drive to cut costs in the 1980s led to outsourcing and this increased in the 1990s. Further cost cutting was undoubtedly a major impact on profits being restored. In 1997 the Derby Cycle Corporation was sold for £125 million to a group of venture capitalists in Washington, DC. The Americans were inexperienced in bicycle manufacture and the company once again hit financial difficulties. They rehired Finden-Crofts as a consultant and in 2000 sold the factory site to Nottingham University, who leased it back to Raleigh on a 3-year contract.

The USA group's mounting debts led them to sell back the company in 2001 to Finden-Crofts for £48 million, a price that included considerable stock and orders. The search for a new factory site for Raleigh bikes in Nottingham began, in preparation for the end of leaseback arrangements in 2003 by the University, which had plans for a new Jubilee campus. Proposals for a new factory in Nottingham were stalled by the local authority planning process but other more significant factors were at work. With the manufacture of Raleigh bikes substantially cheaper in overseas locations, the decision to end production at Nottingham was inevitable. For example, the bikes could be made in Vietnam at 75 per cent of the cost of a bike

◀

made in Nottingham. The manufacture would now be shifted to Vietnam, South Korea and Bangladesh and the Nottingham presence would be retained only as a design centre. The last Raleigh bike made in Nottingham came off the assembly process on 27 November, 2002. The company abandoned its plans to open a new factory in the Nottingham suburb of Bulwell and rehoused its design and marketing function outside the city in Eastwood. Further restructuring took place in 2003 and the marketing function was subsumed in an all-embracing department that also included sales, design and product sourcing. The UK market had been static since 1998 and price cutting to maintain market share had led to a serious decline in the value of the market. In April 2003, Finden-Crofts took a more direct role as the new MD.

Source: Seaton, 2002; *Marketing*, 6 February, 2003; *Nottingham Evening Post*, 11 April, 2003

Questions

1   What does the case tell us about the difficulties of operating a successful manufacturing industry in a global economy?

2   Should we be concerned about the end of manufacturing in such firms as Raleigh?

Does manufacturing matter?

To some, the growth in the services sector of the UK economy is seen as compensation for the decline in the manufacturing base and simply part of the process of evolutionary economic change. However, several arguments are put forward for the importance of manufacturing in a healthy economy. Only manufacturing can add value to raw materials and, in doing so, can provide jobs in numbers that can never be matched by the service sector. While most, if not all, of manufacturing output can be traded as exports, this is not the case for services. Some estimates put the extent of tradeable services as low as 20 per cent of the total. As Bowen (1992) writes, 'you cannot pay for Japanese cars with British hairdressing'. In many other countries, the health of the service sector depends ultimately on the health of the manufacturing industry. In Germany, some 50 per cent of the demand for services comes from the manufacturing sector itself (Hahn, 1993).

It is for reasons such as these that successive British governments have been urged to lend greater support to the manufacturing industry. It is to this and other aspects of the state's involvement with business that we now turn.

The state and business

Taking his lead from Max Weber, John Scott (1979) defines the state as that body which has a monopoly over taxation, money supply, and the legitimate use of violence. The state is normally thought of as comprising the executive, parliament, civil service, judiciary, and armed forces and police. It would be wrong to perceive the state as a united body.

Tensions can and do occur, as between parliament and the civil service or between parliament and the judiciary. Variations in policy often result from differences in political ideology.

Key concept 3.1 The state

The state comprises parliament, the judiciary, civil service, police and armed forces, and so on. Traditionally, there have been tensions between the state's need to direct the economy and regulate business and the wishes of the business community to pursue their interests with a minimum of state intervention. Nevertheless, state intervention is a feature of business life and is inevitable in a country such as the UK where the state is a major employer. Intervention occurs through the legal regulation of market transactions, inventions and employment contracts and through the state's attempt to influence demand both as a consumer and via government economic policy. The business community, in turn, attempts to influence the state by adopting the various tactics associated with pressure groups. Increasingly, business comes under the influence of the policies of supranational bodies, such as the EU.

The World Bank has identified five core responsibilities of the state in any modern society (World Bank, 1997):

- establishing a legal framework;
- developing economic policies;
- building basic services and infrastructure;
- protecting the vulnerable;
- protecting the environment.

All these responsibilities have an impact on business in some way. We have already noted that the state interacts with business through its management of the economy.

In this section we will deal with aspects of the state's activity at both national and local levels in terms of the state's attempt to intervene in business and the efforts made by business managers to influence the workings of the state. It will also link back to the models of economic systems outlined in the previous section. The issues relating to state intervention will be illustrated through Case 3.3, which examines historically the various attempts by UK governments to influence and direct business decisions. This section closes by examining the issue of international political and economic integration and focuses on two supranational bodies, the EU and the WTO. Throughout this book the interaction of the state and business is illustrated by examining the relationship through its impact on the various business activities in Chapters 9 to 13.

Before the relationship between the state and business is examined more closely it is important to consider the broad ideological underpinnings that have informed state involvement in business in the UK and in many other democratic countries in the 20th century. The dominant ideology has been that of **liberal pluralism**.

For liberals, the state is concerned with the maintenance of order and with providing conditions so that business can prosper. The state is seen as a neutral umpire in a pluralist society dominated by voluntary cooperation and exchange, where differences are never fundamental. Under a liberal view of the state, intervention is necessary for the following reasons:

- To protect the workings of the free market against forces that might otherwise disrupt it, such as excessive monopoly power of either business or trade unions.

- To provide and/or control goods and services to individuals such as defence and education, where provision by other means would be impossible or inappropriate.

- To take a longer-term view of economic, social and environmental change than individual businesses are capable of doing.

The liberal perspective allows wide variation, as we saw in our different models of capitalism, from a highly directive economy to one in which the free market is encouraged to operate unfettered by government controls.

Those criticizing this perspective argue that the state tends to operate to preserve the *status quo*, that groups in society rarely have equal power to support voluntary cooperation and exchange, and that ultimately the state is not neutral. Marxists take this view a stage further and argue that the state is the instrument of the ruling class in an essentially exploitative society, where massive inequalities exist. Under a Marxist view of the state, intervention is necessary to maintain the *status quo* in favour of the dominant class. The state will therefore intervene to protect investments or prevent strikes.

State intervention under different economic systems

You are referred here to the discussion of different economic systems in the previous section of this chapter. Under each system the state's relationship with business is different.

- Under systems of **state control and central planning** the state has total ownership of business and controls production via targets, and controls both supply and demand and wages and prices. Such a system typified the old regimes of the former Soviet Union and China. Such total intervention is now rare, existing only in a handful of countries such as North Korea and Cuba. Nearly all former state-controlled economies are in transition towards a free market system. This means that private ownership of business has been introduced and managers will have more freedom to act. The extent of state involvement in such a **transitional** economy varies. For example, although China allows private companies and joint ventures with foreign firms, business activities are still tightly managed by the state operating at both national and regional levels.

- The **Anglo-Saxon** systems of the UK and USA are based around the notion of a free market and non-intervention of the state. Yet here the state is still active in business and polices laws and regulations that have a significant impact on the way business is done and on internal business practices. There is much debate within the business communities of both countries that despite the rhetoric of the free market, the state is often seen as too interventionist in the affairs of private businesses. For example, in the UK the owners of small businesses have complained that employment laws relating to part-time work and maternity leave are disadvantageous to their competitive position. A complication here for the UK is that many laws governing business are not the product of the UK government but emerge from the EU, where several leading member nations operate under a social market system.

- The **social market** capitalism system, as has been seen, has a number of variations. The state plays a key role in protecting the social welfare of its inhabitants. There is considerable investment in such areas as health and education supported by high rates of taxation. Laws are enforced to limit mergers and takeovers, which might affect jobs, and to facilitate employee involvement in business decisions. For example the Anglo-Dutch steel firm, Corus (an amalgamation of British Steel and Hoogovens) announced significant losses in 2002–3 with the inevitable threat to jobs. Far more job cuts are expected in the UK, as Dutch workers will be better protected through their system of employee involvement. However, as we saw in Table 3.7, significant job losses can occur in social market economies. Such state direction in business has been labelled as corporatism. This is essentially an attempt by the government to achieve stability by integration, involving representatives of business and trade unions in the economic decision-making process. However, as we noted in the previous section, some social market countries, including Germany, have become more Anglo-Saxon in their approach to business.

- Under the **Asian** capitalism model the state is directive but not in terms of social welfare, which is very much the responsibility of individuals. The state tends to be pro-business and assists in business growth. In Japan, key sectors have been targeted to receive government support and R&D has been facilitated by the establishment of government-backed centres involving representatives from several firms working in the same sector (these issues are explored later in this chapter). In Singapore, the government actively encouraged the inward investment of foreign firms (see Case 4.3).

Case 3.3   State intervention and British business since 1990

For the early part of the 19th century the state attempted to facilitate business but intervention as such was minimal. The main areas of intervention were law and order, taxation and currency protection. The primary concern was for the smooth operation of the market. Three factors emerged to challenge this policy: an increase in industrial concentration resulting in large firms being able to over-ride market competition; increasing economic crises of the 1920s and 30s with sharp rises in the level of unemployment; and, ultimately, the Second World War.

Economic crises, in particular, led to the state adopting a much more supportive role towards business. State policies followed the **Keynesian** belief that the free market was unable to solve the problems of unemployment and that increasing state intervention was required to redistribute wealth and create employment. The policy was ultimately challenged by a progressively weaker industrial base and the rise of international competition. The state therefore took upon itself to pursue a more directive line.

Increased direction in the 1960s gained broad support, even from groups not normally associated with such a policy, like the Federation of British Industry (a predecessor of the Confederation of British Industry (CBI), and the Conservative government in its setting up of the National Economic Development Council (NEDI) in 1962. Directive policies included attempts to restructure business, the promotion of mergers to encourage both economies of scale and innovation, and incomes policies. However, attempts at directive policies have tended to fail either through the refusal of management or labour to participate or a lack of consensus. Such a failure occurred when the Labour government of 1974–9 launched its 'social contract', a device to control the economy with the cooperation of the trade unions through wage restraint. The plan ultimately failed (and the government along with it) with rising inflation being met by ever-increasing wage demands.

A new series of economic problems emerged in the 1960s and continued through the 1970s. The problems included: rising levels of inflation, wage claims and unemployment; low productivity; and a worsening balance of payments deficit. The Labour government of the 1970s was embarrassed first by the intervention of the IMF in the conduct of its economic affairs and second by a series of strikes, especially in the public sector, during the winter of 1978–9. The latter, in particular, saw a weakening of the traditional alliance between the Labour Party and the trade unions, challenged the 'social contract' referred to above, and did much to bring about a change of government.

The first government of Margaret Thatcher introduced an economic doctrine (later called **Thatcherism** by the media) that owed much to the free market ideas of Hayek and Friedman. State involvement with business was seen as being incompatible with efficiency and freedom and measures were taken to 'get the state off our backs' and to control those elements that were likely to interfere with the freedom of both markets and individuals. A number of policy measures were introduced to achieve the government's goals and included the following:

- Monetarist policies were used to tackle inflation, comprising the gradual reduction of money supply and the cutting of public expenditure to reduce the excess of expenditure over taxation and hence the **public-sector borrowing requirement (PSBR)**.

- A number of **supply-side** measures were taken with the primary objective of stimulating economic growth. Taxation was cut between 1979 and 1988 with the base rate falling from 33 to 25 per cent and the top rate moving from 83 to 40 per cent. The tax cuts were intended as an incentive for those out of work to return to the job market on the assumption that the extra funds available would be invested in business growth. The work incentive was further strengthened by a series of welfare benefit cuts. In addition to these measures, steps were taken to reduce the power of the trade unions, to deregulate and privatize a number of industries and to encourage entrepreneurialism through the growth of the small business sector.

In a number of areas the policies achieved their stated objectives. Inflation fell from 18 per cent in 1980 to around 2 per cent in the first quarter of 1993 and has remained at around 3 per cent or under ever since. Policies on trade union reform, privatization and deregulation were carried out as planned. However, any assessment of government policy is difficult. To ask whether policies have been successful begs a number of questions. We must ask successful for whom, by what criteria, and at what price? The policies have attracted their critics, who feel that they have done little to enhance UK competitiveness. The critics further claim that the policies contributed directly to the demise of the UK manufacturing industry and to a rise in unemployment although these were, in part, the product of globalization and the rise of cheap labour economies. However, there is sufficient evidence to claim that while some have gained, the lower-income groups have experienced a worsening of their standard of living.

The neo-liberal policies established under the governments of Margaret Thatcher were continued under her successor, John Major. In 1997, 18 years of Conservative government came to an end with the election to power of the Labour Party. The party relaunched itself in order to attract a wider group of voters and rebranded itself as 'New Labour'. It was a conscious attempt to broaden its appeal and move away from its traditional working class and trade union base. Some of its more traditional supporters, hoping for a return to the social democratic traditions of the redistribution of wealth and power, have argued that its policies are little different from those of the previous government. For them, New Labour has simply continued the agenda of market deregulation, privatization, low levels of personal taxation, new managerialism in the public sector and support for the values of self-sufficiency and entrepreneurialism (Hall, 1998).

Moreover, its policies in education and training have been viewed, not as instruments of social democracy, but as a means to the creation of a flexible labour force for multinational corporations (Hall, 1998). Others take a less pessimistic view. Held (1998) argues that, while the global economy places constraints on policy, governments are far from powerless, and policies such as privatization were policies of the state and not necessarily the product of globalization. He further maintains that the role of the state throughout the world is being transformed through the development of regional and global policies and the growth of supranational organizations and inter-government agencies, as in the cases of the WTO and the EU, which we discuss later in this section.

Questions

1 Identify the different stages of state intervention in business since 1990 in the UK.

2 What major changes occurred with the election of the 1979 Conservative government?

3 Identify the continuity and change following the election of the Labour government in 1997. What role has globalization played?

4 Should the state attempt to control and influence business?

Difficulties with state intervention

There are a number of reasons why state intervention in business is difficult:

- The impact of government policy upon business activity is often difficult to measure and direct relationships can be difficult to prove owing to the large number of other variables which can, and do, affect the situation.
- Governments change and, with them, policies. Differences both between and within political parties can result in different approaches to intervention.
- The business community may oppose attempts by governments to control it. The majority of owners and managers of business have an ideological attachment to *laissez-faire*.
- As we saw in Chapter 2, many multinationals tend to have a greater allegiance to their own corporate goals than those of any single nation state.

Despite such problems the state does intervene in business in a variety of ways.

Types of state intervention

Collective provision   The most obvious form of state intervention is through the provision of those goods and services that would otherwise be too expensive, too dangerous, or just ineffective if left to private control. Such aspects would include defence, the police, health, welfare and housing. The extent and nature of such collective provision is a matter of political and ideological debate. The British government, since 1979, has pursued a policy of reducing its collective provision, as we saw in Case 3.3 and will discuss under privatization in Chapter 5.

The state as employer   In the UK, the proportion of the working population employed by the state rose from 2.4 per cent in 1851 to 24.3 per cent in 1975. Policies of privatization since 1983 have led to reductions in those directly employed by the state, but it remains a major employer with a profound effect on the labour market. For example, successive governments have attempted to hold down wages in the public sector as part of the policy of reducing public expenditure. In the past, this has resulted in major confrontations with such groups as the miners, nurses, teachers and the fire brigade.

The state as consumer   The state operates as a consumer of many products and services. As a major employer, the state is a major purchaser of office equipment and many businesses rely on government contracts as a major source of revenue. The state, through its involvement in defence, health and education, has a significant influence on the direction of innovation (Chapter 9 has a more comprehensive review of this aspect).

Legal regulation   The legal regulation of business is extensive and complex. The law of contract is used to regulate the market place. Company law deals with such issues as the protection of consumers through the regulation of monopoly power, rules governing the provision of company information and so on. Labour law deals with both the protection of the individual worker and the regulation of collective bargaining. Patent law exists to encourage innovation by granting monopoly rights to patent holders. Illustrations of such legal provisions may be found in the chapters dealing with specific business activities.

Some laws operate as constraints while others exist specifically to aid industrial development. With privatization, new forms of regulation have been added to protect the consumer and, in the UK, regulatory bodies have been set up for all those public utilities now under private control.

Demand management   All governments attempt to influence and control economic growth, the balance of payments, wage and price stability and the level of unemployment. A variety of measures are used including fiscal measures, such as taxation, monetary measures, such as the control of credit, and direct measures, such as import controls and assistance to specific firms. We have seen already in Case 3.3 how the 1979 UK government attempted to stimulate economic growth through monetarist and supply-side policies.

Through taxation and monetary policies the government is able to raise revenue to finance its activities and also to achieve specific objectives, as through the lower rates of taxation levied on food as opposed to tobacco. In the UK, successive governments have given aid either for specific purposes, such as innovation (Chapter 9 contains a full discussion of this), or to assist a particular firm or an entire industry. In the 1960s, the Labour government targeted the nuclear, motor vehicle, and electrical industries for special assistance, while the 1970 Conservative government targeted the machine tool and woollen textiles industries. Similar policies are pursued by other countries, notably France and Japan. Historically, UK governments have assisted specific firms such as British Leyland and Rolls Royce. However, such support for individual firms is ideologically incompatible with the free market economic policies and constrained by policies of the EU. Whether it wishes to or not, the UK government is forbidden under EU competition law to favour UK firms over those in the rest of Europe. However, funds are available within the EU, through its Social and Regional Development Funds, to stimulate the growth of firms in designated deprived regions and to retrain the workforce.

Training   Government concern about skills shortages and the lack of adequate training in the UK has been a recurrent theme since 1852 and a number of studies have pointed to the greater attention devoted to training by our competitors (e.g. Handy, 1987). Successive governments have attempted to redress this balance by such measures as the Education Act 1944, the Industrial Training Act 1964, the creation of a series of Youth Training schemes, and, the introduction of the National Curriculum in schools and the move towards a national system for the accreditation of vocational skills (NVQs). We deal with some of these issues in the section on labour in this chapter.

Protection   Governments have to varying degrees attempted to protect their industries against what is viewed as unfair competition from overseas firms and, indeed, other governments. One direct measure is the use of import tariffs and controls such as quota restrictions. Government representatives will also attempt to influence the policies of supranational institutions, such as the EU or WTO, to ensure a level playing field for the conduct of international trade.

Marketing   Most governments actively support their own businesses in exporting goods and services. Diplomatic services will inevitably involve a trade function and embassies will act as host to trade delegations as well as influencing foreign governments and businesses through a range of diplomatic connections.

Advisory services　In addition to its policies of regulation and assistance, the state offers various types of advice to business people. Such advice ranges from overseas trade, as identified above, to dealing with industrial relations problems.

The business community as a pressure group

So far this section has concentrated on the way the state attempts to influence business. We now turn our attention to the ways in which the state can be influenced by the business community acting as a pressure group or, more correctly, as a series of pressure groups.

We have already noted that businesses in this country are traditionally resistant to state control and are generally committed to a *laissez-faire* economy and that, as a pressure group, businesses tend to be fragmented with no powerful central body to coordinate policy. Indeed some evidence suggests that British industry is a singularly unsuccessful pressure group because of this fragmentation, and tends to exert pressure only in response to crises.

However, as with all pressure group activity there is a difficulty both in observing it and in measuring its effect. We can only make deductions based upon open, formally reported attempts to influence. The business community tends to be secretive and many attempts to influence government policy are undoubtedly covert and informal. Nonetheless, the business community represents an important source of revenue via taxation and borrowing to enable the state to fund its activities and, this alone, constitutes an important political lobby.

We have suggested that, for the most part, managers tend to be reactive rather than proactive as far as the state is concerned and seem more concerned to predict changes in the political environment than to initiate those changes for themselves. In this way, the tobacco manufacturers predicted increased government regulation of their industry and took measures both to diversify and to transfer attention to growing Third World markets. The same companies reacted successfully to further restrictions on tobacco advertising by expanding their interests in sport sponsorship to maintain a high public profile. Some companies, of course, are more successful than others in resisting state intervention. Multinationals can use their protected status as members of another sovereign state to limit the extent of intervention in those countries in which they operate, and by transferring funds from country to country can minimize tax liabilities. The Swiss pharmaceutical company, Hoffman-La Roche, successfully defended itself against the probing of the British Monopolies Commission in 1971 on the grounds that the British government had no legal right of access to information belonging to a Swiss company. The case was considerably hampered by a lack of vital financial information.

Political risk assessment is a technique or series of techniques used by some firms operating in an international environment particularly where there is considerable investment planned, as in the establishment of a new manufacturing plant. Risk assessments would be built into the strategic plan and assess the stability of the country as well as the chances and likely impact of a change in regime. At a more detailed level, risk assessment will attempt to predict policy changes and their impact upon operations. There have been a number of well-documented cases where a change of government has resulted in the expropriation or nationalization of assets, as has occurred in such countries as Chile, Egypt, Iran, Iraq and Nigeria. Other risks can incorporate such diverse events as civil war, the kidnapping of key personnel and associated ransom demands, restrictions on borrowing, trades union activities, and policy changes concerning the hiring of local staff.

Such assessment is far from easy. Governments can change without any fundamental shift in economic policy and the nationalistic rhetoric of some politicians may threaten foreign investment in the run-up to an election, but be entirely supportive once power has been achieved.

Once genuine risks are forecast, management will wish to take some measures to prevent them. Real pressure group activity exists where the business deliberately attempts to control the political environment in which it operates.

In the UK there are a number of ways in which groups and individuals attempt to influence government policy.

- Professional groups such as the British Medical Association and employers' associations such as the Engineering Employers' Federation attempt to influence policy. The **CBI** addresses a range of economic and business issues, although its impact as a national body is often weakened by the rather fragmented demands of its constituent industrial groups.

- Industry groups lobby government bodies to secure some kind of advantage or to protect themselves from what they see as unfair competition. Thus, the fishing industry in both Britain and the rest of Europe is persistently lobbying for increased protection through the extension of territorial waters.

- Some firms seek political influence through their donations to political parties. In the UK, these have tended to favour the Conservative Party and, in the 1990s, there were well-publicized donations from such firms as United Biscuits, Glaxo, British Airways (BA), Rolls Royce, Hanson and Forté. An element in the repackaging of 'New Labour' has been to broaden its appeal to business and to increase the proportion of funding obtained from corporate sources. As a result large donations have been received from the supermarket chain, Sainsbury.

- Multinationals and the major firms in any country will make some attempt at influencing government policy and may even be consulted.

- Individuals, too, represent an important channel of influence. Many references are made to the 'old boy network' that operates in government and business circles and several firms take more direct action by enlisting the services of a member of parliament on its board of directors. British Airways, prior to privatization, set up a powerful lobby to protect its own position. The Civil Aviation Authority had published a report recommending that BA should give up some of its routes to its competitors, particularly local routes to provincial airlines and international routes to its main competitor, British Caledonian. The report also recommended that BA should move some of its services from Heathrow to Gatwick Airport and allow its competitors to move into Heathrow. The lobby was successful and a government White Paper on airline competition policy favoured BA. Some sources indicated the active role played by the then BA chairman, Lord King, who was a personal friend of the then prime minister, Margaret Thatcher. The government decision effectively prevented British Caledonian from expanding and did much to prepare for its eventual takeover by BA following privatization.

In recent years a number of firms that operate as professional lobbying consultants have emerged. Clients include not just private sector organizations but also local authorities who wish to influence government policy on such issues as the dumping of nuclear waste and who are resisting proposals to create nuclear waste sites in their area.

We can see that businesses attempt to influence the state in a variety of ways: through personal influence, by gaining media coverage for their views, by taking out expensive advertisements, by hiring consultants, and by submitting letters to the press often enlisting the support of other interested parties. The timing of such attempts to influence can be crucial. In 1987 two studies emerged with the expressed intention of influencing government policy on the training of managers. The publication of both reports coincided with a general election campaign, with a substantial loss of impact.

So far in this section focus has been on the way the state exerts its influence over the business community and vice versa. Chapter 2 noted the growing trend of political globalization through trading blocs and supranational political organizations. Such organizations and their activities increase the complexity of the interaction between the state and business. In the next section the general issue of international economic and political integration is dealt with and focuses on two such organizations, the WTO and the EU.

International economic and political integration

International economic and political integration can take a number of different forms. There are essentially two types, **global integration** as with the UN or WTO and **regional integration** as with the EU. There are at least 30 regional groupings and they operate across all continents. The major types are listed below and are placed in ascending order of integration.

- **Free trade areas**. Nations within these areas agree to remove barriers to trade such as tariffs and quotas, e.g. NAFTA.

- **Customs unions**. These are extensions of free trade areas in that members operate together to set a common tariff for all non-member states, e.g. the EU operates as a bloc in negotiations over trade with non-member states.

- **Common Market**. This is like a free trade area and customs union with the added freedom that people and capital can move freely between member countries as well as traded goods and services. The EU is a classic example.

- **Economic Union**. This involves the integration and harmonization of economic policies. It is a goal of the EU but has proved to be difficult to achieve with the unwillingness of some members to surrender their sovereignty on certain issues such as rates of taxation or a common currency.

- **Political Union**. This involves not just economic integration but the integration of political systems. The former Yugoslavia achieved such a union after the Second World War. The difficulties of both creating and maintaining such systems in the face of different demands was in evidence with the break-up of Yugoslavia in the 1990s.

Such types of regional association and integration have had a significant impact on management decisions and business behaviour. The operation of such a region can influence the location of production, the targeting of markets, and lead to increased FDI and joint venture activity.

The World Trade Organization

The World Trade Organization (WTO) began its life as GATT (General Agreement on Tariffs and Trade). It was founded as a supranational body shortly after the Second World

War. Alongside the World Bank and the IMF it was set up as part of the **Bretton Woods** system for the management of the post-war economy. Although the initial concern was for trade in goods, this was extended to include services. GATT was always seen as a temporary stage in the creation of the WTO, but it was not until the conclusion of the Uruguay Round of GATT talks in 1993 that this became a reality. The WTO, with its headquarters in Geneva, opened for business on the first day of 1995.

GATT was originally founded on the twin assumptions that trade is associated with wealth and that an increase in trade between nations means a reduction in the risk of war. These assumptions were born out of the experience of the 1930s when many nations sought to protect their own economies during depression through the imposition of high import tariffs and through the experiences of global war in the 1940s. In 2001, when China joined, the WTO comprised 143 member countries. The issues surrounding the membership of China are explored in more detail in Case 3.4.

Key concept 3.2 World trade organization

Emerging from GATT, the WTO is a global organization of some 140 plus nations concerned with the establishment of rules of trade between member states. This it does within the framework of liberalizing world trade and offering assistance to the developing world. The full achievement of its objectives has been thwarted by the continued existence of trade restrictions by many nations and by the activities of some multinationals in moving operations to avoid WTO regulations.

Agreements between members are reached through a series of 'rounds' of which there have been eight since 1945. Each round seeks to pursue the basic objectives by furthering the liberalization of trade. In general the WTO operates by:

- establishing rules which govern trading behaviour between nation states;
- attempting to liberalize trade through tariff and quota reduction;
- offering a facility and a legal framework, including a court, for the settlement of disputes;
- monitoring trade agreements and government policies, especially those which may contravene the WTO objective of further liberalization;
- providing technical assistance and training for developing countries.

The WTO offers a more formal structure for the furtherance of trade agreements than existed under GATT. Senior ministers of member states and regions meet once a year and ongoing business is dealt with by the Council of Representatives which meets around nine times in any one year. The Council's work is further supported by a series of standing committees. Members should adhere to rules governing the trading of goods and services and they have a duty to apply these rules and the same tariffs to all other members. Furthermore, members must not discriminate between domestic and imported goods and services. The WTO members embrace well over 90 per cent of world trade. Its supporters point to the dramatic reduction in tariffs and the equally dramatic increase in world trade since the war.

Others are more sceptical, highlighting the continued presence of trading blocs as proof of the continued existence of protectionism, the success of countries, such as Japan, in resisting foreign imports, and the growth of informal agreements outside the jurisdiction of the WTO. Such an agreement would include the 'gentleman's agreement' between Britain and Japan and between the USA and Japan to unofficially limit the import of Japanese cars. Such agreements are contrary to the spirit of the WTO. Others have criticized the WTO for taking a weak stance on social and environmental issues, including child labour and global warming. The USA government banned the import of tuna from certain countries, on the grounds that the fishing methods used killed large numbers of dolphins and were a threat to the species. The WTO declared the ban illegal in 1991. Many USA firms manufacture in Mexico, thus avoiding more stringent USA laws on pollution, and there are many cases of multinationals exploiting cheap labour economies and sanctioning the use of child labour. The WTO draws a distinction between the traded goods and services and the methods of production, which critics regard as a flaw in its rules. The only exception is the imposition of trade restrictions on scientifically established health grounds. The perceived ambivalence of the WTO towards social and environmental issues has seen recent summits of WTO members targeted by anti-globalization protest groups, who forced the premature closure of the Seattle summit in 1999.

The most recent 'round' of talks began in Uruguay in 1986 and took 7 years to reach its conclusion at the end of 1993. This particular round concerned itself with the usual tariff issues, but also tackled foreign investment, patents and copyright, trade issues concerning service industries, and agriculture. It is this last issue, among others, that resulted in the Uruguay talks taking so long to reach a conclusion. Throughout the world, agriculture is the most highly subsidized of all industries and any proposal to reduce subsidies and hence liberalize trade have met with stern opposition and ultimately deadlock, resulting in the talks exceeding their deadline date. Even though the Uruguay round was completed at the very end of 1993, it was done amid much last-minute compromise. After talks, agreements must then be ratified by the respective governments, a process that can take years. This lengthy process and the difficulties in reaching an agreement has led many to question the ability of the WTO to regulate international business and trade effectively.

| Case 3.4 | China and the WTO |

China was admitted to the WTO on 11 December, 2001. China was one of the original 23 members of GATT in 1948, but withdrew in 1950 after two revolutions, a civil war and the creation of the People's Republic in 1949. China applied for re-admittance in 1986 during the Uruguay round of talks and was given observer status in 1995.

Although not a member of WTO, many foreign goods had been readily available in China for many years, and China emerged during the 1990s as the world's seventh largest exporter. Its status as an exporter and that of having the largest trade surplus with the USA, ahead of Japan, is in part due to the USA opening its doors to Chinese imports while demanding no reciprocal arrangement. Membership of the WTO will mean that China must open its doors to foreign goods and foreign competition.

China's membership has been especially welcomed by the poorer and developing country members of WTO, accounting for 70 per cent of the total membership. They see a large power, such a China, as a counter to the traditional domination of WTO by the USA, EU, Japan and Canada. Particular issues for the developing countries are:

- The agricultural subsidies given to farmers in the USA and Europe, which work against agricultural exports from poorer countries.
- The expense of patented drugs, in particular those to combat AIDS and other epidemics. Drug companies, invariably from the West, have, through their governments, blocked the sale of cut-price goods to the Third World.

Membership of WTO will bring China a number of potential benefits, but with those benefits will be a number of threats. The benefits and threats are not just economic, but political and social as well.

- While the immediate impact of membership is seen as largely symbolic, it is believed that market reforms, already continuing at a pace, will be locked in. As a consequence, China will move more quickly towards a free market economy. However, with that change the whole structure of the Chinese economy will be altered.
- As a consequence of membership, China will have to make a number of legal reforms and many believe that the rule of law will be strengthened in the country.
- There will be an increased flow of goods, information, people and ideas. This will have the impact of weakening the power of the state over individuals and, together with other economic reforms, will have the inevitable consequence of a move towards a more democratic political structure.
- There will be more privatization and deregulation with the consequence of greater freedom for individual firms.
- WTO membership will lead to still greater inflows of FDI and technology transfer.
- The bureaucracy and government machinery will need to be streamlined with faster and more transparent decision-making processes. Such streamlining will inevitably mean significant job losses of officials.
- As well as government workers, those in all sectors of the economy will be threatened as greater efficiency is sought to improve competitiveness. Many jobs in many areas of the economy are currently protected and full employment policies have resulted in chronic overstaffing.
- Currently 800 million people in China depend on agriculture. Western agriculture is more efficient and a reduction in tariffs on imported agricultural produce will be a severe threat to the agriculture sector.
- The four largest commercial banks in China have debt problems and will not be able to compete with foreign banks who will have equal status in 2006.
- Hong Kong, currently a Special Autonomous Region (SAR) within China may benefit through increased port activity. However, as mainland businesses flourish and duplicate activities in Hong Kong, WTO membership could be

seen as a threat to some in Hong Kong. It may, however, lead to more rapid integration and an ultimate end to SAR status.

● Relationships between China and Taiwan have been tense for many years. At the same time that China was given membership of WTO, so was Taiwan.

Source: *South China Morning Post*, 12–16 November, 2001; *Asian Wall Street Journal*, 12–16 November, 2001

Questions

1 Given China's successful involvement in import and export markets over a number of years, what are the advantages to China of WTO membership?

2 What are the potential threats to China of WTO membership?

3 In an increasingly global economy, what effective role can the WTO play and does membership really mean anything?

The European Union

At the beginning of 2003 the EU embraced 15 nation states. In Table 3.8 the stages in the growth of the EU since the 1950s are identified. The EU was formed out of post-war idealism as a means of putting an end to war between European nations and to assist in the post-war political, social and economic reconstruction of Europe. Politically the EU originally saw itself as a third major power bloc alongside the USA and the USSR. With the break-up of the Soviet Union, its political position has almost certainly been enhanced. Economically there was a desire to capitalize on the largest market in the advanced industrial world. Protectionism was sought both against a buoyant Japanese export trade and in response to increasing protectionism on the part of the USA. By 1999, the EU comprised 380 million people, compared to 270 million in the USA and 125 million in Japan. From

Key concept 3.3 The European Union

The EU, which began life in 1952 as the European Coal and Steel Community, now embraces 15 member states, with others, notably from Eastern Europe, wishing to join. The key objective of the EU is the maximization of advantages associated with the free movement of goods, finance and people and to capitalize on a large internal European market. In achieving these objectives it is intended to bring the peoples of Europe closer together and operate a single market using a single currency. Key landmarks have been the Treaty of Rome (1957), the Single European Act (1987), the Treaty on European Unity (1992), the Treaty of Amsterdam (1997) and the introduction of the 'euro' in 1999. There are still serious concerns by some member states, notably the UK, about the timing of the introduction of a single currency and its impact on sovereignty and there still remain considerable differences in wage rates and standards of living between member states.

a UK perspective, the incentive to join lay in the potential of a growing European market to compensate for declining Commonwealth markets.

While the initial impetus for the creation of the EU was economic (it was originally known as the European **Economic** Community), the EU has also formally embraced social and legal issues. Social issues pertaining to the workplace have been grouped together under the collective banner of the Social Charter, to which the UK was unable to subscribe in full at the time, the only EU member so to do.

The political changes that took place at the end of the 1980s and into the early 1990s are likely to change the face of European business and, with the reunification of Germany, a former communist state was brought into the EU for the first time. Others will join in 2004.

Discussions, which took place in the Dutch town of Maastricht in 1992, to produce the Treaty on European Unity and the Treaty of Amsterdam in 1997 both set out to strengthen the EU provisions to achieve even greater unity. The Maastricht Treaty dealt with the workings of the EU institutions, economic and monetary union, social policy, and foreign and security policy. The Treaty of Amsterdam was concerned also with making EU institutions more effective and efficient, and, in addition, addressed issues relating to citizens' rights, employment and the role of the EU in world politics.

In this section on the EU we will examine its objectives, the mechanisms through which those objectives are achieved and focus on specific key issues. Competition issues will be briefly touched on and monetary union and employment issues will be dealt with in more depth.

Table 3.8	Stages in the development of the European Union
Year	*Development stage*
1952	The European Coal and Steel Community formed by Belgium, France, West Germany, Italy, Luxembourg and the Netherlands
1957	The above six countries sign the Treaty of Rome and establish the European Economic Community. The UK is invited to join but withdraws from talks at an early stage
1958	The European Economic Community comes into being
1973	The initial six members are joined by Denmark, Ireland and the UK
1981	Greece joins
1986	Spain and Portugal join
1987	The Single European Act is passed to create a single market by 1992
1992	The Treaty on European Unity, also known as the Masstricht Treaty
1995	Austria, Finland and Sweden join
1997	Treaty of Amsterdam
2002	The Copenhagen Summit invites ten new members to join
2003	Treaty of Accession signed by Czech Republic, Cyprus, Estonia, Hungary, Latvia, Lithuania, Malta, Poland, Slovakia and Slovenia, for entry in May 2004

EU objectives and instruments

The key objectives of the EU include:

- the maximization of the advantages accruing from the free movement of goods, finance and people;
- the increase of competition and demand;
- the maintenance of stable prices and high levels of employment;
- the coordination of the policies of individual governments and their central banks.

Such objectives rest on a number of assumptions.

- First, it is assumed that the reduction in trade barriers will lead to increased competition, which will drive more efficient methods of production and result in better quality products at cheaper prices. This in turn will lead to an increase in demand.
- Second, it is assumed that a united Europe will offer considerable economies of scale and eliminate the waste associated with nation states operating independently.

The main instruments through which these objectives are to be achieved are contained within the Treaty of Rome 1957, the Single European Act 1987, the Social Charter and the Treaty of Maastricht, the Treaty on European Unity 1992 and the Treaty of Amsterdam 1997. In general terms, the instruments comprise 'directives', which are binding but give member states flexibility in operation, and 'regulations', which are binding and directly applicable.

A primary objective of the EU is the removal of obstacles to free trade, and hence there are proposals to eliminate frontier controls and work permits and to harmonize both taxation policies and technical standards. The creation of a single European technical standard for car manufacture would, for example, eliminate the need to produce different types of headlamps for the same model of car to meet the various legal requirements in different European countries. The elimination of such differentiation would reduce costs and likely lead to increased demand.

The degree to which such instruments have been introduced has varied according to the nature of the proposed change and between member nations. Not all countries have embraced the proposals as readily as others. The UK has failed to agree to the provisions of the Social Charter and opted out of the Social Chapter of the Maastricht agreement (although as we have seen, subsequently agreed to opt in). A particularly contentious issue is that of monetary union. It is to this and other issues we now turn.

EU issues

Businesses have been influenced by a certain harmonization that has taken place in company law, employment law, accounting practice, taxation, and the role of financial institutions. There has been significant cooperation over policies concerning industrial development, regional aid and environmental protection. In the same way that business interests lobby national governments, attempts are made to influence EU policy. Nonetheless, there would appear to be a number of major problems for businesses in dealing with the EU:

- There are many concerns expressed about the bureaucracy and somewhat protracted decision-making mechanisms of EU institutions.

- As the number of members increase decision-making becomes more cumbersome. The increase of members from 15 to 25 in 2004 will not help this process.

- There is a conflict of interests between constituent nation states. At the root of this conflict is the key issue of sovereignty. The EU will assume powers that formerly belonged only to democratically elected governments of individual nation states.

- Significant differences exist within the EU between member states. These include considerable differences in geographical size, population, resources, living standards and a whole range of economic variables that present difficulties in the move to a level playing field. Nonetheless, such convergence is a prerequisite of monetary union. Such issues are likely to be more apparent when ten new countries join in, eight of them from East Europe. The additional ten states will increase the EU population by 20 per cent and its land area by 25 per cent, but will add less than 5 per cent to the GDP. There are fears that many businesses in those countries will be unable to withstand the competitive pressures that membership will bring or that the richer members will be subsidizing these countries to unacceptable levels.

We will illustrate some of the difficulties by focusing on competition policy, monetary union and workplace issues.

The **competition policy** of the EU has the avowed aims of preventing cartels, of controlling monopolies, especially state-controlled monopolies, and of restricting state aid to certain industries thereby creating unfair competition. Despite such aims there are many cases of protectionism and unfair competition within the EU. One reason for the demise of the British coal industry lay in the availability of cheaper coal elsewhere and the subsidies offered to coal producers in Germany.

Monetary union had as its initial instrument the **European Exchange Rate Mechanism (ERM)**. This was an attempt to keep the exchange rates of currency between member countries within fixed limits. While the ERM had its detractors, the major objections are usually reserved for the proposals associated with **European Monetary Union (EMU)** and the creation of a single European currency. Those in favour of EMU see advantages in terms of increased competition and trade, the reduction of transaction costs, increased certainty in planning, the reduction of inflation and the necessity for greater political cooperation. Detractors have pointed to the problems of maintaining comparable interest rates, as seen within the ERM in 1992 and 1993, and say that there would be unequal costs and benefits. For the British government EMU is seen as a loss of sovereignty and hence political control and democratic accountability. For this reason Britain has acted as the chief opponent to full-scale monetary union.

A form of single European currency, the 'ecu', has been used for some time, but mostly only as a paper transaction between member states. In 1999, the new single currency, the 'euro', was introduced by 11 participants. Denmark, Greece, Sweden and the UK opted out for various reasons, although all see themselves as potential future members and Greece did opt in soon afterwards. At first the euro was confined to paper transactions, with coins and notes used for the first time in 2002. The plans to introduce the euro were made at a time of some economic confidence within the EU. Its actual launch, however, coincided with a decline in the economic fortunes of most of its participants, with a resulting fall in the value of the euro against the dollar and sterling. The fall against the dollar was almost one third over the first two years due, in part, to the strength of the USA economy, although the euro had recovered by mid 2003.

The development of the EU has been a major reason why trade between member countries has grown much faster than trade with other nations. Its supporters see the euro as a key instrument in strengthening unity between member states and a means to enhance the role of the EU on a world stage.

The claimed advantages of the euro   These are seen in terms of the following:

- For the consumer it will be easier to shop, as differences in the prices of goods between EU members will become transparent. There is a view that prices will eventually converge. This may be good news for the UK car buyer, given that prices are 40 per cent more expensive than in the rest of the EU, but this could have an impact on UK jobs.

- Currency exchange, with its expensive transaction costs and the uncertainty owing to fluctuations in the exchange rate, will become a thing of the past. This will benefit trade between firms within the EU as well as obviating the need for travellers to change money. Ford's chief executive has argued that the failure of the UK to opt in adds 25 per cent to the cost of operating Ford in the UK.

- The inevitable strength of the euro and the conditions of membership within the single currency will create greater economic stability and end volatile inflation and interest rates. This will enable the EU to withstand severe fluctuations in the global economy, as with the recent Asian crisis.

- The introduction of the euro is seen as part of a package of measures, which include the reduction in the social security element of wages. This has the intention of bringing down labour costs and enhancing labour flexibility.

The claimed disadvantages of the euro   These are seen in terms of the following:

- Opponents of a single currency view it not so much as an economic measure, but as a political one; a major step on the route to a federal Europe. This appears to be less of a problem for some members than others, the UK being the major speaker for the opposition.

- A single currency is incompatible with the management of a large economy. It reduces the freedom of individual governments to respond to economic changes that may have a greater impact on their economy than that of other EU states. For instance, governments will be unable to use devaluation as a means of increasing competitiveness.

The arguments given by the UK government for initial non-participation are based around the notion that the currency will only work given the necessary convergence of economies across Europe in terms of economic structures, business cycles and interest rates. The UK government claimed that, by 1999, the economy had not met the necessary tests of convergence. Supporters of the euro have argued that, at the time of introduction, the UK economy was closer than ever before to the other major economies of Europe, but in the long run, the single currency will be impossible to avoid. It is interesting to note that whereas the EU's own conditions of entry to the EMU are clearly set out in terms of performance measures, the UK objection based on its own tests of entry are highly subjective.

The UK public has responded with an apparent lack of interest. Only 27 per cent of the UK electorate voted in the 1999 elections for European members of parliament. This was the lowest turn-out in the entire EU and compared with 50 per cent in Germany and 75 per cent in Greece.

Employment issues were central to the Social Chapter of the Treaty on European Unity, which built on the 1989 Social Charter and dealt with issues relating to wages and workplace conditions. There was an attempt to harmonize practices, not only on wages and conditions, but also on equal opportunities and mechanisms for consultation between management and labour. The UK alone opted out of this element of the Treaty, an act which has provoked much criticism. The problems of unequal wages and conditions were highlighted by the decision of Hoover in 1993 to move 450 jobs from its factory in Dijon, France, to Cambuslang, Scotland. This was done on the basis that wages and, in particular, associated benefits are up to 30 per cent cheaper in the UK than in parts of the EU. Around the same period, Philips moved 150 jobs from Holland to the UK at Blackburn. Such transfer of labour for cost advantages has been dubbed 'social dumping' and threatens to undermine one of the key elements of European harmony.

Focus on the initial opt-out of the Social Chapter and cases such as Hoover tend to divert attention from the impact of EU directives and regulations on UK employment practices. In many cases the EU has ruled that UK legislation does not go far enough and, as a consequence, several UK labour laws have been amended. Through EU intervention, UK employees now have greater protection in terms of equal pay for equal work and in terms of continuous employment when firms change ownership. An issue of continuous employment that EU intervention helped resolve concerns the contracting out of public sector services in the UK. Case law has determined that public-sector employees who lose their job when the service is contracted out, and are then hired by the contractor, must be treated as if the employment is continuous. The EU has also had an impact via the Working Time Directive, which restricts the working week to a maximum of 48 hours, and by the establishment of European **works councils**.

Employment issues, particularly those concerned with global competitiveness and unemployment, were central to the agenda of the Treaty of Amsterdam, 1997. Ministers subscribed to what they defined as the 'four pillars of employment'. These are employability, **entrepreneurship**, adaptability and equality of opportunity. Issues of flexibility and entrepreneurship are dealt with in the next chapter.

Technology

Technology is probably one of the most widely used and least precisely defined terms in business. It is, however, something that affects business in all its forms and activities. We hope to shed some light on what technology represents and where it stands in relationship to the firm in its environment.

Traditionally, the concept has been popularly used to imply some form of process, invariably machinery based, so we think of lathes, assembly lines, computers and cash dispensers. In this way technology represents the application of science and engineering for use in business. However, technology not only refers to the artifacts themselves but also to the way they are used and the theories governing their application. Human knowledge is therefore an essential ingredient of technology. We often distinguish between manufacturing firms according to the nature of the product, especially its constituent materials and its level of sophistication. One can, therefore, speak of material and product technology. On a much broader scale we distinguish between societies according to their sum total of knowledge and skills and the application of these for the benefit of that society. This, too, is known as technology. From a business perspective we can therefore speak of technology as the application of available knowledge and skills to create and use materials, processes and products.

Key concept 3.4 Technology

Technology is a broad concept referring to the application of available knowledge and skills to create and use materials, processes and products. Technology is often accorded a dominant role in business and is often viewed as determining products, processes, organization structure and the individual's attitude to work. While there are situations where the prevailing technology is undoubtedly influential, it is the product of human endeavour and many managers do have a choice.

Key concept 3.5 Information and communications technology

ICT refers to the convergence of technological development in microelectronics, computing, telecommunications, fibre optics and lasers. This has enhanced quantity, quality and speed of transmission, enabled the development of a globally linked economy and given managers and some workers greater potential flexibility in and control over work operations. Developments in ICT have acted as a key driver in the rapid growth of globalization since 1980.

Technology is closely associated with operations systems, representing both an input and a transformation device. It is also central to the process of innovation and has considerable influence on the structure of organizations. These concepts are developed further in Chapters 5, 9 and 10. In this section we look at more general issues in the way technology and business interact, and focus on issues associated with information and communications technology.

Technology: determinant or choice?

A classic view of technology is that it exists as an environmental constraint, which becomes the dominant feature of all businesses. Firms operate within certain technological imperatives, which shape not only the products and the processes they use, but the structure of the organization, relations between people, and individual job satisfaction. Galbraith (1972) painted a picture of markets being dominated by technological considerations rather than consumer choice.

Joan Woodward (1965) has been very influential. Her classification of small batch, mass and process production has featured in most textbooks on management and organization since the 1960s and this book is no exception (Chapter 10 also refers to her work). To Woodward, technology not only determined organization structure, but the relationship between individual departments and the focus of each business.

- In small batch firms, product development and technical sales were key issues.
- In mass production organizations, fragmentation led to tensions between departments, a source of potential conflict.
- In process organizations, once the system had been created, high volume sales became the key issue.

The relationship between technology and structure was, according to Woodward, crucial to the success of a business. In her study of manufacturing firms in south-east Essex she found that the most successful firms financially were the ones that conformed to the organizational type most appropriate for their technology.

Joan Woodward viewed technology as a determinant of both organization structure and the range of possible strategy alternatives. Woodward has been labelled a contingency theorist. However, as we saw in Chapter 1, the contingency approach puts forward a view of business whereby activities at the level of the firm result from the interrelationship of a number of variables such as technology, the behaviour of competitors, the role of the state and so on. The end result is supposedly strategic choice for the individual manager following from an analysis of relevant variables. Woodward's view of technology would appear to give the manager no choice at all. Technology is dominant and managers fail to adapt to it at their peril.

We offer two challenges to this view of technology. First, we look briefly at its relationship with organizational size, and second, we view technology as an element of strategic choice.

- The first challenge to the notion of an all-pervasive technology is offered by those who champion size as a more influential variable than technology (e.g. Hickson *et al.*, 1969). Studies such as these conclude that technology may well be an important determinant of the structure and work patterns in smaller plants, but as firms increase in size, it is size itself that becomes the more dominant influence. We examine the variable of size more fully in the next chapter.

- Technology is believed by some to determine the structure and processes of business, just as the climate and weather determine agriculture. The knowledge, skills, artifacts and processes that make up technology are, unlike the weather, products of the kind of people who operate technological systems. The assembly line is not a technological imperative, but a device created to satisfy the pressures of mass markets and a product of the foresight of entrepreneurs, like Henry Ford, and the skill of designers who made the process work. Viewed in this way, technology is not a determinant of business but rather a product of the way managers respond to other environmental influences. Furthermore, the kind of technology employed by businesses may be a matter of strategic choice. The application of **socio-technical systems** analysis offers managers the possibility of changing the prevailing technology to suit the needs of their own particular workforce and the prevailing social situation in which they operate. Increasingly, technology and, more especially, information technology (IT) are used as strategies for competitive advantage. We see this to good effect in Case 3.5, Thomson Holidays, where an online computerized booking system was established, linking individual travel agents to the central booking facility, thereby giving Thomson the edge in the market place over its rivals. Developments in electronic commerce supposedly offer opportunities for new business and hence competitive advantage. Electronic commerce is discussed later in this section.

We may conclude that the relationship between technology and business is highly complex. It involves the interrelationship of other variables such as size, management choice, available finance, industrial relations, the intervention of the state and culture. It cannot be reduced to a simple notion of determinism. This was seen in the discussion of News International in Chapter 1. Management wished to introduce computerized photocomposition into its newspaper operations in the UK, USA and Australia. The technology was available and the strategy was clear, yet the speed of the introduction varied in the three countries as a function of government attitude, industrial relations, finance and culture (Marjoribanks, 2000)

An analysis of the role of technology in many organizations offers us insights into a highly dynamic process. A rival tour operator to Thomson Holidays may well feel it necessary to develop its own online reservation system to maintain competitiveness. In this case, the rival management is confronted by the twin forces of technology availability and competition. Management must then evaluate the costs of introducing the new reservation system against the costs of not introducing it, the kind of system to buy and precisely how it will be used in their organization. Thus far, technological and competitive determinism have interacted with management decision-making and choice. Once a decision is reached, the new technology assumes a new dynamic, that of reshaping the organization and offering possibilities of new ways of working. At this stage the new technology must interact with the prevailing organization culture and organization politics. This explains why, in some organizations, groups may resist technological change, as in the case of the Fleet Street newspaper industry.

Information and communications technology

For many years, textbooks defined the application through computers of miniaturized electronic circuitry to process information as 'new technology'. A more specific term for the last 25 years is that of 'information and communications technology', more popularly known as ICT. This has changed the way in which, not only business, but social relations are conducted, as the following illustrations show:

● We now email and text one another rather than send letters or even make a telephone call.

● Instead of visiting the library, we access the information electronically from our desk at work or, more frequently, at home.

● In banking and finance, it has enabled money markets all over the world to be linked with instant access to information and especially market changes. The speed of information flow, the accessibility of that information around the world and the subsequent speed of response were major factors in money and stock market falls in all major markets during the latter part of 1987 and the fall of the Asian tiger economies in 1997 (see Case 3.1).

● In retailing, electronic point-of-sale systems (EPOS) provide instant information on sales trends, cash flows and stock levels.

● In manufacturing, computer-controlled machines, robotics, and entire computerized flexible manufacturing systems have greatly enhanced a firm's response to changing market demands and improved product quality. More significantly it has enabled manufacturing operations to be linked around the world and led to the growth of joint ventures.

- In the office the introduction of word-processing systems originally revolutionized typing and, in many organizations, has led to the elimination of the role of typist altogether, as people type their own letters and reports. Email systems can reduce the amount of paperwork in circulation.

- As we see later, electronic commerce has potential to change the way we all do business.

Without doubt developments in ICT have transformed social relations and business and been a key driver in the process of globalization. Castells (1996) sees developments in ICT as a convergence of related technologies and include:

- **Developments in microelectronics.** In particular, microchip technology paved the way for smaller and more powerful personal computers sold at a price that made them accessible to an increasing proportion of the world's population. Developments in chip technology and especially their capacity reduced the need for large mainframe computers.

- **Developments in computing.** In particular there was a convergence of developments in the 1970s and 1980s. In the 1970s Apple launched its first microcomputer based on the development of the microprocessor. In 1981, IBM introduced the term personal computer (PC) with its new product. This was not based on IBM's own technology and was soon cloned by manufacturers around the world leading to an explosion in PC ownership and use. This was facilitated through software developments and the creation of effective operating systems, the first and most influential of which became known as Microsoft.

- **Developments in broadcasting and telecommunications**. These include the proliferation of satellite television and use of emails, the possibility of video-conferencing and the development of the Internet. Not only has this resulted in dramatic increases in the volume of information and its availability to increasing numbers, but has changed the nature of communication. We can now have 'virtual meetings' with any number of participants around the globe, development engineers in different continents can work together on the same project at the same time and have access to information around the world instantaneously. As we saw in Chapter 2, such developments have made possible the creation of the globally linked economy and have led Castells (1996) to refer to the post-1980 era as 'informational capitalism'. He views the developments in ICT as significant as those in the industrial revolution of the 18th century.

- **Developments in optoelectronics.** Such developments include fibre optics and laser transmission. Developments in fibre optics have led to the increased carrying capacity of wire-based systems. The creation of broadband systems has enhanced not just capacity but also speed and quality of information delivery. Laser technology has facilitated the use of CDs and DVDs as sources of information and is paving the way for the replacement of cables as a means of transmitting information.

At the outset we said that the key development was the convergence of the above technologies. A student from India at a UK university, using her own laptop computer, can pick up emails from the university system when visiting home. She can send an essay to her tutor as an email attachment; an essay that has been researched by remote access to the university's library collection stored electronically and by access to the Internet. The software in her computer was installed using CDs and, as a reward for all her hard work, she can use the same laptop to play her favourite music CD or watch her favourite movie on DVD.

In business such developments have been made possible as a result of:

- The availability of cheaper and more powerful computers, which have improved productivity, performance and quality.
- Increased global competition, which has necessitated increased efficiency through reduced operating costs and reduced staffing levels and resulted in increased cooperation across borders.
- The creation of new forms of more flexible organization and management structures.

The changes brought about in business offer a number of advantages to different stakeholders.

- For management, there is the possibility of cost reduction and increased competitiveness and profitability and instant response to changes in the operating environment.
- For the workforce, there are opportunities for increased job satisfaction and career development.
- For the customer, there are better-quality goods and services at competitive prices.
- For suppliers there is the opportunity of forging closer longer-term relationships with manufacturers and service providers.

Many of the above opportunities were sought and largely gained by Thomson Holidays in Case 3.5.

Case 3.5 Thomson Holidays

This case deals with the introduction of the Thomson Open-line Programme (TOP), a computerized reservation system giving travel agents instant and direct access to the company. In this way, customers are able to book their holiday through their local travel agent and obtain immediate confirmation. Such systems were not new. Computerized reservation had been used by airline companies for some 15 years before Thomson's decision to adopt the technology. Thomson were not even the first tour operator, as a similar system was already operated by Olympic Holidays. However, Thomson were the first major holiday company to introduce a direct access computerized booking system that was adopted by a large number of travel agents, and which became the industry standard.

Thomson Holidays is part of the International Thomson Organization. The company, with interests in newspapers, publishing and oil, did not enter the travel business until 1965 with the acquisition of Universal Skytours and Britannia Airways. After a shaky start and several managerial changes, the company emerged as one of the UK's largest operators, mainly as a result of a vigorous price-cutting campaign in the early 1970s, backed by attention to customer feedback and quality improvement. With the collapse of Clarksons, its major rival, Thomson Holidays became the top company in 1974 and now commands a market share in excess of 33 per cent, far ahead of its closest rival, the International Leisure Group. As well as being a tour operator, the company has developed in all aspects of the travel industry. In Britannia Airlines, it controls the largest holiday charter company in the country. Portland Holidays is one of the largest companies selling holidays direct to the public and, in Lunn Poly, the company owns one of the largest multiples of travel agents.

Prior to the introduction of a computerized system, holiday booking was done either by telephone or entirely on the basis of a booking form. This information was handled centrally and all booking data was kept on a card index. The first technological change came in 1976 with the introduction of the Thomson Reservation and Administrative Control System (TRACS). TRACS established a computer network linking head office with ten regional centres, through which bookings were made by travel agents. The company bought existing software used by the airline KLM but had underestimated the degree of customization required and the software was almost completely rewritten.

TRACS was viewed by management as a success and was seen as a major factor in the company keeping ahead of its rivals in the turbulent environment of rising oil prices in the 1970s and the subsequent impact on the cost of air travel. Errors in bookings and administration were reduced, credit control was improved, and the system was popular with travel agents. Central booking staff were reduced by approximately two-thirds and those remaining in post had their jobs enhanced as they now operated as a direct interface between the company and travel agents. The person heading the introduction of TRACS was promoted to Systems Director, recognition by the company of the strategic importance of IT.

When TRACS was introduced in the mid-1970s, networking technology was relatively unsophisticated. By the end of the decade, the Post Office had launched Prestel, a nation-wide online processing system with low-cost terminals. This effectively paved the way for a considerable growth in national computer networks. Thomson extended TRACS to a large number of travel agents through TOP. The relatively low cost of the online system did not limit its use to just the larger multiples in the travel agency business. The accessibility to the small independent travel agency of its computer booking system was an important strategic objective for Thomson.

The company hoped to build upon the efficiency and effectiveness of TRACS, not least the cost savings. TOP became a corporate priority receiving direct top management support and a project team was set up drawing upon staff from all parts of the organization as well as recruiting staff with specific expertise from outside. This was vital given the decision to develop the company's own network, based largely on its experience with TRACS. Travel agents were closely involved throughout the development stage and all participating agents received comprehensive training. TOP was widely publicized by Thomson and the company received a great deal of favourable press coverage. The intended image was created of a company that was not only a leader in the holiday business but also a leader where technology was concerned.

TOP was introduced in 1982 with 2200 participating travel agents. Within a year 3584 agents were involved covering 61 per cent of all bookings. Telephone bookings were withdrawn altogether in 1986 and, by 1988, 95 per cent of all bookings were made through the online system. The overall cost of introducing TRACS and TOP has been estimated at a little over £20 million. Between 1978 and 1987 there was a 400 per cent increase in business and Thomson's market share rose from 18 per cent to 29 per cent, with a further rise to 33 per cent by 1990. Throughout this period staffing had remained fairly constant at around 800 and Thomson estimated that savings directly attributable to the new system were of the order of £28 million.

By 1998, Thomson were ready to enter a new phase in their use of IT. They had introduced BACWAY for Windows, a new computerized system for collecting direct debit payments from travel agents and were planning to use the recent development of interactive digital television to sell holidays. Interactive television bookings had been pioneered in the USA, by such as the travel channel. Thomson decided, with BA, to become the two launch partners for Microsoft's interactive holiday booking service, Expedia. As well as its work with Microsoft, Thomson have developed their own innovation team, under an Innovation Manager to plan and oversee new applications of information technology, e-commerce and digital interactive television.

Sources: Peltu and Land, 1987; Daniels, 1991; *Marketing*, September, 1998; *New Media Markets*, October, 1998.

Questions

1 How did Thomson use technology to gain competitive advantage?

2 What are the opportunities and threats in the maintenance of competitive advantage using technology?

3 Assess the impact of the new technology on the internal workings of Thomson.

There are, however, a number of problems which may be created by the introduction of new technology. While desktop computers and word-processors can be relatively cheap labour-saving devices for the office, the introduction of entire manufacturing systems based on new technology can be prohibitively expensive. In general terms, the introduction of new technology in the office incurs much lower costs than in manufacturing. The availability of a wide variety of software has considerably reduced the cost of establishing computerized systems. However, the costs of adapting the software to meet local specifications can add greatly to the cost of implementation. Considerable costs were borne by Thomson Holidays in adapting existing software already being used by airline companies.

Before leaving the topic of technology, we focus on two areas, both of which have attracted controversy. These are electronic commerce or e-commerce and its current and future impact on business, and the relationship between changing technology and jobs. We deal with each in turn.

Electronic commerce

> Today's business interests sit on a fault line of the greatest seismic shift since the invention of the printing press . . . e-business. We are embarking on a journey of such magnitude that it has the capacity to change the course of our entire social order.
> (*PricewaterhouseCoopers, 1999, p. 5*)

Such statements as the above reflect the hype that surrounds developments in **electronic commerce**, also known as e-commerce and **e-business**. While there is no internationally agreed definition of e-commerce, it is generally held to incorporate any exchange of information at any stage in the supply chain. It thus involves suppliers and manufacturers and service providers and firms and their customers. Commentators such as those at PricewaterhouseCoopers believe that the way we do business will be revolutionized and that it will level the playing field between large and small firms. In this section we will explore the concept of electronic commerce, its impact on business and the issues it raises.

For many companies electronic commerce is little more than the creation of a web site to provide information to customers, while to others it is a means of selling goods and services on an international scale. Essentially, electronic commerce is a transaction involving goods, services and information in which the parties to the transaction do not meet, but interact electronically. Much of that interaction is carried out using the Internet. This has led to the growth of Internet companies, such as Amazon.com, one of the pioneers of electronic retailing. Amazon offers a large catalogue of books, which are offered over the Internet, often at much cheaper rates than in retail outlets. An order can be made and paid for by credit card electronically and the book is sent by post. In addition to retailing, information can be accessed using the Internet. Much of the information is free to anyone with the means of access, as with versions of many local, national and international newspapers. Some databases, such as collections of academic journal articles, require a subscription fee, and can be accessed by means of a password.

In the above cases, both the supplier and buyer gain through reduced transaction costs. Retailers are able to shorten the supply chain to the customer, thereby reducing costs, as well as gaining access to a global market. Consumers benefit through reduced prices and

Key concept 3.6 E-commerce and e-business

Such approaches connect suppliers and buyers directly through computer-based systems. E-commerce generally relates to trading activity involving information, goods and services. The initial point of contact is electronic although, in the case of goods and services, delivery is made using more conventional systems. E-business generally refers to a much broader range of activities, incorporating all business activities. It enables the various elements of global firms to work more closely together and can form the basis of much business-to-business activity. The growth of e-commerce and e-business is directly associated with the development of the Internet and company-wide intranet systems. Doing business electronically reduces the supply chain and hence increases convenience, reduces costs and improves speed of delivery. It is predicted that it will revolutionize business, although at present take-up rates are quite low, costs of entry are high and there are still some unresolved issues related to privacy and security.

access to a range of products globally. In the late 1990s, book buyers were the favourable recipients of a price war as Barnes and Noble, and Borders attempted to gain market share from the market leader, Amazon. Those seeking information have access to a much wider range than hitherto, all of which can be accessed from the home or the office.

A large range of goods, from CDs to cars, can be bought in this way, although as we saw in our case study in Chapter 1, there are some restrictions and some reluctance to making major purchases such as a car via the Internet. E-commerce has enabled home access to personal bank accounts and, with some banks such as Barclays and First Direct, a full range of banking services. The Internet has made possible ticketless air travel, a system used by many USA airlines for internal flights and now used extensively by BA on all flights. An airline seat can be purchased electronically and the customer simply produces identification at the check-in desk to pick up a boarding card. Applications for some university courses can be made over the Internet. Supermarket shopping orders can be placed via the Internet with guaranteed delivery times.

It is not only shoppers who benefit from enhanced services. Some supermarkets, such as Tesco, use e-commerce as the basis of their sales ordering system with suppliers. As with most supermarkets, items scanned at the check-out provide vital information for stock reordering levels. In the case of Tesco, the information is transferred automatically to a central computer system, which automatically raises orders to suppliers, which are then despatched to the appropriate store. This version of retailing JIT eliminates the necessity for Tesco to hold stock in central warehouses, thereby reducing costs. Ford Motor Company moved to a global organization, creating cross-national teams in management and the key functions. In support of this, the company has developed its own intranet system incorporating databases and email and linked to a video-conferencing system. In this way, design teams, working from different country bases, can collaborate on complex design issues.

Companies, such as Ford Motor Company, are part of a group of pioneers in the use of e-commerce and e-business. According to an *Economist* survey, others include Cisco Systems, Dell, General Electric and Visa (*The Economist*, 26 June–2 July, 1999). While the media focus is on the impact for the general public, the size and value of business-to-business transactions far exceeds the use of e-commerce by the ordinary consumer. Businesses have shown themselves much more willing to use the Internet for transactions than the general public, even in the USA, which has the highest proportion of Internet users per head of population in the world. Firms such as those listed above regularly use e-business to deal with both suppliers and customers. The rate of take-up of such methods by businesses would appear to be linked to the level of competition and whether Internet trading is done by major competitors. It is a system that has enabled some companies to come from nowhere to be leading players in their field, as in the case of Dell Computers.

There are, however, a number of barriers to overcome before the seismic shift of PricewaterhouseCoopers' claim can occur.

- A major constraint is one of access to the Internet. In this respect, as we can see in Tables 3.9 and 3.10, there is variability.
- Even with access, many in the USA as well as Europe are reluctant to make purchases over the Internet using a credit card. Evidence suggests that fraud and fear of potential fraud are problems operating against both the seller and the buyer.
- Even when the system works there are frequent complaints of delays in accessing the Internet and in the processing of orders. In order to circumvent a clogged

Table 3.9

Internet penetration

Country	% of population
USA, Canada, Sweden	40
UK	18
Japan	15
Germany	10

Source: EITO, 2001, http://www.eto.org.uk

Table 3.10

PCs per 100 population

Country	Quantity
USA	68
Sweden	44
UK	35
Germany	25
Italy	12
Spain	11
Portugal	8

Source: EITO, 2001, http://www.cto.org.uk

Internet system, many firms in the USA have resorted to sending information through the post in the form of a CD-ROM, thereby adding to the cost of the transaction. A frequent complaint in business-to-business transactions in the USA is the proliferation of 'junk' CD-ROM mail.

- The costs of setting up an effective e commerce system are considerable, which poses particular problems for smaller firms. This has led to transnational initiatives by the G7 nations to encourage the use of e-commerce by smaller firms.

- Surveys of smaller firms reveal there is often significant customer pressure behind the decision to use e-commerce. The advantages are identified as improved competitiveness and enhanced service. However most **SMEs (small- and medium-size enterprises)** when surveyed see it as making a greater contribution to internal communications via the introduction of email systems than they do to attracting new customers (Quayle, 2002; Daniel and Wilson, 2002).

Undoubtedly, privacy and security are key issues and banking services are at the forefront of developing secure firewall and filtering systems. As well as developments in security systems, e-commerce has led to the creation of new laws to protect electronic transactions. Such legal rulings become particularly important where the transactions occur across national borders and hence, across different legal systems. Electronic transactions pose particular problems where there are differences in contract law, consumer protection, sales tax and customs duty. In 1999 the EU began to develop laws to clarify such issues and which country's law would apply in the case of cross-border purchase. Some countries, such as China, Singapore and Saudi Arabia, have already used their legal powers as well as available firewall and filtering technology to limit access to overseas Internet sites. Such censorship is attacked by those who see the Internet as the main instrument for the creation of both a borderless world and the spread of democracy. In fact, the reliance on cabling technology probably offers a greater limitation to the use of the Internet than local censorship, since it favours urban areas and follows existing cabling patterns. However, this may change when fibre optics can be replaced by laser technology.

As with many well-publicized developments in business, we find that the reality is neither as extensive nor as simple as the image. We may stand on the threshold of a revolution, but the threshold would appear to have a larger entrance than e-commerce supporters envisaged. Undoubtedly there is potential for growth, underlining the developments in globalization that are a part of modern business. Consumers have the potential to access a much wider range of goods and services from a much wider range of suppliers. Given that the use of electronic exchange is more prevalent in business than among the general public, business organizations are bound to experience change in their structures and functions. There will also be repercussions for the labour market, to which we now turn.

Technology change, jobs and labour

There would appear to be three perspectives on the impact of technology on jobs and labour.

- First, we have the kind of view associated with such writers as Braverman (1974). Technology change, particularly ICT, is seen as a deskilling agent reducing the amount of discretion an individual has over his or her job, at the same time increasing management control over both work process and worker. The thesis associates technology change with job cuts and rising unemployment, and the greatest impact of both deskilling and job losses is felt by skilled craft workers.

- The second perspective offers an optimistic scenario. New technology is seen as creating new opportunities for the workforce in the form of new and different types of labour with opportunities for existing workers to learn new skills.

- The third perspective is also optimistic, viewing new technology as a liberating device, eliminating the need for human labour in repetitive, dangerous or unpleasant tasks and, in some cases, freeing people to engage in socially beneficial work.

The evidence supporting these three perspectives is mixed. We will view the effect on the numbers employed, on the types of jobs involved, and on the content of those jobs.

- The impact of new technology on **job numbers** received much attention in the 1980s. A comprehensive survey in the UK, by Daniel (1987), revealed that job losses had occurred in manufacturing, but that it was difficult to isolate the impact of new technology from other changes, notably declining markets. He also found that actual dismissals were very rare and that reductions were generally met by redeployment, early retirement and (in some cases highly attractive) voluntary redundancy schemes. In terms of the service sector, Daniel found job gains associated with the introduction of word processors and computers. The introduction of new technology has been used to increase productivity and provide an improved service through retaining existing employment levels. In Case 3.5, Thomson's computerized booking system resulted in staff reductions when it was first introduced. However, over time the increase in the volume of bookings meant that staffing was restored to its former level, with the staff handling a far greater volume of work than previously.

Similar findings were made in an extensive study across the (then) 12 member states of the EU (Gill *et al.*, 1992). In a study of mechanical engineering, electronics, banks, insurance and retail, they found that new technology had created jobs. However, they acknowledged that job losses could well be felt in those firms not employing new technology and thus losing competitive edge and market share. Woodall (1996) points to the case of the USA and Japan; both are countries that have invested more than most in computerized manufacturing yet, compared to their counterparts in Europe, they have not suffered the same levels of unemployment.

- The impact of new technology has been shown to vary according to the **type of job**. In general, the demand for unskilled labour has fallen while that for skilled labour has risen. Routine, repetitive jobs have been eliminated in both manufacturing and service work and some workers have been empowered through having direct control over processes. Far from causing mass unemployment this has led to job shortages in some areas, notably in highly skilled and specialized work. While jobs have disappeared, new jobs, particularly in IT and financial services, have emerged. This uneven impact has in some cases led to a transfer of skills from one group of workers to another. Wilkinson (1986) found that the introduction of the computer control of manufacturing equipment shifted work from the craft jobs on the shop floor to computer programmers and analysts. In many firms this represents a shift in the location of power within the organization and a subsequent impact on organization structure. In many organizations the numbers of middle and supervisory level managers has been greatly reduced. In her study of changes brought about by the 'information age' Stanworth (1998) concluded that the impact of new technology on structure was far more significant than its impact on jobs.

More pessimistic views on the impact of new technology on employment levels emerged in the mid-1990s. Some estimates in the USA suggest that 2 million jobs are being lost annually, and, where replacement is taking place, it is in the form of part-time or temporary work (Rifkin, 1995). The same author sees job losses in manufacturing and service sectors alike. In the latter, banking has experienced numerous branch closures and considerable staff reductions in the face of automatic teller machines, telephone banking and electronic commerce.

Unlike previous types of technological change, IT in particular affects all kinds of jobs and places fewer restrictions on location. Using the advantages offered by IT, such as global networks and the capacity to re-route telephone calls, the same job can be done equally well in Mumbai as Manchester. In this respect, both BA and Lufthansa have centralized their ticket accounting function in India, taking advantage of cheap labour. RCI, the world's largest company dealing in time-share holiday exchanges, has established its European operations centre in Cork, closing down smaller offices in other countries. Where the job involves telephone sales or telephone information, it matters little where the jobs are located. These operations are known as 'call centres', and in 1997 it was estimated that there were 3500 in the UK alone, employing 163 000 people (Davis, 1999).

USA hotel chains have operated such centralized systems for years and many other businesses have followed suit. In Europe, Cork has established itself as the leading 'call centre' with firms taking advantage of Irish government grants and the language skills of the local population. BA has centralized its flight information service in Newcastle, where office rentals and labour are cheaper than in London.

However, as Daniel had found a decade earlier, it is difficult to isolate the impact of new technology from that of other influences. In the 1990s there were considerable changes related to the impact of economic globalization, including increased competition and the transfer of jobs to lower-cost labour markets. Under such competitive conditions, new technology could have been introduced to reduce operating costs and thus preserve jobs in the face of such competition. Such a position is compatible with our view of business as a set of complex interactions.

- The debate about job numbers is matched by that concerning **job content**. We may conclude from the findings of the 1980s research in the UK that, on balance, new technology enriched the jobs of those affected in both manual and office settings, with greater possibilities being afforded the latter group. In deference to Braverman, the surveys do make the distinction between enhanced satisfaction in terms of job content and reduced autonomy through the centralization of management control. Research in the 1990s confirms these earlier findings. New technology would seem to be replacing 'mass labour' with 'elite labour' (Rifkin, 1995), emphasizing more creative knowledge-based work. In manufacturing, automation has greatly enhanced the work environment of jobs such as paint spraying. In the office, the use of word processors has reduced the drudgery of typing numerous addresses. Nevertheless, the benefits derived through the introduction of such advanced systems can be offset by the cost in manufacturing, and by the time taken to encode information in the office before such benefits can accrue.

The main point to be taken from all the studies is that the introduction of new technology should not be viewed deterministically. Its impact is based on a number of different factors, including the nature of the product and service, the type of organization involved and the competitive environment in which it operates, the management strategy employed, and the position taken by trade unions, employees and governments. The majority of studies in the 1980s and 1990s are all fairly inconclusive on the impact of new technology on jobs. We may conclude that the job losses arising directly from the introduction of new technology are less than originally envisaged and must be viewed in the context of job losses resulting from other causes, such as global competition. However, several points need to be made.

- The introduction of ICT, if not directly causing job losses, changes the nature of employment for most people. Some groups gain while others lose.
- In general, there has been a polarization of the labour force. For an educated group in skilled work, their jobs have often been enhanced. For many semi-skilled and unskilled workers their jobs have been downgraded. This latter group is typically in low skilled, low paid, often temporary work and is over-represented by women and ethnic minorities.
- As well as an occupational polarization in most industrial societies, the global organization of production has brought about a geographical polarization. Low skilled, labour intensive work is located in low wage economies such as India,

China and Indonesia, while higher skilled work predominates in the advanced industrial nations.

- As a consequence, in terms of job losses the hardest hit group is the low skilled male workers in advanced industrial nations.
- While there was an initial transfer of jobs from the manufacturing to the service sector, some areas of the service sector, notably banks, suffered significant job losses in the 1990s.
- ICT is generally associated with growth industries. Rather than focus on job losses, perhaps we should be more concerned about the lack of job gains (a point made by Daniel, 1987).

Many of these points are summed up by Woodall (1996):

> The worst thing governments can do is to try to slow down the process of adjustment through regulation, subsidies or protectionism. They may save a few people from pain but they will depress living standards and employment growth for the country as a whole . . . Both information technology and globalization favour the highly skilled. For the unskilled the future could be bleak. (*Woodall, 1996, p. 23*)

Labour

Labour interacts with business through the workings of the labour market and through the activities of trade unions. Aspects to consider are the changes in both the level and nature of employment, the impact of globalization and the role played by trade unions in the operation of business. We have already noted in this and the preceding chapter how the forces of globalization, technological change and changes in both the ideologies and actions of the state have had an impact upon labour markets and trade unions. In the next section we will see how both types of employment and **employee relations** can be influenced by cultural factors. Managers influence the workings of the labour market through various strategies of recruitment, training and payment. Variations in management strategy also account for the way different companies handle issues of employee relations. In this section we will look at four aspects of labour. These are employment trends, the impact of globalization, links between education and training and the power of trade unions in influencing management decisions. A more detailed discussion of human resource and employee relations strategies may be found in Chapter 12.

Employment trends

Jobs in the labour market can be put into one of five groups:

- The **primary** sector, which includes agriculture and mining;
- The **manufacturing** sector;
- The **construction** sector;
- The **retailing** and **distribution** sector, which includes wholesalers, shops and garages;
- The **service** sector, which includes a wide range of activities such as catering, banking, education, health and social care, computing and the professions.

Manufacturing and construction are often grouped together as are retailing, **distribution** and services. The latter grouping is referred to as the **tertiary** sector. The following points will identify the changing trends involving these sectors, not just for the UK but globally as well. We will then present an overview of the influence of globalization on employment trends.

- **Shift out of the primary sector.** In the 1960s and 1970s considerable job losses were experienced in the primary sector (mining, agriculture, fishing etc.). During that period the primary sector workforce was cut by one half in the UK, although, largely through mechanization, its share of total output was increased. In the 1990s further employment losses were incurred by the primary sector through an extensive programme of pit closures in the coal-mining industry; 440 000 jobs have been lost in mining alone since 1981 (Labour Market Trends, 1998). Similar patterns were found in other developed countries, although agriculture still has an important presence in Japan. In the less developed world the reliance on the primary sector is still evident, as we saw in our discussion of the role of agriculture in China (see Case 3.4).

- **Shift out of manufacturing.** The process of **de-industrialization** has led to considerable job losses in the manufacturing sector in most developed countries. Table 3.6 (p. 94) shows how manufacturing industry in the UK shed 40 per cent of its labour between 1971 and 1991. We have noted that this was partly as a result of government policy, but mainly the effects of global competition. A fuller discussion of the de-industrialization process is offered in the first section of this chapter. The trend has been worldwide with a 10 per cent fall in manufacturing employment across all developed countries between 1970 and 1992. However, over the same period, manufacturing employment in the UK fell from 8.5 million to 4.9 million (ILO, 2003). Some countries have maintained levels of manufacturing employment, most notably Japan with the strong presence of a craft labour force.

- **Gains in the service sector.** Job gains have been experienced in the tertiary sector of the economy, particularly in the financial sector, catering, the professions and professional services, and health and social care. Since 1981 the greatest gains in the UK have been in computing and IT with 916 000 extra jobs and social work with 450 000 extra jobs (Labour Market Trends, 1998). Similar patterns are found across most developed economies, although, as we have seen, with less of a shift out of manufacturing. Among the ten most developed economies, service employment rose from 127.4 million in 1970 to 216 million in 1994 (ILO, 2003).

- **Impact on unemployment.** In most developed economies, unemployment rates have risen with the longest increase in Europe. In 1996, the OECD average was 7.5 per cent, while that of Europe was 10.5 per cent. Within most regions there are variations. In Europe, unemployment rates have fallen in the UK but risen in France, Germany and Spain. Unemployment has also declined in the USA and Canada since 1995, and it remains low for much of the developing world. Rates for most Asian countries in 1996 were less than 3 per cent (ILO, 2003). Three trends can be seen:

  - There has been a rise in long-term unemployment among males, mainly those displaced by job losses in primary industries and in manufacturing.
  - There has been a rise in female unemployment. This is a consequence of more women entering the labour force (we deal with this issue later in the section) and hence registering for employment. It is also a consequence of the introduction of

new technology in the service industries and the displacement of lower skilled work, which was done mainly by women.

– There has been a rise in youth unemployment. In some countries this is severe. In Spain in 1997, 40 per cent of under 25s were unemployed (ILO, 2003).

● **Impact of technical change.** As we see in the above examples, some of the changes in the nature of employment are attributable to changes in technology. References to this are made throughout this book and aspects of new technology and ICT have been dealt with earlier in this section.

● **Increase in flexibility.** Across all developed countries labour markets have become more flexible both in terms of the nature of the employment contract and the hours worked. There has been an increase in part-time work, fixed term contracts and self-employment. Figures for the EU show much variation. Part-time working is highest in the Netherlands at 36.5 per cent of all jobs and lowest in Italy with 6.6 per cent (ILO, 2003). Part-time working dominates in the service industry and employs a high proportion of females. In the UK, 86 per cent of all part-time jobs are occupied by women and similar statistics prevail for Belgium, Germany and Switzerland. In the USA, Canada and Japan, while females still predominate in part-time work, the proportion is not nearly so marked as in Europe (ILO, 2003). Flexibility is also increasing in the patterns of attendance. There may have been a decline in traditional manufacturing shift work, but many service industries have moved to 24-hour, 7-day operations. This is particularly the case in some forms of retailing and catering. A fuller discussion on flexibility is presented in the following chapter. While many firms express a clear preference for part-time employees, changes in EU laws have increased the cost of employing part-time workers and may lead to a decrease in this form of employment.

● **Increase in female employment.** Table 3.11 reveals the increase in the number of women in the labour market since 1970. Women are still over-represented in certain types of employment, notably health, education and local government, and they are significantly under-represented in management in all sectors of employment. Indeed, in the UK, the proportion of women managers is about the same in both the private

Table 3.11	Women in the labour force as a % of women aged 16–64, 1970–90	
	% of women in labour force	
Country	1970	1990
USA	49	69
UK	51	65
Japan	55	62
Germany	48	61
France	48	59
Italy	34	43

Source: OECD, Main Economic Indicators, 1995, adapted from Castells, 1996 and the public sectors, despite the much higher proportion of women working in the latter (Cully *et al.*, 1998). We have already noted that women are over-represented in both low skilled and part-time work. In the EU, 32 per cent of all women in employment are in part-time jobs and in the Netherlands the figure is 69 per cent. In all forms of employment in all developed countries, women earn less than their male counterparts (ILO, 2003).

- **Polarization of the labour market.** Both Castells (1996) and Dore (1997) have noted changes in job allocation associated with the growth of 'graduate calibre' jobs and the raising of the educational entry requirements for jobs across the board. The prediction is that this will lead to a polarization within society. There will be those with good education and scarce skills who will obtain challenging jobs, although the impact of global competition and technological change will end the concept of a job for life. However, an increasing proportion of the population will be faced with either poor jobs or unemployment, with little chance of acquiring the necessary skills to move into more challenging work.

Globalization and the labour market

> While capital flows freely in the electronic circuits of global financial networks, labour is still highly constrained and will be for the foreseeable future, by institutions, culture, borders, police and xenophobia. (*Castells, 1996, p. 232*)

The view that globalization has resulted in an increase in the flows of goods, services, capital, ideas and people, is challenged if we examine global movements in the work force. Overall migration figures across the world have been increasing at an annual average rate of just under 2 per cent, although the biggest growth has been within countries in the developing world (ILO, 2003). However, the proportion of the world's work force operating outside its own country is relatively small. In 1996 it was 1.5 per cent of the total working population, with half of those working in Africa and the Middle East. In Europe, with no barriers to the movement of labour, only 2 per cent of workers operate outside their country of origin (Castells, 1996).

An explanation of this is that globalization actually leads to a decrease in labour migration as increased flows of FDI and trade create jobs in most developing countries, although those that do migrate are often the well-educated. There is a fear that multinationals have shifted the manufacture of goods and services and hence labour to lower cost countries, thereby creating increases in unemployment in many countries of the developed world. This view is challenged by the IMF. They argue that globalization contributes to employment growth everywhere, whereas unemployment is a function of government macroeconomic and labour market policy (IMF, 2003). Direct links between globalization and labour migration on the one hand and employment levels on the other, are difficult to prove, because of the interaction of so many variables.

However, despite the relatively low levels of global labour mobility an interesting statistic emerged in 2002. World Bank figures for 2002 revealed that money sent home by migrant workers from developing countries with jobs in developed countries, was greater than the combined total of government aid, bank loans, IMF and World Bank aid (quoted in *Observer* 20th April, 2003). The figures are even more remarkable given that the majority of those workers are among the poorest paid in those countries. India and Mexico received the largest contribution from migrant workers at around US$10 billion each and the Philippines received US$6.5 billion. Such money transfers also accounted for 37 per cent of the entire GDP of Tonga.

Education and training

One way of changing the composition of the labour market and thus addressing some of Dore's and Castells' concern regarding the polarized labour force is through education and training. We offer a brief summary of the history of UK concern for its relatively poor performance in training and education against that of its major competitors, and examine the approach to vocational training in Germany.

> The British entered the twentieth century and the age of modern science and technology as a spectacularly ill-educated people. (*Hobsbawm, 1968, p. 169*)

Hobsbawm's view reflects that of many commentators in the final half of the 19th century. The Samuelson Commission of 1884 accused the UK government and industry of falling behind its major competitors in the adaptation to economic and technical change. The Commission singled out education and training as the key drivers of change. From 1850 to the present day there have been a number of studies and reports, each drawing similar conclusions. Government policy reacts to these findings from time to time in response to falling competitiveness and technology lag.

In the 1980s there was considerable work carried out by the National Institute for Economic and Social Research (NIESR), focusing largely on comparative studies of education and training between the UK and Germany. The reports concluded that the UK workforce was poorly trained, which resulted in the production of poor quality goods and services with an adverse effect on the nation's economic performance. Such findings were confirmed by Handy (1987) in a major study of managerial training across five countries. In general, competitors such as France, Germany, Japan and the USA have a much greater proportion of the population educated to a higher level, more finish training with recognized qualifications and there is greater integration between education in schools and the training system. In addition, the Handy Report points to the poor quality of much of UK management training.

A number of reasons have been given for the shortcomings of vocational education and training in the UK. These can be summarized as follows:

- Many have commented on the apparent divorce between education and training, compared to the integration found in such countries as Germany and France. The UK education system has been heavily influenced by the traditional public schools and their historical emphasis on non-vocational education. A continuing debate among educationalists is that of education of the whole person versus more job-related education. This has re-emerged in the current Labour government's emphasis on skills and employability.

- Traditionally the government in the UK has tended to see training as the responsibility of individual companies. Despite this there have been a large number of initiatives over the past 25 years to tackle specific problems such as youth unemployment and falling competitiveness. Such initiatives, however, have tended to be isolated responses without the framework of an overall long-term strategy.

- Many managers in the UK regard training as a cost, which, given the short-term orientation of many strategies, results in the reduction of training budgets at the first signs of financial reversal. This lack of a long-term approach is one reason for the continued decline in apprenticeships in the UK, despite several attempts to reform the system.

Germany: a training ethos

The findings of the NIESR and the Handy Report have already been noted, which compare the UK unfavourably with Germany. Handy (1987) found that approximately 80 per cent of German managers were graduates, while Britain boasted fewer than 50 per cent. In Germany, the degrees are vocationally oriented with engineering and other technical subjects predominating. It is the norm for better educationally qualified German managers to hold the more senior positions in the hierarchy and to have risen through the ranks rather than by switching companies, as is the case in the UK and USA (Lawrence, 1980; Child *et al.*, 1983). It is not uncommon to find German managers with a degree and a technical apprenticeship.

Germany lays great store by its system of youth training referred to as the '**dual apprenticeship system**'. A very high proportion (around 85 per cent) of all school leavers who do not go on to higher education enter a three-year apprenticeship across a range of occupations (Casey, 1986). The apprenticeship involves training in a mixture of job-specific and general work skills with one day a week spent in a specialist vocational college. The scheme has been successful in supplying the labour market with skilled workers who are easy to retrain because of the presence of general work skills and the emphasis on attitude training. The scheme is highly regulated by the state and is administered by national and local government, employers and the trade unions. The scheme is also supported by the broader education system. Support also comes from the trainees themselves, whose acceptance of low wages in the first few years helps fund the scheme. For example, a 16-year-old trainee in Germany can expect to receive only 25 per cent of the adult wage for the job, compared to 50 per cent in Britain (Casey, 1986). It is this social acceptance of training costs against likely future benefits that does much to underpin the system. No such ethos exists in Britain, and attempts to introduce youth training schemes have met with a consequent unenthusiastic response. The result has been that Germany boasts three times the number of skilled workers as can be found in the UK.

Such differences between Germany and the UK have been used by some studies to explain the differences in strategies, export performance and profitability of German and British industries. Training and skills were particularly significant in explaining such differences in the German and UK kitchen industries (Steedman and Wagner, 1987). However, more recent reports, from such as the German Federal Labour Authority, indicate problems arising from the mismatch between the qualifications of apprentices and the skills needs of employees. There are also indications of rising unemployment upon the completion of apprenticeship. This is due partly to a marked rise in general levels of unemployment in Germany but also to a growing preference for employers to prefer graduates from the higher education system. It is too early to assess the impact of such developments on the system as a whole.

Trade unions

Trade unions are formally organized groups of employees with the aims of job protection, the improvement of pay and conditions, and the widening of industrial democracy, among others. Such aims often bring unions into conflict with their employers, a conflict normally resolved by a process known as collective bargaining. We will examine first the changing nature of trade union membership before assessing the power unions can use to influence business decisions.

The power and role of trade unions varies considerably across the world. In the USA overall membership is low and union strength has tended to be concentrated in the industrial north in older manufacturing industry such as automobiles. In Germany, trade unions are supported by laws relating to co-determination and employee involvement and, historically, have played an important role in decision-making on both national economic and corporate strategic issues. In Japan, as in many parts of Asia, trade unions have little power and are often controlled by management. The exception to this is South Korea. The reasons for such differences are to be found in history, culture, politics, economics and the role of the state.

In this section we focus on trade unions in the UK and chart the changing nature of both membership and influence.

Key concept 3.7   A trade union

A trade union is a group of employees who formally come together to achieve mutual goals. Such goals normally include job protection, improving pay and conditions and attempting to influence management decision-making. In the UK, trade union membership cuts across individual firms and entire industries, although different patterns exist in other countries, notably industrial unions in Germany and company unions in Japan. There is considerable ideological debate concerning the influence of trade unions in business decisions.

Trade union membership has both grown and declined considerably in the UK in the 20th century, as we see in Tables 3.12 and 3.13. A number of key changes indicated by the tables are summarized as follows:

● The major change since 1980 has been the overall marked decline in membership. Between 1979 and 1991, trade unions lost 3.7 million members, some 25 per cent of the total (Bird *et al.*, 1993) and between 1991 and 2001 membership fell a further 1.3 million, a fall of 15 per cent (Brook, 2002). In each year since 1979 there has been a consecutive fall in total membership. Table 3.13 shows the changes in membership of the largest unions from 1991–6. In all cases unions have lost members, including the public sector and white-collar unions. Indeed the most dramatic decline over this period is in the white-collar union MSF, losing almost 30 per cent of its membership. This has been attributed to the loss of white-collar jobs in manufacturing and to the introduction of the check-off as a legal requirement. Under this requirement members must periodically re-register their membership and it is assumed that many have simply failed to do so.

● Along with the decline in membership there is evidence that collective bargaining has also declined (Millward *et al.*, 1992). This is the traditional mechanism used by unions to negotiate wages and conditions with management and many firms are clearly seeking alternative ways of wage determination.

Table 3.12	Trade union density of employees as a percentage of the working population 1913–92	
	Year	*Density (%)*
	1913	23
	1920	45
	1933	22
	1945	38
	1964	44
	1974	50
	1979	55
	1983	50
	1985	46
	1988	42
	1992	36
	1996	31
	1999	30
	2001	29

Sources: Price and Bain, 1983; *The Labour Force Survey*, 1998, 2001

- *The Labour Force Survey* of 1998 reported the first increase in union membership for 19 years, with a 4000 increase on the previous year, although overall density still fell marginally as those in employment also increased. In fact, since 1997 there has been a slowing down in the rate of decline in membership density. The largest increases have occurred among women, part-time workers and those of Asian origin. In 2001, there remained a marked difference between the public and private sectors; density in the public sector was 59 per cent and in the private sector, 19 per cent (Brook, 2002).

- We find marked variations in union membership in different types of employment. A high union density has traditionally been found in such industries as coal mining, which consistently achieved membership levels of over 90 per cent. High densities are also associated with local government and the engineering industry. Low levels of membership are found in retailing, and in hotel and catering. The changing pattern of union membership is illustrated in Table 3.13. The table shows that not only has membership declined in even the strongest unions, but that traditional strongholds of unionism, such as the miners do not appear in the figures for 1996. This is a clear reflection of the changing patterns of UK industries and employment.

- The number of unions has declined from 1323 in 1900 to 393 in 1983 and to 275 at the end of 1991. This change is attributable to a mixture of amalgamation and structural changes in the economy. De-industrialization has accounted for the loss of a number of specialist unions in manufacturing. The amalgamation process has meant that the growth of the firm was, for a time, matched by the growth of the large trade union. At the peak of membership, in the late 1970s, the biggest union, the Transport and General Workers' Union (TGWU), almost topped 2 million members. Table 3.13 shows the top ten trade unions affiliated to the Trades Union Congress (TUC) in terms of membership. Currently, the largest union is UNISON, formed through the amalgamation of three unions in the public sector, the National Association of Local Government Officers (NALGO), the National Union of Public Employees (NUPE) and the Confederation of Health Service Employees (COHSE). Almost all the unions in Table 3.13 have been formed by merger, the majority of which have occurred in the past 20 years.

● Taking a broad historical perspective, unions in older established industries, such as coal mining and the railways, have suffered large membership losses as employment has declined, while union growth has been most marked in the white-collar sector and among public employees. More recent membership increases are to be found among part-time workers and female employees of all types. Between 1990 and 1991, a time of general membership decline, female trade union membership rose by 20 000. Despite these growth trends there is clear evidence that trade unions are failing to secure members in many new areas of employment. They are also failing to attract young people. The largest group of union members are aged 40 or more. Among the under 20s, union membership is only 5 per cent (Brook, 2002).

Union growth and decline have mirrored economic, political and social changes. Increasing levels of unemployment have not only led to a reduction in trade union

Table 3.13	Top ten unions affiliated to the TUC by membership, 1996		
Union		1996 000's	1991 000's
UNISON		1355	1526*
Transport and General Workers Union		897	1127
GMB		740	863
Amalgamated Engineering and Electrical Union		726	980**
Manufacturing Science and Finance Union		446	604
Union of Shop Distributive and Allied Workers		282	341
Communication Workers Union		275	N/A
Graphical Paper and Media Union		217	282
National Union of Teachers		175	N/A
National Association of Schoolmasters/ Union of Women Teachers		157	N/A

Source: Kessler and Baylis, 1998

Notes:

*In 1991 this figure represented the combined membership of NALGO, NUPE and COHSE.

**In 1991 this figure represented the combined memberships of EETPU and AEU.

membership but, undoubtedly, weakened their bargaining power. Two other developments may be noted. First, the influence of unions has been further weakened by the removal of unions from the political arena and the development of economic policy. Second, following the pattern set by American and Japanese multinationals, it is not unusual to find firms with no trade union representing the workforce, or where a union does exist, it operates under single union, no-strike agreements. These strategies are analysed in Chapter 12.

Trade union power

At an obvious level, trade unions do have influence. For example, wage rates in general are higher in unionized firms than in non-unionized firms in the same industry and certain groups, such as the Fleet Street print workers, were able to resist technical change in their industry for many years. The union supporter would doubtless claim that the trade union acts as an important check and balance in management decision-making, preventing management from acting unreasonably and improving the quality of the decisions made.

Some, however, regard trade unions as being too powerful. Their belief is that unions disrupt the mechanisms of the free market, particularly by pricing jobs according to bargaining strength rather than demand. This favours only a minority, pricing jobs out of the market and adding to the problems of unemployment. In addition, individual freedoms are challenged by strikes affecting the supply of goods and essential services. This was the view of the Conservative governments from 1979–97, resulting in a series of laws to restrict union action and, ultimately, to weaken their position.

There is a view that argues that unions have never been particularly powerful and have been concerned only with marginal improvements in pay and conditions without ever seriously challenging management control. By contrast, management are seen to wield considerable power, which is actually strengthened by the formal procedures used in dealing with unions. (A further analysis of this position may be found in Hyman (1972) and Goldthorpe (1977)).

Many of the above arguments have their roots in different values and party politics. This influences not only the position taken, but the way facts are selected and interpreted. As with all influences on the management decision-making process there are insuperable problems of measurement. Even then we have to be content with observing the formal procedures when so much influence is undoubtedly the product of informal communication.

Whichever view is taken it is clear that, since the early 1980s, management's hand against the unions has been strengthened by rising levels of unemployment and changes in labour law. In addition, an increasingly competitive product market has led firms to seek greater flexibility both in the labour force itself and in working practices. Unions, weakened by dwindling membership and fearing job losses, have agreed to many such changes. Some view this state of affairs as permanent, while others see reasons for the decline of unions as a temporary phenomenon linked to specific factors that will change over time.

Summary

In this chapter we have identified four aspects of the environment, namely the economy, the state, technology and labour. For each of these we have selected issues that highlight the interaction between those four elements and between business enterprises and the environment in which they operate.

- The **economy** is viewed as a product of its constituent business activity as well as exerting considerable influence upon the way businesses operate.
- Different **models of capitalism** were reviewed as was their relevance for economies in transition from state control and the different roles of the state in each.
- The issue of **de-industrialization** and its impact on developed economies was examined.
- The **state** was examined from the perspective of the opportunites and difficulties of increasing intervention as an employer, a collective provider, an advisor, a legal regulator and, most significantly, for business as a demand manager.
- The ways in which businesses could influence government policy through **pressure-group activity** was assessed.
- With globalization, the growing trend of **economic and political integration** was examined and illustrated with reference to the WTO and EU.
- **Technology** was viewed both as a constraint and an opportunity as well as a product of innovation by business.
- **Information and communications technology** was seen as a major change agent in business and the impact of technology change on both job content and levels of employment was found to be mixed.
- **E-commerce** was seen to offer significant opportunities but was viewed within a number of limitations.
- The relationship between business and labour markets was seen through the workings of the labour market, issues in education and training and the influence of trade unions.
- Changing **employment trends** were identified and linked to changes in the economy and technology and the impact of globalization.

Discussion questions

1   In what ways can a business influence its immediate economic environment through its R&D, operations, marketing and human resource strategies?

2   Using the illustrations of (a) a mass producer of cars, (b) a university, and (c) a small accountancy practice, examine how a firm interacts with its economic environment at the local, national and international level.

3   Examine Tables 3.3, 3.4 and 3.5. What do these tables tell you about the state of the world in 2003? What changes do you envisage over the next few years?

4   Identify the key differences between Anglo-Saxon, social market and Asian models of capitalism. Which would be the most appropriate model for a country such as China to follow?

5   In what ways does the state assist and constrain business?

6   Using the illustrations of (a) a mass producer of cars, (b) a university, and (c) a small accountancy practice, examine how the management of each of them can attempt to influence state policy and the directions this influence might take.

7   Assess the impact of the EU on the businesses in a single-nation state. Is the expansion of the EU to 25 members likely to strengthen or weaken its impact?

8   Identify the various types of change that are likely to occur from the introduction of business systems based around ICT. What opportunities and threats exist for management and the workforce? What problems will be created and how may they be overcome?

9   Assess the opportunities and constraints associated with e-commerce and e-business.

10   Examine the major employment trends in the global labour market over the last 20 years. What have been the major drivers of change? What has been the impact of globalization?

11   Assess the changes that have occurred in UK trade union organization and membership over the last 30 years. What lies behind the statistics?

Further reading

The changing nature of the interaction of business and its environment means that the best sources of current material are inevitably the better newspapers and the more reflective magazines. The references provided below will offer a useful overview and starting point.

The relationship between the economy and business can be found in a number of books such as Haslam, C., Neale, A. and Johal, S. (2000) *Economics in a Business Context*, 3rd edn, Thomson Learning, London, and in Mercado, S., Welford, R. and Prescott, K. (2001) *European Business*, 4th edn, FT/Prentice Hall, Harlow. The latter text offers a good review of issues relating to the EU. An account of different economic systems is offered by Dore, R. (2000) *Stock Market Capitalism: Welfare Capitalism: Japan and Germany Versus the Anglo-Saxons*, Oxford University Press, Oxford. A view of the state in the wider perspective can be found in World Bank (1997) *The State in a Changing World*, Oxford University Press, Oxford. An excellent account of technology change and its impact on jobs as well as links with globalization can be found in Castells, M. (1996) *The Rise of the Network Society*, Blackwell Publishers, Oxford. Castells book is densely packed with information, which sometimes make it difficult to read, but it is worth persevering. A good review of global trends in the labour market is presented in International Labour Organization (2003) *Labour Market Trends and Globalization's Impact on them*, ILO, Geneva. Recent changes in trade unions in the UK is offered by Brook, K. (2002) 'Trade union membership: an analysis of data from the autumn 2001 LFS', *Labour Market Trends*, July: 343–54. Morrison, J. (2002) *International Business*, Palgrave, Basingstoke, offers a broad coverage of many of the topics covered in this chapter.

4 Cultural influences and business

| Learning objectives | At the end of this chapter you should be able to: |

- Define culture and explain its different forms.
- Assess the relative impact of convergence and cultural diversity on business practices and their relevance to the modern manager.
- Assess the links between convergence and globalization.
- Critically assess the contribution of Geert Hofstede to an understanding of culture and business.
- Assess the value of culture in explaining business behaviour.
- Assess the relative importance of those factors, which have contributed to the growth and decline of the Japanese economy and the lessons they hold for managers generally.
- Explain the process of Japanization.

Introduction

In the previous chapter we examined four aspects of the business environment. These were the economy, the state, technology and labour. In this chapter we focus on the fifth variable in our Business in Context model, culture. In Chapter 2, we noted how globalization was having an impact on cultures around the world. At a superficial level we are exposed to the same television programmes, movies and music and our news is presented to us through media controlled by a small number of large firms. At a more fundamental level we noted shifts in basic values. With globalization there was a tendency for people around the world to become more universalistic (guided by rules rather than relationships) and more individualistic. There is a view that around the globe, cultures are converging. We address this issue by looking at two different perspectives relating to convergence on one hand and cultural diversity on the other. We examine the impact of both perspectives on business.

The second half of the chapter presents a treatment of 'Japanese management'. Despite the relative decline of the Japanese economy in the 1990s, the issues of Japan and Japanese management remain highly relevant for a number of reasons. Japanese methods have had considerable influence in many areas of business, most notably in operations management. The issue of the rise of the post-war Japanese economy provides us with insights into the relative significance of cultural, economic and political variables. Moreover, Japan represents a fascinating case study of a business community being shaped by and shaping its environment.

However before these issues are discussed it is important to examine the concept of culture itself.

The concept of culture

In our discussion of joint ventures in Chapter 2 and in Case 2.1, Beijing Jeep, we noted that a number of problems were attributable to cultural differences. Management interest in culture stems from four factors:

- The interest in the 1970s in the post-war growth of the Japanese economy and in Japanese management practices.
- Cross-cultural research in the 1960s and 70s following the popularity of the convergence hypothesis; a claim that the imperatives of industrialization would eventually cause all industrialized liberal democracies to become more like one another.
- The influential work of Geert Hofstede.
- The idea that managers can make comparisons with practices in other countries to solve problems.

Each of these four factors is covered in this chapter. We examine how managers have imported ideas and practices from other countries and used cultural differences to solve problems. We refer to this as **culture free** and **culture specific** approaches. The influential work of Geert Hofstede will be examined and his name will appear frequently in this section. At the end of this section we explore Japanese management. This is highly relevant to our discussion of cultural differences but more significantly it touches upon all aspects of the interaction of business with its environment and acts as a suitable end-piece to this chapter.

Culture has been defined by many writers. We offer two definitions; the first from the famous anthropologist, Margaret Mead, and the second from the most influential writer on the subject of culture and business, Geert Hofstede.

Culture is a body of learned behaviour, a collection of beliefs, habits and traditions, shared by a group of people and successively learned by people who enter society. *(Mead, 1951)*

Culture is the collective programming of the mind, which distinguishes the members of one group or category of people from another. *(Hofstede, 1994)*

Culture comprises ideas through which we perceive and interpret the world, symbols we use to communicate these ideas, and institutions which enable individuals to become members of society and satisfy their needs. Several writers have used the analogy that culture is like an onion with several layers.

> ### Key concept 4.1 Culture
>
> Culture represents all human activity that is socially, as opposed to genetically, trans-mitted. It includes norms, values and beliefs that manifest themselves in behaviour, practices and institutions. Culture pervades all areas of business life. A particular interest is the extent to which we can learn from the business experiences of other cultures and transplant ideas developed by one culture and use them in a different cultural setting.

- At its most visible it represents those artifacts, goods and institutions that most readily distinguish one culture from another, such as architecture, food, ceremonies, language, and the different emphasis placed by different cultures on aspects of the educational system.

- At a deeper level, it comprises our notions of 'right' and 'wrong', our norms, our notions about what is 'good' and 'bad', our values, things we hold to be true and our beliefs. Many problems associated with the relationships between people of different cultures stem from variations in norms, values and beliefs.

- At its deepest level, however, culture comprises a set of basic assumptions that operate automatically to enable groups of people to solve the problems of daily life without thinking about them. In this way, culture is that which causes one group of people to act collectively in a way that is different from another group of people.

Culture is a highly complex subject and interacts with business in three different ways.

- Our socialization, the influences which shape our behaviour in a particular social setting, will determine our individual orientations to work.

- We tend to see organizations as societies in microcosm with their own specific cultures and ways of transmitting these cultures to their members. In some companies, like Hewlett Packard (HP), as well as in many Japanese and Korean firms, the creation of a corporate culture is seen as a priority and a great deal of time, effort, and expenditure is given to induction and training. We use HP as a case to illustrate aspects of corporate culture in Chapter 5.

- We use culture as an analytical device to distinguish one society from another.

We often tend to equate culture with nationality. While most nation states have their own national cultural characteristics, some countries are typified by two or more cultural groups. A relatively small country, such as Malaysia, has two main cultural groups, Malay and Chinese and several other smaller groups, including Indian. Each of these groups has their own customs and behaviour. Hofstede (1994) has identified six levels where cultural differences can be discerned. These are as follows:

- At the national level we can discern broad cultural differences between countries such as those aspects that make Americans think and behave differently to Japanese.

- Beneath this level we can discern differences: regionally, such as between Northern and Southern Italians; between ethnic groups, as in Malaysia; between religious groups, such as Christians and Muslims or Catholics and protestants; and between different language groups as in parts of the USA where Spanish has become the dominant language. Culturally different groups within the same country are sometimes referred to as sub-cultures.

- Cultural differences can occur between genders, leading in some countries to distinctive male and female roles, as in Japan, where there is a marked absence of women in senior positions within companies.

- Differences occur between different generations, where the values of the older generation are challenged by those of the younger emerging generation. This is sometimes referred to as the generation gap.

- In some societies, social class determines key differences in such things as attitudes to education and consumer preferences.

- Cultures can also vary between organizations as a result of differences in history, ownership patterns, technology, the type of work, leadership style and levels of employee skill. Such differences are often referred to as corporate or organizational culture.

We deal with the concepts of organizational and corporate culture in Chapter 5. In this section we focus on culture at the national and regional levels. Culture is the most pervasive of the five environmental factors in our model. Many aspects of the state, the application of technology, the nature of the labour force and their orientations to work are all culturally determined. However, influences are not just one way. Business organizations can and do influence cultures wherever they operate as we can see from our analysis of multi-nationals operating in transitional and emerging economies.

Culture free and culture specific and the implications for business

The Tower Records store in Kuala Lumpur, Malaysia, stands opposite an Islamic girls' high school. Pupils from the school can often be seen during their lunch break or after school in the store listening to the latest CDs or watching the latest music DVDs of Western popular music. Young people in Japan have developed similar musical tastes and slavishly copy the casual dress sense of American teenagers. A Western observer may be tempted to draw the superficial conclusion that, among young people at any rate, cultures are converging. While this may be true in terms of musical taste and dress preference among teenagers, there exists considerable diversity in underlying core values. An Islamic Malaysian girl and a Japanese boy may have some things in common with their USA counterparts, but there are significant cultural differences as well.

The contending views of convergence versus cultural diversity are often referred to as the 'culture free' versus the 'culture specific' debate. In the following sections we examine briefly the main points in that debate and attempt to draw some conclusions. It is important to note at the outset that these are not alternative models and that aspects of both convergence and cultural diversity are present in businesses in all societies.

The culture free hypothesis

A visitor to the Ford car plant, at Halewood in the UK, will find many features in common with a GM car plant in the USA, a Renault factory in France, a VW operation in Germany,

Key concept 4.2 Culture free versus culture specific

This lies at the heart of the debate about transferring business practices and ideas from country to country. A culture free perspective suggests that culture has less influence over business practices and ideas than, for example, technology and economics. Culture free advocates argue that practices and ideas across the world are converging and that businesses can borrow ideas from their counterparts in other nations. A culture specific perspective suggests that business practices and ideas are rooted in specific cultures and that transference is only possible between nations displaying similar cultural characteristics. This is not an either/or debate and elements of both perspectives can be found in business.

a Toyota plant in Japan, and the Proton factory in Malaysia. Such features include a common technology, similar types of organization structure, individuals with similar skills and job titles, and work being carried out in much the same way. The culture free hypothesis argues that businesses in the same sector in all countries are converging on similar types of technology, strategies, products and forms of business organization. Moreover, some believe that the speed of this convergence is increasing as a result of the growth of global travel and global communications. We examined many of these arguments in our discussion of globalization in Chapter 2.

For the manager, the key advantages of convergence are threefold.

- First, it enables manufacturing and services to take place on a global scale through the creation of global technologies, practices and products. This creates economies of scale to reduce costs and, in manufacturing, makes possible globally integrated supply chains.

- Second, managers and other staff of multinational companies can be moved around the firms' global operations and find themselves instantly at home with the operating systems.

- Third, ideas and techniques developed in one cultural or national setting may be transferred to another and used effectively. Furthermore, developing nations are able to learn from those more advanced countries and thus benefit from the mistakes of others. Such thinking is clearly behind the adoption by British and American firms of Japanese techniques, such as quality circles and just-in-time and the focus on American theories of motivation by British management trainers. Belief in the transferability of techniques has led management to turn elsewhere for solutions to problems such as organization structures, new market entry, product design, controlling labour and cost reduction.

In the late 1980s, management at the Ford plant in Dagenham wished to reduce the average time for resetting the presses and turned to international comparisons for assistance in tackling the problem. The time taken to change the set-up of metal presses at the beginning of the production process is a key element in the overall efficiency of that process. Such changeovers are frequently necessary given the large number and variety of metal parts in a modern motor car and delays at this stage have an impact on the entire process. It was found that Ford workers at the Genk factory in Belgium could, with similar technology, achieve the changeover in approximately half the time of the Dagenham workers.

As a result, a massive training exercise was undertaken and every member of the line-setting teams (those responsible for setting the presses) at Dagenham was sent to observe the Belgian operation. Lessons were learnt and the time was improved in the UK. However, the improvements did not match the time taken by the Belgian workers, which suggested that there were less tangible cultural factors accounting for the difference in the set-up times in the two countries.

The underlying theory behind all the above is that convergence on a particular type of technology and business organization is more significant than the cultural features of a particular society. The key elements in the convergence process are technology, the growth of big business and professional management and the impact of multinationals. There are similarities here with globalization, as we saw in Chapter 2. The arguments were first developed by Kerr *et al.* (1973) and Harbison and Myers (1959). The main imperative of all nations was seen as efficient production and the key elements were developments in science and technology that were available to all. Businesses in all nations, faced with the same problems, adopted the same solutions. These included increasing size, increasing specialization and formalization, the development of similar systems of authority, occupational types and structures, and adopting similar systems of education and training. To Kerr and his colleagues, the ultimate development was that industrialism, as they called it, would transcend differences formerly ascribed to culture and political economy.

Support for the convergence hypothesis may be found in the universality of similar forms of productive technology, in the growth of big business, the multinational and professional management. The assumption is widely held that the theories and approaches to management and organization were universal, and that the same recipes (usually American) could be applied irrespective of the cultural context.

The culture specific hypothesis and the work of Geert Hofstede

Many, including such influential voices as Hofstede and Trompenaars, believe that there are significant national differences in the way that people approach work and organizations (Hofstede, 1980a, 1980b; Trompenaars, 1993). Hofstede's major work was based around a survey carried out between 1967 and 1973 of 116 000 employees of IBM across 40 different countries. The survey was an attempt to measure a number of cultural variables and hence determine the extent to which business activities were culturally defined. IBM is noted for its distinctive corporate culture and the deliberate strategy of developing that culture irrespective of national boundaries. Hofstede was dealing with an organization, which had the same technology in all locations, the same organization structure and jobs, and pursued the same strategies. The conditions were ripe for convergence. However, Hofstede found differences, which could be explained by reference initially to four variables. Table 4.1 sets out these differences for a group of selected countries. The key differences related to values. Further work in South-East Asia with a colleague led to the development of a fifth variable, which explained more fully differences found between operations in the West and in Asia.

- **Power distance.** Power distance is the extent to which members of a society accept that power is distributed unequally. In all societies there is inequality between people be it based upon physical, economic, intellectual or social characteristics. Hofstede found that societies like France, Mexico and Hong Kong – where the power distance is large – formed the basis for social relations. In those societies,

Table 4.1	Differences in cultural values for selected countries following Hofstede's findings				
Country	PD	I	UA	M	LT
Great Britain	35	89	35	66	25
Germany	35	67	65	66	31
France	68	71	86	43	na
Italy	50	76	75	70	na
USA	40	91	46	62	29
Canada	39	80	48	52	23
Brazil	69	38	76	49	65
Japan	54	46	92	95	80
China	78	10	38	44	118
Singapore	74	20	8	48	48
South Korea	60	18	85	39	75
Australia	36	90	51	61	31

Key:

PD **Power distance**. The larger score = more power distance.
   Highest score = 104 (Malaysia); lowest score = 11 (Austria)

I **Individualism.** The larger score = greater individualism.
   Highest score = 91 (USA); lowest score = 6 (Guatemala)

UA **Uncertainty avoidance.** The larger score = more risk averse.
   Highest score = 112 (Greece); lowest score = 8 (Singapore)

M **Masculinity**. The larger score = more masculine.
   Highest score = 95 (Japan); lowest score = 5 (Sweden)

LT **Long-term orientation.** The larger score = longer orientation.
   Highest score = 118 (China); lowest score = 0 (Pakistan)

Source: Hofstede, 1994

such as Germany, Sweden and the USA, the power distance was small and such societies were noted for their attempts to reduce inequality. For example, societies with a 'low' power distance usually have high rates of personal taxation as a means of redistributing wealth in the form of education and healthcare benefits for all.

- **Individualism versus collectivism.** Individualistic societies, such as the USA and the UK, are depicted by a preference for looking after yourself or your immediate family group, a belief in freedom and a tendency towards a calculative involvement with work organizations. Collectivistic societies, such as India, Singapore and Mexico, show concern for a much wider group and emphasize belongingness, which can extend to organizations.

- **Uncertainty avoidance.** Uncertainty avoidance is the extent to which members of a society feel uncomfortable with uncertainty. Members of societies displaying strong uncertainty avoidance, as in Argentina, Switzerland and Japan, tend to be anxious about the future and have an inability to tolerate deviant ideas. In Japanese organizations, uncertainty avoidance is reflected in lengthy and detailed planning and decision-making procedures. Weak uncertainty avoidance, as displayed in Hong Kong, USA and Thailand, is associated with a willingness to accept new ideas and take risks.

- **Masculinity versus femininity.** Masculine societies, such as Japan, USA and Germany, tend to display a preference for achievement, assertiveness and material success and display a strong belief in different gender roles. Feminine societies, like Sweden and Holland, place more emphasis on the quality of life, care for others and equality, more especially between the sexes. For example, Scandanavian countries were among the first to introduce paternity leave.

- **Long-term versus short-term orientation.** Hofstede and Bond (1988) identified a fifth variable through their work with firms in South-East Asia. They found that some societies, particularly those influenced by Confucian philosophy, were much more future oriented, valued perseverance and savings, and were more adaptable than many societies, especially those in the West. They called their variable 'Confucian dynamism'. Regarding **long-term versus short-term orientation**; the difference between is that there is long-term orientation of managers in Japan, Singapore, South Korea and Hong Kong as opposed to the more short-term strategies of the UK, USA and Canada. A long-term orientation was also found in Brazil and a short-term orientation in Pakistan and Nigeria.

These variables shape the values and hence the behaviour of people operating in work organizations and enable us to explain differences in the way different countries conduct their business affairs. They may also explain why work systems developed in one country will not work in another. For example, Hofstede reported that American car workers from Detroit working at the Saab–Scania plant in Sweden disliked the work system, which placed a great deal of emphasis on group work. The Americans, with the exception of one woman, were much happier with a system which stressed individual achievement.

Hofstede noted that many management theories originated in the USA. The USA is typified by ratings that are below average for power distance and uncertainty avoidance, above average for masculinity, and has the highest rating on measures of individualism than any other country in Hofstede's survey. American motivation theory has been particularly influential and, in particular, the approaches of Maslow and Herzberg reflect typically American values. These are, the need for individual achievement and performance (high individualism and masculinity) and to involve the acceptance of risk (weak uncertainty avoidance). The implication is that such theories will not work so well in societies that are more collectivistic and feminine and whose people are risk avoiders.

The culture specific hypothesis claims that cultural influences in different societies will result in different styles of organization behaviour and different patterns of organization structure, as well as variations of influence in the business environment, such as the role of the state or trade unions.

The implications of a culture specific approach are threefold:

- First, we must be extremely cautious in the way we borrow business and management ideas from other cultures. A management technique developed in one country may only work in that country because it is based upon a particular set of cultural values. The failure in the UK and the USA of many attempts to introduce Japanese-style quality circles was due, in the main, to an incomplete understanding on the part of the adopters of the particular cultural values underpinning such an approach. The technique could be transposed but the conditions necessary for healthy growth could not.

- Second, in our dealings with people from other cultures we must recognize that differences do exist and be prepared to adjust behaviour and expectations accordingly. This is the theme of many recent initiatives in training for international management.

- Third, the policies of multinational corporations may well need to vary in different countries, and managers operating out of their home environment need specific training in cultural differences.

Hofstede's major work with IBM has been criticized for its methodology and for its Western bias, although the latter was rebuffed in the later work with Bond. However, several have questioned whether a survey, which began in 1967 can have real relevance for a very different world at the beginning of the 21st century. Hofstede himself returned to this theme in a later article (Hofstede, 1999). He argued that while management practices may change, cultures and the core values remain constant over time. However, he did acknowledge that movement had occurred on the **individualism/collectivism** dimension, as societies tended to shift from collectivism to individualism with increasing economic affluence.

The contribution of Fons Trompenaars

Fons Trompenaars produced his first book *Riding the Waves of Culture* in 1993 and has continued to develop his ideas, working with Charles Hampden-Turner. Trompenaars, like Hofstede before him, believes that much of management behaviour is culturally determined and that the key to successful international management lies in the understanding of these cultural differences. Trompenaars uses an anthropological approach and attempts to examine cultural differences

- in the way we relate to others;
- in our attitudes to time; and
- in our attitudes to the environment.

The few examples presented below offer a flavour of this type of approach.

In terms of how we relate to others, Trompenaars focuses upon five variables relating to how we use rules, individualism, how public and private we are, the extent to which we show emotion and the extent to which we are an achievement oriented. For example, in countries such as the USA, Switzerland and Germany, the prevailing culture is much more universalistic and rules are applied irrespective of the situation. On the other hand, cultures such as those found in Malaysia and Indonesia tend to apply rules in a much more particularistic fashion and personal relationships can be more important in some situations than the rules governing conduct. In such universalistic cultures greater use is made in business of lawyers and contracts, and in multinational operations the head office plays a more directive role.

Cultures also differ in the way they display emotion. Neutral cultures, such as those in Northern Europe and Japan, tend to keep feelings hidden and debate and argument are seldom personalized. On the other hand, emotional cultures, such as those found in Italy or Latin America, show their feelings and find it difficult to distinguish between issues and personalities. In some societies, such as Japan, much more emphasis is placed upon age, seniority, status and professional qualifications whereas in others, like the USA, respect tends to be earned on the basis of job performance. There may also be very different approaches to policies of pay and promotion.

Such differences, as illustrated above, can have a significant influence on doing business with people from a different culture and on the operation of multinational corporations. Trompenaars believes that effective international management can only occur through the understanding of cultural differences. Problems do arise in international business through misunderstandings arising from cultural differences. However, rather than trying to reduce the differences, cultural variations can be used by international firms as a strength to gain competitive advantage. Different cultures offer new perspectives on problems and different approaches working together can find innovative solutions. This approach is key to the concept of managing diversity.

The difficulties involved in using culture as a variable

Culture remains a fascinating concept but a difficult analytical tool. The following points attempt to give some indication of the difficulties involved.

- Many studies, which use culture as a central concept, tend to define culture in rather broad, generalized terms. In many instances it is a kind of residual variable, a catch-all to explain away differences that cannot be explained by differences in the economy, technology, role of the state, size of the firm and so on.

- In many studies, the impact of cultural values on economic performance is only identified with hindsight. For example, one explanation of the rise of the Asian tiger economies (see Case 3.1) in the 1980s and 1990s was the so-called Asian values, a set of characteristics that marked these countries out, especially from the West. However, such a view fails to explain why the same cultural characteristics appeared to have less influence on the economy before this time, nor can it account for the economic crash that befell many Asian countries in 1997. Such links between culture and economic performance tend to be highly selective, ignoring evidence, which does not fit. In this way, accounts of Japan may be biased in that they focus on the successful but not the unsuccessful firms. The accounts also focus on large firms, such as Toyota, and ignore the very important small firms sector of the Japanese economy.

- Comparisons with other countries are often difficult because of the different rules governing the collection of data. Thus, strike statistics are notoriously difficult to compare because different countries use different yardsticks to define and measure a strike. Accounting practices vary widely across many countries with the subsequent difficulty of comparing financial information.

- Cultural comparisons tend to be made from the perspective of one culture only. We may make conclusions about another culture based on our own values. A study of the car industry worldwide showed that European and USA manufacturers outperformed the Japanese on criteria they deemed most relevant: profitability measured by accounting ratios. The Japanese, however, laid greater store by market penetration and growth, and on these criteria easily outperformed the European and American manufacturers (Bhaskar, 1980).

- In many cases language presents a serious barrier to full understanding. Certain concepts do not translate easily. *Technik* is a central concept to German manufacturing, yet has no direct translation in English.

- We have seen that we possess preconceived notions about other cultures, often expressed as stereotypes. These can creep into our analysis and become self-fulfilling prophecies; we see what we expect to see. Our ready acceptance of such stereotypes prevents us from digging more deeply. For instance, an analysis of German management will reveal a much greater formality in superior–subordinate relations than exists in Britain or the USA. We may conclude from this that the Germans have less interest in man-management, when all evidence points towards good working relations existing in German firms. Such stereotypes are often deliberately used in training, when preparing managers for cross-cultural management. Clearly, such approaches need to be used with considerable caution.

- Cultures can and do change over time and our perceptions can become dated. For example, management students in Singapore are keen to challenge Hofstede's classification that scores Singapore low in terms of uncertainty avoidance, typified by a willingness to take risks. They claim that while that may have been true in the early stages of independence in the late 1960s, the prevailing culture of the 1990s is much more risk averse and conservative.

Culture free and culture specific revisited

While convergence as an idea represents a somewhat superficial analysis, we have seen that its practical implications are that because industrialized societies are moving in the same direction we may learn from the mistakes of others further along the route. We have seen, also, that the supporters of the culture specific hypothesis believe that specific aspects of business are especially susceptible to cultural and national influences. The most likely aspects to be influenced by culture are attitudes to work, management behaviour, organization structure, industrial relations, and recruitment and training. If we accept the culture specific hypothesis then we need to be cautious in our approach to managerial panaceas. Useful ideas and methods may be transplanted but care must be taken to see that they have been adapted to the new cultural setting and that there is an understanding of the supporting conditions needed for their development.

Reality, of course, never fits neat conceptual explanations. Both our models may be used to explain the rapid emergence of Japan as an industrial nation. Elements of its business organization, management techniques and state machinery have been imported from other cultures, while other elements are clearly products of its own cultural past. Its late start to industrialization enabled businesses to learn from the mistakes made in more advanced countries, such as Britain, the USA, and Germany. The specific elements of the Japanese culture undoubtedly gave these ideas a fresh impetus so much so that the West, in the 1980s, became fascinated by Japanese business methods. This is the reason that books on business and management have, since the 1970s, paid homage to the phenomenon we call Japanese management.

This mixed view is taken by Ronald Dore (1973) in his comparison of a British and a Japanese factory in the electronics field. He found similarities in the technology and in the complex nature of work organization. In the case of Japan, he noted the impact of **late development** and that ideas had been borrowed from the UK, Germany and the USA.

However, significant differences were found in motivation, recruitment, training and supervision. Dore noted that late developers can overtake their mentors when they, in turn, become the focus of attention for would-be copiers. This is clearly the case with Japan.

Such a mixed approach can also be found in Case 4.3. The development of Singapore owes much to both the traditional cultural values associated with the Chinese and the impact of foreign multinationals and expatriate workers. Such an approach may explain why some Japanese methods such as JIT have found favour with Western manufacturing firms while others, notably quality circles, struggled to gain acceptance in the West.

When we speak of culture free and culture specific, it is important to recognize that they are analytical frameworks and that we can look at business in any country using both perspectives and find examples of both.

The British and business

A popular topic that emerged in the 1980s, and has continued ever since, is the search for an explanation of Britain's economic decline (Wiener, 1981; Gamble, 1985). Wiener uses cultural variables to explain an economic phenomenon. He believes that the British are not good at business because their hearts are not really in it. The prevailing values in Britain are those espoused by the land-owning gentry and, as a consequence, business and especially industry are rejected as being representative of something fairly unpleasant. The consequences of this prevailing attitude are that the pursuit of economic gain is half-hearted and talent is directed away from industry. Government and the professions are favoured as occupational routes, capitalists aspire to be land-owning gentry, and the education system is dominated by a public-school ethos which shuns science, technology, business and industry. While university graduation rates are comparable to those in the former West Germany, only 0.7 per cent of British students are engineering graduates compared to 19 per cent in Germany (OECD, 1993). Moreover, almost 40 per cent of German managers have an engineering degree. Our half-hearted approach to business is consolidated by leaving management to the sometimes gifted but, most times, untrained amateur.

While it is not the job of this text to examine contending theories of Britain's economic decline, views such as those expressed by Wiener have a certain appeal. They are easy to understand and focus on easy targets, such as the public-school system and the land-owning gentry. However, the hypothesis is highly speculative, difficult to verify and probably represents an exaggerated and idealized view. There is no explanation for the success of British entrepreneurs, the energy that accompanied the industrial revolution, nor the economic growth of the banking and finance industries in the post-war period. While it is true that the best products of our education system tend to be attracted not to industry but to the civil service and the professions, that situation is also true of Japan, a country we tend to hold as our economic role model.

Despite such criticisms, there are cultural elements that seem to have a significant impact on business. The class structure of this country provides us with greater insights into the relationship between management and workers. Certainly we assume that anyone with the 'right' background and a reasonable level of education can assume managerial responsibilities with no professional qualifications or training. Wiener's hypothesis might also explain the popularity of accounting as a profession and the leading role played by many UK financial institutions.

Japanese business and management

Management literature since the late 1970s has been preoccupied with Japan. Serious and popular newspapers alike have jumped on the bandwagon and television documentaries have followed the fortunes of British recruits to Japanese multinationals as they exchange Newcastle Brown Ale for sake. Despite such exposure, our knowledge of Japanese management, while much greater, appears to have done little for our real understanding. In many respects the following quote from Endymion Wilkinson is still valid:

> I examine the European image of Japan and find it composed of an arsenal of stereotypes founded on the shifting sands of indifference, ignorance, prejudice, and fear, rather than on any effort to seriously understand the Japanese. *(Wilkinson, 1983, p. 17)*

The stereotypes to which Wilkinson refers have changed dramatically over the years from a manufacturer of cheap, unreliable products to a menacing military and then economic imperialist to a view of Japanese methods as the panacea for the ills of Western capitalism and, currently, to a nation in decline. Within each of these stereotypes we find a number of divergent views.

Even allowing for the difficulties of comparing the economies of different nations it is clear that Japan has emerged in the post-war period as the world's second largest economy behind the USA. There is a widely held view that this is some kind of post-war miracle in which a modern Japanese economy arose from the ashes of a completely devastated country. A similar view is often proffered for Germany. In both cases, the foundations of a strong economy were laid much earlier. Nevertheless, post-war growth has been significant and in Japan's case particular advances were made in the decade from 1955. Despite the marked reduction of that growth in recent years, or even because of it, there remains a fascination in the way that the Japanese organize their business affairs. We offer a flavour of the complexity and paradoxes of that area known as Japanese management. We will do this by looking at various explanations that have been offered for Japanese economic growth since 1945 and for the decline of the 1990s. We examine, also, the investment and experience of Japanese firms in other countries, notably Britain, and the process known as Japanization.

According to Williams *et al.* (1992a, 1992b), the simple explanations for the growth of the Japanese economy in the 1950s and 1960s are:

- The cost advantage Japanese firms had over major competitors in manufacturing. The cost advantages were derived initially from a labour force that worked long hours for low wages. This enabled Japanese manufacturers to make significant inroads into the markets of key competitors,
- The Japanese control of imports enabled the same firms to dominate the home market.
- Firms became cash rich, which enabled them to invest in new methods and new technologies to reduce the build time of their products. As wages rose and hours of work reduced, competitive advantage was maintained by further investments.

Behind these simple economic facts lie a number of interrelated factors, which embrace cultural, political, economic and managerial explanations. It is to these that we now turn.

Cultural explanations

Below we examine the Japanese in terms of Hofstede's values model (see Table 4.1) and how these values translate into business practice.

- The Japanese have moderately high **power distance** and consequently attach considerable importance to vertical relationships, which are typified by loyalty, dependence and a sense of duty. This is reflected in lifetime employment, the absence of job-hopping and the seniority principle, all discussed later in this section. The existence of these values, alongside collectivism, explains the Japanese loyalty to the group, be it the country, the family, or their company.

- The Japanese score very high in terms of **uncertainty avoidance**. Their unwillingness to take risks is reflected in many aspects of business life. It explains both the time taken in the planning process and the detailed content of the plans themselves. It is also demonstrated in the lengthy decision-making processes in many Japanese firms. It may also explain the preference of the Japanese for incremental product development.

- **Collectivism** is a feature of the Japanese and is reflected in the importance placed upon harmony and teamwork in all aspects of working life. Peer group recognition is very important to the Japanese worker. Consultation is a feature of decision-making in Japanese firms and, with uncertainty avoidance, explains the time taken in the decision-making process.

- The Japanese score very high in terms of **masculinity**. This may explain why their alliance partners in other countries often view them as assertive. It may also explain the absence of women in senior positions in Japanese firms, in that a masculine society favours traditional gender roles.

- The **Confucian dynamism** or **long-term orientation** echoes both the conservatism and adaptability noted in Dore's earlier work. Both historically and emotionally Japan is a closed society, due largely to a sense of isolation and a lack of resources. This has resulted in the Japanese placing more emphasis on bank savings than their counterparts in other industrial nations, their willingness to adapt to changing conditions for survival and their preference for seeing things in the longer term. The planning horizons of Japanese firms are much greater than those of their Western counterparts and, in some of the larger companies, it is not unusual to find a 250-year plan.

The role of the state

Historically, the state has always had a significant role in the development of the Japanese economy. The big five companies, known collectively as the *Zaibatsu*, which dominated the Japanese economy in pre-war times, developed with the specific assistance of the government. Their legacy today is in the *Kigyu shudan*, groups of companies around a major bank and in other forms of large conglomerates, known as the *Keiretsu*. These corporate forms lie at the heart of the Japanese economy.

Political stability?   For many years Japan has enjoyed a highly stable political framework. The Liberal Democratic Party (LDP), formed by the merger of two conservative parties, was in power from 1955 to 1993, when it lost its majority to a seven-party coalition. Since then there has been a period of political instability with four coalitions in 3 years, some of which included the LDP and the ultimate restoration of the LDP to power.

The state in Japan represents a network of influence between politics, the civil service and business operating a system of targeted development and trade protection at home, with selective investment overseas. Top civil servants often become top executives upon retirement in a process known poetically as *amakudari* (literally, descent from heaven).

However, conflict does exist: between government and the civil service, between business and the state, and also between companies themselves competing for the same markets. The ruling party, the LDP, is far from a cohesive body, and it consists of different factions competing for power. The credibility of the party has been stretched by the banking crisis of the 1990s, which will be dealt with later. Senior politicians in the LDP and in other parties have been linked with accusations of corruption in the financial sector. The 1990s, with the rise of opposition parties and the demise of successive coalitions, saw a rapid turnover in prime ministers.

The civil service   A central feature of the state's influence is the role played by the civil service. There are similarities with the UK in that the civil service recruits top graduates from the best universities. In terms of business, the two most influential departments have always been MITI (Ministry of International Trade and Industry) and MOF (Ministry of Finance). Traditionally they have helped to coordinate and direct Japan's economic strategy.

- An important role for **MITI** has been the targeting of those industries that are internationally competitive as in the case of cars and micro-electronics. Industries operating in preferred sectors have been offered prime locations, were allowed to expand, and received tax relief on modernization programmes. MITI also ensured that such industries received priority in foreign investment. The department has been especially active in encouraging cartels both for purposes of rationalization and for exploiting world trading conditions, both occurring in the case of the shipbuilding industry. In Chapter 9 we examine the role of the state in R&D and the establishment of research cartels among major manufacturers in a given sector. The other side to this strategy has been a marked lack of assistance for those businesses operating in non-designated sectors of the economy. Despite this, industries outside the favoured sectors, such as hi-fi, pianos, televisions and, above all, motorcycles, have enjoyed considerable success, suggesting that state support may be only one of several factors.

- **MOF** traditionally has controlled the Bank of Japan which, in turn, has significant influence over the major commercial banks and, hence, the direction of investment. In Japan, banks are the major shareholders in industry and commerce, with direct individual investment playing a minor role. This system has been actively encouraged by the intervention of MOF. Additionally, with MITI, MOF assisted in the process of channeling foreign investment to high priority companies, especially when capital was short, and in targeting Japanese investment abroad, in particular to those areas rich in the kind of natural resources and business opportunities coveted by Japan.

Undoubtedly, the state has played a major role in the development of the Japanese economy, more especially by accelerating market forces. However, the role of MITI and MOF have been questioned during the economic changes of the 1990s, including recession and globalization.

● During the 1990s MITI was increasingly in conflict with the major political parties and blamed, by some, for the failure of government industrial policy since 1980, thereby contributing to the problems of recession (Berggren and Nomura, 1997).

● The banking sector came under both national and international scrutiny. Both a cause and consequence of the economic problems of the 1990s have been bankrupt financial institutions and bad loans. Several major financial companies were found guilty of illegal trading. Nomura, one of the largest and most successful financial companies in the world, was found guilty in 1991 of dealing with a gangster syndicate and making illegal payments to favoured clients to cover their losses. A similar scandal occurred in the company in 1997. In 1995 the Daiwa Bank, in the USA, attempted to hide losses illegally and was barred from trading in the USA by the US Treasury and found guilty of fraud in the USA courts and fined US$340 million. Yamaichi, the tenth largest securities company in the world, was forced into liquidation in 1997 with overall debts of £14 billion. The management was found guilty of illegal deals in which some losses were placed in offshore accounts, while others were shifted from one company to another in an attempt to keep them hidden. At best, MOF was accused of weak control and, at worst, was implicated in the Daiwa scandal. The government reforms of 1999 placed greater control of the banks with the government and MOF was effectively down-graded to a treasury ministry.

● Historically the big firms have clearly benefited from their influence with MITI and MOF. However, Callon (1995) feels that, with increasingly complex technologies and the rise of the global economy, major companies have now outgrown MITI. He acknowledges the debt the major firms owe to MITI, particularly for protectionist and growth policies during the 1960s and 1970s. He charts the decline of MITI influence by focusing on the failure of MITI-led consortia in computing. Paradoxically, he sees MITI's failure as a product of market forces and Japan's economic success. Companies so dependent upon MITI in an earlier time had become self-sufficient and viewed MITI's attempts to establish consortia as unwarranted government interference. The market had become less protected as a result of USA pressure and Japanese companies emerged as market leaders, forced to become more innovative in a highly competitive environment. Callon's study exposes the limitations of state intervention when companies are dealing with state-of-the-art research. He also debunks the myth of Japan as a consensus society. His study of the MITI consortia in computing is a study of warring bureaucracies and private firms, and, ultimately, conflict between the state and business.

Economic organization

Several aspects of economic organization are discussed here: the economic system itself, the role played by large corporations, the significance of sub-contracting and the role played by banks.

● The **economic system** is known as *kaisha dynamics*. Berggren and Nomura (1997) define it as follows.
  – The rapid launch of new products.

- The continuous expansion of capacity.
- Focus on cost reduction.
- Continuous increase in output.
- Increased market share.
- Continuous search for better products and processes.

This results in a virtuous circle and is a further explanation of the expansion of the Japanese economy in the period 1960–90.

- Historically, the Japanese system is dominated by the **large corporation**. The pre-war *zaibatsu*, which included Sumitomo, Mitsubishi and Mitsui were broken up by the USA government of occupation. These companies re-emerged as **kigyo shudan**, large conglomerates organized around a major bank. These and other large conglomerates are often known collectively as **keiretsu**, which tend to be highly diversified horizontally and link both suppliers, distributors and retail outlets in an integrated supply chain. The Sumitomo Group has divisions dealing with mining, cement, chemicals, electrical goods and heavy industries, and the Mitsubishi Group deals with chemicals, glass, rayon, paper, automobiles, steel and heavy industries. Additionally, both these groups along with the other large holding companies have banking, insurance and real estate divisions.

- **Banks** operate as major shareholders of many of the major companies. However, here we have a case of banks both as shareholders and a part of major conglomerate empires. This not only gives such firms access to sources of investment but also places them at the centre of a network of information. The relationship with subcontractors is further cemented in that the bigger firms, often through their banks, are major shareholders in the smaller companies. Japanese banking is not only influential in the investment process, it plays a major part in survival of some firms under threat of closure. In the mid-1970s, Toyo Kogyo, the producer of Mazda cars, faced bankruptcy. The Sumitomo Bank, a major shareholder, stepped in and initiated a major turnaround operation, taking control and installing new management with new strategies. The company not only survived, but it developed a new range of models, which enhanced its export performance and world standing and attracted Ford as a major shareholder. The Sogo case study, at the end of this section, demonstrates that in present day Japan, banks owned by foreign investors may be less likely to support ailing Japanese firms.

- **Sub-contracting** is a major feature of Japanese manufacturing industry. Every large firm in Japan uses a large number of smaller firms as sub-contractors and it is not unusual, for a firm employing 1000 workers, to have 160 sub-contractors (Armstrong *et al.*, 1991). In this way a hierarchy of manufacture is built up, with larger firms **sub-contracting** to smaller and so on. In every case, the relationship between the firm and its supplier is carefully specified, with deliveries being requested not by the week or even day but by the hour. This is a central feature of the JIT system, discussed in more detail in Chapter 10. Furthermore, it is quite usual for the purchasing company to get involved in work organization and job design in the sub-contractor's factory, often in an attempt to reduce costs and hence the price of supplied parts. In general the relationship is very close and 'parent' companies tend to be very loyal to their sub-contractors. In recession it is not unnatural for sub-contractors to be supported and protected by the major company, who will often reduce its own labour force to cut costs rather than sever the link with its supplier. The idea of a close relationship between manufacturer and supplier is now embedded in much of manufacturing strategy throughout the world, a lead undoubtedly given by the Japanese.

● Despite the focus given to the conglomerates, **small firms** play an important role in the economy, both as suppliers and in the service industry. Small firms employ a large proportion of the Japanese labour force.

In Figures 4.1 and 4.2 we reveal the connections between large and small firms subcontracting and relative rates of pay. The data offers a very specific view of the competitive advantage offered by the traditional system of sub-contracting in the Japanese manufacturing industry. It can been seen from Figure 4.1 that, compared with the UK, smaller Japanese firms pay less in wages than their UK counterparts. In Figure 4.2 it can be seen that a much larger percentage of Japanese labour operates in smaller firms. Given that the smaller firm predominates in the Japanese sub-contracting network, there are substantial cost benefits derived from lower wage costs.

The labour market

A great deal of publicity has been given to the Japanese concepts of lifetime employment, seniority payment systems and the use of temporary workers.

Lifetime employment and **seniority payment systems** are, alongside company unions, regarded as the cornerstones of Japanese employment practices. An employee will expect to join a large firm on leaving school or college and remain with that firm for his entire working life. Moreover, pay rises and promotion occur incrementally with age and seniority within the company. A number of points need to be made:

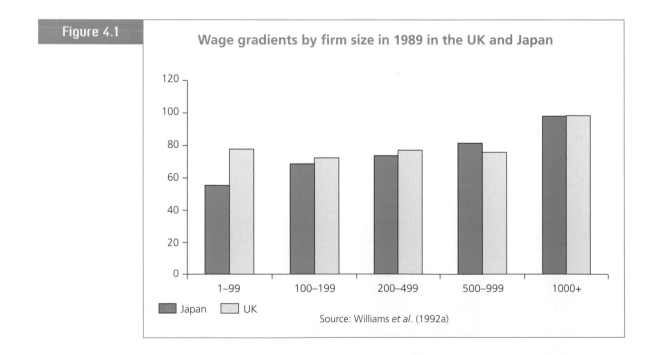

Figure 4.1

Wage gradients by firm size in 1989 in the UK and Japan

Japan UK

Source: Williams *et al.* (1992a)

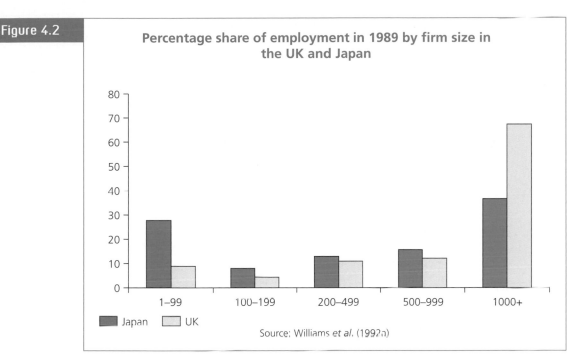

Figure 4.2

Percentage share of employment in 1989 by firm size in the UK and Japan

Source: Williams *et al.* (1992n)

- The system is limited to larger firms only. Employees in smaller firms do change jobs or leave to establish their own businesses.
- The system is almost exclusively for men. Very few women enjoy such such benefits.
- The system is based largely on the assumption of economic growth and has been challenged by the recession of the 1990s as firms have closed and workers laid off.
- Promotion on an annual basis usually occurs only for the first 5 years. Thereafter, promotion tends to be merit-based.

Despite the recession the concepts are embedded in the values attached to employment in Japan and the depth of that attachment may explain the reluctance of many Japanese firms to shed labour, in contrast to many European or American counterparts. Considerable media attention has been paid to those Western firms operating in Japan, such as SAS, which attempted to lay-off large numbers of employees and were forced by the courts to make large compensation payments.

Interest in the **flexible firm** in the West was partly attributable to a similar system that had operated in Japan for some time. A proportion of Japan's workforce has always operated a part-time or temporary workers. Many temporary workers were also seasonal as agricultural workers from the north migrated to the factories of the south during the winter. This flexibility allowed large manufacturing firms to respond to changes in demand at low cost and without threatening those with lifetime employment. In the automobile industry the number of temporary workers fell from 8 per cent in 1990 to less than 3 per cent in 1994 (Berggren and Nomura, 1997).

Temporary workers have no such security as lifetime employment and annual pay rises, have few employment rights and enjoy none of the benefits of their permanent counterparts. Many 'temporary' workers operate in a largely unregulated small firms' sector.

Precise statistics concerning the proportion of workers in each category are difficult to obtain but various accounts estimate the 'permanent' group to represent around 35 per cent of the total workforce, although this varies considerably according to the size and nature of the organization. No farm workers and very few women in Japan have permanent status.

From the point of view of the country's economy there would appear to be some advantages to this economic and labour market organization, not least of which is a built-in elasticity to cope with changing demand. A firm like Nissan has in the past coped with increased demand by taking on more temporary workers and either increasing its number of subcontractors or placing greater demands on its existing suppliers. Reduced demand will be met by lay-offs of temporary workers, as experienced by many such workers in the 1990s. Such is the importance of the relationship with suppliers that it would be rare for subcontractors to be dropped in times of reduced demand, and assistance may even be given to help them out. The system would appear to succeed because of the privileged position and economic strength of the larger companies and the ready supply of temporary workers, a proportion of whom aspire to 'permanent' status, and a proportion who are basically farm workers seeking seasonal work. Such a model of a flexible labour force has found favour with many Western employers and it is an issue we will discuss in the next chapter.

Management and management strategies

Management   Studies such as those by Storey *et al.* (1991) suggest that 95 per cent of Japanese managers are university educated and most do not reach management status until they reach 35–40 years of age. While there is considerable mobility within the same function, fewer than 5 per cent of managers in the survey by Storey and his colleagues had ever worked for another firm. There would seem to be little in the way of structured training, and most of the training that does occur is both on-the-job and instigated by the individuals themselves. There is regular performance appraisal and considerable importance is attached to role models and mentors. Management, in Japan, is still male dominated despite changes in the law to promote equal opportunities. Apart from cultural values, which stress differentiated gender roles, a major obstacle to more female employment is the dearth of child-care facilities. Employment with a major corporation is for most Japanese, management and worker alike, an important source of social status.

Decision-making   Much attention has been focused on consensus and collective decision-making in Japanese firms when, in practice, there would seem to be considerable initiatives and decisions taken by top management alone. However, the consultation process is very important and large numbers of workers do in fact participate. The consultation process is part of a corporate culture, which is reinforced by the trappings of egalitarian society, including company uniforms for all, compulsory exercises at the start of the day, and a sharing of the same canteen facilities.

HR policies   These are often the most publicized aspects of Japanese firms but, as we have seen, they only really apply to those working on large corporations. They include lifetime employment, pay based on seniority, an attention to employee welfare, and fringe benefits such as company housing and holidays. As Beardwell (1997) points out, lifetime employment should really be termed lifetime commitment, in that employees can be transferred to another company in the group or even to a supplier. Reward linked to seniority is an important strategy in strengthening the ties of the individual to the firm. Recruitment and selection tend to be rigorous even for comparatively low-level employees. As we see in Nissan (Case 4.1), the selection of supervisors is a highly competitive affair, candidates being subjected to a battery of tests and strenuous interviews. The selection process for all workers is followed up by an equally rigorous training programme where employees are expected to master most aspects of a particular process. The emphasis is clearly on flexibility reinforced, in most cases, by an absence of organization charts and job descriptions. An important element in the pay of most Japanese workers is the annual bonus. In good years this has been the equivalent of 6 months salary and even during the recession of the 1990s rarely dropped below 5 months in the major firms.

Industrial relations   All Japanese trade unions are **company unions** and employees have no choice as to which union they join. The particular system of company unions has its origins in a 4-month dispute in 1953 involving workers at the Nissan car factory. The dispute led to a lock-out by management that was backed by the major shareholder, the bank, and the USA authorities. The stipulation for a return to work was the acceptance by the work force of a company union with the motto 'those who truly love their union love their company' (Hetherington, 1986). Other companies took Nissan's lead and set up their own unions. Not surprisingly, plant-level industrial relations are comparatively harmonious and are more akin to joint consultation than collective bargaining. Disputes do occur at national level, but they tend to be highly predictable affairs based on annual pay and bonus negotiations. Since the early 1980s the unions have been increasingly concerned with **industrial relations** and the protection of weaker groups of workers, and have been opposed to Japanese investment overseas, on the basis of its impact on jobs in Japan. However, on such issues unions carry little political clout to affect policy.

Manufacturing strategy   For many, the key to Japanese export performance and economic success has been the strategies adopted by manufacturing industry. Attention in the West has focused on just-in-time and lean production and we discuss these in more detail in Chapter 10. However, a number of elements make up successful Japanese manufacturing strategy, which we may identify as follows:

- A meticulously planned, integrated system.
- Attention paid to detail by a disciplined workforce.
- The importance attached to quality and continuous improvement.
- Process and product innovation, the latter paying particular attention to the needs of the customer.

A pivotal figure in the manufacturing system is the first-line supervisor, which perhaps explains the attention paid to his selection. Dore's comparison of Hitachi with English Electric noted, in the Japanese case, the emphasis placed on attendance and timekeeping and the willing participation by Japanese employees in the widely found practice of sacrificing holidays in favour of the company (Dore, 1973). British companies dealing with the Japanese for the first time are often astonished at both the time spent in planning and the inordinate level of detail involved in the planning process. Despite the emphasis on manufacturing, there has been a considerable growth of the service sector, both in Japan itself and in Japanese operations overseas. By the mid-1990s, the service sector, rather than manufacturing, had emerged as the preferred destination for Japan's university graduates.

`An investment in R&D`   In Chapter 9 in we show the extent of innovative activity through a series of patent indicators. There is clear evidence to suggest that the Japanese place a higher priority on new product development than any other nation. Furthermore, companies are encouraged to collaborate in joint **R&D** ventures. These too will be discussed in more detail in the chapter on innovation.

Japanization

In recent years the concept of Japanization has emerged, referring to two related phenomena. First, it refers to the process of Japanese FDI, by which Japanese firms set up operations overseas. Second, it relates to the process whereby Japanese business and management methods are practised in other countries either as a direct consequence of FDI or through the process of cross-cultural transference, as mentioned earlier in this chapter. The former are referred to as 'transplants' and non-Japanese companies pursuing Japanese methods are known as 'adopters' (Elger and Smith, 1994).

Key concept 4.3 Japanization

Japanization refers to the process through which Japanese business practices are incorporated in the businesses of other countries. This occurs directly through Japanese multinationals, where business practices from Japan are transplanted in a host country and have an impact both on the internal workings of organizations and on relationships with suppliers. A more indirect form of Japanization occurs when Japanese methods are adopted by non-Japanese managers and firms. Examples of such adoption include the widespread use of just-in-time methods in manufacturing industry across the world. There are difficulties in operating Japanese methods outside Japan and these are linked to cultural differences.

As far as the UK is concerned (and perhaps other countries as well), the favourable reception given to Japanization in the manufacturing sector by government, employers, employees and, in some cases, trade unions appears to rest on two assumptions.

- First, it is believed that Japanese manufacture overseas will increase the value added in the host country by stimulating economic growth and employment and by reducing the number of Japanese imports.

- Second, there is a belief that Japanese manufacturing methods set the kind of examples that the rest should follow.

In the case of the latter, it is certainly true that just-in-time methods of production are standard practice among manufacturing firms in many countries. (A further discussion of this may be found in Chapter 10.) However, in focusing upon manufacturing we should not forget that the majority of Japanese FDI is in non-manufacturing, particularly in financial services and much, during the '**bubble economy**', in land and property speculation. While the adoption of Japanese methods is apparent in manufacturing, it is less so in the service sector.

A relatively early series of studies of Japanese manufacturing plants and financial concerns in the UK concluded that many features associated with Japan, namely a stable, highly committed workforce, complete cooperation in change and low levels of conflict, simply did not exist in the UK (White and Trevor, 1983). Nevertheless, the Japanese firms did exhibit higher levels of productivity than their British counterparts. In achieving these levels of productivity, White and Trevor found that typically Japanese employment practices, such as the lifetime employment and the seniority principle, were not used but that great attention was paid to selection and training. They found no real difference in levels of employee satisfaction, but the real distinction lay in certain work practices. These were identified as:

- a highly organized approach with an emphasis on fine detail, especially in the planning process;
- the elevation of quality as the top priority;
- a much greater sense of discipline throughout the various organizations;
- a quite exceptional acceptance of management authority, which tended to be more favourable the greater the Japanese presence, almost as if employees were more willing to legitimize the position of Japanese managers than their British counterparts. White and Trevor attributed this to the greater egalitarianism displayed by the Japanese and the greater willingness on the part of the Japanese manager to get involved in the operations.

Although the study was carried out almost 20 years ago and in a different era as far as UK industrial relations are concerned, the conclusion that successful transfer of certain Japanese methods is possible remains today. The main elements would appear to be a careful attention to detail in the planning process, incremental product design, focus on low costs, focus on quality systems, a greater investment in training and a much more egalitarian approach to management. There may be elements which are too embedded in the cultural values of the Japanese and which will be difficult to transfer. These include the stability of employment, the strong company identification and work ethic and the ability of Japanese managers to employ a management style that is a mix of paternalistic, disciplinarian and egalitarian methods. This may explain why many UK and USA firms found difficulty in introducing Japanese-style quality circles.

Such perspectives on the advantages of Japanization are not shared by all. Williams *et al.* (1992b) are particularly sceptical. They produce evidence to show that 70 per cent of Japanese overseas investment is in non-manufacturing areas such as financial services and the purchase of land, activities that do not create jobs. They claim that the influence of Japanese firms has been exaggerated by the media since Japanese firms employ only 0.6 per cent of the UK workforce and only 1.1 per cent in the USA. Moreover, the value of Japanese exports is 40 times that of goods produced by Japanese firms in the UK. Contrary to popular belief, they found that Japanese manufacturing in the UK, especially among the car companies, was not particularly profitable. In a re-examination of Japanese manufacturing effectiveness in the car industry they claim that, Toyota excepted, some European manufacturers such as BMW perform better than the Japanese in such areas as stock turnover and work in progress – traditional measures of manufacturing effectiveness.

While the expansion of Japanese multinationals in Britain is part of the general process of the internationalization of the Japanese economy, two additional factors stand out.

- First, the interest Japanese firms have shown in Britain is seen as a mechanism to circumvent EU trade restrictions on Japanese imports. This has resulted in many joint ventures between British and Japanese firms, as existed between Austin Rover and Honda in the development and manufacture of the Rover 800 series.

- Second, those Japanese firms that have established themselves in Britain have tended to favour development areas where government grants and other advantages are available. Such areas include the north east of England and Scotland, where there are high levels of unemployment. It is undoubtedly much easier to ensure the compliance of a workforce and the cooperation of trade unions, even to somewhat alien work practices, when the alternative is long-term unemployment. There is no doubt that the situation also favours the company in its relationship with its local suppliers. When suppliers are struggling to survive in a harsh economic climate, it is much easier for the purchaser to negotiate contracts that are highly favourable to him in terms of price and delivery.

However, there is evidence in the north east of England that many of the workers taken on by Japanese firms are neither unemployed nor refugees from the most depressed industries, such as mining and shipbuilding. There is also little evidence to suggest that the Japanese are treating English suppliers any differently from those in Japan, where exacting cost, quality and delivery requirements are the norm. Moreover, there is significant evidence that Japanese companies are giving customers what they require, with a growing trend towards the customization of products for local markets.

Further insights into the Japanese in Britain may be found in the Nissan case.

| Case 4.1 | **Nissan UK** |

Nissan, the major Japanese car manufacturer, produced its first British-built car at its Sunderland plant in April 1986. The firm was coveted by several county councils seeking to stimulate business and employment in their areas and competition to attract a major company like Nissan was fierce. Tyne and Wear in the north east, an area of de-industrialization and high unemployment, was selected.

The plant used robots for welding and had a fully automated paintshop, but these are hardly unique features in modern car manufacture. For many the real difference at Nissan lay in its approach to industrial relations and its personnel policies.

Acknowledging the traditional labour relations problems with the car industry in Britain and a strike frequency of over seven times the norm for manufacturing industry, the company, on the advice of personnel director, Peter Wickens, opted for the recognition of a single union only. The policy alternatives of either a non-union shop or the recognition of several unions were felt to be recipes for antagonism and chaos respectively. The competition for union recognition among trade unions hungry for members was considerable. Nissan represented a potential 2700 new members when the plant opened, when most trade unions were losing members at an alarming rate. Recognition was eventually achieved by the Amalgamated Union of Engineering Workers (AUEW) and a deal embracing terms and conditions of employment was signed between the union and company representatives before production started in 1985. The deal was unique both for the car industry and for the AUEW.

The agreement between the union and the company listed certain key principles upon which it is based. These included mutual trust and cooperation; a commitment to quality, productivity, and competitiveness, using modern technology; a need for change and flexibility to maintain the competitive edge; and a belief in open and direct communications. Most significantly there was an adherence to the avoidance of any action that interrupts the continuity of production and the union's recognition of management's right to make the final decision in the best interests of the company.

These principles were reinforced by several mechanisms. First, terms and conditions formed part of a 2-year agreement, which was binding on both sides and included a no-strike clause for the duration of the agreement and during any negotiation or arbitration. Second, in exceptional circumstances, when agreement cannot be reached ACAS would be called upon to arbitrate, but a straight choice must be made between the two alternatives in a system of **pendulum arbitration**. Third, negotiations are to made between the company and the Works Council, not the trade union. The Works Council is made up of elected representatives, each representing part of the plant. Although the election is supervised by the union, representation is open to all employees. In fact one estimate has put union membership at only 18 per cent. As well as negotiating salaries and conditions, the Works Council concerns itself with issues of productivity, quality and planned change.

The personnel practices were also new to the car industry. All employees are treated as single status, share the same canteen, wear the Nissan blue uniform, and receive annual salaries paid in equal monthly instalments. Employees are not required to clock on and are only asked to clock off when overtime is being worked so that a record may be kept. Workers are paid a guaranteed week of 39 hours. Management has retained the right to review both the clocking-on procedure and the guaranteed week in the light of operating experience, and to lay workers off without notice should production be disrupted by industrial action either at Nissan itself or one of its suppliers.

Competition for jobs at Nissan has been high. In an area of 20 per cent unemployment an estimated 3500 applied for the first 22 supervisory positions. An estimated 11 000 applied for the 240 production jobs. Selection processes were exacting. The potential supervisors were all put through a series of psychological tests, while the production workers were narrowed down through successive hurdles, including pencil and paper aptitude tests and at least two interviews for short-listed candidates. The emphasis was on seeking employees with a strong positive commitment to the goals of the company, thereby reducing future potential conflict. Apart from the management, nearly all recruits were under 40 years old, few had previous experience in the car industry and only a minority was unemployed. By comparison, the senior management nearly all had motor industry experience and were recruited from such companies as Ford, Austin Rover and Rolls Royce. In total the company started with three British and four Japanese directors.

Peter Wickens has claimed that Nissan's policies are not peculiarly Japanese, and feels them to be a distillation of American, German and British as well as Japanese methods. Indeed, he operated similar policies in his previous employment with an American company based in North Wales. Whatever the origins, the novelty of

▶

Nissan's approach lies in its single union, **no-strike deal** and in its insistence upon absolute commitment to the goals of productivity, quality and continuity. The approach has formed the basis of its advertising campaign, orchestrated by Saatchi and Saatchi under the slogan, 'They don't half work'.

The Sunderland plant continued its success in the 1990s and was in profit even when Nissan were making overall losses. The annual survey on car industry productivity, produced by the *Economist Intelligence Unit*, has identified Nissan, Sunderland, as the most productive plant in the UK since 1995. By 2003 it had been ranked the most productive car plant in Europe for 7 years running. In 2001 it was 40 per cent ahead of its nearest rival, Toyota at Derby, for cars built per employee. The plant at Sunderland established a strong reputation within the Nissan group for high productivity and, unusually for the Japanese, its cars were being exported back to Japan. Despite this, profits have fallen owing entirely to the strength of the pound.

In 2001 there were considerable fears that the high cost of cars coming off the line at Sunderland, due to the strength of the pound, would lead to the production of the new Micra to be switched to the Renault factory in northern France. This was a particularly strong threat given that the French had a controlling interest in Nissan via Renault's 37 per cent share of the company and that Nissan's CEO was from Renault. The switch was headed off for a number of reasons. Although Renault productivity was high by European standards it could not match Sunderland and the Renault factory lacked sufficient staff to cope with the increased demand. The workforce at Sunderland agreed to a new 24-hour shift system with even greater built-in flexibility. Finally, the European Commission cleared the way for the UK government to award the Sunderland plant a grant of £40 million for investment in the manufacture of the new Micra.

Nissan management in the UK ascribes the plant's success to three major factors. First, they believe that a major source of success is the willingness of staff to embrace change. Their selection and employment practices have done much to eliminate more traditional 'resistance to change' cultures. Second, each department operates a *Kaizen* (continuous improvement) system that is both self-funding and involves all employees. Finally, supervisors are given considerable freedom and responsibility, including the hiring of staff.

Sources: Burrows, 1986; Tighe, 1986; *Guardian* and *Financial Times*, 1998, 1999; news.bbc.co.uk, 15 January 2001; www.nissan-global.com, accessed April 2003

Questions

1 What are the main reasons for Nissan locating its operations in Sunderland?

2 What are the main differences between the Japanese and UK practices in manufacturing industry as illustrated by this case?

3 To what extent is it either feasible or desirable for such practices to be transferred to non-Japanese firms?

4 Assess the current strengths, weaknesses, opportunities and threats of the Nissan plant at Sunderland.

Japan and the problems of the 1990s

Japan has suffered the characteristic consequences of opportunism in the good time. Management has become careless, the banking system over-optimistic and both the economic and the business structure overly bureaucratic. *J. K. Galbraith (Observer, 21 June, 1998)*

The Japanese economy had suffered recessions in the 1970s caused by the **oil shocks** and in the 1980s caused by the high value of the yen. As a response, firms became even more competitive through quality improvement and reducing costs still further. However, the seeds were sown for the recession of the 1990s, which was ongoing in the first part of the 21st century. Massive trade surpluses during the boom years had forced up the value of the yen. This in turn led to the easy credit of the late 1980s, which created in Japan a 'bubble economy', typified by land and property speculation and wasteful investment by major manufacturing corporations. In terms of the labour market, Japan had moved from a low- to a high-wage economy. In manufacturing industry, efficiency gains had kept pace with wage rises but, to some, many of the leading firms had reached the limits of cost reduction. A number of factors came together at the same time, which we identify as follows:

- The high value of the yen, apart from paving the way for easy credit, caused Japanese exported goods to be more expensive and export sales fell. In order to maintain market share many firms held prices thereby reducing or eliminating profit levels.

- The availability of easy credit led to speculation and the subsequent overvaluing of both equities and real estate. When the 'bubble economy' burst in the early 1990s there was a dramatic fall in land, property and share price. Companies, including some banks and individuals were left with massive debts that they could not repay and the banking system was left with large amounts of bad debts.

- This in turn led to a crisis in the financial sector. Banks were mistrusted and people withdrew their savings. Savings were not being channelled into the economy as previously. Confidence was not helped by the previously discussed scandals at Daiwa, Yamaichi and Nomura.

- The population reacted cautiously and domestic spending fell dramatically. This stimulated further price-cutting by the department stores and the influx of cheaper imports, many from China.

- The state, blamed for over-regulation and over-protection in the boom years, was now blamed for its failure to regulate and control the financial sector. Porter *et al.* (2000) believed the state to be too concerned with export performance and failed to stimulate the domestic markets.

- There was increased competition globally, particularly with the re-emergence of a strong USA economy. Low-wage economies also posed a threat to the high-wage Japan.

There were signs of recovery in 1997, which were dashed as Japan was plunged into the South-East Asian crisis in the latter half of that year. The cultural characteristics of the Japanese, particularly the importance attached to saving face, loyalty to the group, a distrust of outsiders and a preference for dealing with difficulties internally, have meant that there was a tendency to hide or even cover up problems. This was apparent in the scandals associated with the finance companies Daiwa and Yamaichi.

The following facts and figures give an indication of the extent of the problems. They have all been taken from editions at the time of the *Financial Times*, *Guardian* and *Asian Wall Street Journal*. The Sogo case illustrates the problems facing a major department store.

- The home market in Japan in the 1990s fell by 20 per cent overall. In 1998 alone, retail sales in department stores fell by 25 per cent and home car production fell from 13 million vehicles in 1991 to 9 million vehicles in 1996.

- During the period 1992–5, most major companies posted losses, including Toyota, Mitsubishi, Mazda and Nissan. The 1997 crisis caused losses the following year for such as NEC and Mitsubishi, while Nissan and Toshiba saw a fall in profits from 1997 to 1998 of 97 and 85 per cent respectively.

- Between 1991 and 1999, Nissan saw a fall in its global market share from 6.6 to 4.9 per cent. In 1999, with its CEO seconded from its partner, Renault, Nissan announced global job cuts of the order of 21 000, which would include the closure of three manufacturing plants and two power train plants in Japan itself.

- By 1998 unemployment had reached 4 per cent. While this is not high by European standards it was by Japanese, and it undermined Japanese confidence in their own system.

- Overtime was invariably cut and in many cases eliminated, thereby depriving many workers of an important component of their wages. Bonuses were also reduced by up to 20 per cent.

- Many manufacturing firms placed an embargo on the hiring of temporary labour and placed pressure on older workers to take early retirement.

- In Nissan, new 'non-Japanese' practices were introduced, including merit rather than seniority-based promotion and share options for senior management. Restructuring occurred in most major companies. In some cases this eradicated the over-staffing of many management hierarchies but it also resulted in job losses.

- From 1992 bad debts held by the banks rose significantly, when in 1996 they outstripped operating profit. By 1998, total bad debts in the banking system were approximately the GNP of Canada. Sogo alone, in 2000, had liabilities of US$16 billion (see Case 4.2). Many of the bad debts were associated with loans to buy land and property.

- The property and land boom of the late 1980s was followed by a price collapse in the 1990s. Commercial land prices in major urban areas increased sixfold between 1979 and 1989 to fall below twice the 1979 figure by 1996 (Porter *et al.*, 2000). The collateral upon which many of the loans were based had disappeared and banks were left with little hope of recovering their debts.

The lack of confidence in the banking system has directed savings away from investment, once a cornerstone of the Japanese economic system. The attack on job security and, by implication, lifetime employment through plant closures and job cuts is a potential threat to the stability of the Japanese employment system. For many years salaried, lifetime employees, referred to as 'salarymen', had enjoyed job security for life. However, as we have noted earlier, so embedded is the value of lifetime employment that many firms have been slow to restructure.

As a direct consequence of problems in the financial sector, the government created the Economic Planning Agency attached to the office of the Prime Minister and removed the planning role from MOF. This is one of a set of proposals aimed at tackling a declining economy, a banking system perceived as corrupt, rising unemployment and skills shortages in key economies, notably telecommunications. The measures include:

- the reform of the financial system by deregulation, which will effectively remove government protection from the traditional banks and finance houses and expose them to the scrutiny of the market place;
- a review of state bureaucratic procedures to confront the problems of corruption and to lead to more effective and efficient government decision-making;
- a move away from lifetime employment with the same company through the creation of a more flexible labour market;
- a series of tax reforms which will cut personal taxation and therefore increase spending power;
- investment in education, science and technology to address skills shortages and, regard to health, to face the problems of an ageing population.

By 2003 the recession was still affecting the domestic economy. However, the major car firms were all declaring big profits, with Toyota announcing the largest profits in its history (*Financial Times*, 4 March, 2003). However, 80 per cent of the profits were from sales in the USA, taking advantage of the growth of the USA economy, favourable exchange rates and a preference in the USA for Japanese cars, which are perceived as better quality and better value for money.

| Case 4.2 | **Sogo** |

In July 2000, Sogo, one of Japan's largest department stores, declared bankruptcy after the Japanese government pulled out of a proposed rescue package. Sogo became the largest bankruptcy at that time in Japan. Sogo filed for court protection against its **creditors** in an attempt to launch a rescue package. Paradoxically, this gave creditors some hope of retrieving at least some of their money. The company had liabilities of $US15.9 billion that it declared in April 2000. It owed money to 73 creditors, mainly banks, and had asked them to write off loans worth $US9.2 billion. The largest creditor, the Industrial Bank of Japan, agreed. The head of Sogo, Hiroo Mizushima was well-connected politically and was once a senior banker with the Industrial Bank of Japan. However, the second largest creditor, the Shinsei Bank, refused to go ahead with the Sogo proposals. The Shinsei Bank had recently been acquired by a USA consortium and, as a consequence was less sympathetic to the plight of Sogo.

However, the real nail in the coffin came when the government did an about-turn on its proposed rescue package. The change of mind came largely as a result of public pressure. There was intense public criticism of the proposal by the government to write off Sogo's loans. The LDP was returned to power in the 2000 elections but had lost a sufficient share of the votes to fear a return to the political upheaval of the previous few years. In a bid to regain public confidence Sogo was sacrificed. Lawyers, appointed by the court, were given the task of developing a restructuring plan and a sponsor was sought to take over the stores. The worst-case scenario involved job losses of 10 000, further bankruptcies among the 10 000 or so Sogo suppliers and fear in other firms that they would soon suffer the same fate.

By the early 1990s, Sogo had emerged as one of the biggest retailers in Japan. As well as stores across Japan, it had major stores in Taipei, Singapore, Hong Kong and most major Asian cities as well as in other countries, including London. The stores in Japan were badly hit by the downturn in consumer spending in the 1990s, when department store sales fell by 25 per cent in 1998 alone. Its business in Asia was also hit by the crash of 1997. A catalyst for the bankruptcy was a fall in sales in the summer of 2000. The summer period is traditionally a time of sales increase and is known as the gift-giving season as friends and business associates exchange presents. However, this summer sales were down 14 per cent on the previous year. It was felt that consumers were shunning Sogo as a result of the shame attached to it by its parlous financial situation. While a fall in sales was a contributory factor, the seeds of Sogo's bankruptcy had been sowed much earlier.

Sogo, under Mizushima's stewardship, was as much a real estate business as it was a department store. Large assets had been accumulated through the purchase of land, the development of the department store and the subsequent letting of retail space in the stores to tenants. Furthermore, Sogo frequently bought more land than it needed, land which was then sold at a good profit once the store had been built. During the bubble economy, Sogo accumulated vast paper assets in this way. When the bubble burst, the value of Sogo's assets fell dramatically as land and property prices crashed and the company was left with huge borrowing debts. Even during the good times, Mizushima made some poor decisions. In the search for real estate gains, several Sogo stores in Japan were in poor locations. In particular, Sogo was a pioneer store in the new Tokyo suburb, Tama New Town. This was intended to be a large new housing development, but its distance from the city centre made it unpopular and the planned developments were scaled down. The Tama New Town store lost Sogo considerable money both in its development and operation.

The lending banks had been aware of this problem in 1994 and alerted Sogo. However, the warnings had been ignored and Mizushima continued the policy of opening new stores, mainly in complex cross-shareholding deals.

The bankruptcy of Sogo has wider implications for the Japanese economy. The refusal of the foreign-owned Shinsei Bank to participate in the proposed rescue package may be part of a new trend in the financing of Japanese companies. Foreign capital may be less sympathetic to the plight of debt-ridden Japanese firms, however large and famous they may be. The government, under public pressure, displayed its willingness to let major companies fail, with the implicit acceptance of the job losses that would occur. As a result of the government decision, shares fell heavily in banks, construction and real estate companies. Small banks were particularly placed under threat of extinction. Large construction firms, such as Kumagai Gumi and Hazama, had watched the events at Sogo with keen interest. The large construction firms had seen the government plans for the rescue of Sogo as setting a trend which they would follow. The withdrawal of government support sent worrying messages to a construction industry that accounted for 10 per cent of total employment in Japan.

In an attempt to save the business, Sogo formed an alliance with a rival department store group, part of the major company Seibu. Seibu acted as the corporate sponsor for Sogo. By February 2003, Sogo were still under court protection, had closed failing stores, sold off nine stores in Japan and either sold or liquidated assets in 150 companies both in Japan and around the world. Around 3300 staff, directly employed by Sogo, lost their jobs, although many went on early retirement. In February 2003, largely as a result of these measures, Sogo announced an operating profit of US$50 million and appeared to be doing better than its sponsor, Seibu. Sogo also announced the opening of a new department store in late 2005 in Osaka, built on the plot of the former Osaka Sogo store.

Source: *Asian Wall Street Journal,* 13–16 July, 2000; Hong Kong Trade Development Council, June 2003

Questions

1 To what extent does the case illustrate the problems of the Japanese economy since 1991?

2 To what extent does the case illustrate the changing nature of the Japanese economy?

Japan and Japanese management: some conclusions

The specific nature of Japanese culture, state intervention, the economic system, the organization of manufacturing industry including the sub-contracting system, innovation, the flexible labour market, management strategies and practices, company unions, and even exploitation have all been used individually or in combination to explain the post-war growth of the Japanese economy. Most contain elements that are highly plausible, and the real explanation is a complex interaction of all factors, with some factors being more important than others at particular times.

Hayes and Wheelwright (1984) have argued that there is nothing peculiarly Japanese about the way they run their businesses. The emphasis on high growth rates, market penetration, low costs, careful planning, long-term as opposed to short-term profits and quality is good business sense in any culture. Three factors temper this enthusiasm.

● First, the elements mentioned above may well represent excellent management practice, but their successful application in Japan may be due to a supportive state, a particular form of economic organization, and draw upon specific characteristics of the Japanese people.

● Many **Japanese transplants** in other countries have never been especially profitable as profits were traded for market share.

● Most significantly, as we have seen in the previous section, the system would seem to be under threat in Japan itself as management adapt to changing economic circumstances. Many of the proposed changes such as deregulation, the removal of lifetime employment and pay tied to seniority would appear to be moving Japan more towards Anglo-Saxon practices.

Japan is clearly in a state of change. The 1990s saw an end to 40 years of impressive economic growth and the start of the longest post-war recession in Japan's history. The growth of the global economy has challenged Japan's position both internationally and domestically, and it has threatened Japanese labour markets and employment practices. The banking system appears to be in a state of chaos.

There are a number of views on what happens to Japan and the Japanese system from here on.

- For some there are already signs that the events since 1991 have changed irrevocably both Japan and the way it is viewed by Western managers. The influx of foreign investment into Japan will change both the banking system and the behaviour of individual firms. Major Japanese firms, such as Nissan and Mazda, are already controlled by foreign interests (Renault and Ford respectively). Investors have lost confidence in banks and employees in the lifetime employment system. There will be an introduction of Anglo-Saxon investment and employment practices. Interest in Japanese management practices will wane as Western managers see a system failing to stem the tide of declining fortunes.

- For others, notably Dore (1997, 2000) and Berggren and Nomura (1997) the Japanese system has an underlying resilience that will see it emerge from recession with renewed strength. There will be a mixture of continuity and gradual change.

- Porter *et al.* (2000) also predict a healthy economic future. They believe that Japan has already demonstrated that it can compete very successfully and they stress its record in the development of innovative processes and products. However they see a number of catalysts for change that they list as follows.

  - An increase in foreign investment and shareholding, e.g. 45 per cent of Sony shares are held by foreign investors.
  - The growth of foreign companies operating in Japan as joint ventures or having taken over Japanese firms. The latter has happened in the cases of Cable and Wireless and IDC, Renault and Nissan, and Ford and Mazda.
  - The mergers among the major banks will affect the structures of the *kigyo shudan* and company groupings will change.
  - The government reforms of 1999 will lead to a reduction in the number of ministries and bureaucracies and a much reduced role for such as MOF.
  - There has emerged a new brand of CEO, in companies such as Sony, Honda and Toyota, all with significant overseas experience.
  - A new group of entrepreneurial companies have emerged that are highly dynamic and profit-oriented.
  - There is evidence of changing values among the younger working population in that they may not expect lifetime employment.

| Case 4.3 | ## Business and management in Singapore |

For many years Singapore stood out from the other Asian tigers in terms of the strength of its economy, particularly its GDP per capita, and the economy was relatively resilient in the face of the 1997 East Asian collapse. Table 4.2 shows the Singapore economy at the peak of its success. In 2000 it was the best performing Asian economy with a 9.9 per cent annual growth. The growth of the economy has

Table 4.2	GDP per capita, 1996		
Country	$US	1996 ranking	1990 ranking
Switzerland	42 350	1	1
Japan	38 120	2	2
Norway	35 710	3	5
Denmark	34 620	4	6
Singapore	32 878	5	17
Germany	30 300	6	7
USA	29 600	7	9
Hong Kong	27 130	11	8
UK	20 900	17	16
South Korea	11 910	24	25

Source: Hampden-Turner and Trompenaars, 1997

been associated with a number of interrelated factors, which include geography, culture, the role of the state and the role played by multinational corporations of several countries. This case will examine all those factors as well as the relative decline that has affected Singapore since 2001.

Singapore is a relatively small island of some 3 million people linked to the Malaysian Peninsula by road and rail. Its geographical position made it an important staging post for world shipping. Singapore was established as a trading post by the British in 1819 and expanded rapidly in the 1860s, as a result of increasing trade with China and Japan and the opening of the Suez Canal. The growth was consolidated by the exploitation of rubber and tin in the surrounding regions, with Singapore operating as a vital export channel. This economic expansion led to considerable immigration to a virtually uninhabited island. The majority of immigrants were Chinese. This is reflected in the current ethnic mix of 76 per cent Chinese, 15 per cent Malay and 7 per cent Indian. A white, largely expatriate population makes up the remainder. In 1959, Singapore achieved self-government from the British and in 1963 joined the Malaysian Federation. The political alliance with the Malay States was short-lived and Singapore became a fully independent nation state in 1965.

Throughout the 1950s and early 1960s there were a number of key problems to be faced. Britain withdrew its bases and hence their impact on the local economy. Relations with Malaysia became problematic. The country had no natural resources and there were insufficient jobs in trade alone to support the population. Its domestic market was small by international standards and the nation faced increasing competition from the growing economies of the region. Politically, at that time, Singapore was far from stable and its businesses were dogged by labour relations problems.

In the mid-1960s a strong government emerged under Lee Kuan Yew and outside help was enlisted. Following the recommendations of a UN Task Force, Singapore embarked on a policy of labour-intensive manufacturing to establish jobs and to substitute imports. Israel, a relatively new state, surrounded by potentially hostile forces and with few natural resources, was seen as an ideal role model, and several visits were made to Israel by leading Singapore politicians. The Singapore government tackled the then regional problem of communism through job creation and the establishment of a vigorous public housing scheme. Trade unions were brought into the system of state capitalism by giving them the island's taxi service to manage and by enabling them to run a major pension and insurance company. A senior government official became head of the trade union movement. Labour problems disappeared. Considerable investment was made in education, to create a unified system and end the division along racial grounds. Most significantly, the government established the Economic Development Board (EDB) to plan and oversee the nation's economic development.

Following the phase of job creation and import substitution, the EDB launched a campaign to attract overseas investment in the form of export-oriented multinational corporations. At the same time there was considerable investment in the port, which is now one of the largest and most modern in the world and certainly one of the busiest. The policies were so successful in terms of job creation that the problem shifted to one of labour shortages and rising wages. The EDB targeted investment that was high-tech, knowledge based and high value added. The country soon became the world leader in the computer disk drive industry. More recent policies have focused on establishing Singapore as a regional centre with outward investment in neighbouring countries, particularly Vietnam.

By any economic measure the policies were successful. From 1985 to 1997 the country enjoyed uninterrupted GDP growth averaging at over 8 per cent per year. Unemployment fell to below 2 per cent in 1991 and became steady at less than 3 per cent until 2001. Inflation has been kept low at around 3 per cent, falling to less than 2 per cent in 1995. Over the same period wages rose by around 9 per cent per annum. A balance of payments deficit in 1980 of minus 3.3 million Singapore dollars was turned into a surplus of 21.3 million dollars by 1995. Output in manufacturing increased over 10 per cent year on year during the 1990s. The problems facing the region in 1997 meant that manufacturing output fell that year by 0.8 per cent overall and labour cuts were announced by major companies such as HP, Philips and Motorola. Nonetheless, the strength of the Singapore economy meant that its problems were less severe than those of its near neighbours.

Three major reasons have been given for this remarkable economic growth: cultural explanations, the role of the state and the part played by multinational corporations. FDI has played a significant role in the economic development of the island, but its attraction has also been a major government policy.

In our discussion of the Asian tigers (see Case 3.1), which include Singapore, we defined the core cultural values in terms of the importance of a number of key features. These include the family, education, hard work, the importance attached to personal savings, perseverance, adaptability and a long-term orientation. The core values originated from Confucianism, which also emphasizes duty and hierarchy, rule by humanity and moral persuasion, meritocracy and the supremacy of ethical standards. In business and economic life, such values are seen in loyalty to the nation's rulers and the support of officialdom, loyalty to the firm by a hard-working

and responsible workforce, the importance of family firms, thrift, adaptable entrepreneurs, and a concern for education and self-improvement.

Undoubtedly, in Singapore there is a commitment to the goals of the government
that is rare in other countries, although high levels of labour turnover as a result of
labour shortages and subsequent spiraling wages suggests that loyalty to the firm can
be compromised. The concern for education is evident in a population eager to accumulate qualifications and by a massive state support of schools, polytechnics and
universities, as well as training for industry. The people are clearly hard working.
Singaporeans save a higher proportion of their income than anyone else, assisted
largely by the state-run Central Provident Fund (CPF), which takes around 20 per
cent of wages, matched by a further 20 per cent from the employer. The CPF then
offers interest on savings, provides finance for home ownership and acts as a retirement pension fund. Withdrawals are also possible to buy blue-chip stock.

Family firms play an important part in the economy of Singapore and there are
many large and powerful Chinese businesses. Some of these businesses are linked to
Chinese clans, to which people belong on the basis of their family origins, traced
back to a particular village in China. Among the Chinese there is also some evidence
that groupings of people who speak the same Chinese dialect are attracted to specific sectors. For example, Hokkien-speaking people tend to dominate in banking,
finance and trade. However, there is also evidence to suggest a weakening of such
traditional networks and value systems. Many of the new generation have acquired
university education, often overseas, and experiences have been broadened beyond
traditional values. In several local firms, family control is being replaced by professional management.

Undoubtedly, the state has played a major role in establishing the conditions for
long-term economic growth to take place and for controlling the direction and pace
of that growth. Its agency, the EDB, has been particularly influential. The state is
viewed as being pro-business, establishing pragmatic policies when needed to support business growth. This has been complemented by a substantial investment in
education and training, particularly technical training, and in housing and welfare.

Since independence, Singapore has been effectively a one-party state, with control in the hands of the People's Action Party (PAP). The government is noted for its
strong social control. Opposition parties do exist but their parliamentary representation is negligible. The November elections of 2001 saw the PAP take 82 of the 84
seats in parliament. State leadership has been highly directive and proactive, particularly in defence, education and training, and the economy. Many Singaporeans work
directly for the state and government employment tends to attract the most talented
from the population. Its government ministers are the most highly paid in the world,
reinforcing a strong desire for stability and incorruptibility. The economic policies
embrace the attraction of foreign direct investment and the establishment of a number of government-linked companies. Some of these, like Singapore Airlines, are
highly successful and pursue policies that are both aggressive and progressive. As
well as the government-linked companies, the state plays a part in local investment
through the Development Bank of Singapore. In more recent years economic policy
has involved a closer relationship with Malaysia and Indonesia, to broaden both the
product and labour market. Much of Singapore industry's unskilled labour travels

◄

daily across the causeway linking Singapore to Malaysia and the government has backed offshore manufacturing in both Malaysia and the nearby islands of Indonesia.

For many years Singapore has been an attractive location for multinational investment and many leading firms from the USA, Japan, Germany and the UK have manufacturing operations on the island. There are now over 3000 foreign firms operating in Singapore, attracted by a number of features. Singapore is viewed as a very safe and relatively attractive posting for expatriate employees. The EDB has been behind several initiatives to improve the social amenities of the city in ways favoured by expatriates. The redevelopment of the areas around the river to provide areas of restaurants, bars and entertainment is one such initiative. There are tax incentives and state provision of factory shells and related infrastructure. The Singaporean government has been quite selective in its dealings with multinationals, favouring high-tech, capital-intensive firms. Such companies have also been attracted by the political stability of the country and the absence of effective opposition either from political parties or from hostile trade unions. The available local labour force is generally well educated and well trained, although there are labour shortages and competition for highly-skilled managerial and technical talent is fierce.

The very success of Singapore and the increasing prosperity of its population have been recognized as a problem. There are fears that the country, like Japan, will become too expensive, with a widening gap between rich and poor. The signs are there in the form of escalating salaries and rents for office and factory space. These have pushed up significantly the cost of operating in Singapore. Increasing affluence has brought with it increasing individualism, which poses a threat to traditional values, and, perhaps, social and political stability. Labour shortages, labour mobility and continuous annual wage rises have both increased workloads and resulted in a workforce with high expectations. For some, Singapore is still too dependent upon foreign investment and foreign managerial talent. Moreover, its very success has acted as a role model for others in the region with the consequence of increased competition, more especially from lower-wage economies, notably China and India.

Such problems were highlighted in 2001. Unemployment rose to 4.5 per cent, the currency weakened against the USA dollar and there was a substantial decline in orders in those firms manufacturing microchips and disk drives. In general, the economy was seen to be too dependent on an increasingly volatile electronics sector. GDP fell and a recession was declared. Fears were expressed that an ageing population would become a strain on public finances as many had invested their savings in a property market that had fallen substantially. In 2003 estimates for the GDP placed Singapore fourth in the region behind Japan, Australia and Hong Kong and with a global rating which was back at the level of 1990.

For many, the strength of the state and the strength of the national systems will overcome such potential problems. For others the 1997 slowdown and the recession of 2001–2 will act as a catalyst for change.

Sources: The Singapore Yearbook (various years); Chong Li Choy, 1990; Wong Kwei Chong, 1991; Schein, 1996; *Asian Wall Street Journal*, July 2001, July 2002

Questions

1 What factors do you attribute to the successful growth of the Singapore economy? Which do you see as the most important of these factors?

2 To what extent are the strategies followed by Singapore a key to the economic growth of other nations?

3 What threats does Singapore face in the early days of the 21st century and what are the possible remedies?

4 In what ways does this case illustrate both convergence (culture free) and cultural diversity (culture specific)?

Summary

- Culture was viewed as a pervasive factor shaping the entire environment of business, however care should be taken in using culture to explain business behaviour.

- Culture operates at different levels, including corporate and within any society there are a number of sub-cultures.

- Almost all business behaviour displays aspects of convergence (**culture free**) and cultural diversity (representing **culture specific**).

- The most influential writer on culture and business is Geert Hofstede. He identified a number of key cultural values that can be used to explain differences in business practices and worker behaviour.

- The rise and fall of the **Japanese economy** was examined through a combination of cultural values, social, political and economic organization, and specific business strategies and practices. The examination of Japanese business is not only illustrative of the cultural debate but also represents an extended case of the way businesses in a particular environment interact with key elements of that environment.

- The transferability of business ideas and practices was examined through a review of **Japanization**. Lessons to be learned here are applicable to the transfer of business ideas and practices generally across cultures.

Discussion questions

1 What do you understand by the concept of culture? Identify the various forms of cultural difference (national, ethnic, age, gender, corporate, etc.) that you can see in your own environment?

2 What do you understand by the concept of convergence? What is the link between convergence and globalization?

3 How useful is the concept of culture in explaining the way businesses operate in different countries? To what extent can business ideas and management techniques developed in one cultural and national setting be transferred to another?

4　Assess the contribution of Geert Hofstede to our understanding of business.

5　Examine Table 4.1 differentiating a number of countries according to the findings of Hofstede. What conclusions can you draw from the table?

6　What are the reasons for the growth of the Japanese economy post the Second World War? Are any factors more significant than any other?

7　Assess the contribution of Japanese practices and ideas to Western management?

8　What changes do you predict for the future the Japanese economy following a decade or more of recession in the 1990s and early 21st century? Assess the likely impact on both government policy, and business and management practices.

Further reading

Excellent sources for culture and business in general are Hofstede, G. (1994) *Cultures and Organizations,* McGraw Hill, London and Trompenaars, F. (1993) *Riding the Waves of Culture: Understanding Cultural Diversity in Business,* Economist Books, London. An approach focusing on cross-cultural communication and negotiation is offered by Adler, N. (1997) *International Dimensions of Organizational Behaviour*, 3rd edn, South Western College Publishing, Cincinnati, OH. Holden, N. J. (2002) *Cross-cultural Management: A Knowledge Management Perspective*, FT/Prentice Hall, Harlow, offers a slightly different perspective but covers the basics well and has some good cases. An interesting account of the impact of culture on business in Britain can be found in Wiener, M. J. (1981) *English Culture and the Decline of the Industrial Spirit 1850–1980*, Cambridge University Press, Cambridge. A good treatment of Japanese management, dated but still relevant, is Dore, R. (1973) *British Factory–Japanese Factory,* University of California Press, Berkeley. A good review of Japanization can be found in Elger, T. and Smith, C. (1994) *Global Japanization? The Transnational Transformation of the Labour Process,* Routledge, London. Min Chen (1995) *Asian Management Systems: Chinese, Japanese and Korean Styles of Business*, Routledge, London, gives good accounts of business systems in three countries and traces their origins. Porter, M. E., Takeuchi, H. and Sakakibara, M. (2000) *Can Japan Compete?*, Macmillan, London, examines Japanese practices in the face of a long recession and argues for Japan's economic resilience.

5 Organizational aspects of business

Learning objectives   At the end of this chapter you should be able to:

- Illustrate the interrelationships between goals, structure, ownership, size, and organizational and corporate culture.
- Explain the nature of goals, the role they play, and the causes and consequences of goal conflict in organizations.
- Identify the factors influencing organizational structure, explain the different types of structure and assess the suitability of different types of structure in different situations.
- Critically assess the relationship between structure and performance, and recent trends in structure, including delayering, down-sizing and the flexible firm.
- Explain the different forms of ownership and articulate the relationship between ownership and control.
- Assess the differences between management and control in the public and private sectors and the impact of privatization.
- Explain the impact of organizational size on business behaviour.
- Define the small firm and assess its role in relation to owners, customers and the economy.
- Explain the difference between organizational and corporate culture, and critically assess the contribution of these concepts to organizational performance.

Introduction

In the previous two chapters we have examined aspects of the environment that interact with business. Such aspects constitute the outer level of our model. In this chapter we examine a second level of interaction and influence belonging to the organization itself. We will consider five aspects in our model:

- goals
- structures
- size

● ownership

● organizational and corporate culture.

As with other aspects of our model, there is considerable interaction and overlap between these organizational issues. As well as pointing out the areas of overlap in each individual section, the way that issues relating to goals, ownership, structure and size come together is examined in more detail through the concept of organizational and corporate culture. In addition, we highlight two specific issues – the public sector and small businesses – both of which illustrate the complex nature of these organizational relationships. The public sector has been chosen since it is a good illustration of the interaction and tensions within the organizational elements as well as those operating between the organization and its environment. In addition, government policies in many countries of privatization, deregulation and the commercialization of the public sector have meant that the distinction between public and private concerns is becoming increasingly blurred, further justifying our focus. The treatment of small businesses raises key economic and political issues as well as highlighting the very specific nature of business problems found in this sector.

Goals

In this section the nature of goals shall be examined, the purposes they serve and how they emerge. The potential problem arising from a number of different goals operating in the same organization shall also be considered. We often speak glibly of organizations like WalMart, British Gas, Microsoft or even our own college as having goals. However, we should not ascribe behaviour to abstract entities such as organizations. Goals should always be attributable to some person or group.

The renewal of interest in the role played by goals in influencing the behaviour of organization members has been highlighted through the concepts of the 'corporate social responsibility' and of the 'excellent company'. Companies such as Royal Dutch/Shell, Daimler–Chrysler and Levi Strauss regularly publicize their commitment to socially responsible and ethical business. In companies like IBM, HP and Boeing you will find clearly articulated goals which are so dominant that they appear to have a life of their own irrespective of the personnel involved. Closer examination will certainly reveal that such goals are carefully formulated by the chief executives of such companies as part of a policy of establishing a set of dominant values, which guide the behaviour of every organization member.

Goals are not just a means of giving members a sense of direction and thereby reducing ambiguity and conflict, they are also used as statements of ethical intent. The relationship between **ethics** and business is highly topical as each decade throws up examples to place ethical considerations at the forefront. In the 1980s there were the well-publicized cases of Chernobyl, Union Carbide at Bhopal and the *Exxon Valdes* and the late 1990s has the raging debate on genetically modified crops, which has brought the USA company Monsanto to the public's attention. The importance of the relationship between ethics and business in the 21st century is acknowledged in this edition by examining these issues in Chapter 8.

Managers often use goals with the assumption that the clear formulation of goals will influence performance. In the internal management of organizations, this assumption has been translated into a set of techniques aimed at influencing the behaviour of individual members, known as **management-by-objectives** or **MBO** (Drucker, 1964). Where MBO is used, the goals for the organization as a whole are generally broken down into individual goals or targets for each manager, forming an entire network of interconnected and internally consistent goals. The most effective MBO schemes tend to be those where there is some measure of negotiation between manager and subordinate over the precise nature of the goals to be achieved by the subordinate. This raises two points: that goal formulation is part of a political process and that goal achievement is undoubtedly related to the extent to which goals are shared by members of the organization.

However, the evidence on the influence of goals on performance is mixed, and even where such a relationship can be shown, it is unclear how it works. The use of goals to determine performance is easiest to understand where jobs are straightforward so that clear targets can be set and performance measured. Many jobs are more complex and performance measurement is difficult to achieve. Furthermore, employees may be expected to achieve a number of different goals which could conflict with one another or with those of other workers. We shall see that, for some organizations, internal consistency is difficult to achieve in the face of considerable inter-personal and inter-departmental conflict. The extent to which goals can be used to motivate performance is also a function of management behaviour and individual expectations.

Not every company has such clearly identified goals. For many small firms (as well as some larger ones), goals remain the unstated intentions of the owners; they may be thought of only in the vaguest of terms; employees may be completely unaware of them, and may give priority to their own personal goals, sometimes bringing them into conflict with management. A review of most companies' annual reports will reveal that the explicit statement of the goals is usually marked by its absence. Instead, the various missions, objectives and strategies must be extracted, or at best implied, from the various statements by company chairmen and operating reports.

Key concept 5.1 Organizational goals

The stated goals of an organization exist to give direction to the activities of its members. In many companies, goals comprise both an overall statement of intent, sometimes referred to as a mission statement, and a set of more detailed objectives to guide strategic planning. Since many organizations are made up of different interest groups the formulation of goals can be a highly political process. This can cause conflict, but the goals of most businesses are generally accepted as being those of the senior management team. There has been a renewal of interest in the role of goals to shape the culture of an organization. We deal with this aspect in our discussion of organizational and corporate culture.

The nature of goals

> We consider goals to be the ultimate, long-run, open-ended attributes or ends a person or organization seeks. (*Hofer and Schendel, 1978, p. 20*)

Allowing for the contention that organizations can engage in goal-seeking behaviour, this definition sees goals in terms of the future orientation of the company, but stated in rather loose, broad terms. The examples in our case illustrate this point. A popular notion is that business firms should possess some superordinate goal, namely the maximization of profit. This view has been challenged. Some, like Handy (1993), see profit as a by-product of other goals like survival, market expansion and enhancing reputation. Marris (1964) sees profit as less important than growth. The reality is that the goals vary over time and according to cultural differences. The variation of goals over time is best illustrated by reference to the public sector. Historically viewed as a public service organization, with the emphasis on service, more recent changes have widened the goals to incorporate notions of best value and the term 'new managerialism' is used to describe strategic shifts that have taken place in hospitals and universities. As we see below, the concept of goals is used differently by different writers. Some see goals as a generic concept, while others see them as part of a hierarchy of a generic concept that they define as strategic intentions. In this chapter we use the concept of goals in its broadest context.

Hofer and Schendel (1978) make the distinction between:

- **Goals**, which are seen as being unbounded, generalized statements of intent.
- **Objectives**, which represent those intentions that can be measured within a certain time frame.
- **Strategies**, which are seen as the processes by which goals are determined through the adoption of certain courses of action and the allocation of resources. We examine strategies more thoroughly in Chapter 7.

Richards (1978) distinguishes between closed- and open-ended goals.

- **Closed-ended goals** are those that have clearly defined and measurable targets to be achieved within a stated time period.
- **Open-ended goals** are the type that include some broad statement of intent such as the pursuit of excellence.

This broader view of goals has sometimes been defined as a firm's '**mission**', which would seem to equate with Hofer and Schendel's concept of a goal. Richards sees a mission as a master strategy which has a visionary content and which over-rides all other types of goal (Richards, 1978).

Miller and Dess (1996) place concepts such as goals, objectives and mission as different forms of **strategic intentions**, which can be arranged in a hierarchy as follows:

- **vision**
- **mission**
- **goals**
- **objectives**.

Vision relates to the future orientation of the organization and describes the kind of organization it ought to be. Mission is a statement of the key values, which define the purpose of the organization and, perhaps, its distinctive competitiveness. Goals are more specific statements of intent than mission, while objectives are the operationalization of the goals.

Another classification made by Perrow (1961) distinguishes between 'official' and 'operative' goals.

- **'Official' goals** are statements of intent, which occur in official documents.

● **'Operative' goals** on the other hand reflect the behaviour that is actually occurring, and which may, in fact, conflict with the official intention. To Perrow the development of a package of operative goals was the process of corporate strategy formulation.

How goals are developed

Our understanding of how goals develop owes much to the work of Cyert and March and their *Behavioural Theory of the Firm* (1963). They see organizations in terms of individuals and groups who combine to pursue mutual interests as coalitions. The interests need not be shared but the coalition is recognized by all participating interest groups as the most effective way of achieving their goals. This view of the firm reappears in Chapter 7 under our discussion of behavioural approaches to strategy formulation.

An **interest group** may be an entire department, such as marketing or research and development, or it might be a particular section within that department, such as a project team. It may even be a less formal grouping of managers within a department who collectively wish to pursue a specific policy. The creation of such interest groups may be a deliberate structural device. For example, senior management at Procter and Gamble felt that its interests could best be served through the creation of teams based around a single product or groups of products. The aim was the creation of healthy competition between product teams, and a competition and justification of resource allocation which would operate in the best interests of the firm as a whole. A more detailed discussion of the relationship between goals and structure may be found in the next section.

Interest groups can emerge owing to the complexity of the organization's task and/or its environment, requiring a degree of internal specialization, to deal with specific problems, such as product development, or external bodies such as banks. Interest groups may also develop informally, cutting across formal structures.

Each interest group will determine its goals by reference to the information it collects. Such information generally includes comparative data on other organizations on such issues as price, product design, and criteria for success. Many interest groups, for example, establish their goals in relation to competing groups in the same organization. The important point made by Cyert and March is that groups deliberately limit strategic choice by selecting information from the range available and, having decided upon a course of action, often fail to consider alternative strategies. This is perfectly understandable given the range of information and the time available to make decisions. Such a process is sometimes referred to as **bounded rationality**.

Interest groups combine to form **coalitions** and in any one organization there will be a number of such coalitions. They are created by a process of influence, negotiation and bargaining between different interest groups. It is out of this process that the goals that guide the behaviour of organization members emerge. However, in any one organization there is usually a group that may be identified as a **dominant coalition**. Once established, the dominant coalition will set up procedures to ensure that their goals are pursued by the organization as a whole. Such criteria will normally include establishing the procedures for staff selection, promotion and reward as well as laying down the rules of operation. The dominant coalition usually comprises, therefore, the senior management of an enterprise. However, certain groups align themselves with top management to ensure their goals are well represented. Even in those organizations where decision-making proceeds along more democratic lines, as in institutions of higher education, the various coalitions will compete for membership of key committees at which decisions about such issues as resources are taken.

In short, the ability of groups to pursue their goals depends upon the power they wield in the organization, which may depend on a number of variables. These may include their position in the hierarchy, the skills of group members, the resources they command and whether or not their role is seen as legitimate by the rest of the organization members.

It is inevitable that different coalitions will pursue different interests and that some will compete. The process of influence, negotiation and bargaining may be termed organizational politics. Such a concept tends to be viewed pejoratively and political activity in business firms is often seen as a problem. Yet, if we subscribe to the views of Cyert and March the process is an inevitable prelude to goal setting. Nonetheless, the potential problem of goal conflict will now be explored through the examination of **multiple goals**.

Multiple goals

In any organization made up from different interest groups some conflict over goals is inevitable. Later in this chapter we examine goal conflict emerging from the separation of ownership and control, and that arising in the public sector. Marris (1964) found that, while shareholders were concerned primarily about profitability, the professional managers, acting as the directors of companies, were more concerned with growth. In this instance profitability is a by-product, for it is growth that expands the director's sphere of influence and hence his or her personal power and reward. Despite such potential conflict between director and shareholder goals, some compromise is usually made by directors to protect their own position. Handy (1993) presents several examples of goal conflict, including that between the sales and production departments. The goals of the sales department are normally measured by volume turnover, while those of the production department are measured by cost-efficiency. We return to this particular problem in Chapter 10, when we depict the classic dilemma of the production department as that of satisfying the twin demands of customer satisfaction and operating efficiency.

In some cases such conflict can be seen to operate against the best interests of the organization. A study by Selznick (1949) of the Tennessee Valley Authority is viewed as a classic of its kind. An emerging organization, formed to solve the problems of irrigating and redeveloping a vast area in the Tennessee Valley, tackled its job through delegation and specialization. In this case, each specialist division within the organization (Selznick refers to these as sub-units) developed a greater commitment to its own sub-unit goals than those of the organization as a whole. This fragmented the total effort and resulted in groups devoting a great deal of their time to legitimizing their activities and competing for resources. This set up conflicts with other groups which further strengthened the resolve of each sub-unit to pursue its own goals. Selznick referred to this process as the 'bifurcation of interests'. Burns and Stalker (1966) noted how a similar conflict developed between the production and research and development departments in certain Scottish electronics firms, with the subsequent decline in their competitive standing. In Pettigrew's (1973) study, computer programmers saw their status threatened by an emerging group of systems analysts. In response they attempted to control information to preserve their exclusive position and prevent their work being downgraded.

In such cases, activities move away from dealing with customers or even coping with external changes in the market to focus on the resolution of internal tensions and management becomes the management of internal coalitions. Case 5.1 illustrates issues of goal conflict in London Zoo that were brought to the surface at the time of financial crisis in the early 1990s. In many organizations conflict often remains hidden, emerging only when problems get out of hand. In most situations conflict can be contained and managed. A similar situation occurred within the BBC during the summer of 1993. Viewing figures revealed that BBC1 was achieving only 29 per cent of the television audience against ITV's 41 per cent. This created a much-publicized debate about the future direction of BBC programming and there was a belief among senior managers at BBC1 that it was catering for an elite upper-income, middle-class audience and needed to widen its appeal. This debate led to further allegations of autocratic management and a stifling of creativity, which led to conflict between different factions within the organization. This would appear to be an on-going debate within the BBC.

We can see that it is quite normal for multiple goals to exist in most organizations. Conflict does occur as can be seen in Case 5.1 and the illustrations above. However, not all conflict of this kind is necessarily a problem. It would appear to be limited by four factors:

- Most groups in an organization will agree to those goals formulated by senior management as a means of achieving their own goals. This is the result of the bargaining and negotiating process between interest groups.
- Most organization members would appear to accept the goals of top management with little question. This would seem to be an implied element of the employment contract.
- The dominant coalition normally sets up a series of controls to ensure compliance to their goals. Such controls have been alluded to earlier and include selection procedures, induction and training to ensure that rules are followed. In addition, management can use technological controls in the form of work design and job allocation, and financial controls in the form of budgets and reward systems. In such ways as these, the management of organizations ensure at least a minimum level of compliance with their chosen goals.
- In many firms senior management acknowledge that different groups may have their own goals which need to be satisfied.

Case 5.1

London Zoo

London Zoo in Regents Park, in the centre of London, faces many of the problems of urban zoos; relatively cramped and inappropriate conditions for keeping large animals in captivity, little prospect of expansion, falling attendance and increasing opposition from a variety of animal welfare groups. From its heyday in the 1950s when the zoo regularly attracted 3 million visitors a year, the attendance figures were around 1 million in 2001. Further drops in attendance were associated with a major UK outbreak of foot and mouth disease and a significant fall in tourism resulting from terrorist attacks in the USA and the Iraq war. Furthermore, the zoo has pursued a policy of removing its larger animals to its sister zoo, Whipsnade. These were a particularly popular attraction. There are fears that the increase of admission prices by 10 per cent in 2003 would lead to further reductions in attendance.

▶

This case focuses on London Zoo and the events of the early 1990s. In 1991 London Zoo faced a financial crisis and closure was imminent. The surrounding debate between the owners, the managers and employees was a good illustration of goal conflict within a complex organization faced with considerable external problems. The case also examines subsequent changes and their impact on the future of the zoo.

London Zoo and its sister zoo, Whipsnade, are the property and responsibility of the Zoological Society of London, a body made up of fellows elected on the basis of some special interest and expert knowledge in zoology and its related fields. The zoos had experienced financial problems for a number of years and, in 1988, the Society commissioned a consultancy report. It recommended that the two zoos be run on a much more commercial basis and, following the publication of the report, the zoos were put under the control of a separate organization, Zoo Operations Ltd. A process of commercialization began which included a reduction in the number of animals, a marketing campaign to attract more visitors, the introduction of a more business-oriented approach and a number of organizational changes. Among these were wholesale changes in the terms and conditions of employees. Zoo staff were put on a consolidated pay scale and for the first time were faced with **appraisal** and performance-related pay. At the same time the problems facing the zoo were cushioned somewhat by a government backing of £10 million.

Despite the changes, the recession in 1991 caused a decline in paying visitors and news of closure was leaked to the press. Paradoxically, this led to a sharp increase in visitors to the zoo, perhaps sensing their last chance to see the animals. An appeal was launched and the management embarked on a number of fund-raising and cost-cutting exercises. A panda was borrowed from China in an attempt, amid much publicity, to mate London's own panda and a version of the popular television programme, Blind Date, was used to gain maximum coverage. It became particularly important to focus on specific attractions since parts of the zoo had been closed as they were unsafe and policies to reduce the number of animals kept were well advanced. Almost every day saw more animals leave the zoo for other destinations or to be destroyed. This was a harrowing experience for most of the keepers who had built up a close relationship with their charges. At the same time, staffing levels were being cut and employees were reduced by one-third. This necessitated jobs being combined and keepers, who were used to specializing in a particular area, were asked to take on a range of tasks with different types of animals.

These changes highlighted a number of differences between various groups associated with the zoo. Goal conflict has never been far from the surface. As with any zoo there is a basic tension between those who see the zoo as a focus and means of academic research into zoological matters and those who see it primarily as a form of entertainment for the public. Some of the cruder attempts at commercialization were anathema to the former group. In general, the shift to a business management approach brought a number of tensions to the surface and several factions emerged. The members of the Zoological Society were one group, the management of the zoo another, and a third comprised those keepers and researchers who made up the majority of the zoo's employees. Within these groups there were differences. Some fellows saw commercialization as the only means of survival. Others, however, banded together as a 'Reform Group' opposed to blatant commercialism and questioned the policies of the zoo's management. There was a general debate about the role of zoos in society and the role governments might play. The £10 million grant was unusual for a UK government intent on creating a non-subsidized free market society. Despite this financial gesture, many of the fellows were openly critical of the government and cited a much greater financial backing given to zoos in other countries. There was a strong belief that no longer could zoos support themselves. The Reform Group formed a coalition with a group of employees who had established themselves as a 'Survival Group', and who were a useful source of information to the fellows on the daily events at the zoo. Within the employees, a number of different issues emerged. The primary concern of one group focused on changes in their terms of employment. Another group expressed the greatest concern as the loss of animals and the difficulties of providing adequate care for those remaining. Some researchers saw the crisis as an ideal opportunity to further their claim that greater attention should be paid to academic research and the furtherance of zoological knowledge.

The financial appeal and various marketing ploys were partially successful but the impact was essentially short term and when, in 1992, the zoo made further losses and failed to achieve its targets for the number of visitors, closure seemed inevitable once again. The zoo was saved by a donation from the Emir of Kuwait as a gesture of gratitude to the British people for their part in the Gulf War. The publicity surrounding this donation and the plight of the zoo led to still further donations. The basic divisions persisted. There were still those who wanted the zoo to become a profit-making theme park, with animals placed in realistic sets to mirror their natural habitat, with a later addition of a state-of-the-art aquarium. On the other hand, there were those who saw that the zoo's only chance for public support, and hence survival, lay in the preservation and breeding of endangered species. This battle for the ideological heart of London Zoo was dubbed by the media as the 'suits' versus the 'beards'.

In the event, the theme park and aquarium concept, at a joint estimated cost of £95 million, were deemed too expensive. The zoo focused, instead, on conservation work and launched an extensive marketing campaign around the concept of 'Conservation in Action'. Part of the campaign was the introduction of an animal adoption programme, in which members of the public and organizations could sponsor particular animals. The campaign attracted a great deal of media attention through the support of national celebrities and through a BBC programme, Zoowatch. In addition the zoo attracted a sponsor, who donated £1 million a year specifically for marketing purposes.

In 1997 the zoo announced an operating surplus of over £1 million. Since then the zoo has attracted lottery funding and government support for special projects such as the '21st Century Tiger Project'. Such funding has been relatively small and the zoo continues to be dogged by problems.

At the end of 2001, a keeper was crushed to death by one of the elephants during a public exhibition. The elephants and other large animals such as the rhino were transferred to the more spacious grounds of Whipsnade. The zoo came under attack from the Royal Society for the Prevention of Cruelty to Animals (RSPCA) and other

▶

animal rights and welfare organizations over its treatment of animals. They cited the reduced life expectancy of most zoo animals, which in the case of elephants was less than 50 per cent of animals in the wild. Part of the problem was the inappropriate nature of many of the buildings. Several of the buildings in Regents Park are of considerable architectural interest and the zoo contains 12 listed buildings. For example, the penguin pool, designed by Lubetkin in 1934, is hailed as a masterpiece of modernist architecture, yet is far from the ideal habitat for penguins. A new form of conflict has emerged, that between building conservation and animal conservation.

Continuing attempts have been made to refocus the zoo around conservation but use this to attract the paying public. At the end of 2001, the structure of the zoo's senior management was changed and Regents Park and Whipsnade were brought under the same senior management team. This comprised a commercial director, a zoological director (responsible primarily for the welfare of the animals) and a director of research. The key was the bringing together of entertainment, conservation and research and in 2002 a re-branding exercise generated the slogan 'Engaging hearts and minds'. This was a clear attempt to move away from the image of a learned society to that of engaging the public in issues of conservation. Around the same time, the 'Web of Life' project was introduced to tell the tale of the conservation of biodiversity.

The zoo, ever concerned for publicity and income from a variety of sources, was keen to stress the feature of the Reptile House in the first Harry Potter book and film and its use as a location in the popular film *About a Boy*.

Sources: *Personnel Management Plus*, July, 1993; *Management Today*, July, 1993; *Marketing*, April, 1994; *Financial Times*, various 1995–8 and 7 February 2002; *The Times*, 27 March, 2002; *Design Week*, 13 June, 2002

Questions

1 Identify the various interest groups in London Zoo and the nature and origins of the of goal conflict between them.

2 To what extent are the financial problems affecting London Zoo since the early 1990s a product or a cause of the goal conflict? What other factors were at work?

3 What strategies may be most suited for London Zoo over the next 10 years? What should be the main goal of the zoo and what issues of goal conflict may arise?

In this section we have depicted the formation of goals as a complex process involving the resolution of external influences and internal politics. As such, the system is highly dynamic and changes in the goals will occur with changes in the external environment, such as market demand, technology and government policy, as well as changes that take place between interest groups within the organization. A change in ownership or top management may lead to a shift in emphasis of the firm's operations. The acquisition of the department store chain Debenhams by the Burton Group led to a change in operation as well as image. More franchises were awarded to established retailers to operate within each Debenhams store and there was considerable investment on internal refurbishment in all locations. In the late 1990s, Ford Motor Company used a revised statement of goals as a means of re-orienting staff in the face of decline in traditional markets and increased global competition. The process was dubbed 'Ford 2000' and seven goals were set out to add value to the firm, as can be seen in Figure 5.1.

Goals are not formalized, meaningless statements but the products of a highly interactive and dynamic process. The changing of goals in the face of external and even internal changes is seen to be a prerequisite for the survival of the organization. Those managers who cling to inappropriate goals would appear to place their companies at risk. However, the assumption that the existence of explicit statements of intent, such as goals, is linked to superior company performance has not been widely researched and when it has been, the findings tend to be inconclusive. Bart and Baetz (1999) in their study of links between mission statements and performance among large Canadian firms concluded that there was no automatic connection between mission and performance. However, there was evidence of superior performance where a firm had a mission statement to which management subscribed and also where the mission statement had been produced as a result of some form of employee involvement. There would appear to be clear links here to issues of commitment and corporate culture, issues we deal with later in the chapter.

In much of our discussion of goals there are clear implications for organization structure and it is to this we now turn.

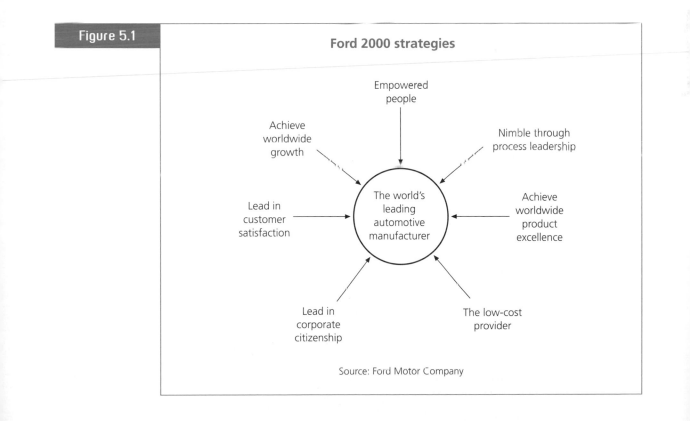

Figure 5.1

Ford 2000 strategies

Source: Ford Motor Company

Structure

A dominant theme in our discussion of goals was that organizations are made up of different interest groups formed as coalitions. One of the factors that may facilitate or inhibit the way these groups pursue their goals and whether such goals may be achieved is the structure of the organization. In this section we will examine how structures develop, the variations that occur in structural type, and their impact on performance. You should note, however, that any discussion of structure is biased towards the large firm, and most of the studies in this area are of large corporations. This is inevitable in that structural problems tend to be associated with size and complexity. The balance is redressed later in this chapter when we devote an entire section to issues in small businesses.

A structure is concerned with the grouping of activities in the most suitable manner to achieve the goals of the dominant coalition. It is concerned with:

● the organization of work around roles;

● the grouping of these roles to form teams or departments;

● the allocation of differential amounts of power and authority to the various roles;

● job descriptions, mechanisms for coordination and control, and management information systems.

In much of the writing there is an implicit assumption that senior management seek a structural elegance for their organizations to enhance performance. This, in turn, assumes that managers have a choice and that structures can be deliberately created to affect overall performance. We will now examine those factors that can influence a firm's structure to determine the extent to which structures can be manipulated by management.

Key concept 5.2 Organization structure

An organization structure is a grouping of activities and people to achieve the goals of the organization. Considerable variation is possible in the type of structure employed and the influences at work include technology, size, the nature of the environment, management strategy, the behaviour of interest groups, the firm's history and wider cultural factors. In general terms, a particular structure emerges to maximize the opportunities and solve the problems created by these various influences. In practice, however, the evidence concerning the influence of structure and performance is very patchy indeed.

The factors that influence structure

There are a number of factors that may influence the structure of an organization. We have identified them under six main headings, placed in no particular order of importance.

Technology   For some, technology is the most important, if not the sole, determinant of a firm's structure. This is part of the concept known as 'technological determinism'. Much of the work in this area is indebted to Joan Woodward's (1965) work on the impact of technology on a hundred manufacturing firms in south-east Essex (also mentioned in Chapters

3 and 10). She and her research team found that differences in manufacturing, from small batch to mass production to process technology, resulted in corresponding differences in a number of factors. These included the size and shape of the management hierarchy, the proportion of management to other employees, the proportion of direct to indirect labour, and the number of subordinates controlled by any one manager (the span of control).

Size   Other researchers find size to be a more significant variable in influencing structure than is technology. This was a particular theme of a group of academics at Aston University in the 1960s and 70s (see, for example, Pugh, 1969). As firms increase in size, additional problems are created in terms of coordination and control, often necessitating structural changes. For example, as the business expands the owner of a small business often faces increasing pressures on his or her time. No longer is he or she able to maintain a close control of operations and act as the focal point for customers, as well as managing administration and wages. In such cases some formalization and delegation is inevitable and a stage is reached when small businesses take their first steps towards bureaucratization. Such changes in structure with increasing size can be viewed in large as well as in small firms. We can see with Dow Corning in Case 5.2 that significant structural changes were made as the company expanded its product range and its markets. The way firms respond to size may vary, resulting in different types of structure, which we identify in the next section. While there are obvious connections between size and structure, the complexity of an organization's operations may have a more significant impact on its structure than sheer size.

Changes in the environment   In our discussion of the contingency approach in Chapter 1 we saw how organizations need to adapt to their environment in order to survive. An important feature of that adaptation is structural. Burns and Stalker (1966) noted that technological and market changes in the post-war electronics industry were best served by a less bureaucratic, more flexible kind of organization. Such organic structures were an essential element in the firms' ability to cope with a highly changing environment, and firms that retained their traditional bureaucratic or mechanistic structures were much less successful. The IBM case in this section illustrates the relationship between structure and a rapidly changing product market.

This theme of the structure fitting the dominant aspects of the firm's environment is the major plank in the work of Lawrence and Lorsch (1967). They believe that different tasks in the organization are confronted by different environmental problems and demands. These differences should be reflected in the structures of the departments carrying out those tasks. In their study of the plastics industry they found a highly uncertain technological environment which called for a flexible R&D function, while the demands imposed on the production department were more predictable, enabling a more traditional, bureaucratic structure to operate. The structural implications of Lawrence and Lorsch's analysis do not end with what they term the 'differentiation' of functions. In order to operate effectively, all organizations so differentiated must establish integrative devices, which might include a committee structure or designing special coordinating roles.

Strategy   The influence of strategy on structure is related to the way management perceive their environment. A firm wishing to be a product leader in a technologically sophisticated product market will have a correspondingly large R&D department in terms of both investment and employees. A firm that places a great deal of emphasis on cost controls may have a larger than average accounting department.

The relationship of strategy to organizational structure owes much to the work of Alfred Chandler (1962, 1977). He based his first work around an in-depth case study of the development of four companies, DuPont, General Motors, Standard Oil and Sears Roebuck. His work, however, had a much broader perspective, that of charting the development of American capitalism and especially the role played by the professional manager. One of the major conclusions of his work is that structure is a product of managerial strategies. The relationship between the two is more complex than many summaries of Chandler acknowledge. He found that structure did not automatically follow strategy and that managements often needed a crisis before they would agree to structural change. This point emerges in Case 5.3 with IBM.

As might be expected of an economic historian, Chandler viewed the relationship between strategy and structure as dynamic and evolutionary. He identified several stages in the development of American capitalism. These were cycles of growth and consolidation, each with its own implications for the organizational structures of the emerging large corporations in his study.

- The growth of mass markets and the development of the techniques of mass production were accompanied by vertical integration to ensure the supply of materials and secure distribution channels, and by horizontal integration through takeovers to maintain growth.

- Expansion brought its own problems of coordination and control and subsequent inefficiency. These were solved by the growth of professional management and the development of organizations structured around specialist functions, such as marketing and finance.

- As existing markets became saturated and the benefits accruing from organizational restructuring slowed down, new markets and products were vigorously pursued by overseas expansion and R&D respectively.

- Once again these developments brought their own problems of coordination and control. This time a new form of structure emerged. All four firms in Chandler's study had adopted a multi-divisional structure by 1929, with DuPont and GM leading the way. The essential qualities of this structure will be identified in the following section.

Similar cycles of expansion and consolidation through structural change can be found in studies of British companies (see, for example, Channon, 1973). While such works offer strong evidence for the influence of strategy over structure, we have already noted the complex nature of the relationship. Chandler noted that the motivation for structural change emerged not only from changes in strategy but that it needed the catalyst of an organizational crisis. We can see cases where structural change may be unnecessary or at least delayed by the sheer market power of the firm, as in the case of IBM. There may even be a case for arguing that structure can determine strategy. For example, once a company has adopted a multi-divisional structure, this could well give divisional managers the incentive, confidence and resources for even greater expansion. This interplay of strategy and structure reappears in Chapter 7 and is illustrated by changes in the USA multinational 3M.

Culture   The influence of culture on structure should not be underestimated. There is evidence that different structural forms are favoured in different countries. For example, American firms developed initially through the adoption of divisional structures, while the UK favoured the **holding company** (Channon, 1973). Firms in different countries often reflect different emphases. For example, American firms tend to stress the legal, finance and marketing functions, while those in Germany tend to feature operations. Studies on such aspects as the shape and extent of the management hierarchy have also noted differences between countries (Brossard and Maurice, 1976; Trompenaars, 1993). For example, the hierarchies in French firms tend to be steeper than in the UK, and much steeper than in Germany. Structure may also reflect specific organizational cultures; for example, those firms favouring the involvement of employees in decision-making may set up participative forums to facilitate this.

Interest groups   Although Chandler noted the resistance on the part of some managers to structural change, the whole issue of interest groups and organizational politics was largely overlooked. The preferences of the dominant coalition can exert considerable influence on the structure, as can the demands of major stakeholders. Those firms where the owners play a major role in management tend to be highly centralized. In the public sector, the pressure for accountability often results in elaborate financial control mechanisms and bureaucratic procedures. In some manufacturing firms, the pressure from banks on lending may in times of recession lead to reductions in development activities, with a corresponding impact on the size of the R&D function.

Cases 5.2, 5.3 and 7.2 all show structural changes following management changes. While size, market and other environmental influences inevitably played a major role in Dow Corning, IBM and 3M, the catalyst for new structures in all cases would seem to be changes at the top.

Two important points emerge from our consideration of the six influences above.

- First, there is considerable overlap between the various factors. For example, the structural changes of firms like Dupont and GM link technology, size and strategy; the different structural routes taken by firms in different countries are a function of both cultural differences and variations in environmental factors. In short, the structure of an organization can only be explained by reference to a number of interrelated factors. Once again, this is amply illustrated in both the Dow Corning and IBM cases.

- Second, our analysis raises the issue of the extent of choice senior management have in determining the structure of their organization. Are structures creative innovations to implement changing strategies or are they the inevitable consequences of adaptation to prevailing influences? Such issues are raised in the shipping industry Case in Chapter 9 (9.4); structural changes were an important factor in the implementation of strategic change in a highly competitive environment, but they were also determined by technical innovations in such areas as cargo handling and telecommunications. In short, the structure of the shipping companies would appear to be the result of both prevailing economic and technological conditions and management choice.

| Case 5.2 | **Dow Corning** |

Dow Corning was formed in 1942 from Dow Chemical and Corning Glass. The original focus of the firm was R&D, and the firm was highly centralized around technology and products. At this stage of its development the products were closely related and the firm operated under a traditional functional management structure.

By 1962, several changes had taken place. The company had grown, largely through product diversity, and central control of product development was no longer appropriate. In addition, there had been a change in top management and the new chief executive established five product divisions as profit centres, each with its own functional structures. The new structure was seen as successful in integrating the functions, and a contributory factor in the firm's continued growth and increased profitability.

Within a short time, further international expansion brought its own problems. There was conflict between the demands of the home and foreign markets. Conflict also arose over the central supply of raw materials and the mechanisms for **transfer pricing**. The impact of an economic recession meant that profit levels fell. These problems were met by a further change in management along with a major structural change to a matrix organization.

The ensuing matrix comprised two major elements: specialist functions and ten business profit centres, newly created from the existing five divisions. Employees reported to a business centre manager and a functional vice-president. Each business centre comprised different product boards. Each product board was led by a particular functional manager and leadership tended to change with the product life-cycle, from R&D at the early stages to marketing as the product moved through each stage of the cycle.

Structures and processes were developed within the matrix to enhance coordination and deal with conflict. A great deal of attention was focused on modifying individual behaviour by such techniques as MBO and group goal setting and the firm was assisted in its search for goal congruence by having a management structure dominated by chemical engineers. As the businesses developed it became clear that the firm needed to rethink the basic components of its matrix structure. In addition to organization by function and by business product, there was also organization by geography, to satisfy the increasing international dimension of Dow's business. In part the focus on area management was made to solve a major problem attributed to the original matrix, that of building too many new plants and failing to capitalize upon economies of scale.

Problems with the matrix persisted. Area managers were seen to have too much power within the organization and were accused of empire-building, employees complained of too many bosses and the matrix created a cumbersome **bureaucracy** with a great deal of time consumed in meetings. Dow, unlike many other organizations, did not retreat from the matrix in the face of these problems. An expansion into the pharmaceuticals sector through a number of acquisitions meant that some form of flexible, semi-autonomous structure was required. Senior management decided to refocus the evolved matrix structure. A small team of senior executives were given the task of supervising all operations. They also had the responsibility of ensuring that only one of the three elements of function, business and geography took the lead in any venture, thus avoiding conflict and duplication of effort. In addition, considerable attention was paid to employee communication, with the result that the matrix was viewed as a more open, less secretive form of organization structure.

By the end of the 1980s the company operated in 32 different countries and was responsible for the manufacture of 1800 different products. The success of its flexible organization structure, particularly the growing interchange of ideas and practices across regions, gave management the confidence to seek out more areas for expansion. More business unit teams were created and were given autonomy to develop new products and encouraged to innovate.

One of the profitable growth markets had been in silicone breast implants. These were found to have caused serious health problems for large numbers of women and the company was sued in the USA courts. The damages and potential future damages were so great that the company filed for **Chapter 11 bankruptcy** in the USA. Under Chapter 11 a company may retain its assets but must develop a payment plan to the satisfaction of its creditors. In other words, the firm is pledging future cash flows against its debts. By 1999 new claims were still being made by those injured as a result of breast implants some years earlier.

Dow Corning were also hit by the financial crisis in Asia, which had a particular impact on its core silicone business. Despite this the company had begun to move out of Chapter 11 bankruptcy. It had closed plants in Asia, Europe and the USA and had begun to reorganize around product groups rather than geographical areas, and had set out plans for a consolidation of its global supply chain.

Sources: Galbraith and Nathanson, 1978; *The Economist*, August, 1988, pp. 61–2; *Financial Times*, 1998–9

Questions

1 What were the key factors involved in Dow Corning changing from a functional to a divisional and then to a matrix structure? How do these influences relate to the six influences identified earlier in this section?

2 What problems did Dow Corning encounter with the matrix organization? How might such problems have been minimized?

3 What structure would be most appropriate for the company to aid its recovery post Chapter 11 bankruptcy?

| Case 5.3 | IBM |

In 1988 the senior management at IBM implemented significant structural changes, following the appointment of a new chairman in 1985. These changes were seen as a product of several interrelated factors, not least of which was an unacceptable fall in profits since 1984.

Before 1988 the organization structure reflected a high degree of specialization between the various functional departments (known somewhat confusingly for our purposes as divisions). Clear distinctions were drawn between the technical division, with responsibility for design, the manufacturing division, with responsibility for making the computers, and the marketing division, responsible for sales. In addition, IBM had no separate department concerned with software development. As a result of this type of structure, management concluded that counter-productive internal conflicts were set up, new designs were delayed by as much as two years, and new models, when they were introduced, lacked supporting software enabling competitors to increase their market share in key areas.

In a way IBM had been lulled by its dominant market position and early technical leadership in the field. The company firmly established its leading position throughout the 1960s and 70s. Current management thinking suggests that the company became complacent, highly bureaucratic, ultra-conservative and missed the essential entrepreneurial spirit associated with its early days.

While IBM still dominated the mainframe market, helped significantly by its USA government contracts and supplies to many major companies throughout the world, it had not responded to important changes in other markets. The computer market had become technically very diverse, and there had been many aggressive new entrants. Such new entrants were not held back by a large bureaucracy; they operated with flexible organization structures that enabled them to respond more effectively to technological change and be sensitive to the needs of the customer. The resulting market became highly fragmented and price competitive. IBM mini-systems lost out to Digital and the personal computer market was swamped by IBM compatibles, like Amstrad, selling at considerably cheaper prices and offering a more comprehensive range of software.

The structural response of IBM was divisionalization and decentralization. Five divisions were created: mainframes, minicomputers, PCs, telecommunications and new technology. Each division became an autonomous unit, and was responsible for its own product design, manufacture, sales, and ultimately profits. By the end of 1991 the company had restructured yet again, creating 14 areas of business, ten concerned with product lines and four with marketing.

In 1998, the trend towards semi-autonomous units, in the UK at least, was reversed. Increased competition, especially from new entrants in the PC market, meant that a consolidated response was needed. The various UK units were brought together under one banner of a Personal Systems Group bringing together the PC division, the network computing division and the consumer division.

Sources: Cassidy and Holmes, 1988; *Business Week*, December 1992; *Marketing*, January 1998

Questions

1   What factors led IBM to change its organization structure? What advantages and disadvantages did the new structure have?

2   Why is structural change so often the response to poor financial performance? How influential is structure in changing the performance of a business?

Types of structure

In this section we present a brief review of the major structural types and examine some trends in organization structure. In examining more recent trends we cover, albeit briefly, the debate on the flexible and de-structured firm.

Very few organizations conform precisely to a particular structural type. In some organizations a particular kind of structure predominates, while others display a variety of types. We will explain the basic characteristic of each type and present in Figure 5.6 a summary statement of the supposed advantages and problems associated with each one. In Figure 5.6 we group the divisional and holding company types together, since they are both structures to achieve decentralization. However in the text there is a section for each. As we mentioned earlier, structure does not emerge as an issue until a firm reaches a certain size. Many small firms have no apparent structure at all, beyond a centralized control system, but even this is not inevitable, as in the case of partnerships between professional people. We identify five main types of organization structure.

Functional

The main criterion guiding this type of organization is functional specialization. There are clear links here with classic forms of bureaucracy. As we can see from the illustration in Figure 5.2, employees performing related specialist tasks are grouped together under a single management structure. Most firms, as they develop, adopt this form of structure and it is especially suited to single-product firms. The structure was widely used by British firms, even very large companies, up to the 1960s, but became less common in larger firms, especially, as it was superseded by **divisionalization** (Channon, 1973).

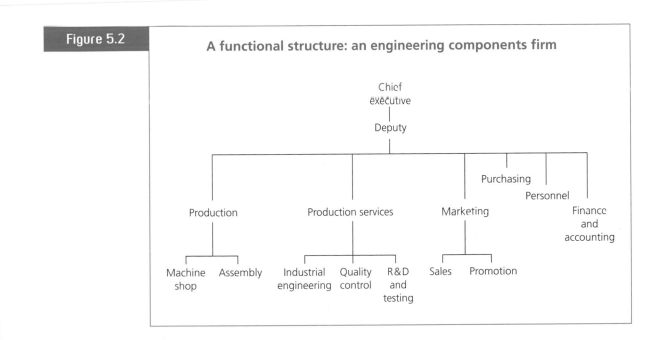

Figure 5.2   **A functional structure: an engineering components firm**

Divisional

The development of the divisional or, as it is sometimes called, the multi-divisional company is associated with market expansion and product diversification. In both these cases traditional functional structures showed themselves to be inadequate in coordinating and controlling the firm's activities. Divisionalization was a particularly American development and is associated with 'pioneer' companies like GM and DuPont in the 1920s and with the multinational expansion of American firms in the 1930s (Chandler, 1962).

An illustration of a divisional structure is shown in Figure 5.3. Under such an organization structure each division is self-contained and operates as a profit centre. Divisions can be grouped around products or markets or a combination of the two. The activities of the various divisions are directed by a central headquarters unit who take a global view of corporate strategy. Depicted in Figure 5.3 are a number of central activities, including various types of planning, communications and intellectual property. In many divisionalized structures, R&D and purchasing are often centralized activities to benefit from economies of scale, especially given the high costs associated with R&D. The dual existence of divisional profit centres and central units is a source of tension for many firms operating this structure, especially in the allocation of the costs of these central units to the individual divisions. In one case, a divisionalized engineering firm operated a central foundry, which also had to act as a profit centre in its own right. As well as serving the needs of its own organization, the foundry, having spare capacity, was encouraged to seek contracts outside

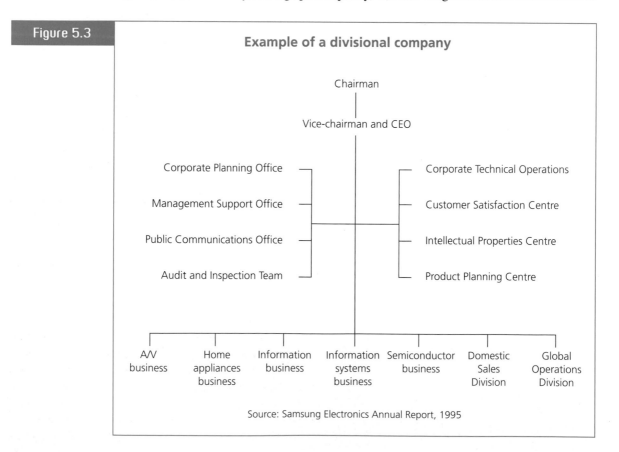

Figure 5.3

Example of a divisional company

Source: Samsung Electronics Annual Report, 1995

the firm. This set up two sorts of tension. First, the various divisions complained about having to pay the 'going rate' for foundry products, and second, the divisions always demanded priority over external contracts, which hampered the foundry from achieving its own profit objectives.

Once divisions have been established, a decision still has to be made about grouping within each division. In some cases this is done along traditional functional lines, whereas in others staff are organized around products.

Key concept 5.3 The multi-divisional company

A multi-divisional company comprises a number of different business units which may pursue markedly different types of business acitivity. The various business units operate as profit centres and are centrally coordinated by a corporate headquarters, which may also control certain central services, such as research and development, and finance. This kind of structure was developed in the USA in response to business growth. In Britain many large, diverse organizations have tended to favour a somewhat looser holding company structure with possibly less central coordination of strategic planning. In reality, there is much overlap between the two kinds of structure.

The holding company

This form of organization is associated with the growth of the firm by acquisitions and a high degree of product diversification. It may comprise a group of independent companies controlled by a coordinating group, usually made up of the chief executives of the constituent companies. At its extreme form, as exemplified by a company such as Lonhro, this structural type represents as much a form of ownership and investment as it does a kind of organization. Hanson Trust is one such company that has been subjected to considerable criticism for pursuing policies of short-term financial gain at the expense of company development through its selective policies of corporate acquisition and sales. Hanson's attempt to buy ICI in 1991 generated considerable speculation concerning major job losses and future investment in ICI. Amid growing opposition, the takeover was eventually thwarted by the ICI board (a fuller account of this debate may be found in Adcroft *et al.*, 1991).

Figure 5.4 offers us a different form of holding company, which is made up of constituent companies all bearing the name of the group, in this case the Korean giant, Hyundai. Large Korean firms, like those in Japan, usually comprise a grouping of highly diversified businesses. In the case of Hyundai they are placed in industrial groupings.

As we saw in the previous chapter, the holding company is the prevalent structural form for large Japanese companies. It has also been described as the peculiarly British route to divisionalization (Channon, 1973). There are similarities between divisionalization and the holding company, although in the UK the holding company arrangement is, in many cases, a function of stock market behaviour and the high number of mergers and acquisitions. The holding company is a looser arrangement than the divisional company and may lack the focus.

Figure 5.4

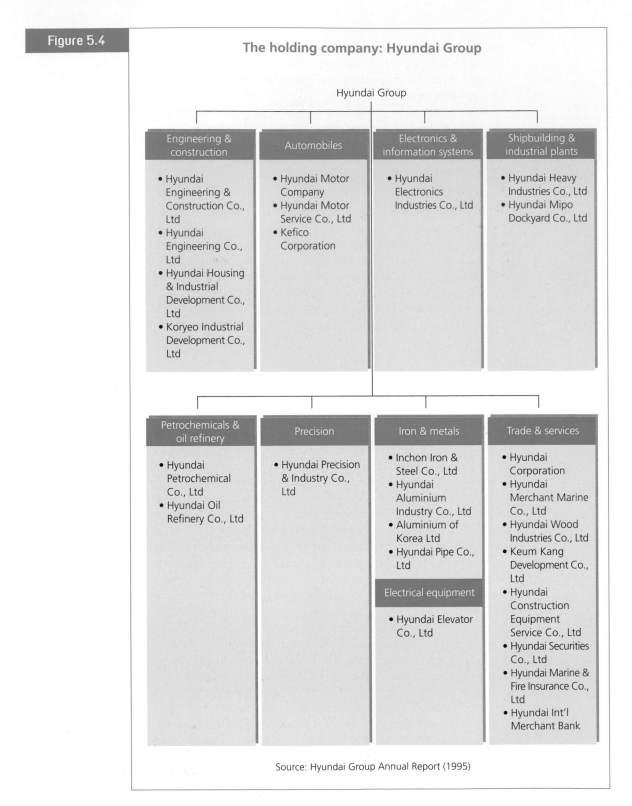

The holding company: Hyundai Group

Hyundai Group

Engineering & construction

- Hyundai Engineering & Construction Co., Ltd
- Hyundai Engineering Co., Ltd
- Hyundai Housing & Industrial Development Co., Ltd
- Koryeo Industrial Development Co., Ltd

Automobiles

- Hyundai Motor Company
- Hyundai Motor Service Co., Ltd
- Kefico Corporation

Electronics & information systems

- Hyundai Electronics Industries Co., Ltd

Shipbuilding & industrial plants

- Hyundai Heavy Industries Co., Ltd
- Hyundai Mipo Dockyard Co., Ltd

Petrochemicals & oil refinery

- Hyundai Petrochemical Co., Ltd
- Hyundai Oil Refinery Co., Ltd

Precision

- Hyundai Precision & Industry Co., Ltd

Iron & metals

- Inchon Iron & Steel Co., Ltd
- Hyundai Aluminium Industry Co., Ltd
- Aluminium of Korea Ltd
- Hyundai Pipe Co., Ltd

Electrical equipment

- Hyundai Elevator Co., Ltd

Trade & services

- Hyundai Corporation
- Hyundai Merchant Marine Co., Ltd
- Hyundai Wood Industries Co., Ltd
- Keum Kang Development Co., Ltd
- Hyundai Construction Equipment Service Co., Ltd
- Hyundai Securities Co., Ltd
- Hyundai Marine & Fire Insurance Co., Ltd
- Hyundai Int'l Merchant Bank

Source: Hyundai Group Annual Report (1995)

Project teams

These comprise units specially created to cope with a highly unstable environment. In essence they are temporary structures formed around a particular task or problem and reflect technical expertise rather than any notion of management hierarchy. Such structures are commonly found in high-technology firms and some types of service organizations, especially consulting firms. In advertising agencies, teams are usually created to deal with specific client accounts. In R&D departments the research work may be organized around several teams, each handling a different problem. In construction companies project teams may be created to deal with a particular job such as the building of a new office block. The membership of teams can be highly fluid; different specialists may be brought in at different times and one employee may be a member of several teams.

The approach reflects a close identification with the needs of the client and is an extension of the kind of client-based structure found in professional firms such as solicitors, accountants and the like. However the use of teams has become more common in firms of all sizes as they search for flexibility and responsiveness.

While focusing specifically on the needs of the client does have its advantages, there can be some unnecessary duplication of resources and there may be scheduling and logistics problems. These become more severe as the organization gets larger, and a stage may be reached where project teams need to be supported within a functional or divisional framework. The matrix structure was developed especially with such problems in mind and it is to this we now turn.

The matrix

Essentially the matrix is an attempt to combine the best of all worlds: the customer orientation of the project team, the economies of scale and the specialist orientation of the functional organization, and the product or market focus of the divisional company. The matrix is an attempt to devise a structure that can effectively manage at least two different elements, be they size, products, markets or customers.

The essence of the matrix is presented by the Dow Corning case; the work was controlled originally in two directions, by a functional specialism and by a product grouping. Committees are set up to coordinate the two orientations, and attention is given to training the staff towards goal congruence. Further developments in the matrix at Dow added a third dimension to the structure, that of geography. The illustration of a matrix in a university business school is presented in Figure 5.5.

The matrix became very popular in the 1970s and owed much to the work of Lawrence and Lorsch (1967) and Galbraith (1971). It was embraced by companies such as Dow Corning (see Case 5.2), General Electric, Ciba Geigy and Citibank. The popularity was short-lived and of all the structural types the matrix has attracted most criticism. In a later work, Paul Lawrence referred to the matrix as an 'unnecessary complexity', which was only justified in certain situations (Davis and Lawrence, 1977, p. 21). These were:

- If two or more of a firm's dimensions, like products and markets, were especially critical to its performance.
- If employees needed to carry out highly complex, interdependent tasks in an uncertain environment.
- If economies of scale were needed, especially in the use of scarce or expensive resources.

Unless such conditions are present the matrix can cause more problems than it solves. Some of those problems are depicted in Case 5.2, which also illustrates the changes made by Dow to counteract such problems. Trompenaars (1993) has argued that the effectiveness of the matrix may be limited to specific cultures. Matrix organizations are not successful in Italy where, Trompenaars argues, bosses are seen as father figures. Since matrix organizations often require people to have two bosses, Italians find it difficult relating to two 'fathers'.

For many years, matrix management was a by-word for inefficiency, conflict, delay and cost. However, it was seen by some companies in the 1990s as the structural form that is made for the company wishing to act globally and transnationally. In the case of Ford Motor Company, the creation of a matrix organization was an integral part of the Ford 2000 strategy (see the previous section on goals). The structure was based around five vehicle centres, four in the USA and one in Europe. These vehicle centres are served by cross-national teams in most of the functional areas. In this way, a buyer at the European supply headquarters in Basildon, in the UK, could report to a manager in the USA and be part of a team embracing buyers in Germany and Spain. The system is supported by the company's extensive video-conferencing facilities and its own airline company, which facilitates regular meetings between team members. The new structure was introduced by senior management, mindful of the problems of matrix organizations in other companies. Considerable attention was paid to setting clear objectives, having clear definitions of roles, appointing and promoting those people who could operate transnationally and investing heavily in public relations (PR) and training. The advantages of matrix management were stressed. The then CEO, Alex Trotman, saw its advantage in breaking down the 'chimneys' of the functional structure, which act as barriers, and opening up people to new ideas. Trotman defines the new structure as 'more like jazz than a structured orchestra' (quoted in Lorenz, 1994).

Students should always remember that the structural types identified above represent fairly broad categories. In reality a firm may display a mixture of structures. We have already seen how many divisionalized companies have functional specialisms within each division. In a functional organization we may find that different departments are organized along different lines; the operations department may well extend the functional structure, while the R&D staff may well be organized as project teams. New structural forms are emerging all the time, adapting the traditional approaches to suit their own needs.

Trends in organization structure

A cursory review of the management literature of the last 20 or so years will identify a number of recurring themes and phrases. Numerous references are made to the flexible firm, the boundaryless organization, the flat organization, the lean organization, the down-sized organization, delayering, empowerment, outsourcing, networking and even the virtual organization. These concepts represent two major trends.

- Large organizations are being broken down into smaller units accompanied by a reduction in the number of employees (**down-sizing**) and a reduction in the numbers of level of management (**delayering**). There is a shift away from more rigid structures often associated with functional, divisional and even matrix organizations.

- Instead the focus is upon the creation, through decentralization, of more flexible forms of organization, that empower employees and are more responsive to the needs of the customer.

Figure 5.5

Matrix structure: University Business School

Head of School

Deputy Head of School
(academic programmes)

Deputy Head of School
(subject areas)

Course directors

Course leaders

	Strategy & international business	Marketing	Economics & finance	Operations	HRM
MBA					
MSc Finance					
MSc Marketing					
MA HRM					
BA Business Studies					
BA Accounting & Finance					
BSc Business Economics					
Professional courses					
Short courses					

Such 'new' organizations are championed by such as Peters (1992), Hammer and Champy (1993) and Ashkenas *et al.* (1995).

The ultimate form of new organization is **networking**, sometimes referred to as the **virtual organization**. This type of structure has been made possible by developments in computer technology whereby computer systems can interact. Such a system enables people to operate from home and has been heralded as the organization structure of the future. Networking has attracted considerable publicity in both academic journals and the popular press. This attention, however, tends to exaggerate the real extent of networking.

Figure 5.6	A summary of advantages and problems associated with different types of organization structure

Advantages	Problems

1. Functional organization

Advantages	Problems
• Specialization • The logic of custom and practice • A clear chain of command	• Conflicting departmental objectives • Conflicting management values • A lack of coordination • A lack of consumer orientation

2. Divisional organization and Holding company

Advantages	Problems
• The operation of businesses as profit centres • The encouragement of entrepreneurship • Reduces upward dependency on top management • Economies of scale by centralization of common features like R&D	• Cooperation and interdependence • Accounting procedures, especially transfer pricing • Increasing diversity of operations • Overall management control

3. Project teams

Advantages	Problems
• The ability to cope with an unstable environment • The use of individual expertise • The ability to cope with diverse problems • Deal directly with the customer	• A costly duplication of services • Scheduling • The participants have no functional home • What happens when the project is finished?

4. Matrix organization

Advantages	Problems
• Emphasizes the strengths of the functional and project types • Flexibility of labour • The ability to transfer expertise where it is most needed • Dual control via function and project • Closeness to the customer	• Coordination and control • A proliferation of committees and meetings • Too many bosses • Conflicting loyalties for staff • Can be slow to adapt

Even in pioneer networkers such as Rank Xerox, those employees operating under this system are but a very small percentage of the total employed.

While the numbers of firms switching to this form of organization is exaggerated, computer-based interaction has become commonplace in global organizations, where employees in different countries can work together using telephone, email and video-conferencing.

Of course, a form of networking has been around for some time in certain types of manufacturing industry in the form of home-working. In this case, individuals or even families engage in simple assembly work (as with electrical components) or in such activities as dressmaking and alteration. Home-working has become a way of life in some countries such as Japan and is a particularly low-cost form of labour.

We focus on two related trends; down-sizing and delayering and the flexible firm.

Down-sizing and delayering

If the flexible firm was the structural concept of the 1980s, down-sizing and delayering emerged as the key features of the 1990s. Delayering is defined as:

The planned vertical compression of managerial levels of hierarchy. (*Littler* et al. *2003*)

Whilst down-sizing can occur without delayering and vice versa, the two tend to go together. The group of employees that have been affected most is middle management. We referred briefly to this in the last chapter in our discussion on the impact of ICT on jobs. The assumptions behind down-sizing and delayering are set out as follows.

- Large bureaucracies are inefficient and ineffective. They are expensive, slow to respond to change, and focus on internal processes rather than on the needs of the customer.
- Delayering will create more flexible and responsive organizations that will empower employees and bring the firm closer to its customers.
- While cost-cutting is not a primary objective, this will be an added benefit as labour costs are cut.

The findings of a number of studies have been summarized in Littler *et al.* (2003). These findings tend to be supported by their own study of 2964 firms in Australia, New Zealand and South Africa.

- Delayering is happening in a high percentage of firms around the world and challenges the classical principles of organization and management, particularly with reference to the span of control (the number of employees effectively controlled by a single manager).
- The reduction in the number of levels of management reduces the promotion and hence the career prospects of many managers. As a consequence there has been an increase in managerial job changes between firms.
- The subsequent redesign of those management jobs that remain has resulted in increased responsibility and increased work-loads. While some managers are positive about this, others feel more stress and job dissatisfaction. In general, there are greater numbers expressing dissatisfaction than satisfaction.
- With the removal of management levels, the workforce is empowered and take on more responsibility. As with the management group, there are mixed views of enrichment versus stress and anxiety increases.
- The impact of redundancies and increased labour mobility is a reduction in the levels of loyalty and commitment to the organization.
- There is a certain cynicism about the real objectives of down-sizing and delayering. There is some evidence to suggest that in many organizations service levels have not improved, but have actually worsened. This reinforces the belief that cost-cutting may be the primary objective.

The flexible firm

The concept of the flexible firm emerged from work carried out by the Institute of Manpower Studies and associated largely with the writing of John Atkinson (his 1984 article offers an excellent summary). The main assumptions behind Atkinson's model are that new forms of organization are required as a strategic response to the combined effects of market stagnation, job losses, technical change, increased uncertainty and reductions in the working week.

In the 1990s the focus shifted to emphasize flexibility as the key strategic response to globalization. Murton (2000) argues that in the global economy a premium is placed on responsiveness and adaptability, with the manipulation of labour costs as the easy option. The 1990s has also seen the growth of critical literature surrounding flexible labour market trends, with many of the critics focusing on issues of insecurity and exploitation.

Atkinson's original model identified three types of flexibility:

- **Numerical flexibility**. This is achieved through management's ability to make rapid alterations to the headcount of the firm to meet changes in demand. A growth in part-time work, temporary contracts and sub-contracting were the expected consequences of numerical flexibility.

- **Functional flexibility.** This is achieved when employees are able to perform a range of jobs and can move between them as the need arises. In many organizations this will see an end to demarcation between trades and result in multi-skilling. Historically, especially in the UK, demarcation has often been viewed as the cause of inefficiencies as well as industrial relations disputes.

- **Financial flexibility.** This is required to reflect changes in the supply and demand of labour and to enhance the operation of functional and numerical flexibility. This can be achieved through the creation of differential rates of pay for full- and part-time workers, introducing the link between effort and reward for a greater number of workers and the use of incentives to encourage workers to become multi-skilled.

Sparrow and Marchington (1998) argue that there are not three but seven types of flexibility observable in modern organizations and that these flexibilities are both discrete and parallel. In addition to the three defined by Atkinson, they recognize **temporal, geographical, organizational** and **cognitive** flexibility. Temporal flexibility is concerned with changing the time patterns of work, as with the introduction of shift work. Geographical flexibility involves the increased mobility of groups of workers as in the introduction of transnational teams. Organizational flexibility relates to structural and systems changes and cognitive flexibility to the changing mindset of the workforce. Beatson (1995) draws the distinction between micro-flexibility, which occurs at the level of the

Key concept 5.4 The flexible firm

Flexibility within organizations occurs in a number of different ways. These include the employment of part-time workers, those on short-term contracts and the use of out-sourced contract work. It also involves getting employees to do a range of different jobs, introducing variations in pay and times of attendance and increasing the geographical mobility of labour. Such changes are seen to be on the increase as a result of globalization, higher levels of competition and the need for most firms to reduce costs. There is clear evidence that all forms of flexibility are on the increase. While the impact is often viewed positively from the perspective of the organization, certain negative outcomes have been noted for the individual worker.

firm, and macro-flexibility, which deals with changes at the level of the labour market in general.

In all its forms the 'flexible firm' will break up traditional organization structures. For Atkinson, the key outcome will be the establishment of two groups of employees; core and peripheral. Core employees are those on permanent or long-term contracts and who hold key skills and positions within the organization. Accordingly, core workers are well rewarded and often have the security of lifetime employment. Peripheral workers comprise two groups. It is envisaged that there will be a group of full-time workers, who will be less skilled and not enjoy the security of the core worker. The second group will comprise part-time and contract workers hired in direct proportion to the demand or to deal with non-core business such as cleaning and catering. The distinction between core and peripheral workers has long been a feature of the Japanese labour market and is referred to in Chapter 4.

There has been a great deal of research into the impact of the flexible firm on organizations in the UK and the rest of Europe and good summaries can be found in Legge (1998) and Murton (2000). The main points are:

- Part-time work has increased in all sectors. In the UK between 1984 and 1996 it increased 31 per cent and it is estimated that approximately 25 per cent of the UK labour force are part-timers. The highest proportion of part-time workers are still found in the service industries and among female employees, although more recent trends suggest that part-time employment for males is growing at a faster rate than that for females.

- The use of temporary contracts has also increased by over 30 per cent since 1984, with the largest increase occurring since 1992 and in the public sector. The popularity of temporary contracts in the public sector is as a management response to variations in the budget. For example, the use of such contracts has grown in the university sector where budgets are tied to student numbers, which may be unpredictable.

- There is clear evidence of the increasing use of sub-contractors across a range of public and private organizations. Historically a classic feature of the construction industry, this is now used by many local authorities, largely as a direct result of government regulations insisting on competitive tendering for services such as rubbish removal. In the private sector there is increasing use of sub-contracting in the production of parts in manufacturing, owing to both globalization and the development of modular manufacturing processes. Many large firms use sub-contracting not only for cleaning and catering, but also for key HR functions such as recruitment, training and payrolling and in marketing for promotional and advertising activities.

- Multi-skilling has occurred but the weight of evidence suggests that much of this is as a result of job enlargement and the intensification of work as opposed to a focus on job enrichment for the individual.

- In terms of temporal flexibility, there has been a spread of shiftworking to the banking sector and the growth of call centres and e-commerce will probably lead to further increases. Part of the growth is around the concept of 'customer care', particularly in the service industries, where firms have increased their times of operation to meet customer need, as with the Sunday opening of shops or, in some cases, the 24-hour opening of supermarkets.

Pollert (1987), in an early critique of Atkinson's work, accuses the Institute of Manpower Studies of offering vague concepts and of producing a model that is not supported by current evidence. She argues that elements of the flexible firm model can be seen in many organizations, but they have been introduced as cost-cutting exercises rather than a strategic response to a changing market environment. This is particularly true of local authorities and other public sector organizations. She goes on to claim that many of the elements are far from new, citing multi-skilling as a feature of 1960s productivity bargaining initiatives. In some industries, notably fast food, she cites core workers as anything but the skilled, highly paid elite of Atkinson's flexible firm. Finally, she fears that the adoption of the flexible model could lead to more problems than it solves. Such problems as the growth of part-time employment have certainly attracted the interest of trade unions, where it is viewed as a part of the process of decreasing job security.

These themes reoccur in work throughout the 1990s. Dore (1997) sees flexibility in terms of a not necessarily appropriate response to increased shareholder pressures. Legge (1998) questions whether an increase in labour flexibility is a sound strategy and offers a clue as to her position in the title of her work, 'Flexibility: the gift-wrapping of employee degradation?'. She argues that within Western culture we tend to associate flexibility with positive images, yet for the core worker the outcome is often work intensification and stress and for the part-time or temporary worker it means insecurity. However, she does accept that there are advantages for employers in terms of cost reduction and the regulation of industrial relations. For some employees there are advantages. In the case of parents, part-time work provides the opportunity of combining work and child-care and for some it has been an important route of re-entry into the labour market.

There are other issues. The distinction between core and peripheral workers forms part of the debate about inclusion and exclusion in society. The very term peripheral suggests a group on the edge of society and the overall growth of part-time and contract work may lead to a lessening of importance of the firm as a source of identity in society. Hakim (1996) contends that the workforce has polarized into a primary labour market dominated by males and a secondary market typified by part-time jobs and high rates of labour turnover, dominated by females. His research suggests that the female secondary workforce accounts for as much as 40 per cent of the total labour market in the UK.

Ultimately the links between the introduction of the different forms of flexibility and economic success at either the micro or macro levels is still unproven. We end this discussion of structure by extending this theme with a brief look at the relationship between structure and performance.

Structure and performance

We can see from Figure 5.6 and our discussion of the various structural types that some structures are more suited to some situations than others. Conversely a firm that adheres stubbornly to a structure that is totally inappropriate to the contingencies that it faces may be creating problems for itself. However, the evidence on these matters is far from convincing. The major difficulties in establishing a correlation between structure and performance would appear to be first, identifying appropriate measures of performance and second, proving causality. We can make some general points:

● Whatever the relationship between structure and performance, once a structure has been installed it is often very difficult to change it. Equally, frequent structural changes could be damaging in terms of the disruption that takes place and the requirement on the part of staff to learn new systems.

- It is extremely doubtful whether structure alone can lead to improvements in performance. However sound the structure may be, it is unlikely that it can totally overcome problems created by staff incompetence or even divisive internal politics. In some cases a high degree of specialization or divisionalization can lead to a worsening of relationships. We might even speculate that there is more evidence for suggesting that structure can affect performance in a negative way than there is for its having a positive impact. There is some evidence that structure in harness with other variables can lead to improvements in performance. This point was taken up by Galbraith and Nathanson (1978), who argue that effective financial performance is obtained by achieving some kind of congruence between strategy, structure, processes, rewards and people.

- We have noted elsewhere in this book that performance can influence structure and systems (see the discussion on 'organizational culture' later in the chapter). More successful companies are likely to be less bureaucratic, while less successful firms tend to have more controls, particularly cost controls. This fits in with the one of the key assumptions of our Business in Context model: that influences operate in more than one direction, and while organizational factors, such as structure, can affect the outcome of a firm's activities that outcome, in turn, affects the organization.

Ownership

We might assume, quite logically, that ownership is an important variable in that the owners of a business will wish to determine the goals and the way that business operates. In support of our assumption we could cite illustrations of influential founders, such as Henry Ford, Bill Hewlett and Dave Packard in the USA, and the Sainsbury and Cadbury families in the UK. We could also refer to numerous cases of small firms where the owner, often single-handedly, controls the destiny of the business. In the case of the small firm the owners can be clearly defined and their impact easily assessed. Discovering who actually owns and controls businesses becomes much more difficult with large corporations like the major oil companies, or even an organization like British Gas, where privatization has been accompanied by widespread share issue at least in the first instance. It would appear that the greater the size of the organization and the greater the dispersal of share ownership, the more we can question our original assumptions and need to examine the relationship between the ownership and the control of businesses.

The degree of private and public ownership is another issue that holds significant interest for students of business. Organizations that are wholly or partly state owned, or those that have been privatized raise important issues of management control and public accountability. Issues related to privatization have become increasingly important in many countries as the state has divested itself of its public corporations. This is particularly the case in those economies in transition from state control to a market economy, as in many countries in Eastern Europe (such transitional economies were dealt with in Chapter 3).

In this section we will focus on the following three aspects of ownership and examine the implications for business operation. First, we identify the various types of firms that exist, largely from the perspective of their legal structures. Second we explore the traditional debate about ownership and control. Finally we examine the issue of the public ownership of organizations and the trend of privatization. The two elements were brought much closer together in the latter half of the 1980s in Britain. Traditional public sector concerns, such as hospitals and local authorities, have been urged to take a more commercial approach. Since 1983, many organizations like British Telecom, BA, British Aerospace, and utilities, such as gas, electricity and water, have passed from public to private ownership or to a mixture of public and private ownership. The phenomenon is not confined to the UK as privatization has occurred in such countries as France, Germany, Canada and Australia. In most cases, privatization has been accompanied by a massive increase in the proportion of the population owning shares and, in the initial phases at least, a highly dispersed ownership pattern for those concerns. It is this dispersal that is at the heart of the ownership and control debate. However, first we identify the various types of organization from an ownership perpsective.

Types of ownership

- **Sole trader**. This is the term used in the UK to define the most common form of business ownership. A **sole trader** can, and often does, employ staff and a better term would probably be that of sole proprietor. This is a common route for entry into business and is found in most small business start-ups in most countries around the world. Sole traders can be typically found as electricians, plumbers, hairdressers, shop owners and consultants. A key feature of sole traders is that of unlimited personal liability, in that any debts accumulating are the responsibility of the owner. This is a common reason for small business failure. In most countries such firms are relatively easy to set up and have considerable attraction in that ownership and control are combined and, although personally responsible for all losses, sole traders take all the profits. Many of the key issues affecting sole traders are discussed in the section on small firms later in this chapter.

- **Partnership**. In common with sole traders, a **partnership** has unlimited personal liability and partners may have their personal assets placed at risk to cover losses or if the firm is sued. This may be a particular problem in the case of professional malpractice, where sums can be large. As a consequence some partnerships become companies with limited liability. This is not a popular trend, particularly among professional firms, and, in recent years, a new form of organization has emerged, the **limited liability partnership**. This is a hybrid organization with elements of both a partnership and a limited company and can be found in larger law firms and accountants in the UK. A similar type of organization exists in the USA. In essence the firm must register its accounts and while individual members are liable, that liability does not extend to other members of the firm. Of course, to limit liability, most partnerships will take out professional indemnity insurance and, in some cases, this is a requirement of the profession.

  Partnerships are found most particularly in the professions such as in law practices, accountancy firms and medical practices. Partnerships are essentially combinations for the mutual interest of partners. Ownership is shared on the basis of each partner putting capital into the firm, which is then taken out when the partner leaves or retires. Such input of capital is a means through which partnerships can expand. In most partnerships, income is derived by partners through a share of the profits. Not all partners may have an equal share of the business and the profits are divided accordingly.

The role and responsibilities of partners tend to be controlled by law and many professional partnerships are controlled further by a professional body, such as the Law Society in the UK. Key management and control issues in partnerships tend to be decision-making and the management of staff. Decision-making can be an issue where individual partners pursue their own interest rather than that of the firm as a whole. Managing staff becomes an issue in professional firms, where partners are the key practitioners and fee earners and, while technically skilled, are not necessarily trained managers. In many professional firms, a partnership or practice manager is appointed to manage the non-professional staff activities and usually the accounts, thereby creating a limited separation of ownership and control.

- **Limited companies**. In the UK there are several types of **limited company**. The main types are **public limited company (plc)** and **private company**, which carries the suffix, limited (ltd). The main difference between the two is that a plc has shares that are available for the general public to buy and the company is quoted on the stock market. In the private company the shares are not openly available and may be owned by the founders, family interest and/or the current management. A **company limited by guarantee** is owned not by shareholders but by a number of members, whose liability is limited to the amount of contribution. Companies limited by guarantee are most commonly found in the not-for-profit or the voluntary sector, but Network Rail is one such company that operates to make a profit (see Case 5.4).

Public limited companies tend to be larger firms and private companies are generally found among the small and medium-sized enterprises, although this is not always the case and some larger companies are still private. However, both forms of companies exist as legal entities that are separate from the people who own shares and all assets are owned by the company and not by individuals. In both cases the owner's liability is restricted to the amount they have invested in the company, usually in the form of shares. A common exception to this is found in the small business sector, where owners are frequently asked to give personal guarantees to banks for loans.

All limited companies must conform to the requirements of the Companies Act. Both plcs and private companies have directors elected by the shareholders. In general the company is run on a day-to-day basis by a chief executive officer and a set of executive directors, who are normally paid employees. Non-executive directors may be appointed from outside if they have some special attribute to bring such as experience, skills or connections or all three.

Some form of public limited company and/or private company exists in most other countries. In Germany, there are the exact equivalents in the form of an *Aktiengesellschaft* (AG), the equivalent of the UK plc, and a *Gesellschaft mit beschränkter Haftung* (GmbH), the equivalent of the UK private company. The GmbH predominates in Germany and forms most of the influential *Mittelstand*, a group of mid-sized companies, many of which are family owned. However, unlike the UK system, corporate governance in Germany is strictly controlled by law and all firms over a certain size must abide by the co-determination laws, which lay down requirement for a two-tier system of boards and employee representation on the most senior board (the *Aufsichtsrat*) and via the works council (*Betriebsrat*). Such differences between the UK and Germany are features of the difference between Anglo-Saxon and Social Market systems of capitalism identified in Chapter 3.

- **Public sector organizations.** Many variations in ownership and control exist in the public sector. This is a broad area that covers central government departments, local government departments, universities, schools, hospitals and public sector corporations. The final type is essentially business organizations, which are nationalized. In most countries the number of public corporations have declined significantly in the last few years with the increase in privatization in most countries and the liberalization of former state-controlled economies. Key issues in both nationalized and privatized organizations alike include effectiveness, efficiency and public accountability, issues that are dealt with later in this chapter, when we deal with ownership and management in the public sector.

Ownership and control

The issue of ownership and control is one of continuing interest for academics, more especially among economists and sociologists. It is also a debate that raises significant questions for businesses in practice. How committed to the future of an enterprise are managers who have no stake in its ownership, or shareholders who have no interest beyond a return on investment? Are the resulting strategies in the best interests of all concerned: owners, managers, employees, the state, the public at large? How much freedom do managers have in developing business strategies?

Key concept 5.5 Ownership versus control

The ownership versus control debate is concerned with potential conflict of interests between the owners of business organizations and those who manage them on a day-to-day basis. The issue is a product of the creation of the joint stock company and the emergence of the professional manager to replace the owner-manager. The key issue is the extent to which company goals are pursued in the best interests of all stakeholders or that of a group of shareholders with no direct involvement with the firm. This issue becomes especially significant in volatile share markets with a large proportion of institutional investors, where high levels of share trading can lead to large numbers of mergers and acquisitions. There is a fear that pressure from shareholders for dividend leads to short-term management decisions that may not be in the long-term best interests of the firm.

The debate around these issues originates from the separation of ownership and control through the creation of the joint stock company and the subsequent dispersal of share ownership. With increased investment businesses grew in size and complexity and control by professional managers became a necessity. The complexity of such growing businesses led to a specialization within the management group and the separation of the firm into different specialist functions and activities. Bureaucratic rules and procedures were developed to coordinate and control such activities. Both the specialization and the bureaucratization reinforced the control of the management group with a supposed weakening in the power of the owner to influence decisions. The owner's main source of control was through the possession of capital stock.

This phenomenon was highlighted in the seminal study of Berle and Means (1932) and developed in later work by Berle (1954). Berle and Means in a study of the 200 largest non-financial corporations in the USA classified the firms by their mode of control. They concluded that 44 per cent of the firms were management controlled and that this trend was increasing. The Berle and Means study has been replicated in both the USA and Britain with similar results, although both the data and conclusions of such studies have been the subject of significant controversy (Child, 1969 and Scott, 1979 have a reasonable summary of these studies).

Berle and Means used their data to develop and support their own view of a 'managerial revolution'. To them management control was 'better' in that it resulted in more effective decisions both for the profitability of the firm and for the general good of society; it was more professional and more socially responsible. The concepts of a 'neutral technocracy' and a 'soulful corporation' have stemmed from such value assessments of management control. We can see a clear link between Berle and Means's notion of 'managerialism' and the earlier work of F. W. Taylor on 'scientific management'. For both Taylor and Berle and Means, management should use a professional approach based on the application of science to solve the problems facing the firm. According to Berle and Means, management control would be truly professional in that strategies would be guided more by scientific analysis and be more answerable to society than the potentially narrow self-interest of the owner-manager.

This concept of a managerial revolution was popularly espoused by Burnham (1941), whose ideas have attracted perhaps more attention than his analysis deserves. Burnham, writing at the time of Roosevelt's 'New Deal', saw similarities in many nations through the increased state control of the economy. He believed that, through this, managers, as the controllers of capital, would be able to assume a powerful role in society and direct businesses to serve their own ends.

There is a tendency to view such debates as purely academic. This would be wrong, since the questions that emerge are central to the way businesses operate and the control of organizations has implications not only for the survival and prosperity of the organization itself but also for the people who work for it, firms who deal with it, and society at large. We therefore examine some key issues in the ownership and control debate and raise a number of questions around the conclusions drawn by Berle and Means.

● **Do managers really have more power and control than shareholders?** Even with a dispersal of share ownership, shareholders' needs still have to be satisfied, which may place constraints on management decisions. There is always a danger that shareholders, in the face of what they perceive as unpopular management decisions, will sell their shares, creating instability in the firm's stock market position. This is often the reason given for dividend pay-out in the UK being much higher than in the USA, Germany or Japan (see Chapter 13 for a fuller account). Managers keep dividends high to protect the firm against the threat of hostile takeover.

In any case the distinction between managers and shareholders has become increasingly blurred. While in many companies there clearly has been a separation of ownership and control, there is an increasing tendency, especially in the larger firms, to offer senior management shares in the company as part of their annual remuneration deal. In this way, managers may well identify with shareholders' own aspirations. This argument has been extended by the Marxist analysis of ownership and control, which views shareholders and managers not as being separate but as different forms of the same animal; no real distinction is drawn between managers and capitalist owners. In addition to such arguments we can see that management freedom to make decisions is often held in check by banks, governments and trade unions. This complicates the ownership and control debate and we return to the role of the financial institutions later in this chapter and in Chapter 13.

- **Many large and influential companies are both family-owned and controlled** and no separation has in fact occurred. In the retail trade in Britain such family-run businesses as Sainsbury and Dixons have grown and prospered in relatively recent times. Empirical work from the USA suggests that family ownership and control of major businesses is still a significant feature.

- **Has the ownership of shares really been dispersed?** The data presented by Berle and Means (1932) showed that 86 per cent of the largest 200 USA companies had a minimum of 5000 shareholders, with 22 per cent having over 50 000. Putting such data in perspective, Miliband (1969) cited evidence which revealed that in Britain in 1961 only 4 per cent of the population owned shares and 1 per cent of the population owned 81 per cent of all shares. Others, notably Child (1969), interpret the evidence that while there may be some evidence of share dispersal, the majority of shareholders own relatively small numbers of shares and tend to be extremely passive. This can result in minority shareholders owning a substantial proportion of all shares, with considerably more interest and potential influence in management decision-making. It is not just the dispersal of shares that should concern us, but the pattern of that dispersal.

Most of these data are of course fairly old, and the entire pattern of share ownership, in Britain at least, has been confused by the large number of share issues in the 1980s and 1990s resulting from the government's policy of privatization. Many of the earlier share issues, such as British Telecom, were oversubscribed to a significant extent. While it is undeniable that large numbers have been brought into share ownership for the first time, it is, however, much too early to assess the situation. Many of those who have bought shares have done so with the prime intention of a quick sale for profit. This whole business has been summed up by the humorist Miles Kington as follows:

> … the British public has learnt how to fill in forms they didn't quite understand, send them off at the last possible moment, receive negligible numbers of shares in public companies they are not interested in, flog them off immediately for a tiny profit. (*Independent, 30 July 1987*)

There is evidence that the shares of such public sales find themselves consolidated among a much smaller group of traditional shareholders, particularly financial intermediaries, such as banks, pension funds and investment companies within a relatively short space of time.

- **Are professional managers more effective and more socially responsible than the traditional owner-manager?** Recent assessments of management in Britain have raised serious doubts about the competence of those managers. Degrees of social responsibility are particularly difficult to gauge. In any case there is some logic in suggesting that the career-motivated professional manager would show less not more paternalism towards staff and less concern for social issues in general than the traditional entrepreneur, who would often have strong connections with the local community.

The contemporary plausible interpretation of the ownership and control debate focuses on the role of financial institutions. We can always cite the case of small firms and even large corporations where owner control is the norm. However, in both Britain and America a substantial shareholding of many of the major firms has passed into the hands of financial institutions, including banks, insurance and pension companies. Their presence changes the nature of the Berle and Means debate. There is an acknowledgment of a separation between shareholders and managers, but a serious challenge to the concept of the passive shareholder. Such financial intermediaries not only tend to hold a significant minority stockholding, which gives them both power and influence, but they also take an active interest in important strategic decisions. Their credibility with their current clients and their ability to attract future investors rests upon the ability of their investment managers to ensure that yields are both attractive and secure. The sale of large numbers of shares by a bank or pension fund could well undermine the confidence of the stock market in a particular firm and result in a **hostile takeover**. Large financial investors have become the dominant type of strategic control in British companies. They possess the mechanisms to be well informed and the power to make their views known to management. They become particularly active in crises and may be instrumental not just in dictating the policy of top management, but in determining the composition of that group.

The clear inference from such an examination of the stockholding role of financial institutions is that the envisaged separation of ownership and control has not taken place. However, the influence of financial institutions on business is far from being just financial. The representatives of financial institutions are elected or appointed to the boards of directors of those companies where they hold a substantial minority interest. The senior officials of a bank may each hold a number of such directorships, as do the senior officials of other financial institutions. A pattern is thus built up of interlocking directorships representing a very important network of information, which supersedes finance as an instrument of power. Such directors will influence the recruitment of other directors and will inevitably favour those with access to vital information.

We can see that management decisions in a single firm may be influenced and even significantly constrained by directors representing the interests of other institutions altogether. A similar pattern of influence and constraint occurs in the management of public sector organizations and it is to this we now turn.

Management and control in the public sector

We often refer to the public sector as if it were a homogeneous group of organizations. This is highly misleading, for the public sector in most countries encompasses a wide range of institutions. At least four broad types may be identified:

- **Industries that are wholly owned and controlled by the state.** These were the dominant type of business organization in the former communist countries of Eastern Europe and in China. In the non-communist world such industries comprised utilities such as gas and electricity, and former private industries that had been nationalized, such as the coal industry in the UK. In most parts of the world such state-owned industries have reduced significantly in number as a result of economic liberalization and privatization.

- **Companies that the state controls as majority shareholder.** Such companies existed in many parts of the world, as with Renault in France and British Leyland in the UK. In many UK cases such companies had been bought out by the state to prevent their closure. This was seen to be important in key sectors such as the car industry or where a closure would have occurred in an area of high unemployment. As with wholly owned state enterprises, such ownership patterns are rare as more countries adopt more market-driven systems.

- **Services to the population.** These include such as the health, education and social services, where state provision is an historic duty and which are funded through the taxation system. Once again, in many countries, there has been a shift towards private provision in many of these areas. However, it is considered imperative that other services such as the police and armed forces remain under state control.

- **Other government departments at local and national level.** These would include such as the foreign office and local government planning departments.

    The rationale for a public sector can be explained in political, economic and social terms, although we can make a broad distinction here between the business and non-business institution. In terms of the provision for health, education, social services, and especially the police and armed forces, there is a broad consensus that public ownership and control is socially and indeed politically desirable. Even here there has been considerable debate about the extent of public provision in areas such as health and education. The major political contention concerns a public sector business presence, brought sharply into focus by the privatization of many public sector concerns in the 1980s and 90s in the UK and elsewhere.

Problems with the public sector

Traditionally the public sector has always faced a number of serious problems arising from the tensions between public ownership, political control and day-to-day management. These tensions may be viewed in terms of goals and objectives, finance, control, management and organization. We identify below some frequently held views about the public sector.

- **The goals of public sector organizations have often been ill-defined and conflicting.** For example, in the UK, there was never a clear policy coordinating the activities of the coal, gas and electricity industries, when all three were under public ownership. Moreover, many public sector operations have found conflict between the provision of a service and the necessity to break even, the UK railways being a good illustration. Such confusion over the goals led Sir Peter Parker to comment on his time as Head of British Rail,

    I'd never before been in a job where no-one could tell me what winning means. (*quoted in Foy, 1983, p. 68*)

A major problem here is the presence of a large number of stakeholders resulting in multiple, often conflicting goals. As a result public sector managers may respond by being cautious and lacking in innovation. Procedures are seen as more important than customer focus and, as a consequence, strategy formulation tends to reinforce the status quo.

- **The superordinate goal of the public sector to operate in the public interest is itself open to question.** Who defines the public interest and is it possible to satisfy all elements of the public at the same time? British Steel suffered radical cuts, including a loss of 40 per cent of jobs between 1981 and 1984. Radical restructuring followed, which placed the company in a profitable position just before its privatization in 1987. There has been such a radical pruning of the coal industry and the wholesale closure of collieries that the industry barely exists. Such cuts have had significant impact on levels of unemployment and affected local economies adversely.

- **Financially the public sector operates under considerable constraints.** Pricing policies are often dictated by government in attempts to tackle inflation, as under an incomes policy, or to direct consumption, as in the case of energy use. Public sector enterprises often find investment difficult; they are often prevented from borrowing from the government to hold down the PSBR, and the sources of external funding are severely restricted.

- **Excessive intervention** has been a frequent complaint among public sector managers. The very structure of the public sector means that it is answerable to different groups within government itself, to politicians, civil servants, appointed governing bodies, and various consumer groups, all of whom may have differing expectations and impose conflicting demands upon management. The whole issue is invariably complicated by the organizational politics that develop in the relationship between the heads of public sector organizations and their respective government masters. Such relationships are rarely stable as a result of political change.

- **Decision-making is slow and complex.** This results from long chains of command and the constant need to refer upwards or to committees to satisfy the need for public accountability.

- **Management autonomy and motivation are limited.** While procedures stifle initiative, pay is not linked to performance. As a result the public sector attracts less ambitious managers to 'safe' careers.

However, Parker (1995) believes such problems exaggerate the differences between the private and public sectors. He feels that flexibility and inflexibility can be found in organizations in both sectors and that bureaucratic 'red tape' is more a function of size than it is of public versus private. He argues also that many private sector management fashions such as total quality management (TQM) and business process re-engineering have found a ready audience among public sector managers.

Nonetheless, in response to such problems, many governments have embarked upon a policy of privatization, deregulation and the introduction of a commercial approach in the public sector. It is to these issues we now turn.

Privatization

We introduced privatization in our discussion of the transitional economies of Eastern Europe and China in Chapter 3. The claimed advantages of privatization may be stated as follows.

- It creates increased competition, which leads to increased efficiency, higher productivity, quality improvement and, ultimately, growth and profit.

- Shareholders have a financial interest in the effective management of the enterprise. Managers' performance is therefore closely monitored and controlled.

- Since customers have a choice, there will be a focus on customer care and service levels will improve.

- Costs will be reduced as a result of competition. In particular there will be a reduction in labour costs as organizations seek greater efficiencies.
- There will be improved awareness of and adaptation to changes in local, national and global environments.
- There will be greater incentives for staff through more flexible pay arrangements and profit-sharing schemes. Managers will be encouraged through incentives to be more innovative and proactive.
- For the newly privatized organizations there would be greatly increased opportunity for raising revenue which could be reinvested in the operation. It was assumed this would stimulate innovation to the benefit of all.
- For the state there will be a reduced public sector deficit and borrowing requirement. Privatized businesses will attract more inward investment.
- Society will change as more people are given the opportunity to own shares.

Key concept 5.6 Privatization

Privatization refers to the government policy of selling off public assets to private ownership and control, usually by share issue. The policy was prevalent in the UK in the 1980s, driven largely by an ideological belief in the workings of the free market. The policy extended to the deregulation of certain public services, thereby ending public monopolies over the provision of such as public transport and refuse removal. The process has also been pursued in other countries such as France, Germany, Australia and Canada. The policy is driven by the belief that private firms are both more effective and efficient, and free managers from the constraints of political control. In the UK the impact of privatization on service levels and cost is mixed and the process has generated considerable political and ideological debate.

The privatization policy in the UK was vigorously pursued by the Conservative governments of 1979–97. Its roots were in an ideological commitment to the free market, and a belief in the inherent inefficiency of the public sector. This has not only resulted in the selling of entire industries, but in the privatization of certain services within the public sector, such as the laundry in hospitals and rubbish collection in some local authorities. Could such a policy liberate management from excessive constraints on their freedom to manage and create the kind of advantages illustrated above?

We examine the UK case by looking at the development of the policy and its underlying rationale, before attempting some kind of evaluation.

In the first 4 years of the government's reign following the 1979 election, no clear policy emerged beyond a support for the deregulation of certain services, such as public transport bus provision and the sale of council houses to sitting tenants at favourable prices. The period 1983–9 was one of major activity, with a mixed approach including share flotations, either in whole or part, and the selling of public companies either to their management or to the private sector. During this period such concerns as British Aerospace, Cable and Wireless, British Telecommunications, British Gas, BA, the British Airports Authority and British Petroleum passed either wholly or partly from public to private ownership. These were followed in the 1990s by the electricity boards, the electricity generating industry and the water boards. The UK government became a leading consultant in the process and its advice was eagerly sought by the French, Australian and Canadian governments embarking on similar policies.

It is clear that share ownership has been broadened and the over-subscription of some issues indicates public support, and some firms, notably British Aerospace and the National Freight Corporation, showed a marked increase in profits. Critics argue that the privatization of vast concerns such as British Telecommunications and British Gas seems not to have influenced the market place at all, but merely changed the ownership status of a **monopoly**. Further criticisms have been levelled against the pricing policies of newly privatized companies, the inadequate provision for regulating large monopolies and the short-term strategy of 'selling off the public silver'. More cynical critics have pointed to job losses and the large pay awards to those former heads of public corporations.

Even 20 years after the beginning of the privatization boom in the UK it is still difficult to assess the impact. First, it has varied across the different organizations. Second, many have changed the nature of their operations to such an extent that it is difficult to make before and after comparisons, particularly where there have been acquisition and changes in ownership since privatization. Finally, there is considerable difficulty in disentangling the ideological, political and economic aspects of the argument. Apart from the social issues at stake there is, at the moment, mixed evidence to suggest that the private sector is any more or less efficient or effective than the public sector. The following examines some of the available evidence in the UK:

- After the original dispersal of the share issue, most of the individual shareholders sold their shares to make a quick profit. Ownership patterns have consolidated and concentrated, with most shares held by institutions. A mixture of a low initial share price and radical cost-cutting following privatization meant, for most companies, a rise in share value. As maturity sets in that share value has stabilized and in the 1990s there were criticisms against such as British Telecom that its share price had under-performed.

- Consumers benefited from price reductions in some cases. Gas prices fell 20 per cent from 1986 to 1993 and telephone prices fell 29 per cent from 1984 to 1995. Against this the cost of water has risen at twice the rate of inflation since privatization.

- The restructuring and cost-cutting exercises that accompanied privatization, in almost every case, have resulted in significant job losses and a delayering of management. BT moved from 245 000 employees in 1990 to 137 000 in 1995.

- BT claims improved service levels in terms of response to customer problems and complaints and the company has also increased its range of services. In some cases, notably the water companies, complaints have increased and in others services have been cut as part of restructuring. The withdrawal of the facility to pay gas bills at gas showrooms has been one such change. For the utilities, privatization has brought new priorities, notably a focus on achieving greater efficiencies. The knock-on effect has been a reduction in R&D expenditure. In British Gas this was reduced by 32 per cent between 1993 and 1997. In 1989 the Central Electricity Generating Board (CEGB) spent £200 million on R&D, but only £178 million in 1997, explained in part by a reduced emphasis on nuclear power.

- After a number of years as private companies, the former public sector organizations have become the target for acquisition by other companies, including those from overseas. The French and the Americans have been particularly active in this respect, to the extent that, by 1999, seven of the 12 electricity companies in England and Wales were owned by USA businesses. British Steel has moved in with the Dutch steel firm, Hoogovens. Privatized companies have pursued acquisition strategies themselves, notably BT. Key drivers for this have undoubtedly been globalization, developments in communications technology and the need to pursue growth in the face of a stagnant home market in the early 1990s. For example, BT acquired MCI, the second largest long-distance telephone company in the USA. While it is understandable that privatized companies should pursue business growth in this way, there are concerns that secondary trading of shares could operate against the public interest by focusing on the share price, rather than public service.

- Public criticism of privatized businesses has tended to focus on the utilities and particularly the impact on household bills, how the utilities are regulated and the dramatic salary rises of senior management.

New public management

While there has been considerable focus on privatization, significant changes have been taking place in the remaining elements of the public sector, particularly those services provided by local authorities, in a number of different countries, especially in the EU. The changes are often summed up by the phrase 'new public management'. Such changes include aspects of privatization and have blurred the boundary between the public and private sectors. New public management comprises some or all of the following.

- The use of the private sector to deliver services either wholly or partly. This is sometimes referred to as externalizing. In a study of major cities in 11 EU countries Torres and Pina (2002) found that the private sector was most involved in the care of the elderly and of children. In the UK there has been an encouragement for the public sector to seek private finance to provide services. This was known as the 'private finance initiative', expanded in 1996 via the **public private partnership (PPP)** scheme. The schemes were based on the belief that contracted-out or franchised services offered greater value for money.

- The devolution of services away from a system of centralized control and provision. This compliments externalizing and is sometimes referred to as de-concentrating. It involves the delivery of public services by smaller, more responsive and flexible units. In some parts of Europe this represents a shift away from a social market to a more Anglo-Saxon model of capitalism (a fuller explanation is offered in Chapter 3).

- Such changes have resulted in the down-sizing and delayering of the public sector (see the structure earlier in this chapter).

A consequence of such changes is that many of the activities carried out by local authorities are contracted out and are not directly controlled by them. Critics argue that as a result, these activities are not scrutinized and not as publicly accountable as they were when wholly performed within the public sector. Supporters of PPP suggest it offers the best of both worlds by providing greater flexibility and effectiveness, yet retaining public accountability via public sector involvement. Considine and Lewis (2003) argue that we may be witnessing a new era in the public sector in a number of different countries. They argue we have shifted from *procedural governance*, in which services were provided by large public bureaucracies. The first shift was towards *market governance*, in which services were privatized or contracted out. They view the latest trend as a move towards *network governance*, comprising a strong strategic partnership between public and private sectors with the potential to link effectively as never before, clients, suppliers and producers.

Case 5.4

Railtrack

The British government of the 1980s pursued a relentless policy of privatization and most publicly owned companies and public utilities went into private ownership via share issue. The organizations involved include BT, BA, British Gas, British Petroleum and the various water boards. Alongside this, public housing was sold and local authority functions were put out to tender and many went to private firms. The railways industry, under British Rail, emerged from the 1980s still in public control.

In 1994, British Rail, while still in the public sector, was broken up. As a result of the 1993 Railways Act, 25 operating companies were formed as train operating units to run the trains, control the routes and set the timetables. These were organized on a regional basis. A single organization, named Railtrack, was formed and was responsible for track, signals, stations, tunnels, bridges, viaducts and level crossings for the entire UK rail network. Many forecast that this was the precursor to privatization, and they were proven correct.

In 1996 Railtrack was privatized and the shares were floated at an initial price of £3.80. The privatization was carried out on the same basis of many of the flotations of the previous decade. Shares were offered to the general public, the company was to be run on profit lines and a regulator was appointed to safeguard the public interest. The train operating units were offered as franchises to companies who could demonstrate their competence to the newly formed Office of Passenger Rail Franchising. Most of the franchises went to established companies such as Stagecoach, Virgin and National Express, although a company called Prism was set up with the sole intention of winning franchises. Some of the franchises went to management buy-outs, as in the case of Thames Trains and Great Western Trains, although the latter was later sold on. The privatization was one of the last significant decisions of the John Major government before losing the election in 1997. Many consider that the privatization was rushed through and insufficient thought had been given to the new structures.

Railtrack's main source of funding was to come from the train operating companies who would pay to use the track, stations and so on. Railtrack also received income from its property portfolio, in addition to the funds it received from the government to assist with major projects.

In 1998 all seemed to be going well. The share price had risen to £17, the company was valued at £17 billion and it was widely publicized that it was making £1 million per day profit. By May 2001, Railtrack announced losses of £534 million and from January to September that year the share price fell from £9.25 to £2.80. On 8 October, 2001 the company had debts of £4.5 billion and went into administration at the request of the government. The Transport Minister, Stephen Byers was quoted,

Our action will see the end of Railrack. In my judgment the time had come to take back the track and put the interests of the travelling public first. (*quoted in* the Guardian, *8 October, 2001*)

Ernst and Young, a major accounting firm, were called in to act as administrators and run the company and effectively create the conditions for the launch of a new organization. The government refused to put in money to save Railtrack. Their argument was that too much public money had already been spent on Railtrack projects and the company had shown itself ill-equipped to operate an effective service and manage its own budgets. It was thought at the time that any further money put into Railtrack would jeopardize plans for increased spending on health and education. The action of the Government was seen by some as re-nationalization.

The problems, which led to the demise of Railtrack, were several:

- Throughout the 5-year existence of Railtrack as a private company there had been continuous requests for government funding. Railtrack became known as a private firm that was reliant on public funding and was seen by the government as a company that had no effective strategy for controlling costs. Undoubtedly, major projects had spiralled out of control. The modernization of the West-coast mainline was budgeted at £2.2 billion. By 2001 costs had already reached £7 billion, with further rises estimated. Thameslink, a project to improve cross-London rail travel, had been scheduled for completion in 2000, a forecast revised to 2007.

- Despite the publicity given to major projects, there was a serious lack of investment in the infrastructure. The company was criticized for the high amounts of dividend paid to shareholders and for ignoring the public interest. Indeed the lack of investment was seen as the cause of the Hatfield rail crash in 2000 (see below).

- There were a number of well-publicized disasters, all of which implicated Railtrack. In September 1997, seven people were killed in a rail crash at Southall, when safety equipment was found to be at fault. In October 1999, two passenger trains collided as they approached Paddington station in London, with 31 deaths. The main cause of the collision was signal failure. In October 2000 a train crash at Hatfield killed four people. The cause was found to be a disintegrating track, which had been scheduled for renewal 12 months earlier.

- There were frequent customer complaints about delays and Railtrack was invariably blamed by the train operating companies. Railtrack quickly acquired a reputation for unreliability and had to pay out large penalty payments to the operating companies. Customers were also highly critical of the increased cost of rail travel and placed some of the blame for this with Railtrack.

- During the late 1990s many key staff left the company. A criticism was that they were replaced by people with little or no experience of running railways. In addition there was criticism of the large salaries paid to top management, a frequent complaint in newly privatized companies.

- The regulatory mechanism was accused of weakness and of ignoring the lack of investment and consequently the safety implications. There were many people involved in regulation and the system was felt to be confusing. In an attempt to sort out the regulatory system, the government appointed Tom Winsor as the new regulator just prior to putting Railtrack into administration. One of his first acts was to commission an independent report, which exposed the significant lack of investment, while the state of the track was deemed to be in a worse condition than it was before privatization.

The immediate impact of administration was a bitter dispute between Railtrack and the government. The chief executive of Railtrack, Steve Marshall, resigned and accused the government of unacceptable behaviour and going back on its promises. This accusation was directed partly at the government's refusal to back the company with further funds and partly to the government's attempt to freeze £350 million, which Railtrack had in its bank accounts. Railtrack insisted that this was income derived from its property activities and not directly related to the rail business. In the end, the government relented and much of the money was paid to existing share-holders. Many of the institutional shareholders saw the administration as a government take-over tantamount to re-nationalization. However, the government were keen to avoid this due to the high cost involved in paying off the shareholders (which, by law, had to be based on an average share price of the last few years). Shareholders did receive some compensation, mainly from the sale of assets and the bank account of the Railtrack Group.

The collapse of the company had an immediate knock-on effect in other sectors. Many major construction companies, such as Balfour Beatty and Jarvis, were heavily reliant on Railtrack for much of their revenue, e.g. Railtrack contributed 40 per cent of the turnover of Jarvis. Share prices in the construction industry fell immediately and many companies feared that work would slow down and that outstanding payments would not be made.

The process of administration led to the creation of a new company and a new brand, Network Rail. The new company would assume all the responsibilities previously undertaken by Railtrack: the maintenance, renewal and enhancement of the rail infrastructure. Network Rail was set up as a private company to operate on a commercial basis. However, it was established as a company limited by guarantee (CLG). Such a company is often found in charitable organizations. A CLG has no shareholders but is owned by members, who hold the Board accountable. The liability of the company is limited to the amount each member guarantees. Network Rail has 116 members drawn from industry partners and from the general public. As there are no shareholders, no dividend is paid and all profits are reinvested. Network Rail claims that all its senior management have either engineering experience or experience of railway operations either in the UK or overseas.

Source: *Guardian*, *Financial Times*, 8–11 October, 2001; www.networkrail.co.uk accessed in August 2003

Questions

1 What rationale can you give for the privatization of British Rail?

2 What, in your view, were the key factors that created the problems in Railtrack?

3 In what ways will Network Rail differ from Railtrack? What similar problems will it face?

Size

The influence of size as an organizational variable interacts across all levels of our Business in Context model. Many of the issues relating to size are dealt with elsewhere in this book and in this section we simply present a summary of those issues. We do however develop the concept further by examining the issues relating to small businesses.

We have already seen earlier in this chapter how size is an important determinant of structure. Hickson *et al.* (1969) noted that, with increasing size, the technological imperative gives way to the size imperative. Increasing formalization and bureaucratization are inevitable consequences of the growing firm, and the organization structure and management procedures are shaped by the need to coordinate and control large numbers of people. In our earlier discussion we saw how the growth of firms, especially through diversification, was an important element in companies such as GM adopting a divisional structure.

With size comes the development of specialist activities. In Chapter 12 we see how the development of personnel or human resource management as a specialist function is closely related to the increasing size of organizations. The employment of large numbers of people invariably calls for specialist expertise in the areas of recruitment, training, job evaluation, payment systems and industrial relations. In Chapter 9 we see a relationship between size and the R&D function. In this case, it is not simply a matter of the numbers employed but also a function of the need to maintain a powerful market position through investment in both product and process development and, of course, the ability to attract that investment.

Size is also related to dominance in the market place, as illustrated by the brewing industry in Britain. The industry is dominated by a handful of very large firms who maintain their market position not just by their ability to invest in product and process development, but also by the amount they are able to spend on nation-wide advertising campaigns. Their position is further strengthened by their strategy of acquiring smaller independent breweries, which find themselves unable to compete. The growth of lager sales at the expense of the traditional bitter beers has attracted the attention of the international brewing industry who are investing heavily in the British market. Most of the big brewing firms have grown by merger and acquisition, creating trans-European conglomerates such as Allied-Domecq, Grand Metropolitan-Guinness and Carlsberg-Tetley. A similar pattern can be found in the music industry. By 1993, the industry was dominated by four companies controlling over 70 per cent of the market. These were Warner, Thorn EMI, Sony and PolyGram. A key element in concentration in the music industry has been the growth in sales of compact discs (CDs). Not only do these require considerable investment in technology for their manufacture, favouring the big firm, but the public demand for re-issues of old vinyl records in CD format has led to the larger firms buying up smaller independent producers to acquire their catalogues.

The big four CD producers dominate the sector, not just in terms of market share. There is a clear correlation in this industry between size and profitability. The biggest companies announce the biggest profit margins. There is a view that, in some industries, as with the illustration of the CD market, size is important. There is a considerable fear that the decline of the UK manufacturing industry in the 1980s has resulted in a lack of critical mass that is unable to compete in world terms. We have already discussed this issue in Chapter 3.

The ability of the large firm to dominate the market place is only part of its relationship with its environment. The size of a firm may be an important buffer in dealing with the demands imposed by its environment. We saw in Chapter 2 how the multinational corporation is able to dominate its environment, including influencing and in some cases over-riding the policies of nation states. Size has also been a factor in attracting government support, not only in terms of R&D investment; the numbers employed by such firms as British Leyland have necessitated government rescue attempts during financial crises for political and social reasons as much as for economic ones. In the 1970s, in particular, size was often a vital protection against enforced closure.

An important rider to this discussion is the influence of technology. Developments in technology, and more specifically information technology, have meant that, in some industries, size is less significant. The growth of e-commerce and the proliferation of call centres has meant that business activities can be concentrated in smaller units (see Chapter 3 for a fuller account).

Size, structure and market position are themselves important variables in the determination of organization culture, which we deal with in the next section. At the micro-level there has been a great deal written about the impact of organizational size on the individual by focusing on the concepts of bureaucracy and alienation. Large organizations can undoubtedly present behavioural problems in terms of both management control and individual motivation. Such problems have been tackled by a range of devices, including the creation of autonomous work groups in an attempt to break up the organization into more easily managed units. Despite such behavioural problems it should not be forgotten that, at the management level at least, many employees actively seek out large firms for the career opportunities they offer.

While there is considerable evidence supporting the dominant position of the large firm, the problem of control in particular questions whether large firms actually make the best use of their resources. The relationship between size and performance has been challenged by the small firms' lobby, elevated from a 'small is beautiful' campaign in the early 1970s to a near political crusade for the future of Western capitalism in the 1980s. We now deal with the issues and arguments surrounding small firms.

Small businesses

The small firm has played a key role in the development of the business enterprise, particularly in the 19th century when economic growth owed much to the activities of individual entrepreneurs. The role of the small firm was overtaken by the development of mass production, mass markets and, above all, the creation of the joint stock company which created investment and effectively removed a major constraint to the growth of businesses. Throughout the 20th century the focus has been on the increasing size of businesses and the market domination by big business and the multinationals in particular. In this section the focus will be on the UK experience, but comparisons will be drawn with other countries.

In the UK, the watershed came in 1971 with the publication of the *Report of the Committee of Inquiry on Small Firms*, generally referred to as the Bolton Report, after the Committee's chairman. The Committee's investigation was born out of a concern that the small firms' sector was being neglected, but also out of a disillusionment and fear of the economic and social consequences of domination by big business. The conclusion of Bolton and his colleagues may be summarized as follows.

● The small firms' sector in Britain was in decline, in terms of both its size and its contribution to the nation's economy.

- The decline was more marked in the UK than in its major economic rivals.

- Despite the decline the small firms' sector 'remains one of substantial importance to the United Kingdom economy' and that 'the contribution of small businessmen to the vitality of society is inestimable' (*Report of the Committee of Inquiry on Small Firms*, Bolton, 1971, p. 342).

The Report's importance lay not just in its conclusions but as the first serious and, subsequently, influential attempt to define the small firm and in its stimulus to later research, much of which takes Bolton as its base point. The stimulus of the 1970s became the academic growth area of the 1980s, with many business schools setting up special small firms' units, both for the purposes of academic research and to provide support for the regeneration of the small firms' sector. The stimulus was fuelled in the 1980s by a government increasingly determined to publicize the small business as the key element in the nation's economic revival. A report published in 1983 by a group of Conservative MPs and researchers stated,

> A high small firms ratio is consistent with high levels of growth and output. The malaise of our small business sector is a symptom and a cause of our comparative decline as an industrial nation. (*Bright* et al. *(1983) p. 15*)

Key concept 5.7 The small firm

A firm is defined as small on the basis of the numbers it employs and its turnover, although definitions based on such data alone are open to debate. Generally small firms are dominated by the values of the owner-manager, operate in relatively small markets with a limited range of products and services, have difficulty in raising capital and many lack formal management systems. There are problems associated with measuring the size of the sector and the evidence is mixed in terms of the contribution of the small firm to the economy, its benefits to the individual and as a provider of jobs.

Such statements as those of Bright *et al.* (1983) were reinforced by a host of measures aimed at supporting small businesses, including special loans for business start-ups and special extension of welfare benefits to stimulate self-employment. In addition changes were made in the stock market through the creation of the **Unlisted Securities Market** whereby small firms could raise investment capital. The entrepreneur became the hero figure for the 1980s and people such as Alan Sugar and Richard Branson became household names. The rationale for government support was more than a belief in the economic importance of the small firm. At a time of high unemployment the small business start-up offered a practical and, to some, a highly attractive solution. Moreover, it was a solution that was ideologically compatible with the government's views on economic management, welfare and self-help.

There is no doubt that the government's promotion of the '**enterprise culture**' in the 1980s resulted in the dramatic growth of small business start-ups. There were other related factors. Increasing unemployment and reductions in welfare benefits pushed many into self-employment. At the same time, developments in information technology made small firms in some sectors more viable, such as specialist travel agents.

In this section we will look at the extent and nature of the small businesses in the UK and assess their value, focusing particularly on the economic arguments for continued state support. Many of the points are illustrated by Case 5.6, which summarizes a study of several small firms in the Nottingham area. Although the study was carried out some years ago, many of its findings are still valid today. A more detailed discussion of entrepreneurship is included in Chapter 9, which examines innovation.

What is the small firms' sector?

The small firms' sector is notable by its lack of accurate data. Any student of small businesses is immediately confronted with two problems:

- There are serious difficulties in defining a small business.
- There are difficulties in estimating the size of the small business sector.

Definitions

The **Bolton Report**'s working definition included those firms employing fewer than 200 people. The Committee identified three primary characteristics of a small firm; these were having a small market share, being owner-managed and being independent of any larger concern. The Committee, while acknowledging the difficulties, recognized the need for a numerical definition of a small business, but also recognized that the criterion used for manufacturing (numbers employed) would be inappropriate for construction, where much smaller firms were the norm, and for retailing, where the totally different criterion of turnover was seen as more appropriate. Some kind of quantitative definition is essential to the effective administration of government support and the law, small firms being exempt from certain aspects of employment law. The criteria used by Bolton are shown in Table 5.1.

Storey (1994) argues that the criteria used by Bolton no longer have relevance, particularly definitions based on output, which are affected by technological change. He prefers the EU classification as shown in Table 5.2.

Table 5.1	The Bolton Report definition of the small firm
Industry	*Statistical definition of small firms*
Manufacturing	200 employees or less
Retailing	Turnover £50 000 p.a. or less
Wholesale trades	Turnover £200 000 p.a. or less
Construction	25 employees or less
Mining/quarrying	25 employees or less
Motor trades	Turnover £100 000 or less
Miscellaneous services	Turnover £50 000 or less
Road transport	5 vehicles or less
Catering	All excluding multiples and brewery managed houses

Source: Bolton, 1971, 1.9 p. 3

Table 5.2	EU classification of small firms	
Size	*Classification*	
Small and medium-sized enterprise (SME)	Fewer than 250 employees	
Small business	Fewer than 100 employees	
Micro business	Fewer than 10 employees	

While this offers a simple definition, there are still problems. What may be a small firm in one type of business may be a relatively large firm in another.

Because of the difficulties with quantitative measures, some have attempted to distinguish small businesses by identifying characteristics that are special to them (Bolton, 1971; Bridge *et al.*, 1998; Burns, 2001).

- Small firms generally operate with a limited range of products and have relatively few customers in relatively small markets. They tend to have limited market share and generally have little influence on price. However, some small firms operate in niche markets with a wide customer base and have considerable influence on price.

- Small firms are independent and have little in the way of outside controls.

- Small firms are influenced greatly by the owner-manager and owner values tend to dominate. Management is carried out, in many cases, by one person, who performs all or most of the functional roles. Most small firms have an absence of functional managers and specialists.

- Small firms tend to be perennially short of cash. They are reliant on personal investment and are unable to raise capital as easily as large firms. This results in a lack of investment in new technology and in training and development.

- Strategies tend to be reactive and short-term, the latter often being a function of cash-flow problems.

- Business systems are rarely formalized and tend to be based on the experience of the owner-manager. There is some evidence in the UK that this is changing, through the influence of such bodies as **Business Link** and **Investors in People**. There is now greater interest among the small firm community in setting up business systems through a process sometimes referred to as capacity building.

The extent of the small firms' sector

In the UK, official statistics are incomplete as far as small firms are concerned. For example, the Census of Production excludes firms of less than 20 employees and has only limited data on those of less than 100 employees. In addition, there is a marked preference on the part of some small businessmen to remain outside official statistics for the purposes of tax avoidance.

Because of these problems, the estimates of the extent of small business activity and the contribution to the economy can vary considerably. However, in all countries there does appear to be an increase in the number of small firms. Two main reasons are given for this growth.

- There has been a shift from manufacturing to the service economy in most countries. Small firms tend to predominate in the service industry.

- Developments in information and communications technology and the reducing price of that technology have enabled smaller business units to function independently and it is now viable to operate as a small firm in many sectors of the economy.

Recent statistics indicate that 95 per cent of all businesses in the EU come under the definition of small and that they generate 66 per cent of employment across the EU, with 62 per cent in the UK and 79 per cent in Italy. Estimates of the USA economy suggest that firms, employing less than 20 people, contribute 50 per cent to the GDP and account for 50 per cent of exports (Burns, 2001).

In addition to the increase in the number of firms, the survival chances of small firms appear to have improved. Although the problems of data accuracy are as acute here as elsewhere, estimates of the failure rate of business start-ups in the 1970s ranged from 50–75 per cent within the first two years (Bannock, 1981). More recent data, based on VAT registrations, suggests 50 per cent for the first 3 years. Most studies note that the chances of survival increase with time. Daly (1991), basing his analysis on VAT de-registrations, found that while the annual failure rate was around 20 per cent in the second and third years of existence, the rate fell to around 10 per cent when businesses are better established. There would therefore appear to be a clear correlation between failure rate and the age of the concern.

The main reasons for failure would appear to be finance, including cash-flow problems, poor products and inadequate marketing and **market research**. However, small business owners are not always the best people to offer an objective analysis of the failure of their own business. It must be acknowledged that not all small firm closures are the result of failure. The success of some firms means that they are bought by larger concerns. Other reasons for closure can be related to the retirement or death of the owner.

International figures confirm the view that the small business start-up is a risky venture. A survey of small firms across the world from 1980 to 1990 revealed that, on average, 50–60 per cent of start-ups fail within the first 5 years. The same report highlighted that in some countries, notably Singapore, the failure rate was as high as 70 per cent (El-Namiki, 1993).

However incomplete the database on small firms may be, there is considerable evidence that the UK has fewer self employed than many other comparable industrial nations, and it has fewer small firms making far less of a contribution to the economy. The small firms' sector here is smaller than that in the USA and Germany, and significantly smaller than that in Japan, where small firms play a significant role in the manufacturing economy. (Chapter 3 has a fuller discussion.)

Types of small firm

Burns (2001) identifies two broad types of small firm:

- **The lifestyle firm** typifies most small firms. It is the preferred alternative for many to working for someone else. It is not seen as a route to growth and fortune and operates to provide an adequate level of income. Such firms are rarely dynamic and the owners wish them to remain small. Examples of such businesses would include the neighbourhood newsagent, the local plumber or jobbing builder.

- **The growth firm** represents those entrepreneurial businesses who offer innovative products and services or who seek rapid growth. The most successful of these rapidly move out of the small firm category. Examples of such businesses include those developed by entrepreneurs such as Bill Gates and Richard Branson.

Others have distinguished between the family firm and the non-family firm. The **family firm** has been the source of considerable academic interest in recent years. Typically it is a firm established within a family and managed by family members. A Barclays Bank Survey (2002) found that 60 per cent of all businesses in the UK with a turnover of less than £5 million were owned and managed as family firms. Their survey further indicated that family firms are both smaller than most small firms and are generally more productive.

The **advantages of the family firm** may be identified as follows:

- Through family members there is a culture of trust, commitment and support. The strength of family support is particularly important during difficult times for the business.

- Family firms can operate more flexibly. Family members are often prepared to give a great deal of their own time and are willing to fulfil a number of different roles within the business.

- Finance may be easier than in other forms of small business, by drawing on the resources of a family network.

- The family often wants the business to continue and future generations are groomed for succession. In this way family firms tend to take a longer term view than most small firms and key areas of knowledge about the business are handed down to successive generations.

- Decision-making is relatively straightforward and quick.

However research has identified a number of specific **problems with family firms**, that are not found in other small firms (Kets de Vries, 1996; Leach and Bogon, 1999).

- Family firms are often a source of role conflict, when family and business interests clash. Frequent problems include the difficulties of dismissing family members for poor performance and those arising from disagreements over goals or strategic direction.

- Many family members occupy management positions for which they have received no preparation and for which they lack even basic skills of management.

- Family members with no direct involvement in running the firm often wish to influence decisions. This is a frequent source of conflict among those managing the firm.

- There are frequent problems with succession. The next generation may be unsuitable, not interested or may clash with their parents about how the firm is run.

The value of small businesses

The value of small businesses may be viewed in terms of the benefits to the owners, their impact on economic growth, the number of jobs they provide, and their service to the consumer. We will deal with each of these aspects in turn.

Benefits to owners   In terms of the individual, the small firm offers a number of assumed advantages. A Gallup Poll finding in 1986 cited the desire to 'be your own boss' as the main motivation behind small business start-ups, and more significant than unemployment (*New Society*, March, 1986).

- Certainly self-employment offers the individual far greater opportunities for control, and perhaps greater satisfaction through direct involvement, than working for someone else.

- The small business has for many been the pathway to real wealth, social mobility, and perhaps political power in the local community.

- Some owners doubtless see their own business as a source of security for their family and as a kind of immortality via family succession.

Against such values is the very real risk of failure and serious financial loss for the owner and his or her family, and romantic tales of individualism, wealth and job satisfaction should be set alongside the long working week, the frustration and the stress that many small business owners inevitably experience. The reality for many is that self-employment is less lucrative than working for someone else, and those that are successful either become prime candidates for a takeover bid by a larger firm or fear a loss of control that inevitably comes with growth.

The contribution to economic growth   The evidence for this is patchy. The 1996 Pulse Survey (an Arthur Andersen/London Business School collaboration) concluded that small firms were less likely to grow than larger firms but when they did it was at a faster rate. We have already noted that many governments see the small firm as an essential ingredient of a healthy economy.

- The most obvious role for the small firm in this respect is to act as a 'seedbed' for future big business and in so doing secure the future of the economy.

- The small firm is seen as filling gaps in the market place by offering specialist products that would be uneconomic for the large firm to offer.

- More significantly the small firm is seen as a force for change by being inherently more flexible and innovative than the larger business. This image of the small firm was strengthened in the 1980s by the publicity given to the success and growth of certain small firms in the computer industry, although the majority of small businesses are decidedly 'low' rather than 'high' tech.

- In particular the small firm is seen as a useful vehicle in a recession; small firms are seen as price-takers and therefore offer no threat to inflation rates, and they are able to plug the gaps left after larger firms have rationalized their operations. In the UK, the rationalization of bus routes by the major companies together with the government deregulation of bus services paved the way for a number of smaller companies to enter the market, especially in rural areas and on the larger housing estates. These bus companies were able to operate routes that were uneconomic for the larger companies.

Many writers (for example Scase and Goffee, 1980; Rainnie, 1985) are more sceptical of the economic contribution of the small firms' sector, feeling that the small firm is exploited by big business and the main economic advantages of a small business presence accrue to the larger company. Certainly large manufacturing concerns could not survive without the components supplied by a host of smaller companies, and the extension of sub-contracting in manufacturing has been a factor in the growth of the small business sector. The relationship may not be exploitative, although, as we saw in our examination of Japanese methods in the last chapter, the purchasing power of the large firm can have a significant impact on the profit margins of smaller companies. Certainly there is evidence of larger firms taking over markets created by smaller companies when those markets prove successful. For example, IBM only entered the PC market once the market had been established by a number of small firms. IBM then dominated that market for many years.

There is an assumption that small firms are first to the market place because they are inherently more innovative. Supporters of this view cite inventions such as air-conditioning and cellophane, which originated from individual entrepreneurs, and that small businesses often emerge from ideas for new products or clever adaptations of existing products. Big business, on the other hand, is often accused of channelling R&D along predictable lines and being less cost-effective in its use of R&D expenditure. Apart from the difficulties of measuring such things, the evidence for these claims is very mixed. Research suggests that even if small firms are inventive they often lack the development capital for successful innovation. (The distinction between **invention** and **innovation** is drawn more fully in Chapter 9.)

There is evidence to suggest that a high proportion of small business start-ups do not involve new products but involve the owner in replicating his or her previous employment. This trend becomes especially critical where buy-outs are concerned and may be a primary cause of small business failure among buy-outs. In this case an ailing firm either sells out or divests part of its operation to a group of existing employees, usually management. Their experience and skills give them the optimism to continue operations in the same product market, perhaps ignoring the lack of demand or excessive competition operating in that same market, and they merely repeat the failure of the original firm.

`Job creation`   We have already noted that the small firm sector employs a large percentage of the work force in most countries. The small firm makes a number of contributions towards job creation.

- As we see in Case 5.5, redundancy and unemployment are big push factors towards self-employment.

- Self-employment is a valuable source of work for those groups, such as ethnic minorities, who are discriminated against in the labour market.

- In certain communities an over-dependence on a few large firms for employment can have serious consequences when those firms close, as with many mining communities following the pit closures of the 1980s and 90s. Under such circumstances, a healthy small business presence may provide employment diversity and help counter the worst effects of mass redundancy. This view was taken by the government when faced with mass redundancies at the pre-privatized British Steel Corporation in the Sheffield area. The company took advantage of tax advantages by providing venture capital to business start-ups in the area.

However, there are decidedly mixed views on the small firm as a provider of jobs. Storey (1994) maintains that small firms create jobs more consistently and at a faster rate than larger firms and that job creation is a particular feature of the fastest growing small firms.

Storey does acknowledge that such firms represent a very small proportion of the sector. Others paint a different picture. A study of the high-tech industry, one of the flagships of the small-firms lobby, in the Cambridge area from 1971 to 1981 concluded that only 800 new jobs had been created during the entire period (Gould and Keeble, 1984). However, whatever number of new jobs are created, they can easily be overshadowed by job losses in a large organization. Moreover, we have already seen from the high proportion of start-up failures that small firms are a source of job losses too.

Whatever the arguments for the quantity of employment provided by small firms, there have been several critical accounts concerning the quality of such jobs. Before it was disbanded, the Greater London Council (GLC) was especially critical of the small firm as an employer, citing exploitation through low wages, long hours and an absence of trade union recognition as the main reason for their lack of support for small business development in the area (GLC, 1983). Obviously, not every small firm exploits its workforce, and many employees prefer the informal and often harmonious working environment that the small firm can provide.

Benefit to the consumer   There are a number of assumed benefits:

- We have already seen in our example of the deregulation of the bus industry how the small firm can benefit by filling the gaps left by the larger company.
- There is also the argument that the smaller firm is also closer to its customers and can provide them with a more personalized, responsive and specialized service.

There are certain highly specialized product markets, such as precision scientific instrumentation, which tend to favour the smaller concern. Whether the smaller firm offers a 'better' service to the consumer is impossible to generalize or even judge. When buying expensive wine for 'laying down' for several years, a small specialist firm may be the most appropriate consumer choice, while a supermarket chain may offer the best value on less expensive purchases. The situation becomes particularly blurred when you consider that a number of larger firms of all types pay particular attention to customer sales and after-sales service. At a broader level, a small firms' sector may be of considerable benefit to the consumer in challenging the power of monopolies.

Many of the above benefits of the small firm have been challenged by Bennett Harrison (1994). Citing a study of firms in the USA, Western Europe, and Japan, he argues that the shift in emphasis towards the small firm is not supported by the facts. The findings suggest that large firms dominate capital, markets and employment. Moreover, as mentioned earlier, large firms dominate SMEs financially, commercially and technically. He sees that the small firm is less able to innovate and is inherently less technically advanced than the large firm.

Case 5.5   ## Small firms in the Nottingham area

A survey was carried out of 100 small firms in the Nottingham area. The firms were all wholly new businesses that had come into existence since 1977 and were independent, owner-managed and engaged predominantly in manufacturing. The main findings concerned the motivation behind setting up, the choice of product, the advice sought by small businessmen, and the labour costs involved.

▶

The attraction of setting up in business was seen in terms of both pull and push factors, often operating together. The main push factors in order of significance were: redundancy; job insecurity and unemployment; disagreement at a previous firm; and the closure of a previous venture. The main pull factors in order of significance were: the desire for independence; the possession of specialist knowledge; the development of a product idea; and the incentive of financial reward.

The product chosen by the new company was invariably derived from the owner's previous experience, hobby or working skill. Seventy-eight per cent set up in businesses that were the same or similar to a previous employment and only 4 per cent were classed as having innovated a new product or process. The advice available to small business concerns was seen to be not particularly helpful or attractive to the potential entrepreneur. Over 40 per cent took no advice at all prior to starting up, and only 4 per cent attended any type of training course. Labour costs were typified by the owners working long hours for little remuneration, especially in the first 2 years, and the relatively low wages accepted by employees. The labour cost policy was related to a competitive pricing policy for market penetration.

The researchers conclude that such small-firm growth in manufacturing is a response to economic recession and occurs in established industries with little contribution to product or process innovation and, as such, is unlikely to contribute towards economic recovery and growth. Moreover, the pricing and wages policies of the new entrants is likely to have a depressing effect on the local economy by threatening the livelihood of established enterprises. As such, government policies aimed at increasing the number of small firms 'may simply be increasing the throughput of firms rather than the stock'.

Source: Binks and Jennings, 1986

Questions

1 What main conclusions about the small firms sector do you draw from this study?

2 How relevant are these findings today? In what ways has the small firms' sector changed?

3 What does the case tell us about individual motivation to set up a small firm? What other factors can you identify that are not mentioned in the study?

The small firm as a case for government support

We believe that the health of the economy requires the birth of new enterprises in substantial number and the growth of some to a position from which they are able to challenge and supplant the existing leaders of industry . . . We cannot assume that the ordinary working of market forces will necessarily preserve a small firm sector large enough to perform this function in the future. (*Bolton, 1971, 8.5, p. 85*)

Bolton and his committee were clear that government support was necessary to secure the future of the small firm and hence the economy. Since then, successive governments have revealed their support of the small business by a large number of different measures. Despite this apparent attention, many critics still see a gap between government rhetoric and effective action. There would appear to be a need for an effective overall government strategy for the SME and small firms' sector, justified on both economic and social grounds, as in the case of inner city regeneration. As Storey argues,

> The small firm sector in the United Kingdom has now reached a size and importance in which public policy towards it cannot be left entirely to those with a vested interest in the smaller firm. (*Storey, 1994, p. 303*)

One of the intentions in our analysis of small businesses was to look behind the current popular support for the small firms' sector and attempt to challenge the view that the encouragement of small business development is a valid strategy for economic recovery and growth. It is indeed difficult to draw any firm conclusions at all, for despite the growth of research data and the space devoted to small businesses in the serious as well as the popular press, many difficulties remain.

Confusion still reigns over an agreed definition of what actually constitutes a small business and the evidence that we do possess is highly contradictory in its findings. A major problem involves politics and ideology, which were as much a part of the Conservative government's support as the GLC's condemnation.

What we do find is that the small firm provides some jobs, offers some hope for the unemployed and meets the sub-contracting needs of big business. However, there is very little evidence that a policy of support for the encouragement of small firms will either solve the problems of long-term unemployment or result in substantial economic growth. Behind the rhetoric of politicians there is considerable criticism aimed at those very measures designed to support the small firm. The sheer number and complexity of such measures and the different sources of advice have been shown to be as confusing as they are helpful. Moreover, the cost of government measures, such as the Loans Guarantee Scheme, has proven much too expensive for many small firms. Outside the government schemes the banks appear keen to provide services for the small firm, but even here the picture must be seen in perspective. Among the EU countries, the UK banks have been singled out for criticism of their over-cautious approach towards the funding of small firms. Bannock (1981) found that German banks on average lend twice as much for longer periods and at lower interest rates than their British counterparts. The closer relationship enjoyed between banks and small firms in France and, particularly, in Germany may account for the larger small business and SME sectors in those countries.

Bannock's vision of a healthy economic future involves small and large businesses in a kind of optimal balance, with small firms as the 'motivators of growth' and large firms as the 'consolidators and accelerators'. In this way the small firm may play a significant role in the recovery from recession. Others are less optimistic. However, we can say that small business development is important in the future of any economy, but political interest owes as much to ideology as it does to sound economic argument. For our purposes, the case of the small firm is again an excellent illustration of the interplay between the various elements of our Business in Context model.

Organizational and corporate culture

We have already encountered the concept of culture in our treatment of the environmental context of business in Chapter 4. There we focused on broad cultural distinctions between different groups of people, particularly in the comparisons of businesses in different countries. In this section we focus upon culture in a more localized setting, that of the organization itself. The goals, structure, patterns of ownership and size of an organization both reflect and are reflected in its culture. Other influences on the culture of an organization include its history and all those aspects we have identified as belonging to the environmental level of our Business in Context model. The importance of the organizational culture is that it sets the scene for the determination of strategy and hence the operational aspects of organizational life. The concept assumes, therefore, a central position in our model of business.

Interest in organizational culture can be traced back to the early sociological works of Durkheim through Elton Mayo and the Human Relations Movement to **'organizational development' (OD)** and HRM. Interest was heightened in the USA during the 1970s as American companies, searching for a solution to the problems of the economic recession, looked to the role models of Japanese firms and the more successful firms within their own country. In turn, academic research in business shifted its focus away from individual management techniques to examining the business as a complete entity and viewing the way people responded to their own organization. This was reinforced by the changes in political economy that were taking place in the UK and the USA at the time and by developments in HRM, which focused on culture change at the level of the firm (see Needle, 2000 for a more detailed review of the historical development of organizational culture).

The terms 'organizational culture' and 'corporate culture' are used interchangeably in the literature. In our review we draw a distinction between them in much the same way as Smircich (1983) differentiated between 'analytical' and 'managerial' perspectives on culture. In this section we will define culture at the level of the firm and examine further our concepts of organizational and corporate culture. We examine the concept of a strong culture and its relationship to notions of the 'excellent company'. We assess its value as a business tool and offer a critique. We will illustrate these points by reference to Hewlett Packard, the American computer and electronic instrument firm, presented as Case 5.6.

Key concept 5.8 Organizational and corporate culture

These two terms are often used interchangeably, but in this book they are defined differently. Organizational culture represents the collective values, beliefs and practices of organizational members and is a product of such factors as history, product market, technology, strategy, type of employees, management style, national cultures and so on. Corporate culture, on the other hand, refers to those cultures deliberately created by management to achieve specific strategic ends. The concept came to prominence in the 1980s with interest in so-called excellent companies and the idea that specific types of corporate culture were a template for success. Such views have been challenged by much of the evidence, although certain cultures can make a significant contribution to coordination and control and levels of employee satisfaction.

The terms defined

Culture at the level of the firm has been defined as:

The way we do things around here. (*Deal and Kennedy, 1982, p. 4*)

> The pattern of beliefs, values and learned ways of coping with experience that have developed during the course of an organization's history and which tend to be manifested in its material arrangements and in the behaviour of its members. (*Brown, 1998, p. 9*)

> a) A pattern of basic assumptions, b) invented, discovered or developed by a particular group c) as it learns to cope with problems of external adaptation and internal integration, d) that has worked well enough to be considered valid, and e) is to be taught to new members as the f) correct way to perceive, think and feel in relation to those problems. (*Schein, 1990, p. 111*)

The quote from Deal and Kennedy is frequently used in both managerial and academic treatments of the subject. It is in fact not the authors' own, but a quote from Marvin Bower, the then managing director of McKinsey, for whom Deal and Kennedy were consultants. Their definition is typical of the language used in many of the managerial texts and is sufficiently broad to add little to our understanding of the concept. Brown and Schein attempt to detail the key elements, which are:

- beliefs and values that are developed in an organization over time;
- learned by its members;
- used to guide their behaviour and solve their problems;
- manifested in the language used and in every aspect of organization life.

We have already identified that, in this book, we make a distinction between organizational culture and corporate culture. We explain that distinction as follows.

Organizational culture sees organizations in terms of a unique combination of variables. These include history, technology, product market, type of employees, type of ownership, leadership and strategy. Other influences include the broader culture of the country or region, the prevailing political economy and the behaviour of the stakeholders. Many attempts have been made to simplify this range of variables through the use of models attempting to draw distinctions between generic types of organization. An early and highly simplistic attempt was made by Harrison (1972) who classified the character or ideology of organizations under four categories: power, role, task and person. This same classification was popularized by Handy (1993), who referred specifically to these categories as cultures.

Corporate culture focuses on the use of culture as a control device to enhance performance through the development of greater commitment and the integration of all employees at all levels in the organization. It is this perspective on culture at the level of the firm that attracts the greatest critical attention. Some writers, notably Willmott (1993), view the manipulation of culture in this way as highly questionable, referring to it as the 'dark side of the force' and likening it to Orwell's *1984*. Others, such as Thompson and McHugh (2003), while offering similar criticisms, also see some benefits to employees through the more paternalistic strategies of employers. The idea of a management-led corporate culture lies at the heart of the notions of a 'strong culture' and 'the excellent company', to which we now turn.

Strong cultures and the excellent company

The concept of corporate culture is most apparent when we examine those companies with strong cultures. Strong cultures are associated with those organizations where the guiding values of top management are clear and consistent and are widely shared by the employees. Such cultures are typified by a set of strong values passed down by senior management. The values are strengthened by rituals, which emphasize and reward appropriate behaviour, and a cultural network, comprising a system of communication to spread the values and create corporate heroes. A feature of strong cultures is their association with hero figures, who exemplify the key values. Ray Kroc of McDonald's, Bill Hewlett and Dave Packard of Hewlett Packard and Anita Roddick of the Body Shop are examples of such corporate heroes.

The processes of creating such a 'positive' organizational culture would appear to operate as follows:

- The senior management of a company set goals and issue guidelines, which promote strongly held shared values; common emphases are enthusiasm, diligence, loyalty, quality and customer care.

- To ensure that such guidelines are passed on to all employees there is usually a high investment in the procedures of communication and integration.

- A number of techniques are commonly used to create and maintain a specific corporate culture. Some firms pay particular attention to the physical environment, and some like, HP, attempt to create a corporate style that is recognizable wherever they operate. In their case the focus is the facilitation of communication. In IBM a layout that facilitates communication is equally important, as is the use of a corporate colour: blue.

- The goals of the company are invariably written down, explicit, communicated to all employees and tend to stress the contribution that employees can make to the firm. Heroes and myths play an important role in communicating the core values as illustrated by the 'Bill and Dave stories' in Case 5.6.

- The same importance is ascribed to rituals, which take the form of team meetings or out-of-work social activities, where participation is the norm.

- The organization structure strengthens the culture by a common focus upon autonomous units to enhance group identity and loyalty.

- Recruitment and selection methods tend to be rigorous to screen out unsuitable candidates and ensure a fit between the recruit and the prevailing culture.

- Considerable emphasis is placed on induction and training as primary vehicles for cultural socialization. All these processes and procedures can be found in firms such as IBM and HP. A study of three electronics firms in South Korea, Hyundai, Samsung and LG, revealed considerable investment in induction and training as a means of transmitting corporate values (Needle, 2000). All three companies had a separate training centre, where new employees spent up to four weeks focusing exclusively on corporate values. More intensive education around corporate values followed promotion and every employee spent a few days each year at the centre for purposes of reinforcement.

Such strong cultures are a central feature of the so-called **excellent company**. Peters and Waterman (1982) may not be the only writers to attempt to identify the features of the excellent company (Ouchi attempted much the same a year earlier), but their attempt proved to be the most successful by far with their book *In Search of Excellence*. Several million copies have been sold since its publication in 1982 and the book arguably ranks alongside Taylor's *Scientific Management* (1947) as one of the most influential manage-ment texts of all time. Peters and Waterman carried out an investigation of 62 top-performing American companies. Six measures of long-term productivity were devised and only those firms that ranked in the top 20 of their industry on four out of the six cri-teria were included in their in-depth study. Their final sample numbered 43 firms, includ-ing IBM, HP, Boeing, Digital, Caterpillar, Eastman Kodak, Walt Disney and 3M. The sample was not intended to be representative of all types of firm and banks are notable by their exclusion.

In all, eight attributes of excellence were identified. These were, using Peters and Waterman's own terminology, as follows:

- **'Bias for action'**, being typified by clear objectives and a marked absence of committee procedures.
- **'Closeness to the customer'**, typified by processes and procedures aimed at identifying and serving the customers needs.
- **'Autonomy and entrepreneurship'**, which are best achieved through the creation of small cohesive teams.
- **'Productivity through people'**, with workforce involvement at all times.
- **'Hands on; value driven'**, involving the fostering of a strong corporate culture by top management who are seen to be in touch with all employees.
- **'Stick to the knitting'**, which involves limiting activities to what the firm does best and avoiding diversification into unknown territory.
- **'Simple form, lean staff'**, avoiding complex hierarchics and large administration sections.
- **'Simultaneous loose–tight properties'**, which means that organization structure should display a combination of strong central direction with work group autonomy.

Throughout their work, Peters and Waterman stressed the importance of socializing and integrating individuals into a clearly defined corporate culture. The firm becomes much more than a place of work.

> . . . by offering meaning as well as money, the excellent companies give their employees a mission as well as a sense of feeling great. (*Peters and Waterman, 1982, p. 323*)

At its most influential the corporate culture is seen as having replaced organized religion and the family as the most important focus in a person's life (Ray, 1986).

Case 5.6 **Hewlett Packard**

Hewlett Packard (HP) is an American multinational operating in most major coun-tries of the world. It was founded in the late 1930s in Palo Alto, California, by Bill Hewlett and Dave Packard, both of whom have had considerable influence on com-pany philosophy, although Dave Packard died in 1986 (Bill Hewlett died in 2001). Traditionally the firm has operated in four main divisions each representing differ-ent product groupings. These divisions are: the Computer Systems Group, the Measurement Systems Group, the Medical Products Group and the Analytical

▶

Instrumentation Group. The company now employs over 120 000 people in more than 110 countries worldwide and has manufacturing and R&D in 52 of them. Its philosophy as a global company is based around a unified corporate culture irrespective of location.

By the end of the 1990s the management had become aware that as a company they needed to change their focus. They recognized that most of their clients were operating in a rapidly changing world. They wanted more than the purchase of hardware systems. Rather, they needed someone to guide them through a period of rapid and confusing change, of which e-commerce was but one element. HP decided to offer a complete service to customers, which they called 'HP Consulting'. This required a change in approach not just for HP employees, but for their customers as well. The methods they used in effecting these changes were based on a central element in all their activities they had used since the beginning. This central element became known as the 'HP Way'.

The 'HP Way', a set of beliefs, objectives and guiding principles, is described by Bill Hewlett as follows:

> . . . the policies and actions that flow from the belief that men and women want to do a good job, a creative job, and that if they are provided with the proper environment they will do so. It is the tradition of treating every individual with respect and recognising personal achievements . . . You can't describe it in numbers or statistics. In the last analysis it is a spirit, a point of view. There is a feeling that everyone is part of a team and that team is HP. As I said at the beginning it is an idea that is based on the individual. It exists because people have seen that it works, and they believe that this feeling makes HP what it is.
> (*quoted in Peters and Waterman, 1982, p. 244*)

The HP Way is probably best illustrated from a number of words and concepts extracted from HP's own publications. These are love of the product, love of the customer, innovation, quality, open communication, commitment to people, trust, confidence, informality, teamwork, sharing, openness, autonomy and responsibility.

It is not just the communication of such sentiments that appears to be important in HP but that such sentiments appear to be shared by a majority of employees and felt with a certain intensity.

The sentiments are reinforced by a series of processes and procedures, which we identify below:

- Communication is the key underlying theme behind all activities in HP and is an important ingredient of the company's attitude towards innovation and quality. Informal communication is encouraged between all employees of different levels and functions. The physical layout of the offices and work stations has been deliberately created to encourage *ad hoc* meetings and brainstorming. The use of first names is almost obligatory and is the norm, even in the German operations where employees are used to a much greater degree of formality in personal relationships. Management assists the informal processes by engaging in what HP term MBWA (management by wandering around). At a more formal level there are frequent announcements to the workforce on such matters as company performance and all employees are given a written statement of the company goals stressing, as they do, the contribution that individuals can make. Regular team meetings are obligatory for groups within the organization and once a week all employees meet for a briefing session by senior management. Less formal channels of communication are still guided by the company, in that employees are encouraged to participate in coffee breaks signalled by a bell. The communication policy is assisted by the company's commitment to decentralization.

An important aspect of communication in HP is the various stories and myths that are a continual feature of management training, retirement parties, company speeches and in-house journals. These stories generally tell of key moments in the company's history, or recount the exploits of the corporate heroes, usually Bill Hewlett and Dave Packard. These stories serve an important purpose of stressing a collective identity and underlining the goals of the founders.

- Quality, according to Peters and Waterman, is pursued with zealotry. The company certainly sees its prime objective as a commitment to the design, manufacture and marketing of high-quality goods. Commitment to quality is viewed as ongoing with continual product improvement as a major goal. All employees are involved in the definition and monitoring of quality, a process reinforced by procedures such as MBWA and ceremonies to recognize, reward and publicize good work. The company has a stated policy and associated methodologies of continuous improvement.

- Innovation, like quality, is regarded as the responsibility of all employees. Following the espousal to 'stick to the knitting' there is a clear commitment to products related to electrical engineering and the company's existing product portfolio. Openness is encouraged and prototypes are often left for other employees to test and criticize. Employees are free to take company equipment home with them. In relations with their customers the company is guided by yet another principle and mnemonic, that of LACE (laboratory awareness of customer environment). A central strategy in R&D is the design of products to customer specifications and the LACE programme gives customers the opportunity to make presentations to the company. Such procedures stress the strong emphasis on customer service. The 'HP Consulting' initiative is a further attempt to link new developments with the needs of customers. It is also an attempt to assist customers to deal with innovations occurring in their business environment, such as e-commerce.

- Personnel policies are carefully designed to reinforce the HP Way as well as ensuring that it works. Most HP employees have no requirement for clocking-on and many operate on flexible working hours. All employees attend a detailed induction programme with communication of the HP Way as a key ingredient. In terms of selection, care is taken to select only those who meet the criteria of being high calibre and possessing flair, adaptability and openness. Most recruits are young. As we have seen, considerable attention is paid to the environment and the general well-being of employees is a major consideration. Employee commitment is reinforced by a highly structured system of objective setting.

Objectives are mutually set at all levels and are cascaded down throughout the organization. Salaries are reviewed every three months for each employee through an evaluation based on the achievement of objectives.

● There is a somewhat traditional and conservative approach to finance and accounting. There is an emphasis on careful management of assets, self-financing investment, and minimal long-term borrowing.

The overall impression is often that HP is too good to be true.

> We tried to remain sober, not to become fans. But it proved impossible. (*Peters and Waterman, 1982, p. 246*)

Certainly on most measures of performance and employee satisfaction, HP emerges as a highly successful company. The net profit has never been less than 3 per cent of net turnover and R&D expenditure never less than 10 per cent of turnover. More than 50 per cent of the turnover is generally attributed to products developed in the previous two years. A measure of the employees' commitment occurred in 1970 when, in the middle of a recession and bad time for the company financially, a 10 per cent pay cut was agreed rather than lay people off.

The downturn in the computer industry towards the end of the 1990s and the early part of the new millennium had a serious impact on HP sales and profits. Other established firms were also affected and HP announced a merger with Compaq. The two products would continue to be marketed separately but the future impact on the distinctive HP culture will be interesting to observe.

Sources: Peters and Waterman, 1982; Beer *et al.*, 1984; Needle, 1984; Feurer *et al.*, 1995; Greenly, 1999; *Financial Times*, *Guardian*, September 2001

Questions

1 What are the key elements of the HP culture and how are they implemented?

2 What are the strengths and weaknesses of this approach?

3 Assess the impact of the HP culture on the performance of the company. What other factors may be significant?

4 Why did the company merge with Compaq and what impact is this likely to have on the corporate culture?

Culture and performance

Those who subscribe to this kind of vision of organizations argue that companies displaying such characteristics are invariably more successful than those that do not (Peters and Waterman, 1982; Deal and Kennedy, 1982). We examine this claim by reference to a number of studies that have been carried out examining the impact of culture on strategy and on performance.

Brown (1998) sees the link between culture and strategy as inevitable. He argues that the culture of an organization will determine key strategic elements, including how the environment is perceived and interpreted, how information is analysed, and how the main players react. This echoes the earlier work of Miles and Snow (1978). They identify three types of organization: defenders, prospectors and analysers. Each of these is culturally different and each pursues different strategies.

The notion of a culture–strategy fit also underpins many studies on culture change, where culture is manipulated to achieve the desired strategic ends. At best, this represents an understanding by management that successful implementation of a strategy requires consideration of behavioural and culture change and a corresponding investment in training and other processes. The case of BA is a good illustration of this kind of change process (see Case 12.3). At worst, however, it represents a vague hope on the part of management that simple exhortations to culture change will bring about the desired strategic change.

BA is often cited as an example of how culture, or more specifically culture change, can lead to improved performance. Goodstein and Burke (1991) attempted to provide links between culture change and the conversion of a US$900 million loss into a US$435 million profit. Even more measured accounts, such as those of Höpfl et al. (1992), point to some success factors and argue that the 'new' culture at BA enabled it to withstand subsequent pressures on business such as those associated with the Gulf War and the deregulation of transatlantic routes.

Links between culture and performance were also postulated by Gordan and Ditomaso (1992), who found some correlation between the strength of a widely shared culture and short-term financial performance. In Whipp et al. (1989) an analysis was made of Jaguar, a blue-chip car producer with a sought-after product and strong export market. The placing of Jaguar under British Leyland (BL) management in the 1970s resulted in a performance decline, explained as a clash of cultures between Jaguar employees and BL management. It was a case of a specialist versus volume car manufacturer, where energies were diverted as Jaguar management engaged in political battles to retain a distinctive corporate identity. Performance at Jaguar improved dramatically in the 1980s when, free from the restrictions of BL, a new management team attempted to recreate the values of the company's most successful era through a focus on costs, quality and incremental quality improvements. When Ford acquired Jaguar in the late 1980s, Jaguar were allowed to operate with considerable independence and the relationship and integration was carefully planned to avoid the earlier mistakes.

Yet the studies by Gordan and Ditomaso (1992) and by Whipp et al (1989) also point out the dangers of linking culture and performance too directly. Both acknowledge the likely interference factor of a whole range of variables. In the case of Jaguar, the performance of the company, especially in its main export market, the USA, was aided significantly by a favourable sterling–dollar exchange rate. Such limitations have led many to question its utility as a concept. It is to these issues we now turn.

How useful is organizational culture as a concept?

The more analytical perspective of organizational culture attempts to view culture as a complex collection of many variables. The problem with such analyses is the isolation and measurement of variables. It is hardly surprising that so many articles and books are dependent upon anecdotes from key participants as the major form of data. However, an attempt at such an analysis may be useful to management attempting a strategic change. An assessment of the prevailing influences on the culture of the firm may indicate the likely success of a strategic initiative in terms of its fit with the culture.

If for nothing else, an analysis of organization culture may assist us in gaining fresh insights into the realities of organizational life and obtaining a richer picture. For example, a focus on culture and, in particular, subcultures, as large public organizations, such as universities and hospitals, undergo change, may lead to a greater understanding of the underlying issues. In hospitals, there are tensions between the medical staff and budget-conscious administrators. In universities similar tensions exist between academics and senior management. Academics see traditional freedoms being eroded by management initiatives responding to a harsh financial climate and government funding, increasingly tied to performance indicators. Such external pressures are challenging the traditional values that underpin the culture.

How useful is corporate culture as a concept?

A number of problems have been identified with the use by managers of a strong culture to guide and control the behaviour of organization members.

● **Official versus unofficial cultures.** The exhortations of corporate literature and of top management can appear markedly different from the realities of organizational life. In this vein, Watson (1994) makes a clear distinction between official and unofficial cultures existing within organizations at the same time. He argues that each has its own particular discourse, in that while the official culture talks about 'empowerment, skills and growth', the unofficial reflects upon 'control, jobs and costs' (Watson, 1994, p. 112)

● **The rigour of much of the research** into the so-called excellent companies is challenged. For example, Hitt and Ireland (1987) argue that the excellent companies of the Peters and Waterman study performed no better on stock market valuation than other 'non-excellent' companies appearing in the 'Fortune 1000' listing.

● **The use of corporate culture as a management tool is not feasible.** A number of limitations in the management use of culture have been identified:

  – Some authors believe that the significance of culture is overstated, and that variables such as product/market, size and monopoly power are more important (Carroll, 1983). The case of IBM frequently appears in the literature where it is questioned whether their dominance of the market was a function of culture or monopoly power. The excellence guru himself, in a later book, used market changes to explain the fall from grace of some of his original sample (Peters, 1987).

  – Willmott (1993) argues that changing economic conditions have much more impact on a firm's performance than culture. The strong culture of the three Korean electronics companies, previously cited, made little difference in the face of the economic crisis in Asia in 1997 (Needle, 2000).

  – The kind of culture seen in firms such as HP and IBM may simply not be appropriate in certain types of organization. Dawson (1986) argues that Peters and Waterman have not uncovered a set of universal principles, but strategies that only work under certain conditions.

    Their 'slim, consensual organizations' of the future are probably applicable to firms employing professionals and technicians from the primary labour market in the development and operation of new technology or highly fashionable

products and processes. They may however be less successful in other
technological, product or labour market conditions. (*Dawson, 1986, p. 137*)

One may conclude from this that certain types of culture, notably that associated
with the 'excellent' companies, is incompatible with certain types of company,
specific types of work, and, almost certainly, the presence of an active trade
union movement.

- There is clearly conflict here with the concept of the flexible firm. It may be
difficult to establish corporate values and gain commitment among a growing
number of part-time and contract employees. Labour market issues are clearly
important here, particularly when combined with employee characteristics related
to job mobility. In Singapore, job changing is frequent and an accepted route to
career and salary enhancement. As a consequence, firms have difficulty
sustaining a particular culture.

- Even where conditions are 'favourable', cultures may be very difficult to change.
Scholz (1987) maintains that culture change can take anything from 6 to 15
years. This is in stark contrast to those managers who regard instant culture
change as the panacea for all that ails their company.

- Ultimately, as we have already shown, the utility of the concept is brought into
question by the continued difficulty in establishing any meaningful links between
culture, strategy and performance. Dawson (1986) raises the fundamental
question as to whether culture is a cause or a consequence of a firm's success. In
other words, is a firm like HP successful because it has a particular kind of
culture, or does it have a particular kind of culture because it is successful? It is
much easier to gain employee consensus when profits are healthy, bonuses are
good and job security is guaranteed.

- **The use of corporate culture as a management tool is not desirable.**

  - The key issue here is one of ethics. At worst corporate culture is seen as a form
of brainwashing or conditioning and at best it sends out conflicting messages to
employees. It is true that in companies such as HP, employees are encouraged to
be creative, yet are expected to conform; to be individualistic within a corporate
image of a vast collective; to exhibit freedom, yet be subject to considerable
expectations as to appropriate behaviour. The whole issue is probably best
summed up by Peters and Waterman's notion of 'simultaneous loose–tight
properties'. Under such conditions individuals were encouraged to operate as
free, creative individuals, within a cloak of tight collective corporate control. For
Willmott the contradictions are part of the use of corporate culture as a control
mechanism.

  - A number of writers, notably Silver (1987), are concerned about the exploitative
potential of corporate culture. The essence of such criticism is that the emphasis
on the moral commitment of the workforce is simply a means of achieving high
productivity on the cheap. Silver singles out McDonald's for particularly harsh
criticism.

    The lively, people-oriented culture is but a complement to the speeded up,
    Taylorized assembly line production of food. . . grease burns, irregular hours,
    autocratic bosses, sexual harassment and low wages all come with the quarter
    pounder. (*Silver, 1987, pp. 109–10*)

- Ethical or exploitative, corporate culture may be undesirable simply because it prevents change. In Rank Xerox, middle management were so cast in an identical mould of strong corporate values that they were dubbed 'xeroids'. Their programmed thinking and successful company, built on the patent protection of the photocopying machine, rendered them impervious to a changing business climate and, ultimately, unable to respond to increased competition (Williams *et al.*, 1989).

Culture as a useful concept

Thus far in the critique we have focused on the problematic aspects of organizational and corporate culture, yet even some of the more critical writers have identified some benefits. Of course, one must always add the rider, benefits for whom and at what cost?

- For Ray (1986), corporate culture offers management coordination and control via a moral involvement of the workforce. It is also claimed to reduce conflict and uncertainty, particularly through the emphasis on clear guidelines and effective training (Deal and Kennedy, 1982).
- Peters and Waterman (1982) stress the benefits to employees, notably a sense of belonging and good pay.
- Culture has also been viewed as a vital link between the rational and the subjective aspects of determining strategy and is seen as the element that turns strategy into a reality (Whipp *et al.*, 1989).
- The continued success of firms such as HP is used as evidence that strong cultures are not necessarily as dysfunctional as the critics suggest.

Summary

In this chapter we focused our attention on the organizational elements of business which we identified as goals, structure, ownership, size and organizational and corporate culture. As befits our model, all elements interact not just with each other but with aspects of the environment, business strategy and operations.

- **Goals** are viewed as the products of a highly interactive, dynamic and political process, involving influence, conflict and compromise between different interest groups. Goals give a sense of direction to a firm's activities but a number of goals may operate at any one time and may conflict.
- We identify the factors that influence **structure** and examine a number of structural types. The relationship between structure and performance is of obvious interest to businessmen, but as yet the evidence is inconclusive.
- **Structural trends** are examined, including delayering, down-sizing and flexibility.
- **Ownership** is seen as important because of its potential impact on the way businesses are managed and we examine the relationship between ownership and control.

- The relationship between **public and private sector management** is explored including a review of the issues relating to **privatization**.
- We examine the influence of **size** on such factors as structure, market power, relationship with the state, and the impact on the individual.
- The case for government support of the **small firm** is examined in light of the potential contribution of small businesses to the economy and society.
- **Organizational culture** is viewed as the product of a number of variables that distinguish organizations from one another. **Corporate culture** is viewed as a strategic device created by top management.
- In terms of the relationship between culture and performance, culture may be less important than technology or the product-market and we question its usefulness in terms of the feasibility and desirability of culture change at the level of the firm.

Discussion

1 How are goals formed and what are the major difficulties encountered in goal formulation and implementation?

2 View the web sites of some companies with which you are familiar. What can you learn from their mission statements and statements of corporate objectives?

3 What are the major causes of goal conflict and how might they be resolved?

4 Assess the relative importance of the various strategic, organizational and environmental factors, which influence organizational structures?

5 Assess the advantages and disadvantages to both management and employees of flexible labour markets and the creation of the flexible firm?

6 How significant is the separation of ownership and control to the way businesses operate?

7 Examine the advantages and the prime beneficiaries of privatization. To what extent does privatization solve the problems of managing public sector organizations?

8 Examine the rationale behind government support for the small firms' sector. To what extent and in what ways are small firms economically relevant today?

9 To what extent do the terms organizational culture and corporate culture represent different concepts?

10 What is the relationship between the type of corporate culture envisaged by Deal and Kennedy and by Peters and Waterman and company performance in terms of profitability and job satisfaction? Can the internal culture of an organization act as a buffer against environmental influences?

Further reading

Barry, J., Chandler, J., Clark, H., Johnston, R. and Needle, D. (eds) (2000) *Organization and Management*: *A Critical Text*, Thomson Learning, London offers useful contributions on many of the issues raised in this chapter, particularly organizational culture and the flexible firm. Those students seeking an historical perspective on structural issues are advised to look at Chandler, A. D. (1962) *Strategy and Structure*: *Chapters in the History of American Capitalism*, MIT Press, Cambridge, MA. Probably the best summary of the ownership and control debate is offered by Child, J. (1969) *The Business Enterprise in Modern Industrial Society*, Collier-Macmillan, London. A good summary of research and debates about the role of the small firm is found in Storey, J. (1994) *Understanding the Small Business Sector*, Routledge, London and in Burns P. (2001) *Entrepreneurship and Small Business*, Palgrave, London. No examination of organizational culture would be complete without a look at Peters, T. J. and Waterman, R. J. (1982) *In Search of Excellence: Lessons from America's Best-run Companies*, Harper and Row, London, although a sounder academic treatment is offered by Brown, A. (1998) *Organizational Culture*, 2nd edn, Financial Times Pitman, London.

6 Management and leadership

- Define management and articulate the difficulties inherent in such definitions.
- Assess the wide range of management roles and managerial behaviour.
- Explain the reasons for the 'manager's right to manage'.
- Recount the various models of management and explain the reasons for their change over time.
- Explain the contribution of key writers and offer a critique of the main theoretical models.
- Assess management activities and explain their link to the theoretical models.
- Articulate the differences between management and leadership.
- Explain the significance of leadership to modern management.
- Assess the different theories of leadership in the context of modern organizations.

Introduction

The authors of several management texts are fond of telling us that management can be traced back to the building of the pyramids and even beyond. It is undoubtedly true that many management functions that we see today were performed by those responsible for projects like the pyramids, running the economy in Elizabethan times and sailing a ship to discover the New World. However, none of the people performing these tasks in historical times were recognized as managers. The emergence of the manager as an identifiable occupation is a relatively recent phenomenon and is related to a number of factors:

- industrialization;
- the creation of the joint stock company and the subsequent separation of ownership and control;
- the increasing size and complexity of organizations leading to specialization;
- the growth of bureaucracies leading to the development of organizational hierarchies;

- notions of professionalism and the development of management education;
- the above combining to result in the development of a management class.

In this chapter we will explore several dimensions of management and leadership. We will attempt to define management and explore the basis upon which managers can claim the right to manage. We will contrast the classical theories of management with what we know about management behaviour and attempt to link the two. We treat leadership as a separate section, acknowledging its current popularity among those who seek to influence management development. The various theories of leadership are examined in the light of the needs of modern organizations.

Management

What is management?

> You know, you start off doing a real – I mean a – you know, an actual job and then you end up getting promoted. And then you're the manager. (*Manager quoted in Watson, 1994, p. 29*)

This accords with the view of Charles Handy, who once said at a presentation that 'management was something that happened to nice people at a certain stage of their lives, like getting married and having children'. These quotes highlight the vague nature of management to many people. That vague nature is due to a number of factors concerned with the difficulty of identifying the role of the manager. As we can see below there are obstacles to finding out what management is, many of which are related to the broad and varied nature of managerial work.

- Many definitions of management are prescriptive and idealized and can be challenged by research studies into what managers actually do.
- Managers control access to information about their role in organizations and many are defensive and secretive.
- We can see different management roles in different contexts. A public sector manager may take a different approach from a private-sector manager. Managing a small business is different from managing a large global company. A section manager in a bank may have different priorities to his counterpart in a firm making tyres.
- Within the same organization there are differences between managers. Such differences exist first at different levels. A chief executive officer has a different role to a manager in charge of a small administrative team. Second, managers in one function, such as operations, may have different objectives and display different behaviour to a manager in accounts or human resource management (HRM).
- Some managers are effective by performing their role in an assertive, extrovert fashion, while others are equally successful 'leading from behind'.
- In the discussion in Chapter 4, we have seen how management priorities vary across cultures, affecting the way managers choose and plan their strategies.
- In our discussion of organizational culture we have seen how management style may vary between companies as a result of the prevailing culture.

- Furthermore, in accordance with our Business in Context model, different influences at different stages in the life of an organization will have a significant influence on the way managers behave. Managers in different environmental and organizational contexts will act differently.

Nevertheless, if we are to make sense of management and what managers do, then some kind of definition is needed. A popular definition is 'getting things done through other people', ascribed to various people from Mary Parker Follet to Rosemary Stewart. It is a succinct definition and links management clearly with a leadership role. A more detailed definition is offered by Tony Watson.

> Managing is organizing: pulling things together and along in a general direction to bring about long-term organizational survival. (*Watson, 1986, p. 41*)

To support this definition Watson speaks of 'strategic exchange', in which the manager shapes a team of people to result in efforts to match and meet the external demands placed on the organization. In this sense, the strategic exchange takes place both within the firm and between the firm and its environment. Within the firm the exchange occurs between individuals in the same department, and between managers of different departments. The exchange occurs externally between the firm and its suppliers, the firm and its customers and the firm and its shareholders. In this way management lies at the heart of our Business in Context model.

- Shaping the functional, strategic, and organizational contexts and, at the same time, being constrained by them.
- Coping with the demands of the external environment.

We can illustrate this by looking at some of the jobs performed by a university head of department. He or she must shape and organize the academic staff to fulfil the teaching requirements for the academic year and do the same for the administrative support staff. He or she must liaise with other departments, where courses are shared by students and with central services over budgets, time-tabling and room bookings. He or she may talk to school and college teachers and heads about students who have applied but not made the grades required and to employers about placement opportunities for students. He or she may negotiate with firms to provide in-company courses, with other colleges, both home and overseas, about franchising a degree programme and to suppliers to obtain the best deal on the latest computer equipment. All this is done within a framework of a strategic plan informed by student target numbers provided by the government and an income generation target set by the vice-chancellor. The overall aim is the satisfaction of the various stakeholders and the long-term survival of the institution.

Key concept 6.1 Management

Management is a broad term that is applied to a wide range of people in different types of organization and in different contexts. In essence, management is the balancing of external and internal influences, the coordination of activities and of people to achieve the goals of the organization. There is often some discrepancy between definitions of management in theory and management practice.

In addition to this definition of management we can view management in a number of different ways (Child, 1969; Watson, 1994):

- Management is an economic resource that performs functions to direct the work of an organization.
- Management is a set of activities involved with achieving its main functions.
- Management is a system of authority within an organization.
- Management is a team of people within an organization.
- Management is an elite group within society.
- Management is an employee group within the organization.

Whichever definition or whatever perspective of management we favour, a key aspect of the manager's role is the legitimacy they have to do their job. In the next section we explore their right to manage.

The manager's right to manage

The legitimacy of the manager rests upon several factors.

- The manager may own the business and the right to manage is legitimized through property ownership. The majority of managers do not own the business, but control the capital assets of those who do.
- The manager's right to manage is enshrined in law. Managers of public limited companies (plcs) have a legal duty towards their shareholders. All managers have a set of legal duties towards their employees but, more significantly, employees have a legal obligation to obey reasonable orders and fulfill the requirements of their contracts.
- The right to manage is reinforced by the various types of power in the possession of the manager. These are:
  - **Position power**. This is sometimes known as **legitimate** power and is derived from the manager's formal position in the organizational hierarchy.
  - **Reward power**. This derives from the ability of the manager to reward subordinates for obeying orders, performing the task and achieving the goals. The reward can be direct in the form of payment or bonus or less obvious in giving employees time, freedom or access to interesting jobs. There is a negative side to this in that the manager can withhold such rewards from those employees not performing as required and the ultimate sanction is dismissal.
  - **Charisma power**. This is sometimes referred to as **referant** power and relates to the ability of the manager to get subordinates to follow him or her by virtue of the strength of his or her personality.
  - **Political power**. This is sometimes known as **connection** power. The right to manage rests on the ability of the manager to create a favourable situation for employees and the organization by negotiating with others inside the organization as well as external stakeholders. Managers are often seen in a favourable light by their subordinates if they can access scarce resources or win highly competitive contracts.

- **Expertise power.** This rests on the manager's specific knowledge of the technical aspects of the job or on the know-how to get things done within the organization. Linked to these aspects is the access to information to enable the group to complete their task. This is sometimes known as **information power**.

● The right to manage is part of a widespread value system and is accepted by the workforce and rarely questioned. This view has been supported in more radical accounts of management (Nicholls, 1969) and in accounts of industrial relations at a time of widely publicized strikes in the UK (Hawkins, 1978). The conclusion of such authors is surprise that there is so little conflict and challenge to the manager's right to manage.

We can therefore see that the legitimacy of management rests upon a number of factors, most of which lend considerable support to the manager's position and actions. Despite the view that there is little challenge to the manager's legitimacy a number of points should be made, as follows:

● Recent surveys of UK managers have uncovered a widespread belief that the majority of their managers lack competence and certainly lack leadership skills (Horne and Stedman-Jones, 2001; Council for Excellence in Management and Leadership, 2002). A traditional view of UK managers is that they spend too much time on man mismanagement and insufficient time on strategic issues.

● The delayering that has occurred in many organizations throughout the world, creating flatter structures has undermined the manager's position power.

● The rapidly changing global competitive environment has given manager's considerable problems in just keeping up with the changes that are occurring. Many lag behind and, as a consequence, their expertise and knowledge power is undermined. However, this situation may favour those managers who are particularly adept at managing through their connections within and outside the firm.

● The various stakeholders of the firm may restrict the manager's freedom to act in a number of different way. Banks to which the firm owes money may dictate strategic direction. As we see in Case 6.2, shareholders can rise up to block management decisions. The state through its legislative devices can restrict the freedom of managers to act as they wish. Finally, in some organizations there is the countervailing force of the trade unions.

What managers are supposed to do

A review of most management textbooks will offer us a list of activities that purport to define the role of the manager. As we shall see in the next section, studies of management reveal a different picture. Nonetheless, we continue our exploration of management by examining those activities and the various historical models of management that underpin them.

The most frequently identified activities of management are:

● forecasting
● planning

- organizing
- coordinating
- communicating
- motivating
- controlling.

The sequence of these is deliberate, implying a logical progression. A manager must forecast before a plan can be made and planning must precede organizing and so on. These activities derive in the main from the earlier models of management that focused on rational approaches. It is to these we now turn.

Models of management   In examining the models of management that have been developed over time, we will use the classification set out by Boddy (2002) with some modifications. These are:

- rational goal models
- internal process models
- human relations models
- motivation models
- open systems models
- responsive management models
- fashions, fads and gurus.

Our treatment of these models is selective and more detailed accounts, especially of 'scientific management', 'bureaucracy', 'human relations' and 'motivation theory' can be found in good textbooks on organization theory and behaviour (see, for example, Martin, 2001; Fincham and Rhodes, 1999; Thompson and McHugh, 2003). We close the section by offering a critical reflection on such models of management.

Rational goal models   These models assume that management is a scientific and rational process moving employees and the organization towards some stated goal. Its chief exponent was Frederick Winslow Taylor (1947), whose work in the earlier part of the 19th century had considerable impact on the way organizations, more especially in manufacturing operations, work. His work dealing with operations is reviewed in Chapter 10.

Taylorism   Like many management models **Taylorism** was a product of its time. Taylor (1856–1915) was, for most of his working life, an engineer and manager. His later life was spent promoting his ideas on scientific management. In the USA, in the early part of the twentieth century, there was a shortage of skilled workers, as well as a need to increase efficiency, to coordinate the work of organizations that were growing ever larger and deal with the growing issue of trade unionism. In essence Taylorism encompasses:

- The use of scientific methods to find the best way of doing the job and the best equipment to do it with. If possible, jobs should be reduced to a series of routine, predictable tasks.
- The need to ensure that the best person to do the job is selected.
- The training of those selected to follow the procedures derived scientifically.

- The provision of financial incentives for following the procedures and achieving targets.

- The separation of 'doers' (the operators) and 'planners' (the managers).

The introduction of scientific management under Taylorist principles was shown to increase efficiency in many organizations, although initially it met with opposition from both the USA government of the day and the trade unions. Its widespread acceptance as a set of guiding principles, particularly in the manufacturing industry, around the world was an important part of the process of the creation of the semi-skilled worker to replace the craftsman and the introduction of a new breed of planner/managers.

Taylor's work was extended by contempories such as Frank **Gilbreth** (1868–1924)**,** in the field of work study and by Henry **Gantt** (1861–1919), a one-time colleague of Taylor, in the field of incentive schemes.

The scientific approach underpinned the development of **operations research (OR)** during the Second World War. OR is essentially the development of mathematical models to manage complex situations. During the 1960s there was a resurgence of interest in scientific methods, particularly those related to measurement and mathematics and a key competence of management at that time was numeracy. The use of mathematical models is present in most organizations today and the capacity for their development has been enhanced greatly by developments in management information systems (MIS) and the use of computer programmes.

Internal process models   Whereas Taylor's approaches focused on the needs of manufacturing industry (although applications can be seen in office work) the internal process models were applicable to all types of work and involved the whole organization. Internal process models are sometimes referred to as **administrative management** or **classical organization theory** and are also based on rationality and the scientific method. Indeed the applications of the ideas of Weber and Fayol, as outlined below, were intended to complement scientific management.

Weber and bureaucracy   Max Weber (1864–1920) was a German, initially an economist and later a sociologist. He was interested (among other things including religion and the development of capitalism) in the difficulties of managing large complex organizations, particularly government organizations. He felt that the problems found in large organizations – a relatively new phenomenon at the turn of the century – could be solved by the application of bureaucracy. This involved:

- The application of rules governing the conduct of all workers in carrying out their duties.

- A division of labour allowing individuals to specialize and become expert in a particular field.

- An authority structure arranged in a hierarchy of jobs ranked on the basis of the authority needed to carry them out.

- Rationality and scientific method.

- Impersonality, particularly in choosing strategic options and in the selection and promotion of staff. All these activities should be done scientifically.

Fayol and administrative management   Henri Fayol (1841–1925) was born in France and, like Taylor, was a practising engineer for much of his life but spent the later part of his life promoting his management ideas. His original work, *Administration, industrielle et générale* was first published in 1916, but the English version did not appear until 1949 as *General and Industrial Management* (Fayol, 1949). The work was extremely influential and taken up in the UK by Lyndall **Urwick** (1891–1983), who assisted in the UK publication of works of not just Fayol, but of Taylor and Follett as well. Fayol's chief contribution to the development of management lies in the identification of the basic management tasks and in the creation of a series of principles of management.

He identified the core management tasks as:

● planning

● organizing

● commanding

● coordinating

● controlling.

His principles of management are presented in Table 6.1. They were written at a time when there was a theoretical void in management, that was to be filled part by Fayol and part by Taylor. His principles were an important guide to practising managers and formed the basis of management training for many years. In contrast to Taylor's machine approach to management, Fayol viewed the organization much more as a living organism and, in some ways, prepared the way for a systems view of organizations.

Human relations models

Like the rational goal models, human relations models emerged at the beginning of the 20th century and were a response to a particular social and economic context, particularly in the USA. It was a time of rapid industrialization and increased mobility, which was breaking up traditional society. As a consequence, there was a search for an element of stability and security through work organizations. It was almost as if the work group would become the replacement family. It was also a time of increasing organizational size, inexperienced managers and growth of trade union opposition. Management was seeking ways to ensure the compliance and commitment of their workforce. The advocates of human relations at the time of the publication of F. W. Taylor's book *Scientific Management* saw little that was contradictory in the two schools and saw human relations as adding to the theory provided by scientific management. Interest in human relations developed strongly throughout the 1950s and 1960s, due largely to the late publication of the findings of the Hawthorne Studies, particularly in the UK, and subsequent work by **Likert** and his team at the University of Michigan, encapsulated in his book, *New Patterns of Management* (Likert, 1961). The human relations model had significant impact on the training of managers, particularly at supervisory level.

Follet   Mary Parker Follett (1868–1933) started from the assumption that, for the good of society, the group was more important than the individual. Much of her thinking on the subordination of the individual to the needs of the group had echoes of early socialism. For the management of organizations, she emphasized the importance of teams to get the job done and in particular their contribution to the creative process. She was supportive of

Table 6.1	Fayol's principles of management

Principle	Definition
Division of work Essentially greater specialization would lead to greater effectiveness	**Centralization** The organization is like a living organism and the degree of centralization versus decentralization depends on the organization's needs
Authority Should always be linked to responsibility	**Scalar chain** The hierarchy of authority and the line of communication. Speed of decision is important and delegated authority may be needed to avoid delay
Discipline Could take different forms but all involved the agreement between the firm and its employees. Employees should be obedient within the terms of the agreement and managers should impose sanctions where necessary	**Order** Essentially 'a place for everything and everything in its place'; includes the right place for materials at the right time and the filling of posts by the right people
Unity of command Orders should come from one manager only and there should be no conflicting instructions	**Equity** Treating people fairly on the basis of both justice and kindliness
Unity of direction There should be one plan led by one head	**Stability of tenure of personnel** A particular problem in large organizations and needed to be addressed by attention to induction, staff development and motivation
Subordination of individual interest to general interest The interest of the firm should be paramount at all times	**Initiative** The ability to develop plans and see them through to success. This was seen as a key ingredient in the motivation of employees
Remuneration of personnel A fair price for services rendered and paternalistic considerations such as health, education and social welfare	**Esprit de corps** Team-building based on harmony

many elements of scientific management but was critical of the concept of the division of labour, as this could break up teams.

Mayo   Elton Mayo (1880–1949) was born in Australia (where he was mainly educated), and where his earlier works on the political and social problems of industrialization were published. His move to the USA, in the 1920s, coincided with his developing interest in the application of psychotherapy to problems of conflict at work (a theme taken up by the Tavistock Institute somewhat later). His fame, however, derives from his time at Harvard University and his membership of the team that carried out the Hawthorne Studies. These were a series of studies carried out at the Hawthorne plant of the Western Electric Company in Chicago. A series of experiments were set up between 1927 and 1932 that led to the discovery that favourable social relations and social situations were more significant to workers and had more of an influence on performance than physical conditions. The work stressed the importance of the work group, leadership and communication. The main findings of the Hawthorne Studies were published by others but Mayo emerged as the chief publicist and has been forever associated with them.

Motivation models

The human relations researchers continued their work on groups and communication, some of which we discuss in the section on leadership later in this chapter. In the main, the focus of human relations models was the group. A new approach to human relations emerged which instead of focusing on the group based its approaches on the individual. This owed much to the work of **Abraham Maslow** (1908–70) and his theory based on a **hierarchy of needs**. His work was echoed by **Frederick Herzberg** (1923–2000), whose **motivation–hygiene theory** led to the development of job enrichment techniques.

The essence of these theories and much of the motivation theory that followed (expectancy theory, for instance) is the importance of the individual. To Maslow and Herzberg, good group relations and good relations with supervisors are seen only as the rock upon which real motivation occurs. Real motivation lies in goal-seeking behaviour that stretches the individual in a sense of personal achievement. Such theories, which focus on the individual, are often criticized for being culturally biased and specifically American (see Chapter 4 for further details).

Open systems models

Open systems models are also discussed in detail elsewhere in this book. At the end of Chapter 1 we introduced both open systems and contingency models and in Chapter 10 (Operations) we examine the use of the open systems model in operations management.

In essence this approach to management argues that management can only be understood in terms of the context within which it operates. This is a major theme of this book. Management activities are a product of:

- Interaction with the external environment including suppliers, customers, labour supply, banks, prevailing technology, governments, culture and so on.

- Interaction with the organizational environment, including influences relating to size, structure, organizational culture, interaction with employees and other managers and so on.

As a consequence management is part analysis, part negotiation and part adjustment.

Responsive management models

There has been increasing uncertainty as a result of rapid technological and social change, increasing global competition, globalization, more demanding customers and employees and so on. As a result of this uncertainty management can respond in two ways:

● By recognizing that there is no magic formula for management in all situations and management is essentially an iterative process. Effective management is what works in a particular situation at a particular time and managers build up a repertoire of appropriate behaviours as they encounter each new situation.

● By being flexible and adaptable and by developing skills in communication and in their handling of uncertainty.

The former is similar to the 'science of muddling through' that we introduce in the next chapter as a device for the formulation of strategy. The latter response presupposes that managers can be flexible and adaptable and that the ability to deal with uncertainty can be trained. This may not always be the case and, as such, the latter approach has much in common with the trait theories of leadership and their drawbacks discussed under leadership models later in this chapter.

Fashions, fads and gurus

In the last 20 years the book stores (in particular those at airports) have been dominated by a new wave of management books, which offer advice and above all solutions to the practising manager. The more successful of these include *In Search of Excellence* (Peters and Waterman, 1982), *7 Habits of Highly Effective People* (Covey, 1989), and *5 Disciplines of the Learning Organization* (Senge, 1990), but new titles emerge each month. Such books are sold in millions and their authors assume the status of gurus, enjoying lucrative careers as consultants and conference speakers.

The approaches of *In Search of Excellence* have been considered in our discussion of corporate culture in the previous chapter. The problem with most of these books is that they present ideas that are very much the fashionable product of their time. The effectiveness of the ideas is almost impossible to prove and most lack any critical reflection. At best they present common sense in an embellished form and some confuse the reader with elaborate concepts, as with Peters and Watermans' *'simultaneous loose-tight properties'*.

Nevertheless, the influence of such works should not be underestimated. Senge's ideas on the learning organization were embraced by the top management of many organizations, including the Ford Motor Company and used as part of management training. Ultimately, however, such ideas are transient and are influential only until the next fashion comes along.

Critique of management models

● In general there is no real body of scientific knowledge to underpin so-called management theory. This questions both the value of any model to the practising manager and also claims that management is indeed a profession.

- Many of the approaches have come under severe criticism by many researchers. Taylor's system of specialization, prescribed tasks and payment by results has been criticized as 'deskilling' and even inhuman. The **Hawthorne Studies** have been criticized for the their flawed methodology and poor science. Weber's principles of bureaucracy have been shown in many situations to be counter-productive to the effective achievement of goals. The fashionable theories of the modern era are seen to lack substance.

- Many of the models (Fayol excepted) have their origins in the USA. As such they reflect USA culture, which is individualistic, risk-taking, fairly assertive and is more likely to accept authority than those cultures in other advanced industrialized nations (Hofstede, 1980a). As such these models may not apply to management in other cultural settings, although using Hofstede's measurements, USA culture is fairly close to that in the UK.

- The manager is neither scientific in his or her approach nor is he or she a disinterested professional. The Marxist argument is that the manager is the agent of capital and will always take the side of the owners. Even if one disagrees with this perspective, there is plenty of evidence to suggest that managers pursue behaviour and strategies that are in *their* best interests and not necessarily those of their employees or organizations. For example, studies reveal that managers favour takeovers where their position will be secure (not unnaturally) and resist takeovers that would threaten their position, even though it may be in the best interests of the long-term survival of the organization.

- Managers do not always behave in an objective, rational and scientific fashion. They operate politically, balancing conflicting interests, negotiating, persuading and selling ideas to others. In this respect the 'open systems' and 'responsive' models come closest to incorporating this kind of reality.

- Thomas (2003) believes that managers use magic and their equivalent of religious symbols to get people to follow them. He argues that managers have developed sets of techniques, which have the appearance of science, but are in fact no such thing. An example of this may be personnel selection techniques involving tests and interviews, the interpretation of which is highly subjective. This is magic, and the chief magicians are the consultants who offer solutions based on incomplete and non-scientific analysis. Religious symbolism comes in where shareholders, the company and the market are almost supernatural entities that must be worshipped.

- There is little evidence to suggest that managers perform their tasks as depicted by the models and it is to this we now turn.

What managers actually do

There have been a number of studies about the work that managers do. These include studies by Carlson (1951), Stewart (1967), Mintzberg (1973), Luthans (1988) and Watson (1994). The studies have much in common in that they all conclude that management rarely conforms to the kind of models we have just discussed.

Rosemary Stewart, for example, asked 160 senior and middle managers to keep a diary of their work lives. Henry Mintzberg drew heavily on the earlier work of Carlson and Stewart and added his own in-depth study of five executives. Fred Luthans, and his team of researchers, observed 292 managers in four organizations over 2 weeks. Tony Watson spent some time among managers at a firm in the Nottingham area.

The conclusions drawn from all these studies may be summarized as follows:

- The managers displayed a wide variety of behaviours, and their roles varied greatly. Equally a variety of styles was identified. If this is the case, can we identify transferable behaviour in managers that can be carried over into the next job? Does this also question the value of generic courses such as the MBA?

- During the week, and even during the day, managers play a large number of roles and engage in a large number of activities. Many of these are not planned and seldom do they follow any kind of logical sequence.

- Managerial work is highly fragmented, typified by constant interruptions.

- Managers spend most of their time talking to others, giving and receiving information; in formal meetings, telephone calls and informal, social interaction. The studies found that managers show a distinct preference for verbal over written communication. However, managers also considered that they spent a great deal of time on paperwork. Were such a study carried out today, the use of email may be a significant feature.

- Managers see themselves as part of a network of relationships both within the organization and outside. As such, political and networking skills are viewed as essential.

- Managers tend to rely on habit and intuition rather than theory.

- Managers are reactive and engage in firefighting rather than follow carefully formulated strategic plans.

- More senior managers perform a great quantity of work at speed.

- Managers have a preference for current, specific and non-routine tasks.

New models of management?

Based upon such studies some of the writers have attempted to classify management behaviour, as shown below.

Rosemary Stewart (1967)   identified five types of manager:

- **Emissaries** were outward facing and spent a great deal of their time with customers and other organizational stakeholders.

- **Writers** adopted a solitary approach and either spent most of their time on their own with their paperwork or in one-to-one situations.

- **Discussers**, on the other hand, spent most of their time with others.

- **Troubleshooters** tended to operate in a highly fragmented way, spending little time on any one task and moving between them quickly.

- **Committee members** were mostly seen in formal meetings.

Henry Mintzberg (1973)   identified ten manager roles, which he placed in three categories as presented in Table 6.2. Mintzberg argued that all managers play a combination of these

Table 6.2	Mintzberg's manager roles	
Roles	*Function*	
Informational roles		
Monitor	Seeks out and analyses information to understand the organization and its environment	
Disseminator	Shares information with members of the team and others in the organization	
Spokesperson	Represents the organization to the rest of the world. Outward-facing communicator	
Interpersonal roles		
Figurehead	Symbolic representative of the organization	
Leader	Focuses on communicating with and motivating subordinates and colleagues	
Liaison	Focuses on making contacts outside the organization	
Decisional roles		
Entrepreneur	Initiates change	
Disturbance handler	Deals with unexpected changes	
Resource allocator	Chooses between competing demands for resources	
Negotiator	Reaches agreement particularly over the allocation of scarce resources	

roles, although their importance varies with the level of the manager in the hierarchy, the type of business and the personality of the manager.

Fred Luthans (1988)   The problem with classifications, such as those of Stewart and Mintzberg, is that they may add to our knowledge of what managers do and what roles they play, but they offer little guide to managers themselves on the key activities that may make the difference between success and failure. As well as classifying activities, Luthans measured managers' performance in terms of :

- **Success** – whether managers had been promoted.
- **Effectiveness** – measured by reference to the team's performance and their level of satisfaction.

Luthans identified four types of activity.

- **Communicating**
- **Traditional management** seen in terms of planning, decision-making, controlling and so on.

- **Networking** especially outside the organization and engaging in organizational politics.
- **Human resource management** in terms of staffing, motivating, handling conflict and so on.

Luthans concluded that successful managers, i.e. those that got promotion, spent most of their time as networkers and least of their time dealing with HRM issues. Effective managers, on the other hand, spent most of their time communicating and engaging in HRM.

Reality versus theory?

Hales (1986) was critical of the studies of Stewart, Mintzberg, Luthans *et al.* He believed that they were based on the flawed assumption that we could learn about managers from observable behaviour or even diaries. To Hales the missing piece was how the managers themselves interpret their behaviour. He felt that the activities identified by managers could be reclassified in terms of the classical principles of such as Fayol. This position is admirably summed up by Thomas (2003).

> When the findings of studies of managerial behaviour are recast in terms of the categories defined by classical writers, their much maligned analysis turns out to be surprisingly robust. (*Thomas, 2003, p. 42*)

Watson (1994), in his study of managers at ZTC Ryland (a disguised name of the real company), made a number of interesting comments in an attempt to link the classical models with the studies of managerial behaviour.

- He agreed that managers rarely conformed to the classical interpretation of their role.
- Yet he accepted that the survival of any organization does depend on someone planning, organizing, coordinating and controlling, and needs the compliance of its employees. He argued that the classical writers should not be dismissed, rather that they provide a broad template for managerial activity.
- Managers view their primary role as contributing to the overall performance of the organization and what they do or how they do it is secondary to this.
- All organizations need management, but how this is carried out is a choice.
- Most managers accept that they 'get things done through other people'.
- Despite an aversion to theory (and particularly fashions and fads) what managers regard as intuitive behaviour is, in fact, guided by broad models about how things should work.

Leadership

The differences between management and leadership

Management and leadership have often been used to mean the same thing. However, in recent years leadership, while part of the job of management, has been identified as the determining factor in the success of the organization. In this section we will examine this contention as well as looking at the various approaches and theories to leadership that have developed over the years.

Several writers have made the distinction between management and leadership. Martin (2001) distinguishes between management and leadership in a number of different ways and the following classifications draw heavily on his work:

- In terms of the **role**, he views leadership as a component of management and argues that leadership is what managers do to be effective. A person can be a leader and not the manager. In certain situations, as in the work of a team on a highly technical project, the leader of the project may not be the most senior person in the team in terms of hierarchy. In terms of role, Martin argues that managers tend to be outward focused, while leaders tend to be inward focused.

- In terms of **situation**, leaders tend to be more situation specific. Whereas managers are appointed to a position in the organization and their job is defined by contract and job description, different leaders may emerge at different times as the situation demands. Some have called this the 'Admirable Crichton' approach based on a play and film of the same name, in which a shipwreck transforms the normal social order and the group, for the duration of the shipwreck, is led by one of the servants.

- In terms of **context**, some organizations place more emphasis upon leadership than on management as such. Martin cites the armed forces as one such context, in which roles are so clearly defined and role holders drilled in the tasks required that the main role for officers is to lead.

- In terms of **what managers and leaders do**, management activities tend to be focused more on routine procedures. Leadership skills, on the other hand, are necessary under conditions of change.

The above classifications have been reinforced by other writers such as Kotter (1990) and Boddy (2002). We may draw the following conclusions, as shown in Table 6.3. However the creation of such lists can be misleading in that they set up artificial distinctions between management and leadership. It could be argued that effective leaders need to be outward as well as inward-oriented. Spotting an opportunity in the market before everyone else fits many of the above characteristics of a leader. Managers cannot only be concerned with the routine. We therefore return to the view that leadership is an essential ingredient of successful management.

Key concept 6.2 Leadership

Whereas management focuses on coordination, leadership is concerned with influencing the performance of individuals and groups and inspiring them to higher levels of performance. There are links between leadership and innovative thinking, and leadership is currently thought by many to be the determining factor in the success of the organization.

Why leadership?

Leadership lies at the heart of management in that managers can only get the job done through other people (indeed this is one of the oldest definitions of management). In this way John Adair (1983), an influential writer on leadership, sees leadership in terms of the interaction of:

Table 6.3	Management and leadership classifications	
	Classification	
Management	Concerned with formal authority in an organization	
	Balances the complexities of the external environment with the availability of internal resources	
	Focus on managing complexity	
	Operation of current procedures	
	Achieving goals	
Leadership	Concerned with influencing the performance of a group within an organization	
	Inward orientation on the performance of individuals and teams	
	Focus on bringing about change	
	Innovation	
	Inspiring people towards a higher level of performance	

- achieving the task;
- building and maintaining the team;
- developing the individual.

To Adair, these three factors are the essence of leadership and no one element can be achieved without the other two.

Many argue that leadership is an essential ingredient of modern management and the difference between organization success and failure. There are several reasons offered for this.

- Through downsizing and delayering, old hierarchies have been changed radically. Most organizations are now much flatter and old systems of power and authority, based on a manager's position in the hierarchy, are no longer appropriate.
- Most organizations face rapid, significant and constant change. Managers need to respond by being creative, visionary and, above all, leading.
- Managers have seen the significance of controlling members of the organization through a set of strong values within the creation of a corporate culture. As we saw in our discussion of corporate culture in Chapter 4, leaders have an important role to play in this process, by embodying the core values of the organization.
- More demanding employees.

Such changes, especially those within the competitive environment, have been at the heart of recent initiatives to place leadership at the centre of the management agenda. Two such studies have been carried out in the UK. These are those of The Institute of Management (Horne and Stedman-Jones, 2001) and The Council for Excellence in Management and Leadership (2002).

| Case 6.1 | **The Institute of Management study** |

The study was based on a survey of 1500 practising managers and a number of interviews, involving ten established leaders from different organizations, ten middle-managers and ten who were part of the government scheme to support voluntary involvement of young people.

Horne and Stedman-Jones (2001) point to the context of the need for organizations in the UK to recruit 400 000 new managers by 2006 and that such managers would need to operate in an internal and external environment of growing complexity. Such complexities include continuous change, increasing competition, more demanding employees and customers and flatter organizations. They argue that such changes challenge traditional notions of management and leadership, and the new focus needs to be around vision, values, communication and interpersonal relations.

Their survey of UK managers revealed the following:

- UK managers are generally unimpressed with the qualities and the abilities of their leaders, in particular, although viewed as knowledgeable, they are seen to lack the ability to inspire others.

- There is a link between increased turnover as a measure of organizational performance and the priority given by organizations to leadership development. In general, however, low priority was given to leadership development.

- A strong emphasis was placed on a leader's role to shape goals and unlock the potential of their people to achieve them. Relationships with others was seen as the key to leadership success.

- UK managers' preferred characteristics of ideal leaders were identified as follows:
  - inspiration (identified by 55 per cent of respondents)
  - strategic thinking (41 per cent)
  - forward-looking (36 per cent)
  - honesty (26 per cent)
  - fair-mindedness (23 per cent)
  - courage (21 per cent)
  - supportiveness (20 per cent)
  - knowledge (19 per cent)

The recommendations of the report urged organizations and their managers to take a proactive approach to leadership development, which included:

- The recognition that leaders need to take action to make managers feel they are well led and, in this respect, the survey reveals they have much to do.

- There should be a systematic and consistent framework for reward, promotion and leadership development.

- The focus should be on new forms of leadership development suitable for flatter organizations. In particular there should be an emphasis on 360 degree appraisal (where subordinates are not only appraised by their line manager but line managers are also appraised by subordinates) and on self-managed careers.
- All people at all levels need mentors.
- Leadership opportunities can be given to all as through project leadership.
- Leadership should be based on acceptance and participation and not authority systems.
- Leaders should take control of their own learning and development.

Source: Horne and Stedman-Jones, 2001

Questions

1 Can you sum up the approach to leadership taken in this report? To what extent do you agree with this approach?

2 To what extent do you agree or disagree with the list of leader qualities and skills identified by the report.

3 Assess the recommendations of the report.

Theories of leadership

A brief review of a number of texts dealing with leadership reveals a remarkable consistency in their approach of leadership theory. Most identify three types of theory:

- theories based on traits and/or skills;
- theories based on the leader's behaviour or style;
- situational or contingency models.

We will use these categories and add a fourth, which we will term 'more recent approaches'.

Theories based on traits and skills

These are some of the earliest attempts to define and identify leaders and have their origins in the notion that leaders can be selected on the basis of some personal characteristic. Early attempts to identify leaders even took into account physical characteristics, particularly height. Such theories have tended to be discarded for many years, yet the identification of traits and skills has been an important feature in more recent attempts to identify leadership development as a priority. See, for example, Case 6.1 and the Report of the Council for Excellence in Management and Leadership (2002). The latter identifies 83 different factors, a combination of traits, skills and tasks that contribute towards leadership excellence.

Commonly cited traits and skills include:

- vision
- decisiveness
- creativity
- courage
- social skills
- well-organized
- emotionally stable
- sensititity to people's needs

- intelligent
- initiative
- enthusiastic
- dependability
- self-confident
- inspirational
- tough minded
- lead by example.

A more modern approach to trait theory was taken by Kirkpatrick and Locke (1991). They identified six traits, which they found to differentiate leaders from non-leaders. These were:

- ambition and energy
- desire to lead
- honesty and integrity
- self-confidence
- intelligence
- job-relevant knowledge.

However, they add a warning that the possession of such traits will not guarantee success as a leader and are merely an indication.

Those approaches, based solely on personal traits or characteristics, assume that the selection of leaders is more important than their training (leaders are born and not made). Those approaches which combine both traits and skills at least allow some scope for leadership training. With all such approaches, however, there would seem to be a number of difficulties.

- The lists appear to be endless and it would be impossible to find all the characteristics in any one person.
- We do not know which traits are more important than others and which work best in what situations. Many believe that there are no universal traits for all leadership situations.
- Some of the lists appear contradictory. For example, can leaders be tough minded and sensitive to the needs of others both at the same time?
- Is leadership a product of these characteristics or do these characteristics develop with experience of leadership? For example, some people grow in self-confidence and their ability to make decisions when given leadership responsibility.

Despite such criticisms we can still see trait and skills approaches being used today:

- They are often used by the media to describe management success or failure.
- They feature heavily in the person specifications, which guide many management selection processes.
- They have reappeared under the more fashionable heading of 'management competencies'.

- Adair (1989) acknowledges that while leadership can be trained there must be certain qualities present to make this possible.
- The approach has re-emerged in its modern version as 'charismatic leadership'.

Theories based on behaviour and style

The early rejection of the trait theories led researchers to seek other factors to explain leadership. Much of this research was conducted in the USA from the 1930s onwards, centred around the Universities of Iowa, Ohio and Michigan. The appeal of this approach to managers was that if a style or type of behaviour could be identified that was associated with effective leader behaviour then managers could be trained to behave accordingly. Much of the work is associated with the 'human relations' school of management.

The impetus for much of the work came from researchers at the University of Iowa who studied leadership styles in boys clubs. Leaders were identified as authoritarian (directive, impersonal and non-participative), democratic (discussion and contribution from the group) and *laissez-faire* (complete freedom given to the group). The democratic style was found to be the most successful.

The Ohio Studies   These were carried out in the immediate post-war period and involved both military personnel as well as managers from a range of organizations, including student leaders. The studies are presented in Stogdill and Coons (1957). Two significant leadership styles emerged:

- The **considerate style** emphasised concern for the employee's well-being and the building up of respect and rapport.
- The **initiating structure style** focused on getting the job done and emphasized goal attainment by setting standards and allocating resources.

The studies found that leaders could score high on both styles, low on both styles, or high on one and low on the other. It is generally agreed that scoring high on both consideration and initiating structure was the most effective form of leadership. However, the researchers acknowledged that other combinations could be equally effective dependent upon the situation. The study therefore ushered in the situational or contingency approach to leadership, discussed in the next section.

The Michigan Studies   The initial leadership studies at the University of Michigan took a similar approach to the Ohio team. Here two factors were also identified:

- The **employee- or relationship-oriented** leader was concerned for people and demonstrated a broad rather than a detailed approach to supervision.
- The **task-oriented** leader was concerned for task completion and was involved in planning, organizing and controlling rather than doing.

The studies found that dissatisfaction and labour turnover were highest where managers saw the task as more important than people and on the whole favoured the employee-centred style. However, as with the Ohio studies, the researchers did acknowledge that there were some situations in which a task-oriented style might be more effective.

The Ohio and Michigan studies were highly influential in the development of the human relations school of management thinking. A good summary of the Michigan studies can be found in Likert (1961). Likert himself took the studies a stage further in his development of the four systems of management/leadership. These were:

- **System 1 – exploitative autocratic**. The leader has no confidence and/or trust in subordinates.

- **System 2 – benevolent autocratic.** The leader has some confidence and trust and will occasionally seek opinions but ultimately makes all decisions.

- **System 3 – participative**. The leader shows confidence and trust in subordinates and seeks their opinion before making the decision.

- **System 4 – democratic**. The leader has complete trust in subordinates, seeks their views and makes use of their opinions in formulating decisions.

Likert's research in successful and unsuccessful teams concluded that Systems 3 and 4 were more likely to be associated with successful teams.

The managerial grid of Blake and Mouton   The work of Blake and Mouton (1964) was an extension of the Ohio studies. Their work culminated in the production of the **managerial grid,** identifying management styles according to concern for people and concern for production (see Figure 6.1)

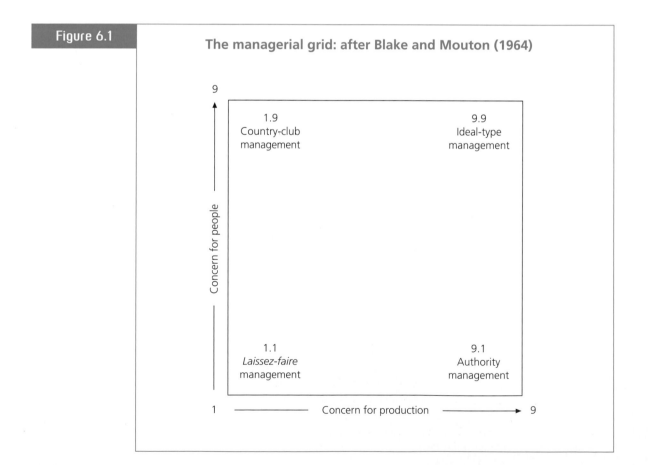

Figure 6.1

The managerial grid: after Blake and Mouton (1964)

Blake and Mouton argued that managers had one dominant style but that style could be varied and most had a back-up style if their preferred style failed to work. They argued that the preferred style was a function of the manager's own beliefs, their background and experience and the organization structure and processes. As such Blake and Mouton's grid could be classed as situational theory, which we introduce in the next section.

The conclusion drawn from Blake and Mouton was that the most effective leadership style was 9.9; the team management approach. Moreover, they developed training techniques to move managers towards a team management style.

However, there is little hard evidence to suggest that the 9.9 approach is the best for all situations and certain situations may favour a concern for people while others a concern for production.

Situational or contingency approaches

Almost all the work of the behavioural or style 'school', while suggesting that one approach to leadership may be the best for most situations, acknowledges that situational variables play an important part. The situational or **contingency approach** takes this a stage further by suggesting that leadership style and effectiveness may be contingent upon the factors in the situation within which it is practised. This does illustrate the difficulty of fitting theories into neat classifications.

Tannenbaum and Schmidt (1973) These researchers took the classification of leadership styles identified in the Iowa studies, namely autocratic (authoritarian), democratic and *laissez-faire* and identified how each approached decision-making in a different way. Thus:

- **Autocratic** leaders make the decisions and announce them to the groups.
- **Democratic** leaders involve employees much more in the decision-making processes.
- *Laissez-faire* leaders give employees complete freedom of action.

The researchers argued that there were three main influences on this process:

- The background, experience and confidence of the manager.
- The characteristics of the employees
- The nature of the task, the time available for its completion and the culture of the organization.

The introduction of situational variables extends the work of the behavioural/style school and this study is really a cross-over between that theoretical school and the situational/ contingency approach. Tannenbaum and Schmidt's argument was that the most effective leadership style was a function of the situation. However, their approach has its critics. A common criticism accuses the model of being a self-fulfilling prophecy, in that an autocratic leader may behave that way because he believes the employees to be incapable of contributing to decisions. This has the result of de-motivating employees, their performance drops still further and the opinion of the manager is confirmed.

Fiedler's contingency theory Fiedler (1967) found that effective leadership was a combination of four factors:

- **The leader's preferred style.** Fiedler believed that the leader's style was a function of his or her view of the least preferred co-worker (LPC). If this view was favourable then the preferred style was a concern for people, and if unfavourable the preferred style was a concern for the task. Fiedler believed that the style was a function of the leader's personality and could not be changed.

- **Leader–member relations.** These were identified as either good or poor. Good relations exist when the leader is confident, accepted by the group and has their loyalty. This places the leader in a strong position to influence group members. When relations are poor the leader resorts to getting things done by using his or her authority or position within the organization.

- **Task structure.** This is identified as being either structured or unstructrured. Structured jobs tend to be routine and simple and offer considerable power to the leader. Unstructured jobs tend to be more complex and favour a more democratic leadership style.

- **Leader position power.** This is identified as being either strong or weak. In general, the stronger the position power the more autocratic behaviour is tolerated by the group.

Fiedler believed that different kinds of leaders performed best under certain situations. For example, the leader has most control when leader–member relations are good, when the job is highly structured and when position power is strong. Fiedler identifies such situations as 'favourable'. On the other hand, when relations are poor, the job is unstructured and position power is weak, the leader struggles to maintain control and the situation is 'unfavourable'. Fiedler believed that task-oriented leaders performed best in situations that were either very favourable or very unfavourable to them. People-oriented leaders were most successful when the situation was neither favourable nor unfavourable.

However, given that the leader's style is fixed, if the style does not match the situation then either the leader must be changed or the situation must be changed, generally by attempting to change the relations between leaders and their groups.

Fiedler's theory has been generally supported by research but, in common with many contingency theories, it is difficult for the practising manager to apply.

Path-goal model This was developed by House and Mitchell (1974) as an attempt to add to the work of the style approaches. It is based on the belief that effective leaders assist their subordinates to learn appropriate types of behaviour, so that the subordinates are able to gain rewards for the satisfactory completion of a task.

Four styles of leadership are identified:

- **Directive.** Group members are offered specific guidance, given specific targets and a set of rules for the completion of a task.

- **Supportive.** Group members are shown concern and friendliness by the leader and assistance in achieving the task.

- **Achievement oriented.** Group members are persuaded to to accept challenging goals. The leader expresses confidence in the group.

- **Participative.** The leader consults with the group about what to do and how to do it and takes the group's views into account.

The appropriate style under this model depends upon:

- the group members abilities and personal needs;
- the nature of the task and the authority structure of the organization (termed as the 'environment').

Different styles work best in different situations. For example, directive leadership works best where the task is ambiguous or stressful and the group is generally inflexible. It works less well with high ability groups. A supportive style tends to work best where jobs are boring and repetitive or unpleasant. A participative style works best where the group is confident in their own abilities and the task is complex. However, House and Mitchell are keen to point out that there is no magic formula and managers must work out their most effective style given the prevailing situation. Some believe this to be less of a theory and a reliance on the manager's own intuition.

More recent approaches

The more recent approaches have tended to focus the need for leadership in complex, competitive and changing environments and the need to involve the group in the leadership process.

Transactional-transformational leadership   Kuhnert and Lewis (1987) see the standard approach to leadership as transactional, whereas the changing environment of business calls for a transformational approach. Much of traditional leadership theory has focused on transactional situations whereas modern organizations require a transformational approach.

- **Transactional** leaders allocate work, make routine decisions and monitor performance. The approach tends to work best where conditions are relatively stable, tasks are unambiguous and the employees have fairly traditional orientations to work in.

- **Transformational** leaders have the skills and personal qualities to recognize the need for change and identify the appropriate course of action. Transformational leadership is associated with charisma, vision, inspiring the group to change and achieve high performance. Transformational leadership works best under conditions of uncertainty and change.

Both the above approaches can be seen in the work of the Council for Excellence in Management and Leadership (2002). This body was established in 2000 by the UK government. Its report *Managers and leaders: raising our game* recognizes that the effective performance of organizations depends upon having management systems to deal with the complexities of the internal and external environments and having leaders to motivate and inspire employees to improved performance levels. The council has established a framework of 83 management and leadership abilities and has set out to establish research to uncover an improved theoretical base and a framework for leadership education and training that involves secondary schools, business schools and business organizations.

Is leadership necessary?

Thomas (2003) concludes that from all the many studies on leadership there is little in the way of useful conclusion and there is no real evidence that any of the researchers have demonstrated the key to leadership effectiveness. He feels that too much emphasis has been placed on groups and their performance and insufficient attention has been paid to the organizational and social context within which leaders operate. While his conclusions may be a little sweeping, he raises issues that lie at the heart of our Business in Context model, namely the organizational and environmental contexts.

Whereas the situational and contingency theorists saw the contexts of leadership as helping to shape outcomes, Thomas sees them simply in terms of constraints. He identifies a number of organizational constraints. However, as we see below, not all are constraints and it is probably best to define them as **organizational factors**.

- **Age.** The age of the organization may inhibit intervention by leaders to change. Leaders tend to be most effective in the early stages of an organization but those that follow later have difficulty in changing entrenched views and attitudes. We have seen in Chapter 4 that many of the policies of Hewlett Packard are directly attributable to its founders Bill Hewlett and Dave Packard.

- **Size.** The size of the organization affects the extent of the leader's influence. Large organizations are much more difficult to influence and change than small ones. Large complex organizations tend to have a complexity of tasks in different locations and requiring different expertise. These may all limit the ability of the leader to influence performance.

- **Structure.** This may facilitate or inhibit a leader's influence. In highly centralized structures, local leaders may have difficulty bringing about change or influencing performance, but those at the top may wield considerable influence on procedures throughout the organization.

- **Operating situation.** This can vary between stability and crisis. Thomas argues that leaders are seldom needed in stable situations and are most needed in times of crisis. The need for leaders in times of crisis accords with the modern view of the importance of leadership in complex, changing organizations. However, leaders may also be needed in stable situations where the motivation of the employees is an issue.

- **Employees.** They can resist attempts by leaders to influence them. This can be done through absenteeism or union action but most commonly through inertia.

In terms of the **environmental context** many factors lie outside the control of leaders. This was discussed in Chapter 3, when we examined the manager's ability to influence the environment of the firm. Our conclusion now is the same. The environment can be difficult to change, but managers can lead the organization in its adaptation to its environment and may even be successful in bringing influence to work to shape the environment to the advantage of the organization.

Case 6.2	**Executive pay in the UK – a review of current issues**

Each year the *Guardian* newspaper publishes a report on UK executive pay. This is based on the annual reports and accounts of companies in the FTSE-100 list and calculates the entire remuneration package including pay, bonuses, benefits, share options and so on. The findings of the 2003 report were published not long after headlines were grabbed by the decision of GlaxoSmithKline (GSK) to increase the remuneration of its chief executive, Jean-Pierre Garnier by 70 per cent a year and to guarantee him a pay-off on leaving of a package worth £22 million. Many newspapers referred to this as a 'platinum parachute'. The GSK case made the headlines because, in an unprecedented move, the shareholders voted against the proposals at the annual general meeting of the company. The vote was part of a new procedure requiring shareholders to vote on remuneration issues. Opposition was also voiced at the AGMs of HSBC, Barclays, Reuters and Granada, but in none of those cases was there a 51 per cent vote against, as in the case of GSK. The GSK shareholders were angry that the share price of the company had fallen and that it had underperformed alongside its major competitors. However, their vote could not force the company to change since the decision and policy had already been made. The purpose of the vote appeared to be intended simply to ratify a board decision. The force of the rejection did, however, force the company to review its policy.

The issue at GSK is not unique. J.-P. Garnier was only the 11th best paid executive according to the *Guardian* report. For the year 2002 the average remuneration package of executive directors was £1.7 million with a basic salary average of £600 000. One hundred and ninety directors were paid in excess of £1 million and in some companies, such as BP, Unilever and Tesco, several executives earned more than £1 million. The highest paid director earned £9 million. In 2002 executive director pay rose 23 per cent against an average earnings increase of just over 3 per cent and an average fall in the share price of the FTSE-100 of 24 per cent. Since 2000, executive director pay has risen by 84 per cent on average while the share price fell 50 per cent during the same period.

There are arguments why senior executives should be paid such large amounts. The remuneration packages are not out of line with those paid to USA executives. This was an argument used by GSK in comparing itself with Merck and Pfizer. It is argued that high levels of pay are required to recruit the best international talent, which is in short supply and to prevent the best UK talent from being poached by overseas competitors. An argument, often put by chief executives themselves, is that innovative inspirational leadership with responsibility for shareholders, employees and customers is high pressure, high risk and should be commensurate with high rewards. J.-P. Garnier of GSK did not consider himself overpaid. In an interview with the *Daily Telegraph* on 21 May, 2003, he stated, 'I didn't seek this contract . . . I accepted it . . . I'm not Mother Teresa. This is a highly competitive business.'

The argument over top executive pay raises a number of issues.

- The size of the pay award compared to that received by others in the organization, especially the shopfloor.
- The pay-offs promised or made to directors of poor performing companies such as GSK, Royal Sun Alliance and Abbey National.
- The amount companies invest in the pension pots of existing and retired directors. For example, the retired chief executive of GSK, Sir Richard Sykes, has £15.2 million set aside to yield an annual retirement income of £729,000. Such pension payments are approved by existing directors, who are doubtless seeking such payments when they retire.

- There is also the issue of general principle, whether anyone is worth pay in the millions.

The events of 2003 have caused considerable concern from a number of stakeholders. The issue must be viewed against a wider background. As well as the debate over executive pay, there have been accounting and corporate governance scandals at ENRON and WorldCom, many have lost their jobs in corporate down-sizing initiatives and many have seen their own pension funds significantly eroded by the dramatic fall in the stock market.

Shareholders are normally passive. They have always been able to vote against the annual report and accounts but have rarely done so. The majority, the institutional shareholders are rarely concerned with corporate governance and executive pay and rarely vote, preferring the direct route of selling their shares when there is something they do not like. However, the all-round fall in stock market prices and the opportunity to vote on remuneration issues has made them keener, less disinterested stakeholders.

There would also appear to be a widening gap between directors and the shopfloor. The MORI annual poll in June 2003 showed that the majority of employees, including managers, believed that the directors of large companies were untrustworthy and overpaid. Moreover 75 per cent of those polled feared that their pensions would not be honoured when they retire. A 2002 report by Mercer Human Resource Consulting found that only 40 per cent of employees trusted their management and, significantly, the lack of trust increased with length of service. Caulkin (2003) sees a paradox between the lack of trust expressed by employees and the rhetoric of corporate social responsibility. He states, 'the higher you go the less managers understand about the work and the more likely their interventions are to destabilize it.'

The UK government has expressed its concern over executive pay but so far has restrained from legislation. The view of the then Trade and Industry Secretary, Patricia Hewitt, was that companies must put their own house in order. A recently commissioned report on non-executive directors (the *Higgs Report*) recommends that the setting of pay of senior executives should take into account what shopfloor workers are paid. GSK has taken some steps to put its house in order. A number of non-executive directors have been removed and Deloitte Touche have been asked to review the whole issue of executive pay. A spokesperson for the company admitted that GSK had 'misjudged the *zeitgeist*'.

Source: *Guardian* Report on Executive Pay 2003; Caulkin, 2003; www.guardian.co.uk/executivepay

Questions

1 If leaders are to inspire and innovate and are in short supply should not the salaries of top executives reflect this?

2 What arguments can you give in terms of management and leadership roles and functions to support the claim that senior executives should be well rewarded?

3 To what extent is it fair that the price of shares should be used as an argument in the determination of executive pay?

4 To what extent do you agree with the Caulkin argument that a gulf has been created between board members and the rest? What can senior management do to restore trust?

Summary

- While management is 'getting things done through other people' and 'pulling it all together' to meet organizational and environmental demands, there are difficulties associated with any definition. This is due largely to the weak body of knowledge and the large variation in the types of management work.
- The legitimacy of the manager is based on a number of things including property rights, law, various forms of power and an underlying value system.
- A number of different theories and models of management have emerged at different times. However, for the most part we can question their rationality and their untility.
- There have been many attempts to identify what managers do and construct models around this, but several linkages can be found to the more classical approaches.
- Leadership is considered a key element of modern management and is especially important in times of rapid change and intense competition.
- There have been many attempts to develop an appropriate theory of leadership, most of which have only limited application.
- In keeping with the Business in Context model, we may conclude that both management and leadership are best viewed within an organizational and environmental context.

Discussion questions

1 Consider the roles of the chief executive of a major global corporation, the canteen manager at a manufacturing plant and a university head of department. To what extent can these three be called managers? What roles and activities do they have in common and how do they differ?

2 Why should we do what manager's tell us to do? What kinds of power do the three examples in question 1 possess?

3 Critically examine the various models of managers. Which do you consider the most relevant and why?

4 Why do managers seek gurus and follow fashions in management practice?

5 What conclusions do you draw from the studies on the work managers do? Contrast these findings with Fayol's principles of management' in Table 6.1. Do such studies invalidate much of management theory?

6 To what extent is leadership different from management?

7 Why is leadership such a focus of concern amongst management professional bodies and with governments?

8 Critically assess the various theories of leadership. Which do you find most relevant and why?

Further reading

Reasonably good reviews of the various approaches to management and leadership can be found in Boddy, D. (2002) *Management: An Introduction*, FT/Prentice Hall, Harlow. Sheldrake, J. (2003) *Management Theory*, 2nd edn, Thomson, London offers an excellent tour through the various management writers and their models and theories. An interesting study of management with some excellent illustrations and thought-provoking comment is found in Watson, T. J. (1994) *In Search of Management: Culture, Chaos and Control in Management Work,* Routledge, London. A critical account of most aspects of management and leadership can be found in Thomas, A. B. (2003) *Controversies in Management: Issues, Debates, Answers*, 2nd edn, Routledge, London. Robbins, S. P. (2003) *Organizational Behaviour*, 10th edn, Prentice Hall, Upple Saddle River, NJ offers good summaries of the various theories of leadership.

7

Management strategy

Learning objectives At the end of this chapter you should be able to:

- Explain the strengths and weaknesses of the different approaches to strategy and how they interact.
- Assess the uses of strategy in different organization contexts.
- Use simple models to assess the general and immediate competitive environments of an organization and demonstrate the limitations of such models.
- Illustrate the links between strategy, goals, structure, ownership, size and culture at the level of the firm.
- Explain the concepts and assess the value of resource analysis, core competence, value chain and portfolio analysis.
- Explain the various kinds of strategic option and demonstrate the basis for the selection of a particular strategy in different situations.

Introduction

Management strategy as a linking process between environmental and organizational variables is a fundamental aspect of our Business in Context model. We can examine the various business functions, R&D, the production of goods and services, marketing, HRM, and finance and accounting through their relevant management strategies. In Chapter 1 of this book we highlighted the cases of the European car industry (Case 1.1) and News International (Case 1.2), both representative of the exercise of strategic options in the face of external and internal opportunities and constraints in the two industries concerned.

Management strategy contains a number of interrelated elements:

- It involves consideration of environmental changes which bring about new opportunities and pose new threats.
- It is concerned with the assessment of the internal strengths and weaknesses of the institution and, in particular, its ability to respond to those opportunities and threats.
- Management strategy is the product of a decision-making process influenced by the values, preferences and power of interested parties. We examined some of the issues involved in this in our discussion of management in the previous chapter.

● Management strategy is concerned with generating options and evaluating them.

Management strategy is, therefore, an all-embracing term dealing with goals and object-ives, the firm's environment, its resources and structure, the scope and nature of its activities and ultimately the behaviour of its members. Given the large number of variables involved and the considerable subjectivity of the decision-making process, strategy for-mulation is a highly complex process. The approach used by management texts (including, to a certain extent, this book) is to reduce such complexity to a series of steps. While this is understandable, it can both oversimplify and give the impression that management strategy is a logical process. Whittington notes that in 1993 there were 37 books in print in the UK with 'strategic management' in the title. He writes,

> There is a basic implausibility about these books. If the secrets of corporate strategy could be acquired for £25, then we would not pay our top managers so much . . . .
> (*Whittington, 1993, p. 1*)

In this chapter we deal with the various elements of management strategy and attempt, wherever possible, to draw attention to the more subjective and political aspects. We begin by examining the nature of strategy, through the way strategy is formed. We refer to this as the strategic process. We then look at the different contexts in which strategic decisions are taken, and go on to identify the various environmental and organizational aspects of management strategy. We end the chapter by examining a number of common strategic options, and a brief look at the criteria for strategic choice.

We prefer to use the term 'management strategy' since most strategies in organizations originate from the management group. The concept crops up in many guises and is some-times referred to as 'business policy', 'corporate strategy', 'corporate planning' and so on. Although attempts have been made to formulate distinctions between such terms, the general interchangeability of their use indicates a similarity in approach.

The strategic process

An examination of how strategy is formed gives us useful insights into the nature of strat-egy itself. We identify five different approaches, which we have termed rational, flexible, creative, behavioural and incremental, and a sixth which suggests that some managers operate without a conscious strategy. We deal with each in turn.

Key concept 7.1 The strategic process

The strategic process refers to the way in which management strategy is formed. In most organizations this involves a mixture of scientific and rational analysis together with more subjective and political considerations.

The rational approach

This is the classical approach to strategy and is typified by the work of Ansoff (1968) and Porter (1980, 1985). Strategy formulation is portrayed as a scientific and highly rational process, assisted by a range of techniques such as technological forecasting, portfolio

Figure 7.1	An analysis of the strengths, weaknesses, opportunities and threats of Swot United, a Third Division football club

Opportunities	Threats
Promotion to other divisions	Seven other professional clubs operating in a 25-mile radius
Increased revenue from success in cup competitions	Rising costs of wages and transfer fees, bank interest charges, policing, equipment
Sale of town-centre site and redevelopment on the outskirts	Local authority refusing planning permission
Development of a membership squash club and fitness centre attached to the ground	Best players may leave
Use of ground for other functions, e.g. rock concerts	Competitions for spectators' time and money from other sources, e.g. cinema, DIY
Development of retailing activities	Increased levels of unemployment in the area

Strengths	Weaknesses
The club owns its own ground and car parks in a good town-centre site	Large bank overdraft
Good housekeeping and relatively low wages	Ground facilities in poor order, especially seating and toilets
A hard core of 2000 loyal supporters	Insufficient funds to invest in higher wages and transfer fees
A successful and well established youth development policy	A relatively small population to support so many clubs in close proximity
The image of a 'friendly' club with good connections in local history	Poor image compared with First Division neighbours

analysis, environmental impact analysis and sensitivity analysis. The aim of such techniques is generally profit maximization (Whittington, 1993). The rational approach owes much to the development of contingency theory. In Chapter 1 we noted that the contingency approach stressed the importance of a strategic fit between the firm and its environment. Analyses are made of a firm's environment to assess likely opportunities and threats, and of its internal resource position to identify strengths and weaknesses. This process is sometimes referred to as **SWOT analysis**, an acronym for strengths, weaknesses, opportunities and threats. An illustration of the kind of analysis that can be made is offered in Figure 7.1. There are disadvantages with this kind of approach.

● The approach is based upon the assumption that information is readily available to the strategist and an accurate assessment can be made of its likely impact on the firm. In reality, knowledge is often imperfect.

- The environment of modern business is often highly complex and dynamic. This makes assessment of opportunities and threats difficult.

- Complexity and lack of information do not just apply to the environment. Management can often be unaware of the real strengths and weaknesses of their own organization.

- In scanning the environment, management is often collecting the same information as rival firms. As a result, similar strategies occur and there may be a lack of truly innovative solutions. The focus is on the environment rather than on the creation of distinctive competencies and on the needs of the individual customer.

- As we saw in Chapter 5, processes of decision-making are both subjective and political, attracting the criticism of 'pseudo-science'.

Despite these criticism the rational approach can be useful in that it collects relevant data, it can give direction, it has a certain face validity and, as Whittington (1993) argues, it can serve as a form of group therapy. Despite such criticisms the rational approach to strategy is popular and is the basis of many texts. It can be a useful starting point, provided managements are aware of its limitations.

Key concept 7.2 SWOT analysis

SWOT stands for strengths, weaknesses, opportunities and threats. It is normally associated with more rational approaches to strategy formulation but perhaps its greatest contribution lies in providing the management strategist and student of business a broad framework for analysing the position of a firm at a particular moment in time. It can also be useful in the development of a number of strategic options which attempt to tackle opportunities and threats, build on corporate strengths and avoid weaknesses. An important consideration is that for most management there is a choice of strategy.

In the 1960s and 70s the emergence of an increasingly complex and turbulent business environment called for modifications in the rational approach.

The flexible approach

The complexity and volatility of the environment may mean that a detailed SWOT analysis is both difficult and inappropriate and profit maximization may be an inappropriate strategy. The environment may be changing so rapidly that many of the historical and current data are meaningless. This kind of situation led the oil companies, like Shell, to adopt a different approach to strategy formulation known as 'scenario planning'. The approach recognizes that uncertainty can never be eliminated, but it can be reduced by plotting different scenarios, each responding to alternative visions of the future. Managements are therefore prepared for a number of possible changes that may occur. Writers such as Williamson (1991) argue that, under such conditions, the best that managers can hope for is to maximize the chances of survival by cutting costs to become more efficient (survival of the fittest) and by playing the market. A good example of the latter is offered by Whittington (1993) citing Sony, who, in the 1980s, produced 160 different models of the

Walkman for the USA market, but retained only about 20 models on the market at any one time (survival of the most popular).

The creative approach

This takes the flexible approach one step further by stressing the importance of imagination in the strategic process. The idea that such an approach to strategy formulation is actually better has been taken up by management writers in the 1980s. Peters and Waterman believe that the more formal approaches to strategy formulation with the emphasis on complex environmental and organizational analysis can lead to 'paralysis through analysis' (Peters and Waterman, 1982, p. 31). The resulting policies are often too conservative, insufficiently adventurous or positive, and ignore the human contribution. Their 'excellent' companies are typified by a strategic planning approach which recognizes the values of the decision-makers as one of the driving forces giving the firm its competitive edge. The more complex and changing the business environment and the more difficult the problems facing managers, the more creative they need to be.

The behavioural approach

There is strong support for the view that strategy formulation is far from being a rational, logical process (Cyert and March, 1963; Mintzberg and Quinn, 1991). Instead, strategic choice is the product of the organization's dominant coalition, invariably senior management, and is based upon its values, ideologies and personalities, and upon the process of organization power and politics. The process invariably involves some negotiation between senior management and other groups. The most overt of these processes take place at shareholders' meetings and in collective bargaining with trade unions. However, the most significant negotiations generally take place between competing factions within management itself, over such issues as the allocation of scarce resources, and are consequently much more difficult to observe. Behavioural analyses of the strategy formulation see management values and objectives as more than individual inputs to the planning process. They influence the way the environment is perceived and, hence, the choice of opportunities and threats and the assessment of strengths and weaknesses. Because of the bargaining processes involved, the outcomes of the behavioural approach to strategy are likely to be satisficing rather than maximizing.

The incremental approach

This approach has much in common with the behavioural approach. Strategy is not a carefully prepared plan with clear goals, but a process by which management in the organization gradually come to terms with the firm's environment. Limited objectives are constantly modified in the light of experience and through the process of negotiation between interested parties. As a consequence, strategies are continually being changed. The incremental approach has been put forward as a more realistic and more effective method of dealing with complex and changing situations. The concept originated from the work of Lindblom (1959) in an article appropriately titled 'The science of muddling through'. Although his work was mainly concerned with large public sector organizations such as hospitals and universities, there are strong parallels with larger private sector firms. Mintzberg (1990) has sympathy with this perspective and sees many strategies emerging as opposed to being consciously planned. This gives rise to notions of strategic learning as management builds up a repertoire of effective strategies on the basis of what has worked in the past.

An absence of strategy?

Finally, we present the view that strategy formulation is not a conscious management activity. Strategy is not an issue when firms appear to be operating to the satisfaction of management. It becomes an issue only in times of crisis when any attempt at strategy formulation may be too little and too late. There may be several reasons for this. Management may be complacent and reluctant to rock the boat or they may have myopic vision and hence a limited view of alternatives (see Levitt, 1960, and a discussion of the concept of 'marketing myopia' in Chapter 11). It may be that managements are too distracted by the daily business of survival and see themselves too weighed down by resource constraints to contemplate strategic options.

The various approaches we have identified reveal a mixture of rational and non-rational approaches to the formulation of management strategy. Nevertheless, strategies are more than management hunches played out in an information vacuum. More likely, management select what information is appropriate for their purposes, and this invariably involves consideration of both environmental and organizational variables. Management values and organization politics are important not only in the choice of strategy but in the selection of information upon which that strategy is based. All six of the approaches we have identified may operate together in the same firm. The following illustration reveals this mixed approach to strategic decision-making.

Partners and office staff in a firm of solicitors have experienced a number of problems with their computerized client record and accounts system. The firm were one of the first to install such a system, but the growth of the firm and the increasing complexity of its growing international business have meant that the existing software cannot cope. One of the newer partners joined the organization from a rival firm, and he was particularly impressed with the system used there. He spends several months persuading his fellow partners that it may be a good idea to change systems. The process of persuasion is accompanied by the gathering of information to show the growth of the firm over the past few years and illustrations are well chosen to show the advantages of the new system in terms of faster information retrieval and better management information on the current status of client accounts. Information is also collected on the cost of the proposed software and the new hardware needed to support it. The office practice manager also presents information on the cost, strengths and weaknesses of rival systems. Quotations are sought from a few computer firms with experience of installing such systems and in servicing professional firms. The partners agree to go ahead with the proposal. A more recent convert to the idea, one of the senior partners, uses his influence to promote and eventually engage a firm of computer consultants. This firm has been set up by the brother of a senior partner in another law firm and he has successfully installed the chosen system in that firm.

The above illustration reinforces the notion of strategy as both an intellectual exercise in information gathering and presentation and a political exercise involving values, power and influence. In this case, the situation was a relatively straightforward investment decision with implications for office practice. Strategic decisions to enter a new product market or change radically the structure of the organization involve even greater complexities.

Figure 7.2	Approaches and styles of management strategy		

Approach	Style		
	Formalized planning	Entrepreneurial	Negotiation and consultation
Rational	X		
Flexible	X	X	
Creative		X	X
Behavioural			X
Incremental			X

Apart from these six approaches, we can identify three broad planning styles: formalized planning, negotiation and consultation, and entrepreneurship (a similar model is offered by Mintzberg, 1973). In Figure 7.2 we show how these different planning styles interact with the first five of the strategic approaches.

The suitability of a particular planning style may depend on the size and nature of the firm. For example, a formal planning system is more likely to be found in a large firm. Smaller firms by their very nature will favour an entrepreneurial style, and a high degree of consultation will be found in larger public sector organizations. Moreover, different styles may be appropriate for different functions. While formalized planning may be a key feature of operations strategy, an R&D strategy may benefit more from an entrepreneurial approach. Where trade union influence is considerable, management may need to proceed more through consultation.

Both the approaches and styles may change over time. A university which has operated through a mixture of an incremental approach and a consultative style may, when faced with the kind of threats identified in Case 7.3, need to operate in a much more entrepreneurial way. Indeed, at certain stages of their development, all organizations may require such entrepreneurial inputs to survive (Mintzberg, 1973). The role of the entrepreneur is usually associated with discussions of small businesses. It is our contention that entrepreneurial activity is equally important in large firms too, a theme we develop in Chapter 9.

Strategic contexts

We have identified how managers may employ different approaches to the task of strategy formulation. In addition we can identify various contexts in which the strategic process operates.

● Strategy is not the sole preserve of the profit-making organization. All organizations have strategies, formalized to a greater or lesser extent. We can see strategies at work in such diverse organizations as businesses, schools, the police, charities, professional football clubs and the church. In recent years there has been a focus on management strategies in the public sector. The health service has actively recruited its area managers from industry and commerce in an attempt to introduce a more businesslike approach, including a greater emphasis on strategy formulation. In Case 7.3 we present the case of the new universities. For a number of years they have operated in a changing environment and have needed to formulate a different kind of strategy.

- We may differentiate between those strategies pertaining to entire industries, such as shipping or **machine tools**, strategies employed by firms operating in a number of different business markets, such as Unilever and GM, and strategies pertaining to those operating in a single or restricted product market. Cases 7.1 and 7.2 illustrate the strategic process at the level of an entire industry and within a multinational corporation respectively.

- The distinction is sometimes drawn between a **corporate** and **business** strategy. A corporate strategy is employed by those firms operating in a number of different businesses; it focuses on issues relating to the overall business mix and helps identify the type of businesses management could pursue. A business strategy deals with a single business and concentrates on issues relating to successful competition. A multi-divisional firm like GM therefore operates both corporate and business strategies.

- We may identify strategies operating at different levels of the organization from broad strategies at the top, moving through a series of successive stages towards strategies for specific functional areas like HRM and marketing, and finally to individual targets and budgets.

The uses and value of strategy

We can identify several reasons for management to engage in strategy formulation:

- Strategy assists in the formulation of goals and objectives and enables them to be modified in the light of information and experience.

- Strategy is a form of management control. It is a plan that guides behaviour along a predetermined route. At the operational level it results in budgets and targets.

- A clear strategy both assists in the process of allocating resources and may provide a rationale for that allocation so that it is perceived to be fair by organization members.

- It enables management to identify key strategic issues that the firm may face in the future and prepare appropriate action.

- Strategy performs a useful role in guiding the action of the constituent parts of the organization as well as acting as an integrating mechanism ensuring units work together. The integrating power of strategy is a central feature of 'strong' corporate cultures as illustrated by firms such as IBM and HP.

- Leading on from that, strategy formulation can be an important element in the process of social change. Strategic objectives are achieved by changing the behaviour of employees. This is the essence of organizational development programmes used by such companies as Shell and part of the current vogue for the creation of a strong corporate culture.

- The formulation of strategy is seen as a useful training ground for the development of future managers.

We have already questioned the extent to which formalized strategy is used by firms. An even more important consideration is the extent to which the existence of a formalized strategy contributes to organizational success. Studies suggest that those companies using some form of strategic planning process perform better than those who do not, and where data are available they tend to show that the introduction of strategic planning methods leads to improvements in performance. (A good summary of a number of studies in this area is presented in Hofer and Schendel (1978)). However, Greenley (1990) in his review of the link between strategy and performance, found very few studies showing a positive correlation. There would appear to be two problems:

- The difficulty with all such studies is the problem of isolating and measuring the effect of strategic planning on performance, be it return on investment (ROI), market share or some other criterion. A firm's financial and market performance, even over time, may be influenced by so many variables outside the control of management that causal links between strategy and performance may be difficult to show.

- The relationship is complicated in that performance may well influence strategy rather than the other way around. A firm that has been highly profitable may be stimulated into seeking new investment opportunities either through new product development or acquisition. Conversely, a firm incurring significant losses may well be limited in its strategic options and have them determined by people external to the firm such as bank managers or liquidators. In this case the firm's performance is the reason for pursuing a divestment strategy, involving the closure or sale of the least profitable parts.

The environmental aspects of strategy

In the last section we suggested that it was often difficult to establish a clear link between strategy and performance because of the great number of influences at work. Much of that complexity may be attributed to the firm's environment.

The firm's environment is of course a key aspect of our Business in Context model. In Chapter 1 we introduced the notion of contingency theory and the belief that a firm's performance was dependent upon it achieving a strategic fit between itself and the environment in which it operates. In Chapters 3 and 4 we identified, with the use of selected examples, significant aspects of the business environment. We noted how these aspects influenced and, in turn, were influenced by businesses. We further suggested that these elements not only interact with business but with each other, resulting, for most firms, in an environment that is highly complex and changing. In this and the previous two chapters we have already noted how that complexity is further complicated by the values of decision-makers and the internal structures and politics of organizations. The strategist's task of making sense of the environment is therefore a very difficult assignment.

We can identify two aspects of the environment that may influence strategy as follows:

- There are those issues that affect all firms operating in a given business environment. These are many of the issues we raised in Chapters 3 and 4 and may include the state of the economy, the nature of the labour force, changing technology, government policy and social and cultural influences. This is called the **general environment**.

- There are those factors that have direct bearing on the firm's competitive position, which we will call the **immediate competitive environment**. An analysis of both these environments will enable management to arrive at some assessment of the major opportunities and threats facing the organization.

The general environment

An analysis of a firm's general environment is sometimes known as **environmental scanning**, and usually comprises some sort of assessment of the key environmental influences, how they interact with the firm and with each other and how they change over time. There are many difficulties with such an analysis. Some managers tackle the sheer complexity of the environment by generating masses of information, not all of which is relevant and not all of which is accurate. The use of computers has increased the capacity for information handling and, in some firms, managers can be submerged in a sea of data, much of which has only marginal relevance to their needs. At the other extreme there are those who either ignore the environment completely or who have a very blinkered perception of the firm's relationship to it. In such a situation key trends can be missed, and the firm either cedes opportunities to its competitors or is unprepared for changes when they occur.

Our analysis of the general environment is based on a model that classifies the environment as simple and static, dynamic, or complex (Johnson and Scholes, 2002). We deal with each in turn.

Simple and static

Firms operating in a relatively simple and static environment can generally rely on management strategies that are based on historical data. Customer needs and hence sales forecasting can generally be predicted from past records. A company producing Christmas cards knows precisely that demand will peak at the end of the calendar year and will have a good idea of the size of that demand. Similarly, fireworks manufacturers in the UK knew that demand would peak before bonfire night in November each year. However, there is a danger that managers become complacent and the survival of the business may be jeopardized by sudden and unexpected changes, as with a change in the law making the sale of certain types of firework illegal. Other changes can creep up on management. The Christmas card market has become highly competitive, with many new entrants, including charities and societies. The fireworks market has changed too, with a movement towards public displays and a more general use in celebrations all year round. Even simple and static environments may not be so simple or so static.

Dynamic

A dynamic environment changes quickly and frequently. Managers operating in this environment generally need to be sensitive to the environment and predict those changes that are likely to occur. The home computer market has been particularly dynamic. In the UK, Sinclair was first to the market but failed to maintain the required product development and found its market taken by such as Amstrad, which initially was sensitive to, and even helped create, changing consumer needs. In its turn, Amstrad has been replaced by such as Packard Bell, offering attractive all-in packages and forging important alliances with the major computer superstores. Newer entrants, such as Dell, have based their rapid growth on selling directly to the customer through mail order. In such a dynamic market household names quickly come and go. Businesses that fail in dynamic environments are generally those where managements have failed to see the changes which are occurring or are either unable or unwilling to take appropriate action.

The case of professional soccer in England and Wales is one where an entire industry lost ground to a variety of competitors for its customers' time and money, and the general trend towards declining attendance and hence revenue seemed irreversible 10 years ago. The football authorities tackled the problem, in part, by the creation of an elite Premier League and by insisting on major ground improvements for the top clubs, including the creation of all-seater stadiums. A lucrative television deal for the Premier League was struck with a leading satellite television company and the clubs imported a variety of international stars from other countries. The result has been a major turnaround for the leading clubs, with capacity attendances for most matches and a vast increase in profits. This, in turn, has led to a rise in wages and much greater mobility among players. Increased mobility is a function of an EU ruling giving players freedom of movement at the end of a contract, where previously clubs could demand a transfer fee. In the main, clubs have had to make rapid adjustments to rising costs through increased prices and the growth of merchandising club shirts and other products. Some of the larger clubs have shops on the scale of mini-department stores. For the other, non-elite clubs the position has worsened. Attendances have continued to fall and the importing of overseas talent has reduced potential transfer revenue. With falling revenue, such clubs are unable to make the necessary investments to offer an acceptable product to an increasingly demanding clientele. In Chapter 13 we examine football finances as a case in accounting and finance.

Dynamic environments require entrepreneurs who have the vision to spot opportunities and the motivation to pursue them. They are also suited to more creative approaches to strategy. However, there may be a danger that management could respond unnecessarily to changes in a dynamic environment. For example, some firms, when threatened by new entrants offering much cheaper products in the same market, respond by launching a cheaper version of their own product. This not only shows a lack of faith in the quality of the firm's original product, but it will inevitably take sales away from that product and have a potentially damaging effect on the firm's reputation.

Complex

A complex environment is one in which different demands are placed upon different aspects of the firm's operation. A firm producing a range of different products for different markets could be said to be operating in a complex environment. Most firms in such situations reflect this complexity in their organization structures. We saw in Chapter 4 how the development of the multi-divisional firm was a direct response to the problems faced by emerging multinational corporations like GM in the 1920s. The problem facing firms in a complex environment is the extent to which the complexity needs to be accommodated by organizational changes. Some firms attempt to reduce the complexity by restructuring, which may include selling off some of its constituent units. Such action is a common feature of mergers and acquisitions and will be dealt with later in this chapter.

In the case of dynamic and complex environments a firm faces a number of interconnected problems related to the degree of change, the speed of change, the complexity of
its environment and the corresponding complexity of the organization. Managers tend to
seek to reduce such uncertainty as much as they can by a variety of measures.

● The uncertainty may be reduced by collecting relevant information. We have already
  noted the problems associated with collecting accurate information and with
  information overload.

● As we saw in Chapter 3, managers will attempt to influence and control the
  environment. This can be done by a variety of measures such as technological
  innovation, forming coalitions with other organizations, political lobbying, acquiring
  raw material suppliers or retail outlets, stockpiling materials and equipment, training
  staff in rare skills, and so on.

● New structures and procedures, such as planning and forecasting, may be set up to
  cope with uncertainty. There are, however, dangers with setting up new structures.
  The establishment of specialist units can create its own problems of cooperation and
  integration. In the early days of computing in business, the creation of specialist
  groups of programmers and analysts led to tensions and conflict (Pettigrew, 1973).
  In Chapters 4 and 9, we can see how attempts by the Japanese to set up research
  consortia for each industry have not been an unqualified success.

The immediate competitive environment

We will attempt to locate a business in its immediate competitive environment using the
model devised by Porter (1980), as shown in Figure 7.3. Porter has identified five forces,

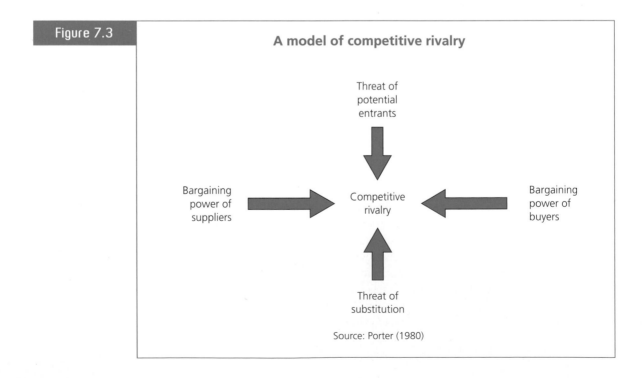

Figure 7.3

A model of competitive rivalry

Threat of
potential
entrants

Bargaining
power of
suppliers

Competitive
rivalry

Bargaining
power of
buyers

Threat of
substitution

Source: Porter (1980)

which have immediate bearing on a firm's competitive position. We explain and illustrate these forces in turn.

The threat of potential entrants

The threat of entry is related to the ease with which a new business can establish itself in the same product market. The relative ease with which new restaurants emerge in a large urban area like London suggests that the threat to existing restauranteurs is very real. However, the ease of entry means increased competition and can result in a highly volatile market, to which the death rate of new restaurants will testify.

The threat posed by potential entrants is reduced if there are barriers to entry. These can operate in a number of different ways, as follows:

- Equipment and associated capital requirements place heavy burdens on investment and firms may have to withstand considerable unit cost disadvantages initially. Such difficulties would be presented to firms attempting to enter mass car production or oil refining. It would be difficult for newcomers to achieve sufficient economies of scale to recover their outlay in a reasonable time.
- These difficulties can be increased where access to raw materials is an additional problem.
- In some types of industry, breaking into a market is difficult owing to the considerable customer loyalty to existing products and brands. A soft drinks manufacturer attempting to launch a 'cola'-type product would have considerable difficulty persuading the market to switch from Coca Cola or Pepsi Cola.
- In the industrial components industry, getting customers to switch may pose the additional difficulties of part compatibility.
- Such barriers may be further compounded by the difficulty of obtaining access to channels of distribution. Our soft drinks manufacturer may have considerable difficulty persuading the major supermarket chains to stock its products.
- Patents held by existing manufacturers can pose a significant obstacle to those wishing to enter the market with imitative products. The patents on the drugs librium and valium owned by Hoffman-La Roche have enabled the firm to establish a monopoly position in the tranquillizer market. Similarly, patents held by Poluroid posed difficulties for firms such as Kodak to enter the instant camera market.
- In a more general way the operating experience gained by existing firms over a number of years can place the newcomer at a significant disadvantage.

Apart from the threat of new entrants, competitive rivalry can be heightened among existing competitors if the general growth rate of the industry is slow and if there are many firms of similar size with a relatively undifferentiated product range.

We should not forget that there are barriers to exit as well as barriers to entry. A large manufacturing company with considerable operating losses, but with many employees and a significant investment in plant and machinery, will undoubtedly face pressures to stay in business. Such pressures will be related to the extent of the firm's assets, which may not be recoverable if the firm closes. This fear of lost investment may only be one factor. Senior management may be particularly attached to the company, emotionally as well as financially, and place a high value on its survival, despite market and financial evidence to the contrary. Pressures will undoubtedly come from the local community and, in the case of some firms, from the national government, fearing the effect of closure on local and national economies and on levels of unemployment. In the case of some firms such as British Leyland and Rolls Royce, in the UK during the 1970s, government pressure was accompanied by significant government investment to ensure the survival of these companies. Barriers to exit operate in small firms as well, where there is likely to be an even greater ego involvement on the part of the owner-managers and a subsequent reluctance to accept forced closure in the face of market forces.

The threat of substitution

Substitution occurs where a consumer is able to replace your product with a different type of product performing the same service or satisfying similar needs. The cotton textile industry in Britain was not only threatened by new entrants from cheap labour economies but also by the development of substitute products in the form of man-made fibres. We have already identified some of the threats facing the professional football industry. A major threat has been the growth of substitute activities such as sport on television, active rather than passive participation in sport, and the growing popularity of DIY. Rail travel in the USA declined as airlines opened up local networks and assisted in the establishment of local airports. The size of the country meant that air travel was perceived as a more effective means of covering large distances. Distances are less of a problem in the UK, yet rail companies face competition from bus companies, competing on price and from a growing network of local air traffic, competing on the basis of speed and comparative price.

The bargaining power of buyers

Buyer power increases where there are a large number of firms offering the same or substitute products, especially where there is little or no cost involved for the buyer in switching from one supplier to another. A restaurateur in central London faces considerable competition from the large number of other restaurants operating in that area, as well as other attractions competing for the potential client's disposable income. In such situations the product/market strategy of the restaurant becomes of utmost importance. Such strategies will include considerations of product differentiation and quality, market segmentation, price and promotion (Chapter 11 has a fuller account of these strategies). In the industrial components industry, particularly where specialist components are involved, the relationship may be different. There may have been a mutual accommodation of product changes over a number of years and such a strong relationship forged that the cost of switching would be high. Components suppliers often invest time and energy building up such relationships with customers. In such situations a threat still exists if the customer firm's acquisition strategy takes in a similar components supplier.

The buyer–supplier relationship is highly complex and involves most facets of our Business in Context model. The complexity of the technology plays a major part, as does the competitiveness of the market. We saw in our discussion of Japanese management, in Chapter 4, that a mix of cultural and economic factors was also significant. As part of their normal business strategy, Japanese industrial firms operating in Britain rely heavily upon sub-contractors to supply components, and tend to build up close relationships with these suppliers. With British government backing, Japanese manufacturing companies have tended to locate in areas of low economic activity. This automatically places such firms in a strong bargaining position with respect to the local components industry.

The power of a buyer generally increases the more he or she buys. This power can be exercised in the demand for discounts or the expectation of preferential treatment in the supply of goods. A factor to consider here is the relative size of the two parties. Buyer power normally exists only if the volume purchased forms a high proportion of the selling company's total sales. The larger supermarket chains have considerable buyer power, particularly over such as the smaller food suppliers. Smaller foodstores have attempted to secure greater buyer power by banding together for bulk purchases, as with associations like Spar, Mace and VG.

The bargaining power of suppliers

Our illustration of the bargaining power of buyers in the industrial components industry works equally well for suppliers. In this and other cases, supplier power is stronger where the component is highly specialized and few suppliers exist. Supplier power is also strong where the cost to the buyer of switching allegiance would include major product adaptations. A computer manufacturer can gain additional market power where it develops popular software that can only be used on its own machines. A case of supplier power in the computer industry emerged in the late 1990s around the monopoly power of Microsoft, the creator of the Windows operating system for PCs. The system is sold as the standard operating environment with most PCs and Microsoft has a 90 per cent share of the market. However, Microsoft came under criticism and was eventually taken to court under USA anti-trust law. The company was accused of abusing its monopoly power in its attempt to control the market for access to the Internet via its browser system, *Internet Explorer*. Microsoft was accused of putting pressure on its main rival, Netscape, and of attempting to force the manufacturers of PCs, such as Compaq, to use Microsoft's system alongside the Windows operating system.

Most firms act as both suppliers and buyers and the bargaining power can be a two-edged weapon. A restaurant operating in an affluent area where there are no other restaurants probably does not face strong bargaining power from its customers and therefore maintains a strong competitive position. However, if there are equally few suppliers of meat, fish and other foodstuffs then these firms have supplier power over the restaurant.

Competitive rivalry

Competitive rivalry lies at the heart of Porter's model and is depicted by Porter as firms jockeying for position. Particularly intense rivalry is found in such situations as a large number of competitors of equal size, where the market has slow growth or where exit barriers are especially high. Such situations exist in the European car industry, as we saw in our case study in Chapter 1. Intense rivalry can also be found among UK supermarkets, particularly those like Sainsbury, Tesco, Safeway, Asda and Waitrose, operating in the same general market segment. Such companies employ staff whose sole job is to monitor the competition through regular product and price checks. Intense rivalry in the IT industry often takes the form of poaching key staff.

The strength of a model like Porter's is that it focuses on the immediate operating environment of the business and avoids prescription by enabling management to examine the forces acting upon their firm. We have seen how cost is an important factor as a barrier to entry. The relative cost of switching is also a factor in determining the relative power of buyers and suppliers and the threat of substitutes.

There are, however, a number of criticisms of Porter's model. (Lynch (2003) also offers a good summary.)

- The analysis depends upon a level of knowledge about the competitor, which may not be so easy to obtain as with competing supermarkets.
- As we have seen earlier in the chapter, the model portrays a rational approach to strategy which may not match reality.
- The model sees customers as one of several factors, when several current approaches elevate the customer to a more central role.
- Porter also views buyer–supplier relationships in terms of power and that they pose a threat, when, in some industries, the prevailing trend is towards greater partnership and long-term relations.
- The model assumes that once the analysis has been made, an appropriate strategy can be found. We have already noted that strategy is much more complex.

Managements can make use of Porter's model by establishing a position for their firms in the market to maximize defences against competitive forces and, where possible, turn them to best advantage. Porter identifies three generic strategies of particular advantage in this respect. These are **product differentiation, market segmentation** and **seeking to obtain the lowest costs**. Discussion of these strategies pervades our analysis of operations and marketing in Chapters 10 and 11 respectively.

Environmental threats and opportunities

An assessment of the general environment and the firm's immediate competitive position should enable management to identify the major threats and opportunities facing the firm. In Table 7.1 we present an illustrative list of the environmental opportunities and threats using the elements of the Business in Context model. This is usually the first stage in selecting appropriate strategic options. For a firm like Orlake Records (Case 10.3), producing gramophone records in a declining market, or a restaurateur opening in central London, the threats and opportunities may be very clear. However, we can identify several complicating factors.

- A threat to one part of an organization may represent an opportunity to another. Thus in the 1970s, when the post and telecommunications services in Britain were part of the same organization, a postal workers' strike led to increased revenue through telephone calls. The closure of some courses in a university, owing to falling student demand, may divert resources to other areas.
- Defending yourself against a threat or capitalizing upon an opportunity is a function of both the firm's standing in its environment and its internal resource position. Survival in a declining market may be easier if you have a large market share to begin with and raising finance to invest in new products is often easier for larger established firms than the small business. Small firms often face the particular dilemma of spotting a market opportunity but lacking the resources to take full advantage. Laker Airways was relatively successful at breaking into the charter airline market by offering cheaper flights than those currently available. As the firm

expanded by introducing flights to the USA it faced direct competition with the larger state-financed airlines. Laker was ultimately unable to compete with the larger firms, who adopted price-cutting tactics, and the company over-reached itself financially through the purchase of a large number of new aircraft in anticipation of increased revenue from the new routes.

● Managements differ in their ability to identify opportunities and threats. The management of a firm doing particularly well in a declining market may ignore the longer-term implications of their position. Even when opportunities and threats have been identified, managements may differ as to their relative importance and may develop different perspectives, based perhaps on their attitudes to risk. Careful analyses of market opportunities may come to naught in the face of a preference for inaction rather than entrepreneurial risk-taking. Failure to take action in the light of environmental change is one form of management myopia. Perceiving the environment as presenting more of a constraint than it need is another.

Table 7.1	Examples of environmental opportunity and constraints using the Business in Context model, as they affect a small manufacturing firm		
Aspects of the environment	**Opportunity**	**Constraint**
Economy	Growth in the market and increased demand	Increased foreign competition. Rising interests rates at home and unfavourable foreign exchange
State	Tax concessions for small manufacturing firms	New laws on pollution and safety necessitating costly product redesign
Technology	The availability of substitute raw materials at cheaper prices	The high-cost equipment modernization to meet increased demand
Labour	Local supply exceeds demand and there is a good supply of part-time and contract staff	A shortage of workers in certain key skills and high wage demands among those groups
Culture	A traditional small-firm community with a tradition for hard work and company loyalty	An influx of new workers in the community from areas of industrial decline and with a history of management–worker mistrust

We can therefore see that the perception of an opportunity or threat is a highly subjective process. It is partly for this reason that strategy formulation is as much a behavioural and political process as it is analytical. There is another important point. We have tended to focus on the environment as offering the management decision-maker opportunities or constraints. A major contention in this book is that the manager can influence and shape the environment. It is not simply the analysis of the environment that provides the answer but the ability of managers to see more in that environment than their competitors and in so doing create their own opportunities.

Case 7.1

Strategic options facing the UK machine tool industry in the 1980s

The machine tool industry provides manufacturing firms with the means by which the products are made, including tools for such operations as metal cutting, stamping and drilling. Larger manufacturing companies with highly specialized machining needs, such as a major car producer, will make some of their own tools, but most will buy from specialist machine tool manufacturers for at least some of their requirements. According to Hayes and Wheelwright (1984), a healthy machine tool industry is an essential prerequisite for a successful manufacturing industry. It is only by using custom-designed tools that innovative products can be made, and only through such products can firms gain a competitive advantage.

The machine tool industry in Britain had been in decline for a number of years. Its share of the world market fell by 50 per cent from 1965 to 1982, while imports rose from 26 per cent to 61 per cent over the same period. A number of reasons have been forwarded to explain the decline. These are as follows:

- the general decline in the manufacturing industry;
- the competitive threat posed by Japan and Germany;
- a lack of graduate engineers in Britain;
- over-diversification resulting in short production runs;
- a general lack of automation and computer application;
- a vicious circle of decline resulting in a lack of investment;
- poor marketing;
- low-volume production at high cost.

Several strategic options for the industry have been identified:

- **Industry extinction.** This involves allowing the industry to die a natural death by starving it of investment and relying solely on imported machine tools. Such a strategy may be detrimental to manufacturing for the reasons outlined above.
- **State intervention.** Attempts had already been made at state intervention, including special provisions for the development of state-of-the-art tools in computer-aided design (CAD) and manufacture and flexible manufacturing systems. Other measures had included attempts to encourage merger among smaller manufacturers to pool development ideas and achieve some economies

of scale. The problems of state intervention lie in possible policy changes with shifts in political ideology and a danger of management complacency. The ultimate form of state intervention would be nationalization, a somewhat remote possibility in the political climate of the 1980s. The government could impose some form of import control, but this could be a dangerous strategy in that other countries may retaliate and, despite its declining market share, British industry does depend on its exports. Furthermore, import controls may speed up the process of Japanese machine tool firms operating from British or other European bases.

- **Rationalization.** Not surprisingly, this was the most common strategy. The suitability of such a strategy would seem to depend on a number of mergers also taking place. This may achieve some kind of product standardization, longer production runs and subsequent cost reductions. However, in a rapidly declining market, this may lead to short-term survival, but it could be a route to eventual industry extinction.

- **Foreign investment.** This had already occurred and British firms had been bought by USA and Japanese interests. However, FDI would only be attractive in the case of highly specialized firms with attractive market niches or to get around the kind of import controls suggested in the second option.

- **Licensing.** Under this arrangement, British firms would manufacture products designed by firms in other countries. The current success of the Japanese machine tool industry, supported by a large manufacturing base, would make the Japanese attractive partners in such joint venturing. It is not clear what the Japanese would gain from the licensing arrangement beyond a fee for British firms manufacturing Japanese patented products. Licensing can be valuable if it generates innovation on the part of the licensee. The Japanese, however, are very restrictive on what they will allow licensees to do, and this would almost certainly preclude innovation.

The UK machine tool industry was unable to stem the tide and continued in sharp decline throughout the 1990s. The industry was still dominated by the Germans and Japanese with some USA firms doing especially well in certain niche markets. Taiwan and South Korea posed a threat to the world order through their ability to manufacture at much lower costs. Their progress was halted by the regional economic problems of 1997. The Germans maintained their reputation as the world's leading exporter of machine tools. The reputation had been built on a strong customer focus stressing product quality and reliability, enabling them to maintain premium prices. In the UK there were some acquisitions, particularly by USA interests, but the strategies of most of the firms were largely defensive and concerned only with short-term survival. The UK industry continues to decline. In 1998, output in the UK fell by 8 per cent, when that in the rest of Western Europe rose by 7 per cent. In 1999, a downturn of 25 per cent was predicted for the industry.

Sources: Eilon, 1985; Lane, 1985; *European Journal of Marketing*, 1994; *Professional Engineering*, 1998–9

◄

Questions

1 Examine the factors which have been held responsible for the decline of the UK machine tool industry. In what ways have they contributed to the decline? Which factors may be more significant than others?

2 Assess the strengths and weaknesses of each of the strategic options?

The organizational aspects of strategy

In this section we will explore the relationship between management strategy and the organizational aspects of our model, and focus on particular issues of resource assessment such as **core competences**, **value chains** and **portfolio analysis**. Organizational analysis is traditionally an integral part of strategy formulation and serves a number of related purposes for management.

● Some kind of resource profile is needed to establish whether the various opportunities, threats and management expectations can be met by the organization in its present state. A knowledge of the resources an organization possesses, and what can be done with them, is a prerequisite for determining future plans and establishes whether a gap exists between what management would like to do and what they can do. This is sometimes referred to as **gap analysis**. For example, the management of a manufacturing firm would need to know if it could accept and meet a new, large order using its existing product range and its existing machine and labour capacity. The gap analysis will identify for management those resource aspects that may be lacking and that will have to be rectified if opportunities are to be realized or threats are to be successfully fought off. The completion of new orders by the manufacturing firm may be dependent upon product modification, the purchasing of new equipment and the hiring of new staff. This, in turn, may involve the raising of new loans from the bank and setting up programmes for the recruitment and training of staff. Expansion of this nature has further implications for the size of the supervisory and maintenance teams.

● The way resources are used by management and how various resource elements of the organization link together can create competitive advantage. Examples of this include focusing on efficient low-cost internal systems or a niche market producer developing and maintaining good customer relations. Such issues are dealt with later in this section as core competences and value chains.

● An internal analysis will enable management to assess the attractiveness of the organization, its activities and its products in its current markets and assess their potential for future investment. This is the particular contribution of portfolio analysis.

A rather narrow, traditional view of strategic planning sees strategy as the result of environmental analysis and the organization factors are seen either to facilitate or inhibit the chosen strategy. Such a view runs counter to the major contention of our Business in Context model, which sees all elements as interacting with one another. Organizational changes are brought about by changes in strategy, but strategic changes are also the product of aspects of the organization. We have already noted in Chapter 5 that it is possible for structure to influence strategy. We can also see that expansion plans will undoubtedly build on strengths or core competencies, a case of the firm focusing strategy around a key resource, such as the skills of a particular group. We deal with more general issues of strategy and organization before turning to the more practical questions of resource analysis, core competencies, value chains and portfolio analysis.

The interaction of strategy and organization

All the organizational elements of our model – goals, ownership, structure, size and culture – interact with the process of strategy formulation.

We have already seen how the **goals** of an enterprise set targets for strategy to follow. We have also emphasized the behavioural nature of this process in that both goal and strategy formulation are the products of management values, and the processes of organizational power and politics, which have a major influence upon management decision-making.

The process of goal setting and strategy formulation is greatly influenced by **ownership** variables. A group of professional accountants in partnership may each have their own views about the growth of the firm, the recruitment and training of new staff and so on. In a partnership these views are generally resolved by discussion or through the dominance of a particular partner. The discussion of ownership and control in Chapter 5 showed that for larger companies, with diffuse share ownership and professional managers, strategy formulation was more complex and often dependent upon the influence of some shareholder groups. There are numerous illustrations where small business owners may deliberately resist growth strategies in order to retain personal control over the firm. However, the reverse is also true in that strategies involving merger and acquisition have a significant impact upon patterns of ownership and control. Managers may actively pursue acquisitions, which give them more power and enhance their own career aspirations.

We noted in Chapter 5 that, according to Chandler (1962), **structure** followed strategy, and this was a dominant feature in the expansion of American multinationals and in particular the development of multi-divisional structures. It was also suggested that strategy may be influenced by structure. For example, a company with a large and active R&D department would almost certainly pursue vigorous strategies of new product development. The 3M Case in this chapter shows how top management were concerned that their existing procedures for strategy formulation were inadequate and set about creating a new structure precisely to give the firm a new strategic impetus. At the operational level the organization structure can facilitate or inhibit strategy formulation and implementation. Two aspects appear to be important here: the authority structure of the firm and the procedures for making decisions. Burns and Stalker (1966) studied the post-war electronics industry and saw differences in the strategic responses of firms to changing market conditions. Those firms that had responded most effectively to changing market demand were firms typified by a more flexible, open structure, which they termed organic. The firms that struggled in the changed environment and failed to adapt were by contrast more bureaucratic, with often lengthy and inappropriate procedures for making decisions, and where structural divisions between departments inhibited cooperation. Organizations, particularly those in the public sector, which rely heavily on committees for the formulation of important decisions, may find the process too cumbersome when a quick strategic response is needed. In a similar way, participation, which can facilitate employee motivation and commitment, may inhibit decision-making through the inherent slowness of the procedure. We noted in Chapter 4 how this, in part, accounted for the slowness of the decision-making process in some Japanese firms.

The Chandler approach to strategy and structure falls within the classical, rational tradition of strategy formulation. There are two further positions. To some, structural change is so difficult that the disruptive effects may be counterproductive in achieving strategic goals. An alternative approach suggests that strategic change in a highly competitive environment may only be possible by radical organizational change, which could involve replacing the management team or selling off parts of the business.

Such considerations of structure are inevitably linked to **size**. In very large organizations strategy formulation may be cumbersome because of the reasons given above. There is also a danger that strategy can become fragmented through the diverse nature of operations and locations. It was these conditions that led 3M to reconsider its procedure for strategy formulation, as illustrated in Case 7.2. Another handicap of large size involves the control of a strategy once it is formulated. The larger the organization, the more filters there are to interpret and perhaps distort a central strategy.

We have already discovered that an important element in the core management strategies of firms such as IBM and HP is the creation of an **organizational culture**, with an emphasis upon shared values. We have stressed the importance of management values in both formulating and evaluating strategy. In this case the creation of a value system to embrace the entire organization is seen by some to be more significant than strategy itself. We have already noted how traditional approaches to strategy have been downgraded by such as Peters and Waterman (1982). Nevertheless, the care with which such firms as HP have embarked upon staff recruitment, selection and training to develop such shared values (Case 5.6) would indicate the influence of a very distinctive strategy indeed. Feurer *et al.* (1995) noted that a strength of HP lay in extending strategic ownership to all parts of the organization. Employees at all levels were engaged in strategy formulation and implementation, giving the company a distinctive edge. The culture of a particular organization may act as a constraint against strategy implementation. For example, strong trade union organization may resist management's proposals to sell off part of the organization in an attempt to safeguard the jobs of its members.

Case 7.2

Minnesota Mining and Manufacturing Company

The Minnesota Mining and Manufacturing Company, better known as **3M**, operates in over 50 different countries producing around 50 000 different products using many different technologies. By most definitions it is regarded as a very successful company. It is truly multinational and multi-divisional, although the company was relatively slow to diversify both internationally and in terms of its product range.

The company was founded in 1902 to mine corundum, but quickly switched its attention to the manufacture of sandpaper, its only product for 21 years. In 1923, the company developed masking tape for paintshops in the car industry and this was followed by domestic adhesive tape and other tape products, such as sound recording tape. Tape products account for some 17 per cent of output, but the company also produces office and photographic equipment, pharmaceuticals and chemicals. Only in 1951 did the company set up operations outside the USA, which remains its biggest market.

It fitted Peters and Waterman's model of an excellent company along several dimensions:

- It was a highly innovative company supported by a corporate goal that 25 per cent of annual sales should come from products developed in the past 5 years, and a senior management dominated by scientists, who encouraged R&D staff to follow through their own ideas.
- The company was committed to high-quality goods design to fulfil customers' requirements.
- A considerable emphasis was placed upon communication throughout the company and management processes were dominated by a network of meetings. In Peters and Waterman's terms it was a 'loose, consensual organization'.
- 3M was based around a strong central culture based on a traditional USA mid-west work ethic. Wherever they operated, small-town locations were favoured as best embodying the core values and management recruited staff who best fitted the culture.

In best Peters and Waterman tradition, the company had no complex planning mechanisms. By 1980 the firm was undergoing change. The firm had grown considerably in a short period, especially in terms of overseas expansion. A new chairman was appointed and there was a belief that the company had become too committed to short-term goals. In particular, the environment in which the firm was operating was changing in a number of different ways, which included an increased variability in interest rates, high rates of inflation in some operating countries, shorter life cycles for some products, scarcer and more expensive resources, and a declining demand in its traditional markets of office products and magnetic tape.

A major discontinuity was occurring involving changed senior personnel and both organizational growth and an increasingly threatening environment. The priorities identified by management were as follows:

- an even greater effort to be expended on product innovation;
- an improved control and coordination of the firm's global resources;
- a greater concern for the future by establishing a more comprehensive approach to long-term planning.

It was decided that new arrangements for strategic planning would accompany a major structural reorganization. This is shown in Figure 7.4.

The main elements of the new system may be identified as follows:

- It is an attempt to build upon the existing loose consensus by emphasizing the exchange of information and ideas, but facilitating this by more formalized systems. A database was set up to generate information about the company. In particular, managers were encouraged to analyse and discuss the strategic options pursued in other parts of the company. This enabled managers to learn from the actions of others as well as being an excellent method for training new managers.

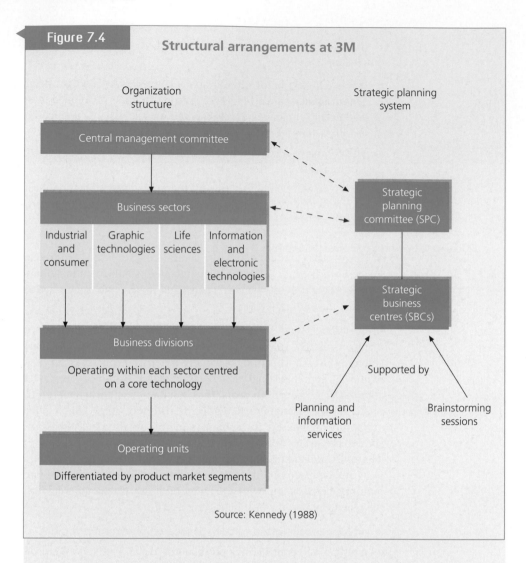

Figure 7.4 Structural arrangements at 3M

Source: Kennedy (1988)

- A new formalized planning system was introduced whereby global strategies were worked out by the Strategic Business Centres (SBCs), the Strategic Planning Committee (SPC) and top management and individual business strategies were worked out by each division using the global strategy as a template. The division was able to set realistic performance measures based on detailed knowledge of its own product market.

- The SBCs acted as centres for the generating of ideas by integrating information and ideas from each of the operating divisions. It was hoped that some form of synergy of ideas would take place. The SBCs focused specifically on product development issues. The generation of ideas was supported by an annual event, during which each operating unit must submit plans outlining where it will be in 15 years time. This event acted as a forum for creativity outside the normal planning framework and deliberately adventurous ideas were encouraged. In addition to these systems the firm holds regular brainstorming sessions throughout the year. This interactive style of strategic planning became the hallmark of the company.

The new system immediately facilitated greater international activity. In the 1980s, 3M operated in 30 or so countries and by 1995, its activities were across over 50 countries. There was an expansion of R&D work in Japan and Europe through the establishment of new laboratories and joint ventures with universities. Several unproductive businesses were sold and the company attempted to establish a higher international profile through corporate advertising and the sponsorship of the 1988 Olympics. However, the new arrangements also attracted some internal criticism on the basis that while the company had a greater knowledge of and direction over its existing businesses, no significant new ideas had been generated.

By the 1990s, 3M had consolidated the Graphic Technologies and Information and Electronic Technologies divisions to form the Information, Imaging and Electronics Sector. In 1991, many of the industries supplied by 3M were in deep recession. Nonetheless, the company persisted with a strategy of continuous innovation and established 'Challenge 95', a campaign to reduce concept to customer time by a third and reduce costs by 10 per cent. Business growth was boosted by 3M's success in Asia. The company had operated in Japan for almost 40 years (rare for a Western firm), and was the first to establish a wholly owned operation in China. Sales doubled in Asia between 1988 and 1993, attributable to the company's reputation in the region and the tailoring of its products to meet local market needs.

In 1995 3M failed to make its own financial targets for the first time in its history. The company announced job cuts worldwide of 5000, the disposal of all peripheral activities and $650 million worth of businesses in computer diskettes, videotapes and audiotapes.

Sources: Peters and Waterman, 1982; Kennedy, 1988; *The Economist*, December, 1991; *Fortune*, February, 1996

Questions

1 What were the reasons that led 3M to change its approach to strategic planning in the 1980s?

2 What was the relationship between strategy and structure and were the structural changes successful?

3 In the light of events post 1990, what alternative strategies might 3M have pursued?

Resource analysis

At the beginning of this section we explained the importance of the current resource position to the formulation of management strategy. A manager needs to know what resources the organization possesses, how those resources are used and how they are controlled. The analysis will cover physical resources such as land, plant and machinery, financial resources and human resources. The analysis should also cover the key relationships in the operating system. These exist between the firm and its suppliers and the firm and its customers as well as the relationship between parts of the same operating system. These issues are dealt with in more detail under core competencies and value chains later in this section and under supply chain management in Chapter 10.

For example, the staff running a business course at a university may wish to change the curriculum to give much greater time and emphasis to IT. An analysis of the current position may reveal a shortage of available PCs and terminals, a shortage of funds to increase the provision, and staff with insufficient skills and experience to teach this subject. Even if funds could be diverted or revenue raised from running extra courses, there may be physical constraints on the establishment of new computer laboratories, in part owing to claims on available space from other departments. In addition, recruitment of appropriate staff may be difficult, so the management may need to seek substitute skills from its existing workforce. It may be possible to use courses offered by the engineering faculty or import engineering staff with spare capacity. However, there may be concern that the approach used by another faculty would be inappropriate to the needs of business students. In other words, the linkages in the system would not be sufficiently strong. In this case, an analysis of the resources may reveal that achieving the goal of increased provision by expansion is not possible. Consequently the utilization of the existing provision needs to be examined to reveal where more effective changes could be made and to see what could be achieved using the existing resources. Rather than expand in a different direction, an alternative scenario may be to develop an existing area of competence and build the course around that.

In many firms, resource analysis is accompanied by the use of a variety of accounting ratios such as return on capital employed, profitability and so on. Different ratios have more relevance at different stages of the firm's development than at others, so that while profitability may be appropriate for established firms, productivity and sales may be more useful for newly established companies and cash flows may be more significant when firms are in decline.

The value of resource analysis lies not only in assessing the viability of a particular strategic proposal but also in assessing the ability of the organization to adapt to change. Can the firm deal with changes in demand or can it withstand increased competition on a global scale? Has it the financial backing to invest in new technology? Do employees possess the necessary skills and is the age profile of its staff sufficiently balanced to ensure succession? Competing through resources is a key theme of both core competencies and the value chain.

Case 7.3

The new British universities

Between 1989 and 1992 the British higher education sector, comprising the polytechnics and colleges of higher education, experienced a number of significant changes, brought about as the result of government education policy and accompanying legislation. These can be summarized as follows:

● Polytechnics and colleges of higher education achieved corporate status, disassociating them from the control of local authorities and causing significant changes in the way they were funded and managed.

- The government abolished the division between the old university sector and the polytechnics by granting the polytechnics, along with some of the colleges of higher education, university status and with it, the power to award degrees. Those polytechnics and colleges achieving university status became known as the 'new universities'.

- The third change concerned the creation of the Higher Education Funding Council (HEFC), a new body responsible for funding, and the Higher Education Quality Council (HEQC) with responsibility for quality control and enhancement. After 1992, HEQC became the Quality Assurance Agency for Higher Education (QAAHE) and all universities have been subjected to a number of audits, of finance, teaching and research. The Research Assessment Exercise (RAE) and the Teaching Quality Audit (TQA) have resulted in scores being awarded each university, which, in the case of the RAE, has funding attached in line with the score.

The environment in which the colleges operate was also changing. A declining population of school-leavers was predicted to affect traditional patterns of student recruitment. In fact, the effect has been uneven as some courses, such as law and business studies, continued to grow in popularity, while others, such as economics and some engineering courses, declined. However, the proposed decline in the numbers of school-leavers was overtaken by the government push to expand student numbers in higher education. The expansion of the sector has been so rapid that the target enrolment for the year 2000 was achieved by 1993. Much of that expansion has occurred in the new universities. At the same time, continued government pressure to hold down public sector expenditure has resulted, in some cases, in reductions in staffing and the resourcing of facilities, such as libraries, setting up conflict with the increased demand from larger numbers of students. The league table culture, that is now a part of the public sector, has incorporated the universities. Frequent publication of university league tables in a variety of national newspapers, all using a variety of criteria, has intensified competition between universities. The older universities have tended to gain higher league table positions than the new universities. This is in part a function of the criteria used and in part due to their greater resource base in the form of finance, buildings, student accommodation and research-active staff. In addition, a government decision to alter the structure of funding by levying a fee on students themselves has added to the tensions.

Many of the new universities are unsure about their role. They were established in the 1960s to offer different courses with an emphasis on vocational relevance. Do they continue with a strategy of pursuing different types of courses to the old university sector or do they attempt to compete on similar terms? Do they attempt to compete for research funding, despite the resource advantage enjoyed by the older universities? The research advantage includes staff with fewer teaching hours and more time to engage in research and consultancy.

The new universities, therefore, face a rapidly changing environment. Many have responded by creating new administrative posts in finance and marketing to meet the new challenges. Most have placed an emphasis on income generation through the winning of research grants, hiring out staff as consultants, and setting up courses to bring in extra fees. For example, the government policy of charging full-cost fees for overseas students has resulted in many universities, old as well as new, seeing such groups as an important source of income and actively searching for new overseas markets. Some colleges have established special units to maximize opportunities in these areas. More attention is being paid to the marketing of courses and the attraction of students from non-traditional sources, especially mature students, to achieve expansion targets and to counteract the impact of falling school rolls. Some see their futures in becoming like the older traditional universities, and have invested in research activity and used this as the single most important criterion in the recruitment of new staff.

The environment continues to change. Competition for overseas students has intensified as the economies and the currency of some Asian countries went into steep decline in 1997. Countries such as Malaysia had traditionally sent many students to the UK. New markets were sought in India and South America and franchise operations were established in Malaysia to retain the student market but at a lower cost for the students. Many of the old universities have been active in the overseas student market and are able to use the league tables as leverage. At home the government has renewed its policy of widening participation by setting a target that 50 per cent of the population will be educated to degree level.

While the environment may be similar for all new universities, there is considerable variation in the way each is responding. Colleges differ in their financial position, their resources, their own particular areas of excellence, and their perceived attractiveness to potential students, to businesses and to their central government paymasters. This may cause some to seek greater strength through merger and others to consider their portfolio of courses to build on strengths and eliminate weaknesses. The route that each goes down will inevitably be decided by a mixture of careful analysis, inspirational management, ideology, value judgement, pressure brought by interested parties, and good fortune.

Questions

1 What are the major changes that have affected higher education in England and Wales since 1990?

2 What are the opportunities and threats facing the new university sector? How are they positioned to face them?

3 What are the opportunities and threats facing the older established universities?

Core competences

The idea of core competences is associated with the work of Hamel and Prahalad (1990, 1994) and Kay (1993). Core competences refer to those activities of a firm that make a difference and give the firm a competitive edge. This could be the development of efficient internal operating systems, as with Toyota whose core competences became a model for other car manufacturers to follow. In certain specialist markets, such as fine wine, a merchant like Lay and Wheeler has built its reputation on good customer relationships and continuing business. A university may develop a reputation in particular subject areas. It can build on that reputation through the attraction of students, bringing increased revenue, and maintain that reputation through the attraction of leading academics in the field.

Key concept 7.3 Core competence

Core competences refer to those activities of an organization that give it an advantage over its competitors. Such advantages could derive from such as an effective R&D department, an efficient operating system, good internal and external communications, the presence of key individuals, reputation and a loyal customer base. The strategic relevance of core competences is the opportunity they provide management to build upon such specific advantages.

To Hamel and Prahalad, core competences represented the integration of knowledge, skills and technology to give the customer added value in terms of cost and customer value, differentiation from competitors or innovation of new products and processes. They also argue that the core competences should not be tied to a specific range of applications such as an existing product range. They should be extendable beyond their current application to give the firm a sustainable competitive advantage over time.

Kay (1993) identified three areas of core competence. These were:

- **Architecture.** Referring to relationships both within and around the firm, including those with customers and suppliers. A key component of architecture is information exchange between the various parties.
- **Reputation.** For quality goods and services and for such as the dependability and speed of delivery.
- **Innovative ability.** The ability to develop new products and processes to gain competitive advantage through differentiation.

The notion of core competences enables a firm to focus its competitive advantage around its resources rather than focusing exclusively on the market. However, it is important that such core competences are difficult to copy by rival firms, otherwise the basis for competitive advantage is eroded. Toyota maintained a competitive advantage for many years despite numerous attempts by its competitors, both inside and outside Japan, to copy its production system. While some core competences do lend themselves to measurement and analysis, as with stockholding and retention, many others are vague and may only be assessed subjectively.

The value chain

The concept of core competences is closely related to notions of the value chain. We present a brief overview here and return to this topic in Chapter 10. The value chain concept owes much to the work of Porter (1985) and at essence is about the way resources are organized to give **value added** to the end user. Porter's value chain is illustrated in Figure 7.5. The key element of the value chain is not just the added value that the various resources bring to the whole, but added value that derives from the linkages between them, which to gain competitive advantage should be greater than the sum of the parts.

The value chain thus views the firm as a system and a process. Porter identifies five primary activities, which individually and, more importantly, collectively contribute towards adding value for the customer. The end result for Porter is defined as margin, which is the difference between the cost of providing the activities and the total value they generate. For the company, margin may be translated into profit while the customer may see it more in terms of value for money.

Key concept 7.4 Value chain

The value chain offers a view of the organization as a cumulative build-up of added value for the customer through the interaction between key operations activities. The end result is greater than the sum of its parts and, for profit-seeking organizations, means increased margins. Porter identifies key elements of the value chain in terms of primary and support activities. Like the Business in Context model, the value chain sees organizations in terms of key interactions between the various parts.

- **Inbound logistics.** This refers to those activities concerned with the receiving and handling of goods from suppliers and transporting them within the organization.

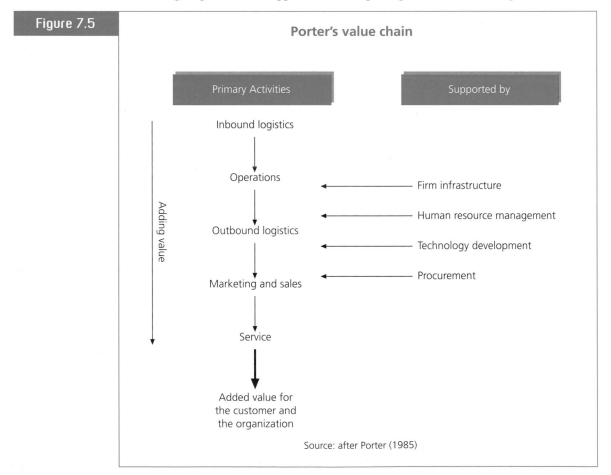

Figure 7.5

Porter's value chain

Source: after Porter (1985)

- **Operations.** Transform the goods into the final product and may comprise a number of different stages and extend across a number of specialist departments.
- **Outbound logistics.** This deals with storing finished items and distributing them to customers. In the case of services it is concerned with all those processes involved in bringing the service to the customer or the customer to the service.
- **Marketing and sales.** Help identify customer needs and, through advertising and promotion, make potential customers aware of products and services.
- **Services.** Covers all those processes involved in before- and after-sales activities such as requirements planning and the provision of customer help lines.

The five primary activities are supported by four other types of activity, referred to by Porter as support activities.

- **Procurement.** Deals with those activities engaged in the acquisition of the various resource inputs to the primary activities. In manufacturing this can occur at a number of stages. Buyers are responsible for obtaining dependable supplies at high quality and at the best possible price. The transport department is responsible for ensuring the most cost-effective delivery of goods to customers, which may involve sub-contracting to another firm, or using the post or rail services.
- **Technology development.** Occurs in all primary activities. It covers product and process development, which can occur in inbound and outbound logistics as much as in operations. It also involves the development of know-how throughout the organization and the transfer of such know-how via training.
- **Human resource management.** Concerned with the recruitment, selection, training and reward systems which support all activities.
- **Firm infrastructure.** Relates to the various systems used throughout the organization. It can include materials planning, logistics, **operations planning**, finance and budget systems as well as the overall strategic plan.

The value chain has drawn criticism for focusing attention on the improvement of existing resources and the linkages between them, when a more radical approach may be required. However, analysis of the value chain can draw attention to major weaknesses in the resource profile and the way the primary activities link together. The concept supports the Business in Context model by viewing the firm's activities as a set of interactions. While the focus is upon internal resource arrangements, the model incorporates elements that exist outside the internal system of the organization, namely suppliers and customers. In doing so it raises the impracticality of defining elements purely in terms of internal or external.

Another approach, which combines internal and external factors, is portfolio analysis. In this case the elements are products and markets. Portfolio analysis could be dealt with in our discussion of strategic options. We deal with it here as an illustration of the interaction between internal (resource) and external (environmental) factors.

Portfolio analysis

Portfolio analysis is a technique normally associated with those firms operating in a number of different businesses and markets, as is the case with the larger multinational corporations. It may also be applied to those firms who operate in the same market with a number of different products. The technique enables management to assess the attractiveness of their businesses and products in their current markets and assist decisions on the direction of future investment. Through such an analysis the manager may reach conclusions on the particular mix of products and markets, the growth and profit potential of those products and markets and the level of risk involved with each one. As a result, a clearer idea emerges regarding priorities for corporate effort and resource allocation.

Key concept 7.5 Portfolio analysis

Portfolio analysis is a technique that can be used by firms operating in a number of different markets and/or with a number of different products. The technique enables management to assess the relative attractiveness of products and markets to assist decision-making on future directions and resource allocation. There are several methods and models available, the most famous of which are probably the Boston Consulting Group Matrix and the General Electric Business Screen.

There are several models that may be used in portfolio analysis and two are illustrated in Figure 7.6. The most famous portfolio technique is the matrix developed by the Boston Consulting Group (BCG). The **BCG matrix** was specifically designed to analyse individual businesses in a company with a range of different business interests. The matrix enables the analyst to plot the position of that business (or product) with reference to the growth of the market and the company's share of that market. We can see from Figure 7.6 that the matrix has been divided into four sectors, each with different product/market characteristics. The products located within these sectors have been labelled question marks, stars, cash cows and dogs respectively. We will deal with the characteristics of each:

- **Question marks** represent products that have a low market share in a market of high growth. The market offers clear potential but the firm invariably needs significant financial and other resource inputs to compete. This may involve product modification, increasing output capacity, increasing promotional activity, recruiting extra staff and raising the level of bank borrowing. Investing in question marks carries a high level of risk, as can be seen through the British government's excursion into microchip development by funding the firm Inmos (Case 9.2). The gains may be significant but the market tends to be highly competitive and the costs of improving market position are invariably high.

- **Stars** are those products that have achieved a high share of a still expanding market. A company with a number or even one of such stars is generally envied by its competitors. Nevertheless, the cost of maintaining this position is usually high. A growing market tends to attract a number of competitors and stars usually need continuing investment in product development and promotion. The PC market in the past few years has maintained a high growth but the increased competition, particularly in terms of product development and price, has meant that several of its stars have risen and fallen in a relatively short time. Other markets where stars have risen and fallen rapidly include cameras and video cassette recorders.

- **Cash cows** are products with a high market share but market growth has stabilized. These provide the firm with its greatest ROI. The market is generally much less

Figure 7.6

Illustrations of portfolio analysis

(a) The Boston Consulting Group matrix

(b) The General Electric business screen

Source: Hofer and Schendel (1978)

competitive and the market position is generally less costly to maintain than with stars. Overall costs are generally lower and economics of scale can be achieved. The surplus funds generated by the cash cows can be used to provide funds for the development of question marks and the maintenance of stars. Zantac, GSK's drug for the treatment of ulcers, was for many years the cash cow that enabled the company to maintain high investments in R&D (see Case 9.5). Such a pattern is typical in the pharmaceutical industry, where development costs are especially high. The pattern has been repeated in other companies such as Hoffman-La Roche with librium and valium.

● **Dogs** are products with the poorest profile on the matrix. Such products tend to be a drain on resources and can be candidates for being dropped altogether or being sold off. This was the reason behind the TI Group's sale of Raleigh Bicycles to Derby International. Dogs are not necessarily worthless. Product ranges and indeed entire companies can be revitalized by, perhaps, a change of management and some fresh ideas. A dog to one company may experience a new lease of life when sold to another. For example, a highly diversified company may find itself unable to devote sufficient attention to those products that are more peripheral to its central activities, as in the case of a manufacturing firm with a subsidiary whose primary activity is property development. The property business could be enhanced if it were sold to a firm specializing in that area.

The BCG matrix implies that management should seek to establish a balanced portfolio and carries with it a notion of progression. It assumes that question marks should become stars which will eventually turn into cash cows to fund the next generation of developing product/markets. Plotting a firm's products in this way may be a useful guide to acquisition and divestment strategy. These options will be discussed in the next section.

The BCG matrix is not without its critics. Much of the criticism is concerned with the imprecise nature of the four categories. For example, stars can differ considerably in their rate of growth and size of market share and the positioning of some products may be an inaccurate reflection of their value, simply because the category may be too broad. Mercedes-Benz has a low share of the total car market, but a high share of the luxury car market. In this case a number of matrices will have to be plotted to represent the different market segments. Nonetheless, such an analysis is perhaps the reason for Mercedes-Benz broadening its market appeal through the production of the smaller, lower-priced A series and the launch of a competitively priced sports model, the SLK. More complex matrices have been developed so that products can be plotted more usefully. An illustration of the General Electric business screen is shown alongside the BCG matrix in Figure 7.6. In this case the concept of industry attractiveness is used instead of market growth and nine categories have been identified to achieve greater accuracy.

In spite of the problems of plotting and measurement, such methods of portfolio analysis are not only of use in planning future product/market strategy but also in raising important questions about how business interests are handled. We have already seen that by analysing a dog changes may be made to improve its position. One company to make use of this type of analysis is 3M. They have developed a matrix to analyse both products and markets, as illustrated in Figure 7.7. The management of 3M is concerned that each of its products and markets are capable of being maintained or improved. It was this method of analysis that led the company to sell off its photocopying equipment business (Kennedy, 1988).

Strategic options

So far in this chapter we have discussed the various components of strategic analysis: the environment, resources and dominant values. We have also suggested that strategy may be formulated by a variety of methods, which may involve a highly formalized planning procedure or may simply be no more than the stated preferences of the chief executive. Whatever the process, the outcome is a particular strategic option or range of possible options. In this section we examine a number of strategic options including diversification, strategies to change the competitive position of the firm, deleting operations and consolidation. When there are several options to choose from, some criterion is needed to select the most appropriate strategy and we end this chapter by identifying examples of such criteria. Case 7.1 examines the type of strategic options that may be available to declining industry (machine tool) and should be compared with Case 10.3 which examines the types of strategies employed by a firm in a declining market (vinyl records).

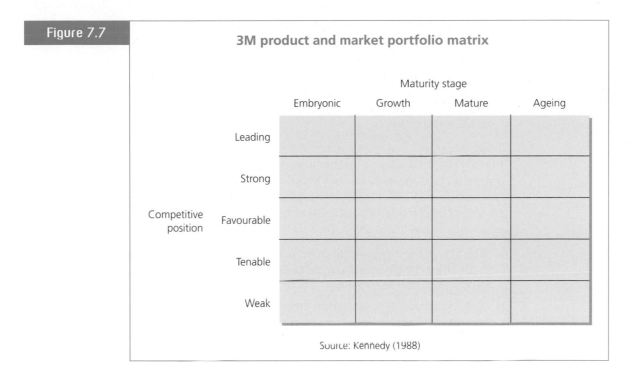

Figure 7.7

3M product and market portfolio matrix

Maturity stage

| | Embryonic | Growth | Mature | Ageing |

Competitive position: Leading, Strong, Favourable, Tenable, Weak

Source: Kennedy (1988)

Types of strategic option

There is an assumption in many management texts that the superordinate goal of most businesses is survival and this may only be achieved by pursuing strategies of growth. While it is difficult to argue against the first assumption, it is clear that not all businesses pursue growth strategies, and, for those like the British steel and coalmining industries, drastic contraction may be the only chance of survival.

Miles and Snow (1978) offer four main types of strategy that competing organizations can adopt within a single industry. They classify firms as defenders, prospectors, analysers and reactors

- **The defender organization.** Tends to have a limited product line. By focusing on a niche market the defender can achieve market leadership, although the key focus of most defenders is improved efficiency through low-cost operations. The defender is unlikely to innovate and is best suited to stable environments. Because of the focus on costs, accountants tend to thrive in such organizations.

- **The prospector organization.** Operates with a wide range of products in a growing and usually fast-moving market. Prospectors tend to focus on innovation and new market opportunities. Such organizations tend to be flexible and decentralized and while efficiency is important, creativity is more important. Prospectors tend to emphasize R&D and marketing as the crucial functions.

- **The analyser organization.** Rarely will this be the first to the market, but will follow others after a thorough analysis of the market and competitor behaviour. Analysers can be found in both stable environments where they tend to emphasize cost reduction and in changing environments, where they emphasize product differentiation. The approach to change is usually cautious and the planning function and planning teams play a key role.

- The **reactor organization.** Tends to have a mismatch between its strategy and the environment in which it operates or it seems to have no strategy at all. Such organizations find it difficult to adapt to new situations and their strategic response is often inappropriate.

While Miles and Snow are concerned with corporate strategies within the same industry, Porter (1985) focuses on **competitive strategies**. These competitive strategies can be applied in any one of Miles and Snow's organization types. Porter presents a relatively straightforward view of competitive options within a single industry. To Porter competitive advantage is a product of positioning within that industry and he identifies two basic types of advantage and hence competitive focus.

- The first of these is competing on the basis of **cost leadership**. Firms pursuing this must aim to be the lowest-cost producer, but still be able to compete in terms of product function and quality.
- The second of Porter's generic competitive strategies is **differentiation**. Firms pursuing this strategy must aim to produce goods and services that have certain unique dimensions that make them attractive to customers. In aiming at product differentiation, competitive advantage can only be achieved by maintaining cost parity or cost proximity.

Porter's approach appeals on the basis of its logic and simplicity. However, business life is never so simple. Furthermore, there are constraints on the effectiveness of such generic strategies. Firms continually strive to reduce their costs and copy each other's methods, as in the case of JIT. In some industries such as car manufacture, there may be limits of cost reduction, which are being approached by the better firms. Differentiation may be short-lived as competitors attempt to emulate each other. BA introduced beds as part of their first-class service on long-haul flights. They were soon followed by Singapore Airlines, and Virgin announced plans to offer double beds as an option!

Our classification of strategies depicts different approaches to growth and contraction. These options are not discrete categories and in many cases the distinction between them can be blurred. They also recognize the complex nature of the strategic process and incorporate discussion of both rational and more subjective factors. We examine diversification in some detail before looking briefly at other types of strategy.

Diversification strategies

Diversification is one of the most far-reaching growth strategies open to management, in that it represents a deliberate attempt to change the nature of the business by increasing its portfolio of products and/or markets in a variety of ways. We can identify two types of diversification, related and unrelated. Related diversification can be further classified into backward, forward and horizontal integration.

Related diversification

Related diversification occurs when the new business is related in some way to the old one.

Several firms have sought to gain greater control over the source of raw materials or the supply of components by some form of **backward integration**. As we saw in Chapter 4, the larger Japanese manufacturing firms depend on a network of sub-contractors for the supply of components. In many cases the larger company has a controlling financial interest in the supplier. In the restaurant business it is becoming more common for some restaurant owners to grow their own herbs and vegetables and bake their own bread, to ensure both the quantity and the quality of the supply. This also provides the restaurant with an additional promotional strategy.

Forward integration occurs when producers diversify to control the onward processes of delivering their goods to the consumer, as in the case of a manufacturer setting up a transport or retail operation or a group of actors leasing a theatre to stage their own work. Post Office letters and parcels were always transported by rail. Before privatization, British Rail extended its own delivery service, Red Star, and took business away from the Post Office by offering a speedier and guaranteed delivery service.

An integrated system of backward and forward integration is known as **vertical integration**.

Horizontal integration occurs most commonly when a firm adds to its portfolio of products by acquisition. Belgo is a successful restaurant in London specializing in traditional Belgian food. Its success led to the opening of a second restaurant in a more central location utilizing the premises of a former restaurant. The group then expanded by purchasing two famous, up-market restaurants and establishing another food-theme restaurant, this time featuring food from Alsace. A related strategy to horizontal integration is the move for **economies of scope**. This occurs when the product range is extended to incorporate similar items, as with the case of a firm supplying fitted kitchens diversifying its operation to include fitted bathrooms and bedrooms as well. Laura Ashley began by selling furniture fabrics, moved into dress fabrics and eventually diversified into selling dresses themselves. The economies of scope include shared central functions such as finance. Horizontal integration may be a valuable way of using a firm's spare resources or capacity. The fibreglass operations of Pilkington Glass found that the waste created in cutting standard widths of fibreglass could be put to good use through the setting up of another operation which compressed the material into insulating bricks, thereby creating a different but related product. Case 10.3 shows how a record company has used related diversification into specialized products as a major strategy of survival in a declining market.

Key concept 7.6 Diversification strategies

These are strategies that move the organization in different directions involving products or markets or both. Related diversification refers to new activities that are directly related in some way to existing operations, such as a hotel opening another hotel in a different location or acquiring a catering business. Unrelated diversification moves the organization in a totally new direction, such as a hotel chain acquiring a newspaper. Highly diversified firms can spread risk across a number of products and/or markets. However, there may be problems associated with coordination and control. Related diversification can lead to benefits of economies of scale and scope.

Kwikfit presents a good example of a number of kinds of related diversification. The company was formed to offer a speedy, low-cost service to motorists in tyre fitting and exhaust system replacement. The opportunity presented itself as a result of the modular manufacture of cars and the ready availability of standardized parts. The reduction of operations to a series of highly specialized routines meant that low levels of skill were needed and hence labour costs were low. Central buying and computerized stock control were other contributory factors to low costs. As a result of low costs and a while-you-wait service the company became very successful and expanded geographically. The company also expanded its product and service range to include shock absorber and brake replacement. The success of the company in terms of profit and market share made it an attractive acquisition for Ford Motor Company, who thus diversified into after-sales service and parts sales.

Key concept 7.7 Backward and forward integration

Backward integration is a diversification strategy to gain control of activities and/or firms further back in the supply chain, such as raw material or components suppliers. Forward integration is a strategy to gain control of activities further forward in the supply chain, such as distribution and retailing. Both backward and forward integration can be achieved by acquisition, joint venture or strategic alliance. Backward and forward integration, either singly or together, are often referred to as vertical integration.

Unrelated diversification

Unrelated diversification occurs when management expand their business into a totally different product market. Marks & Spencer have ventured into the selling of financial services, a totally different operation from their core business of clothes and food retailing. Many diversified companies have a mixture of both related and unrelated products. The London Rubber Company's main product range of contraceptives has been augmented by a range of surgical and household rubber gloves, based on the same technology. The company also produces soap and cough medicine. As with many forms of classification, the difference between related and unrelated diversification is often a matter of degree. The 3M case in this chapter is a good illustration of both types. The company switched from the mining of corundum (an abrasive) to the manufacture of sandpaper (using abrasives as a raw material). The company then began producing masking tape, which led to the related products of adhesive tape and all other kinds of tape product. In recent years the most profitable arm of Ford Motor Company in the UK has been Ford Credit, a company formed to provide finance for car buyers. A similar picture emerges with most car producers.

The concept often associated with unrelated diversification is **synergy**. This refers to the collective influence of the various activities of the company producing an overall effect that is greater than the sum of the parts. Synergy is often cited as a major benefit of diversification, although its impact is often difficult to identify and measure.

We have seen how diversification can provide managers with greater control over supplies and distribution and exploit resources. A highly diversified firm may also be one where risks are spread across a range of products and markets. The motives for diversification may be complex and may include the desire of senior management to extend their power and influence as the firm grows larger. In the USA, the diversification of many companies into totally different areas of business was a direct response to anti-trust laws, which put severe restrictions on the creation of monopolies. There are problems with diversification strategies. A highly diversified company often presents special problems of communication and control and resources may be duplicated. It is for this reason that many diversified companies have adopted a structure involving a mixture of autonomous units sharing some central services, such as R&D. (A fuller discussion of structural devices may be found in Chapter 5.) While extra efficiency gains can result from related diversification, unrelated diversification brings extra costs associated with coordination and control.

Joint ventures, mergers and acquisitions

Many of the illustrations of diversification presented above represent activities that have grown out of the firm's existing business. Firms may also add new products and markets through joint ventures and through mergers and acquisitions. This has the advantage of being a much faster method of diversification than internal development. The company is gaining an 'off-the-peg' business with the experience, knowledge, resources and markets already in existence. Much has been written about acquisitions and mergers and such activity presents consistently good copy for financial journalists, particularly when it is accompanied by boardroom battles and accusations of insider dealing on the stock market. Joint ventures include licensing agreements, particular arrangements with suppliers, joint R&D projects and the creation of an entirely new company as an offshoot of two or more independent parent companies. A fuller account of joint ventures is presented in Chapter 2, where we identify joint ventures as an increasing trend that is directly related to globalization.

Many mergers, more especially in **emerging markets**, are political in nature, as in China and India. Until 5 years ago, in order to operate in India a company had to establish a joint venture with a local company, with the Indian partner taking a 60 per cent share. Changes, such as those in Indian law, reflect the growing influence of globalization on joint venture activity and the need for more flexible arrangements. In Figure 7.8 the differences between mergers, acquisitions and different forms of joint venture in terms of ownership are shown. These various forms of ownership also reveal possibilities for variations in control.

Evidence in the UK has suggested that acquisitions and mergers tend to occur in cycles (Channon, 1973). Channon's view was supported by the events of the 1980s with another round of mergers taking place, particularly involving firms in retailing and in the food and drink industries. Why such cycles occur has not been fully explained and may represent yet another business fashion. In the UK there are a large number of mergers and acquisitions compared to other countries. This is explained in part by the behaviour of the stock market and the massive turnover in shares (Chapter 13 contains a fuller explanation). Germany has a much more stable stock market, yet mergers and acquisitions are on the increase, particularly with overseas companies. Some of the acquisitions have represented very high stakes indeed, as with the acquisition of the USA publishing company Random House by Bertelsmann and of the Westinghouse Corporation by Siemens. The key drivers for German companies include high labour costs, high rates of taxation, a business climate that is highly regulated and shareholder pressure for increased dividend. Such issues were presented in our comparison of Anglo-Saxon and social market economic systems in Chapter 3.

Figure 7.8

Ownership patterns in mergers, acquisitions and joint ventures

Wholly owned
single venture — Merger or acquisition

Partially owned
joint venture

Joint ownership with total control by one party

Joint ownership with shared control

Third company jointly owned and/or controlled

Non-owned
joint venture — Licensing
Franchising

The German case is fairly typical of the modern context of joint venture activity around the world. It has grown significantly as a product of globalization, increased competition, the attractiveness of emerging markets in developing nations and, for advanced economies, declining growth rates and the increasing cost of home operations, particularly in terms of labour and R&D. The impact of globalization has resulted in some interesting cross-national ownership patterns. The famous USA gun-makers Smith and Wesson are owned by Tomkins, a UK company, London Electricity by a company in New Orleans, Northumbrian Water by the French, William Hill, the bookmakers, by Nomura of Japan and Burger King has been in British hands for many years and is currently part of the Diageo stable. Such is the fast-moving nature of global ownership that many of these examples could well be out of date by the time this book is published.

The key factor in the success of any joint venture, merger or acquisition is that there is a strategic fit between the parties concerned. The merger between Guinness and Grand Metropolitan (Case 7.5) was made on the basis of a good strategic fit between the two companies. For example, Guinness brought with it a large number of whisky brands and was strong in the Far East, whereas Grand Metropolitan was weak in these areas but strong in vodka and in Eastern Europe, where Guinness was relatively weak. As we see from Case 7.4, the proposed merger between Renault and Volvo, the strengths of each company were complementary. Volvo was strong in large cars, Renault in small; Volvo was strong in North America, while Renault had a larger market share in South America. However, as the failure of the proposed merger between Renault and Volvo shows, strategic fit may not be sufficient to sustain the relationship in the face of other constraints. Medcof (1997) argues that strategic fit must be accompanied by a long-term alliance strategy. What might appear to be a good strategic fit initially may not be sustainable in the longer term. He cites the case of BA, who bought a 25 per cent share in US Air, only to switch allegiances to American Airlines on the basis that they were better positioned as a long-term partner.

> ### Key concept 7.8   Strategic fit
>
> Strategic fit is an important ingredient of successful mergers, acquisitions and joint ventures. Successful joint activities occur when each party complements the other in terms of their relative strengths and weaknesses. The concept is normally applied to products and markets, but it can apply equally to resources and other forms of core competence. The strategic fit should be compatible with long-term strategic plans, otherwise the partnership may be short-lived or prove to be a costly mistake.

The evidence concerning joint ventures is very mixed. Medcof (1997) cites evidence that successful alliances outperform single businesses, but he does point to a high casualty rate among joint ventures. Peters and Waterman (1982) present a rather negative view, especially of acquisitions. They cite the case of ITT and the difficulties the firm encountered when it diversified out of telephones by acquiring banking and hotel interests. They claim that synergy rarely happens through acquisition, and the whole exercise takes up a disproportionate amount of management time and effort. As befits two proponents of firms adopting a strong central image and consensus culture, Peters and Waterman see great difficulties in achieving a cultural fit between two different enterprises and advise managers to 'stick to the knitting'. Other research echoes Peters and Waterman's concern and tends to warn against unrestrained diversification. A study of 200 companies in the USA from 1949 to 1969 concluded that the poorest performers were those operating in a number of unrelated businesses and those that had attempted vertical integration. The best performers were those that had diversified only in related areas around a set of core activities and skills (Rumelt, 1974). It is interesting to note that while vertical integration is a complementary extension of a firm's core activities, it often requires totally different skills from that core activity. For example, a successful manufacturer of domestic electric appliances may turn out to be a very poor retailer and provider of repair services.

Case 7.4   The failed merger between Renault and Volvo

In 1993 merger talks finally broke down between Renault and Volvo. A merger between the two companies had seemed the inevitable consequence of a number of years of collaboration and the plans seemed well set.

Cooperation between the two firms had begun in 1990 when Renault took a 25 per cent share in Volvo cars and a 45 per cent share in their truck division. Volvo, for its part, took a 20 per cent share in Renault. The early collaboration took the form of an exchange of engines, the joint purchasing of components and joint developments in quality control. The cooperative arrangements between the two companies were a constant source of internal criticism, which focused on the highly bureaucratic procedures that had been established. In this sense a full merger was seen by both parties as the more favourable option.

The strategic fit between Renault and Volvo seemed ripe for merger. Volvo had strengths in the large car market, where Renault had consistently failed to make an impact. Renault's strengths lay in the manufacture of small cars and in diesel technology. In terms of market, Volvo was stronger in Northern Europe and especially North America and Renault had a larger market share in Southern Europe and South America.

Both companies were probably too small to survive in a globally competitive volume-car market. In Europe and the USA merger was a route for survival, particularly in the face of increasing Japanese competition. The major markets had stagnated and both companies had experienced a fall in profits. In the early 1990s Volvo was the more vulnerable of the two companies. It had cut almost a quarter of its workforce and had closed manufacturing plants at Kalmar and Udevalla owing to excess capacity. Its focus on high-priced models made its sales variable with the economic cycles. The size of Volvo's export sales, especially to the USA, made it vulnerable to exchange rate fluctuations. Renault too had reduced its labour requirements, but had done so on the back of a 50 per cent improvement in productivity between 1985 and 1991. A merger seemed to make sense in terms of reduced costs, increased economies of scale and the opportunity to share increasingly expensive R&D costs. The costs of developing new products in the car industry had risen dramatically, necessitating high-volume sales to obtain a return on investment and hence the reason behind much of the merger activity in the industry in the 1980s and 1990s. The senior management of the two companies supported the merger, as did the Swedish and French governments. In any case, Renault was part-owned by the government and, despite plans to privatize the company, would never have allowed merger talks to begin without their support.

The reasons for the merger not taking place were several, involving economic, social, political and cultural aspects. To the surprise of many in Sweden, the alliance would favour French ownership to the ratio of 65–35. In return for its 65 per cent share of the new company, Renault would pay nothing in cash. The ownership ratio would come about simply on the basis of share redistribution. The CEO of Renault, Louis Schweitzer, was to be the CEO of the new company, which would have its headquarters in Paris. The Swedes were suspicious of this arrangement, especially when French newspapers spoke openly of a Renault takeover and Schweitzer predicted in the press a profound restructuring of Volvo's Swedish operations. In part, the unease of the Swedes could be traced back to their ambivalence about EU membership, which they eventually took in 1995.

Opposition mounted in Sweden among several groups of stakeholders. The merger was to take place before the privatization of Renault. The French government had no published timetable for the sale and Swedish shareholders feared either a nationalization by the French of Volvo or a fall in share price. They believed that the share price would be devalued, fearing that the French government would underprice the company to ensure a successful sale. Volvo employees, including many of the less senior managers, became increasingly convinced that a merger would mean a loss of Swedish jobs. Renault had already demonstrated its ability to make significant productivity improvements and there was a belief that such methods would be transferred to Sweden, resulting in yet more restructuring. This fear was understandable given the difference in labour costs in the two countries. Swedish workers enjoyed the highest wages and lowest working hours of any in the European auto industry. In 1991, hourly labour costs in Sweden were 169 Swedish kronor compared to 96 in France. The inevitable conclusion was that jobs would migrate from Sweden to France, and the Swedish government, even if they wished, would be prevented from giving special assistance to Volvo by EU competition policy, even though Sweden was not a member at the time. Eventually these fears found expression in the Swedish media and public opinion turned against the merger.

While the strategic fit between Renault and Volvo was good, the cultural fit was less so. Significant differences exist between French and Swedish management styles. The French are more hierarchical, less flexible and less open. The Swedes are much more likely to delegate and push responsibility for decisions down the organization. As a consequence, Swedish organizations tend to have fairly flat structures while the French reflect their belief in hierarchies through a greater number of levels. Swedish managers tend to be much more international in their perspective and the French more parochial. Surveys of consumer attitudes reflect a Swedish preference for safety, quality and environmental friendliness in their products, while the French score more highly on design and style. Such cultural differences undoubtedly contributed to the failed merger, as did incompatibility in terms of language.

In the face of such problems, the merger collapsed. Since then both companies have sold their respective shares in each other's company. The French government delayed the full privatization of Renault and moved instead from 75 to 50 per cent ownership. Volvo has cut back yet further and closed more plants. In 1998, the Volvo car division, but not the truck, became part of Ford Motor Company. For its part Renault acquired a 37 per cent controlling share of Nissan.

Sources: Williams *et al.*, 1994; Medcof, 1997; Brown, 1998; Hampden-Turner and Trompenaars, 1993

Questions

1 What were the key drivers that led Renault and Volvo to consider a merger?

2 What were the factors that led to the breakdown of the relationship between the two companies?

Other strategic options

Strategies to change the competitive position of an existing business   Whereas diversification and joint ventures represent fundamental changes in the nature of a firm's business, strategies in this category attempt to improve the market position of the existing range of products and services. There are a number of strategic options available, most of them are discussed more fully in the chapters focusing on the functional areas:

● **New product development.** (Chapter 9).

● **Improved market penetration.** By deploying the various elements of the marketing mix, such as promotion or price strategies, market penetration can be improved (Chapter 11).

- **Seeking new markets.** Seek new markets by aiming the product at new market segments or by export (Chapter 11).
- **Improving the quality.** Improving the product or service (Chapter 10).
- **Seeking cost reductions.** Through an improved utilization of resources, such as improvements in productivity, cost reductions may be found (Chapter 10).

Many of these strategies are related. A firm that wishes to move 'up market' and aim its product at a more quality-conscious but less price-sensitive consumer group may need to accompany product changes with an intensive promotion campaign. We pursue this theme in more detail in our discussion of marketing strategies in Chapter 11.

Attempts to change the competitive position of the business can be made through acquisitions which improve the product range and gain access to new markets. Such strategies carry the same advantages and disadvantages outlined above. A growing type of competitive strategy involves franchising ('Structure' in Chapter 5). Through franchising its products or services to individual small businesses, a firm can reach a wider market and, at the same time, spread the risk of that expansion.

All the above options improve the competitive position of the firm by focusing on existing products and services. The strategies can therefore be achieved by internal change strategies. Expansion into new markets may be accompanied by increased promotional and sales activity in that area. However, the more successful change strategies take time and involve more than simply exercising another strategic option. Moves to effect changes in product quality and productivity may involve HRM strategies (Chapter 12) and attempts to change the organizational culture (Chapter 5).

Deleting operations

The decision to cut back and/or sell off part of the operations of a firm is referred to as rationalization or divestment. At its ultimate level this will include liquidation and closure. Such strategies can pose enormous difficulties for the firm involved. The cutting back of activities such as R&D and training to achieve short-term savings may have damaging long-term repercussions. Reducing product lines and services may alienate customers. Cutbacks and closures are generally vigorously opposed by trade unions. The National Coal Board's plans in 1984 to close the Cortonwood Colliery in Yorkshire precipitated one of the longest and most bitter disputes in the history of the industry. On a more general level, rationalization strategies may cause a lowering of employee morale to such a level that existing operations are endangered.

Nevertheless, for some firms, rationalization is the only viable option and may, as successful management buy-outs have shown, offer a new lease of life to part of an organization. In 1981, the shoe manufacturer Norvic was forced to go into liquidation, and one of its subsidiaries, the Mansfield Shoe Company, was faced with closure and most of its workforce were made redundant. The Mansfield subsidiary was saved by a management buy-out which raised extra capital from local industry and from employees exchanging their redundancy payments for shares in the new company. Freed from the financial burden of helping to support an ailing parent company, the newly formed organization found new markets and became reasonably successful, expanding its operations by acquisitions in other parts of the country. However, by the late 1990s, increased competition from lower-cost producers once again placed the company's survival at risk. One of the responses was renewed rationalization through divestment of its previous acquisitions.

Consolidation

A consolidation strategy involves the firm operating in the same product market at existing levels. It is, however, far from a 'do nothing' strategy. Even to stand still firms must keep pace with their competitors. This may involve all the kinds of strategies outlined above, and will certainly involve considerations of product development, quality improvement, marketing and cost reduction.

Strategic choice

Faced with a number of strategic options a manager must make a choice. We have already indicated that the process involves consideration of a number of factors, which we may summarize as follows:

- an analysis of environmental threats and opportunities;
- an analysis of company resources;
- the stated objectives of the company and those of the management team;
- the values and preferences of management decision-makers;
- the realities of organizational politics.

The various options must be tested for their suitability, feasibility and acceptability. The suitability of a strategy would include such considerations as its ability to tackle major problems, improve competitive standing, exploit strengths, and the extent to which it meets corporate objectives. The feasibility of a strategy is the extent to which that strategy can be achieved given the financial, physical and human resource base of the company. Even if a strategy is both suitable and feasible it must still be acceptable to various interested parties, such as management, employees, shareholders and customers. Shareholders may be particularly sensitive to strategies of acquisition. The ultimate acceptance of a particular strategy might depend on the attitude of senior management to risk.

The Strategic Planning Institute in Britain and the USA offers assistance in strategic choice by identifying those strategies most likely to result in increased profit levels. They have set up a scheme known as Profit Impact of Market Strategies (PIMS). In essence PIMS is really a huge database generated by those companies participating in the scheme. A record is kept of strategic options and their links to profit levels. Firms participating in the scheme have access to the data generated by other companies and may therefore learn from their successes and failures. Analysis of the information to date suggests a positive relationship between profitability and market share, but a negative relationship between profitability and the intensity of investment. Surprisingly, PIMS data have uncovered that investment is not such a safe option as many assume. Intense investment usually occurs in highly competitive businesses and companies tend to engage in damaging price wars or find that excessive investment proves a barrier to exit (Beasley, 1985).

The way a strategic choice is made will depend very much on the power and authority structure of the organization. In some firms the strategy may be highly detailed with little scope for interpretation by functional managers. In other firms a great deal of freedom is given to functional management to develop appropriate strategies within broad guidelines. We deal with specific functional strategies in Chapters 9–13. A theme stressed throughout is that R&D, production, marketing, HR and financial strategies should achieve a high level of internal consistency, irrespective of where in the firm the strategy was formulated.

A key factor often overlooked in the choice of strategy is its **sustainability**. This refers to the extent to which the strategy is difficult for others to copy. Such a concept has much in common with core competence, discussed earlier in this chapter. Product and process innovation can lead to a sustainable competitive advantage that persists for many years, especially when protected by **patents** and **trademarks**, as in the case of Rank Xerox. Toyota achieved sustainable advantage over rival car manufacturers both within and outside Japan through continuous refinements in its system of lean production. Coca Cola's sustainable advantage lay in its secret formula and branding policies. However, the history of strategic initiatives is littered with examples of non-sustainable advantages. An excellent illustration of this may be found in the rivalry between UK supermarkets. Each major supermarket chain rigorously monitors its rivals so that any product and price advantage is quickly countered. All followed one another to introduce petrol stations, cafeterias and loyalty cards and as one announced diversification into financial services, it was followed quickly by the others.

Key concept 7.9 Sustainability

Sustainability is the extent to which an organization's strategy is difficult to copy and is therefore the source of competitive advantage over time. This concept is linked to that of core competence (Key concept 7.3).

Case 7.5

Guinness and Grand Metropolitan

In June 1997 a merger was agreed between Guinness and Grand Metropolitan (Grand Met) to create the world's largest drinks company. The two companies could claim 24.7 per cent of the world market, with the nearest rival, Allied Domecq, coming in at 10.8 per cent. The 1996 sales of both companies combined amounted to £12.9 billion with profits of £1.6 billion, 60 per cent of which came from the manufacture and sale of spirits. The merger was completed in December 1997 after approval from the UK government, the EU Commission and the US Federal Trade Commission. The terms of acceptance required the companies to sell Dewars Whisky and Bombay Sapphire Gin and reduce their market power in some smaller European countries. The company surprised everyone by announcing the new company name as Diageo, when the expectation was for the more obvious choice of Grand Metropolitan Guinness.

Ownership was split 52.7 and 47.3 per cent in favour of Grand Met and four new divisions were created. These were Guinness Brewing Worldwide, Burger King, Pillsbury, and United Distillers and Vintners, the last being the largest division by far.

There was a clear strategic fit between the two partners. Guinness brought considerable strength in whiskies, with such brands as Bells, White Horse and, the world's best-seller, Johnnie Walker. In addition to whiskies, Guinness possessed household-name brands such as Gordon's Gin, Harp Lager and Kilkenny Beer, as well as its famous dark stout. Its 34 per cent stake in LVMH, the French luxury goods firm, incorporated Hennessy Cognac and Moet and Chandon Champagne. Grand Met's strengths lay in vodka and white spirits generally. It owned the world's best-selling vodka brand in Smirnoff and had led the market in the production and sale of popular spirit combination drinks such as Malibu and Baileys. Whereas Guinness was predominantly a drinks firm, Grand Met owned Pillsbury, the US-based dough and cake makers, Burger King and Häagen Dazs ice cream. Guinness had particular strengths in the Far Eastern markets where Grand Met was weak, and Grand Met was strong in Eastern Europe, where Guinness was weak. Grand Met also brought significant strengths in the USA market through its vodka sales and its food interests. The joint venture served both interests in a declining world spirits market and growing competition from supermarket and retail chain own brands. Global sales teams now had more to offer their customers.

Neither party was new to joint ventures. Grand Met has had a fairly volatile history in this respect. The company began life as a hotel chain, which it then sold off. Most of its brands were acquisitions such as Burger King and Pillsbury. The company has owned and subsequently sold Watney Mann Truman, Mecca Bingo Halls and Express Dairies. Guinness, for its part, acquired the Distillers Company and Cruz Campo and obtained a large share in LVMH (Louis Vuitton Moet Hennessy). The merger was initially opposed by Bernard Arnault, the head of LVMH, whose company owned a 14 per cent share in Guinness. He was a member of the Guinness board and feared losing his place in the new order of things. He preferred a three-way deal, which was rejected by the two heads of Guinness and Grand Met, both of whom were reported in the press as being highly compatible.

The drinks industry has a long history of considerable merger activity and the deals that preceded and followed the creation of Diageo illustrate the highly volatile nature of merger activity in the UK and beyond. When Watney Mann Truman was sold by Grand Met it became part of the Courage group. Courage then merged with Scottish Newcastle Breweries to form Scottish–Courage. A rival company, Carlsberg Tetley, wanted to merge with Guinness. The strategic fit was good in that Carlsberg Tetley brought with it a large number of public houses and strength in bitter and lager beers. However, the company's interest in Guinness came after an unsuccessful attempt to merge with Bass. That proposed merger was blocked by the government as being against the public interest on the forecast of price rises and job losses. This had a knock-on effect for Allied Domecq who saw any merger involving Carlsberg Tetley as a means of extricating itself from an expensive supply agreement with the company. Bass, unsuccessful in its attempts to merge with Carlsberg Tetley, then turned its attentions to the bookmakers William Hill, given that Bass already owned another major betting firm in Corals. In the event, William Hill was bought by the Japanese firm, Nomura.

Sources: *Financial Times, Guardian, Observer*: various editions 1997–2000

Questions

1 What are the strategic advantages gained from the creation of Diageo?

▶

2   What issues does the merger raise for the management of the company and for the state?

3   What reasons can you give for the large number of mergers in the food and drinks industry?

4   Identify future strategic directons Diageo might wish to take.

Summary

In this chapter we have portrayed the formulation of management strategy as a complex process involving the consideration of environmental and organizational factors as well as management values and organization politics. As a result the process is a mixture of rational techniques and subjective decision-making processes, including a consideration of management values and negotiations between interested parties.

- We have identified a range of approaches and styles, which may operate at the same time, although at different stages of the firm's development one type of strategy may be more appropriate than another.

- The formulated strategy has several functions, not least of which is to anticipate the future by coordinating activities and focusing resources towards chosen objectives.

- We note that the links between strategy and performance are difficult to prove.

- An analysis of the general environment and a focus on the immediate competitive environment will enable management to identify significant opportunities and threats, although how these are interpreted is a function of the values and creative ability of management.

- We identify four kinds of resource: product, physical, financial and people. All are important in enabling management to formulate strategy around the organization's strengths. These strengths may be examined through an analysis of a firm's core competences and its value chain. Portfolio analysis offers both an analysis of resources and an insight into strategic options.

- We examine a number of strategic options, and suggest that each option should be assessed in terms of its suitability, its feasibility and its acceptability. The final criterion stresses a central theme of this chapter: the importance of management values and organization politics in the strategic process.

Discussion questions

1   Examine the role of the scientific method in the process of strategy formulation. Is there a place for subjectivity and creativity?

2   What is the purpose of strategy and how might a particular strategy be evaluated?

3   Identify the major environmental opportunities and threats faced by a city centre restaurant, a large retail store, a high street bank, a university, and a firm manufacturing television sets.

4   Using Porter's **five-forces** model, identify the specific competitive forces operating in the five situations defined in the previous question.

5   In what ways can management use resource analysis and portfolio analysis to guide strategy? What are the major strengths and weaknesses of the models for portfolio analysis identified in this chapter?

6   Assess the usefulness of core competences and the value chain in analysing resources and developing strategy.

7   Make a critical analysis of the different approaches to diversification.

8   Identify the opportunities and threats associated with a merger.

9   What strategic approaches, styles and options would best fit your college or your firm for the twenty-first century? What problems do you foresee with these approaches, styles and options?

Further reading

There are three popular texts, all of which have features to commend them. They are Johnson, G. and Scholes, K. (2002) *Exploring Corporate Strategy: Text and Cases*, 6th edn, Prentice Hall, London, Lynch, R. (2003) *Corporate Strategy*, 3rd edn, FT Pitman, Harlow and de Wit, B. and Meyer, R. (1998) *Strategy: Process, Content, Context: An International Perspective*, 2nd edn, International Thomson Business Press, London. While covering much of the same ground, they approach the subject in slightly different ways. They possess a wealth of illustrations and there are some good cases in all of them. An added feature of de Wit and Meyer is its inclusion of a number of classic journal articles. A number of key articles can also be found in Mintzberg, H., Lampel, J. B., Quinn, J. B. and Ghoshal, S. (2003), *The Strategy Process: Concepts, Contexts and Cases*, 4th edn, Prentice Hall London. A different and interesting view of strategy is taken by Whittington, R. (1993) *What Is Strategy – And Does It Matter?*, Routledge, London. At a more specific level, a good analysis of the competitive environment is offered by Porter, M. E. (1980) *Competitive Strategy: Techniques for Analyzing Industries and Competitors*, Free Press, New York. Some still rate this as his best book.

Business ethics and corporate social responsibility

- Define business ethics and corporate social responsibility and explain the relationship between them.
- Explain the historical and theoretical origins of business ethics.
- Explain and illustrate the complexities involved in doing business ethically.
- Identify and assess the issues involved in corporate social responsibility between the firm and its numerous stakeholders.
- Assess the arguments for doing business ethically.
- Identify and explain the various mechanisms used in organizations for ethical business and corporate social responsibility.

Introduction

> Some companies have acknowledged that there is enhanced corporate reputation to be gained through recognizing that capitalism will be most successful when it cares for its customers, its producers, the environment and the communities in which it operates. (*McIntosh, 1998, p. 3*)

The quote by McIntosh represents a growing concern by commentators from inside and outside business that the goals and activities of business should be concerned with:

- conducting business in an ethical manner;
- treating people who come into contact with the business (suppliers, customers, employers, etc.) fairly;
- being socially responsible;
- looking after the environment.

A number of labels have been attached to such intentions, including business ethics, corporate social responsibility and green business. In this chapter we will address the issues under the twin headings of business ethics and corporate social responsibility. We consider business ethics to be the broader of the two concepts. It is concerned with making choices about right and wrong courses of action. Corporate social responsibility is more pragmatic and deals with key issues in the relationship between the firm and its stakeholders and the firm and its environment.

The issues covered by business ethics and corporate social responsibility are wide-ranging. They cover macro issues such as pollution reduction, the responsible exploitation of raw materials and corporate fraud and micro issues such as fair pay, sexual harassment and cheating on expenses. Some issues fall between these two extremes as with the growing concern over child and forced labour in some countries of the world. These issues cover every business activity.

- In R&D, larger pharmaceutical firms have established committees to oversee the ethical aspects of drugs testing.

- In terms of product development and operations the emphasis has been on safe, non-polluting products and working environments. The Ford Pinto was withdrawn from production in the USA after several accidents involving the explosion of the petrol tank. The Pinto was launched by Ford in 1971 and the design, while conforming to the standards of the day, failed to anticipate incoming legislation that cars should be able to withstand a collision at 30 mph. Exhaust emissions from car engines have been the subject of legislation, leading to the development of new technologies.

- In marketing, many countries have banned or restricted tobacco advertising and set up commissions to monitor advertising and sales promotions to ensure honest representation.

- HR policies have been designed to improve working conditions and enhance the involvement of employees in the decision-making process.

- In finance and accounting, standards have been established about public accountability and, for multinationals, their contribution to the local communities in which they operate.

Undoubtedly our current interest in ethical issues and responsible business stems from a growing public and corporate disquiet about a number of disasters and scandals. In 1984 in Bhopal, India, at the Union Carbide Plant there was a leakage of toxic pesticide gas. This resulted in an estimated 2500 deaths and 200 000 injuries. A resulting criminal case for culpable multiple homicide was brought against the company executive. The company has since been sold to Dow Chemicals.

The Chernobyl nuclear reactor disaster in the Ukraine attracted similar attention, as did the massive oil spillage from the *Exxon Valdes* in Alaska. Many well-known names and figures have hit the headlines. Guinness executives were tried and found guilty of corporate fraud. The Maxwell empire collapsed as a result of the illegal misappropriation of pension funds, leaving many thousands in danger of losing their pensions. The established bank, Barings, was brought down by the illegal activities of one of its traders in Singapore. In Chapter 4 we have already noted the scandals in the Japanese financial sector involving such established firms as Nomura, Daiwa and Yamaichi. We examine one such case, Enron, and the issues involved in this chapter. There are current concerns over genetically modified (GM) crops and the massive pay rises given to managers in recently privatized firms or poor performing firms (see Case 6.2).

As a result of such incidents, Wild (2003) believes that action groups focusing on social responsibility have replaced trade unions in the championing of good work practices. The success of such organizations as Global Exchange and Greenpeace lies in their ability to target global brands rather than individual companies in individual countries. Consumer and environmental pressure groups operate globally in a way that trade unions have never achieved.

In this chapter we will define business ethics and corporate social responsibility, examine the historical background and related theoretical perspectives. We will then put the case for ethical and socially responsible business and examine a number of problems and issues. Finally, we will look at some mechanisms used by companies to support doing business ethically.

Defining business ethics and corporate social responsibility

Ethics is a branch of moral philosophy and there is considerable debate within philosophy over its true nature. In simple terms, it is the study of morals and principles governing the rights and wrongs of human conduct. Marshall (1993) identifies three different approaches:

- **Transcendental ethics** assumes that there are absolute concepts of right and wrong, which apply across all societies. Most world religions claim a universal moral code, which is a form of transcendental ethics.

- **Social ethics** assumes that ethical standards will vary between societies reflecting different histories and influences. Hence, social ethics are demonstrated by the fact that the death penalty is acceptable in some societies but not in others. There are those who maintain that all ethical standards are socially constructed and that no absolute standards exist.

- **Tactical ethics** assumes that people pursue ethical standards because it suits them so to do. Drivers who slow down when they see a speed camera not out of any conviction in the law but to avoid getting caught and paying a fine are practising tactical ethics. In business, managers can produce codes of practice and corporate statements identifying ethical intentions. In some cases this is simply a public relations exercise to gain reputation, when the reality is that such issues are ignored in the practices pursued by the company.

Business ethics

This is concerned with those moral issues and individual choices of right and wrong and good and bad within the conduct of business affairs. The relationship of ethics to business is a highly complex issue and incorporates all three approaches identified above. We can illustrate some of the complexities in a number of different ways:

- Within business there are widespread beliefs about how customers or employees should be treated. However, we can see from examples around the world, and even between firms in the same area, that practices vary significantly. Business ethics would appear to conform to the concept of social ethics, identified above, in that standards in business are a function of:
  - the values of individuals working in organizations;
  - the corporate culture created by top management;
  - codes of conduct operating in individual organizations;

- the social norms of the society within which the organization is located;
- the prevailing laws.

● We can see variations in values across societies. In some societies the use of bribes is an essential part of getting business done, while in others it is considered unacceptable behaviour. The dilemma occurs when employees of an organization in a country where bribes are unacceptable must do business in a country where bribes are expected. Often such bribes are dressed up as corporate gift giving and in many situations there is a fine dividing line between a gift as a token of cooperation and goodwill and a bribe. In some organizations many business people adopt a stance of 'moral relativism', in that they acknowledge that things are done differently elsewhere and it is acceptable to operate to those different standards in that setting. In other organizations there are strict codes about the giving and receiving of presents.

● We can also see that such standards change over time. We in the West decry the use of child labour in such countries as India, yet it was commonplace in the mining and textile industries of 19th century Britain. Our attitudes, and hence our standards, have also changed on issues such as equal opportunities although, some would argue, not nearly enough.

● Managers are presented with many dilemmas. To save the business and hence jobs in one location, it may be necessary to close operations and shed jobs elsewhere. In many situations such dilemmas are resolved by behaving fairly towards those adversely affected. In this case there would be redundancy, early retirement, and retraining packages and counselling for those losing their jobs. Nonetheless there are many decisions in business, while favourable to one group are less favourable to another.

Mahoney (2002) identifies three strands on business ethics.

● **Corporate accountability.** Corporations are accountable for their actions to the general public. In this case companies that transgress socially acceptable standards can expect to be punished, usually by the imposition of fines. In some cases board members can be held responsible and prosecuted as individuals. This happened in the case of fraudulent behaviour at Guinness when three board members were imprisoned; as was Nick Leeson in the case of Barings Bank in Singapore. In most cases of **corporate accountability** the focus is upon big business.

● **Social responsibility.** This is where corporations take responsibility for society at large and, through their actions, attempt to make the world a better place in which to live. In this way large hotel chains, such as the Shangri La group in the Far East, encourage customers to re-use towels in their bathrooms rather than washing and replacing them each day. A study of the corporate culture of Korean electronics firms, Hyundai, Samsung and LG, noted the importance they placed in corporate literature on the dignity of the individual, their life outside work and on the aim of creating a better world for all (Needle, 2000).

● **Stakeholder theory.** The **stakeholder theory** identifies the various groups in society to whom the organization is responsible. We deal with this in greater detail in the next section.

> ### Key concept 8.1 Business ethics
>
> Business ethics is the concern for moral standards and individual choices of right and wrong in the conduct of business affairs. Business ethics is a function of individual values, corporate culture, prevailing social norms and the laws of the land. As a result we can see variations between cultures and changing standards operating at different times. Business ethics sets the framework for the operation of corporate social responsibility and attention to both are believed to contribute towards business success.

Mahoney's classification demonstrates the interconnected nature of business ethics and corporate social responsibility. One might argue that business ethics is the philosophical underpinning for corporate social responsibility. It is to the latter we now turn.

Corporate social responsibility

The concept of corporate social responsibility (CSR) already presents us with a dilemma. We have noted elsewhere in this book how organizations are often treated as entities with minds and actions of their own when, in fact, it is people who make decisions and take actions. In the same vein we would argue that only people can be responsible and we cannot ascribe responsibility to inanimate objects such as organizations. Nonetheless, while the organization's representatives can be imprisoned or fined, fines are levied too on organizations as the responsible corporate entities.

CSR highlights ethical issues in business by defining those groups to whom the company and its representatives are responsible and those areas for which responsibility is taken. In the following list we identify a number of such groups and related activities and focus upon one area – the environment. Organizations such as the UK Business in the Community argue that corporate social responsibility is not just about prevention but about actively doing good (http://www.bitc.org.uk). However, as the following examples show, there are dilemmas:

- **Shareholders.** Some, like Friedman (1970), argue that shareholders are the prime responsibility of companies. However, there are important issues. Many shareholders, particularly institutional shareholders, are concerned above all for a rising share price and a good dividend. In some cases this leads managers to focus on short-term gains over long-term growth, possibly to the detriment of the company and its responsibility to other stakeholders. Moreover, in volatile stock markets, such as in the UK, shares change hands frequently. It is, therefore, sometimes difficult to identify the shareholders and their motives. In contrast to the view of the selfish and fickle shareholder, there is evidence of the growth of shareholders who are concerned to invest only in those businesses with clear ethical standards and which demonstrate social responsibility.
- **Financial institutions.** Many of these are shareholders but some, like banks, lend money to companies. They have an expectation that their money will be paid back in a timely fashion. In cases of corporate insolvency decisions must be made about the relative priority of stakeholders in terms of receiving payments owed to them. In this respect banks tend to have priority. Banks can also have considerable influence on

management decisions which may conflict with the needs of other stakeholders. In soccer, the UK premier-league team West Ham was relegated at the end of the 2002/3 season. The bank instructed the club to sell its most valuable assets (its young, star players) to the dismay of its fans (the paying customers), to balance the books.

- **Customers.** In most cases a customer wants quality goods and services at reasonable prices. In order for firms to keep prices down, costs must be cut. In some cases this has resulted in the firm cutting out safety features to keep costs down. In the case of the Ford Pinto, managers made the decision that the alteration of the design to accommodate proposed changes in safety law would be too expensive once production had begun. Cost reduction often means making people unemployed or, in the case of global companies, switching operations to low-cost economies, creating problems of unemployment at home and facing accusations of exploitation overseas. As with shareholders, not all customers are selfish and calculating and there is evidence to suggest that customers will actually choose and pay more for those goods and services produced ethically.

- **Employees.** If we view employment as a calculative arrangement then employees offer their services in return for wages. However, the modern employee expects much more from employers. Employers are expected to provide not just a means of making a living but a safe working environment, job security, rewarding work, fair treatment, equal opportunities and so on. Many of these are key human resource management issues, such as how long should employees be expected to work and how much should they be paid. As with other stakeholders there are dilemmas. For example, take the case of a firm that pays for the private medical care of its employees, including an annual medical check. If the medical reveals that the employee is HIV positive has the firm the right to know or has the employee the right to privacy?

- **Suppliers.** In recent years there has been increased focus on treating suppliers not just fairly but as members of the corporate family. Cut-throat competition between a number of suppliers has, in many instances, given way to the emergence of a small number of suppliers enjoying close working relationships with their customers. Much of the lead for this has come from Japanese management practices (see Chapter 4). In times of recession a Japanese firm is keen to behave honourably to its key suppliers and maintain contracts, seeking to cut costs in other areas. The relationship works both ways. When Mazda experienced severe difficulties in the 1970s, they benefited from suppliers extending credit for several months (Pascale and Rohlen, 1983).

- **The community.** The relationship between firms and their local community can be significant. A major employer not only provides jobs for many people in the community, but indirectly supports the local housing market and provides revenue for shops and local services. In some cases, in many parts of the world, a single firm dominates a community. This happens in such industries as mining, steel, shipbuilding and with some major car plants. In such circumstances does the firm have a responsibility to the community to stay in business in that location? The impact on communities of coal mine closures in the UK in the 1980s has been significant, not just in terms of rising unemployment at a local level but in terms of the prosperity of other businesses dependent on coalmining, such as suppliers, outsourcers and local shops. Some argue that the reliance of communities on single employers has diminished with increased geographical and labour mobility and community policies of economic diversity.

- **Society in general.** A company, its managers and employees must conform to the prevailing social norms. However, we have already seen how these vary with cultural differences as well as over time. Moreover, there would seem to be a remarkable tolerance within society to a range of permissible business behaviour.

- **Government and the law.** In many cases, prevailing social norms are codified in law. In this way we have laws controlling the safety of products, permissible forms of advertising, the disclosure of financial information and conditions of employment. In addition, governments may set policies which it expects firms to follow. Such policies may restrict the firm doing business in certain countries, as was the case of many governments during apartheid in South Africa, or it may set voluntary limits on pay awards.

- **The environment.** Although not an individual or a group in the sense of the above, most believe that the firm has a responsibility not just to the environment in which it operates but also to the global environment. To many, this area is the most obvious and visible face of corporate social responsibility. It involves the environmental impact of the firm's activities and, as we shall see in subsequent sections, often carries the highest public profile, is used as a focus of public relations and carries the highest risk in terms of cost. For example, the oil spillage from the tanker *Exxon Valdes* is estimated to have cost Esso over US$7,000 million dollars in clean-up costs and compensation. More recently there has been a recognition that environmental concerns are global rather than local, as with the emission of greenhouse gases and its impact on global warming. As a result governments have become actively involved. The Rio de Janiero Earth Summit of 1992 involved leaders from some 120 nations, who signed up to measures to improve the planet through the reduction in the emission of greenhouse gases and to reduce the poverty gap between rich and poor nations. However, the agreement of the Rio Summit was non-binding on the parties and the Kyoto Summit of 1997 attempted to introduce regulations.

The Kyoto Summit illustrates some of the dilemmas facing both firms and governments in acting responsibly towards the environment. The key differences

Key concept 8.2 Corporate social responsibility

Corporate social responsibility (CSR) involves the application of business ethics. CSR is concerned predominantly with the firm and its relationship to its various stakeholders such as shareholders, customers, employees, suppliers, and the community and its relationship to the environment. The assumption is that in all these relationships business decisions are influenced by moral and ethical considerations. While the emphasis is corporate and organizations can be held to account, we should always remember that decisions on ethical issues are made by individuals. CSR, as a concept, is linked to the broader notion of business ethics and the belief that 'good' CSR is also good for business.

were between the USA, the EU countries and emerging industrial nations such as China and India. The EU nations favoured restricting the emission of greenhouse gases to the same level for all. Emerging economies, such as China, argued that such a proposal was unfair since it penalized poorer countries by forcing them into high-cost remedial action, when richer countries had been emitting greenhouse gases at unacceptable levels for years. The USA argued that countries like themselves should give technological assistance to poorer nations and gain 'carbon credits' for so doing, which would count towards their reduction target. By the end of 2003 agreement had still to be reached.

There are a number of problems and issues concerned with the stakeholder approach to corporate social responsibility, many of which are recurring themes throughout this chapter:

● There are so many stakeholders that conflicts can and do arise with the conflicting priorities of different groups. Do consumers pay more to keep local workers in a job? Do banks forgo what is owed them so that suppliers can get paid? When such conflicts occur, which stakeholder has the priority?

● Many of the stakeholders, such as community groups and even shareholders and employees, represent very broad groups. Within each group there will be several different needs, which are likely to set up conflicts.

● Satisfaction of the needs of different groups of stakeholders requires their representation in company affairs and adequate disclosure of information. In many cases, managers have shown reluctance to provide detailed information or allow involvement in decision-making processes.

● The stakeholder approach becomes even more complex in global companies, when the number of stakeholders is likely to multiply as are the differences between them (especially cultural differences). In such situations companies either follow an ethical code of the home nation, irrespective of setting, or adopt a position of ethical relativism. For many years, firms in several countries did not trade with South Africa while apartheid was practised. USA firms were prevented from trading with Vietnam for many years following the Vietnam war. Such ethical positions of the home nation were reinforced by legal sanctions imposed by the respective governments for transgressions. However, before China joined the WTO, many Western and Japanese firms embraced the Chinese in joint ventures, despite expressing reservations about China's record on human rights violations. The argument used here is one of ethical relativism and an acceptance of different practices in different societies.

Theoretical and historical background

In the last section we noted how notions of ethical behaviour change over time. In this section we examine the historical antecedents of modern business ethics and corporate social responsibility, and link the historical development to a number of different theoretical perspectives. Pirie (2000) sees the development of interest in ethical issues as a reflection of political and economic trends. Davies (1997) argues that particular views of business have emerged and been influential at certain times.

We can identify a number of historical stages:

- Ethical approaches to business can be traced back in the UK to the early paternalism of such employers as Cadbury and Rowntree, although the focus was mainly on the treatment of employees. Many of these employers established model villages to house their workers. One of the earliest was at Saltaire, around the textile mills of Titus Salt, near Bradford. Cadbury established Bournville and Lever, Port Sunlight. Many of these early paternalists were influenced by their Quaker ideals.

- Such **paternalism** was threatened by the separation of ownership and control (see Chapter 5). The early paternalists were both owners and managers. The growth of the size of the firm with the emergence of the joint stock company created a new breed of 'professional' managers, with the need to keep shareholders happy.

- Earlier, in the 20th century, concerns arose out of the growth of big business and the need to curb the power of large corporations, as with the anti-trust legislation in the USA, and as a reaction to the depression of the 1920s and 30s. Lobbying for improved terms and conditions at work arose from the growth of the trade union movement around the same period.

- In the post-war era interest in ethical business was related to the 1960s reaction to materialism, the activities of some multinationals in the Third World and increasing concern and publicity about pollution. Further developments were undoubtedly a backlash to the events of the Thatcher and Reagan era with its emphasis on deregulation, privatization and the enterprise culture.

- More recently, business ethics has entered the political agenda through issues related to globalization and fears for the future of the planet. At the same time the public agenda has been stimulated by increased news coverage of environmental and other issues. There are now groups of consumers who demand environmentally friendly products made by employees working under fair conditions.

Davies (1997) offers five different perspectives on business ethics each with an historical perspective:

- According to the Western, Christian theological perspective, business is seen as a god-ordained vocation. There are clear links with Christian ethical principles and an assumption about how business should be conducted. Undoubtedly such a view influenced the early Quaker paternalists.

- Business is also seen as an upholder of the democratic ideal. This is linked to belief in the operation of the free market, where all have a right to compete.

- Business is predominantly a creator of financial wealth from which society and its members benefit.

- Business is a means by which we can leave the planet in a good state. It is not in the interests of business to exploit resources to extinction nor to pollute the atmosphere to make life impossible.

- Business is essentially a means for the development of people.

Davies accepts that, while all these views have been put forward from time to time, the perspective of business as a wealth creator has been the dominant paradigm. Such a view is often ascribed to Friedman (1970), an advocate of the free market who believed that the primary purpose of business is to increase profits. He believed that the real social benefit of business was in its wealth creation and that any other concern was not in the best interests of the shareholders. However, Friedman also believed that managers should operate within the law and adhere to basic social norms. Friedman's view was similar to the more forthright views of Carr (1968). He compared business to a poker game and even a Wild West shoot-out, where ethics mattered less than winning. He felt that managers could separate business and private life in terms of behaving ethically. Both perspectives are the products of a traditional American view of the sanctity of the free market and the role of law to police the transgressors.

Such views as those expressed by Friedman and Carr are challenged by those who believe that business is part of society and should therefore respond to the needs of society and reflect its ethical principles, and that ethics should be just as important as profit or growth. Friedman would argue that businesses do reflect the ethical values of society and that profit and growth provide the platform for the application of ethical standards.

Why should businesses be socially responsible?

The ethical approach to business was once the province of a small number of firms, like the Body Shop, famous for its sourcing of environmentally friendly products from non-exploited labour and establishing its own 'ethical' manufacturing operations. The same company expanded its social responsibility role by backing the *Big Issue*, a magazine produced and sold by the homeless throughout the world. However, there is considerable evidence of a shift in expectations, even in the USA, led by such firms as Levi Strauss. In Europe many companies now publish, as well as an annual company report, an annual environmental report. Here companies set out their goals. For example from Daimler–Benz:

> Even in economically difficult times, a responsible attitude towards the natural foundations of life remains a long-term corporate commitment for Daimler–Benz . . . we would also like to establish an open forum – for an external and internal public alike – where environmental questions may be discussed in a critical but constructive manner by representatives from society, politics and science. In short we are always looking for new impulses towards improving environmental protection within the framework of the economically feasible. (*Daimler–Benz*, 1996, p. 2)

In their 1998 report, 'Profit and Principles – does there have to be a choice?', an appropriate theme in a debate about business ethics, Royal Dutch/Shell explain

> This report is about values. It describes how we, the people, companies and businesses that make up the Royal/Dutch Shell Group, are striving to live up to our responsibilities – financial, social and environmental . . . It is a matter of pride and reassurance to us that throughout the years these core values have endured. They represent an unshakeable foundation on which to build at a time when society has rising expectations of business. (*Royal Dutch/Shell, 1998, p. 2*)

Shell identifies seven principles, which address a number of financial, economic and social goals within an ethical framework. The company regards that it has a responsibility to shareholders, customers, employees, those with whom they do business and society at large.

It is interesting to note that, in both these examples, the firms concerned stress that they are concerned with both ethical and socially responsible behaviour and profit-seeking behaviour. There are a number of points that support the view that 'ethical business is good business'. Wilson (1997) emphasizes the part played by discerning customers, job seekers, investors and employees. We explore the contribution of all these groups as well as other issues below:

- **Ethical business is profitable business.** A few years ago Nike linked their worsening financial performance to a fall in sales, which they attributed directly to well-publicized allegations of the mistreatment of workers in their operations in the Third World (Wild, 2003). There are a number of reasons put forward to support the claim that ethical business is good for business:

  - Ethical business gains favour with consumers, gives them satisfaction and is likely to result in repeat purchases.
  - The highlighting of corporate social responsibility attracts the interest of the media. The coverage attracted is not only good public relations, but may be more effective than costly advertising campaigns.
  - In the same way, the branding of goods as 'ethical' or 'socially responsible' is good public relations and can lead to greater awareness and increased sales. Increased sales can mean increased profits.
  - There is the argument of long-term self-interest that ethical behaviour is conducive to good performance. For example, numerous studies of motivation have shown that if workers are paid minimum wages and have to work in poor conditions then the quantity and quality of their output will fall.

However, with most of these points there are problems of measurement and correlation. In addition there is the presence of strong countervailing forces. Many managers face considerable pressure to cut costs to stay competitive and to focus on profit, growth and dividend. Such pressures can push ethical issues into the background.

- **Attracting bad publicity.** While good practice in corporate social responsibility can attract the right sort of publicity that is good for business, companies can attract bad publicity and become the target of action groups such as Greenpeace. Shell suffered a particularly bad press over its attempt to dispose of Brent Spar, a North Sea oil platform, in deep water in the North Sea. The company admitted that, whatever the rights and wrongs of the issue, it could have been better handled by them.

- **The cost argument.** The costs of not behaving responsibly can be considerable. It is claimed that 22 per cent of the total operating costs of Amoco are attributable to environmental costs (Thomas and Eyres, 1998). The oil spillage from the tanker *Exxon Valdes* cost Esso a reported US$7250 million. The tragedy at Bhopal cost Union Carbide an estimated US$4700 million. Civil actions over the loss of life resulting from accidents in Ford Pinto cars cost Ford US$250 million, although had the actions been taken today the sum would have been considerably higher. The cost to Ford was not just in civil action. All Ford Pinto cars built and sold between 1971–6 were recalled and had their petrol tanks refitted at considerable cost to the company. It is interesting to note that the whole Ford Pinto case arose from an initial company decision that a change in the design at a late stage in the development of the car would be too expensive.

- **Government influence.** There are increasing government pressures on firms to confirm to national and international standards on social and environmental matters. The UK government launched an Ethical Trading Initiative, and an international standard, SA 8000, covers such areas as working hours and the use of child labour. In some cases the pressures are backed by legislation. There are links here to the cost argument for ethical business, in that failure to comply with laws on pollution or conditions of employment may result in prosecution and subsequent fines. There is also a view that, when cases are brought, courts are more lenient if a strong ethical stance has been demonstrated by the company.

- **Ethics and the supply chain.** In order to do business with some companies, such as Toys 'R' Us, Timberland and Levi Strauss, suppliers must comply with a code of ethical conduct. There is also a belief that doing business ethically attracts both buyers and suppliers. In broader terms, the relationship between buyer and supplier has become an important ingredient of business success, especially in manufacturing. An important element in that relationship is trust and the need to behave openly and honourably towards each other.

- **Ethical consumers.** Wilson (1997) argues that, even during a recession, there is a growing band of consumers who seek out goods and services that are both environmentally friendly and have been produced ethically. He cites the example of the Cooperative Bank, which announced that it would not be involved with tobacco companies, firms with poor environmental records or those engaged in factory farming and animal testing. As a result the bank claims an increase in the number of new accounts. Research by Mintel (1994) demonstrated that consumers were willing to pay more for ethical products.

- **Ethical investors.** There are investors, known as **ethical investors**, who seek out ethical companies in which to invest, but evidence is relatively sparse. Some investment companies have responded by establishing investment portfolios of ethical companies. There are difficulties. Who decides which company is ethical and which is not, and on what criteria? Many investors lack detailed knowledge of the ethical code and behaviour of the companies in which they seek to invest and focus on financial performance as a priority. We know that in most countries a large proportion of shares are in the hands of organizational investors. Some of these groups may be concerned where their investment is going. For example, it is estimated that the voluntary sector in the UK has £20 billion under investment at any one time. Many voluntary sector organizations are very concerned where their money is being invested. Stock markets have responded in the publication of such indexes as FTSE4Good and the Dow Jones Sustainability Indexes. In the UK a government directive has meant that pension funds must now have a statement about ethical principles in investment strategy.

- **Ethical employees.** In general terms, most firms will seek to establish some sort of match between corporate values and those of employees to gain commitment from them and to retain their services. Many firms use induction and employee development programmes to reinforce corporate values. Employees are clearly attracted by fair pay, security of employment and benefits such as travel season ticket loans and child-care provisions. There is some evidence to suggest that an ethical stance taken by and employer contributes towards the job satisfaction of its employees (Koh and Boo, 2001). Equally firms have noted an increase in job seekers who are concerned about ethical issues and social responsibility. Many firms now highlight such issues in their recruitment literature.

Some problems and issues

In the previous section we identified a number of points to demonstrate why being ethical and socially responsible was good for business. As the following points demonstrate there are also a number of problems and issues with this view:

- **Weak evidence.** We have already indicated that it is difficult to prove conclusively that concern for ethical business and social responsibility will improve the performance of the company. Many of the above points fall into the category of beliefs rather than hard evidence. For every study claiming a connection there is another offering a more sceptical perspective. For example, Verschoor (1998) did a study of the USA Fortune 500 companies with a management commitment to ethical and socially responsible business, which was backed up by practices. He found there was a statistical relationship between such practices and the financial performance of the company. Van der Merwe *et al.* (2003) argued from their research finding that whereas those companies whose performance was excellent had strong ethical codes and practices, there were other companies that had such codes where performance was anything but excellent. Having ethical codes was not a guarantee of excellent performance. Many companies possessing such codes and practices did not perform well at all. In our discussion of corporate culture, in Chapter 5, we made a similar comment in suggesting that strong cultures were the products of success rather than the other way around. Firms that are performing well have the luxury and financial capacity to engage in social responsibility programmes.

- **Structural barriers.** Many firms operate in highly competitive markets with demanding shareholders. Under such conditions the pressures on managers to cut costs and maximize profit are considerable. However, there is evidence to suggest that cost cutting can lead to serious problems. In the three cases we have mentioned – Ford Pinto, Union Carbide (Bhopal) and Esso (*Exxon Valdes*) – the resulting problems were partly the result of attempts to cut costs.

- **How widespread is the concern?** While awareness and acceptance are widespread among large firms like Daimler–Benz and Shell, there are still many traditional managers who still believe there to be a basic conflict between ethical business and profitable business. This is particularly true among small businesses. In many firms changing well-entrenched attitudes is difficult and takes time.

- **Ethics as a sham.** In some cases the greening of products has been a marketing ploy, and consumers are deliberately misled into thinking they are buying a 'green' product when this is not the case. Some commentators refer to this as 'greenwash'. In the section on corporate culture in Chapter 5, we illustrate how some firms use values, not as a means of involving employees, but as a way of controlling them. Many companies are fond of stating in their corporate literature that 'employees are our most valuable asset' when employment conditions and work practices would suggest otherwise. The fast-food chain McDonald's has been at the centre of much criticism both for its attitude to the environment and to its employees.

- **High cost.** In some cases the costs of environmentally friendly business can be expensive, resulting in unacceptably high prices. There may also be contradictions. For example, in car manufacture, the switch from solvent-based to water-based paint is indisputably better in terms of the environment, yet it increases drying time and, with it, energy consumption that both pushes up the cost and is environmentally unfriendly.

- **Cultural variations.** Different standards, both legal and cultural, apply in different parts of the world. Firms that operate in a number of markets may have the increased cost of ensuring their products fulfil the requirements of each country. Products that can be legally sold in one market may be illegal in another, as with hand-guns, legal in the USA but not the UK.

- **Stakeholder differences.** Different stakeholders may have different requirements as we have seen in our section on corporate social responsibility. In the Brent Spar case, the dumping of the oil platform was acceptable to the UK government, but opposed by some other European countries, such as Germany, and environmental groups, such as Greenpeace.

Such problems as the above create dilemmas for management in their attempts to pursue an ethical business strategy. Survival of the most ethical of companies depends upon achieving financial targets. In 1999, many believed that the Body Shop stood at the crossroads. Its business performance left much to be desired and the company underwent restructure. This involved bringing in fresh blood, but also making people redundant, including the closure of its manufacturing operations. Optimists believed the company's ethical stance would emerge yet stronger and its reliance on a wider group of suppliers would see its value spread to other companies. Pessimists feared that the company would become just another company, undifferentiated from its competitors in its unique ethical stance.

Mechanisms for ethical business and social responsibility

Strategically in terms of ethical business and social responsibility managers may operate at any point along a continuum as we can see from Figure 8.1.

There are a number of mechanisms a firm may use. We identify some of them below:

- **Ethical audit.** An important foundation to behaving ethically is for management to carry out an audit of all the firm's activities and relationships to assess shortfalls in practice and to establish action plans. Key areas for the **ethical audit** are products and services, processes, terms of employment and conditions for employees and the firm's relationships with its suppliers, local community and the environment. Issues may be raised about the safety of products and processes, how customers are treated before during and after sales, how employees are treated and so on.

- **Codes of practice.** These outline the firm's general stand on ethical business in terms of a mission. Most codes of practice also contain policy and operational manuals that attempt to establish appropriate decisions and courses of action in specific circumstances as, for example, with the receiving of gifts from potential customers. Such codes of practice exist not only for employees but also for suppliers. For example, Levi Strauss, Reebok and Nike all challenged the practices of some of their suppliers in Asia and refused to do business with those where there

Figure 8.1

Strategic positions on ethical business and social responsibility

Reactive–defensive

- Only takes action when a problem arises
- Minimal coverage of legal obligations to avoid prosecution

Proactive

- Initiates ethical and socially responsible policies
- Sets industry standards in ethical and socially responsible policies

was evidence of the use of forced labour and/or child labour. As a result, Levi Strauss established a code of practice for suppliers on employment practices, pay and health and safety.

The growth of global business has led to the publication of a number of international codes by such organizations as OECD and ILO, and the UN Commission on Transnational Corporations. Such codes cover a broad range of issues dealing with human rights and work practices. These include statements about the disclosure of financial information, levels of pay, the right of employees to unionize and the length of the working week.

Despite the widespread publication of such codes across a large number of organizations, little is known about their impact on employee behaviour or the firm's activities. While such codes exist, it is reckoned that knowledge and application of them is far from widespread within individual organizations.

- **Ethics department.** Some organizations have institutionalized ethics and social responsibility within the organization structure. In 1980 the World Bank established an ethics function and a few years later incorporated it as the ethics office within the HR department. Since 1990 it has operated as a stand-alone department and has developed an ethical tool-kit to assist decision-making in different cultural settings wherever the bank operates. A separate department was established in 1997, the department of institutional integrity, with the primary task of investigating and advising on fraud and corruption in bank projects (Johnson, 2002).

- **Employee induction and training.** For many firms this is an important mechanism for transmitting values and practices about ethical business and corporate social responsibility. Employees joining one of the major Korean corporations, such as Samsung, Hyundai and LG, will begin their employment with up to 3 weeks induction, which focuses on the values of the organization, including their commitment to social responsibility (Needle, 2000).

- **Whistleblowing.** Some firms, such as the World Bank, have set up **whistleblowing** hot-lines. Employees may phone in, without fear of reprisal, to report any practice or incident where members of the company have been behaving unethically. Such a vehicle has been established for employees in higher education in the UK via the publication the *Times Higher Education Journal*. This reports stories of unethical behaviour among academic staff, such as plagiarism, or by employers in their treatment of staff.

● **Non-executive directors.** The theory behind the appointment of **non-executive directors** is that they have no direct involvement in the management of the enterprise and are able to provide experience from elsewhere and can operate as an impartial voice in influencing strategic direction. As people with an interest outside the organization, they are often considered as an important agent of social responsibility. The 'Higgs Report on the Role and Effectiveness of Non-executive Directors' (reported in Garratt, 2003) sees their function in terms of:

  – widening diversity of board membership to prevent corrupting practices;
  – providing critical and independent thinking in board level decision-making;
  – providing a vehicle for the greater shareholder access to the board.

However, the independence of non-executive directors has been questioned. They have to be closely involved in the workings of the company to be able to offer any critical input. This means they must work closely with management, making it more difficult to maintain distance and retain independence. Moreover, many are appointed because they are well-known to existing executive directors, thereby compromising their potential for independence still further. The Higgs Report noted that only 4 per cent of non-executive directors were formally interviewed before appointment.

● **Implicit mechanisms.** In addition to the explicit mechanisms identified above, there are a number of more implicit measures to champion ethical practice. These operate through corporate culture, management leadership, performance appraisal and incentive schemes. For example, ethical business and socially responsible practice could be part of employee job descriptions and form an important factor upon which performance is judged.

| Case 8.1 | **Enron** |

Enron was founded in 1985 as the result of a merger between Houston Natural Gas and InterNorth, both relatively small regional players in the USA. The Chairman of the new company was Kenneth Lay, who remained in post until Enron's bankruptcy in 2001. The company grew rapidly and had become by the 1990s, the largest energy trading company in the world and the USA's seventh largest company. Every year from 1996–2001 the company was ranked by *Fortune Magazine* as the 'most innovative company' in the USA. Between 1996 and 2000 sales value increased from $US13.3 billion to 100.8 billion. The company was praised by Wall Street and the White House alike. Enron's growth generated considerable wealth for both investors and employees, more especially a small number of senior staff, some later accused of fraud.

Enron portrayed itself as a highly competitive, global business, strongly in favour of the free market and deregulation. It also portrayed itself as a socially responsible organization through its concern for the environment (it had won awards in the USA and in other countries and supported the Kyoto summit on greenhouse gas emissions), its involvement in local communities (it donated generously to schools) and its activities in the Third World (it saw itself as contributing to raised living standards). The company was also keen to stress its empowerment of the workforce in that employees at every level were encouraged to put forward ideas which contributed to the growth of the business. Employees were rewarded handsomely for profitable ideas.

In December 2001, the company filed for bankruptcy with debts of US$15 billion. Later reports estimate that the debt could be even larger. At the time this was the biggest bankruptcy in USA history, a distinction taken over by WorldCom some 8 months later. The demise of Enron was responsible for the bringing down of Arthur Andersen, one of the world's leading accounting firms.

What did Enron do?

Enron was engaged in a number of activities, most of which were related to the energy industry.

- Enron built pipelines, gas plants and power stations around the world.

- It benefited from the deregulation of the energy and utilities industries (those providing energy and water, among other things, to the public) in many countries of the world. As a result, Enron was able to expand rapidly in the 1980s. The company sold energy to a wide variety of industries and utilities in the USA and elsewhere. More significantly it sold contracts to deliver natural gas, electricity and other energy products at some date in the future.

- To support the sale of energy in the future, Enron developed and sold a number of financial instruments to its customers, designed to protect them against large shifts in energy prices. These instruments are known as derivatives in that they are derived from an asset or a product. Their purpose is to allow companies to offset financial risk. The two types of derivative in this case were futures and options. A future is a contract which places an obligation to buy or sell at a set price on a given future date. An option is similar to a future except that the contract offers the right but not the obligation.

- Enron invested in a large number of other activities and business, many of them, particularly in the years preceding bankruptcy, completely unrelated to its core business of energy.

Enron was one of the first companies to take advantage of Internet trading through the creation of Enrononline. Internet business was considerable so that, in the first quarter of 2001 alone, the company was involved in US$27 billion worth of transactions online. Such volume of Internet business had a significant impact on Enron's rising share price and its appeal to investors and the USA government.

By 1999 Enron was involved in a quarter of all natural gas and electricity deals in the world and the company operated in many countries, with large operations in Brazil, India and the UK. In the the UK Enron had bought Wessex Water, several power stations on Teeside and was one of the largest traders on the London Metals Exchange. In all the company employed 19 000, 5000 in Europe, 4000 of them in the UK.

▶

To many commentators, Enron was not an energy company in the traditional sense. The company had capitalized, not only on the deregulation of the energy industry, but also upon deregulation and product innovation in the financial markets. In particular it made a large proportion of its income from derivatives. The complexity of many of these financial products and associated deals meant that Enron's finances were particularly difficult to unravel and even senior employees were not aware of the full extent of the dealing.

What went wrong?

The collapse of Enron happened in a matter of months. In a few weeks, between October and November 2001, the share price fell by 90 per cent and by the end of November three independent credit rating agencies considered Enron to be worthless. Around that time a rescue attempt was made by a smaller, rival energy company, Dynegy. This ended when Dynegy withdrew, claiming that Enron had misrepresented its financial position and its position was far worse than Dynegy had thought.

The market was first alerted when Jeffrey Shilling suddenly resigned as the chief executive of Enron in August 2001. Kenneth Lay, the chairman, took over the role of CEO. From October 2001 onwards, a number of factors came together which led to the bankruptcy of Enron. There have been many accusations of fraudulent behaviour and several senior Enron executives are facing trial. The former Chief Accountant, Andrew Fastow, his wife and seven other executives have been accused and are awaiting trial on charges of fraud, insider trading and the falsification of accounting records.

However, throughout, the company has maintained that it had always operated legally and had simply taken advantage, as had many other companies, of the complexities of the newly deregulated markets in both energy and finance. Several investigating teams have been brought in since bankruptcy, including PriceWaterhouse Coopers. None of the teams has been able to sort out the total complexities of Enron's dealings. The following attempts to give a flavour of Enron's 'wrongdoings'.

- In essence Enron had inflated their earnings through the use of some highly dubious accounting procedures. For example, they included in their accounts derivative contracts at gross rather than net value.

- Enron took advantage of a number of innovations in financial instruments, notably derivatives, to manipulate earnings and avoid regulation. These activities were well-known by the firm's consultants and auditors, Arthur Andersen and by Wall Street investment banks.

- Enron's staff exploited the deregulated energy and derivatives markets to the full. They became involved in a large number of increasingly complex deals with networks of companies (over 3000 were linked to Enron in some way) as well as major banks. The large incentives given to staff to make such deals led to yet more deals, and even some senior managers were not aware of what was happening. The company was unable to control its own staff.

- Enron was borrowing heavily to finance many of its deals. The debts incurred by this borrowing were 'hidden' in a number of companies and did not appear on Enron's balance sheet. This process artificially inflated the value of the company and was a key factor in the increase in share price. This was also a key disclosure in Enron's demise. The company conceded that it had not fully met accounting requirements and, as a result, was forced to reduce its equity by $US1.2 billion. This led to a fall in share price and a loss of confidence in the company.

- The company made a large number of highly speculative and ultimately poor investments, many of them not connected with energy, its core business. Many of these investments were also 'buried' in subsidiary companies and not declared on the balance sheet.

- In the weeks around the declaration of bankruptcy, a number of older accusations resurfaced. We were reminded of accusations of human rights violations against protesters at the building of a power station in Dabhol, India. Amnesty International became involved in the case of the protesters and the World Bank had publicly criticized the cost of the project. Also in India, Enron had been involved in a political corruption scandal concerned with the privatization of energy supply.

- Just prior to bankruptcy, 286 senior staff received bonuses totaling $US72 million. The company argued that the bonuses were to ensure that key staff stayed with them during difficult times. A group representing redundant Enron workers and those that had lost their pension is taking out a lawsuit to recover the $US72 million for the pension fund.

The impact of Enron's bankruptcy

Ultimately the Enron scandal involved both the White House and the UK government. President Bush was an old friend of Lay and had been involved in business deals with him in Texas. Enron had always been active in political sponsorship donating, over a period of several years, more than $US1 million to the Republican party and 500 000 to the Democrats as well as making a contribution of a further half million dollars to various Bush campaigns. Senior White House staff had several talks with Enron during 2001, but the details were not disclosed. Similarly, in the UK, Enron held several talks with the Blair government between 1998–2000. The former Conservative energy minister Lord Wakeham was a non-executive director of the company and the ex-Europe Chairman, Ralph Hodge, was favoured in the UK New Year Honours. It is clear that Enron sought political protection, although the Bush administration has distanced itself from such corporate scandals and has introduced revised laws on pensions and disclosure of financial information.

With the collapse of the share price, many investors lost considerable amounts. These investors included many employees, who had been encouraged to back their own company, particularly in view of its remarkable rise. Many of these same employees were prevented from selling their shares prior to the collapse of the company. Some senior employees, however, did sell their shares before the worst of the collapse, attracting accusations of insider trading. Many of those same employees not only saw their share investments rendered worthless, they lost their jobs and they lost their pensions. Over 20 000 employees are estimated to have lost $US1 billion in a pension fund tied to Enron stock.

Financial institutions lost money and many lost reputation. Credit Lyonnais had $US250 million tied up with Enron. JP Morgan Chase and Citigroup between them agreed to pay $US255 million to settle charges of helping Enron commit fraud. The money will be paid into the pension fund, although the two banks are still liable to private lawsuits brought against them by investors.

The case of Arthur Andersen

Arthur Andersen was one of the 'big five' global accounting firms and employed 85 000 persons worldwide. Andersen was both a consultant to Enron, with a contract worth around $US50 million a year, and also acted as Enron's auditors. The whole Enron case highlighted an ongoing debate within the accounting profession and governments: that of the independence of auditors. The main argument is that firms which as act as both consultants and auditors are likely to be compromised in their auditing duties by their close association with companies, especially where high fees are involved as with Enron.

The Houston office of Andersen admitted to destroying documents relating to the Enron case. Staff were disciplined and the partner responsible was dismissed. More significantly, in June 2002, Andersen was found guilty in a Houston court of obstructing justice. The verdict meant that Andersen was not allowed to audit public companies in the USA and it announced that it would cease practice by the end of 2002. The other large accounting firms have been working with Andersen to transfer their clients. Arthur Andersen still face legal action brought by investors and, if this goes against them, they could be liable for the whole amount wiped off the Enron stock value. This would run to billions of dollars and would bankrupt Andersen. Essentially they are accused of not doing their job by spotting discrepancies in the accounts and alerting investors.

Thus the Enron affair brought down one of the oldest, largest and well-known firms of accountants in the world. There are those who believe that Arthur Andersen deserved all that has happened so far and more. Others see the backlash of a USA government wishing to send out a strong message about corporate fraud.

Endpiece

The new CEO of Enron, Stephen Cooper, sees its future as a scaled-down company of some 12 000 employees. A message on the Enron website in July 2003 stated that: 'Enron is in the midst of restructuring its business with the hope of emerging from bankruptcy as a strong and viable, albeit smaller, company.'

Frank Partnoy, writing in the UK *Guardian* newspaper stated:

> Relative to many of its peers, Enron was a profitable, well-run and law-abiding firm. That does not mean it was a model of corporate behaviour – it obviously

was not. Although the media seized on its collapse as the business scandal of the decade, the truth was that Enron was no worse than Bankers Trust, Orange County, Cendant, Long-Term Capital Management, CS First Boston, Merrill Lynch and many others to follow, including Global Crossing and WorldCom, which collapsed soon after Enron.

Source: www.guardian.co.uk/enron; www.enron.com; Bryce, 2002; *People Management,* 21 February, 2002; Partnoy, 2003

Questions

1 What aspects of corporate social responsibility are represented by the Enron case?

2 In your opinion, did Enron behave ethically and if not why not? How do you place your position on this issue alongside that of Frank Partnoy (stated at the end of the case)?

3 Examine the role of Arthur Andersen in the Enron affair. What impact will this have on the accounting firm? Is it deserved?

4 What steps can be taken and by whom to ensure that an Enron case never happens again?

5 Examine a selection of websites dealing with the Enron case. What has happened to Enron and Arthur Andersen since 2003?

Summary

- Business ethics and corporate social responsibility are both about conducting business in an ethical manner and acting responsibly towards a number of stakeholders and looking after the environment.

- Both business ethics and corporate social responsibility are complex issues and there are numerous issues to be considered in satisfying the needs of a variety of stakeholders and in behaving responsibly towards the environment.

- At the heart of business ethics is a debate about the true nature of business and whether business is the best agent for social responsibility.

- There are however strong business arguments that socially responsible business is successful business although much of the evidence is weak and contradictory.

- Organizations have the choice of a number of strategies and practices to operate in a socially responsible way.

Discussion questions

1 What do you understand by the concepts of business ethics and corporate social responsibility? To what extent can we distinguish between the two concepts?

2 In an organization known to you (firm, college, etc.) identify the various stakeholders. What does corporate social responsibility mean in the case of each?

3 What specific issues emerge when an organization attempts to be socially responsible to a number of different stakeholders?

4 To what extent do you agree with the view that the 'business of business is business' and that social responsibility is best handled by other means?

5 What arguments can you put forward to support the view that socially responsible business is successful business? Support your arguments with evidence and illustrations.

6 What are the pros and cons of whistleblowing?

7 What specific issues in business ethics emerge as a result of globalization?

8 Examine the Railtrack case in Chapter 5 (Case 5.4) and the Executive Pay case in Chapter 6 (Case 6.2). What aspects of business ethics and corporate social responsibility are involved?

Further reading

Chryssides, G. D. and Kaler, J. H. (2002) *An Introduction to Business Ethics*, Thomson Learning, London, offers a fairly broad coverage. Davies, P. W. F. (ed.) (1997) *Current Issues in Business Ethics*, Routledge, London, while offering a philosophical perspective in many of the articles raises a number of interesting issues. A more pragmatic perspective is offered by Financial Times Management, *Visions of Ethical Business*, Financial Times Management, London. A good source of research in ethical issues is the *Journal of Business Ethics*.

Innovation

- Identify and differentiate between the concepts and activities of invention, innovation, entrepreneurship and research and development (R&D).
- Explain how innovation is the product of the interaction of a number of environmental and organizational variables.
- Explain the relationship between innovation and other functional areas of business such as operations and marketing.
- Identify the different types of innovation and forms of R&D.
- Assess critically the meaning of entrepreneurship and the role of the entrepreneur and identify the key variables influencing entrepreneurial success.
- Critically assess the contribution of innovation to a firm's profitability and nation's economic growth.
- Identify the role of state intervention in innovation and assess its contribution.
- Assess the link between innovation and technology.
- Critically assess the relative influence on innovation of organization size, structure and culture.
- Explain and assess the different strategic approaches to innovation.
- Explain the difference between tacit and explicit forms of knowledge and their contribution to innovation.

Introduction

> There can be little doubt that those activities which contribute to the efficient introduction and exploitation of new and improved processes and products are extremely important for the competitive performance and long-term growth of any industrial economy. (*Freeman, 1989, p. 199*)

There is a strong and widely-held belief that innovation is the key to economic growth for both national economies and individual firms. In some cases innovation is the key ingredient for survival in a competitive market. In the electronics industry, where product life- cycles have reduced, constant innovation is essential. Seventy per cent of the products of Siemens, the large German electronics company, are less than five years old, and companies like Siemens must undertake a constant process of product renewal.

Undoubtedly, innovation is a key function of business since it is related to entrepreneurship – the driving force behind business growth and development. In this chapter we attempt a broad-based view of innovation. We will start by examining the differences between the related concepts of innovation, invention, research and development, design and entrepreneurship. We then move on to examine the relationship between innovative business activity and the environmental aspects of the model, in particular its impact on economic growth, the role of governments in stimulating innovation and entrepreneurship, and, especially, differences in government policy and attitudes towards innovation in different nation states. Much government policy focuses upon the encouragement of new technologies, yet it is our contention that the development and design of new products needs to be accompanied by corresponding developments in marketing and in organization. In the latter part of this chapter we extend this view of innovation still further by examining how it operates within organizations, and, in particular, the relevance of organizational structure and culture to innovative activity. The chapter ends by focusing on a number of generic innovation strategies.

It can be seen that innovation is not confined to the technological hardware of products and processes. We believe that successful product and process innovation invariably requires accompanying innovations in marketing and organization structure. These are sometimes referred to as administrative innovations as opposed to technical innovations of the product and process type. Research has pointed to the need to balance both technical and administrative innovation (Daft, 1982; Damanpour *et al.*, 1989). The impact of technical change can be significantly lessened without accompanying changes in administration. For example, the adoption of a new client database in a large organization is of little value unless staff are trained to use it. In Case 9.4 we examine the interrelationship of technical and organizational innovations in the shipping industry. In retailing it is mostly the innovations that the customer cannot see, particularly in the logistics of getting goods to customers, that have given firms their greatest competitive advantage.

There is a particularly close association between innovation and marketing. Peter Drucker sees these two activities as the basic functions of business, as he regards them as the only truly entrepreneurial functions (Drucker, 1968).

The link between innovation and entrepreneurship is important, since it establishes innovation as a function of all businesses. Many people associate innovation with the process of new product design in the manufacturing industry. Yet, examples of innovation can be drawn from every conceivable organizational context. In the financial services industry, banking has been transformed by the introduction of automatic cash dispensers, giving the general public much greater access to their accounts. In an increasingly competitive market the banks have developed mortgage services, and some building societies, which began to offer banking services, eventually turned themselves into fully-fledged banks. In the entertainment industry, the innovation of multi-screen cinemas offers the public a wider choice and has contributed to significant increases in attendance and hence revenue. In the travel industry the booking of airline seats has been revolutionized by computerized booking systems directly accessible by travellers via the Internet. As we saw in Chapter 3, significant claims are made for the impact of e-commerce. In education, innovations occur through the development of new courses or new methods of presenting those courses, such as online learning. In most of the above cases the innovation is viewed as offering the adopter a competitive advantage.

However, these various forms of innovation are not without difficulties associated with management implementation. Such difficulties include the following:

- The cost of the innovation and the raising of the necessary finance.
- Ensuring that the firm is staffed by people with the required skills.
- Persuading the consumer to buy the new product or service.
- Delivering the product or service in sufficient quantity when demand is created.
- Coping with the organization change and the accompanying political processes.
- The time scale required for the change to take place and people to see the returns.
- The attitude of the people involved towards risk and their ability to cope with uncertainty.

A major product change or the installation of new equipment can take 5 years and longer before the development costs are recovered. For this reason alone, major innovations are apt to make both management and financial backers nervous. We examine the management and organization processes related to innovation later in the chapter. First, we make an attempt to define the various terms.

Identifying the concepts

The terms 'invention', 'innovation', 'research and development', 'design' and 'entrepreneurship' are all used in a variety of contexts, often interchangeably. There is a further confusion in that while all are processes, 'research and development' or R&D as it popularly known, is frequently used in an organizational context to identify a department whose primary objective is the creation and development of new products and new ways of making them. We will now look at the concepts themselves in a little more detail.

Invention and innovation

These terms are often confused, yet if we take Schumpeter's line there is a very clear distinction between them:

> As long as they are not carried into practice, inventions are economically irrelevant. (*Schumpeter, 1961, p. 88*)

Tidd *et al.* (2001) remind us that the originators of some of the most famous inventions are not remembered, while those who commercially exploited them are. Thus, few have heard

---

Key concept 9.1 Invention versus innovation

Invention is the discovery or creation of a new product or process, whereas innovation is the process through which inventions and new ideas become a business or operational reality. An innovation can include new products, processes, strategies and organization structures. Innovation is claimed by many as an important source of competitive advantage.

of J. Murray Spengler, the inventor of the vacuum cleaner, yet most know Hoover, initially a leather-goods maker, to whom Spengler sold his idea. In a similar way we associate sewing machines with Singer, yet they stole the invention from one Elias Howe.

Invention is the creation of something new, be it new computer software, a new computer design, a new method for painting cars, a new form of selling, a new university course, or a new form of organization structure. An invention becomes an innovation when the idea becomes a reality, when the new software and computer go into manufacture and start selling, when the new technology for painting cars offers a more efficient system, or when the new university course recruits students.

This reinforces the notion that innovation operates in a variety of forms and in a variety of contexts. We are now able to distinguish three broad categories.

- A distinction can be drawn between **product innovation** and **process innovation**. Product innovation is the development of a new product such as a new model of car, a new form of insurance policy, or a restaurant offering a new vegetarian menu. Process innovation is concerned with how the product is made or delivered to the customer. The development of robots in the manufacturing industry is a form of process innovation, as is a restaurant opening a self-service section in addition to an existing waiter-service operation. In cases like the Toyota production system, process innovations can offer a firm an enviable competitive advantage.

- We have already noted that innovation may occur in every aspect of the organization's operations. We can therefore classify **innovation by function**. Innovations occur in the selection and use of raw materials, in the way goods and services are produced, in the marketing activities and in the way the organization is structured and managed. For example, the introduction of work-group participation in management decision-making is a form of innovation, as are types of job enrichment to enhance worker motivation.

- We can also make a distinction between **basic** and **incremental** innovations. The latter represent innovations that are modifications and improvements on existing products and processes. In fact, the great majority of innovations are not major breakthroughs but modifications, often of a very minor nature. This incremental approach to innovation is pursued successfully by many Japanese companies and is the reason why camera producers, such as Minolta and Canon, bring out a new model at regular intervals.

Illustrations of all these types of innovation are presented in Table 9.1.

In addition to the various types of innovation, we might add a fourth category. This has been termed **pseudo-innovation** (Mensch, 1979). Such innovations are often introduced to revitalize a stagnant market, when, in fact, no real change has taken place. Pseudo-innovations are often the product of marketing campaigns to change the fortunes of a flagging product. The product may be re-launched under a different brand name, repackaged to suggest product changes or advertised as containing a 'new improved formula' when no significant change has taken place. A case in this area is that of the washing powder Square Deal Surf. Its forerunner, Surf, was experiencing a declining market share in a market where every new product appeared to come with a new formula for washing whiter. The company aimed the product at a segment of the market that they had identified as 'anti-gimmick'. To emphasize this point they offered the product with a changed name, which suggested to consumers that they were getting a better deal than

Table 9.1	Different types of innovation	
	Extent of the innovation	
Type of innovation	*Basic*	*Modification*
Raw material	The use of plastic in place of glass in bottles	Changing the components of the plastics in the bottles to make them tougher to withstand the pressure of carbonated drinks
Product	The use of integrated circuits on microchips to replace transistors	Changing the dashboard display in a car to make it easier for the driver to read
Process	Introducing robots to perform the welding operation in a car assembly plant	Increasing the number of stages in a car painting process to gain a better finish
Marketing	Selling computers directly to the consumer rather than through retailers	Using television personalities instead of politicians in a televised political broadcast
Organization	Creating a matrix form of organization in a global company to replace the traditional arrangement based on specialist functions	Outsourcing the payroll function from the HR department

those offered by competitors. The change and repositioning of the product in the market was highly successful and sales increased. We deal with aspects of market segmentation and positioning in more detail in Chapter 11.

The case of Square Deal Surf illustrates the complexity of innovation. To Mensch it undoubtedly represents a pseudo-innovation in terms of product, yet the marketing strategy employed was highly innovative. Moreover, not all innovations are visible. Where washing powders have radically changed their formula this is not instantly apparent to the consumer and the company relies upon its marketing effort to convey this information, reinforcing the importance of an integrated innovation and marketing strategy.

Research, development and design

We can define research and development as **the organization of innovation at the level of the firm.** It is this activity of an organization that both seeks to satisfy a market need by developing new products and methods, and find uses for scientific and technological inventions. This introduces the concepts of **demand–pull innovation** (fulfilling a market need) and **technology–push innovation** (applying existing knowledge). R&D is clearly associated with science and technology, although the R&D function can be performed in all types of industry. We have seen that the process of new product development occurs in non-scientific and technical situations. In many organizations there is a group of people whose primary task is the generation of new business ideas, as in the case of television companies, which have a department for new programme development.

> ## Key concept 9.2 Research and development
>
> Research and development, or R&D, is the name give to the organizational function that is usually the focus for innovation within a firm. R&D can refer to an activity or the name of a specific department. Expenditure on R&D and the size of an R&D department have been used as measures of levels of innovative activity, although they are probably best used as indicators rather than exact measures owing to the presence of other variables which can and do influence innovation.

> ## Key concept 9.3 Demand–pull versus technology–push
>
> Demand–pull and technology–push refer to the sources of innovation. Demand–pull refers to the development of new products and processes as a direct result of market demand. Technology–push is the utilization of known technologies to develop innovative products and processes. Many innovations, for example the CD player, are developed as a result of both demand–pull and technology–push.

In some industries, especially those involved in complex, competitive environments, R&D is a vital part of the business. Firms like IBM and Hewlett-Packard (HP) in the computer industry and Bayer and GlaxoSmithKline (GSK) in the pharmaceutical industry have large teams of staff engaged exclusively in R&D work. The importance of R&D to GSK is shown in Case 9.5. In the case of HP, innovation is part of the organizational culture and is stressed as a responsibility of all employees (Case 5.6). However, the institutionalization of R&D can bring its own problems, which are raised when we look at organizational aspects later in the chapter.

The British government, through the Department of Trade and Industry, now publishes annual league tables of R&D spending. The UK **R&D Scoreboard**, as it is known, has become an important benchmarking device, not just for UK firms but for international firms as well. It lists the top 600 UK firms and the top 600 international firms in terms of their R&D spending and their R&D intensity. R&D intensity is spending as a proportion of sales turnover. Such information is now available for stock exchange listed companies as a requirement of **SSAP 13 (Statement of Standard Accounting Practice)**. Tables 9.2 and 9.3 show expenditure on R&D by companies in the UK and worldwide respectively. Table 9.4 shows the proportion of R&D spending by sector and compares the UK with the overall international data. A number of conclusions may be drawn from the R&D Scoreboard.

● The highest-spending UK companies are both in pharmaceuticals; GSK (featured in Case 9.5) ranks 12th in the world in terms of R&D spending and AstraZeneca 25th. Only five UK firms overall feature in the top 100. With these exceptions, the UK subsidiaries of international companies have a higher listing than the UK companies.

Table 9.2	Ranking of top 20 companies in the UK by R&D expenditure and as % sales 2002		

Company	Rank	2002 R&D spend £ million	% Sales
GlaxoSmithKline	1	2651	12.9
AstraZeneca	2	1915	16.8
BAE Systems	3	994	11.0
Ford	4	738	7.8
Unilever	5	717	2.3
Marconi	6	628	14.6
Pfizer	7	373	39.2
BT	8	362	1.8
Rolls Royce	9	358	5.7
Reuters	10	294	7.6
Shell	11	267	0.3
BP	12	266	0.2
Ivensys	13	265	3.8
Amersham	14	174	11.5
ICI	15	153	2.4
Syngenta	16=	130	15.6
TRW	16=	130	2.7
Vodafone	18	110	0.5
Smiths	19	109	2.2
Nortel Networks	20	105	3.6

Source: DTI, 2002a

- The growth areas of spending internationally are in pharmaceuticals, IT hardware, and IT services and software.
- The UK tends to be dominated by spending in pharmaceuticals, and aerospace and defence. Overall, internationally, the leading spenders are in IT hardware, automotive and pharmaceuticals. Three of the top four countries are leading automotive firms.

Types of R&D

R&D is an incremental process. We illustrate this by using as a framework the classification of R&D developed by Burns and Stalker (1966). Although their classification is biased towards technological industries, it gives us further insights into the innovative process.

- **Pure research** is concerned with advancing the state of knowledge in a particular field with little immediate concern for its commercial application. Very few firms engage directly in **pure research**, and, on the whole, it is generally left to the university sector. Business concerns are involved indirectly insofar as some of them sponsor research activity in some universities.

Table 9.3

Ranking of top 40 companies in worldwide by R&D expenditure and as % sales 2002

Company	Rank	2001 R&D spend £million	% Sales
Ford Motor, USA	1	5109	4.6
General Motors, USA	2	4280	3.5
Siemens, Germany	3	4129	7.8
Daimler–Chrysler, Germany	4	3612	3.9
Pfizer, USA	5	3346	15.0
IBM, USA	6	3189	5.4
Ericsson, Sweden	7	3045	20.1
Microsoft, USA	8	3023	17.3
Motorola, USA	9	2981	14.4
Matsushita Electric, Japan	10	2976	8.2
Cisco Systems, USA	11	2707	17.6
GlaxoSmithKline, UK	12	2651	12.9
Intel, USA	13	2620	14.3
Toyota Motor, Japan	14	2503	3.6
Johnson and Johnson, USA	15	2479	10.9
Lucent Technologies, USA	16	2430	16.5
Nortel Networks, Canada	17	2226	18.4
Sony, Japan	18	2193	6.1
Hitachi, Japan	19	2186	5.2
NTT, Japan	20	2136	3.6
Fujitsu, Japan	21	2122	7.4
Aventis, France	22	2119	15.2
Honda Motor, Japan	23	2079	5.4
Philips Electronics, The Netherlands	24	2016	10.2
AstraZeneca, UK	25	1915	16.8
Alcatel, France	26	1885	12.2
Hewlett-Packard, USA	27	1843	5.9
Nokia, Finland	28	1817	9.6
NEC, Japan	29	1755	6.5
Toshiba, Japan	30	1725	5.5
Novartis, Switzerland	31	1722	13.1
Merck, USA	32	1696	5.1
Volkswagen, Germany	33	1619	3.0
Roche, Switzerland	34	1601	13.3
Pharmacia, USA	35	1562	16.4
Bristol-Myers Squibb, USA	36	1559	11.6
Eli Lilly, USA	37	1543	19.4
Bayer, Germany	38	1514	8.2
Sun Microsystems, USA	39	1391	11.0
Robert Bosch, Germany	40	1384	6.7

Source: DTI, 2002a

Table 9.4	R&D by sector		
		Proportion of total R&D	
Sector		International	UK
IT hardware		25.1	8.2
Automotive		16.5	6.4
Pharmaceuticals and biotechnology		16.3	36.7
Electronic and electrical		10.4	4.5
Software and IT services		6.7	5.1
Chemicals		4.9	3.8
Areospace and defence		3.9	9.8
Engineering		3.0	2.6
Telecomms		2.2	3.0
Health		2.0	1.9
Oil and gas		1.4	3.8
Food processing		0.8	5.1

Source: DTI, 2002b

- In **basic research** firms do get involved since this kind of research is directed at advancing the state of knowledge in a particular applied field with the very real hope that it will prove useful. The managements of these firms hope that such research will lead ultimately to those product and process innovations that will give the business its competitive edge. In some firms, like 3M, the active encouragement of staff to develop their own research projects is an important part of company policy, and many ideas generated from the staff's own programmes have been turned to profitable use by the company (Case 7.2). Other companies, like GSK, have a more organized approach to basic research (Case 9.5). **Basic research** is increasingly important in industries dealing with micro-electronics, biotechnology, genetics, the development of new materials, etc. There has been both an increase in such types of research and an increase in government support in the USA, Japan and Germany. In the UK, basic research, an area of traditional strength, was seen to be in relative decline by the late 1980s (Freeman, 1989).

- **Industrial research** stands in relation to basic research as innovation does to invention. Industrial research attempts to transform pure and basic research into some form of profitable use.

- **Development** takes research a stage further by translating the outcome of research into something more tangible. At this stage in the design of a new product, a prototype or a sample would be produced.

- **Design** is the final stage in the R&D process, which translates the development into the final product for the consumer. The **design stage** attempts to fuse certain elements, which are referred to as the **design mix**. These elements are effective operation, safety, easy maintenance, value for money and aesthetic considerations. These are all focused on satisfying customer needs.

The design aspect of research and development is an obvious area of overlap with both the production and marketing processes, to the extent that product design is seen as an essential element in both fields. Design and styling assume particular importance in industries such as car manufacture, where products are often sold as much on their appearance as their inherent product qualities. A firm like Bang and Olufsen produces televisions and hi-fi equipment to high technical specifications, yet its distinctiveness in the market place owes much more to its visual appeal. Making their products look very different from their competitors is a deliberate Bang and Olufsen strategy.

It is not only in manufacturing industry that design is important. A good illustration is presented by the retail clothing chain Burton at the beginning of the 1980s. The company had always been fairly successful, catering for the needs of a middle-of-the-road male market segment. However, the firm suffered a serious decline of its market share and profitability. The styling of its clothes had not kept pace with the needs of an increasingly fashion-conscious market, particularly those in the younger age group who spend a good proportion of their income on clothes. Moreover, the image of its shops and store layout was decidedly old fashioned and unappealing to the new consumer. As a result of a very detailed research programme to identify and meet the specific design needs of different consumer groups, the management introduced a completely new range of clothes to capture the growing market and invested in a modernization programme to give their stores a new image. This conscious effort in design management was held to be mainly responsible for the profit increase from £16.4 million in 1981 to £80.22 million in 1985.

Entrepreneurship

We noted at the beginning of this chapter that the activities of the entrepreneur were crucial to the process of innovation. Innovation happens because the entrepreneur has initiated it, as illustrated by the work of Ronald Hickman and the 'Workmate' in Case 9.1. The entrepreneur creates new products, new markets, and new means through which products are made and markets reached, based around new forms of organization and new means of managing people. Entrepreneurs have therefore been key figures in business history.

For a time, the role of the entrepreneur in business was understated as the focus turned to the growth and activities of the large corporation. However, in the UK, and elsewhere, the entrepreneur re-emerged in the 1980s as a hero figure. Bill Gates of Microsoft, Anita Roddick at the Body Shop and Richard Branson at Virgin became household names.

The success of certain entrepreneurs to rise above the recession prompted a 1980s UK government, already committed to a free market, to encourage even more entrepreneurial activity in the form of small business development. People were encouraged to develop 'enterprise' as a route to prosperity both for themselves and the nation. The concept of 'enterprise culture' emerged as important government rhetoric supported by a number of significant policy changes to deregulate markets, reconstruct the public sector along business lines, influence curriculum in schools, and to remove impediments to enterprise. Such impediments were seen as an obstructive trade union movement and a welfare state which was seen to offer little incentive for people to be self-reliant.

However, the focus upon small firms and the view of the entrepreneur as the exclusive province of the small firms' sector has detracted from the importance of entrepreneurship in large businesses. In his study of General Motors (GM), Sears, Dupont and Standard Oil, which we referred to in our discussion of structure in Chapter 5, Chandler stressed the importance for managers to be able to see beyond the daily problems of controlling a large corporation and develop new business ideas for the future. More attention is now being paid to the role of the entrepreneur in large firms. However, the qualities that give rise to a successful entrepreneur are not necessarily those of an 'organization man'. This may make entrepreneurs difficult to manage, an issue we discuss later in the chapter.

Key concept 9.4 Entrepreneurship

Entrepreneurship is the activity of entrepreneurs, who are responsible for the creation of new products, processes, services and markets. They develop new ways of doing business, create new forms of organization and new way of managing people. Entrepreneurship is the act of making such changes happen through the mobilization of physical, financial, human and information resources. Such resources are often combined in new ways to achieve improved levels of perfomance. Entrepreneurs are usually willing to lead and take responsibility for their actions.

What is entrepreneurship?

In Chapter 5 we introduced the notion of the entrepreneur in our discussion of small businesses. However, not every small firm is entrepreneurial, since many merely replicate existing forms of business. Becoming self-employed to run a newsagent's shop has little to do with innovation and entrepreneurship. In fact the majority of sole traders and small businesses are not entrepreneurial. Various attempts have been made to define the entrepreneur. Schumpeter presented a somewhat romantic view of the entrepreneur as someone who possessed:

> The dream and the will to found a private kingdom . . . the will to conquer . . . the joy of creating. (*Schumpeter, 1961, p. 93*)

A conference in 1998, sponsored by the UK government, set out the following characteristics of entrepreneurial activity:

- A desire to own and be accountable for one's performance.
- A willingness to engage in a rich and broad network of learning situations and to incorporate learning into one's ongoing activity.
- A fundamental motivation to be successful and make a contribution for one's self and/or other groups within society as a whole.
- The capability and willingness to move beyond the accepted and orthodox if such methods are failing to achieve sufficient value addedness.
- An intellectual and skill-based capability to weigh up the riskiness of innovative courses of action and the ability to manage such risk for the benefit of self and others.
- The capacity to focus activity upon the achievement of tangible and recognized outputs.
- A willingness to move ahead and innovate without being constrained overly by currently available resources. (DTI, 1998)

A model of entrepreneurship

In Figure 9.1 we present a model of entrepreneurship, which serves as a summary of research into the characteristics of successful entrepreneurs and the conditions in which such people thrive (further summaries of this research can be found in Bridge *et al.*, 1998; Burns, 2001; Chell, 2001). The model distinguishes between types of entrepreneur as well as identifying a range of variables which influence successful entrepreneurial activity.

Three types of entrepreneur are identified.

- **Craftsman.** The craftsman focuses on the product, which he or she has invented and/or developed. He or she possesses a specific skill that originates from a trade, craft or engineering background. Craftsmen tend to operate as sole traders or at least in small businesses. They are often characterized as loners.

- **Opportunist.** The opportunist focuses on the market and has the ability to seek out and develop new opportunities. They are often characterized as confident and outgoing.

- **Organization builder.** The organization builder focuses on making things happen and effecting change within organizations. They are often characterized in terms of their strong vision and inspirational leadership skills.

The key variables we identify are:

- **Economic factors.** These include those factors that either present opportunities or drive individuals into new forms of economic activity. Increased competition and globalization can push entrepreneurs to seek new markets. Unemployment can motivate individuals to become entrepreneurs.

- **Political factors.** Such factors will include the ideological commitment of the state towards entrepreneurial activity and the subsequent setting up of policies and regulations to assist entrepreneurs.

- **Social factors.** There are a range of factors which may support or hold back the entrepreneur. These include: social class, level of education, family history and support, and cultural differences.

- **The competencies of entrepreneurs.** A number of competencies have been identified. These include the technical competence to develop new products and services and the ability to manage both external and organizational environments. A successful entrepreneur must be able to assess and react to opportunity and lead organizational change.

- **The personalities of entrepreneuers.** There is a range of personality traits associated with entrepreneurship and the centrality of entrepreneurs to business development has led researchers to seek out those characteristics that make a successful entrepreneur. Many of the characteristics listed in Figure 9.1 are incorporated in the DTI concept of the entrepreneur identified above. McClelland (1961) found that successful entrepreneurs had a high need for achievement and a moderate need for power, while the less successful had a low need for achievement and a positively high or low need for power. The message from this research is clear: entrepreneurs are achievers but those seeking entrepreneurial activity only as a means of achieving power over others are likely to fail.

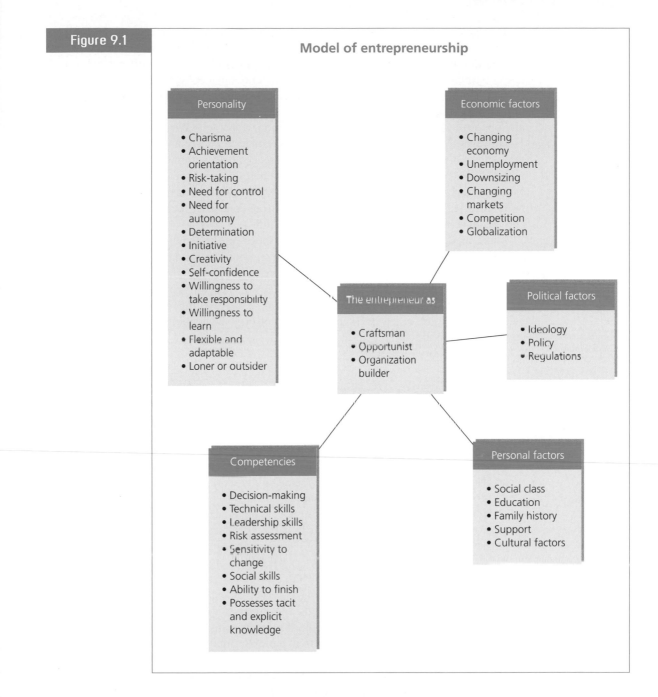

Figure 9.1

Model of entrepreneurship

Personality

- Charisma
- Achievement orientation
- Risk-taking
- Need for control
- Need for autonomy
- Determination
- Initiative
- Creativity
- Self-confidence
- Willingness to take responsibility
- Willingness to learn
- Flexible and adaptable
- Loner or outsider

Economic factors

- Changing economy
- Unemployment
- Downsizing
- Changing markets
- Competition
- Globalization

The entrepreneur as

- Craftsman
- Opportunist
- Organization builder

Political factors

- Ideology
- Policy
- Regulations

Competencies

- Decision-making
- Technical skills
- Leadership skills
- Risk assessment
- Sensitivity to change
- Social skills
- Ability to finish
- Possesses tacit and explicit knowledge

Personal factors

- Social class
- Education
- Family history
- Support
- Cultural factors

The model of entrepreneurship is not predictive and is simply descriptive of the range of variables which can and do influence the entrepreneur. No one factor or even category would appear to be more significant than any other and it is envisaged that the variables interact with one another to create a complex web of influences. This is in keeping with the view of business that predominates in this book and is the basis of the Business in Context model.

The factors identified may vary for each of our three types of entrepreneur. We have already established that the personality traits of the craftsman, opportunist and organization builder may differ. We may assume that the key skills may also differ. Chell (2001) cites research which supports the notion that the craftsman entrepreneur is more associated with a working-class upbringing than the opportunist. We might also assume that the organization builder would tend to be educated to university level, whereas the craftsman and opportunist would be more represented among early school leavers.

However, we may argue that certain characteristics and certain skills could be the prerequisite of all entrepreneurs and that the differences between craftsman, opportunist and organization builder, as illustrated above, are merely stereotypes to be challenged. For example, many successful individual inventors have been both university educated and middle-class. Research in the whole area is far from conclusive, occasionally contradictory and any conclusions should be drawn with caution.

Much of the focus in entrepreneurship has been on the individual or the small firm. It is our view that all firms, irrespective of size, need the introduction of new ideas to survive. In Chapter 7 we introduced the concept of entrepreneurial decision-making as a type of strategy employed by all organizations at some stage. Whether innovation through entrepreneurship is most successful in a small or a large setting, or how it is best organized, are questions we leave to our discussion of organizational aspects. We turn now to environmental issues in innovation.

| Case 9.1 | **The Workmate** |

In 1973 a Design Council Award was made to Ronald Hickman, the inventor of the Workmate. This was only the third time such an award had been made for a tool. The Workmate is a combination of a work bench, a sawing horse and a vice, whose versatility as a tool is much greater than the sum of its parts. It is small, lightweight, and easily stored. The device is bought in great numbers by DIY enthusiasts, but also by professional carpenters and building firms.

Hickman, who had received only a high-school education and possessed no technical qualifications, came to Britain in 1955, working first as a bookkeeper in a music store and then with Ford Motor Company in the styling department. By 1958 he had been doing freelance design work for Lotus cars and eventually joined them as a designer. He was entirely responsible for the Lotus Elan, and in five years had become the design director of the company. He reached the stage where the job was taking all his time, and in 1967 he left Lotus to form his own company Mate Tools.

The idea for the company arose during his time at Lotus. He had moved house and had invented a device to assist him in building fitted furniture to his own design. After various modifications the Workmate Mark 1 emerged, which he patented and sold through mail order, advertising in such magazines as *Do-it-yourself*, *Homemaker*, *Radio Times* and newspapers such as the *Daily Mail*. Sales started in 1968 and the product became an instant success. The demand for the product was greater than Mate Tools could satisfy. As a result several imitators appeared and Hickman began to look for a larger firm to take on the manufacture and sales.

The patent protection saw off the imitators, sometimes after court action when damages were awarded to Hickman. In 1972, Hickman granted Black and Decker an exclusive licence to manufacture the Workmate which was now redesigned as Mark 2.

When the Mark 2 was launched in 1972 the demand was so great that all stocks were immediately exhausted. The Mark 1 had achieved an annual sales growth of 120 per cent and under Black and Decker sales of the Mark 2 were growing at over 138 per cent per year. By 1976 over one million had been sold and by 1983 the product was being manufactured in Britain, France, Italy, Spain, Canada, Japan and Eire. Mate Tools still sold the Workmate itself but bought them ready-made from Black and Decker.

Source: Reports of Patent Cases, 1983

Questions

1 Examine the model of entrepreneurship in Figure 9.1. Which aspects of the model fit this case?

2 What does the case tell us about the strengths and weaknesses of single-person or small-firm inventors?

The environmental aspects of innovation

Four aspects of our model are particularly significant here. We will look first at the relationship between innovation and the economy, which leads logically to a discussion on the role of the state in encouraging innovation. This, in turn, leads to the differences in the way nations approach innovation, which we examine by looking at cultural influences. There is a clear relationship between technology and innovation, which we acknowledge in our assessment of the contending influences of technological development and the market place. We will not discuss the relationship between innovation and the labour market here since we examined the impact of changing technology on jobs at some length in Chapter 3. The relationship between innovation and labour is important, since the skills of the workforce and their attitude towards change, more especially changes in technology, are crucial to the successful implementation of innovation. These themes are developed also in Chapter 12 and the relationship is explored in Case 9.4, which examines changes in the shipping industry. A core element in all these discussions is the role of the economy, and the belief that innovation stimulates economic growth.

The role of the economy

There have been many attempts to link innovation with economic growth. In general, innovation is perceived as the means through which economic regeneration occurs. As such it has held a particular fascination for those who see government investment in R&D as a positive strategy for tackling the problems of economic decline. More specifically economists have attempted to prove links between innovation and such factors as per capita growth and export competitiveness. In this section we will view briefly the general debate which sees innovation as the key mechanism in long-wave economic cycles and then examine attempts to identify more specific relationships.

Innovation and long-wave cycles

The relationship between innovation and economic activity owes much to the work of the Russian economist Kondratieff. He put forward the view that economic activity exhibits regular **long-wave economic cycles** of growth and depression, followed by a further period of growth and so on (Kondratieff, 1935). Each cycle is characterized by a particular form of economic activity; thus the period 1785 to 1842 was dominated by iron ore, coke and the cotton industry, whereas the following period to 1897 centred around the development of the railways. If we extend the cycles to the present day, we can see periods of economic activity based around electricity, chemicals and the automobile, and more recently focusing upon aerospace, electronics and computers.

The explanation for the operation of these cycles has been taken up by a number of economists. For Schumpeter the key was innovation. Each phase of economic recovery can be attributed to clusters of innovations, enabling capitalism to evolve and usher in a new period of prosperity (Schumpeter, 1939). He thought that most innovations occurred when the economic climate appeared more favourable, thus acting as a stimulus for entrepreneurial activity. However, some believe that innovations only occur in the depths of depression, when profits are so low that entrepreneurs are stimulated into risk-taking ventures (Mensch, 1979).

> ### Key concept 9.5 Long-wave economic cycles
>
> Long waves are used to denote cycles of economic growth and decline spanning over 40 years. The idea gained popularity through the work of Kondratieff who saw upswings in the economy related to the development of particular industries over time and downswings as a result of saturated and contested markets. Schumpeter argued that movement out of economic depression is the function of bursts of innovation creating new products and processes, which re-stimulate markets. Long-wave supporters argue that such cycles not only repeat themselves, but are regular in shape and length. Critics argue that the whole approach is far too deterministic.

The notion of economic cycles has generated considerable debate among economists and others, who, despite the absence of hard data, have felt more than capable of contributing to the debate as to when the cycles begin, how long they last, and what the key innovations are. The problems with long waves are the task of identifying and dating the major innovations, and the highly deterministic nature of cyclical activity, leaving some economists to view the theory as convenient rather than meaningful.

> The belief that mankind is in the grip of mysterious forces which it is powerless to change recurs in periods of stress and difficulty. (*Brittan, 1983*)

This may explain the resurgence of interest in long-wave theory in times of recession.

Innovation and specific measures of economic performance

A growing number of studies have been carried out in an attempt to provide hard data linking innovative activity and some measure of economic performance at the level of both national economies and the individual firm. Many of the studies highlight significant differences in measures of innovative activity between nations. We return to this theme when we discuss cultural and national differences later in the chapter. An indication of the types of study carried out is offered below:

- There is evidence to suggest that investments in R&D, particularly those relating to technical change, are the major cause of improvements in productivity and output. Some studies suggest that increasing the quantity of either capital equipment and/or labour are by themselves insufficient for economies to grow and remain competitive and as much as a 90 per cent improvement can be attributed to process innovations (Solow, 1957).

- There is evidence to suggest that the development of new products leads to improved market performance (a selection of evidence is presented in Souder and Sherman, 1994). Analysis of the 2002 DTI R&D Scoreboard (Tables 9.2–9.4) reveals that companies with above average investment in R&D have above average sales growth, productivity and shareholder return. However, this is not always the case. GM was the world's biggest investor in R&D in 1992, spending £3.1 billion, yet, over the same period, made a loss and halved its dividend to shareholders. This illustrates the difficulty of examining R&D in isolation. R&D expenditure by GM may well have contributed to product and process improvements, but these could have been negated by other factors such as the stagnant USA car market or a lack of management strategy to capitalize upon the investment. Furthermore, the time horizon for the investment may be such that the pay-back will be at some time in the future.

- Tables 9.5–9.7 are concerned with patents. As with published expenditure, patents represent an easily measured output of R&D. Table 9.5 examines the number of patent applications per million population filed in the home country by eight manufacturing nations from 1979 to 1989. The same study revealed a correlation between patent applications and GDP and between patent applications and manufacturing output. The clear fact to emerge from the graph is the prolific patent behaviour of the Japanese. In 1989 the Japanese filed 2580 applications per million population, more than the rest put together and five times that of Germany. The dominant market position of GSK's drugs Zantac and Zovirax is, in part, a function of patent protection, and the expiry of the patent resulted in other manufacturers entering the market (Case 9.5).

- A correlation also exists between the number of registered patents and export performance. Between 1937 and 1975 West German patents registered in the USA outnumbered those from any other foreign country. During the same period, the former West Germany was the leading exporter to the USA (Rothwell and Zegveld, 1981). Since 1975, Germany has been replaced by Japan on both counts. In 1987 and 1991, the top three companies receiving patents in the USA were all Japanese (Table 9.6). In fact, eight Japanese companies feature in the top 20 for 1987 and five out of the top nine in 1991. By 1997 the picture had changed. IBM was the leading company in terms of USA patent activity, with Motorola and the USA government prominent. This may reflect the continuing recession in Japan as well as the increase in investment among USA firms. It should not be forgotten that, despite the recession, Japanese firms make up seven out of the top 11 companies. Table 9.7 shows the USA patents granted to automobile firms between 1986 and 1990. Once

Table 9.5	Patent applications filed by residents in the National Patent Office per million population							
Year	Australia	Germany	France	Japan	Korea	Spain	UK	USA
1979	327	502	211	1300	27	51	348	269
1980	448	466	204	1419	32	50	350	273
1981	425	484	202	1629	34	45	369	271
1982	435	497	196	1780	40	43	364	272
1983	451	515	204	1909	40	39	353	253
1984	461	532	206	2135	49	46	337	261
1985	415	528	218	2270	66	38	347	266
1986	361	527	219	2388	88	43	354	270
1987	400	517	228	2546	117	44	350	280
1988	370	519	222	2518	136	47	360	305
1989	407	503	224	2580	166	54	345	331

Source: Needle and Needle, 1991

Table 9.6	Corporation and organizations receiving USA patents by rank order 1987–97					
Rank	1987		1991		1997	
1	Canon	847	Toshiba	1114	IBM	1724
2	Hitachi	845	Mitsubishi Denki	936	Canon	1381
3	Toshiba	823	Hitachi	927	NEC	1095
4	General Electric	779	Eastman Kodak	863	Motorola	1058
5	USA Philips	687	Canon	823	US government	935
6	Westinghouse Electric	652	General Electric	809	Fujitsu	903
7	IBM	591	Fuji Photo	731	Hitachi	903
8	Siemens	539	USA Philips	650	Mitsubishi Denki	892
9	Mitsubishi Denki	518	Motorola	613	Toshiba	862
10	RCA	504			Sony	859
11	Fuji Photo	494			Eastman Kodak	795
12	Dow Chemical	469				
13	E I du Pont de Nemours	419				
14	Motorola	414				
15	AT&T	406				
16	Honda Motor	395				
17	NEC	375				
18	Toyota Jidoshi	375				
19	Bayer	371				
20	General Motors	370				

Sources: 1987 – *Intellectual Property Owners' Inc.*, March 1988; 1991 – *Intellectual Property Newsletter* 16: 1. January 1993; 1997 – US Patent and Trademark Office

Table 9.7	USA patents granted to automobile firms, 1986–90	
	Company	No. grants
	Toyota	1218
	Honda	1218
	Nissan	1054
	General Motors	993
	Mazda	568
	Ford	399
	Mercedes	377
	Chrysler	176
	Mitsubishi	176
	VW	97
	BMW	62

Source: Narin, 1993

more the Japanese dominate despite GM showing a 50 per cent increase on the previous four-year period and Chrysler a 100 per cent increase on the same period.

- There is some evidence to suggest that consumers appear willing to pay more for goods of superior technical quality. Once again Germany features, this time in comparison with Britain. Between 1971 and 1975 Germany's share of exports to OECD countries (an association of 21 leading industrial nations) was 22 per cent compared to Britain's 10 per cent, despite the fact that the unit value of German exports was 40 per cent greater (Rothwell and Zegveld, 1981). The assumption here is that investment in improving the quality of goods will pay back in the form of increased sales.

Despite the research findings and the persuasive pleas for investment in R&D, the links between innovation and economic performance remain speculative. One difficulty is our inability to measure innovation. Indicators that have been used, such as patents and the amount of money a firm has invested in its R&D activities, can at best be considered a

Key concept 9.6 Innovation and economic growth

There is considerable debate concerning the relationship between innovation and economic growth, both at the level of national economies and individual firms. There is a basic assumption that innovation leads to economic growth and it becomes particularly important to lead economies out of recession. Despite the plausability of such claims, it is difficult to measure the precise impact of innovation on the economy. As with many aspects of business, the isolation of a single variable, such as innovation, can present an oversimplified view of the complex nature of business activity. Nevertheless, the importance of innovation to economic growth has resulted in significant state intervention.

Key concept 9.7 Patents

A patent is a legal device that enables the holder to maintain a monopoly in an invention for a stated period, which in Britain stands at 20 years. The state grants this monopoly in return for a full disclosure of the invention. Such a system exists in all industrialized countries. A patent protects the inventor from would-be copiers and enables him or her to exploit the invention for profit and/or the good of society. It is believed that the benefits of such a system will actively encourage invention and innovation. A patent holder may issue manufacturing licences to third parties and thus derive further financial benefit.

rough guide. For example, a patent may be registered and then never used to produce anything of value; improvements in products and processes can originate as much from individual inventors and equipment users as they can from organized R&D departments.

We have already noted in the case of GM that significant expenditure is no guarantee of short-term financial success. More significantly the attempts to isolate innovation may give a false impression. The export success of 'upper range' German cars such as Mercedes-Benz and BMW may well be attributed to the technical superiority of the product when compared to other cars in the same range. Such an explanation fits the research findings identified above. There is another explanation. Both firms have been particularly active in carefully targeted advertising campaigns, which not only stress the technical superiority of their product but also attempt to give the product an image of exclusivity and high status. To what extent are their sales attributable to technical innovation and how much to an effective advertising campaign? This illustration confirms the interrelationship of innovation and marketing that we identified earlier. It also emphasizes a key theme in this book: that business activities are interrelated and there are dangers in viewing one activity, such as innovation, in isolation.

Throughout this section we have made reference to the role of state intervention, and it is to this aspect we now turn our attention. We will view the role of governments in general terms and then explore how governments in different countries operate with respect to the stimulation of innovation, with a specific note on the UK.

The role of the state

In almost every country, the state has a significant involvement in innovation. Three main reasons may be given as motivation for this involvement:

- Using the kind of economic evidence presented in the last section, there would appear to be a clear belief that innovation and entrepreneurship are major factors in economic expansion and export competitiveness.

- We have already noted that investment in innovation is both long term and high risk. The mechanism of the free market may be inadequate in generating those basic innovations upon which economic expansion is based, hence the need for state subsidy when individual companies are reluctant to invest.

- Intervention is often necessary for political and strategic as well as for social reasons. In Britain and the USA defence spending forms a major part of all expenditure on innovation. Many countries have seen space exploration as a goal of national importance and prestige, and the same could be said for the British and French governments' involvement with the development of the supersonic jet airliner, Concorde. Investment in the nuclear fuel industry is viewed by several governments as a desirable energy strategy.

In the UK the state is involved in innovation in a number of different ways. It invests in R&D in individual firms, government research establishments and in universities. It has established the legal protection of inventions through the patent system. The state's financial support is clearly biased towards technological innovation in the manufacturing and defence industries but exhortations for innovation and enterprise are usually aimed at all firms in all sectors.

The activities of the state in subsidizing, protecting and encouraging innovation provide an excellent illustration of the interrelationship between the state and business at a more general level. In this section, we attempt a classification of the types of intervention specifically concerned with innovation and examine the associated problems.

Types of state intervention in innovation

We examine state intervention under six main headings; procurement, subsidies, education and training, patents and licensing, restrictive and enabling laws and, finally, import controls. These types of innovation occur even where the government has expressed its ideological opposition to interference in the workings of the free market.

Procurement

The need of the state for certain products has stimulated research in many areas. UK private industry only funds a half of all R&D activity, but carries out over two-thirds, the difference being linked to government contracts (Bowen *et al.*, 1992). Defence work offers the clearest illustration with implications not only for the armaments industry itself, but also in electronics, computing and aerospace. Businesses in the USA have seen the armed forces as a very large and very stable market for **procurement**. There is a view that the goals of business and the military have become intertwined and form an important part of the image-building that goes on between ideologically opposed nations. In Britain the needs of the National Health Service (NHS) have stimulated developments in the pharmaceutical industry and, in most nations, the fear of disappearing natural resources has led to government-backed research to find synthetic materials.

Subsidies

Subsidies to individual firms occur in the form of investments, grants and tax concessions. We have seen how special policies exist, such as those to encourage innovation through small firms. Most subsidies aim to support a particular form of R&D. For example, EU funding, particularly through the European Social Fund, is biased towards the use of more innovative business solutions, particularly in IT. The development of Inmos, presented in Case 9.2 illustrates the role of British governments in subsidizing R&D and the dilemmas which often accompany it.

Education and training

There is an underlying assumption that state investment in education and pure science will have a significant impact in increasing the level of innovation and thus benefit both the economy and society. The relationship between primary research and the knowledge-based activities of higher education institutions is supposedly one of the key features of the modern age. Galbraith observed of educators and scientists that they 'stand in relation to the industrial system much as did the banking and financial community in the early stages of industrial development' (Galbraith, 1972, p. 283)

There are certain well-publicized developments in both Britain and the USA that lend substance to the post-industrial society thesis. Developments in 'Silicon Valley' in California and, in the UK, the growth of the science parks around major universities, such as Cambridge, show the relationship between industrial research and major universities with a reputation for science. The growth of some American high-technology companies such as HP in Palo Alto, California, is clearly associated with this phenomenon, as is the development of a network of businesses in computing and related fields in the vicinity of Cambridge. We note in Case 9.5 that Glaxo chose to locate one of its USA research laboratories in the midst of universities in North Carolina. Such illustrations support the view that competitive endeavour among firms in close proximity to each other is a spur to economically successful innovations and that there is synergy to be gained both through such competition and through collaboration with the university sector.

In spite of such developments, British institutions of higher education are often subjected to financial stringencies as part of the government's determination to reduce public expenditure. On the positive side this has, in many cases, pushed industry and universities much closer together. Some universities, like Warwick, have generated significant funding from industry. The critics of this type of development see a danger of weakening the primary research base and restricting university research to projects related to the very specific requirements of a limited number of companies. This could restrict opportunities for breakthroughs in basic technology considered essential for industrial regeneration. The experience of Warwick would refute such claims. As well as attracting significant external funding it has established itself as a leading research institution as rated by the UK universities 'Research Assessment Exercise'.

The state sometimes intervenes in skills training. Many ascribe Germany's advantage in product and process innovation to its superior craft training schemes. Clearly a skilled workforce is one that can adapt readily to technical changes. Skills shortages in the UK may have been responsible for the relatively slow adoption of computerized aids to manufacturing, such as **computerized numerical control (CNC)** machines. This aspect illustrates the interaction between innovation and the labour force in our model. The effectiveness of innovation depends upon it being supported by employees with the requisite skills. The development of new processes may prove even more costly if they remain idle waiting for the skills of the workforce to catch up, as Rolls Royce found to its cost in the early 1970s. The development of the high-performance jet engine, the RB 211, encountered many problems. Although the focus was upon the mounting costs of the project, costs which almost forced the company out of business, a contributory factor was the lack of expertise to overcome the many technical difficulties which arose at the development stage.

In the 1970s many firms invested in computer hardware and software in the belief that this would change their business overnight. In some of these companies the systems were under-utilized, as insufficient consideration had been given to training the employees.

Patents and licensing

A patent is a legal device that enables the holder to maintain a monopoly in an invention for a stated period, which in Britain stands at 20 years. In exchange for granting this monopoly, the owner of the invention must make available its details to the general public. The patent system operates in almost every country in the world. The stated benefits of such a system are:

- It actively encourages new developments by offering protection to the patent holder against others copying the invention, as illustrated in Case 9.5 with Zantac and Zovirax.
- By revealing the details of the invention, it encourages further inventions and innovative activity along similar lines.
- It prevents the duplication of research.
- It ensures that the benefits of research are passed on to society.
- A real benefit to the patent holder is the opportunity to issue manufacturing licences, as illustrated in Case 9.1 by the licence bought by Black and Decker to manufacture and sell the Workmate.

A firm holding a patent on a particular type of manufacturing process may allow another firm in the same business to use that process upon the payment of an agreed fee. In the case of major inventions this can be an important source of revenue for the patent holder. The revolutionary method for the production of glass, the 'float process', was developed by the St Helens firm of Pilkington Brothers Ltd in the early 1960s, since when licences have been granted to glass manufacturers all over the world enabling them to use the same process. Licensing is clearly a vital source of revenue for some companies. In 1991 Texas Instruments made US$415 million from licensing its semiconductor patents, while in the same year its manufacturing activities made a loss of US$203 million. In certain cases the law has had to intervene to enforce the issue of licences where it was felt that some companies were operating an unfair monopoly. This occurred in the case of Roche, the Swiss pharmaceutical company. In 1971 the British Patent Comptroller ordered Hoffman-La Roche, as the company was then called, to grant licences to two British firms, Berk Pharmaceuticals and DDSA Ltd, for the manufacture of the tranquilizers Librium and Valium. Despite frequent requests, the Swiss drugs company had repeatedly refused manufacturing licences on the grounds of the safety standards of the finished product. However, the British patent system held that the refusal to grant licences gave the Swiss company an unfair monopoly in the drugs industry.

Since that time, the law relating to licensing has been amended and compulsory licences may now be issued only in the case of the non-manufacture of the product by the patent holder or in cases where the product is not manufactured in this country. The main idea behind such laws in most countries is to stimulate the development and use of the invention in that country and hence assist local businesses.

Restrictive and enabling laws

Most countries possess laws that control manufacturing standards and relate to such aspects as safety and pollution. Not only do these laws ensure that innovations conform to certain standards, but they aim to encourage research into socially desirable end-products, such as car engines with low fuel consumption or car exhaust systems that restrict pollution into the atmosphere. The ends are not only socially desirable but can have an effect on business performance as well. A firm that meets government standards of product quality enters the market place with additional competitive edge.

Such regulations can benefit some firms but handicap others. The determination on the part of the 1993 USA administration to reduce the healthcare budget posed a threat to Glaxo (Case 9.5, p. 400), but may lead to the development of cheaper generic drugs. The use of restrictive laws has been greatest in the USA and there is a lobby that sees a danger that excessive government regulation may hold back technological innovation and hence the country's economic growth. However, as with the relationship between innovation and economic growth, there is a difficulty in establishing a direct causal link between such laws and innovative activity at the level of the firm. As an illustration, we can see that increases in the price of oil in 1973 resulted in both Britain and the USA introducing new laws relating to speed limits and exhaust emission. However, the ensuing trend in the design and manufacture of smaller cars would almost certainly have occurred in response to increased oil prices irrespective of any legislation.

Import controls

The theory here is that restriction on the imports from other countries will have a beneficial effect in stimulating research in the home country or intensifying the search for a substitute product or process. Import controls enforced by Japanese governments has often been cited as the major impetus to considerable innovations by Japanese businesses. There is, however, a danger that other countries may well retaliate and impose their own restrictions. Concern about the trade imbalance between the USA and Japan, in favour of the latter, has resulted in presidential delegations to Tokyo and agreements on import quotas. The Americans themselves have in the past been fond of using import controls and the development of the synthetic fibre industry in the USA owes much to restrictions on the import of woollen products. The **GATT** agreements and the creation of the World Trade Organization have been part of the process to bring an end to such import controls (see Chapter 3 for more details).

Some problems with state intervention in innovation

We have seen that the main motive for state intervention to encourage and support innovative activity is the desire to improve economic performance. We have also seen the difficulties of showing a direct relationship between investment in innovation and economic growth, whether measured at national or organizational levels. There are other difficulties with the state's involvement as identified below:

- An over-reliance upon state funding may have serious repercussions at times of reductions in government expenditure.
- A major difficulty lies in the ability of government employees to make decisions in highly specialized technical and scientific areas, and decisions that are in the best interests of the business community as a whole. Government support may well be important in stimulating innovation but the critical skills and knowledge reside in the firms themselves or the higher education sector.

- For intervention to be successful, extensive consultation is required and there needs to be freedom for individuals to pursue their own research goals, otherwise there is a danger that intervention can be misdirected. Several highly publicized government-backed ventures, such as Concorde or gas-cooled nuclear reactors, have not met with the success predicted for them as a result of these difficulties.

- The issue of freedom raises the most fundamental questions of an ideological kind and is especially troubling for those governments committed to *laissez-faire* economic policies. As we see in the Inmos case, the British government was at the same time pursuing a policy of support through the British Technology Group, while planning to sell the company to the private sector. Such conflict of interests may well be detrimental to innovation since political considerations may come to dominate business development.

- Underpinning many of the difficulties outlined above is the view that governments have the power to constrain innovation and entrepreneurial activity by bureaucratic interference and restrictive legislation.

- The direction of state intervention may raise conflicts within the agencies of the state as well as raising certain ethical issues. Proposals by one department may be opposed by another. For example, new developments in air travel, in particular the increased passenger-carrying capacity of aircraft, have necessitated airport expansion. This can be of benefit to the local economy by stimulating the job market and offering opportunities for local businesses. The same proposals will almost certainly be opposed by local residents and environmentalists. Such debates have surrounded the siting of London's third airport and the expansion of the airport at Heathrow to incorporate a fifth terminal complex. An overemphasis on government defence contracts may result in a neglect and subsequent loss of competitiveness in civil markets.

Issues like these deal with aspects of business ethics and question the purpose, direction and outcomes of innovative activity. Kumar is especially sceptical and he sums up the whole argument most appropriately:

> There are the familiar examples of the atomic bomb, other weapons of the biological and chemical kind, space exploration and large scale capital intensive technology with its propensity to pollute the environment and exhaust the world's supply of fossil fuels. Then there is the ingenious and expensive gadgetry of the mass consumer industry with its built-in principle of planned obsolescence and marginal technical improvements . . . medical research seems equally skewed in the direction of people with power to persuade and pay . . . and 99 per cent of the knowledge effort of the industrial societies is devoted to the problems of the developed world. (*Kumar, 1978, p. 230*)

| Case 9.2 | **Inmos** |

The Inmos saga . . . provides 1980s evidence of Britain's still unbridged 'two cultures' gap, through politicians' ignorance of technology and technologists' naivety about politics. (*Guardian, 3 December, 1985*)

◄

Inmos has been a hostage of political incompetence, City misunderstanding and corporate chaos. (*Guardian, 31 March, 1987*)

In 1978, under a UK Labour government, the National Enterprise Board (NEB), in its role as an industrial holding company, invested £50 million in a newly formed company, Inmos, to develop, manufacture and market semiconductors, popularly known as microchips. The company was formed by a small group of capitalist entrepreneurs, including an Englishman and two Americans, and was based originally in the USA. NEB accepted the proposals of the new company even though it had no product or even design for one at the time. The motivation behind the government's involvement was the desire for Britain to develop its own semiconductor industry, not only because this was seen as a valuable and growing market but also as part of a wider strategy for the development of the government-backed electronics industry. This included at the time such firms as Ferranti and ICL, and the industry was identified as central to the country's economic development through the 1980s. An important factor was the decision to join a race for the development of a new form of microchip, which would perform the functions of several types of semiconductors on a single chip. This creation of a 'minicomputer' on a single chip was seen as the next development in 'very large scale integration' (VLSI) technology.

At the time, the semiconductor market was dominated by the Americans, with Texas Instruments leading the field. The Japanese, however, were launching a collaborative effort by leading companies to develop the next generation of VLSI. By contrast, European firms had a weak position in the market and prospects did not look good. The management of Inmos decided that its main strategy was to push ahead and be the first company to produce the revolutionary chip, its particular version to be known as the Transputer. In the meantime, it was decided to design and manufacture conventional semiconductors and the company set up two production plants: one at Colorado Springs in the USA, designated as the corporate headquarters, and the other at Newport in Wales. The British operation was controlled from a research base in Bristol. Inmos saw its success in a highly volatile industry as being based upon, first, the development of an entirely new product acceptable to the majority of users as the best and, second, on high-volume sales to offset the high development costs.

At the outset Inmos faced a number of difficulties. There was scepticism in the City among the civil servants, some trade unionists and potential American customers wary of a state-controlled company. There was opposition from within the ranks of the Labour Party, especially left-wing members who objected to the three founders acquiring such a large stake in the company and in particular to the large amounts of money being paid to the two Americans. More significantly, several experts in the field felt that insufficient investment had been made, given the nature of the company's strategy. Worse problems were to follow with the defeat of the Labour government at the hands of the Conservatives in the 1979 election. The incoming government were less than enthusiastic about Inmos, preferring to give support to those companies like ICL that were already established in their field. Moreover, there were proposals to limit the activities of NEB and an ideological commitment to privatization. This not only placed the future of Inmos in some doubt, but there were delays in necessary funding at a crucial time in the company's development.

In 1984, after investing an estimated £100 million in the company, the government sold its interests to Thorn EMI for £95 million. This followed a well-established pattern in the microchip industry: that of small innovative companies being bought up by large multinational organizations. In Thorn's case it was seen in the City as a hasty acquisition, after the company had been refused in its attempts to merge with British Aerospace. The following year, the microchip market suffered a downturn and Inmos was forced to cut back its activities by 20 per cent, with lay-offs in both Britain and America. Later, in 1985, Thorn EMI announced that it was looking for a development partner for Inmos, possibly from Japan, and was willing to relinquish up to 49 per cent of its shares.

There can be little doubt that the ideological and political differences, the selling of Inmos at a crucial stage in its development, and the continued uncertainty of its role within the Thorn EMI stable arrested the company's growth. However, the Transputer was developed successfully, it was ahead of its rivals and began to sell well. Thorn EMI did manage to sell Inmos, which became part of SGS-Thomson (now known as STM). In 1992 the company joined forces with QPL International, a Hong-Kong based firm, to develop high-tech digital and mixed signal technology to customize the manufacture of microchips. By 1998, competition, especially from South Korea, oversupply and the fall in demand for microchips led to the company calling in the administrators to run its three factories in South Wales.

Despite the difficulties of manufacture in the USA and UK, STM maintains a strong research presence at the former Inmos laboratories in Bristol. Indeed, much of the microchip industry in the Bristol area owes its presence to Inmos. Many spin-off companies set up by former Inmos designers have prospered, including Morton Media – pioneers in videophone technology. The transputer failed to bring the rewards for Inmos but it left an important legacy in microchip technology and in the creation of a pool of expertise.

Sources: McClean and Rowlands, 1985; *Guardian*, 1985–7; *Financial Times*, 1998–9; *Western Daily Press*, 2003

Questions

1 What were the opportunities perceived by the UK government and by the founders of Inmos in establishing the company?

2 What does the case tell us about the advantages and disadvantages of state involvement in innovative activity in individual firms?

3 Why did Inmos fail?

Cultural and national differences

So convinced have we become of the dependence of the total social, political and economic order on technical development that national output of scientific discoveries and the rate of technological advance have begun to appear as the ultimate criterion of culture and different political and social systems are compared as facilitators of this kind of achievement. (*Burns and Stalker, 1966, p. 19*)

Nearly all governments in the major industrialized countries have attempted to influence the direction of innovation in some way. While there is a danger of creating cultural stereotypes and perpetuating myths, the response of different governments has varied and different areas have been targeted. Not only this but investment in R&D has been taken as an indicator of a nation's economic health and future prosperity. We will explore both these issues.

A key issue is undoubtedly globalization. This has facilitated the diffusion of innovation in ways and at a speed that mark out the last 20 years from anything that has gone before. The creation of global business networks has facilitated information exchange and similar innovations have been taken up in diverse cultural contexts.

National differences

Britain has always been typified as placing emphasis on basic research with its application in defence, nuclear energy and space research. The spin-offs have been few, limited to a small range of companies, and make little impact on the manufacture of commercial products. As Table 9.8 demonstrates the most significant R&D sector is pharmaceuticals. The **USA** too has been criticized for emphasizing big projects in defence and aerospace, usually with government backing, and consequently with a corresponding reluctance on the part of private companies to invest in their own long-term projects. However, as we see from Table 9.8, a different perspective emerges. USA firms dominate global R&D in most sectors of the economy, with only Japan and Germany having higher investments in electronics and electrical R&D. The table confirms the USA dominance of the global economy in 2002. **France** is typified as giving strong central direction and significant financial support to private industry in a bid to achieve scientific and technological independence, by creating a domestic supplier in every major world industry. **Germany** conforms to a less directive model but give specific assistance to those areas where market

Table 9.8	Percentages of total R&D by sector contributed by major countries					
Sector	USA	Japan	Germany	France	UK	Others
IT hardware and IT services	57.8	19.9	0	5.1	1.4	15.8
Pharmaceuticals and biotechnology	50.0	8.9	5.2	8.2	14.4	13.3
Electronics and electrical	16.4	47.6	19.6	3.1	1.2	12.1
Software and IT services	89.8	1.4	3.8	2.9	2.1	0
Health	85.7	1.1	6.5	0	5.5	1.2

Source: DTI, 2002b

success is guaranteed, a policy particularly successful in the machine tool industry. In addition, we have already noted in Chapter 3 how much emphasis is placed on Germany supporting businesses through a national system of training, thus ensuring the workforce possesses the required skills to enable them both to develop and exploit innovations.

Innovation in Japan

Japan has attracted the greatest number of myths and stereotypes (for further details see the section on Japanese management in Chapter 4). Japanese economic success has been linked to the import of key innovations and technologies from other industrialized nations, imperative for such a late industrial starter. The widespread belief soon developed that Japanese businesses could not innovate. While there is little doubt that Japan has gained from bought-in technology, there is also clear evidence that Japan is now probably the world's most innovative industrial nation (Tables 9.5 and 9.6 support this view). The Japanese have made significant advances in machine tool technology and, in particular, in developments in automated plant and robotics, and in modifying existing technologies. While products such as the transistor and the video cassette recorder (VCR) were invented elsewhere, the Japanese have shown considerable innovation in commercializing such products.

Japan has more of its workforce engaged in industrial R&D than the UK, France or Germany (Peck and Goto, 1982). Japanese businesses spend five times the amount on R&D than their British counterparts (Bowen et al., 1992). In addition to private investment, considerable assistance is offered by the Japanese Ministry of International Trade and Industry (MITI). MITI has been active in monitoring trends, in particular those pertaining to foreign investment. It has acted as a channel through which the diffusion of innovation has occurred. At the same time, the internal market has been jealously protected against incursions by foreign suppliers.

The two key strategies pursued by the Japanese are **incrementalism** and **collaboration**. The large number of patent applications by Japanese firms (Tables 9.5–9.7) bear testimony to the importance Japanese firms place upon incremental developments. In terms of collaboration, MITI provided both encouragement and facilities to enable Japanese computer firms to engage in big-budget research in the 1970s in areas such as VLSI. Six of the largest computer companies were organized into two research associations to collaborate on new developments. The early focus of such collaborative ventures was the facilitation of access to existing research rather than the developments of new products. Firms collaborated in reverse engineering exercises to analyse the products of foreign competitors to determine how they were made. As the limits of such technological transfer were reached and as foreign firms became less inclined to license to Japanese firms, the focus of collaboration shifted to the development of entirely new products.

While collaboration has been an undoubted feature of the Japanese approach to innovation, some research has suggested that the approach has not been without its problems. Mowery and Rosenberg (1989) suggest that some collaborative ventures between Japanese firms have been typified by a less than full disclosure by the participants and by some firms sending second-rate researchers. Additionally, firms are less inclined to participate fully the closer the research is to the frontiers of technology. This view is supported by Callon (1995), whose analysis of collaborative research in computing concluded that the major firms had, to a certain extent, outgrown MITI, and wished to retain a considerable measure of independence to protect market advantage. He cites this as a major factor in the failure of Japanese collaborative research in advanced technologies. Further reference to Callon's study can be found in the section on Japanese management in Chapter 4.

An underlying theme in the comparative analysis of national attitudes to research and development is one developed in our earlier section on economic aspects of innovation: that trends in R&D investment are correlated with national economic growth.

Innovation in the UK

In comparison with other major industrial countries, the UK spends less on R&D as a proportion of GDP and employs fewer research scientists as a proportion of its labour force than its main competitors. The pattern of innovation among private sector British firms is one of great concentration. In 1990, 20 UK companies accounted for 64 per cent of civil R&D and 50 companies accounted for 80 per cent.

In some industries, notably pharmaceuticals, the UK has world-class R&D performers in the likes of GSK and AstraZeneca. In other industries, notably chemicals, UK firms have fallen behind. Table 9.9 shows the relative change for the UK leading chemical firm, ICI.

The DTI Scoreboards for R&D in 1998 and 1999 both reveal that, whereas the average expenditure on R&D for the world's top 300 companies was over 5 per cent of sales turnover, the corresponding average for the UK top 100 was just over 2 per cent. These scoreboards show the commanding lead in R&D taken by the USA and Japan. Not only does the UK have far fewer companies among the top 300 spenders but those firms spend less as a proportion of turnover than firms in the USA and Japan.

A number of reasons have been put forward for the relatively low investment in R&D by many UK firms.

- The behaviour of the stock market is frequently cited, more especially the payment of high rates of share dividend linked to short-termism.

- The withdrawal of the state from direct support is also given as an explanation. This was particularly apparent under the free market ideologies of successive governments since 1979.

- The lack of R&D activity in UK firms is also a function of the nation's industrial structure. The USA, in particular, has a much higher proportion of high-tech firms engaged in leading-edge research. UK industry is typified by low-tech firms and the GlaxoSmithKlines are the exception rather than the rule.

- Another reason given for the low investment of UK firms in R&D is an over-emphasis on defence and prestige projects.

Table 9.9	ICI UK and world ranking by R&D expenditure		
	Year	UK ranking	World ranking
	1991	1	35
	1997	12	132
	2001	15	246
	Source: DTI, 2002b		

- Historically, high interest rates and the difficulties of raising investment capital are also cited.

While such comparative data and analyses are revealing, we repeat our caution; it is difficult to show precise links between cultural and national differences, R&D expenditure, innovation and economic growth. Furthermore, while criticism is voiced at the British government for pursuing an apparent selective policy, Japan is often held as a shining example for doing much the same thing.

Our discussion of cultural and national differences has focused almost exclusively on R&D and technology. We should not forget that other forms of innovation exist. While the behaviour of financial markets is blamed for the lack of investment of UK manufacturing firms in R&D, firms specializing in finance have themselves been highly innovative, developing new products to keep one step ahead in a highly competitive business.

We return to the theme of technology, although the theme is used to further illustrate the interrelationship between innovation and marketing.

Innovation and technology

There is an obvious relationship between technology and innovation. Numerous illustrations exist where developments in state-of-the-art technology result in business innovations and the development of new products and processes: the microchip being a good example. There are some, like Schumpeter, who see technical breakthroughs as the force that changes the whole nature of business, and the ability of firms to respond is crucial to their survival (Schumpeter, 1961). The emphasis on the role of technology is referred to as 'technology push'. There is an alternative view in which demand plays a leading role in determining the direction, extent and impact of inventions. While some industries undoubtedly have a richer knowledge base than others, notably chemicals and electronics, the profitability of the application of that knowledge was predominantly a question of demand. This process is referred to as 'demand–pull' (Schmookler, 1966). This was referred to earlier in this chapter (see Key concept 9.3).

Several attempts have been made to support the primacy of demand–pull over technology–push and vice versa and illustrations can be given on both sides. The development of synthetic fibres is clearly a case of **demand–pull**, while the growth of the mass market in electronic calculators is clearly a case of the successful use of developments in integrated circuits and hence **technology–push**.

In most instances, the distinction between technology–push and demand–pull is too simplistic. The growth of sales of the CD is the product of both the application of laser technology to produce consumer goods (technology–push) and a function of rising discretionary income and market segmentation (demand–pull). The two forces would appear to operate side by side. The development and rapid expansion of 'International Direct Dialling' by British Telecom was a direct response to a growing market demand among the business community for telephone communication with overseas associates. Having developed the technology, BT found that the resources were being under-utilized outside peak business periods. The company therefore launched a successful advertising campaign to increase private and domestic use of the available technology. The initial development was demand led, while subsequent developments were clearly a case of technology leading the market, and a company anxious to obtain a healthy return on a not inconsiderable investment.

Another interesting example is provided by Case 9.3 concerning innovations in camera technology and the development of 'Post-it' adhesive note pads. Both illustrations reveal the close relationship between innovation and marketing. In the case of Canon, technical developments are used as a selling feature to give companies an edge over their rivals. For their part, consumers, through the media of persuasive advertising, have come to expect regular product changes, which improve the performance or add on extra features to existing models. The 3M product would not have seen the light of day were it not for some lateral thinking on behalf of some staff, and the product would have failed but for an aggressive marketing effort and a persistent faith in the product.

We can see from these illustrations that the marketing function is both an important guide and support to the direction of innovation. Marketing activity helps in the selection of R&D projects by providing information on the probability of their commercial success. It then assists in persuading the consumer that change is desirable. EMI is a good example of a British firm that has been highly innovative but lacked resources and, perhaps, has focused more on technological developments and less on market application to exploit its technological advantage. GSK, by comparison, has been ruthless in abandoning research on less promising products at a relatively early stage (Case 9.5).

We can see then that invention, innovation, research and development, manufacturing and marketing have a complex relationship that is not always fully explored by those seeking to prove a correlation between innovation and economic growth. The illustration of the development of the railways in Britain is a good example of this complexity. In 1814 the technology for the development of the railways was available. However, it was several years before a number of factors converged. These were the technological know-how, the availability of cheap labour, an expanding export market, the need for rapid access to ports, a growing mobility among the middle classes, and the available investment from the profits of industrialization. In other words, the innovation of the railways was a product of technology, market need and available capital, together with encouraging social and political conditions (Rothwell and Zegveld, 1981).

As well as being the catalyst for innovation, in some cases an established technology can be difficult to change. Whittington (1993) cites a number of examples, the most famous of which is the development of the 'QWERTY' keyboard on typewriters. It is acknowledged that this particular configuration for keyboards is not the most efficient. Its development was a function of mechanical constraints of early typewriters and the insistence of the Remington Company that a keyboard should have all the letters to type 'typewriter' on one line. The system persists despite the fact that the mechanical constraints no longer exist.

Thus word-processors of today use an inefficient system originating in nineteenth century mechanical constraints and a Remington Company sales ploy. (*Whittington, 1993, p. 88*)

The same author cites the dominance of light-water reactors in the USA nuclear industry, based on its use in the 1950's nuclear submarine, despite more efficient and effective systems being available. In many cases the persistence of certain technologies in the face of new developments is linked to the politics of organizational decision-making. In general, organizational factors add to the complexity of the relationship between technology and innovation, and it is to these we now turn.

Case 9.3

Innovation and marketing: two cases

Case 9.3a: The Brownie 127 and Canon Autofocus

Throughout the 1950s and 1960s one of the most popular cameras was the Brownie 127 made by Kodak, the British subsidiary of the American company. Its simplicity and ease of operation made it a market leader. The camera was produced from 1952 to 1964 and underwent just one model change involving a slight modification of the lens. A comparable camera is the Canon Autofocus made by the Japanese company Canon. It has the ease of operation of the Brownie 127 but is much more complex technically. Introduced in 1979, there were five model changes in the first six years of its life. This was deemed necessary not only because of the rapid technological advances in electronics but also because of the intense competition among Japanese camera manufacturers, causing Canon alone to spend 10 per cent of its turnover on R&D in 1985. The market expects regular product changes reflecting new developments in photographic technology and each new technical development, in the form of improved performance, styling and new features, is eagerly paraded through advertising to give camera producers that significant edge over their rivals.

Source: *Sunday Times*, 16 February 1987

Case 9.3b: The 3M 'Post-it' notes

The R&D department of the American multinational 3M had developed a partially adhesive glue, but had found no commercially viable application for it. The development waited 5 years until one of the team devised the idea that a notice board coated with this adhesive would provide a much more convenient means of fixing and removing notices than the conventional drawing pin. This innovation was compatible with 3M's considerable interests in office equipment. The idea failed at the test-marketing stage. One of those responsible for the project then turned the idea around. The glue on the notice board was changed to glue on pieces of paper which could then be used on notice boards and other places where messages were fixed. The product was refined and the end result became the 'Post-it' note, a pad of readily detachable adhesive labels. Once again the marketing test failed, but it was thought that the product was not reaching the potential user. The company persevered, and in a risky marketing venture, introduced a mass trial of the product by giving away large numbers of pads to secretaries, typists, receptionists, bank clerks, and anyone else who might possibly use the product in the company's home town of Minneapolis-St Paul. The 'Post-it' notes soon became addictive and a massive local demand was created which soon spread both nationally and internationally.

Source: Kennedy, 1988

Questions

1   What do these cases tell us about the process of innovation?

2   What do the cases reveal about the links between innovation and marketing?

■■■■ Organizational aspects of innovation

When we examine innovation at the level of the individual organization, the most significant aspects to emerge are those of size, structure and organization culture. Ownership variables do not appear to be particularly significant and, despite the obvious interest of the state in the innovation process, there is certainly no evidence to suggest that innovation in publicly owned companies is any more significant than that in private firms. Indeed, critics of public ownership may well argue, citing the Inmos case as a good illustration, that political involvement slows down the process of innovation. We shall see that the question of goals is invariably tied up with issues of size, and we deal with these aspects together in our next section.

Organizational size and goals

Not only does the impact of organizational size upon innovation present us with some rather conflicting evidence but also, in the UK at least, public policy appears equally confused. From the 1970s onwards we may be forgiven for thinking that the attention of the policy makers has focused largely on small firms, possibly as a reaction to the merger activity of the previous decade. In practice, however, R&D expenditure in Britain is concentrated in relatively few large firms. In 1978 five firms accounted for 41 per cent of all expenditure on R&D and received 76 per cent of all government R&D funding. We saw in the last section how this pattern has continued, with 50 companies being responsible for 80 per cent of all civil R&D. We will examine some of that evidence and attempt to show the relationship of size with changing goals as well as illustrating the dynamic process of innovation at the level of the firm. However, we must remember the major difficulty in our assessment of innovation: that of measurement. While R&D expenditure is clearly some indication of innovative activity, firms can be highly innovative in their products, marketing and organization without having an organized R&D function.

There is a clear line of thinking, going back through such writers as Galbraith to Schumpeter, which believes that developments in technology depend upon expensive research programmes of the kind that can only be found in the large corporation. Accordingly, big firms are deemed to be best and monopolies even better. The complexities of modern technologies and the corresponding development costs set up irrevocable pressures towards the growing scale of organizations. Evidence in the 1960s was fairly clear in that large manufacturing firms spent proportionally more on R&D, had a larger share of innovation and were quicker to adopt new techniques of manufacturing (Mansfield, 1963). Findings such as these led to the assumption that R&D could only be economic once a certain size of firm had been reached. Certainly this line of thinking influenced British public policy in the 1960s with its encouragement of merger activity.

There can be little doubt that the large firm is able to invest in projects that carry a higher element of risk. Furthermore, the large firm has greater access to finance both from external sources and from the internal generation of funds. However, there are two pieces of evidence that appear to favour the smaller company.

● Small firms spend more on R&D as a proportion of total sales and employ proportionally more staff in R&D than the larger firms, though this could be a case of economies of scale operating in favour of the larger firm rather than any significant differences in their innovative capacities. The link to sales is defined by the DTI R&D Scoreboard as **R&D intensity**. Smaller companies do have higher R&D intensities, but this may be because they are in the process of establishing themselves and are in the research phase of their development. It may also be a function of their lower sales compared to that of larger firms.

- Firms of less than 1000 employees account for more than 20 per cent of innovations in Britain, far greater than their share of R&D investment but less than their share of employment or net output (Pavitt, 1983).

Those who subscribe to the small-firms lobby would argue that the smaller company is much more adaptable, much closer to the consumer and, hence, the source of far more significant innovations than the big firm. We deal with such arguments in more detail in the section on small businesses in Chapter 5.

Jewkes has consistently championed the cause of the small inventor but found that size is a far less significant factor than the competitive nature of the market in which the firm operates (Jewkes *et al.*, 1970). We may conclude from this that highly innovative firms are more likely to be found in very competitive markets, as illustrated by the previously mentioned case of Canon cameras, and that this occurs irrespective of the size of the firm.

There are, however, important variations according to the nature of the sector in which the firm operates. Most innovations in the electrical, electronic, food, chemical and vehicle industries occur in large companies. In the case of mechanical engineering, instrumentation, leather and footwear, it is the smaller firm that tends to dominate (Pavitt, 1983). There is a danger with such analyses in that they confine innovation to products and processes. Significant innovations in, for example, retailing and financial services tend to be overlooked.

We may conclude from all this that there is no clear relationship between size and innovation, but we are able to make the following observations:

- The investment required in some types of innovation, and the need for high volume production for a return on that investment, clearly operates in favour of large companies. A good example here would be the chemical and pharmaceutical industries.

- An influencing factor would seem to be the sector of operation. Some sectors, like chemicals, tend to be traditionally dominated by large companies while in others, especially instrumentation, the small firm still plays a significant role.

- There are cases of breakthroughs being made by small firms in all sectors, but they may have to align themselves with larger companies to obtain the necessary development capital, production capacity, or access to markets, the Workmate, Case 9.1, being a good example.

- Where markets are especially volatile, any firm, irrespective of size, may have to keep innovating to maintain market share. It is in such situations that entrepreneurial activity becomes most important.

The main difficulty with analyses of this nature is that they tend to view relationships at one point in time when, in reality, the innovative process and the size of firms can be viewed as highly dynamic. Henry Ford produced five different engines in quick succession, prior to the Model T, in a relatively small, jobbing-based organization. No product change then took place for 15 years, as the emphasis shifted to the development of mass-production process technologies and incremental product improvements (Abernathy and Utterback, 1978).

Examinations of business histories show us that the most fundamental product innovations usually take place at a relatively early stage of a firm's development, when it is still relatively small. As the firm develops, more emphasis is placed on process innovations. A stage may well be reached where the growth of mass markets and the need for economies of scale in the production process mean that fundamental change is resisted as being too costly. In other words the goals of the company change over time with changes in size and the nature of the innovations. A longitudinal study of the development of Computer Aided Design (CAD) systems in manufacturing found that from 1969 to 1974 initial innovations took place in small computer software companies. From 1974 to 1980 the main developments were taking place in much larger companies. Either the original firms had expanded or they had been bought out by firms, such as General Electric, wishing to buy into the new technology. In both cases, size was seen as an important factor in the attraction of venture capital. From 1980 onwards, smaller firms once again entered the market, concentrating on the development of highly specialized CAD systems, with a limited field of application (Kaplinsky, 1983).

We have noted in this section the need for some small firms to align themselves to larger companies for access to development capital and markets. There are some larger firms who pursue a deliberate strategy of innovation through acquisition. This can be a useful strategy where the acquired firm operates in the same product market but, as we saw in the last chapter, difficulties can arise where diversification is totally unrelated.

Innovation and organization structure

> When novelty and unfamiliarity in both market situation and technical information become the accepted order of things, a fundamentally different kind of management system becomes appropriate from that which applies to a relatively stable commercial and technical environment. (Tom Burns, in the Preface to *The Management of Innovation*, Burns and Stalker, 1966, p. vii)

The starting point is appropriate, since it was Burns and Stalker's study of the post-war electronics industry and, in particular, the failure of some of the Scottish firms in their study to set up effective research departments, that has been so influential, not only in the development of organization theory, but as a practical guide to innovative firms on the development of appropriate structures. In this section we will examine why such a 'fundamentally different kind of management system' is necessary, the problems encountered in setting up such a system, and the attempts that have been made to provide solutions to these problems. We illustrate the arguments by focusing on the R&D department in typically science-based industry. The same arguments apply for any group within an organization with the primary responsibility for initiating innovation. For example, in an advertising agency tensions often arise between staff who manage client accounts, and who have to adopt a business orientation, and those whose primary responsibility is the generation of creative ideas.

Burns and Stalker identified two ideal types of organization, which they called the **mechanistic organization** and the **organic organization**. In their view the organic organization was more effective for innovation. The key differences between these two types of organization is presented in Table 9.10.

The R&D function and those connected with it have various claims for different treatment from the rest of the organization.

Table 9.10	**Differences between mechanistic and organic organizations**	
	Mechanistic	*Organic*
	Highly specialized tasks. Fragmentation and differentiation	Contribution of individuals to a collective common goal
	Tasks follow abstract rules	Tasks related to the needs of real situations
	Roles and jobs are defined in a precise way	Roles and jobs are loosely defined and are continuously being redefined
	The structure is very hierarchical with location of key knowledge at the top	Responsibility and authority are delegated throughout the organization. Knowledge exists anywhere in the organization
	Interaction and communication tends to be vertical	Communication flows in all directions. Team-working and networking are encouraged
	Members of the firm are expected to be loyal and obedient	Members of the firm are expected to be committed to the goals
	The focus tends to be on experience and knowledge built up within the organization	The focus is on external experience and knowledge is drawn from a variety of sources
	Innovation strategies tend to be based on rational approaches using SWOT analysis	Innovation strategies tend to be incremental

Source: Adapted from Burns and Stalker, 1966

- There is a fundamental belief that the creativity inherent in the function requires its workers to communicate freely both within and outside the organization and to be free of the kind of bureaucratic controls to which other departments are subjected.
- The very nature of the work demands that there be flexibility as far as the allocation of priorities, patterns of working and normal management control systems are concerned.
- Specifically there is a demand for the relaxation of hierarchical controls and a need to see investment in R&D as a long-term issue.

Those companies where innovation is a key activity have tended to respond by creating special R&D departments. This can create a problem, that tends to arise frequently, in that this sets up a clash of cultures between R&D and the other departments. The need for flexibility, as outlined above, challenges the existing bureaucratic controls and with it the existing power base. The old order with its allegiance to the organization and the *status quo* can be shaken by a group of scientists and technologists with their allegiance to a knowledge base whose source lies outside the organization. In such a situation it is often convenient for top management to isolate the R&D department both politically and sometimes geographically. In this way it presents less of a challenge to the *status quo* and can be conveniently amputated when costs need to be cut. It is not uncommon, in times of economic recession, for firms to cut back or close down altogether their R&D function. This sets up an interesting paradox between the need to reduce expenditure and the central role ascribed to innovation in economic recovery.

However, it is often the scientists themselves who support this isolation within the organization. It absolves them of responsibility and gives them the kind of freedom they seek to pursue their own goals. This can involve role-playing to a widely held image of the eccentric scientist. As Burns and Stalker note:

> a reputation for eccentricity may be helpful not only in creating a complaisant attitude in industry towards the transgression of normal rules and towards a claim for privileges but also in furthering a career . . . also taken to imply in some degree abdication from claims to leadership in the general management of business concerns. (*Burns and Stalker, 1966 p. 176*)

The result for the organization is invariably a lack of coordination between R&D and other activities like production and marketing; a situation which, as Burns and Stalker found, retarded the innovative process and was detrimental to the effective operation of the firm as a whole. A great deal of time can be wasted on internal politics and the situation can lead to a proliferation of committees and intermediaries to operate in a coordinating capacity, creating jobs like methods engineers.

In many ways, the R&D department needs to be different because its goals are different, the time horizon on which it is evaluated is different, and it has different needs with regard to the formality of its operations. An R&D department needs an informal structure because of the uncertain nature of its work and its need for a flexible response to both technological and market changes. Specialists may need to be brought in from outside, possibly on a temporary basis, decision-making and responsibility may have to be decentralized, and there will usually be a very loose specification of jobs and work procedures. Integration may be achieved through the management information system, by creating cross-functional teams, or by using some managers in special integrating roles.

There are dangers with this approach. Catering to the special demands of the R&D function can lead to the kind of isolation we have already discussed and the various attempts at integration can all too often result in paperwork jungles or the creation of supernumerary roles whose sole reason for existence is to act as go-between. In his study of the management of innovation in eight different firms, Parker found that a great deal of attention had been paid to structural considerations, setting up departments, creating special teams, training and coordination. However, he found this to be less important than an effective strategy for innovation, which he found to be lacking in most instances (Parker, 1982). Part of the problem according to Chaharbaghi and Newman (1996) is that innovation is viewed differently by various people in varying functions. This often results in a fragmentation of effort.

Communication and coordination would appear to be key issues. Multinationals that can draw effectively upon a worldwide network are generally more innovative than those who operate as separate national entities. Companies such as GSK and Siemens have established global innovation networks, vital in fast-moving industries such as pharmaceuticals and electronics. As we saw in Chapter 4, many Japanese firms have built up close and effective relationships with their suppliers, which has led to new developments in both products and processes. In all firms a close relationship between R&D and marketing is essential to provide information which reduces uncertainty concerning the acceptability of innovative products.

Firms operating globally would seem to have three options. Innovation can be the prerogative of some centralized unit such as a central R&D division, or it can be a decentralized activity or a combination of both systems. A centralized system offers economies of scale and may offer advantages in the development of totally new technologies. However, where it is important to develop local products for local markets, particularly where supply chains are involved in the development process, a decentralized system may be more effective. Most global firms, such as HP and Ford, have R&D operations in most of their main markets. Tidd *et al.* (2001) argue that the key factors involved in centralization versus decentralization and global versus local are as follows:

- Where basic research is important, as in the pharmaceutical industry, centralization tends to be the norm, as it does where a period of trial and error is needed after a fundamental breakthrough.

- Firms following long-term strategies tend to have more centralized R&D than those pursuing more short-term, market-led strategies.

- There is a tendency for most global firms to locate the majority of their innovative activity in the home country. In the case of Germany, Japan and the USA, Tidd *et al.* (2001) note that as much as 80 per cent of high-spending R&D is located at home. The main use of foreign R&D would appear to be to adapt products for local markets. Of course, in the case of certain complex products, such as passenger aircraft, even this may be unnecessary. Localized R&D would seem to operate best when there is a need to exploit local conditions, as in the case of working with local raw materials or using specialized local knowledge and skills.

Some believe that effectiveness is achieved through the organization of the firm around its dominant competitive issue. In this way, if innovation were identified as the priority then the firm should locate its centre of power and influence around that activity. Successful innovative firms not only see innovation as a priority but build an entire organization culture based on innovation. In the next section we reinforce this theme. Organization changes, which follow technical innovations, can underline the competitive advantage of the innovation. The impact of containerization and advances in telecommunications offered opportunities to shipping companies, but full advantage was only gained following corresponding changes in jobs and organization structure (see Case 9.4 for more details).

The role of organization culture

In the previous section we dwelt at length on the structural issues pertaining to the operation of an R&D function. We have maintained throughout that innovation is not the sole prerogative of science-based manufacturing industry, nor does it depend on the existence of a formally established R&D department. We have already established that innovation applies to all forms of business, and many firms are entrepreneurial and innovative largely because it is seen as a responsibility of all staff irrespective of their function.

A culture of innovation may be built up in a variety of ways. One way may be to recruit innovative and entrepreneurial staff and, by using training programmes, to develop creative thinking. More significantly, the lead normally comes through the activities and energy of senior management, and their creation of an organization to foster innovation. In the HP case and in our reference to excellent companies in Chapter 5 there would appear to be some correlation between the existence of a strong corporate culture and innovative activity. Ekvall (1991) reported on a research programme about creativity and found, not surprisingly, that creative organizations were typified by high trust, freedom, idea support, playfulness and risk-taking. Such supportive climates are typical of Peters and Waterman's 'excellent companies'.

Case 9.4

The shipping industry

The shipping industry is concerned with the transport of goods by sea, and is not to be confused with shipbuilding. The information for the case is taken largely from a study of the shipping industry, titled *Innovating to Compete* (Walton, 1987). Walton examines eight countries: Denmark, Holland, Japan, Norway, Sweden, United Kingdom, USA and the former West Germany. The choice of the eight nations is significant in that they represented the world's traditional merchant fleets and accounted for 74 per cent of the entire world tonnage in shipping prior to the second world war. Since the war, the powerful position of these shipping nations has been challenged by a variety of factors. By 1973 their collective tonnage had fallen to 43 per cent and by 1983 to 26 per cent. The case study identifies those factors and examines the strategic responses of the shipping companies concerned. It should be remembered that, while merchant fleets are invariably linked to nation states, shipping is operated as a business and shipping companies are privately owned.

In Walton's study, two phases were identified: the first 1963–73, and the second 1973–83.

Period 1: 1963–73

For the eight nations listed above this period was one of economic prosperity. The demand for shipping exceeded supply and that demand was increasing throughout this period at a rate of 7 per cent a year. It was also a period in which unemployment was extremely low and the shipping industry faced intense competition for its labour from land-based industries. The lure of seafaring had declined with the prospect of long periods away from home and the increasing development of functional ports in unglamorous locations away from the main centres of urban life. Furthermore, time spent in port had been sacrificed to the fast turnaround of vessels to save cost and maximize operational time. Combined with these factors was a growing resistance to the quasi-military regime of the merchant navy, especially in the face of attractive job opportunities elsewhere. Labour shortages became the norm in the shipping industry of all these nations. Under such conditions the bargaining power of trade unions is substantially strengthened, as was the case in the majority of companies covered by the study. Wage rates were increased to attract and keep labour, with a corresponding increase in costs. Nevertheless, demand for shipping was still high and the industry remained relatively healthy, with increased costs being borne by the customer through increased freight charges.

Period 2: 1973–83

1973 was a watershed for the shipping industry in the eight nations. The problems caused by the high costs of labour were superseded by very high interest rates and a dramatic increase in the cost of fuel. Unfortunately, as far as these developed countries were concerned, price competition within the industry had increased through the activity of two types of new entrant.

- There had been the fast growth of shipping operating under 'flags of convenience'. This shipping is associated with such countries as Liberia and Panama, where the cost of registering and insuring ships is much lower than in traditional shipping nations. The advantage to the ship owner is not just in terms of registration and insurance. The regulations covering shipping operations and shipboard practices tend to be far less restrictive, and labour tends to be cheaper too. A country like Liberia has actively marketed this service and sees it as an important source of foreign investment. Under such a mechanism overheads and labour costs are kept to a minimum, and shipping operating under a **'flag of convenience'** is able to enter the market place offering an attractive price to the customer. It is hardly surprising that the eight nations saw a defection of ship owners from their fleets to such 'flags of convenience'. The bulk transport of the world's oil supply quickly became the prerogative of the Liberian tanker fleet, heavily underwritten and supported by the major multinational oil corporations.

- Certain governments, particularly those of the former Soviet bloc nations and those of developing countries, see their own shipping industry as a means of achieving highly prized international recognition. The industry becomes both metaphorically and literally a flag carrier for its sponsoring nation. Government-backed shipping from such countries has, like the 'flags of convenience', reduced the price and widened the choice for the customer.

The problems facing the eight nations were therefore intensified and by 1983 the entire industry was suffering from problems of over capacity. This became particularly acute as the decade from 1973, unlike its predecessor, marked a decline in the demand for shipping.

The strategic options of shipping companies in the established nations

We can see that a combination of rising labour and fuel costs, high interest rates, cheap competition and over-capacity had seriously weakened the competitive position of the eight developed nations in Walton's study. Those firms still operating were faced with a number of options in order to maintain their competitive position. The strategic options and the problems associated with them may be identified as follows:

- Some firms found that the move towards much larger vessels enabled them to achieve economies of scale and compete on price. Such an option was not

▶

available to all owing to the very high investment costs needed for this type of strategy.

- Some governments decided to assist their own shipping industry by setting up subsidies and by granting generous tax allowances. Protectionist strategies and trade agreements have been used to safeguard the position of national fleets. Such agreements might include the provision that all coastal traffic should use national carriers, or that the exchange of imports and exports must be accompanied by a corresponding exchange of shipping services. While some governments were committed to such policies, others showed a complete disinterest and, in some cases, ideological opposition to state intervention.

- A popular strategy involved product specialization. Some companies decided that they could not compete with developing nations and 'flags of convenience' in the transport of bulk cargoes or in the oil tanker trade. Instead, they opted for those cargoes requiring specialist facilities and handling, such as liquid gases and other dangerous chemicals; or they chose to operate with highly mixed loads in relatively small batches. However, over-specialization can be threatened by the lack of demand, and the cost of transporting loads in small batches raises its own logistics problems.

- A classic response to the problems of labour shortages and increased labour costs was process innovation. Containerization has been a popular option in many cases: cargoes come ready packed in large containers, reducing the need for dock and shipboard handling. Inevitably, containerization was supported by the development of the 'roll on–roll off' process, where the containers are driven directly onto the ship and unloaded by container lorry, obviating the need for cargo handling at all. Such developments have been matched by the automation of shipboard engineering, control and monitoring processes and changes in telecommunications rendering traditional methods of ship-to-shore communication redundant. In all cases, such innovations reduced the need for labour or enabled formerly specialized tasks to be substituted by those with a lower skill requirement. However, such changes carry high investment costs and often meet employee resistance to change, more especially union opposition to both reduced manning levels and more flexible work practices.

- In shipping, as with all industries, technical innovations invariably offer the possibility of organizational changes to underline the advantages of the former. In particular, automation and changes in telecommunications introduced the possibility of flexible manning and, hence, even greater labour savings. Some companies went even further and attempted to introduce permanent crews operating as a team and ensuring continuity of labour: a radical innovation in an industry built on a history of casual hiring. The move towards teamwork was a deliberate attempt to improve the quality of working life and was accompanied, in some cases, by the creation of less hierarchical organizational structures. These new structures offered more opportunity for delegated authority and participation. Some companies saw such moves as inevitable to match conditions in shore-based industries and to change the merchant navy's image of authoritarian man-management systems to attract labour. Bringing about such changes is not without its difficulties. The very structures that are identified for change are likely to provide the biggest obstacle. The shipping industry is typified by highly bureaucratic structures and shipboard relations steeped in naval tradition where ship captains are highly resistant to participative forms of management.

The options are not mutually exclusive and some shipping companies had pursued all five options in an attempt to maintain their competitive position. Far from being mutually exclusive, some of the options were dependent upon the support of others for maximum effectiveness. The major point of Walton's study is that competitiveness can only be achieved when technical innovations are accompanied by organizational innovations.

Source: Walton, 1987

Questions

1 Identify the key competitive issues facing the shipping industry in the eight developed nations.

2 Which of the strategic options identified were likely to be the most popular and why? Which of the options were truly innovative?

3 What does the case tell us about the nature of innovation?

Innovation and management strategies

Throughout this chapter we have seen that both management and representatives of governments have operated on the clear assumption that innovation is linked to increased productivity, market share and profitability, as well as being an indication of the state of a nation's economic health. A strong lobby exists for the promotion of an innovation strategy as the key to competitive advantage. Typical of the lobby is the stance taken by Hayes and Wheelwright. They maintain that firms must innovate to survive, since strategies that depend on imitation and following market trends will ultimately lead to a saturation of the market. While some firms will survive better than others by clever marketing strategies and introducing the kind of 'pseudo-innovations' we discussed at the beginning of the chapter, real growth is dependent upon the development of new products. Hayes and Wheelwright focused on the manufacturing industry and an important feature of the hypothesis is the primacy of innovative machine tool technology. Only through this will firms be able to manufacture products that are distinct from those of their competitors (Hayes and Wheelwright, 1984). Clearly their hypothesis is biased towards manufacturing but has application for other sectors as well. We will return to this argument in the next chapter and refer you to Case 7.1, which deals with the decline in the British machine tool industry.

In this section we will examine two types of innovation strategy, 'first to the market' and 'follower strategies'. Following our discussion of organization structure and culture we will revisit the concept of integrated strategies before closing the section with an examination of some constraints to innovation.

Types of strategy

In Chapter 7 we identified a number of different approaches to strategy formulation that we called the 'strategic process'. We noted that a popular approach to strategy was the rational approach based on an assessment of the firm's environment and of its strengths and weaknesses. We argued that such an approach is unlikely to produce innovative solutions since much of the knowledge is also available to competitors and therefore strategies are likely to be copied.

Whittington (1993) and Tidd *et al.* (2001) argue that an innovative strategy is more likely to arise from an incremental process. This allows strategy to develop in a step by step approach and is constantly amended as new things are learnt about the environment, the organization and the customers. Such a process goes hand in hand with a form of organizational learning, in which the organization members develop a knowledge and understanding that is unique to their firm and situation. Such knowledge is sometimes referred to as **implicit or tacit knowledge** and is a source of competitive advantage. **Explicit knowledge,** on the other hand, is that derived from external source and is available to all.

Key concept 9.8 Tacit and explicit forms of knowledge

These are two forms of knowledge found in organizations. Explicit knowledge is obtained through rational processes of data collection and is often contained in documentation. Such knowledge is often available to all and, as a consequence, is rarely a source of competitive advantage. Tacit knowledge, on the other hand, is the sum total of knowledge acquired by organization members throughout the lifetime of the organization and passed on to subsequent generations of employees. It is rarely documented and difficult for outsiders to penetrate. Since tacit knowledge is unique to a particular organization, it can be an important source of innovation.

As we noted in Chapter 7, no single approach to strategy is necessarily better than any other. However, in terms of innovation, two generic strategies have been recognized. These are 'first to the market' and 'follower'.

'First to the market' strategy

According to Ansoff and Stewart (1967), organizations pursuing this type of strategy display the following features:

- Research and development is viewed as a central part of their operation.
- There is a strong commitment to basic research, technical leadership and hence a willingness to take risks with comparatively large investments.
- Research tends to be close to the state-of-the-art and the organization employs a high proportion of top-rate research scientists.
- There is considerable coordination between research, production and marketing and planning is usually long-range.

The large pharmaceutical companies, like Pfizer, Roche and GSK, fit into this category. They use R&D and a 'first to the market' strategy as a deliberate attempt to dominate the market. As we see in Case 9.5, GSK and its predecessors have always employed large numbers of research scientists, have close links with universities in various parts of the world, and successfully developed the anti-ulcer drug Zantac before its rivals – achieving a very large and very profitable market share.

Being first to the market gives a firm a number of distinct advantages:

- The firm can use the patent system to create a monopoly position and earn income from licensing activities, as we saw earlier with Texas Instruments.

- Those first to the market can control limited resources. The first development in a new beach resort can occupy the prime site and buy land when prices are relatively cheap. Those following, especially if the resort becomes fashionable and popular, are faced with less desirable locations and higher prices.

- Those that are first can set the industry standards that others must follow, as in the case of computer hardware and software. The battle for market share in the UK satellite televison industry was fought between Sky and BSB, with the two companies operating different systems. In some respects BSB operated a technically superior system but being first enabled Sky to gain the largest market share. BSB experienced financial difficulties and were eventually taken over by Sky.

However, being first to patent the invention is insufficient in itself. Sony was not the first company to patent the Walkman but was the first to produce it cheaply and market it effectively. Rank Xerox was first to the market with the photocopying machine and used the patent to create an effective monopoly but failed to compete effectively for several years with Canon and Toshiba when they entered the market as followers. Being a follower can have advantages and it is to this we now turn.

'Follower' strategies

A variety of follower strategies can be identified. Some firms, such as Philips operating in the domestic electrical market, are highly innovative and take state-of-the-art technical knowledge invented elsewhere and use this to develop their own product range. Other firms in the same market, such as Hotpoint, will follow somewhat cautiously behind the state-of-the-art technology, concentrating more on design modifications. In the two cases above, the companies possess R&D departments and, while not first to the market, are still concerned with innovation. By contrast there are some followers who have no R&D function as such. They exist largely on a strong manufacturing base and have the ability to copy others' products quickly and effectively. Successful firms of this type operate on low costs, have a comparatively low selling price and the ability to deliver on time. They rely on being highly competitive as opposed to innovative. Firms operating in this way do not tend to be household names.

Being a follower has its advantages:

- Goods can often be introduced more cheaply as high development costs do not have to be recouped.

- Those coming after can learn from the mistakes of the pioneers. For example, Boeing developed its highly profitable 707 range of aircraft by learning from the metal fatigue problems that dogged the early versions of the British Aircraft Corporation's Comet and, as a result, gained a much larger market share (Bowen *et al.*, 1992).

- Coming second also means that a market with support mechanisms such as knowledgeable retailers, service and maintenance facilities, and complementary products, is already established. In the computing area, later arrivals entered a market place where software standards were established and they could develop their products accordingly.

Follower strategies can be pursued in specific circumstances by otherwise highly innovative and well-known companies. We have noted already that, when Rank Xerox's patent on the photocopier expired, several companies, including Canon, Toshiba and Gestetner, used the available technology to manufacture their own versions. In many cases those coming second not only have the advantages highlighted above but can also build upon their reputations in other fields. In the case of Canon and Toshiba they developed photocopiers that were not only cheaper but more reliable. This, in turn, resulted in Rank Xerox rethinking its own strategy and led to a focus on quality and the development of 'total quality management' (TQM) techniques in an attempt to recapture its former market position.

Integration – strategy, structure and culture

> Although innovation is a primary source of competitive advantage, it is usually an effective source only if it can be deployed in concert with some other sources of competitive advantage, or if it is at least supported by other strategic weapons. (*Kay, 1992, p. 127*)

Our illustrations of the 'first to the market' and 'follower' strategies above suggest that the two are not mutually exclusive and that a firm can pursue different strategies in different product markets. The quote from Kay (1992) suggests that whatever strategy is pursued it is insufficient in itself without the support of the rest of the organization. This reinforces the theme raised in our earlier discussion of the relationship to innovation of organizational structure and organizational culture. We may conclude from the works of Kay, other authors and various case histories that the strategic implications for a firm wishing to be innovative are as follows:

- In general there needs to be a risk-taking ethos that is supported by top management. Such an ethos is an important part of the firm's vision statement, widely accepted by employees.
- There ought to be a willingness to experiment and therefore a freedom to fail. Employees should be empowered, encouraged and supported. Individual contributions should be recognized and publicized throughout the organization.
- This should be supported by the recruitment of people with creative talents and, where appropriate, with good technical backgrounds in the specific industry sector.
- Recruitment policies need to be reinforced by training and development programmes which place emphasis on innovation and the acquisition of the required technical knowledge. Promotion strategies should include technical know-how and a commitment to innovation as key criteria. Development targets should stretch individuals.

- The exchange of ideas should be encouraged, not just within the firm but, especially for those operating in science-based industries, also by fostering links with universities and other research establishments.
- Mechanisms that facilitate communication can be set up, such as suggestion schemes and more radical methods of employee participation, but, more generally, innovation may be encouraged if the organization is flexible and decentralized.
- Effective structures tend to be based on small flexible teams, where employees have broadly defined jobs. Employees should be encouraged to interact with people and ideas from outside their own organization.
- Innovation is about learning and change, and it is linked to the concept of the learning organization. There should be a focus on tacit learning that is used for competitive advantage.
- Whether a special R&D department is created or not, attention needs to be paid to integrating the function of innovation with the rest of the organization's activities. Kay (1993) goes further and speaks not only of the importance of integration within the firm – between departments, management and labour – but also between the firm and its suppliers and the firm and its customers. The close relationship between many Japanese manufacturing firms and their components suppliers illustrates this, as does the policy of HP of consulting customers in the innovation of new products (see the section on Japanese management in Chapter 4 and the HP case in Chapter 5).

Probably the most significant feature to emerge from the points made above is the need to create a particular organization culture or climate that is supportive of innovation. This in turn needs to be supported by an environment where emphasis is placed on developing the skills of the workforce, and where innovation is encouraged by banks and by effective political policies instead of rhetoric. The absence of these features presents the innovative firm with considerable constraints.

Constraints to effective innovation strategy

Despite the central role ascribed to innovation, there are constraints which may significantly limit its effectiveness.

- For any new idea there is a high probability of failure. If we add this to a tendency on the part of many managers to underestimate the costs involved, then it is easy to see why some companies have found innovation a particularly risky strategy. Lockheed and Rolls Royce in the aerospace industry are good illustrations of this.
- Managers in many industries, faced with the pressure for career development and pressures from shareholders for a generous dividend, may opt for safer short-term investments which preclude more radical innovative strategies. Undoubtedly the problems associated with short-termism in general highlight the importance of a supportive financial system for effective innovation.
- The time lags between development and commercial exploitation can be highly variable, a process taking an estimated 22 years as far as television was concerned.
- In addition to all these problems, economic, social and political conditions may militate against effective innovation. We have already seen the importance of a skills infrastructure and supportive political policies. Objections by trade unions fearing

losses in job security, either real or imagined, can set back the introduction of process innovations, as we have seen in the newspaper industry (Chapter 1). High interest rates offered by banks as a result of high inflation can add to the reluctance on the part of managers to invest in new ventures.

Difficulties of the kind identified above have led to the preference of some firms to seek alternative strategies. A common alternative is the use of the patent and licensing system identified earlier in this chapter. Instead of developing products and processes itself, a firm will manufacture a product or use a process that has been developed elsewhere, on the payment of a licence fee to the patent holder. This is not only a strategy for the avoidance of R&D costs but can save a great deal of time in the development process by eliminating duplication of effort. The high cost of development in the electronics industry was considerably reduced for many firms by using, as their starting point, the original patent for the transistor owned by the Bell Telephone Corporation. Licensing may not be totally passive and may, in fact, be a spur to modifications, resulting in a company developing its own innovations.

In addition to licensing, the costs of innovation may be reduced by undertaking joint development with another company, buying in specific research work as needed from a specialist research consultancy firm or even through acquisition strategy. In this way, a firm can add to its stable of new products, processes and patents by purchasing particularly innovative companies that are operating in their chosen direction of diversification. In some cases a spin-off company can be established to focus on a specific project, as SmithKlineBeecham did with Adprotech before its merger with Glaxo Wellcome.

In discussing innovation strategies, students should always remember that the strategies are never as discrete as textbook models would like them to be. We have already noted that a firm can be first to the market place with some of its product range while following other firms in other types of product. A firm may well have a strong R&D department with a record of successful innovation. At the same time it could license developments from its competitors and even pursue an acquisition strategy of buying up certain highly specialized units.

What does appear to be important is an integrated strategy, a theme that appears central to the innovative process. A good idea may be wasted without corresponding policies in operations and marketing, the respective themes of our next two chapters.

Case 9.5   GlaxoSmithKline

In 2000, Glaxo Wellcome and SmithKline Beecham merged to create the largest UK pharmaceutical company. In terms of sales revenue in the industry it ranked fourth in the world behind the big USA firms, Merck, Pfizer, and Johnson and Johnson. The key motivation behind the merger was the creation of a research-led company to challenge the best in the world in terms of its ability to invent and deliver new drugs to the market. The merger was estimated to save the company £1.89 billion. The company operates across 104 manufacturing sites in 40 countries and has 24 R&D centres in seven different countries. The headquarters are in West London and, at the time of writing, the chief executive is Jean-Pierre Garnier, formerly second in command at SmithKline Beecham.

This case focuses on developments that occurred in Glaxo Wellcome before the merger and deals with the recent problems that have arisen since the merger.

Glaxo Wellcome was itself formed by a merger in 1995. With this merger Glaxo Wellcome controlled 35 per cent of the world gastro-intestinal drug market, 25 per cent of the antibiotic market, 25 per cent of the respiratory market and 70 per cent of the anti-viral market. The focus of the company remained the prescribed pharmaceuticals market, despite considerable growth in the over-the-counter non-prescription drugs market. At that time Glaxo Wellcome had a presence in over 50 countries, manufacturing in over 30 of them. Glaxo Wellcome operated in a competitive world market where research plays a highly significant role both in terms of expenditure and in terms of the ever-present need to develop innovative products.

Glaxo had risen to prominence with the development and manufacture of the world's best-selling drug, Zantac, a treatment for ulcers. The drug was launched in 1981 and became the world top-seller by 1986. However, the company did not emerge as a leading-edge researcher until the 1960s when the acquisition of a research-based operation led to the development of Ventolin, a successful drug for asthma sufferers. The company had developed in the early part of the 20th century as a family business selling powdered milk for babies, with a gradual extension into products related to infant nutrition. The real point of entry into the drugs market came with the Second World War when the company began to produce penicillin. Zantac transformed Glaxo from a moderate UK company into a world leader. Wellcome was founded in the late 19th century as a UK company, Burroughs Wellcome, by two Americans. The company developed the rubella vaccine, but its best-selling item, Zovirax, a treatment for herpes, was lauched, like Zantac, in 1981. By 1996, Zantac was the world number one and Zovirax the world number six in terms of drug sales. Overall the company had six medicines in the top 40 best-selling pharmaceutical products.

Before the merger, both Glaxo and Wellcome were noted for their commitment to R&D. Between 1987 and 1992 more than 50 per cent of Glaxo's capital spending went towards equipping research laboratories. In 1992, Glaxo built a large new research complex at Stevenage to employ 1700 research scientists. In 1992, the Stevenage research laboratories were the largest investment project in the UK after the Channel Tunnel and Sizewell B. The laboratories became the research HQ for Glaxo Wellcome. Following the merger, the company was able to rationalize its R&D operations, saving £600 million a year. At the same time, it became the top listed UK company in terms of R&D expenditure, spending £1.14 billion in 1997. By 2001, in world terms, the R&D expenditure of the new company GlaxoSmithKline was second among all pharmaceutical companies, marginally behind Pfizer of the USA.

Glaxo Wellcome had its research HQ in the UK, and research operations in the USA, Japan, Spain, France, Singapore, Switzerland and Italy. Glaxo Wellcome's R&D strategy was an extension of that pursued by Glaxo. The company had a fairly ruthless approach to weeding out the potentially successful from the unsuccessful developments at a relative early stage and the marketing of innovative drugs at relatively high prices. There was a strong belief in different approaches to problem solving and Glaxo Wellcome not only capitalized upon cultural differences in the approach to research but moved its researchers around the various locations. The organization of research was invariably flexible with the emphasis upon small teams feeding into project approval committees. There was a strong support of pure research and links with the university sector were seen as crucial. In 1992, Glaxo supported University Chairs and projects to some £7 million. The location of its laboratory in North Carolina was in the 'research triangle' between three of the state's most prestigious universities and the Stevenage development resembled a university campus. Such a commitment to pure research underlined the long-term view of R&D strategy. This is inevitable in an industry where it is not uncommon for the development process to take between 10 and 15 years. An important feature here was the good relationship that the management of the company had deliberately fostered with City financial institutions.

The development of Zantac by Glaxo owed much to initial work carried out by a British scientist, James Black, whose findings were published in 1972. Black was working for the USA firm SmithKline French, who were the first to the market place with their anti-ulcer drug, Tagamet, in 1978. The scientists at Glaxo were convinced that by reworking Black's studies they could develop their own superior product. An intensive research programme and product trial resulted in Zantac being launched in 1981. The R&D period for Zantac was highly concentrated, with a subsequent shortening of product lead-time. Effective use was made of patent protection to differentiate the product from its main rival.

The success of Zantac as a product was invariably linked to its acceptance in the USA. Apart from its being the largest market for drugs there were fewer price controls than elsewhere and, hence, a greater potential for profits. Zantac was initially marketed in the USA by the Swiss company Hoffman-La Roche, well known in the American market through its own products, Librium and Valium – the world's biggest-selling tranquilizers. Zantac was priced higher than Tagamet and it is widely acknowledged that the marketing campaign was aggressive. Not only were the superior claims of Zantac over Tagamet forcibly made but Glaxo emphasized the negative side-effects of the rival drug. Subsequent pressure by the USA regulatory body, the Food and Drug Administration, has resulted in Glaxo withdrawing some of the claims made concerning the superiority of Zantac. Nonetheless, Zantac took the USA market from Tagamet to become the world's best-selling drug. At its peak, sales of Zantac accounted for some 40 per cent of Glaxo's total sales.

However, by the mid-1990s there were a number of serious threats to the market dominance of both Zantac and Zovirax.

● In 1993 a new administration was elected to power in the USA. A key policy of the new administration was the reduction in healthcare costs, which were the highest of any nation. There was considerable pressure to reduce the costs for the elderly, who generally have inadequate insurance and must pay the full cost of treatment. There was also pressure to bring down health insurance premiums and to reduce the cost of state-funded healthcare. The drug companies, who charged premium prices for their products, became an obvious target. The USA government encouraged the purchase of cheaper generic drugs developed in lower-cost labour markets, such as Puerto Rico. The threat at the time to both

Glaxo and Wellcome was significant given their reliance on the sales performance of Zantac and Zovirax in the American market.

- The above threat was magnified by the expiry of the patents on both Zantac and Zovirax in 1997. This meant that others could enter the market, producing generic versions of the drugs at a much lower price. This, in turn, forces the originator to lower their prices to remain competitive, with the risk of a substantial fall in profits. Glaxo Wellcome attempted a number of legal manoeuvres to retain their patents to no avail. The company also attempted to gain some ground on the generic drugs manufacturers by negotiating a deal with the manufacturer, Novopharm, to produce Zantac ahead of the patent expiry date. Nonetheless, the initial impact of the expiry of the patent was a 3 per cent fall in total sales for Glaxo Wellcome in 1997.

There were a number of factors that mitigated these threats:

- The merger itself had resulted in both Glaxo and Wellcome reducing their dependence on a narrow range of products, and enabled the new company to have a broader product portfolio.
- As well as saving substantially on R&D costs, the merger resulted in a global reduction of labour costs, with 7500 jobs being lost.
- New opportunities had opened up in emerging markets, which by 1997 accounted for 15 per cent of world sales in pharmaceutical products.
- The management considered that their continued investment in R&D enabled them to replace Zantac and Zovirax with other best-selling drugs. Between 1990 and 1997, Glaxo Wellcome launched 24 new products, which in 1997 represented 34 per cent of sales. The company has great hopes for new drugs to treat migraine and AIDS. Other developments included drugs to alleviate the side-effects of chemotherapy and considerable investment in the development of gene guns to deliver vaccines and treat cancers.

Since the second merger in 2000 to create GSK the company, now with even greater investment in R&D, has strengthened the position of its predecessors as one of the world's leading companies. However, there have also been significant problems:

- The sheer size of the new firm has been questioned in some quarters, particularly as new drugs have not been developed at a speed and volume as predicted. To offset this, the company established six specialist drug discovery units. However within a short time the heads of three of these units had left to join rival companies.
- During 2002 the share price fell by 50 per cent. Although the UK stock market fell significantly during this period, the performance of GSK was seen as poor.
- With echoes of Zantac and Zovirax some years earlier, the patent protection of two of its more recent best-selling drugs was under threat from generic manufacturers. The drugs were Paxil, an anti-depressant that outsold Pfizer's Prozac, and Augmentin, an antibiotic.

◀

- The company was criticized for its position on the sale of AIDS drugs to Africa. In common with its predecessor companies, GSK insisted on selling drugs at premium prices. Opponents claimed this put them out of the reach of most African states, where AIDS was a serious problem. The company eventually relented following the intervention of the UN and its Secretary General, Kofi Annan.

- In May 2003, in an unprecedented action, shareholders blocked proposals on the contract of the Chief Executive, J.-P. Garnier. Under the terms of the proposed agreement he was to be promised a settlement of over £20 million, to be paid when he decided to leave the company. The shareholders considered this excessive. The issue arose at the same time as criticism levelled at the appointment of several non-executive directors. The criticisms were based on the poor records of several of those directors with companies in other sectors.

Sources: Fagan, 1991; Connon, 1992; Kay, 1992; Buchan, 1993; *The Economist,* 25 January, 1995; Company Reports, 1998, *Medical Marketing and Media*, May, 1999, *Guardian,* 24 July, 2002; *Observer,* 25 May, 2003

Questions

1 What advantages are to be gained by the merger of Glaxo and Wellcome and the subsequent merger of Glaxo Wellcome with SmithKline Beecham?

2 What conclusions can you draw from the case about product innovation in the pharmaceutical industry?

3 What does the case tell us about the organization of innovation?

4 What are the major threats facing GlaxoSmithKline?

Summary

- Invention, innovation, research and development, design and entrepreneurship are all related concepts.

- For businesses, it is the process of innovation that is the key concept – turning an invention into something profitable. Innovation can relate to products, processes, marketing and organization, and can range from the most fundamental to the most minor changes.

- Evidence suggests that the more successful innovations are those that are integrated, when product, process and organizational change occur together. Integration would appear to be an important theme in innovation.

- We view innovation as the key to increased productivity, market share and, hence, profitability and the firm's continued survival. The theme has been translated to the scale of national economies, and we have seen how some regard innovation as the source of economic recovery out of a recession. These relationships are difficult to prove but there can be no denying that without innovation there can be no new products or processes.

- The importance of innovation has been recognized by governments all over the world, although there are considerable variations in the extent and direction of intervention. Government support for innovation is seen not only for economic reasons, but for political and social ones too, although there can be significant ideological and practical difficulties in the state's involvement.

- There are clear links between innovation and technology, although in practice it is difficult to determine whether an innovation is a result of 'technology–push' or 'demand–pull'.

- Most important innovations in business are the product of a range of different factors. An understanding of the market place is particularly important and innovation and marketing are interrelated activities.

- At the level of the individual firm there is no clear evidence linking the size of a company with its propensity and ability to innovate, although very expensive research tends to be concentrated in large companies. The sector in which the firm operates and the volatility of the market all interact with the size of establishment in a rather complex way.

- What is fairly clear is that firms with an R&D department have special problems in the integration of R&D with other activities and, in particular, production and marketing. The most successfully innovative companies tend to be those that have paid attention to the creation of a particular organization culture and the encouragement to all staff to be creative.

- Some firms clearly see themselves as technical and market leaders and invest a high proportion of their income in developing new ideas, products and processes. Other firms are more content to sit behind the field and rely upon minor developments or strategies of copying. There are a range of possible strategies that can be adopted either singly or together.

Discussion questions

1 Examine Tables 9.2–9.4 relating to expenditure on R&D. What conclusions do you draw?

2 Examine the ways through which the state can subsidize, encourage and protect innovation in private firms. Why should the state get involved, and what difficulties arise with such involvement?

3 Assess the relationship between innovation and economic growth. Which criteria would you use to show such a relationship?

4 Examine Tables 9.5–9.7 relating to patents. What conclusions do you draw?

5 Select a range of consumer domestic products that illustrate the relationship between technology–push and demand–pull. Which of these two is the more significant?

6 What contribution can the size of the firm make to innovative activity?

7 Identify the major problems associated with the existence of a special function responsible for the initiation of new business ideas, such as an R&D department. What structural devices would you employ to reduce these problems?

8 Assess the innovation strategy alternatives for a manufacturer of consumer electrical goods, a major computer firm, a package holiday company, and a university.

9 Critically examine the characteristics of the innovative firm as listed under the heading 'Integration – strategy, structure and culture' on page 398.

Further reading

Tidd, J., Bessant, J. and Pavitt, K. (2001) *Managing Innovation: Integrating Technological, Market and Organizational Change*, 2nd edn, John Wiley & Sons, London, offers a well-researched account which touches upon most aspects of this chapter and is particularly good in its focus on technology, strategy, markets and organizational issues. A strategic approach is offered by the reader edited by Roberts, E. B. (2002) *Innovation: Driving Product, Process and Market Change*, Jossey Bass, New York. The book contains contributions from some leading writers. A broader-based view of entrepreneurship may be found in most of the books written by Peter Drucker, especially Drucker, P. (1985) *Enterprise and Innovation*, Heinemann, London. Although the study is almost 40 years old, there are few better or more relevant books on the organization of innovation than Burns, T. and Stalker, G. M. (1966) *The Management of Innovation,* 2nd edn, Tavistock, London.

10

Operations

Learning objectives   At the end of this chapter you should be able to:

- Identify the key objectives of operations and their contribution to competitive advantage and explain the conflicting nature of those objectives.
- Explain the difference between the operations function in a manufacturing and service organization.
- Define operations as a system and as a transformational process.
- Identify and explain the key actitivities of operations management and assess their contribution to organizational effectiveness.
- Articulate the problems and issues involved in planning and control.
- Assess the different approaches to quality control.
- Explain supply chain management and just-in-time.
- Explain the link between technology, the design of operations systems and the impact of jobs.
- Explain the impact of operations on the size and structure of the organization.
- Identify and assess key operations strategies.

Introduction

The operations function is concerned with the creation of the goods and services offered to consumers. We often associate operations with manufacturing industry but we can also see an operations function in department stores, restaurants, banks, local government, schools and hospitals, in fact in all kinds of organization.

We begin by examining the central role played by operations in all types of organization and examine two specific aspects of that role: the design of operations systems and how those systems work. We deal with the important function of purchasing within the broader context of supply chain management. The operations function is sometimes portrayed as the function that is most isolated from the environment in which it operates. We refute that idea and examine the relationship of operations with its environment by looking at the influences of a changing economy and government policy towards the manufacturing industry, factors pertaining to the labour force, the impact of technological developments and cultural differences in the way societies view and organize operations. A particular reference will be made to Japanese manufacturing industry. Our analysis of organizational aspects also explores cultural differences and their interaction with the other variables of the Business in Context model, especially the role of organization size and structure. We close the chapter by exploring strategic aspects of operations.

A central function

The operations function has a central role in most types of organization. According to some estimates it accounts for some 70–80 per cent of a firm's assets, expenditure and people (Hill, 1991). In addition, it is central to the firm's success by providing what the customer requires either at a profit in a private company, or within budget in a non-profit organization. It is, therefore, concerned with issues that are crucial to the consumer. These are issues of quantity, quality, availability and price. It is also concerned with issues that are crucial to the management of an enterprise. These are issues of productivity and cost.

The growth of the non-manufacturing sector has encouraged our rethinking of the operations concept. We can see clearly that significant operations issues exist in managing an airport as busy as Heathrow. Planes must take off and land safely and on time. In order for this to occur, key operations must be coordinated, including air traffic control, ground crews, baggage-handling, passport control and customs, aircraft cleaning, refuelling and catering. In busy regional hospitals surgical operations must be carefully timed and scheduled, patients transferred to and from wards, equipment prepared and the various support systems, from nursing to catering, properly briefed. Techniques originally developed in manufacturing are now commonplace in non-manufacturing contexts, and senior staff in these organizations assume the role of coordinating operations.

Key concept 10.1 Operations

Operations is concerned with the transformation of a variety of inputs such as information, people, materials, finance and methods into a variety of outputs such as goods, services, profit, customer and employee satisfaction. Traditionally associated with manufacturing production, it is now generally recognized that operations is a key function in all organizations, irrespective of their primary objective. The centrality of the function means that operations has a significant influence on costs and revenue as well as organization structure.

In the past 30 years, operations management has enjoyed renewed attention. A number of factors are responsible for this, including:

- Increased concerns for improved efficiency and effectiveness in operations management have stemmed from the two oil crises of the 1970s and the associated rises in the cost of fuel and raw materials.
- The rising cost of labour.
- The rapidly developing globalization of business has created interest in the development of systems to coordinate operations across the globe. We noted in Chapter 2 that it is now commonplace for manufacturing firms to make products

comprising of parts from around the world, or even locate labour-intensive operations in low-cost countries. The development of the operating systems to enable this to happen has itself contributed to the accelerating pace of globalization.

● This coordination has led to the exchange of ideas and techniques. The success of Japan as a manufacturing nation has led many firms in the West to adopt methods of JIT manufacture, a concept originally developed in Japan. Such developments have elevated operations management to a key role in many organizations and the primary source of competitive advantage.

Competitive advantage through operations is derived from the key objectives of the operations system. It is generally acknowledged (for example, Slack *et al.*, 2000) that these are:

● quality
● dependability
● speed
● flexibility
● cost efficiency and effectiveness.

These objectives recur in our discussions throughout this chapter and a more detailed discussion of their role in operations strategy can be found in the final section.

Key concept 10.2 Key objectives of operations management

Key objectives are acknowledged by many to be quality, dependability, speed, flexibility, cost efficiency and effectiveness. Focus on these issues will result in competitive advantage. It has been suggested that real competitive advantage will come from a primary focus on quality, followed by dependability, speed, flexibility and finally cost. The belief is that attention to the other factors will lead to both a reduction in cost and a customer who is willing to pay more for a high-quality, reliable product. In reality operations strategies vary in the way these items are mixed.

Despite the application of similar techniques, to manufacturing and non-manufacturing firms alike, some differences can be found. We examine these briefly before looking at the various elements that make up the operations function.

Some differences between manufacturing and non-manufacturing industries

Both these sectors are concerned with the production of goods and services, but differences do exist between different types of organization operating in the same sector. A volume car manufacturer, like Toyota, has little in common with a small business making hand-crafted furniture, yet both are lumped together as manufacturing concerns. By the same token, an organization like Barclays Bank would be classed together with a small hairdressing business, as non-manufacturing concerns. We can see that the differences within each of these sectors can be as significant as those existing between them. When we examine the organizational aspects of operations later in this chapter, we make an attempt to classify different types of operation system in each sector. At this stage, however, it is worth pointing to the major differences between manufacturing and non-manufacturing:

- Manufactured goods tend to be more tangible, storable and transportable.

- In a non-manufacturing concern the customer is generally more of an active participant in the process. This is especially true in education and hospitals and those organizations offering a personal service, such as hairdressers, solicitors, financial advisors, and counsellors. The interaction of the customer means that the process is often less predictable, and operation systems correspondingly more complex.

- Unpredictability means that operations are more difficult to control in the non-manufacturing sector. The degree of contact with the customer can affect the efficiency of the operation. For example, doctors may not be able to plan their work as effectively as they would like owing to the variability in the consulting needs of patients. Productivity therefore becomes more difficult to measure and quality becomes much more a matter of subjective assessment.

- The quality of a service tends to be assessed on the basis of not only output but also the way it is delivered. Aspects of delivery can be important for perceptions of quality in manufactured goods, but less so than for services.

We examine the implications of these differences when we look at the various elements of the operations process in the next two sections.

Identifying the operations function

We have seen that an operations system exists to provide goods and services, which it does by transforming inputs into different kinds of output. We can view this as a system comprising inputs, process and outputs, which we illustrate in Figure 10.1. (See also the section on the systems approach in Chapter 1.)

We can see clearly from Figure 10.1 that the operations function transforms the various resource inputs into the required goods and services. Three aspects of the model need further explanation:

- Not all the outputs of the system are necessarily desired outcomes. Waste, in the form of either substandard products or unused raw materials, can be a costly item in manufacturing, while in the form of polluting chemicals it can constitute an environmental hazard. Customer dissatisfaction can be an unintended output. The consequence of diners at a restaurant receiving bad service may well mean they decide never to return.

- The concept of environmental pollution introduces the notion that outputs of one system are invariably inputs to other systems. The manufactured outputs of a car components factory are clearly inputs to other firms. The increasing use of systems of global sourcing and global sub-contracting by manufacturers had led to new developments in operations strategies and placed increasing emphasis on supply chain management. Wages paid to workers will invariably be passed on to shops and supermarkets and also to such as building societies, in the form of mortgage payments, which are then used to fund further investments.

● Outputs may also be considered as inputs to the same system. In this way, information gained during the production process can be used to improve the operation of the system, such as changing the supplier to improve the quality of parts and reduce the number of rejects. A large number of dissatisfied customers at a restaurant or a hairdressing salon is an indication that some element of the process needs attention. This is known as feedback. Another type of relationship can be built up between output and input when materials are recycled. In the manufacture of float glass at the Pilkington plant in St Helens, the smoothing of edges, the cutting of glass to size, and the generally fragile nature of the product mean that there are always quantities of broken glass. While measures are taken to keep this waste to an acceptable minimum, it is broken up to form 'cullet', a vital raw material in glass production.

We can see from the systems model that production is a transformation process resulting in the creation of goods and services. This provides us with a means of classifying different

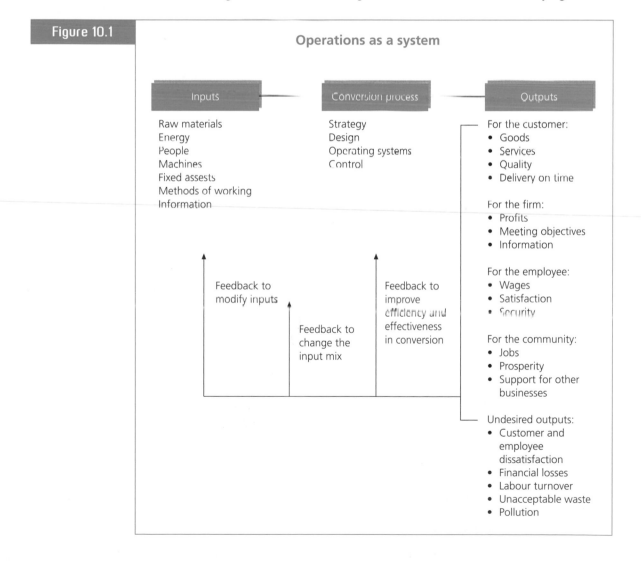

Figure 10.1

Operations as a system

Inputs	Conversion process	Outputs
Raw materials	Strategy	For the customer:
Energy	Design	• Goods
People	Operating systems	• Services
Machines	Control	• Quality
Fixed assests		• Delivery on time
Methods of working		
Information		For the firm:
		• Profits
		• Meeting objectives
		• Information

Feedback to modify inputs

Feedback to change the input mix

Feedback to improve efficiency and effectiveness in conversion

For the employee:
• Wages
• Satisfaction
• Security

For the community:
• Jobs
• Prosperity
• Support for other businesses

Undesired outputs:
• Customer and employee dissatisfaction
• Financial losses
• Labour turnover
• Unacceptable waste
• Pollution

types of production system. Wild has identified four types, each based predominantly on a different kind of transformation (Wild, 1985):

- A transformation in the form of raw materials or components is typified by manufacturing firms but also by such as builders and landscape gardeners.
- A change in the nature of ownership is primarily the concern of suppliers, wholesalers and retailers.
- A change of place is the focus for transport systems such as airlines and road hauliers, postal services and courier firms.
- Service industries, in particular, aim to transform the state of the customer. For example, insurance firms aim to make people feel more secure, building societies lend money for people to improve the quality of their lives and make investments for the future, while osteopaths aim to improve the physical well-being of their patients. However, the attraction of some manufactured goods is that they also induce a change of state. The sales campaigns of certain quality cars or designer clothes stress image and the increased desirability of the owner to members of their peer group.

Many organizations operate all four types of transformation process. A typical manufacturing firm will not only make goods but will sell and transport them direct to the consumer or to an intermediary, such as a wholesaler or retailer, and, in some cases, aim to make the purchaser feel good. We tend to think of restaurants as operating predominantly in the service sector, yet all restaurants have a manufacturing operation that transforms raw material foodstuffs into dishes for consumption. Retailers are not just concerned with ownership change but are involved in place transformation too.

Slack *et al.* (2000) have identified three types of transformation:

- materials processing
- information processing
- customer processing.

Materials processing is similar to Wild's first category, however the second two offer us a slightly different perspective. Information processing occurs among such as accountants, librarians and people engaged in the telecommunications industry. Customer processing covers at least two of Wild's categories and can involve physical processing, in the case of hospitals or hairdressers, accommodating or feeding them, in the case of hotels, transporting them, in the case of airlines, or changing their psychological state by making them feel good.

A systems view of operations identifies the relationship between inputs, processes and outputs. Additionally, viewing operations as a transformation process recognizes that value is added to the various systems inputs, beyond their original cost.

A good illustration of the interrelated nature of both operations systems and the various types of transformation processes can be found in the retail chain Marks & Spencer, whose primary product ranges are clothes and food and drink. Marks & Spencer, one of the most successful retail chains in Britain with branches worldwide, has vigorously pursued a policy of offering high-quality products at an acceptable price to a mass market. It relies on a high turnover of goods. An important output is, therefore, a high level of customer satisfaction with both the product and the service. Three kinds of feedback are important to this process:

- First, there is the customer's willingness to make return visits to the store.
- Second, there is the careful research of customer needs.
- Finally, there is the shop policy of accepting returned goods, which may then be repackaged and resold.

The pursuit of quality is reflected in store layout and staff selection and training but, most significantly, in the choice of suppliers. Marks & Spencer expects a high level of quality in the goods it buys to sell on. In the 1980s this had a remarkable effect on the British textile industry. For many years the company policy was to buy British. The result was that 90 per cent of Marks & Spencer stock was British, and the company took 20 per cent of the total British output of textiles. The demands for quality standards, good design and reliable delivery led to improvements in the textile industry itself and enabled it to increase its competitiveness on a world scale, especially through the introduction of new technology. By the mid-1990s the policy had changed. A strong pound and the rising cost of British goods forced the company to diversify its sources and less than 50 per cent were bought from UK suppliers. In the clothing area many of its product lines were sourced from lower-cost suppliers in other countries, with a corresponding impact on the UK textile industry. The decision of Marks & Spencer in late 1999 not to renew the contract of its main UK supplier for underwear placed around 4000 jobs at risk in the supply industry. Many other UK-based textile firms had closed operations to manufacture in lower-cost labour markets. This was made possible by technological innovations, which enabled quality goods to be produced in most locations. The relationship between Marks & Spencer and its suppliers, not only in clothing but also in food and drink, becomes even more complex in that many of the products are sold under the store's own label yet manufactured by independent producers.

This is a good illustration of the complexity of inputs and outputs as well as demonstrating the fluidity of system boundaries and the involvement of Marks & Spencer in globalized manufacturing. However, its major concern, retailing, is a good illustration of transformations taking place in ownership, place, information and the state of the consumer.

Conflicting objectives and changing solutions

Any operations system is concerned with the production of a certain number and type of goods and services at a designated level of quality. Completion and delivery must be within certain time limits and within acceptable financial and social costs. The price charged must be acceptable to the consumer and must ensure sufficient quantity of sales to secure an acceptable ROI. The entire system should have sufficient flexibility to be able to adjust to changing demands.

Key concept 10.3 Potential conflicts in an operations system

In most operations systems, there is inevitable tension between the needs of management to construct an efficient operation and the needs of customers. The needs of the former tend to focus on costs, while those of the latter focus on design, quality, price and delivery. Many of the techniques in the design, scheduling and control functions aim to resolve such potential conflicts.

Consumers want goods and services to their specific requirements of quantity and quality and perhaps to be tempted by a selection of offerings. The goods and services should be easy to obtain at the time they are needed and should be sold at a price the consumers deem reasonable. If we select an unframed painting at an art shop, we know that a hand-crafted frame in a special material will cost more than framing it ourselves using a ready-made frame, and that we may have to wait some time for the job to be done by an expert. Many consumers are willing to make trade-offs: to pay more for quality, or to wait for made-to-measure items. Many are not willing to do this and managers are left with the task of balancing a number of potentially conflicting objectives to achieve both customer satisfaction and the efficient utilization of resources. This is illustrated in Figure 10.2.

Such conflicts exist in all types of operations systems. We may wish to travel by air from London to Singapore although cannot travel on the day we wish because all seats are booked. We travel two days later but, when we arrive, we must wait 2 hours to get into our hotel room, because the room-cleaning schedule means the room is not ready. In both cases solutions may have been found by upgrading our flight to business class or upgrading the standard of our room to an available suite. However, such options may be at an unacceptable price. We could have re-routed our journey via another European city, but this would have added to the length of journey or required us to fly with a less desirable airline. We could have changed hotel but our original choice was made on the basis of a convenient location and good price. A local authority cleansing department schedules its refuse collection on the basis of a once-weekly collection in each area. The inhabitants of a large apartment find this insufficient for their needs since it leads to an unpleasant build-up of rubbish. An extra collection can be made – but at an additional cost to the residents.

The main reason for conflict goes back to the interrelated nature of the operations system, as the following illustration shows. In an attempt to reduce costs, managers have a number of different options. They can cut back on raw material or staff, which may result in lower-quality goods and a generally poorer service. They can expect the workforce to increase productivity for the same reward or they can gear up for higher productivity by ensuring long production runs (in the case of manufacturing) or reducing the time spent

Figure 10.2	The conflicting objectives of operations management

Customer satisfaction	V	Efficient utilization of resources
Availability of goods and services in the quantity required		Low levels of stock
Best quality for price		Scheduling which meets all demands
Good selection of innovative goods and services		Best price for quality
Fast, reliable delivery		Limited range creating long runs and repeat offerings. Low-cost design
Flexible delivery on demand and easy access		Scheduling to fit resources and constraints. Efficient use of raw material and labour
		Low-cost location. Restricted hours of working and opening

with clients (in the case of the service industry). All these options give rise to potential conflicts. Goods of lower quality may not be acceptable to the consumer, unless the price is cut thus negating the original cost-cutting exercise. The workers may resist attempts by management to increase the tempo of work. In manufacturing, the introduction of long production runs has a trade-off in the form of reduced flexibility and lack of choice for the consumer.

The operations manager needs to balance the opposing forces which are the cause of such conflicts. The development of operational research during the Second World War resulted in the post-war emphasis on the 'numerate manager', a concept which found a ready application in a range of operations management techniques. These included value analysis, developments in work study, linear programming, network analysis, statistical quality control, and the emphasis on specific measures of efficiency such as machine utilization, work in progress, labour utilization and so on. Such techniques are also used in the non-manufacturing sector, as the concepts of staff–student ratios and optimum class sizes in education will testify.

Many of the techniques mentioned above are primarily concerned with efficiency. While efficiency is important, it can distort the system. In manufacturing, the achievement of long runs may be the most efficient use of materials, machines and labour. This can, however, frustrate some customers, who require a quick response to their order, and valuable customers may go elsewhere. A doctor faced with a waiting room full of patients may be more efficient by limiting consultation time but with the attendant danger that a potentially serious problem could be overlooked. Efficiency is often the goal, when greater attention needs to be paid to effectiveness in the form of adaptation and flexibility.

As a result, the application of more complex quantitative techniques can produce a limited focus. In recent years attention has shifted to a greater emphasis on the management of the whole system and its relationship with other systems. Operations managers emerge as mediators, coping with different demands, both within the operations system itself and between that and other systems. This role is sometimes termed boundary management. We develop these themes in more detail in our discussion of operations strategies at the end of the chapter. In the meantime, we look a little more closely at the relationship between operations and the other activities.

The relationship between operations and other functional areas

The centrality of the operations function and the boundary role of the operations manager bring into focus the relationship between the operations function and the other functional areas. Examples of such relationships include the following areas.

Innovation   As we saw in the previous chapter, innovation is at the heart of new product development, with obvious implications for the operations function. In both manufacturing and service industries, production capabilities and capacities must be important considerations at the design and development stage of any product. An innovative product design is of little value if it cannot be made by the workforce within certain cost parameters. Similarly, a new design for a business studies degree course must take into account the skills of the teachers and the capabilities of the students.

Supply chain management   We will deal with **supply chain management** in more detail later in this chapter. As the procurer of raw materials and the guardian of the quality of those incoming materials, purchasing has a key role in the production process for manufacturing, as we saw in the example of Marks & Spencer. Purchasing also makes an important contribution to overall costing. A university sending its lecturing staff to teach on its programmes in China may make significant savings through the bulk purchase of airline seats and hotel rooms. Globalization has extended the concept of the supply chain for many organizations and its management has a significant impact on the efficiency and effectiveness of operations systems.

Marketing   Information about consumer requirements is essential to those in operations. Operations managers need to know the total demand for their products and services and when they will be required. This forms the basis of planning. Feedback from consumers on the utility of the product or service or its value for money can assist both the R&D and operations functions in the design and creation of future products. Holiday companies frequently ask clients to complete a questionnaire about every aspect of their holiday, not only as a public relations exercise but also to improve the product and the way it is delivered.

Finance and accounting   The accounting function clearly interfaces with operations in the development of budgets and targets. In return, operations information is essential to such decisions as pricing and wage determination. The accounting function will also play a major role in decisions to replace major items of capital equipment.

Human resource management   HRM will assist in the recruitment, selection and training of operations staff. Other key activities include industrial relations, the design of payment systems (including incentives), and the control of the safety, health and welfare of the workforce. Traditionally, industrial relations and wage incentives assume a significant role in the manufacturing industry but the role of staff selection and training are crucial to the success of those service industries with high levels of customer contact. Industrial relations is an important element in the public sector which tends to have high levels of union membership.

Case 10.1	## Eberspächer and Mercedes Benz

Eberspächer is a German manufacturer of exhaust pipes that has formed a close alliance with Mercedes Benz, part of the Daimler–Chrysler group, in Sindelfingen near Stuttgart for the supply of exhaust systems for the complete range of Mercedes cars. In recent years Mercedes Benz has formed close alliances with a number of suppliers, including the tyre manufacturer, Continental. The suppliers are all linked by a JIT system and many benefit by their close proximity to the main manufacturing plant at Sindelfingen. The location of suppliers is a deliberate strategy by Mercedes and relocation, where necessary, is often part of a joint venture between the pair. As well has having a close relationship in terms of supply, Mercedes and Eberspächer also cooperate on labour issues. Some of the jobs carried out in the Eberspächer plant are done by workers on temporary transfer from Mercedes – as an alternative to laying them off. This adds to the built-in flexibility in the integrated supply system.

The concept for an integrated supplier of exhaust pipe systems emerged after a period of planning by a multi-functional team from Mercedes Benz, involving staff from assembly, purchasing, materials planning, logistics and product engineering. The planning team developed a modular exhaust system, using interchangeable parts to make 16 different exhaust pipe types for different model variations. Four manufacturers were invited to tender for the supply contract and Eberspächer emerged as the company best able to deliver the concept as well as being the lowest-cost producer. Mercedes then entered into detailed planning with Eberspächer to develop the production system that would supply exhaust pipes, not only to the main plant at Sindelfingen, but also to a smaller plant at Rastatt and to the spare parts depot.

The production system was built around a number of core concepts. JIT principles would dominate, based on optimized delivery from component manufacturers to Eberspächer, where there would be optimized production, assembly and delivery to the final assembly stations on the line in Mercedes Benz. The system had to have built-in flexibility, not just for changes in production volume, but also to cater for the planned expansion of production by Mercedes over time. Both JIT and flexibility were assisted by the close location of the main Eberspächer production facility to the Mercedes final assembly plant. In fact, Eberspächer was part of an industrial park that had grown up around Mercedes: the largest manufacturing plant in the region.

The production system developed was more effective and efficient than any previous system in terms of cost, speed, quality, flexibility and dependability. There was a reduction in the number of types of exhaust pipe from 32 to 16. Production time was reduced by the use of welding robots. The Eberspächer production system is built around nine welding groups. Each welding operation is the same irrespective of the type of pipe, which are all differentiated by a barcode. The manufacture of the exhaust pipes is activated by a computer control system, which sends an order to the line as soon as the safety stock level reaches an agreed level. The stock level is set by Mercedes and may vary according to the needs of the vehicle manufacturer. Once made, the exhaust pipes are stored by type and transported as required either to the assembly line or to the spare parts operation.

Transport is controlled by a separate distribution company acting as a sub-contractor to Eberspächer. The transport drivers are each responsible for loading the exhaust pipes on the trucks themselves.

Flexibility is built into the system in that there is spare capacity at Eberspächer in terms of both physical welding capacity and a spare assembly team. Such flexibility is essential in a JIT system to cope with variations in product, volume, technical specification and in case of machine breakdown. Each assembly line in the main plant at Mercedes keeps a spare exhaust system of each type in case of damage during assembly but, given the proximity of the supply operation, an emergency supply can reach the line in 10 minutes. This backup is supported by a Mercedes requirement that each of the trucks belonging to the transport sub-contractor be fitted with a hand-phone.

Considerable attention was given at the operations planning stage to design quality into the production system. In addition, each employee of Eberspächer has responsibility for quality in his or her area of work. There are clear rules for quality operating between Eberspächer and its suppliers, and quality is coordinated by a member of the management team who liaises regularly with a counterpart in Mercedes Benz.

Sources: Mercedes Benz and Eberspächer KG, 1996

Questions

1 What are the main operations features in the joint venture between Eberspächer and Mercedes Benz?
2 What are the advantages of such a system to both companies?
3 What are the potential disadvantages of such a system to both companies and how might they be avoided?

The key activities of operations management

In Table 10.1 we offer a classification of the main activities of operations managers. A distinction is drawn between the design of the operations system and the operation of that system. In this section we include a review of supply chain management.

Table 10.1	The activities of operations management
Activity	*Classification*
System design	Product design
	Forecasting demand
	Capacity planning
	Equipment design
	Work design
	Location
System operation	Operations planning
	Scheduling
	Quantity control
	Quality control
	Technology control
	Cost control
Supply chain management	Purchasing and supply
	Inventory management
	Logistics
	Distribution

The design of operations systems

This involves the design of the products and services that people require and the design of the processes to supply those products and services efficiently and effectively. As we saw in the last section, this invariably involves operations managers with other functional areas of the organization. We deal in turn with product design, forecasting demand and capacity planning, equipment design, work design, issues relating to location and, finally, the design of operations networks.

Product design

There are two major decisions in **product design**.

- The **styling and function** of the product, sometimes known as the product specification.
- The range of products or degree of **standardization** to be offered.

In manufacturing, decisions will also be made on the type of materials to be used. Design issues clearly interface with innovation (Chapter 9) and marketing (Chapter 11), and issues relating to these aspects of product design are discussed more fully in those chapters. Decisions about both the product specification and the product range involve the kind of conflicts discussed previously. Customers desire goods and services that conform to their expectations of function, quality, reliability and cost. For the operations manager those same goods and services must be both easy and cost-effective to produce and deliver. For this reason, issues of product design also involve issues of process design.

The product design process invariably involves the development of **product concepts**, which are then screened to produce an end result that aims to satisfy the needs of both the consumer and the firm. Concepts can originate from a R&D department or a more informal design team within the organization. Important sources of product ideas also lie outside the organization. They can originate from market research information, through discussion with customers about their needs or from examining what the competition is doing. In the previous chapter we talked about technology–push and demand–pull. In this case we can also talk of **competitor–push**. Information about competitors' products is important in the design stage. Many firms buy the products of their main rivals to see what they comprise and how they have been put together. Academics involved in teaching an MBA at one university might obtain the course outlines and syllabuses from another university to gain ideas about new course development. In the manufacturing industry this can involve the more complex process of **reverse engineering**, where products are systematically taken apart to see how they were made.

The decision on which product design to follow involves considerations of acceptability, feasibility and viability for both the firm and its customers. Will it be acceptable to the market and will it be reliable enough or safe enough for customers to use? Can it be produced at a price that meets company cost and profit requirements and is attractive to the consumer? A variety of methods are available to operations managers to assist in answering these questions.

Value engineering is a process that involves the rigorous analysis of the various elements of the product to investigate where cost savings can be made in the design or manufacture or, perhaps, where the element can be substituted by one of lower cost. The

Taguchi method (named after its Japanese originator) sets out to test the robustness of the design in extreme conditions. A famous example of the Taguchi method at work was involved in the early testing of the Mercedes A Class car on Swedish roads. An infrequent but not uncommon driving hazard in parts of Sweden is an elk straying across the road, at best, forcing drivers to swerve and, at worst, causing an accident. Mercedes set up an experiment, performed in front of the motoring press, whereby its A Class car would have to swerve violently to avoid a model representing an elk. On performing the test the car overturned, forcing the company to cease production and amend its original design to produce a more stable vehicle.

Key concept 10.4 Value engineering

Value engineering is an important technique used in the design of products and services. Essentially it involves the rigorous analysis of the various elements of the product and/or service, with a view to establishing where cost savings can be made in the design or manufacture. The technique also examines where a particular element in the product or service can be substituted by one of lower cost.

In recent years, two systems have developed which focus upon the interface between design and operations in the manufacturing industry. These are **CAD (computer aided design)** and **CAM (computer aided manufacturing)**. Operating together these are known as **CADCAM systems**. CAD enables the designer, through the use of computer graphics and computer memory, to evaluate the consequences of various design alternatives. This has assisted in both the speed and accuracy of the design stage. A linked CAD-CAM system has a memory bank of standard designs and the appropriate machines and tools required for manufacture. In many industries this has assisted greatly in the development of modular production methods. A modular system exists where products are built up by the different combination of a family of standard items. In the car industry, for example, a great number of different models can be offered, yet all are based around different combinations of the same body shells, engines, gear boxes and so on. The development of such systems has had a significant impact on the ability of firms to set up global manufacturing systems with a global network of components suppliers and sub-assembly plants.

Developments in modular systems can simplify the operations process and represent a form of standardization. A lunchtime sandwich bar may appear to have a very large range of products, when in fact all are based on different combinations of a limited range of ingredients and are made using similar production techniques. This is a case of increased standardization giving the impression of increased variety. Many companies see standardization as an important means of cost reduction. A college offering a wide variety of evening courses, some of which are poorly subscribed, may decide to rationalize its operations around the most popular courses, reducing both staffing costs and overheads. For the manufacturer, standardization often means a better utilization of resources, such as longer production runs and the opportunity to obtain discounts on the purchasing of raw materials and components in bulk. For the consumer, however, it may mean less choice, which may be acceptable if prices are reduced. One of the advantages of the modular system lies in the attempt to maximize both standardization and choice. This is the rationale behind the decision of many British universities to offer modular degree schemes. An

Key concept 10.5 CADCAM

CADCAM is a linked system comprising computer aided design and computer aided manufacture and has revolutionized the design process in manufacturing industry. Through the use of a computer software package containing a memory bank of a variety of designs, a design engineer is able to test the feasibility of design prior to manufacture. The same software will also provide options of manufacturing methods for particular types of design. Although such systems are expensive to buy, a CADCAM system can speed up the design process considerably and offer a much wider range of design options for consideration.

important operations decision is the extent of standardization that is both desirable and feasible.

Forecasting demand and capacity planning

These two tasks form the basis of a series of decisions central to operations management, since it is here that the direction for the entire operation is set and resources are acquired and deployed. There is a particular need for market information and accurate predictions of demand. This is obviously much easier where goods are made or services delivered to order, less so when goods are made to stock or services are on demand. In this case historical data is important but even this may prove inadequate in a highly volatile market of changing demand, high levels of competition and variations in supply.

Even where demand can be forecast with some accuracy, **capacity planning** may not be straightforward. It can be especially sensitive to product and process innovation, and it will be affected by decisions on the type of technology used, organization size and structure, the extent of sub-contracting and policies concerning the intensity of labour, the size of the labour force and the hours of operation. Organizing the capacity to meet demand in some kind of sequence is known as scheduling, which we deal with under operations planning.

Capacity planning is especially difficult in service industries. In most instances, the product on offer cannot be stored when the capacity is not fully utilized, as with airline seats and perishable foods. The concern for unused capacity in the hotel industry has led some hoteliers in popular resorts to overbook rooms. This works well given the predicted number of cancellations but can lead to holidaymakers not being accommodated in the hotel of their choice and their subsequent dissatisfaction. In some types of industry there are well-established peaks and troughs.

A number of strategies are used by service industries to reduce the difficulties imposed by capacity planning by attempting to control demand:

● Demand can be channelled or delayed to match available resources. A bus company or an airline will dictate demand and capacity by operating a fixed schedule and, in some cases, insisting that passengers buy tickets beforehand.

● Extra capacity can be laid on in times of known high demand: many department stores hire additional part-time staff during the Christmas period.

● Some services can operate a delayed delivery system to control demand and plan capacity. A garage will attempt to match the cars it accepts for servicing work with available equipment and labour and will delay bookings to times when capacity is available. The system can and does break down, through overbooking, staff absenteeism, and jobs taking longer than planned. In such situations the problem may be solved by overtime work, but this increases cost and any delay can impair the service the customers feel they are getting.

In the case of the bus company and the car service there is a certain flexibility in both equipment and staffing levels. Such flexibility is not available in all situations. A telephone company must establish a capacity to cope with peak demand, which occurs during office hours. At other times the capacity is under-utilized and represents a net cost to the company. In most countries, telephone companies attempt to smooth out demand through the use of cheaper rates for off-peak usage and frequent advertising campaigns to reinforce this in the public's mind.

There are instances where companies have used demand and capacity as a marketing strategy. In this case capacity is deliberately limited, with a knock-on effect on product availability. Some foreign car manufacturers, like BMW in Germany, deliberately limit the number of cars they release to Britain, thus keeping their product fairly exclusive and enabling them to maintain high prices.

Equipment design

Decisions here relate to the selection of the type of equipment to be used, how much of it is to be manufactured in-house, how much is to be bought in, and what equipment replacement strategies to adopt. There is a close relationship with product design, capacity planning, the nature and skills of the labour force and accounting procedures.

Key debates in this area concern the extent of automation and computerization, job security and job satisfaction. The choice of equipment will influence how the work is to be designed which, in turn, will affect organization structure. We will return to these issues in our discussions of technology, labour and organization structure later in this chapter.

Work design

We are concerned here with two types of decision:

● the physical layout of the operations system;
● the design of individual jobs.

Many of the issues pertinent to equipment design also apply, relating to the arrangement of equipment, workstations and people. The dominant considerations here are economic (meeting demand and keeping within cost constraints), technical (product design and utilizing available equipment), and behavioural (fulfilling the needs of both the consumer and the workforce).

Variations in these economic, technical and behavioural factors often result in different types of operations system. We return to this theme when we offer a classification of systems in the section dealing with organizational aspects of operations. Work design is one way management attempts to satisfy those conflicting demands shown in Figure 10.2.

The layout of a department store usually involves the grouping of like products to capitalize on staff expertise and meet customer expectations. The layout caters for both demand and buyer behaviour by locating fast-moving goods and frequent purchases on the ground floor. With goods such as furniture, the purchase is planned and deliberate and the store can afford to locate the furniture department on the upper floors. Staffing policies in department stores often follow such decisions on layout. Permanent, specialist and more highly-trained staff tend to be located where customers require specialist advice, as in buying furniture and carpets. Where goods have a quick turnover and customers generally know what they want, lower-paid temporary staff proliferate. In the self-service cafeteria in the department store, the flow-line of goods will correspond with the order in which people eat their meals.

The minimization of cost is a major management consideration and the technique used is known as **work study**, comprising method study and work measurement.

Method study is 'the systematic and critical examination of the ways of doing things in order to make improvements' (British Standard (BS) 3138). The approach taken is usually highly methodical, with a set sequence involving a detailed analysis of the present method, the careful development and testing of new methods, the training of the workforce, and the installation and regular testing of the new methods. The technique seeks to find more efficient and effective ways of doing work and, as such, embraces equipment design and ergonomics as well as more subjective, psychological aspects of the person/job relationship.

Work measurement is 'the application of techniques designed to establish the time for a qualified worker to carry out a task at a defined level of performance' (BS 3138). The most common technique is time study, in which a trained observer times the job as it is being done, making adjustments for rest allowances and so on. Nowadays, work measurement is greatly assisted by the use of predetermined motion time standards (PMTS). Under this system, the work study engineer has a set of tables which list the times for a variety of motions that form the basis of most jobs. Work measurement can be done by simply piecing together the times of the constituent elements of the job.

Key concept 10.6 Work study

Work study comprises a series of techniques aimed at improving the efficiency and effectiveness of work. These techniques are grouped under two headings. Method study involves techniques which focus on improving how the job is carried out and includes not just the methods involved in the tasks themselves, but also equipment design. Work measurement aims to construct standard times needed for an average worker to complete the various tasks involved in a single job and is thus a vital component in planning.

Work study is useful in planning and scheduling, cost estimation, the determination of maintenance schedules, manpower planning and employee training. It also forms the basis for most types of output-related incentive schemes. The technique is applied to both manufacturing and non-manufacturing concerns. The standard method for administering drugs to hospital patients was changed as a result of work study. The old system involved drugs being kept in a locked drugs cupboard and, for each patient, the nurse had to return to the cupboard, unlock it and retrieve the appropriate drug. This involved most of the nurse's time in walking to and from the cupboard, as well as a safety risk if ever the cupboard were left unlocked. A new system was devised which is now standard practice in most hospitals. The drugs are kept in a mobile trolley, which is moved from patient to patient.

On a more esoteric level, the change from overarm to underarm pitching in baseball to achieve greater speed and accuracy is supposedly attributed to the application of work study by Frederick Winslow Taylor!

Location decisions

The location of the operations system is generally a combination of a variety of factors.

● The availability and the cost of labour are important issues in determining location. The creation of science parks in close proximity to major universities enables firms to have easy access to key research skills. The decision of Hoover to relocate its operations from France to Scotland was made on the basis of lower labour costs in the latter. Wage costs form only part of this equation. The high non-wage costs of labour in Scandanavian countries makes them less than attractive for the location of labour-intensive industries; this was one reason why the employees of Volvo and their trade unions feared job losses in Sweden following the proposed merger with Renault (Case 7.4).

● The availability of raw materials and proximity to energy supplies and transport systems are often key decisions in the location of manufacturing plants. The Ford engine plant in Dagenham (UK) and Ford Germany make use of the Thames and the Rhine respectively for the location of major manufacturing plants for the easy transport of raw materials and finished goods, as well as a source of water.

● The cost of land and property rentals is important for both manufacturing and non-manufacturing organizations alike. This was a factor in the UK government moving many of its services out of London.

● Specific local issues also play a part. These can include the cost of local taxes, the degree of financial assistance available, the ease or difficulty associated with planning procedures and local amenities in general.

Many of the above factors are illustrated in the Singapore Case in Chapter 4. The Singapore government deliberately set out to sell the country as a location for the high-tech manufacturing industry. The Singapore Economic Development Board established sales offices in New York and California to market Singapore as an attractive location. The attraction was based on generous tax advantages, the provision of factory shells, excellent infrastructure, an educated, English-speaking labour force, weak trade unions and a safe location for ex-pats with good local amenities. Globalization has offered many firms potential competitive advantage through location. Cheap labour can be accessed in the emerging markets of Eastern Europe, Asia and Latin America, while know-how and specialist skills can be obtained in the USA and Western Europe.

Location is an important consideration in the service industry, especially where customers are expected to travel for receipt of the service. The location of a hospital on the outskirts of a town may solve the land constraint problems of a central site but the new site must be easily accessible by patients and visitors, otherwise it is failing in its service function. Similarly, large supermarkets located on the edge of towns must make the effort of travel worthwhile in terms of a wider range of produce at cheaper prices. An important consideration here is also the availability of ample car-parking space. Another incentive is offered in the form of cheaper petrol prices at the supermarket's own petrol stations, with even further discounts tied to the amount of purchases bought in the main store. A professional practice, such as a major accounting or law firm, may need to balance the advantages of operating from a Central London site, especially for client consultation and prestige purposes, against the rising costs. A prestigious location, even at considerable cost, can be seen as important for marketing purposes. A number of car showrooms are located along Park Lane in London despite the prohibitive rents and difficulties with traffic and parking. The advantages of prestige and presence on a busy thoroughfare are seen as effective marketing investments for the brand in general even though actual margins on that operation are low or even run at a loss.

The above factors link location decisions with the proximity of customers, their ease of access and their expectations. Proximity to customers is not a factor in the growing industry of call centres and the growth of e-commerce, as discussed in Chapter 3. However, cheap rent, good telecommunications facilities and the availability of labour are important. As well as customers, the proximity to competitors may also be important. In retailing, proximity to other shops means a larger potential population of customers. The same logic also applies to the location of restaurants and cities such as New York and Hong Kong, have streets dubbed 'restaurant row'. In most major cities, areas have developed that are famous for specific activities – such as the legal district, the financial district and so on. Close proximity to rivals is seen as an important source of competitive information and while such firms compete they also collaborate to assist clients. Usually an entire support industry grows up around the firms, including specialist recruitment agencies, specialist book shops and office equipment suppliers.

The design of operations networks

This has become an area of growing importance. The influences at work here include globalization, the need for cost reduction in the transformation process, the management of the supply chain and the influence of Japanese models. Operations are viewed and designed as a network linking suppliers and customers through the transformation process. The traditional view of network design is in the form of vertical integration. Backward or downstream integration involves the incorporation of all or part of the supply chain through some form of joint venture, which may or may not involve acquisition. Forward or upstream integration involves a similar incorporation of the distribution chain.

The claimed advantages for both types of integration are:

- improved quality and dependability through a close association with suppliers and customers, involving an exchange of information and occasionally staff, and a better mutual understanding of requirements;

- an increased potential for both product and volume flexibility as well as speed of operation through the ability to synchronize the activities of all participants in the network;

- costs can be reduced through a sharing of facilities such as R&D or banking, and through the increased speed of the transformation process.

Such advantages are built into the Japanese manufacturing system, which is led by the major firms. Each major firm has several tiers of inter-linked suppliers with considerable cross-ownership between them. Raw materials suppliers are linked to components suppliers who feed into final assembly. The system is supported by a number of shared facilities, which can include technology transfer, transport and energy supply. This close relationship between a manufacturing firm and its suppliers is illustrated in Case 10.1. In this example, Eberspächer, a supplier of exhaust pipes to Mercedes Benz, is a first-tier supplier. The suppliers of components to Eberspächer are second-tier suppliers. In 1997 Ford created a company within a company in Visteon Automative Products. This was made up of four existing component supply divisions, each concerned with a different group of components. Historically there had been little coordination between them. The aim of the new company was to develop an integrated system involving all four groups in information sharing and joint design projects, producing a system solution for all vehicle component needs. Moreover, while Visteon was established under the ownership and protection of Ford as a tier-one supplier, its immediate goal was to establish itself as a supplier to any vehicle manufacturer in the world and earn at least 20 per cent of its revenue from manufacturers other than Ford.

There are questions of how far such integration can be taken and there may be problems of adequate control through acquisition strategies (see Chapter 7 for a further discussion on acquisition strategies and Chapter 2 for a discussion of joint ventures).

Managing the operating system

We deal with two main aspects of operations management:

● operations planning
● operations control.

Operations planning

The aim of operations planning is to ensure that sufficient goods or services are produced to meet demand. The activity determines what the organization can achieve in terms of:

● the quantity of goods and services it produces,
● the quality of those goods and services,
● the timing of their delivery, the cost of production,
● the degree of flexibility the organization has at its disposal.

The key influences are the extent to which management can control the supply side and the demand side of the equation. In manufacturing, known customer demand over time and a dedicated JIT supply system can result in an effective low-cost operation. However, where there are large fluctuations in both demand and supply, inefficiencies are bound to occur with a corresponding increase in the cost of operations. Even where planning is based on accurate information, things can go wrong. A university is able to plan its schedule of lectures for the term, semester or year based on the known numbers of students registered to take certain subjects, the availability of rooms and the constraints of staff and student timetables. However, the sudden illness of a lecturer may mean that the lecture cannot take place, rooms can inadvertently be double-booked or, in the case of open courses, there may be more students than space available.

A basic consideration in manufacturing is whether goods are made to stock or to order. Ford Motor Company has a policy that all cars are ordered before manufacture. On the other hand Chrysler, in the USA, historically made various models which were then sold from stock. The fast-food chain Macdonald's produces hamburgers to stock based on carefully prepared demand forecasts. Hamburgers that are not then sold within a certain length of time are discarded. Macdonald's claim that this system provides greater operating efficiency, and they still have the flexibility to produce goods to order when stocks are inadequate. Making items to stock can mean that goods are always available when needed, but it can be costly in terms of having stock lying around. Making goods to order is more efficient but can mean that the customer has to wait.

Operations planning overlaps with issues of capacity planning which we discussed earlier. In the service industry, problems of manufacturing to stock or order reveal themselves in the provision of standardized or customized items. A hairdresser will offer a standardized service to all customers, such as a haircut and wash, and a customized service in the form of styling. Restaurants often attempt to offer the best of both worlds. An 'à la carte' menu offers the consumer flexibility of choice but within a limited range of dishes. In general terms, the greater the choice the greater the problems for the operations planner. The more dishes the chef must make to order the longer the potential delay for the customer and the greater the difficulty in serving a group of customers at the same time. This is the reason that many restaurants will insist that large groups order from a set menu.

The above examples illustrate the problems of loading, sequencing and scheduling.

- **Loading** refers to the amount of work that can be allocated to a particular work centre, be it a department, unit or person. Effective planning usually aims to even the load through a process known as **load levelling**, both over time and across employees and groups. Where demand is known in advance, as in the allocation of lecturing duties in a university, loading should be a relatively straightforward operation, provided there are agreed rules as to what constitutes a fair load. In certain areas, such as the health service, where resources are tight and demand may be high, demand can be controlled by an appointments system. However, such a system must have the capacity to deal with emergencies, often requiring those with scheduled appointments to wait or have their appointments cancelled.

- **Sequencing** relates to the order in which work is done. The basis of this can vary from firm to firm. A simple method of sequencing is on the basis of first come, first served. In certain departments of large food stores, where demand can build up periodically, this problem is tackled by having a customer numbering system, which ensures that customers are dealt with in order. In some manufacturing firms it may be more appropriate to batch work irrespective of the order date, since this is a more efficient utilization of resources. Some firms may prioritize work by customer.

- **Scheduling**. The aim of scheduling is to balance the costs of production against demands for goods and services, and to ensure that demand is met in the most efficient way possible. This, of course, gives rise to the classic dilemma of operations management, as we saw in Figure 10.2. A whole series of theories and techniques have been developed to deal with such problems. These include Gantt charts, queuing theory, linear programming and the more complex models of operational research.

The problem with all such techniques is that, while they can offer optimal solutions to the problems of production planning and scheduling, they cannot allow for all the constraints operating in a given situation, many of which cannot be measured and many of which are highly subjective. Coping with variations in supply and demand depends upon having some measure of capacity. Manufacturing firms use measures of machine and labour utilization, both hospitals and hotels use beds, universities use staff–student ratios and room size, and so on. Where variations occur between capacity and demand there are three generic coping strategies:

- Variations in demand are simply ignored and activities are constant. This results in stable employment and, in times of high demand, high utilization of resources. When demand falls, however, costs will rise through problems of over-staffing or too much stock being created. In the case of a specialist art or antiques dealer, where margins are high, long periods without customers may be acceptable. In the case of the public sector, where resources are tight, stable levels of staffing mean that customers must queue and wait for the service they require.

- Capacity can be adjusted to meet demand. This is done in manufacturing firms by overtime or hiring temporary labour when demand is high and laying off workers when demand is low. The flexible firm, as discussed in Chapter 4, is a prime example of the use of labour flexibility to adjust to changes in demand. However, overtime can be expensive and hiring extra staff is only possible if spare capacity in the other resources is available, particularly machinery and equipment. Reducing the workforce carries social costs as well as financial costs where redundancy is involved. In the service industry, customer contact often makes scheduling difficult owing to the variations in time demanded by each client. In some banks this kind of problem has been tackled by the introduction of automatic teller machines (ATMs), together with a division of labour into those staff dealing with standard transactions and those dealing with more complex enquiries. The gains of adjusting capacity to meet demand are in the form of increased revenue, although where resources are stretched there may be costs associated with reduced quality.

- Demand can be adjusted to fit capacity. It may be increased to make use of spare capacity through price reductions, advertising and promotional campaigns and even the development of new products. Airlines often cut the price of their fares and hotels the price of their rooms to encourage more travellers in low season. A university may use spare capacity during vacations by hiring out rooms and residential accommodation for conferences. Where there is excess demand this too can be controlled. Most doctor's surgeries now operate appointment systems and football clubs ensure that demand does not exceed capacity by making certain games all-ticket affairs. Alternative strategies here might include persuading the customer to accept a delay in delivery or sub-contracting the work to another company.

Scheduling decisions can be highly sensitive and illustrate the relationship between the firm and the environment in which it operates, which is especially true of the public sector. The provision and scheduling of the railways in the UK was examined in the 1960s by a committee under the leadership of Lord Beeching. The resulting Beeching Plan meant that several lines were closed and certain towns were left with no railway provision. This created widespread political and community opposition. The debate centred around the argument as to whether some public services should continue to operate at a considerable loss or be closed, thus saving the taxpayer money, but depriving some of a service they may need. Similar problems face bus companies in planning their routes, especially in less populated, rural areas. Planning and scheduling problems are also highly contentious in the health services. Hospitals must schedule operations according to their available resources; this means that only a specific number of non-emergency operations can be budgeted in any one year, resulting in a build-up of waiting lists.

All these illustrations take production planning and scheduling out of the domain of programmed decisions and simplistic techniques and involve social, political and ethical considerations.

Operations control

There are various types of control used in any production system. We identify these various forms of control and the mechanisms through which they are achieved in the following list. As with all forms of control, those managing the system must determine the standards that are to operate. In some types of system such standards may be difficult to measure, for example the quality of education or social work. In other situations there may be conflict concerning the appropriateness of certain standards, for example between the firm and its customers over service standards, between marketing and production about delivery times, or between management and unions over levels of productivity.

- **Quantity control.** This is sometimes known as production control and sometimes as progress chasing. **Quantity control** ensures that the throughput of goods and services goes according to the planned schedule.

- **Quality control.** This ensures that the quality of the finished product or service meets the standards set in the design stage and also meets with the approval of the customer. In manufacturing **quality control** involves quality considerations about components and raw materials. It can be especially difficult in services, where standards are both variable and highly subjective. We deal with issues of quality in more detail in the next section.

- **Technology control.** This refers to the maintenance of plant or equipment. While issues of maintenance are invariably linked with manufacturing industry, the use of computers and other types of office equipment places technology control on the agenda of all organizations. The key issue in **technology control** is the determination of when a piece of equipment is in need of service. Many firms solve this problem by instituting a system of planned preventive maintenance. Developments in IT have meant that, in some instances, visual warnings can be installed when maintenance is required. These operate as a function of the number of times the equipment is switched on, its running time, how intensely it is used and so on. Such systems have been installed in some cars to indicate when a service is due. In some firms technology management is sub-contracted through service agreements with suppliers, as in the case of photocopying machines. In many such cases equipment is leased rather than bought outright and, in the case of problems, replacement is automatic. Where equipment is bought, management must make decisions about when to replace it.

- **Labour control.** Issues at stake here include the extent and style of supervision and the nature and use of incentives.

- **Cost control.** There is a strong link with **cost accounting** and budgeting. **Cost control** involves the collection and analysis of accounting information about all aspects of the business and the use of comparisons, which are either historical and/or based on benchmarking against another organization.

We can see from the five types of control that there is considerable overlap. Labour control has a close relationship to quantity, quality and cost control; productivity is a function of quantity, labour and cost control. A key concern in most organizations today is quality. Many organizations have become so preoccupied with quality and a number of related techniques that we examine this phenomenon more closely in the next section.

With all types of control someone must decide upon the appropriate form of action when deviations from the standard occur. Various options are available, as the following illustrations reveal.

In the case of a bottling plant, the decision is fairly straightforward. Empty bottles are washed and then closely inspected prior to being filled; bottles that are cracked or chipped are broken up, bottles that are still dirty are sent through the washing process again. A clothing manufacturer making garments for a quality-conscious retail chain, like Marks & Spencer, has other options. It may be possible to sell elsewhere items that are not acceptable to the original client. Some manufacturers sell slightly imperfect goods to their own staff or to the public as 'seconds'. Such decisions get more complex in businesses such as a restaurant, where overall quality may not be judged until the meal has been eaten, and the only redress is in the form of compensation. Assessments, especially of quality, can be highly subjective and a potential source of conflict between producer and customer.

Quality planning, control and assurance

From an analysis of management literature, mission statements and internal publications of organizations, we might well conclude that organizational life since the 1990s has been dominated by thoughts of quality. Notions of quality pervade all types of organizations. Universities, under new forms of government control, have fallen upon the concept like converts to a new religion. In this section we will attempt to define quality, examine its importance and review both traditional and more modern approaches to it. The latter will take us through benchmarking, business process re-engineering (BPR) and total quality management (TQM).

Garvin (1988) and Slack *et al.* (2000) have attempted to classify what we mean by quality under a number of headings, representing different approaches. These are as follows:

- The **transcendant approach** to quality is the best possible and the best available. In their mission statements many firms strive to be the best but such a goal is subjective: it is difficult to attain, usually comes at a high cost and is accompanied by high prices. Cars such as Ferrari and Rolls Royce take this approach, as do certain expensive and highly-rated restaurants and hotels.

- **Manufacturing approach.** This takes the view that quality is conformance to design specification. This approach to quality is from the perspective of the manufacturer or service provider but may not be the view of the consumer.

- **User-based approach.** This takes a utilitarian view from the perspective of the consumer and is based on the concept of 'fit for purpose'.

- **Product-based approach.** This sees quality in terms of both 'fit for purpose' and 'conformance to specification' and attempts to combine the user-based and manufacturing approaches. As we have seen, there can be conflict between the two perspectives and as with any concept based on the perception of the consumer, different consumers have different expectations.

- **Value-based approach.** This sees quality in relative terms and as a function of cost and price. As we see later in this chapter, the differences in cost of a return flight from London to New York in first class and the cheapest economy are more than £7000. In both cases flight experiences will be judged in terms of the value of the service experienced by the passengers.

- As an extension of the above approach, Slack *et al.* (2000) view quality in terms of **customer expectations versus customer perception**. Where expectations are met, quality is acceptable. Where expectations are exceeded, quality is deemed to be high, but where expectations are not met quality is seen as poor.

The traditional view of a quality product is that it conforms to specification. This is a somewhat narrow approach to quality that has been superseded by a view that focuses much more on the perspective of the customer. This does mean that quality is ultimately subjective. Nonetheless, both manufacturing and service organizations must plan to achieve standards of quality based on their operating experience. Deming (1986) argues that improved quality is a virtuous circle of lower costs, lower prices, increased market share and the provision of more jobs. The importance of quality is thus seen in terms of enhanced reputation, increased sales revenue and a better deal for customers, employees, shareholders and the society at large. In Chapter 9 we pointed to studies that suggested that consumers are willing to pay more for goods of higher quality.

The cost of quality failure can be significant. There are the famous examples of Chernobyl, Union Carbide and the *Exxon Valdes*. At a more mundane level, an electrical fault in a new dishwasher, a battery that does not work or an airline meal that is not the one ordered by the passenger are the kind of quality problems experienced by consumers on a daily basis. In such cases the costs are those incurred by the company in scrap or replacement. However, other costs may be less easy to define, such as the customer buying another brand of dishwasher or battery the next time or changing airline for subsequent flights. Furthermore, stories of poor quality are passed around and reputations can be damaged.

Methods of quality control, assurance and improvement

In this section we compare more traditional approaches to quality, based on the notion of measurement against a performance standard, with alternative approaches, such as benchmarking, business process re-engineering and TQM. Historically, methods associated with quality have moved from control to assurance to, more recently, a focus on quality improvement.

The traditional approach to quality control involves measurement against a performance standard, which is sometimes referred to as **conformance to specification**. A number of steps are involved as follows:

- First, the performance standard or quality characteristics must be defined and specific measures applied. These can relate to such factors as dimensions, appearance, reliability, durability, speed of service, behaviour of staff, after-sales service and so on. Specifications for the paintwork on a car can include the number of coats, the evenness of the finish, the appearance of the finish and how long it will last. For hotel rooms the specification will include the number of towels and toiletries to be provided for each bathroom and the frequency with which they are changed. Macdonald's use a number of specifications relating to the customer ordering process. This involves attempts to define specific measures for customer greeting, taking the order, assembling the order, presenting the order, obtaining payment and thanking the customer. Thirty-five separate steps are identified, each with its own associated measure.

- Once a measurable standard has been set, the next step is to assess goods and service against that standard to determine what is acceptable and what is not acceptable. In most processes, this can be done at different stages. In the manufacturing industry it is common to find quality checks on incoming materials and components, regular checks at each stage of production and then a final examination of the finished product. This kind of process can be vital in ensuring that problems are dealt with as soon as they arise and are not passed on to the next stage in the process. The boundary between acceptable and unacceptable can vary depending on the type of product or service. In certain types of precision engineering there may be no allowable deviation from the standard. In the accident and emergency department of a busy hospital a standard may be set that each patient is seen by a nurse within 15 minutes of arrival. At exceptionally busy times or in the event of a major emergency, the standard will have to be revised. In most cases standards will have a tolerance factor built in. A number of methods are used for measuring performance against the standard. The record company in Case 10.3 uses a mixture of visual and audial checks. A decision must be made whether to check every product or service item or operate a sampling method. Where sampling is concerned, techniques of statistical quality control and statistical process control have been developed to assist the manager.

- The final decision involves the corrective action needed to close or reduce the gap between performance and the standard. This can take a variety of forms. In manufacturing, faulty items can be reworked or scrapped. In retailing, faulty or damaged goods can be replaced or a refund made to the customer. In some service industries it may be difficult to recover the situation and the only remedy may be a refund. Where flights have been delayed by some time, particularly where mechanical problems are concerned, some airlines will offer further free flights as compensation. For many service industries, recovering a problem situation to the total satisfaction of the customer can be a useful way of reinforcing customer loyalty.

- Once corrective action is taken, the process should not end. The information obtained in the quality control process should be fed back to other parts of the operating system, so that quality improvements can be made.

There are two major problems associated with more traditional methods involving measuring performance against a standard.

- The approach tends to be inward-looking and emphasizes organizational criteria rather than customer criteria.

- The approach tends to be historical, in that faults are rectified after they occur.

These problems have led managers to seek alternative approaches. We will examine two of them briefly – benchmarking and business process re-engineering – and a third – TQM – in more detail.

Benchmarking

Benchmarking is the comparison of performance in one organization or part of an organization against that in another, with a view to finding ways of improving performance. This is a common technique used by major car manufacturers. Interest in the success of the Toyota production system led managers from most Western car manufacturers to benchmark their company's performance along several dimensions with that of Toyota and make visits to Japan to see such systems first-hand. Comparisons were made of the hours taken to build a car, the amount of work in progress, stock levels and vehicles made per employee. Much of the interest in these kinds of comparisons gave rise to the focus on 'lean production', which is discussed later in the chapter. In practice, benchmarking can be done in a variety of ways. Comparisons can be made with other departments in the same organization, or with other organizations in the same business – or even in a different kind of business. Quality improvements in some public sector service industries have come from benchmarking against manufacturing firms. Benchmarking can focus on specific measures of performance, as with Toyota (above), or on practices that achieve those performance levels. In many cases the focus is on both.

Benchmarking is used extensively outside the manufacturing sector as well. A service has been established for the legal profession in the UK offering inter-firm data on all aspects of operations, including the number of partners, number of staff, client profile, profitability and so on. The UK government offers benchmarking data to educational establishments in the form of performance league tables.

Benchmarking does not replace traditional methods of quality control and can operate alongside them. What benchmarking does offer is a focus on the market place and on performance improvement. However, transferring the lessons learned from benchmarking exercises is not always straightforward, particularly where cross-cultural comparisons are involved. We must be careful to compare like with like and that differences in performance are attributable to factors other than culture. These arguments are explored in Chapter 4, when we discuss culture and business, and later this chapter in our discussion of lean production.

Key concept 10.7 Benchmarking

Benchmarking is the process of improving quality through comparison with another organization or a different part of the same organization. Quality improvement is achieved through learning from the practices and methods of others and adopting them for use in your organization. There can be limitations in the transfer of such practices, especially where different cultures are involved.

Business process re-engineering

Business process re-engineering (BPR) owes much to the work of Porter (1985) and Hammer and Champy (1993). The aim is to add value for the customer at each stage of the

> ### Key concept 10.8 Business process re-engineering
>
> This is a radical approach to quality improvement with the aim of integrating all activities of the organization to focus on the customer. Invariably it involves the radical rethink of all aspects of operations in terms of cost, quality, speed, and service standard. The results often include a radical restructuring of the organization.

value chain. However, BPR sets out to be deliberately radical and aims at nothing short of dramatic improvements. This inevitably involves a fundamental rethinking of the organization and its operations. In BPR the key performance indicators are cost, quality, speed and service standards. It is an approach that aims to integrate the activities of the organization to focus them more sharply on the customer. BPR recommendations generally incorporate radical restructuring, involving reducing the number of departments, especially those dealing with customers, and reducing the numbers employed. For this reason it is not always popular with employees at any level. It has been criticized for focusing not so much on quality as cost, and its most ardent critics see it solely as a means of reducing the workforce and as a passing fad.

Total quality management

Total quality management (TQM) is a strategic approach to quality that permeates the entire organization. It goes beyond control and assurance in that it incorporates a number of different techniques and approaches, and is linked to culture change in the organization.

While many see TQM as a relatively recent phenomenon, the concept emerged from the work in statistical quality control at the Western Electric Hawthorne plant in the 1930s and was primarily associated with the work of W. Edwards Deming and Joseph Juran, although the concept of **total quality management (TQM)** is attributed to Armand Feigenbaum. The key ideas were introduced to Japan by the Americans as the occupying force in the immediate post-war era and found its greatest expression in the Japanese manufacturing industry. Japanese techniques associated with TQM can be found in the work of such as Ishikawa and Taguchi. The basic concepts and ideas in the development of TQM can be found in Feigenbaum (1961), Deming (1986) and Juran (1988).

> ### Key concept 10.9 Total quality management
>
> TQM is a strategic approach to quality that embraces all members of the organization. The aim is to create a corporate culture that focuses on the needs of the customer by building quality into every aspect of the operation. The claimed advantages are a cost saving for the organization and added value for the customer. It is a method of long-term continuous improvement that is linked to national standards, such as BS 5750, and internssational standards, such as ISO 9000. Common criticisms include its association with the introduction of a cumbersome bureaucracy and the problems of introducing such systems in low-trust cultures.

The essence of TQM incorporates the following:

● It is a top-down management philosophy that focuses on the needs of the customer.

- Key values tend to include 'customer awareness', 'getting it right first time', 'continuous improvement' and 'teamworking'.

- It comprises a quality plan, which offers a structured, disciplined approach to quality and incorporates a number of systems, tools and techniques. Particular emphasis is given to the collection and analysis of information and to employee training.

- It covers all parts of the organization and often also involves those organizations in the supply chain. Relationships between departments in the same organization, as well as those between firms in the supply chain, are governed by detailed service level agreements.

- As we can see from the key values, TQM is culturally based. Involvement of all staff is central to its philosophy. TQM statements abound with references to teamwork and creative thinking and often contain slogans about empowerment as a means of adding value.

- TQM focuses on the elimination of costs associated with control and failure. These are seen as signs of poor quality. Instead the emphasis is on prevention through the involvement of all staff. In this way all costs are reduced.

- Through its focus on continuous improvement, TQM is essentially a long-term approach.

Such elements are incorporated in the mission statement of Akzo Chemicals, a multinational employing around two thousand people in the UK:

> The supply of quality products and services to meet both internal and external customer expectations and to promote the participation and development of all employees in the pursuit of continuous quality improvement. (*Tayles and Woods, 1993, p. 3*)

The classic approach to TQM is the kind associated with worldwide quality standards such as **ISO** 9000. The specific UK equivalent of ISO 9000 is BS 5750, established by the government through the **British Standards Institute (BSI)**. Under BS 5750 quality is defined as an all-embracing concept involving all people and stages in the production process.

In order to obtain BS 5750 firms must prepare a 'quality manual' which sets out policy and procedures on quality assurance. A key element of the policy is that companies must identify their own quality standards. There then follows an assessment process to review policy and procedures, and to ensure that they are being carried out. Successful firms are awarded a certificate which gives them the right to incorporate the standard in their marketing literature. Maintenance of the award is dependent upon follow-up inspections, usually at annual intervals. Many TQM systems go beyond the policy and procedures manual to incorporate a set of instructions associated with each job.

As Hill (1991) noted, there is a widespread belief among managers that they derive benefits from the introduction of a TQM system. These benefits can include a rethink and improvement of existing procedures, a 'badge' such as ISO 9000 and BS 5750, which can be used as a marketing feature, and, of course, an improvement in quality itself. The attraction of TQM to management is also seen by Hill (1991) to incorporate political factors. TQM has increased the participation of middle management, particularly in the decision-making process, and given them more power to get things done.

There are also a number of criticisms associated with TQM as expressed in the studies of Hill (1991) and Wilkinson *et al.* (1992). A summary is offered below:

- Despite the culture of involvement and the slogan of empowerment, the focus is on management control, leading, in some cases, to management by stress.

- TQM systems are bureaucratic, time-consuming and expensive to install and run. When associated with the demands of ISO 9000 and BS 5750, TQM has been dubbed 'quality management by manual'. Furthermore, the notion of a firm setting its own standards has been attacked as subjective and misleading for the public.

- The gains from introducing TQM are often less than those anticipated. This leads to demotivation and lack of interest in systems and procedures. The result is that the impact of the introduction of TQM fades over time.

- Despite claims for the inclusive nature of TQM, its failure is often through a lack of integration. A new set of procedures may be bolted on to existing quality control and assurance systems, which leads to lack of understanding and seen as yet another set of bureaucratic compliances.

- As we saw in our treatment of corporate culture, there is a paradox between a top-down system, which inevitably involves control, and the same system, which urges involvement and empowerment.

- TQM requires high levels of trust across the entire organization. It is, therefore, difficult to introduce TQM effectively in low-trust situations. For this reason TQM is incompatible with the job losses often associated with BPR.

Supply chain management

Supply chain management is a relatively new concept and involves a number of activities previously managed by different departments within the same organization. Purchasing and supply managers were concerned with the interface with suppliers. Inventory or stock control managers were involved with the management of stock once it had reached the organization. Distribution managers were concerned with the interface with customers. Those involved in logistics were concerned with the planning and management of materials flows in the organization, particularly at the downstream end of operations, and as an interface with distribution. The concept of materials management was an early attempt at integration and defined by the Institute of Purchasing and Supply as:

> The concept requiring an organizational structure which unifies into one functional responsibility the systematic planning and control of all materials from identification of the need through to delivery to the consumer. Materials management embraces planning, purchasing, production and inventory control, storage, materials handling and physical distribution. The objectives of materials management are to optimize performance in meeting agreed customer service requirements at the same time adding to the profitability by minimizing costs and making the best use of available resources.

While this could also stand as a definition of supply chain management, the reality of materials management in many manufacturing organizations was a focus on purchasing and internal flows (Slack *et al.*, 2000).

Key concept 10.10   Supply chain management

Supply chain management brings together a number of related activities, including purchasing and supply, inventory management, logistics, materials management and distribution. These are combined as part of an integrated strategy which aims to reduce costs for the organization and enhance satisfaction for the customer. Like many approaches in operations management, it aims to resolve the classic dilemma of both satisfying customer needs and ensuring the efficient utilization of resources (articulated in Key Concept 10.3 and Figure 10.2). Such an approach can involve suppliers and distributors in joint ventures with the organization.

Supply chain management attempts to integrate purchasing and supply, inventory management, logistics, materials management and distribution across the entire organization. In doing so, supply chain management:

● takes a holistic view of the movement of materials, components and information within a single organization and in its relationship with suppliers and customers;

● extends the boundaries of a single organization to incorporate those organizations involved in upstream activities (suppliers) and those involved in downstream activities (distributors, retailers, customers), a key feature of any effective supply chain being the close relationship with suppliers on the one hand and customers on the other;

● takes a strategic view of the supply chain and manages the process to reduce costs for the organization and to create added value for the customer.

A representation of supply chain management can be seen in Figure 10.3.

In any one organization there are likely to be a number of supply chains, which vary in length. A major decision, which must be made in manufacturing in particular, is the extent to which control of a supply chain extends into ownership through various forms of vertical integration. We deal with this concept elsewhere in the chapter as well as in Chapter 7. The supply chain concept can be applied to non-manufacturing organizations as well. In universities, students are part of a supply chain. Full time students are 'supplied' by schools and colleges and part-time students by local employers. The students must fulfil certain quality requirements in the form of qualifications to gain entry. Once they have entered the university they are processed through a number of teaching, learning and assessment stages to emerge with a degree and enhanced career opportunities. While all too few universities take an holistic and strategic view of this process, elements of supply chain management are emerging. Many universities make great efforts to build close relations with certain schools and colleges to ensure a consistent supply of known quality. In the case of the recruitment of students from overseas, universities establish joint ventures with agents in a number of countries to manage the flow more effectively. At the downstream end of the chain, most universities have an established careers service to assist in employment. The creation of closer relationships between universities and employers has emerged as a key feature in the UK government's strategy on employability through education. As students pass through the system there is attention paid to completion rates and the reduction of wastage as a measure of the quality of provision.

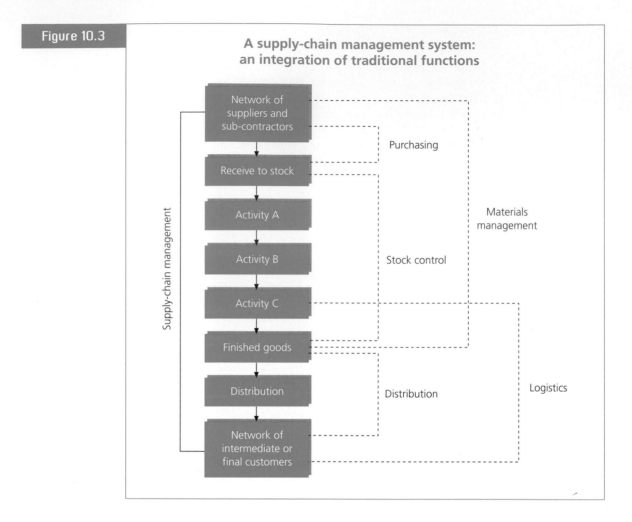

Figure 10.3

**A supply-chain management system:
an integration of traditional functions**

The importance of the supply chain concept is twofold:

- First, from the perspective of this book, it illustrates, more than most activities, the interaction of operations management with its environment. The price and availability of goods are influenced by various environmental considerations, such as the economics of supply and demand. However, management will operate purchasing strategies in order to control supply and demand and hence the environment.

- Second, supply chain management can have a significant impact on a firm's costs and hence its profitability. The 1960s focused on rising labour costs, while the oil crisis of 1973, and subsequent rises in the cost of many materials and components, brought the precarious state of raw material supply into sharp relief. Even modest savings on the cost of raw materials and greater care in the management of those materials as they pass through the organization can have a greater impact on profit than increased sales revenue. The 1990s and beyond have seen a focus on the costs associated with quality and customer care, issues central to supply chain management.

Given that the scope of supply chain management is potentially vast, we will focus on a selected number of issues involved in purchasing before examining some associated techniques, especially JIT.

Purchasing issues in supply chain management

The key variables of purchasing are source, quantity, quality, time and price. We will examine each of these in turn.

Source   Management is faced with a number of decisions concerning the source of the firm's raw materials, components and services. The obvious strategy is one that maximizes the other four variables, obtaining supplies and services in the quantity and quality required, when they are needed, and at an acceptable price. In achieving these aims, managements must decide whether to produce their own materials, components and services or buy them from other manufacturers; and if the latter, whether to opt for a single supplier or buy from a number of different suppliers.

The **make or buy** decision involves consideration of vertical integration. This can be achieved through the acquisition of a material, component or service supplier or by doing it yourself. Either approach will give management greater control over the reliability of supplies, and it may well add a new dimension to the firm as a supplier to others. There are considerable implications to such a strategy, which are not only financial. Consider the case of a firm that sets up its own foundry to manufacture its requirements for cast metal products. The foundry has to operate as a profit centre and, since it operates in an area of declining demand, contracts to do work for other firms. The foundry may be placed in a position of supplying major competitors as well as having a conflict of priorities over the respective demands of its own and other organizations. In more general terms, we noted in Chapter 7 that acquisition through vertical integration may not be very successful owing to the different nature of the industries involved. The trend in manufacturing is that firms make less of the total product and rely much more on suppliers and sub-contractors. We return to this theme later.

There are a number of advantages in using a **single supplier**. A good relationship can be built up over time, which leads to mutual commitment and dependability. Frequent communication enables problems to be solved as they arise and leads to improvements in the quality of supply. A greengrocer supplying a top restaurant will know through discussion and experience that the chef will only accept first-class produce and pre-selects accordingly. The greengrocer will also be able to advise the chef when certain types of produce are particularly good, which may affect the quantity of the order. A single supplier offers potential economies of scale and opportunities for joint development, as in collaborative R&D. However, where a single supplier fails to deliver as required or where variety may be limited, there may be greater security and flexibility in using a variety of sources. Multiple suppliers can offer volume flexibility and a range of experience through dealing with different customers. Where a number of suppliers are competing for the same order, the purchaser may be able to reduce costs through price competition. The relationship between Mercedes Benz and Eberspächer in Case 10.1 is a good example of the advantages of a close relationship between manufacturer and a single supplier.

The relationship between supplier and purchaser is often a question of relative power. This is discussed at length in Chapter 7 and you are referred specifically to Figure 7.3. If the purchaser is in a strong position compared to the suppliers then they may have to bid for the contract, enabling the buyer to obtain the most favourable deal. Such bidding and dealing introduce a highly sensitive variable to the purchasing function, so much so that it has been defined as 'a maelstrom of human relations' (Starr, 1972, p. 271).

The personal relationships between buyers and sellers are an important ingredient in purchasing. A purchasing manager with a supply problem may well be able to solve it by using his or her personal relationship with one of the suppliers. Time, effort and expenditure are regularly involved in building such relationships. There are also cases where personal relationships have resulted in contracts being unfairly secured and even bribery used, as some legal cases over local authority building contracts will testify.

Quantity   The major purchasing decision here is how much to order at any one time. This is a function of cost, storage capacity, and the nature of the operations system. The decision can be difficult. For example, a firm operating complex machinery on a continuous process basis may need to stock expensive replacement parts, even though they be needed only infrequently. A decision model has been developed, the '**Economic Order Quantity Model' (EOQ)**, which establishes a trade-off between the cost of acquisition and the cost of holding stock. Some firms have very precise stock and delivery requirements in an attempt to minimize material costs. This is illustrated by the JIT method, ascribed to the Japanese and examined later in this chapter.

The greater the purchasing requirements, the greater the possibility of obtaining discounts. Some highly diverse organizations operate a central purchasing function to maximize such discounts. The needs of several London boroughs for certain goods is met by a central purchasing function.

Quality   The quality of incoming raw materials, components and services is a vital ingredient in the quality control function. The purchasing department or the materials manager is usually responsible for the acceptance sampling and inspection of incoming materials.

Time and price   The timing of a purchase is, like order quantity, a function of the needs of the operations system, storage capacity and price. Certain commodities are particularly price sensitive which has led to buyers speculating on the price. In the 1970s the price of silver rose dramatically. This was particularly significant for the film-developing industry, which used silver as a major ingredient. Some companies refused to buy in a rising market, preferring to wait for, what they saw as, the inevitable fall. Some of those companies went out of business as their stocks ran out long before prices fell. Some firms, to offset the costs involved in stockholding, engage in hedging, a process of buying materials and stock at the current price for delivery at some future date. This may involve **futures** and **options** trading, although the volatile nature of some markets increases the risk in decision-making. Such trading was one of the major activities of Enron through the sale of **derivatives** (see Case 8.1).

Two trends are particularly noticeable in the manufacturing industry. These are the extension of the manufacturing process down the supply chain and the globalization of the supply industry.

● The nature of the manufacturing industry has changed. A factory that makes the majority of its own components is now a rarity. The large manufacturing plants concentrate increasingly on the final assembly of components made elsewhere. We have already noted this in our discussion of Japanese management in Chapter 4. The advantages of getting suppliers to do the manufacturing are that wages are generally lower in the components industry, and firms operating in that industry are able to specialize, often on the basis of more advanced R&D. There is also the advantage that suppliers can also bring experience gained from working with different manufacturers.

● In our discussion of globalization, in Chapter 2, we noted that global supply chains were now common, taking advantage of lower costs in some cases and specialist know-how in others. In some industries, the twin forces of globalization and increasing sub-contracting has resulted in the emergence of very large supply firms. This was seen in Chapter 1, when we examined the car industry. Two American firms, Lear and Johnson, supply 50 per cent of the total world market in car seats.

Supply chain management techniques

Traditionally techniques associated with supply chain management have focused on stock or inventory control based on the notion that too little stock causes hold-ups and too much stock at any stage in the process is costly. There is also a need to counter supplier and seasonal variations and, where possible, take advantages of economies of scale in purchasing. Techniques such as EOQ, mentioned in the last section, have been developed to balance these seemingly conflicting demands. However, such techniques focus on a limited range of variables in a highly complex area.

Two computer-based systems have been developed to deal with the more complex issues of supply chain management. These are **MRP1 (materials requirements planning)** and **MRP2 (manufacturing resource planning)**.

MRP1 enables managers to determine the requirements for the quantity of materials needed and the timing of that need, where a high degree of complexity is required. MRP2 offers solutions at the level of the operations system and, as well as dealing with materials requirements, deals with capacity planning and scheduling. Both techniques focus on costs.

JIT is a technique that has grown significantly in popularity throughout manufacturing industry. This technique lies at the heart of achieving greater efficiency through the management of the supply chain.

Just-in-time

The origins of this system are ascribed to the Toyota car plant, although similar systems operate throughout the Japanese manufacturing industry. The effectiveness of the system drew the attention of Western managers and its use quickly spread by adoption and by the expansion of Japanese multinationals into other countries. **Just-in-time (JIT)** aims to obtain the highest volume output at the lowest unit costs. The system is based on the simple principle of producing goods and services only when they are needed. Because of this, JIT is described as a 'pull-through' system, as is shown in Figure 10.4. Exact quantities are produced and specific requirements are placed on materials and parts suppliers, as well as each stage in the production process, to deliver just-in-time for the next stage of operations. Materials intake, work-in-progress and finished stock are therefore kept at minimum levels.

Figure 10.4

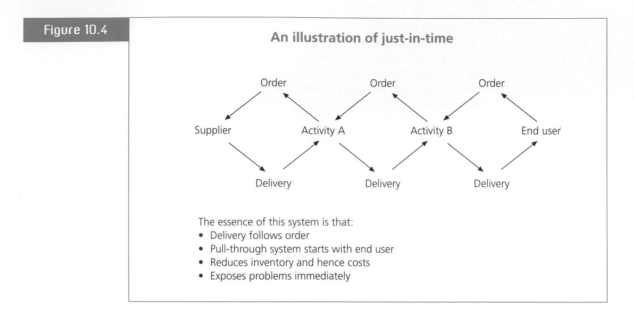

An illustration of just-in-time

The essence of this system is that:
- Delivery follows order
- Pull-through system starts with end user
- Reduces inventory and hence costs
- Exposes problems immediately

Key concept 10.11 Just-in-time

JIT aims for the highest volume of output at the lowest unit costs, based on producing goods and services only when they are needed. Starting with the customer demand for the product or service, the JIT system works backwards. Goods and services are produced for each stage of the operation only as required. For this reason JIT is sometimes referred to as a pull-through system. JIT eliminates the need for maintaining costly inventory and utilizes specific techniques such as Kanban (as discussed later in this section).

Key elements of the system are:

- customer demand;
- implicit notions of quality and continuous improvement;
- the elimination of waste;
- cost-effective operations;
- employee involvement;
- teamwork;
- close links with suppliers and customers;
- the need to balance supplier and user flexibility.

JIT is more than a system of inventory control and involves activities across the whole organization. In the more traditional approaches, buffer inventories are built up at the start of the whole process, between each activity and again at the end. The traditional system protects supply to each part of the organization and to the customer, but does lead to cash being tied up in stock as well as increasing the numbers employed in inventory management. Moreover, a system that relies on buffer stocks will hide inefficiencies in any part of that system. Problems are immediately brought to light and must be dealt with.

For the system to work effectively:

- the operation must exist as an integrated and interdependent whole;
- a high quality of materials and components must be available at every stage;
- materials and components must flow quickly through the system;
- the system must be flexible enough to cope with variations in supply and demand.

The claimed advantages for the system are identified as follows:

- JIT smooths out the production flow and reduces all types of inventory levels and hence costs.
- By preventing production delays it enhances planning and enables the firm to meet its delivery deadlines.
- At the same time, it eliminates time wasted in waiting for components, as well as over-production.
- Through the involvement and interdependence of staff it creates improved teamwork throughout the organization.
- JIT encourages a much closer relationship with suppliers and those able to meet the demands of the system are often offered high-volume contracts, sometimes as the sole supplier. This is a marked contrast to the kind of strategies used by some firms to guarantee consistent suppliers by using a number of competing components manufacturers.
- To obtain the maximum flexibility from JIT, it is often introduced with new multi-purpose machinery, enabling the firm to manufacture a wider range of product types in shorter runs.
- Most significantly, JIT demands cooperation from all stages of the production process and usually requires mechanisms for labour flexibility and teamwork, with implications for the organization structure. An illustration of JIT in operation can be seen in Case 10.1.

At the Toyota factory, the system is controlled by an information system known as 'Kanban'. This is a system of cards or signals that inform Toyota the quantity to be produced by each process and the precise quantity each process should withdraw from the previous stage, which may be either another process, a materials store, or even a supplier. In Toyota, the Kanban system is extended to its sub-contractors, who must conform to the precise delivery requirements of the parent factory. The Kanban system is the most commonly used JIT technique and it lies at the centre of the entire system. Nothing happens unless the Kanban is received.

While JIT and Kanban can strengthen the ties between the company and supplier, as we saw in our earlier discussion, the system can place considerable pressure on sub-contractors who are expected to be at the call of the parent company. The system can only work given the willingness of suppliers to participate. This situation has frustrated some Japanese companies operating in Britain and led to protracted negotiations with British supply companies, some of which find the demands placed upon them too great for the rewards involved. JIT also means that disruptions in supply, for whatever reason, can have a dramatic impact on the entire system. A major earthquake in the Kobe region of Japan severely disrupted road and rail links. Although many manufacturing plants were undamaged by the earthquake, supplies could not reach them and they were unable to operate because they carried insufficient stock.

Operations and the environment

The job of operations management is to produce goods and services for the customer through the most efficient utilization of resources. The achievement of these goals requires a certain amount of predictability in the supply of materials, labour, finance and so on. This may be difficult in a turbulent environment and explains why managers set up buffer systems to protect operations from unexpected changes in the environment. In practice, this is achieved by having certain levels of buffer stock and groups of workers who are available when needed. This can be expensive and more effective operations systems are generally those that can respond to environmental change rather than being isolated from it.

In the past 20 years the changes that have had most impact upon operations management have been globalization, new technology and the diffusion of Japanese manufacturing methods such as JIT. The globalization of business has added to the complexity of operations management. We have noted elsewhere in this book how all business activities are now part of a global network. A single manufacturing firm can be involved in the assembly of components from several countries within several countries. A Hollywood film can be made in the UK using technical expertise from the UK film industry at the same time that a UK film is made only because of USA financial backing. At the same time there are forces for localization, pushing operations managers into alliance with local firms as part of a JIT system.

All the environmental aspects of our model relate in some way to the operations function. In this section we will explore the more significant aspects of that relationship. We deal first with the interaction of operations, the economy and the state, with a focus on the manufacturing industry. The theme of manufacturing also emerges in the examination of operations and technology, where the emphasis is on techniques based on computerization and automation. We look at the interaction of operations and labour, and the section is closed with an examination of operating systems in different societies, focusing on Japan.

Operations, the economy and the state

Given that the operations function is central to any organization, it can be deduced that the value added is central to GDP growth. Until the 1980s, successive British governments recognized the economic importance of manufacturing through policies to encourage its growth, and through its attempts to regenerate flagging industries and firms. Since then, advocates of continued support of manufacturing industry have lost out to those who favour the operation of the free market. The decline of the UK manufacturing industry is examined in more detail in Chapter 3, along with reasons why manufacturing industry is important in a healthy economy.

The state is involved in the operations function in a number of other ways.

- We saw in Chapter 9 how firms can be affected by regulatory laws such as those relating to the purification of waste water or the emission of toxic waste as by-products of the manufacturing process.

- The UK government has established measures in recognition of the role played by quality in international competition in both the manufacturing and service industries by the establishment of BS 5750. The government has stated its intention of giving contracts only to those firms who possess BS 5750 and the Department of Trade and Industry (DTI) has published a register listing those companies that have been quality assessed. There are increasing signs that some industries will only buy goods and components from firms that have been quality assessed, and it is predicted that the future purchasing habits of the general consumer will be influenced by BS 5750. At an international level the same applies to ISO 9000.

- As part of its regional policy, successive governments have attempted to influence the location of both the manufacturing and non-manufacturing industry. This has generally focused on measures to encourage firms to locate in areas of high unemployment by giving them generous grants and tax allowances.

Operations and technology

In Chapter 3 we also discussed the influence of technology on the labour force and upon the way work is organized. We also argued that technological change has an impact not only on the operation of a particular function but also on the entire organization structure. These themes are explored in Case 9.4, concerned with the shipping industry. The impact of technological change on operations can be seen in terms of cost, speed, flexibility, quality and dependability. Slack *et al.* (2000) also argue that a significant impact of technological change is that it forces managers to rethink their entire operations strategy.

When we think of technological change and operations, we tend to think of its application in manufacturing through computerized numerical control (CNC), robotics and other forms of automation. However, developments in computerized MISs have affected all types of organization. In the service industry, developments in customer processing technology and the use of the Internet have changed the way we access information or obtain services, such as the booking of tickets for a rock concert or football match. In banking, the introduction of ATMs and the growth of telephone and computer banking has changed the way we access banking services, which has led to significant changes in the industry. The number of jobs has been reduced and many banks have closed operations. Many of the banks occupied prime corner sites in the majority of UK cities, and they have now been transformed into pubs and restaurants. However, in this section we do focus on manufacturing and examine changes brought about by robotics and flexible manufacturing systems.

Robotics

The nearest analogy to an industrial robot is the human arm to which a variety of tools can be attached to perform a variety of jobs, from metalwork to painting. The majority of industrial robots operate from a fixed position with the restricted movements defined by a computer program. However, in some industries, considerable use is made of automatic guided vehicles. These are used extensively in the newspaper industry to move large paper rolls from store to the printing presses as required.

Robots offer possibilities of fast, continuous operation, improved quality and the liberation of human labour from repetitive, unhealthy and unpleasant tasks, as with paint spraying. They can reduce the need for direct labour and can be programmed to operate flexibly. Very few robots, however, possess tactile or visual capabilities and, while their potential impact on manufacturing systems could be considerable, for many firms the supposed flexibility they offer a production system has been exaggerated.

> Robots cannot be reprogrammed for new models by pressing a few buttons. That is a myth. (*Williams* et al., *1987, p. 439*)

The main handicap to the more extensive use of robotics in industry is cost, involving not just the cost of the actual robot but also the high costs of developing specific software and machine tools. This problem is heightened in times of economic recession or in cheap labour economies when a plentiful supply of cheap labour may lower the motivation for such an expensive investment.

Flexible manufacturing systems

A **flexible manufacturing system (FMS)** brings together the various elements of advanced manufacturing engineering to solve the problem of offering consumer choice and a quick response to market changes using a minimum of working capital. Potentially it offers manufacturing industry a solution to the kind of dilemmas outlined in Figure 10.2. An FMS usually embraces computer-controlled machines, robots and an automatic transport system for moving tools and workpieces, as well as parts and raw materials. The system is supported by a computerized system for scheduling, tool selection, parts selection, fault finding, machine breakdown detection and so on.

Key concept 10.12 Flexible manufacturing systems

Flexible manufacturing systems enable a range of different models to be built using the same assembly line and pieces of equipment. The claimed advantages of FMSs are in terms of speed, flexibility, improved quality and lower costs. Most FMSs comprise a number of linked computer-controlled machines, robots and computerized transport systems. The programmed FMS selects the right tools and components for a particular job and usually has built-in mechanisms for automatic fault finding in the job and the equipment. FMS can be linked to CADCAM (Key concept 10.5) to create computer-integrated manufacture (CIM).

In car manufacture an FMS would enable a range of different models to be built on the same production line, with the necessary tool changes being automatic, and the required parts being delivered automatically to work stations in the quantity and at the time they were required. A typical FMS would incorporate a multiple tool system, a CNC machine with the capability of performing a number of different machine-tool operations. For example, the drilling of a variety of different-sized holes in a single machine part could be achieved in a single sequence of operations. Prior to such multiple tool systems such jobs would require a number of different machines, and the consequent moving of workpieces, or time-consuming changeover of machine tools. FMS is taken a stage further by **computer integrated manufacturing (CIM)**, which links FMS to CADCAM and computer-controlled order and distribution systems.

The claimed advantages of such systems as FMS and CIM include speed, flexibility, lower costs and higher quality as below:

- Higher productivity would be achieved through the better utilization of plant, materials and labour.
- A larger number of product variants would be possible in smaller batches, offering the consumer greater choice and potential satisfaction.
- Reduced set-up times and, consequently, shorter manufacturing lead times with a more flexible response to change.
- The need for less inventory at all stages of the production process.
- Improved operations control and improved quality.

A study of eight cases of FMS in Britain revealed that at constant sales level, a fourfold increase in plant investment resulted in higher productivity, a threefold reduction in inventory and a threefold increase in profit. Further investment in plant, together with an increase in sales, had an even greater impact on profits (National Economic Development Office, 1985).

Despite this potential for variety, the reality for many companies is that the pay-back on such substantial investments as CNC machines, industrial robots and FMS is only feasible on long runs. Automation paid off handsomely for VW because of the high-volume production, whereas the relatively low volume of Austin-Rover's output meant that its automation turned out a poor investment (Williams *et al.*, 1987). Furthermore, as we found with robotics, only a limited range of product variety is feasible before costly programming and tooling changes are required. In any case the quest for product variety may well be a marketing myth. The continued manufacture of washing machines to the same basic design and the purchase of second cars and television sets would indicate that the consumer's need for repeat or supplementary purchases is sometimes greater than the need for variety.

Innovations in operations technology undoubtedly carry the potential for a more effective and efficient operations system. We have seen, however, that such enthusiasm must be tempered by the high cost and a recognition of the limitations of the new technology. Investment is no guarantee of business success and a focus on increasing market share may pay better dividends for many companies.

Further complications are caused by the impact of such developments on the labour force. The same technology that has the potential of eliminating the need for people to do noisy, dirty, dangerous work, that can improve working conditions, and offer interesting opportunities for restructuring the organization, also carries the very real threat of job displacement. It is to such issues that we now turn.

Operations and labour

The impact of the operations system on the labour force and vice versa is such a complex and well-documented area that we can only hope to introduce some of the main issues here. Some of those issues have been dealt with elsewhere in the book, notably supply and demand, labour costs, flexibility and the impact of location. We have seen how labour costs were a central issue in the proposed Renault–Volvo merger (Case 7.4). We have also examined the impact of globalization and the relocation of labour-intensive operations to lower-wage economies. In this section we deal with issues relating to deskilling and pay.

Taylorism and deskilling

The organization of labour in most operations systems is dominated by the work of F. W. Taylor and his treatise on *Scientific Management* (Taylor, 1947). The thoughts attributed to the scientific management school represent an attempt to solve the problems of management incompetence. This was essentially a problem of control owing to the growing size and complexity of organizations and the growth of trade unions. The main principle of *Scientific Management* draws a distinction between planning and doing, with management, as the planners, controlling every aspect of the work process. This involves the design of tasks and work measurement, the careful selection and training of the workforce, target setting and the design of payment systems. The application and, in some cases, misapplication of Taylor's ideas resulted in a tendency towards an extensive division of labour, work simplification and tight managerial control. Much of the manufacturing industry and many of the larger production systems in non-manufacturing throughout the world exhibit elements of Taylorism, and the ideas of F. W. Taylor were popular not only among American capitalists but with Lenin and Mussolini.

Key concept 10.13 Taylorism

Taylorism is a system of work associated with the writings of Frederick Winslow Taylor, more especially his book *Scientific Management*. The system emerged in the early part of the 20th century to solve the problems of management control in manufacturing organizations growing in size and complexity, and to improve both the efficiency and effectiveness of manufacturing systems. The key elements of Taylorism are the distinction between planning and doing, the scientific analysis of work and the application of scientific methods to work itself and to the selection and training of people.

Taylor's work is associated with the development of work study (Key concept 10.6). Taylor's ideas became as influential as those of any management thinker and the principles of Taylorism can be observed in most types of organization both in and outside of manufacturing. His ideas have attracted much criticism, particularly for the impact of his methods on deskilling.

Despite its widespread popularity, the scientific management approach has met with considerable criticism. Taylor's views have been labelled as authoritarian, subjective, unscientific and ultimately unfair. The main thrust of the attack is focused around the deskilling hypothesis encapsulated in the work of Braverman (1974). The extensive division of labour means that work becomes fragmented, the machine becomes more important than the worker, and control shifts from the skilled worker firmly into the hands of management, whose position is strengthened by their virtual monopoly of knowledge of the work process. Braverman saw scientific management as the essential control of labour in the production process. **Deskilling** occurs not only in the manufacturing industry but also in many service industries, such as large banks and insurance companies. In such establishments work has been fragmented in much the same way as in the manufacturing industry, and both the discretion of individual employees and their contact with the public has been reduced by the operation of programmed decisions, the use of standard letters using computer systems and automated telephone answering systems.

Criticisms of Taylor's approach tend to focus on managerial control, the reduction of man to the level of a machine, its crude economic approach and even the eccentricity of Taylor himself. More than most management writers, Taylor has been subjected to much hostile criticism which has tended to mask some of the more enlightened aspects of his thinking: for example, his views on training and participation. Ultimately, the widespread application of scientific management suggests that it offered solutions acceptable to many, even trade unions. Nevertheless attempts have been made to humanize the work environment, as a response either to Taylorism, his critics, or arising from other motivations. These attempts have focused on the problems brought about by deskilling.

Solutions to the problems of deskilling

Several theories and techniques have been put forward to counteract the negative impact of deskilling on the individual worker, such as a lack of job satisfaction and alienation. These attempts include human relations management, job rotation, job enlargement, job enrichment, autonomous work groups, participation schemes and, the current catch-all for many of these and similar approaches, the 'Quality of Working Life' movement. We will deal with just two of these, job enrichment and autonomous work groups.

Job enrichment owes much to the motivation theories of Herzberg (1968). It focuses on the content of jobs and attempts, by redesigning the work, to give workers more responsibility, more control, a greater sense of achievement and ultimately more satisfaction. Applications tend to be more successful among white-collar jobs (where there is more scope for change) and among those who actively seek more responsibility. However, successful application in terms of productivity and job satisfaction was found in a series of experiments with several types of employees at ICI in Britain (Paul and Robertson, 1970).

Autonomous work groups have their origins in the notion of socio-technical systems and, in particular, the work of the Tavistock Institute in Britain, although the application has tended to be given more scope in Scandinavia. The approaches vary, although in essence they involve the creation of an autonomous work group, which is given responsibility for the completion of a part of the operation. The manager thus freed from labour control operates more as a 'boundary manager' dealing with problems of the immediate environment.

As solutions to the problems of deskilling, both job enrichment and autonomous work groups, like the other approaches mentioned, have been successful in certain situations but tend to operate under severe constraints and naturally have attracted their critics. A recurring theme in this criticism is that both approaches have been introduced to solve management problems of absenteeism, high labour turnover, low productivity and poor profit margins, with job satisfaction for the individual as a subsidiary issue. In particular, writers such as Braverman see job enrichment as a reaffirmation of management control. The workforce is offered a palliative but the changes are carefully controlled by management. In most cases radical restructuring has not occurred and scientific management principles still dominate the operations system.

Payment systems

An important aspect of the interaction of labour and the operations system is the issue of pay. Pay acts as an incentive for the individual worker to participate in the operations process and may also be used by management as a control device. These functions operate side by side. We saw in Figure 10.1 that labour is an input to the operations system. The input is bought in and therefore represents a significant cost to the firm, which managements invariably attempt to control. The search for effective means of motivation and control has led to the design of a variety of payment systems.

In the manufacturing industry, the most common form of payment system is some form of remuneration by results. This usually operates in the form of a flat-rate of pay supplemented by a bonus payment directly related to the output of the individual worker or group of workers. **Payment by results** takes many forms but each subscribes to the principle of extra payment for increased output subject to quality, wastage and machine utilization time. Such incentive schemes tend to be most value in certain situations typified by the following conditions:

- in highly competitive markets, where output or a quick response to customer demands may be vital in establishing a competitive advantage;
- where the workplace is large and some form of impersonal control is needed;
- in firms with relatively high labour costs, where some control can be exerted by varying the work flow;
- where workers can control the pace of work either as individuals or members of a group;
- where opportunities for personal involvement with work is lacking and pay is the only motivator.

Many criticisms have been levelled at such methods; nevertheless, their persistence is a measure of their popularity, not just with management but also with employees. Furthermore, some form of payment by results also operates in non-manufacturing firms, such as sales commission in retailing. In its crudest form, where payment is only made for work completed (known as piecework), it is the sole form of payment. This is also the case in some professions such as a barrister or dentist.

The importance of pay in controlling and influencing operations has been recognized by those seeking to change the culture of the organization to gain greater commitment from the workforce. Methods involving some form of direct profit sharing, a system whereby a proportion of pre-tax profits is shared out among the workforce, have proven to be unpopular, at least in the UK. There has, however, been a growth in the use of performance-related pay, whereby employees receive a periodic bonus based directly on their individual contribution to the organization as judged by management.

Cultural influences and operations

We have already explored this theme in some detail in Chapter 4, when we examined the extent to which operations systems around the world have converged as a result of the growth of the large transnational corporation and the associated factors involved in globalization. In our examination of Japan, also in Chapter 4, and in our discussion of JIT, earlier in this chapter, we noted one explanation for the rise of the Japanese economy in terms of well-planned and executed methods of operations management, especially in the manufacturing industry. Four aspects of that process are singled out:

- attention to detail;

- the importance of quality control;

- a totally integrated production system from the delivery of materials and parts to the distribution of the final product;

- support from a labour system that places emphasis on total flexibility and is marked by an absence of job descriptions.

The key issue is the extent to which systems developed in one culture can be transferred to another (much more detail on this debate can be found in Chapter 4). JIT as a system was developed in Japan in response to specific Japanese conditions. These included a scarcity of raw materials, the uncertainty following the Second World War and a manufacturing system comprising of large numbers of smaller firms feeding large conglomerates. JIT also fitted core cultural characteristics of the Japanese. A high level of uncertainty avoidance is met by the JIT requirement for meticulous planning, and JIT builds on values associated with loyalty, dependence, duty and responsibility. Despite these culturally specific features, JIT has been adopted by European and USA firms with some measure of success.

By way of contrast the concept of **quality circles**, while attributed to the Japanese, has a pedigree that can be traced to production committees in First-World-War Britain and participative management in the USA. Nonetheless, it was in Japan where, from their inauguration in 1963, they spread in popularity. The circles comprise small groups of employees who work together and who volunteer to meet regularly to solve job-related problems, especially to discuss ways of improving the production process and product quality. They are supervisor-led and have the authority to implement change.

Key concept 10.14 Quality circles

Quality circles or, as they are sometimes known, quality control circles were developed in Japan in the early 1960s as a result of the influences of USA 'quality gurus' such as Deming and Juran. They work through a small group of employees from the same department or area of work. These employees meet regularly with their supervisor after work has finished to seek ways of improving the job. In Japan such groups have the authority to implement change. Such an idea was attractive to Western managers, but there were cultural barriers associated with the effective transfer of the process in many instances.

Attempts to introduce quality circles in other countries have met with mixed results. Those that fail generally do so because of underlying distrust between management and worker and scepticism on the part of management. In Japan they thrive on more cooperative workplace relations but more particularly, as in Germany, on an underlying ethos that stresses product quality.

◼ Organizational aspects of operations

The centrality of the operations function to an organization means that, more often than not, the nature of the organization is significantly influenced by the nature of the operations system. In this section we will explore the interaction between the operations function and the organizational elements of our model. After a brief review of organization size, we will devote this chapter to the interrelated elements of structure, goals and organizational culture.

Operations and organization size

The size of the firm, expressed in terms of both numbers employed and capital invested, has a close relationship with the operations function. A firm dedicated to mass production is invariably large, in terms of both the number of employees and capital investment. A mass producer of motor cars, such as Ford or GM, will employ many thousands of workers at any one of their assembly plants throughout the world. As with most elements of the Business in Context model, the influence is two-way. The sheer size and complexity of the operating system in a volume producer of automobiles will influence the size of the workforce and the capital employed. By the same token, the size of the firm and its output requirements will determine the precise nature of the operations system and, in particular, the technology employed. For example, only the largest of firms with high outputs are able to invest in highly automated production systems at profit.

The relationship persists in other types of business too. The multinational hamburger chain, Macdonald's, which specializes in the mass production of a limited range of hamburgers, employs thousands in a variety of outlets throughout the world. While Macdonald's investment in production technology may not be as high as a car manufacturer's, the cost of leasing prime sites in urban areas represents a considerable investment. The production technology employed in an oil refinery requires only a small proportion of labour to that employed in mass production technologies, yet the emphasis on sophisticated process technology means that capital investment is generally much higher. A very large insurance firm will almost certainly use a factory-style flow line for the processing of the very large numbers of policies it has to handle.

The relationship between size and the operations system reveals itself most clearly through the way the operations process is organized and its impact upon organization structure.

Operations and organization structure

In Chapter 5, we introduced the popular claim that production technology and size have probably a greater influence on organization structure than any other variable. We argued that the relationship also involved a number of other variables, such as strategy, culture and the behaviour of interest groups. Nevertheless, since the operations function represents the firm's central activity it would be somewhat surprising if the structure did not reflect both the technology and the strategies associated with producing the goods and services of the organization. There are clear overlaps with our discussion of structure in Chapter 5, and you are advised to refer to the relevant parts of that chapter.

We base our analysis in this section around the classification offered by Joan Woodward, to which we have referred to in Chapters 3 and 5. She and her research team studied a large number of manufacturing firms in south-east Essex and identified three main types of production technology:

- unit and small batch
- large batch and mass
- process production.

The three types accounted for key variations in organization structure. Variations occurred in the number of levels in the hierarchy, the span of control of each manager, the nature of job descriptions, the degree of written communication and the extent of functional specialization (Woodward, 1965). For example, a small batch system is depicted by a more flexible structure than a mass production plant. The most important thing to Woodward was not simply the nature of these variances but that structural design should be matched to the nature of the prevailing technology. Woodward was thus one of the earliest exponents of contingency theory (explained in Chapter 1). For instance, a small batch producer could only be successful if it adopted a flexible structure, and business failure could be attributed to a firm adopting a structure that was inappropriate to its production technology.

We will use a slightly expanded version of Woodward's classification to illustrate the relationship between the operations system and organization structure. As we have mentioned, Woodward based her work on the manufacturing industry, but the classification may be used to examine structural differences in other types of business as well.

- **Project.** Project operations is a very specific kind of operations system in which the entire process is committed to the completion of a single task to customer requirements, as in the case of building a ship, fulfilling a major construction contract, developing a computer database, or carrying out an extensive management consultancy exercise. The organization structure usually comprises a project team, specifically created for the project in question. Many large construction companies use this arrangement within a broader matrix framework (Chapter 5 has a fuller discussion of matrix systems).

- **Unit and small batch.** These operations can be classified as 'jobbing' operations. Whereas most projects are carried out on the customer's own site, small batch production is not. It may, like a project, comprise the production of a single item to customer specification. More often it represents the production of a small number of items. In manufacturing, the organization tends to be focused around a number of processes on general-purpose machines, operated by skilled labour. The organization hierarchy tends to assume a somewhat flat shape. Examples of this type of organization would include an engineering company manufacturing precision parts for aeroplane engines, or a high-class restaurant serving a limited number of customers each night.

- **Large batch and mass production.** In manufacturing, the move from small to large batch production usually involves a shift to assembly-line methods. In most types of large batch production, equipment is specifically designed around a particular product or range of products and involves considerable machinery in the movement of goods and materials. At its most extreme, as in a car plant, this represents mass production on a grand scale but most mass-market domestic products are made in this way. The typical mass-production organization is labour intensive, utilizing semi-skilled labour in repetitive jobs that offer little discretion to individual workers. The system is highly bureaucratized with a correspondingly larger number of management levels, inspectors, progress chasers and the like than in small batch production. Firms that come into this category usually have a combination of production types. Components tend to be manufactured in large batches in a scaling-up of typical jobbing arrangements, whereas assembly tends to be carried out using a flow-line method. Similar organization structures can be found in those service organizations catering for mass markets, such as a high street bank, a bus company or a major airline.

- **Process production.** At its most extreme, large batch production represents an almost continuous flow of materials through the process. With such industries as the manufacture of chemicals or the refining of oil, true process production emerges, comprising equipment specifically designed to handle large volumes. In such organizations, the workforce generally operates in small teams dealing with a particular aspect of the process, using cognitive rather than manual skills and having much more discretion than in assembly-line work. Consequently, there tends to be less management engaged in quantity and quality control and, in most cases, these functions are automated. Such organizations are typified by rather tall hierarchies but this reflects complex grading systems more often than management control.

The changes that are typified by a shift from jobbing to process operations are summarized in Figure 10.5.

Organizational goals and culture

Given that operations is the central activity in most organizations, it is hardly surprising that there is a clear connection between the organization of operations, its associated strategies and culture at the level of the firm. The success of approaches, such as TQM and JIT, depends not just on a set of techniques but also on the acceptance of a culture change

Figure 10.5

Variations in operating systems in manufacturing

Jobbing

Increasing

Product standardization

Demand

Break-even as a percentage of capacity

Batch — Layout as a function of the product

Layout as a function of the process

Flexibility

Flow **Increasing**

by employees and those in the supply chain. Firms such as HP use the layout of their operations to reinforce the prevailing corporate culture. In the case of HP an emphasis on open plan offices and facilities for regular meetings strengthen the culture of communication and involvement.

The notion of an organization culture based around operations is the major theme in Hayes and Wheelwright's 1984 analysis of American manufacturing industry. They support the view that a strong manufacturing base is essential to a healthy economy and that a major handicap is often the attitude of management towards the production function. They saw the prevailing culture of the typical American manufacturing firm at that time being dominated by accounting and, in particular, the need for a quick return on investment. Managers were highly mobile and had little interest in developing the technical know-how essential for new product development and improving the manufacturing system before they move on to better their careers. Short-term profit was seen as a measure of success and there was inadequate investment in R&D and plant improvement. Portfolio management, through the buying of other companies, became the substitute for development. Instead of operations, the emphasis was placed on marketing as the key function to stimulate existing markets through advertising and repackaged products.

For Hayes and Wheelwright the solution lay in a greater investment in innovation and, for manufacturing firms, a development of their own machine-tool industry. The development of dedicated machine tools is held to be essential to gain a competitive advantage in the product market. For many firms, this will require a change in the corporate culture that stresses technical competence as its key criterion. This is achieved by the selection and development of technically qualified managers, a much greater investment in technical training, and a much greater focus on quality by all employees.

The Hayes and Wheelwright hypothesis draws heavily upon comparisons with Germany and Japan. While the analysis is appealing, their views of both Germany and Japan are subjective and often idealized. Furthermore, we have already seen in the previous chapter that the relationship between innovation and economic growth is speculative.

Operations strategies

We have already established in this chapter that operations is the central function in all organizations. We have also noted that there is often a conflict between the two objectives of operating efficiency and achieving customer satisfaction. We can now restate those objectives in terms of a number of key strategic elements presented in Key concept 10.2. These are the achievement of:

- quality
- dependability
- speed
- flexibility
- cost.

These strategic objectives have formed an underlying theme to most of this chapter. They also form the link between operations and other functional areas. All the factors are involved with and are dependent upon product design and development, which we dealt with in Chapter 9. We shall see in the next chapter how such factors form the basis of marketing strategy. Achieving operations objectives would be impossible without the necessary finance and accounting control mechanisms (Chapter 13), and without recruiting, training and organizing a workforce with the necessary skills (Chapter 12).

Below we attempt to demonstrate the specific contribution to competitive advantage made by each of the five strategic objectives.

The **quality** of goods and services offers competitive advantage in terms of the dependability and attractiveness to the consumer. From the firm's perspective an emphasis on quality reduces costs and increases value added. We have seen in Chapter 8, and earlier in this chapter, that goods and services of higher quality can often be offered at a higher price. While the introduction of TQM has been shown to reduce overall operating costs, some costs associated with higher-quality goods and services, such as those associated with raw materials, presentation and staffing, can be high and this is normally reflected in the price. For some firms, like Bang and Olufsen, this can be a successful strategy. For Grundig, however, the advantages of a reputation for high-quality goods was eliminated by poor control over production operations (Case 10.2).

Dependability refers to the capability of the firm to deliver its goods or services to the customer's satisfaction, not just to meet consumer expectations of quality, price and durability but more importantly on time. This may be achieved by carrying large stocks, but this can be costly, as once again illustrated in the Grundig case. Inevitably, it involves investment in operating systems such as JIT and TQM. Both applications can reduce time and cost and reduce the need for rescheduling.

Speed of operation involves two aspects:

- First, there is the speed associated with the time between the product idea and its appearance on the market. Considerable advantage can be gained through the delivery of innovative products ahead of the competition.

- Second, there is the speed associated with the time it takes between order and delivery to the customer. This minimizes customer's waiting time, reduces inventory and can improve forecasting. The second approach is implicit in JIT and lean production.

The **flexibility** to alter products and meet volume demands with minimum lead-time are often strategies for survival in highly competitive or, in the case of Orlake Records (Case 10.3), declining markets. Flexibility in terms of product range and volume can offer considerable advantages in terms of the attractiveness of a wide selection of goods and services, the ability to deal effectively with fluctuations in demand, and the ability to deliver on demand at the convenience of the customer. This approach does require a flexible and often multi-skilled labour force, as well as good relations with suppliers. While flexibility can be a distinct advantage, there may be just as great an advantage in going for high-volume production in a single product market. This allows the firm to take advantage of the **experience curve**, which can result in a virtuous circle of expansion. An increased market share leads to greater experience in operating the production system, resulting in lower costs. When these are passed on in the form of lower prices the result is even greater market penetration. Such a virtuous circle can be enhanced by investment in production technology to reduce operating costs still further. This kind of strategy, while potentially successful in an expanding market, has severe limitations when the market is declining.

Cost advantage results from taking costs out of the operations process. These costs are involved in product development, the product itself and in the operating system, and involve those associated with materials, facilities and staffing. The cost advantage of Eberspächer in Case 10.1 was a predominant reason for Mercedes setting up a joint venture with them as a major supplier. As we see in Case 10.2, one of Grundig's major strategies for improving its poor position in the 1980s was a focus on operating costs. In some organizations there can be a trade-off against quality. A restaurant that attempts to reduce costs by buying cheaper raw materials may find that it loses its reputation and trade. A problem faced by managers is that cost cutting is an easy option. However, on its own it may not give competitive advantage unless it is integrated with improved quality, dependability and speed.

| Case 10.2 | Grundig |

Grundig is a well-known German company, which has always had its main manufacturing operations in Nürnberg. It is best known as a producer of high-quality televisions, VCRs, electronic office equipment and computer controls for CNC machines. It has consistently had a reputation for quality and precision which it used as a marketing theme. In the recent past, ownership has involved the Grundig family, the Dutch multinational, Philips, and Swiss banking interests. Philips acquired equity in 1984 and gained management control, but sold in 1997.

As a single company, Grundig represented the post-war economic growth of Germany. In 1979, Grundig employed 38 000 worldwide. However, by 2001 the company was losing 150 million euros a year. By 2003 only 3 800 were employed and, of those, only 1800 in Germany. In April 2003, Grundig filed for bankruptcy. Attempts were made to attract a buyer for the whole business and talks were held with electronics firms in Taiwan (Sampo) and in Turkey (Becko). The company is currently being run by an insolvency administrator assisted by consultants.

For many years the company was the market leader for television sets in Germany. However, as early as 1984 Grundig was operating at an annual loss of DM290 million. The reasons for the company's decline were several:

● In 1983 there were 500 different TV models in stock, some of which had not been made for 5 years. Stocks of all goods were operating at 28 per cent of sales.

● Grundig had invested heavily in the Philips V2000 system of video recording, which proved a marketing failure. As a consequence there was a large surplus stock of such recorders.

● The company had suffered badly in the video market at the hands of low-priced Japanese competition.

● The family control of the company had been highly centralized, traditionally autocratic and somewhat idiosyncratic. Decisions were made that reflected the values of the chairman rather than good business practice in those product markets. Consequently good advice from members of Grundig staff was ignored.

In 1984, faced with these problems and high operating losses, a new chief executive was installed, who came from Philips. The goals of the company under the new

▶

regime were to maintain product quality, but to reduce operating costs, streamline production, and establish greater control over supplies and stocks. This was achieved through a number of measures:

- The model range was reduced quite considerably.

- The company invested in a new automated production line for the manufacture of VCRs, to produce high-volume output at a relatively low operating cost.

- The stocks were reduced to 19 per cent of sales.

- Stocks of raw materials and work-in-progress were cut by 14 per cent.

- Grundig attempted to rationalize its operations through a joint venture with Blaupunkt. Grundig would make televisions for Blaupunkt who would reciprocate by making car radios for Grundig.

- A much greater attention was paid to production planning, cost control and budgeting, as well as a more comprehensive effort to define market sectors.

The new strategies improved turnover per employee by 50 per cent, although the revenue per product was relatively low owing to price competition within the industry. The overall impact was measured by the transformation of an operating loss into a profit of DM50 million by 1986.

Since 1986, the company faced increasing competition. In 1994, it formed a joint venture with Gooding Consumer Electronics and in the same year moved into the satellite receiver and decoder market, led by a former Amstrad marketing chief. The company launched its first advertising campaign for 6 years. In 1995 plans were discussed to move its manufacturing from Germany to South Wales to take advantage of lower costs.

However, none of the measures or plans were sufficient to save the company. For the last 15 years Grundig had failed to compete in the domestic TV and DVD markets. Competition from Asia was selling products at a lower price and had moved into the high-quality market sector that Grundig claimed for its own. Grundig's collapse is also part of a recession in Germany. In 2002 alone there were 37 500 business failures, and in Bavaria, where Grundig were based, large firms such as Kirch (media) and Fairchild Dorner closed down. In terms of television producers, only two remain in Germany, Loewe and Metz, both operating at the specialist, top end of the market.

Source: *Financial Times*, 1986, 1994, 1995; *Die Welt*, May, 2003

Questions

1 What were the weaknesses of Grundig's operations practices in the 1980s and why were the changes brought in by Philips so significant?

2 What are the reasons for Grundig filing for bankruptcy? To what extent have operations management practices contributed to the decline of the company?

Managements need to decide the most appropriate strategy for their organization. It is possible for firms operating in the same industry to have significantly different strategies. Texas Instruments has traditionally opted for high-volume production, reasonable prices and high market share of calculators and measuring equipment. HP, on the other hand, operating in the same markets, has concentrated on low-volume, high-quality, innovative products. Different strategies can even exist within the same organization. The Roux restaurant chain in London operates at the most expensive end of the market in its restaurant 'Le Gavroche', producing highly individual, expensive meals in luxury surroundings. At other restaurants they serve set meals at a fixed price and aim at value for money. They also provide a catering service involving a high volume of pre-prepared vacuum packed meals. These different strategies mix all the elements we have identified above. In the case of the Roux organization there is a link in terms of staff development. The different strategies enable staff to be trained and developed in less exacting situations before the management has confidence in them operating at the highest level.

Most airline companies operate a variety of services on the same route, first class, business class, economy, excursion, stand-by and so on. These are all priced according to the quality of service and the dependability and flexibility offered to the customer. Table 10.2 shows the cost of a return fare from London to New York in June 2003 using BA as the carrier.

Table 10.2 demonstrates that two passengers travelling on the same plane to the same destination, one with a first-class ticket and one with an advanced purchase ticket can pay £7522 and £357 respectively. From an operations perspective, the first-class ticket offers more flexibility, in that it can be used on any flight, while the advanced purchase ticket can be used on specified flights only. The table also demonstrates the price difference between

Table 10.2	British Airways return fare structures London to New York, June 2003
Service	Cost (includes fare less taxes) £
Concorde (discontinued Oct 2003)	8230
First class – fully flexible open ticket	7522
First class – 42-day advanced purchase non-refundable	3592
Business class – fully flexible open ticket	4550
Business class – 28-day advanced purchase non-refundable	2245
Business class – 42-day advanced purchase non-refundable	1745
Premier economy – 7-day advanced purchase non-refundable	1053
Premier economy – fully flexible open ticket	1167
Economy class – fully flexible open ticket	828
Economy class – 3-day advanced purchase non-refundable	357

a fully flexible open ticket, which allows travel at any time and different types of advanced purchase ticket, which restricts travel to nominated flights only. The lower price for advanced purchase encourages the consumer to nominate specific flight times and thus assists the airline with capacity planning and scheduling.

The first-class passenger uses much more of the aircraft's resources in terms of space and staffing levels and receives a much higher quality of service. Greater speed is offered in the check-in process and with the destination baggage handling. There are other less tangible benefits, such as exclusivity and privacy. These factors increase the cost of the product and this is reflected in the price. There are, however, other factors at work, including a price based partly on what the market will bear and partly on that many first-class seats are usually paid for not by individuals but as part of business travel. Such issues of pricing strategy illustrate the overlap between operations and marketing, which is discussed further in the next chapter. The variations in airline ticket prices are compounded by seasonal factors, although these tend not to affect the higher-priced tickets. In addition we have a number of market outlets all offering exactly the same product at different prices, which in turn reflect their own costs and profit goals. It is for this reason that airlines such as BA seldom discount their fares to travel agents.

There are a number of different views on the most effective operations strategy:

- One approach is to group the strategies around a dominant theme, using one of quality, dependability, speed, flexibility and cost. However, it is difficult to view such strategies in isolation. A strategy that focuses on quality will inevitably improve dependability and reduce certain operating costs. There are cases of firms that have pursued cost advantage to the neglect of others with damaging effects on quality, dependability and flexibility.

- For the above reason, it is suggested that operations strategy should not only be internally consistent but also the overall corporate strategy and the strategies of the other functional areas, notably innovation and marketing. This idea of consistency is central to the notion of the 'focused factory' (Skinner, 1974).

- However, such a focused strategy will need to be flexible to respond to the different needs of customers and, if necessary, to match the competition.

- The reality of operations strategies in many organizations is that compromises do have to be made. There may be trade-offs between quality and cost/price, quality and speed, dependability and flexibility, cost and flexibility and so on.

One approach in manufacturing that is based on an integrated strategy is the notion of **lean production** and it is to this we now turn before a brief examination of the evaluation of operations strategies.

Lean production

Lean production is a totally integrated manufacturing strategy based on a set of ideas that emerged from the Toyota production system (Ohno, 1988). The essence of Ohno's ideas at Toyota was the elimination of all waste in the production process from the time the order is taken to the time that cash is received for the product. In this way the elimination of waste will speed up the production process, maintain a flow of work, reduce costs and result in high value added. Ohno's work at Toyota and similar methods used by firms in the Toyota supply chain, as well as elsewhere in Japan, were elevated to celebrity status through the work of the International Motor Vehicle Program at MIT. This was a detailed study, 1986–90, of Japanese techniques focused on the decline of such American producers as GM relative to their Japanese competitors. In the best-selling book which emerged from the study, *The Machine that Changed the World*, Womack *et al.* (1990) claimed that the productivity in Japanese car plants was twice that of their American counterparts and set the standard for the rest of the world to follow. Their view was that lean production, while owing its origins to mass production, was a discretely different and superior system, and if adopted would result in the USA automobile industry closing the gap on Japan.

Key concept 10.15 Lean production

Lean production is a totally integrated strategy for manufacturing that came out of the Toyota factory in Japan and quickly found favour among managers in the manufacturing industry across the globe. It integrates a number of key features. These include value engineering in design (Key concept 10.4), FMS (Key concept 10.12), an integrated supply chain with a close relationship with suppliers and distributors (Key concept 10.10), JIT (Key concept 10.9) and TQM (Key concept 10.11). Lean production also represents a cultural shift for all employees, with an emphasis on flexibility and teamwork. Massive improvements in operating efficiency are associated with lean production, but these are questioned by some writers who feel they may be limited to specific contexts. Nonetheless, the impact of lean production methods in all types of manufacturing has been significant.

Lean production represents an holistic approach to manufacture and integrates a range of methods and philosophies, including JIT and TQM (discussed elsewhere in this chapter). The following represents the key features of lean production:

- JIT manufacture;
- total quality management;
- close contact and joint activities with a limited number of dedicated suppliers, including design and costing, leading to a mutual understanding of expectations;
- close contact with all aspects of the distribution chain;
- focus on costs at all stages of the process, including the use of value engineering in design;
- continuous improvement (which the Japanese call *kaizen*);
- state-of-the art flexible technology enabling fast set-up and changeover times;
- small batch manufacture with the ability to offer considerable variety;
- total preventative maintenance;
- teamwork is stressed throughout the process and no demarcation of duties within teams;
- employees are flexible and multi-skilled with an absence of indirect labour;
- a delayering of management and a dramatic increase in delegation throughout the organization.

Womack *et al.* (1990) argued that the integration of the above represented a fundamental change in manufacturing strategy and covered product design, the organization of operations and relationships across the entire supply chain.

> (Lean production) . . . uses less of everything compared to mass production – half the human effort in the factory, half the manufacturing space, half the investment in tools, half the engineering hours to develop a new product in half the time. (*Womack* et al., *1990, p. 13*)

Womack *et al.* (1990) argue that these advantages were found in plants with similar investment in automation and that the least automated plants in Japan were more efficient than automated plants in the USA. They further argue that the products that emerged from such systems carried half the average defects and used one-tenth of the inventory and one-fifth of the number of suppliers.

Given such evidence, it is hardly surprising that *The Machine that Changed the World* became a best-selling business book and findings, such as those of the research team at MIT, led to the senior managers of the top USA car firms making study tours of Japanese car plants. Undoubtedly, the interest generated led to a change in the way leading Western firms such as GM and Ford attempted to change their operations processes and accelerated the take-up rate of JIT among Western manufacturers.

However, lean production is not without its critics. The claims made by the MIT research team and in Womack *et al.* have been vigorously challenged by Williams *et al.* (1992a). They argue that:

● The difference that is claimed to exist between mass and lean production methods is not empirically sustainable. Their claim is supported by Wickens (1993), a senior manager at Nissan's UK plant and advocate of Japanese methods. He argues that the Toyota-inspired system is, in fact, lean mass production, with elements of both Taylorism and Fordism.

● The 2:1 advantage claimed by lean production cannot be supported by the evidence. They produce data which show that, Toyota apart, the margin of superiority of Japanese car manufacturers is small and, in some cases, bettered by European and USA car manufacturers.

● The MIT study fails to explain how the Japanese take labour out of the system. Williams *et al.* argue that the labour figures of Japanese firms cannot be compared to those of the West, because of the greater reliance of the Japanese on the subcontracting system. The headcount is in effect pushed down the supply chain, giving the impression of the 'lean organization'. Furthermore, they argue that the amount of hours worked by the Japanese worker in comparison to the West, particularly levels of overtime, is evidence of the greater intensification of work in the Japanese firm. Trade unions around the world have been interested in this latter phenomenon. Japanese unions have been critical of a system that leads to exhausted workers and low profits, while Canadian unions have been concerned that the elimination of buffer stocks in lean production leaves workers with little control of their immediate work process (both reported in Wickens, 1993).

In many instances Williams *et al.* (1992a) argue that the MIT data is flawed or that it does not compare like with like. A similar concern has been expressed by Ford Motor Company about the annual publication of statistics on productivity in the European car industry by the Economist Intelligence Unit. Their refusal to participate in the survey is based on the fact that plants differ in terms of age and equipment. The relevance of this to a discussion on lean production is the difficulty of separating the relative impacts of lean production and plant modernizations.

The above debate offers two polarized positions presenting, respectively, the positive and negative sides of lean production. The adoption of lean production methods in whole or part, by many manufacturing firms, is some indication that their management see the investment as worthwhile. Nissan in the UK (see Case 4.1) claim that lean production, as a transplanted operations system from Japan, has contributed to its status as the leading producer of cars in Europe as measured in terms of number of cars built per employee per year. In 1998 that figure was 103, with the next best performance coming from VW at Navarra in Spain and GM at Eisenbach in Germany, each with 76 cars per employee (Economist Intelligence Unit, 1999). However, an aggressive lean production system can threaten the security of many employees and it is understandable that the system has been examined closely by trade unions in many countries, including Japan itself. Wickens of Nissan sees a middle way, which harnesses the efficiency gains of lean production along-side improved working conditions, a distribution of the gains, and offers stable and secure employment.

> Lean production of a type is the way forward, but it must be lean production managed by people who care about people. (*Wickens, 1993, p. 89*)

Evaluating operations strategies

Hayes and Wheelwright (1984) have developed a model for the evaluation of an operations strategy based on four stages of strategic development. The original model focused on manufacturing industry and was adapted to the service sector by Chase and Hayes (1991).

- At Stage 1 the firm is reactive and the operations function is low status in the organization and has less influence than marketing and certainly finance. They term this stage **internal neutrality**.

- At Stage 2 the firm is more outward-looking in that it attempts to benchmark against the competition. The strategy is still reactive in that the firm is a follower rather than an innovator. They refer to this stage as **external neutrality**.

- At Stage 3 the firm introduces the notion of systems improvement to improve its performance across a range of activities. A clear strategy emerges and operations strategy is one of a number of linked functional strategies. This stage is referred to as **internally supportive**.

- At Stage 4 the operations function becomes the driving force behind the organization and its key to gaining real competitive advantage as the firm becomes a product and a process leader. They term this stage **externally supportive**.

We have already touched upon the Hayes and Wheelwright philosophy elsewhere in this book, notably in our discussion of an operations culture earlier in the chapter. Although adapted to apply to the service sector, this evaluation model owes much to Hayes and Wheelwright's criticisms of USA manufacturing industry in the 1980s, where they argued that USA firms were falling behind the competition owing to a lack of process and product innovation and a distorted focus on financial controls and short-termism. Their thesis that operations should be the key strategy fits in with its central role in most organizations. However, many organizations may operate best at Stage 3, where strategies are integrated, yet responsive to external opportunities and threats.

Case 10.3	Orlake Records

Orlake Records makes vinyl gramophone records on an old industrial estate in Dagenham, East London, and represents a classic case of survival in a declining market. The company was bought by the First Sound and Vision Group (FSV) in 1999. Orlake continued to make vinyl discs, but the new company focused on its North London operation selling CDs and cassettes. FSV placed its faith in the development of self-adhesive pads to protect CDs and invested heavily in the project, diverting income from across the group. The new product failed dramatically and FSV along with it.

FSV was placed in administration under Robson and Rhodes on 6 November, 2000. The North London operation was closed but the production of vinyl records was allowed to continue at Dagenham. The company was bought in November 2001 by Portal Space, who since has changed its name to Orlake Vinyl Ltd and traded under the old name of Orlake Records. Around this time, one of its major competitors, EMI, closed its record manufacturing plant in Hayes, West London. The plant and machinery were bought by Orlake and, after a period of cold storage, Orlake established a sister plant in Hayes, trading under Portal Space. EMI shifted its production overseas but since the majority of sales were in the UK and required a fast turnaround, EMI commissioned Portal Space to carry out the production for them. Between them, Orlake and Portal Space have 50 per cent of the UK production of vinyl.

The UK is a major player in the vinyl market as shown in Table 10.3.

From 1979 to 1986, the annual trade delivery of vinyl singles in the UK fell from 89.1 to 67.4 million, and LPs from 74.5 to 52.3 million. Over the same period the sales of cassettes increased threefold to reach 69.6 million in 1986. In the 1990s the sales of vinyl declined still further and CDs eclipsed both vinyl and cassettes in the market place. By the end of 1998, this trend had continued apace, as Table 10.4 illustrates. Competition in manufacture had become intense, not just in this country

Table 10.3	Share of global singles market 2002

Country	%
Japan	29
UK	20
France	15
Germany	15
USA	3
Rest of world	18

Source: *BPI Weekly Newsletter,* 19 May, 2003

but internationally as well. At the end of the 1990s only six manufacturers of vinyl discs remained in the UK, and Orlake had the capacity to fulfil UK market needs in its entirety. In spite of this dramatic decline in the market, Orlake not only managed to maintain its output levels but has seen a dramatic increase in market share. In 1999 Orlake received a substantial order from the major record company, Polygram. Orlake had produced vinyl records for Polygram for a number of years, achieving high levels of satisfaction by fulfilling small orders to quality specifications, flexibly and on time.

The vinyl market itself has changed. A mixed market of 7-inch singles, 12-inch LPs, and variations in the form of shape discs, picture discs and colour discs has shifted to a focus on the production of 12-inch singles aimed exclusively at the dance market. Much of this growth is accounted for by independent record producers and record brokers. The latter represent a one-stop shop for cutting, sleeve and label design. In this respect the BPI figures presented in Table 10.4 under-represent the sales of 12-inch singles by about 50 per cent. Official statistics focus on selected official outlet stores, while the 12-inch market also includes sales from small specialist shops, in clubs and pubs, as well as exports. These do not feature in the UK statistics. Nonetheless, the table still reveals the overwhelming dominance of the CD market. However in a period of CD dominance, the 12-inch singles market has both held its own and increased in value and the real decline of the period has been in cassette sales.

Orlake is able to turn around orders in 7 days for new releases and 5 days for repeat orders. Its largest competitor, Ministry of Sound, sells at higher prices but has a turn around capability of 5 and 3 days respectively.

Table 10.4	Recorded music sales by type as a proportion of the total

	1996		1997		1998		1999		2000	
	Nos	£	Nos	£	Nos	£	Nos	£	Nos	£
Singles										
7"	0.8	0.2	0.7	0.2	0.5	0.1	0.2	0.07	0.18	0.04
12"	2.8	1.4	2.5	1.3	2.2	1.2	2.5	1.3	3.0	1.5
Cassette	7.1	1.9	6.9	1.7	7.1	1.9	7.0	1.7	4.8	1.2
CD	15.9	7.5	19.1	8.6	19.2	9.4	18.9	9.1	15.4	7.6
Total	26.6	11.0	29.2	11.9	29.0	12.6	28.9	12.2	23.4	10.4
Albums										
LPs	1.0	1.0	0.8	0.9	0.8	0.8	0.8	0.6	1.12	0.7
Cassette	17.8	16.1	14.2	13.2	12.2	10.8	6.6	6.2	4.0	3.5
CD	54.6	71.9	55.7	74.1	57.9	75.9	63.6	80.7	71.4	85.2
Total	73.4	89.0	70.8	88.2	71.9	87.5	71.0	87.5	76.6	89.4

Source: *BPI Yearbook*, 2001

▶

The actual manufacture is the following stage from the recording studio. There the final tape is converted to a series of vibrations, which cut grooves into a master disc, known as the lacquer master. Orlake has a plating shop, which takes this master and, through an electro-forming process, makes its own moulds to form the basis of record production. Several moulds may be required depending on the number of presses to be used, the length of the run and the uncertain working life of each mould. The actual record is made in the production department by compression moulding which presses extruded plastic on to the mould on a specially designed machine. This takes around 25 seconds for the average disc. Operations at Orlake is based in two buildings. The smaller building houses the plating shop, the library of production moulds, and acts as storage for labels and sleeves. The larger building houses the production presses and the offices and offers some storage space for the finished product. However, there is not a great requirement for storage, given the fast-moving nature of the business.

Record companies may use a number of manufacturers, particularly on high-selling items. Orlake manufactures for a range of different companies and as a competitive strategy attempts to meet customer requirements of high quality, low cost, and in as short a time as possible. Orlake production is shown in Table 10.5.

Table 10.5　**Orlake production totals**

Year	Million units
1998	2.2
1999	3.5
2000	4.2
2001	4.6
2002	3.8
2003	3.6 (estimated)

The fall in volume since 2002 is attributed to changing economic conditions, but it has not affected the profitability of Orlake. When EMI operated in the UK it had more capacity than it needed and sold at cheap prices to utilize as much capacity as possible. When EMI ceased production, prices were able to rise by a substantial amount but customers remained loyal to existing producers such as Orlake.

The variety of the work means that there are no standard production runs. Very large production runs associated with a vibrant 7-inch singles market are now a thing of the past. The market comprised of 85 per cent 12-inch singles. The largest run in 1998 was 8000 units, but production runs of 500 are now not uncommon and the average run is about 1250 units. The firm uses two types of presses, fully automatic and manually operated. Orlake has 14 automatic presses: two of them for 7-inch singles. In addition the company has five manual presses, more than any other producer, offering Orlake additional flexibility. The presses give Orlake a capacity of around 4.5 million units a year operating with two 5-hour shifts.

Certain products such as 'picture' discs and 'shape' discs can only be produced using manual machines. However, the demand for both products has declined as they were associated largely with the 'heavy metal' boom of the late 1980s. Since 2001 there has been an increase in the production of picture discs with the revival of such bands as Metallica and Iron Maiden. Management sees it as important to retain the capacity to produce special discs on manual machines, and Orlake is the only company offering such a variety of products. It is felt that this offers Orlake both a competitive edge and a means of gaining access to higher-volume business with some companies.

Production planning and scheduling is carried out on a continuous basis at the point of order and is the responsibility of the sales order clerk and the production controller. Schedules are drawn up on the basis of 'first come, first served'.

Quality control is the responsibility of the supervisor in the plating shop – the area where master moulds are made – that determine the quality of the entire operation. Quality control throughout the company relies heavily on visual checks. At the pressing stage, one finished record in every 20 is checked visually. Ninety per cent of all faults can be spotted visually by a trained operator. In addition a particular pressing is checked audibly every hour. Before storage, a further one record in 40 is checked visually, a process that is repeated after 9 hours have elapsed to allow the plastic to cool down. Faults found with the moulds can sometimes be rectified manually. At the pressing stage, if repetitive faults are found in a particular run, the whole batch is destroyed. More recently, management have moved towards a system whereby quality is the responsibility of all employees and is reflected in the bonus scheme.

Orlake operates with a core staff of 50 employees. About 30 of these are full-time staff working a 40-hour week. The rest are part-timers, each operating a 5-hour shift. Two such shifts are run each day. Overtime is used extensively to meet fluctuations in demand. Many of the staff have been with Orlake for several years and the company has a significant pool of experienced, skilled staff. The employees are extremely loyal to the company and have a considerable commitment to and interest in the product.

A benefit of the move to a two-shift day system has been the improved levels of quality with increased levels of management supervision. No job descriptions are used and all staff are expected to work flexibly across a range of tasks. Operators become packers and vice versa, and both supervisors and management help out in the production and packing process. As with other industries operating in areas of declining demand, some skills are difficult to find, more especially those in compression moulding.

Orlake has done well in such a declining market and survived the collapse of its parent company, FSV. The new company plans even more expansion including the establishment of a vinyl theme restaurant and associated shops in London's Soho district. Orlake's survival and success are a feature of several interrelated factors:

● Management have targeted quality and service as key elements in gaining competitive advantage. There is a desire to improve service levels still further.

● Prices have risen with the withdrawal of EMI. Orlake has never chased volume through price discounts and has maintained a niche market with several customers. Ten years ago the company saw price competition as an important strategic tool but this has changed. However, whereas price discussions are held with customers once a year, discussions about quality are held for every order.

- Considerable emphasis is placed on cost efficiency. In the 1990s much of this was achieved through staffing cuts, the elimination of the night shift, improvements in quality, continued staff flexibility and in increased use of automation coupled with a production focus on the 12-inch disc. From 2000, cost reducton has focused on expanded capacity on the automatic presses without increasing staffing. Gross margins have continued to rise despite increased materials costs.

- Speed of response and dependability of delivery times is seen as vital in a business where the life span of the product may be relatively short. The firm has a strategy of fulfilling customer orders for any type of gramophone record in as short a time as possible and a reputation has been built up for low lead-times and prompt delivery.

- While special items such as shape discs, hologram discs and picture discs are much less significant in terms of volume, the company retains the flexibility to produce such items as and when required. Such flexibility has enhanced the company's reputation in the market place.

Sources: Orlake Records, Dagenham, Essex; *BPI Yearbook*, 2001; *BPI Weekly Newsetter*, 20 May, 2003

Questions

1 Assess the market factors that have contributed to the success of Orlake in a music industry dominated by the CD.

2 What conclusions do you draw from the Tables 10.3–5 presented in this case?

3 Assess the operations strategy of Orlake in terms of quality, speed, flexibility, dependability and cost.

4 Why did Orlake survive the collapse of FSV?

5 What does the future hold for Orlake and upon what does its continued survival depend?

Summary

- The operations function is a transformation process, that takes a variety of inputs such as materials and labour and turns them into goods and services.

- The function operates in a variety of industries and settings and is not limited to manufacturing.

- The main activities of operations management involve the design of a system to process inputs and setting up control devices to ensure effective operation.

- It is acknowledged that the operating system has expanded to incorporate all the elements of the supply chain from components to customers.
- The key objectives of any operations system are quality, dependability, speed, flexibility and cost.
- A central problem in operations management is the reconciliation of customer satisfaction with the efficient utilization of resources.
- Traditionally, techniques of operations management have emphasized efficiency. However, there is a growing awareness of other elements, such as the flexibility to respond to changing market demand and a need to focus on quality.
- Effective operating systems and operations management have a significant impact on the economy.
- Globalization has had a significant impact on operations through the geographical extension of the supply chain and the growth of global, interactive operating systems.
- The centrality of the function means that it exerts considerable influence on organization structure.
- Changes in technology have particular relevance for operations systems, in terms of both product and process innovation. In manufacturing and the service sector alike there have been significant changes in the way goods and services are both produced and accessed by the customer.
- Japanese methods, especially in manufacturing industry, have been very influential and include JIT, TQM and lean production.
- For the labour force, operations has considerable influence over employment patterns, wage levels, health and safety, and job satisfaction.
- Operations strategies are a core element of a firm's overall corporate strategy. The most successful strategies would appear to integrate all elements of the operations system, display a clear focus and are consistent with the strategies of the other functional areas.

Discussion questions

1 Examine the similarities and differences to be found in the operations systems of manufacturing and non-manufacturing organizations. How do the operations priorities differ in a firm producing television sets for a mass market compared to those of a large regional hospital?

2 Design a systems model for a manufacturing firm, a retail organization and a university. Show both the types of transformations that are taking place and the other systems with which the firm interacts. What are the key activities and key relationships?

3 Define the objectives of a firm manufacturing television sets, a hospital and a fast-food restaurant in terms of quality, dependability, speed, flexibility and cost.

4   What strategies can be employed to solve the conflicting objectives of operating efficiency and customer satisfaction?

5   What types of impact can product design have on the operations process? How does it affect the key objectives of quality, dependability, speed, flexibility and cost?

6   Assess the impact of globalization on operations management.

7   Identify the operational aspects that influence scheduling in a restaurant, at an airport, and for a major national daily newspaper. What strategies and techniques would you employ to solve scheduling problems in these three situations?

8   Why is supply chain management an important aspect of manufacturing industry? To what extent have techniques imported from Japan assisted this process?

9   To what extent can the techniques associated with JIT and lean production be applied to a department store, a hospital and a university or college?

10 Examine the links between TQM and corporate culture.

Further reading

Probably the most comprehensive text, in terms of coverage and examples, currently available is Slack, N., Chambers, L. and Johnston, R. (2000) *Operations Management*, 3rd edn, FT Prentice Hall, London. Some good cases from both manufacturing and the service sector can be found in the companion volume to Slack *et al.*'s main text, Harrison, A., Harland, C., Johnston, R., Chambers, N. and Slack, N. (2003) *Cases in Operations Management*, 3rd edn, FT Prentice Hall, London. A focus on operations in the service industry can be found in Clark, G. and Johnston, R. (2000) *Service Operations Management*, FT Prentice Hall, London.

11

Marketing

| Learning objectives | At the end of this chapter you should be able to: |

- Define marketing and trace its development as an area of activity.
- Identify the operation of marketing in a number of different contexts.
- Identify the various elements of marketing.
- Explain how these elements form the basis of the marketing mix and articulate how this operates.
- Assess the various approaches to buyer behaviour.
- Critically assess the significance of branding and market segmentation and the value of the product life-cycle.
- Explain the role of marketing in relation to the economy, the state and technological change.
- Assess the factors influencing the operation of marketing in different organizational contexts.
- Evaluate different marketing strategies.

Introduction

In this chapter we will examine the nature of marketing as it applies to different types of organization. We will attempt to define marketing and chart the development of marketing as a concept. The various elements of marketing, research, product, price, promotion, distribution and buyer behaviour will be analysed in turn, as will the key concepts of branding, the product life-cycle and market segmentation. As in our treatment of all functional activities we will use the Business in Context model to look at the environmental, organizational and strategic aspects of marketing. In the two previous chapters we stressed the interface between innovation, operations and marketing. This theme will be taken up in this chapter, particularly in the discussion of product development, the relationship of marketing with operations technology, the place of marketing in the organization structure and, most significantly, when we examine the design of marketing strategies.

Decisions in marketing generally focus on the nature of the markets and on the products and services to serve those markets. In terms of products and services marketing is concerned with design, prices, promotion, and the means through which they are distributed. In most advanced industrial societies individuals are faced with a vast choice of such products and services, which can be acquired in a variety of ways, often at a range of prices. Advertising is a pervasive feature of modern life, often so glamorized by the media that the management decision to change its advertising agency is, for a brand like Guinness or Nike, a matter of high drama to be played out in the national press. For such reasons marketing, probably more than any other business activity, attracts strong positive and negative feelings. Many members of the public as well as many business and management students associate careers in marketing with the glamour and fictional lifestyles of the people portrayed in advertisements. Such a view is misleading, for marketing is much more than advertising and the tasks can involve the much less glamorous work of collecting detailed market information and the problems of transporting metal containers made in Mansfield to a customer's factory in Bromsgrove.

It is this high-profile nature of marketing that attracts its critics. Marketing is variously accused of creating (among other things) an excessively materialistic society, planned product obsolescence, the high-pressure selling of poor-quality products and the excessive political power of the multinational. Borrowing themes from Vance Packard, marketers are seen as 'The Hidden Persuaders' or 'The Waste Makers' or both. The marketers would counter this, listing their credits as the development and supply of products and services demanded by consumers, the provision of essential information for the shopper, and the use of marketing to create public awareness for such socially acceptable goals as improving a nation's health. Given the increasing use of marketing in political elections, it might also claim to be an important part of the democratic process.

Definitions and orientations

Marketing is human activity directed at satisfying needs and wants through exchange processes. (*Kotler, 1983, p. 6*)

Marketing consists of individual and organizational activities that facilitate and expedite satisfying exchange relationships in a dynamic environment through the creation, distribution, promotion and pricing of goods, services and ideas. (*Dibb et al., 1997, p. 5*)

The achievement of corporate goals through meeting and exceeding customer needs better than competition. (*Jobber, 2001, p. 5*)

Marketing is not a specialized activity at all. It encompasses the whole business. It is the whole business seen from the point of view of its final result, that is from the customer's point of view. Concern and responsibility for marketing must therefore permeate all areas of the enterprise. (*Drucker, 1968, p. 54*)

The above definitions introduce a number of different aspects. Marketing is seen as:

- an interactive process;
- being aimed at satisfying (or exceeding) customer needs;
- operating in a competitive and dynamic environment;
- concerning goods, services and ideas (and therefore existing in all types of organization);

- involving activities of design, pricing, promotion and distribution;
- the responsibility of all members of the organization.

Key concept 11.1 Marketing

Marketing is an interactive process aimed at satisfying or even exceeding customer needs. It is concerned with the design, pricing, promotion and accessibility to the customer of goods, services and ideas. It exists in all types of organization and is the responsibility of all members of the organization.

The following approaches to marketing have been identified. They present a generalized view of the historical development of marketing ideas.

- **The production orientation** assumes that consumers will buy whatever is available and the emphasis should be on production and distribution. This approach to marketing works best when demand is greater than supply and goods and services are relatively easy to sell. Its origins lie in the expanding populations of Europe and the USA at the end of the 19th century.

- **The product orientation** assumes that goods and services will sell themselves, usually because of inherent quality and performance characteristics, and that sales promotion is largely unnecessary. This approach also assumes that consumers are generally well informed.

- **The selling orientation** assumes that consumers will not buy sufficient goods and services unless they are persuaded to do so by advertising, sales promotion and incentives to the sales force. This approach is often necessary when supply outstrips demand, or in the case of what Kotler (1983) defines as 'unsought' goods, such as encyclopaedias, or with the promotion of political candidates. The concept emerged with the development of the techniques of mass production and its origin is particularly associated with the depression of the 1920s and 30s, more especially in the USA.

- **The true marketing orientation** shifts the attention to the consumer, whereas the production and selling orientations concern themselves with the needs of the organization. The true marketing approach involves the determination of consumer needs and values and the design and supply of goods and services to satisfy them. The assumption here is that the consumer is sovereign and the survival of any organization depends upon the satisfaction of its customers. In this context, customers can include organizations as purchasers of components for manufacture or office equipment; individuals when they buy a car, go to the supermarket or eat in a restaurant; visitors to a holiday resort; supporters of a particular political party; and even students of a university. Such an approach underpins most modern definitions of marketing, as seen above. The development of the marketing orientation is linked to increased competition, the deregulation of markets and advances in information technology. It is also linked to rational approaches to management that are based on investigation and analysis as the basis of strategy. This, in turn, is linked to the emergence of market research as an important activity. Piercy (1997), while rejecting the effective contribution of much market research and traditional marketing theory, strengthens the case of the marketing orientation. He argues most vociferously that there can be no other legitimate approach to 'going to market' (a phrase he uses rather than marketing) than by satisfying customer needs.

- **Societal marketing** takes the previous orientation a stage further. With societal marketing the attention is still focused on the consumer's needs, but the assumption here is that those needs are satisfied in such a way as to enhance the well-being of the consumer and society as a whole; goods and services should be socially acceptable, non-harmful and non-polluting. This approach arises from the enhanced consumer awareness of environmental issues. In many major supermarkets shelves are dedicated to the presentation of organic foods and new product lines, such as toilet rolls and kitchen towels made from recycled paper, or coffee filters using unbleached paper, have been developed. Washing powder and certain foodstuffs are packaged in refillable containers and recycling bins have sprung up at supermarkets, colleges, parks and car parks. Supermarkets such as Tesco, Sainsbury and Safeway have made considerable investment in the design of new stores to present attractive buildings constructed using environmentally-friendly materials. In many organizations, distribution logistics, which has always been concerned with fuel efficiency, now deals with traffic reduction as a major goal.

While these approaches to marketing do approximate to the historical development of marketing, we can see them working side by side today. Precision engineering tools tend to sell on the reputation of the product and because they are engineered to meet the exact requirements of the customer; while certain double-glazing and kitchen installation firms produce made-to-measure items that tend to be marketed using aggressive promotion and selling techniques.

If textbooks and professional journals are a reliable guide, the most popular view of marketing today as held by its practitioners is one that focuses on consumers and the determination and satisfaction of their needs. This view is not without its sceptics. J. K. Galbraith (1972) challenges the consumer-oriented marketing concept, which he calls the 'accepted sequence'. The growth of big business, the complexity of modern technologies and the correspondingly massive investments in product development have disenfranchised the consumer. 'The revised sequence' has taken over, in which complex products, beyond the understanding of the average consumer, are developed at great cost. The emphasis shifts from the satisfaction to the creation of consumer demand through investment in promotion to safeguard investments in product development.

A discussion that focuses entirely on individual consumers and manufactured products presents a somewhat restricted view of marketing. In the next section we examine the extent to which the marketing is applied in other contexts.

Marketing in different contexts

Marketing as an activity is carried out in a variety of contexts. The most obvious being, of course, the sale of goods and services to individual consumers as end-users. Marketing also occurs when a firm manufacturing petrol tanks deals with vehicle and lawnmower manufacturers and others who use petrol tanks in their products; this is sometimes referred to as industrial or organizational marketing. Equally, it is not only manufactured products that may be marketed, also but services, such as banking and management consultancy. Holiday resorts, such as Disneyland Paris (Case 11.4), have always marketed themselves to attract tourists but in recent years other places, such as Milton Keynes and Telford, have engaged in marketing to attract business development. In the 1980s, the London Docklands Development Corporation used fairly aggressive marketing techniques to attract businesses, property developers and other forms of investment to a hitherto derelict site of the former London Docks. In 1965, Singapore needed inward investment to offset the loss of British bases. The government established the Economic Development Board (EDB) and set up marketing offices in the USA and other countries. The EDB represented a one-stop shop for would-be investors, offering a fast response and eliminating the need for investors to negotiate with a range of government agencies (see Case 4.3 for more details). In addition to the marketing of products and services, some firms actively promote themselves by presenting a corporate image to the public. Marketing is far from being the sole prerogative of profit-making organizations, as governments, political parties and charities have discovered. We will deal with each of these aspects of marketing in turn.

Organizational marketing

The concept of industrial marketing can be misleading since it implies the marketing of industrial components for use in further manufacturing processes, as in the case of our petrol tank. Organizational marketing is a more useful term since it can accurately embrace any marketing exchange between two or more organizations. Retail organizations, like Marks & Spencer, engage in marketing when they buy finished goods from a variety of different sources. In modern times the state has become a very powerful consumer and a very large market in its own right. The state can use this power for social and political ends, by awarding contracts to firms in economically depressed areas or by withdrawing contracts from those firms who do not adhere to government policy, such as wage levels. In general, organizational marketing differs from consumer marketing in a number of ways:

- Whereas consumers buy goods and services for a variety of reasons, which may include less tangible considerations of status, organizational buyers tend to be more concerned with the utility of the product or service as well as its contribution to their costs.

- Organizational buying is institutionalized and is often carried out by professionals using formalized procedures involving quotations and contracts and often as part of a close, ongoing relationship between buyer and seller. In the case of a firm such as Marks & Spencer, buyers will specify in detail quality levels and often how the product must be made. We saw this illustrated in Chapter 4 by the demands made by Japanese manufacturers on their components suppliers.

- The concept of **organizational marketing** has become very important to local authorities both in the UK and elsewhere. The deregulation and privatization of the 1980s and 1990s meant that many local authority services were outsourced, involving processes of competitive tendering from would-be suppliers. In the late 1990s many authorities used a principle known as 'best value', in which organizations marketing their goods and services to them must conform to fairly stringent criteria.

The marketing of services

It is only fairly recently that many service organizations have fully acknowledged the need to consider marketing in any serious way. The historical reluctance of the service industry to engage in marketing may be due to the relatively small size of the many service operations, the intangible nature of some of the products and, in the case of the professions, the constraints imposed by their own professional bodies. Significant changes have taken place. The service industry has grown and become fiercely competitive. The major banks facing competition from building societies and other financial institutions have invested heavily in advertising and other kinds of sales promotion. Many consumers are now deluged by direct mail shots from various credit card organizations. A student opening a bank account for the first time is wooed by a variety of offers such as free overdrafts and gifts. In addition, the banks have been careful to target markets such as students, small businesses, and more recently those needing pensions, as well as extending their distribution network by reintroducing Saturday opening and installing automatic cash machines in a variety of locations. Airline companies have decided to package their products in a much more tangible way; business travellers are now invited to buy BA's 'Club Class' or Singapore Airline's 'Raffles Class' and enjoy a number of distinctive product advantages. On some airlines, economy travel has been repackaged to convey an attractive image. Thus BA's economy class becomes 'World Traveller'. The lifting of advertising restrictions on the legal profession in Britain has led, in some cases, to vigorous promotion of price differentials on services such as conveyancing.

The marketing of images

Organizations such as the Post Office, British Petroleum and ICI have spent heavily to convey a specific corporate image, which may well stress efficiency, experience, breadth of operations, company size, social responsibility or all of these characteristics. Theatrical agents have always existed to promote their clients, but the concept of marketing people has been extended to present any celebrity figure who may be 'packaged' to enhance his or her earning capacity through paid public appearances. The marketing of ideas has also grown in popularity. In 1987 the British government launched a major campaign to inform the population about AIDS, and anti-smoking campaigns by a number of different organizations are now commonplace.

The case of the Post Office represents another broadening of the marketing concept to incorporate the public sector and non-profit-making organizations, such as charities. Political elections in Britain are now fought by parties who invest heavily in marketing an image as well as an ideology. The Labour Party, conscious of a need to widen its appeal after three successive election defeats, targeted the young, professional middle classes as future voters and tailored its appeal accordingly. Even this was not enough to win the 1992 election. This defeat led to the Party repackaging itself as 'New Labour' and aiming its appeal at non-traditional, middle-class voters. The repackaging and subsequent promotional campaign, particularly the use of high-quality image advertising, was seen as a key factor in their election victory of 1997. The marketing of political parties presents an interesting combination of marketing an organizational image, ideas and people.

Governments themselves use marketing. Between the financial years 1986–7 and 1987–8 there was an increase of 90 per cent in UK government expenditure on marketing of all types and a 287 per cent increase in advertising alone. In the first three months of

2001, the UK government spent £62 million on advertising, a 157 per cent increase on the same period the previous year. During the same period, Unilever spent £34 million and BT £24 million. The majority of spending was on campaigns such as benefit fraud and anti-smoking and on the Government web site (*Guardian*, April, 2001). Most government departments have large press and public relations offices.

The use of marketing by governments raises ethical issues: it invariably supports the particular ideology of the party in power, and may be abused by some individuals to promote their own political careers.

International marketing

This is often considered as a separate marketing context requiring adaptations of the product, its price and the way it is promoted to account for differences in cultural expectations or constraints imposed by the governments of nation states. Such differences have led many firms to appoint local agents in different countries to market their products or else engage in a joint venture with a local firm. The Danish brewery Carlsberg engages in such joint production ventures throughout the world, to either ease the problems of distribution or to overcome government restrictions on the operation of foreign firms – or both. International marketing can be seen as part of a continuum which can involve selling goods and services overseas, from a home base, through various forms of equity joint venture, to wholly owned subsidiaries in different countries.

Export marketing involves issues such as global versus local products (see Chapter 2 for a more detailed discussion of globalization). Even where global products exist they tend to be marketed in different ways to account for variations in culture and government policies.

The elements of marketing

We have already seen that the marketing concept focuses on the consumer and his or her needs. Marketing strategy is enshrined in the concept of the marketing mix, popularly referred to as the **4 Ps** – product, price, promotion and place. Consumers constitute an implicit rather than explicit element of the marketing mix but we shall include them under the heading of buyer behaviour. In addition to these considerations, an effective strategy requires information, usually through the process of market research. We are therefore able to identify six key elements of marketing: market research, product, price, promotion, place and buyer behaviour.

The six elements will be treated as separate entities, although in practice there is considerable overlap. The price of a product, especially when higher than comparable offerings, can be used as a product feature and even a method of promotion stressing the exclusivity of the offering; this, in turn, depends upon the consumer perceiving and acknowledging a relationship between price and quality. Packaging is a means of protecting the product, an important form of promotion, as well as a means of facilitating the distribution of the product. The concept of place is concerned with the way the product or service reaches the consumer; in some cases free delivery is presented as a feature of the product to mark it out from competitors. We reinforce these six elements by examining the important concepts of brands and branding, segmentation and the product life-cycle in the next section.

Key concept 11.2   The marketing mix

The marketing mix generally refers to overall marketing strategy which involves the manipulation of four key elements. These are decisions concerning the nature of the product and its design, price, sales promotion, advertising and customer aware-ness, and distribution. These four factors are popularly referred to as the 4 Ps: product, price, promotion and place. Two important aspects of this are not made explicit: market research and buyer behaviour. Decisions about the marketing mix cannot be made without researching the market in all its aspects and that includes a thorough understanding of buyer behaviour.

Market research

Market research deals with the collection and analysis of information about the other five aspects of marketing. Four types of market research can be distinguished, although there is considerable overlap between them, and most firms engage in all types.

- Management needs to possess accurate information about its current marketing activities. This includes the number and value of sales of its current range of products and services, and its market share compared with competitors. Such information can provide useful feedback on sales variations by region or by salesperson, and may well provide the basis for implementing changes.

- Management needs to be aware of developments that are occurring in the market place, which might have a direct or indirect bearing upon the business. Such information may be about new products brought out by other companies, the relative prices of goods in shops, how competitors are promoting their products, or whether changes are taking place in the way consumers buy goods. This second activity is sometimes referred to as market intelligence for it enables management to build up a picture of the market in which they operate and chart the significant changes and trends so that strategies may be initiated and altered as appropriate.

- Market research involves feasibility testing: to assess the market potential of a new product or service; to assess the consumer reaction to pricing policies or price changes; to assess the reaction of consumers to a particular advertisement and so on. When a company like Nestlé launches a new chocolate bar, the product has invariably been tested on a wide range of people, and their reactions to appearance, taste, price, value for money, and, sometimes, the method of promotion are carefully assessed. An essential element of feasibility research is an analysis of the market itself, especially its size and composition in terms of age, sex and occupation. Customer reactions to products are often tested using in-depth interviews with individual consumers or using focus groups. A focus group is a means of discovering more about a particular product through engaging a small group of consumers or potential consumers in a group discussion led by a trained facilitator. Such groups are used in the marketing of industrial as well as consumer goods and are used widely by such firms as HP and British Oxygen.

- The fourth type of research is a mixture of the previous three in that it collects information to evaluate a product and the way it is priced, promoted and acquired by the consumer as an ongoing process after the initial launch. Continuous data of this type are often collected by consumer panels. These are groups of consumers, who may be representative of the population as a whole or some specific segment of the market. Panels are then asked to monitor such things as their purchasing and eating habits, their television viewing, and so on. In 1991, Taylor Neilson AGB launched a Great Britain consumer panel comprising 10 000 households to collect detailed information on most aspects of consumer purchase (Frain, 1999).

Individual organizations, especially if they are large enough, can do their own market research. However, research has developed as a specialist activity over the past 25 years or so, and numerous agencies, such as Mintel and Taylor Neilson AGB, have arisen offering a variety of services. Many such firms operate multinationally and, among their many services offered to clients, provide regular television viewing figures, so enabling firms to target and evaluate television advertising campaigns. Such firms provide their clients with regular market intelligence on market share and trends, tasks often beyond the resources of an individual company. Some market research agencies specialize by product or the type of service offered and some have built up reputations for consumer interviewing.

> ### Key concept 11.3 Market research
>
> Market research involves the collection and analysis of information to gain feedback on current marketing activities, including those concerned with new product launches and testing the market response to new product proposals. It is concerned with collecting and reviewing information about competitors' products, pricing, promotions and distribution policies.

The product

In our discussion of the different contexts of marketing we saw how the term 'product' has a wide connotation and may include manufactured goods, services, people, organizations, places and ideas. A product comprises a number of elements, apart from its more obvious features, which can include a brand name, packaging, after-sales service, delivery, warranty and so on. Marketing needs to consider all these aspects of the product. Free delivery or extended guarantees may be seen as essential product characteristics by some consumers.

A **product line** is the total number of variations of the same basic product, differentiated by quality, cost or extra features. A car manufacturer will make several versions of the same basic model with variations in engine size, type of gearbox, paintwork and so on. BA offers product differentiation both before and during its flights through different levels of service in each class. In response to price competition from companies such as easyJet, BA launched its own subsidiary offering low-cost, 'no-frills' flights to popular European destinations. The breadth of a product line is closely related to the degree of market segmentation, a concept we introduce in the next section.

A **product mix** is the total number of different products offered by the firm, sometimes referred to as the product portfolio. The size of a firm's product mix can have a significant impact on its profitability in that the effect of poor performers may be lessened by the income from better-selling items. However, too broad a product mix can cause problems of control.

Marketing considerations are an important input in the process of developing new products. We saw in Chapter 9 that new product development was not only potentially expensive but that the risk of failure was high. Extensive market research is needed concerning such aspects as the utility and acceptability of a design, the target market and likely acceptable price of a new product. An estimate may be made about likely future sales which, when set alongside likely development costs, is essential in assessing the business viability of a new project. While we tend to associate new product development with manufactured goods, it has become increasingly important in the services sector. A large number of new products have been launched in the financial services sector as a result of deregulation, increased competition, technical change and more knowledgeable and sophisticated consumers.

We will return to consideration of the product in our discussion of branding, segmentation and the **product life-cycle**.

Price

If marketing strategy were based entirely on the analysis of the neo-classical economists then price would be the most significant feature of that strategy and would be based on the concept of the price elasticity of demand. A product is price elastic if changes in price influence changes in demand. All things being equal, an increase in price will lead to a fall in demand and consequently a fall in revenue and vice versa. All things are rarely equal, and consumers can behave in an unpredictable manner. Many factors influence price and pricing strategy and operate at the environmental, organizational and strategic levels of our model. We deal with some of those factors under the following headings.

Cost A business firm wishing to make a profit must use the cost of making a product or providing a service as an important base point in setting its prices. However, the sensitivity of most pricing decisions lies less in the cost of raw materials, labour, and the like, than the understanding of those factors that may determine the extent of mark-up on the basic cost price. These include most of the factors identified below. Moreover, costs can be distorted by accounting methods, particularly those associated with apportioning overheads. For example, should overheads be calculated for individual cost centres or averaged for the whole organization? An idea often propounded by neo-classical economists is that cost and therefore price are associated with the economies of scale and that volume production will lead to price reduction. While this may be true for some products, there are many exceptions which challenge both the notion of economies of scale and the necessity of tying price to volume production. We return to these arguments in our discussion of the product life-cycle and marketing strategies.

Consumer behaviour The price of a product may well be related to what a consumer can afford and to what he or she is prepared to pay. This, in turn, is related to income levels, the consumer's perceptions of quality and value for money, and the consumer's budget for a particular purchase. In purchasing a new camera for a special holiday or a new word-processor for the office of a small business, the consumer's own target price based on what he or she wants to pay may be the primary factor. The range of products considered will then be limited to those priced within a range around or below the target price. A firm aiming at a particular target market may be best advised to discover the budgeting behaviour of its potential consumers before setting the price. Some firms use target pricing to influence product design. For example, where costs are likely to exceed target price, value-engineering methods will be used to reduce costs. However, there can be cases where the consumer's perception of value exceeds the target price. In 1972, Jaguar launched the XJ12 model. Demand so outstripped supply that second-hand cars were being sold for 40 per cent more than the original price. Consumer perceptions can, of course, be influenced by promotional activity. The brewing industry in Britain has focused its attention on the lager market. Many brands are deliberately marketed as highly priced products offering the consumer 'real' quality. This strategy was successfully pursued by the brewers of Stella Artois to establish their product in a highly competitive market. Such strategies depend heavily on 'brand image' (discussed in the next section), fashion and social influences. The lager market is aimed at the young drinker: the attractiveness (particularly to the opposite sex) and the social superiority of drinking a particular brand is stressed.

Economic factors   Price is related to the economy in a number of different ways, all of which have a potential impact on an organization's pricing policy:

- The affluence of consumers will have an obvious influence on their level of budgeting and regional variations may produce differential demand, especially for certain luxury items.

- The role of the state in managing the economy may affect both demand and prices.

- The control of interest rates will influence the extent of consumer credit and hence the size of an individual's budget, as will levels of taxation.

- During periods of high inflation the government may well introduce measures to control prices.

- A major influence on price for exporters is the currency exchange rate which fluctuates according to the state of the economy. In early 1985 the pound and the dollar approached parity which made many British goods highly attractive in the USA giving firms, such as Jaguar, a significant boost to their profits through increased sales. As the dollar weakened against the pound British exports became less attractive and for 1987–8 Jaguar cars announced significantly reduced profit figures due, in no small part, to changes in the exchange rate. As a changing exchange rate brings prices of products more into line with competition from domestic suppliers or other country's imports, criteria other than price become more important. The relationship is far from simple and no matter how attractive the price of imported goods may be, it can be offset by delays in delivery, an inadequate distribution network, or a poor after-sales service.

Competition   Many firms price their products by reference to an existing market, basing their price around that offered by competitors for products of similar features and quality.

Management goals   The price of goods is often related to the extent to which managements wish to optimize profit. Management goals rarely conform to simple economic models and are complicated by considerations of power, politics and personal preference. The desire of a group of managers for a larger market share for their products may result in a low-price strategy to build up demand. In some firms price may be deliberately used as a promotion strategy to create an image of product quality in the eyes of the consumer.

Organizational size   The size of an organization may give it market power and the ability to manipulate market prices. This is especially true of oligopolies. At one time, the Swiss pharmaceutical firm Roche controlled around half of the world tranquillizer market, largely through its products Librium and Valium. This brought the firm to the attention of the Monopolies Commission, who, in 1971, accused the company's British subsidiary of exploiting the market against the public interest by charging excessive prices. We saw in Chapter 9 how GSK's market dominance with Zantac and Ventolin enabled them to charge high prices. A major supermarket chain, such as Walmart or Tesco, is able, because of its purchasing power and stock turnover, to insist on large price discounts from its suppliers.

We began our discussion of price by challenging the all-important view attributed to the price element in marketing by neo-classical economists. A much more detailed account of the relationship between price and demand and, in particular, the limitations of the neo-classical approach may be found in *Economics in a Business Context* (Haslam *et al.*, 2000). The role of price in marketing strategy is, as we have seen, highly complex. Nonetheless it is the only element of marketing strategy that generates income, all other items incurring cost. Pricing policy is therefore a vital strand of strategy which, because of the complexities involved, is often difficult for management to judge. We return to such strategic considerations at the end of this chapter.

Promotion

We can identify five types of promotion; advertising, sales promotion, direct marketing, personal selling and publicity. The significant growth of promotion as a marketing activity is a function of the growth, complexity and competitiveness of markets and the developments of appropriate technology, as in the newspaper and television industries. It was not until 1896 that UK newspapers, following the leadership of the *Daily Mail*, recognized the value of advertising revenue to offset rising costs (Cannon, 1986).

All types of promotional activity use psychological theory and communication models of human behaviour, but the nature of the promotion used will depend on a number of factors, including the strategy of the organization, the available budget and the type of market. While television advertising may be an appropriate medium for the promotion of consumer goods, such as chocolate bars, a specialist magazine may be preferred for promoting expensive camera equipment, and personal selling may be the best way to market industrial goods to other organizations. Some forms of promotion, such as television advertising, are obvious while others, such as shop design, are less so. The Burton Group, on taking over Debenhams, invested heavily in redesigning the department store interiors to project a new image and attract different market segments.

Promotion, like distribution, often involves management working together with representatives of other organizations. Advertising, for example, may involve the marketing manager working closely with an agency as well as representatives of the media. We will return to these aspects when we discuss the organizational aspects of marketing, and turn our attention, for the time being, to the various types of promotion.

Advertising   The management of **advertising** involves four major considerations; the design of the message, the selection of the media, the cost of both production and exposure and the evaluation of its effectiveness.

- The design of the message reflects the three functions of advertising:

- First, it operates to inform the consumer and may be useful in creating initial demand for a product or informing consumers about such things as price changes.
- Second, it operates to persuade the consumer to buy the advertiser's product rather than that of a rival. This form of promotion tends to focus on specific features which distinguish a product from its competitors, and by building up a brand image.
- The third function serves to remind the consumer of the product and encourage repeat purchases. Such promotion is not aimed solely at consumers, but also at wholesalers and retailers to give products shelf space. In general, the nature of the message will vary in all these cases. For example, an advertisement that aims to change the buying habits of consumers will often use images with which the potential consumer identifies.

● Advertisers have a wide choice of media, including national and local newspapers, magazines, cinema, television, radio and posters. In recent years there has been considerable increase in the use of local independent radio and local newspapers, no doubt reflecting the expansion of both types of media. The selection of appropriate media also involves questions of timing and an advertising campaign may be carefully scheduled to use various forms of media, either concurrently or consecutively, to achieve maximum impact. For example, Ford uses press and radio advertising to promote special offers and the television and especially cinema to attract a younger buyer and to build the brand image.

● The cost of promotion will vary with the media selected. In 2003 the daily rate for a full-page advertisement in the *Daily Telegraph* would cost £44 000 for mono and £55 550 for colour. The comparative rates for the *Guardian* would be £17 500 and £20 500 respectively (less than the 1999 price). The variation in price has little to do with the cost of production and is more a reflection on the higher circulation rates of the *Telegraph*. A similar advertisement in a local paper could cost around £2500–3000. Although they have steadied in 2003, rates for national advertising have increased significantly over the past 10 years, although those at the local level have remained roughly the same (an undoubted reflection of increased competition in the sector). The above costs are for exposure only and do not include the cost of producing the advertisement. Each of those prices may vary considerably with the demand for advertising, the positioning of the advertisement, and the extent to which special deals may be struck between the buyers and sellers of advertising space. The major problem with such expenditure is the degree of waste, since much advertising can be ignored by large sections of the population, and the real impact is often difficult to evaluate. We will deal with the problems of evaluation in our discussion of marketing strategy.

Sales promotion   This incorporates a wide variety of different techniques, including free samples, money-back coupons, special offers on loyalty points, contests and so on. Manufacturers promoting goods through the trade often provide attractive point-of-sale displays or product expertise in the form of a specialist salesperson. A furniture manufacturer, such as Grange, a bedding firm like Dunlopillo and many of the cosmetic manufacturers train and pay their own staff to operate in department stores. Exhibitions and trade fairs are popular ways of promoting goods both to the trade and industry as a whole. Such forms of sales promotion apply to services as well as manufactured goods. New restaurants often invite a specially targeted clientele to a launch evening. Railway companies have introduced several types of fare structure to attract off-peak users, in the same way that many restaurants offer reduced-price meals to attract customers outside the hours of peak demand. These examples illustrate the interaction between sales promotion and pricing strategies.

Sales promotion is sometimes referred to as '**below-the-line**' advertising and is often underestimated in considerations of promotion. It is estimated that sales promotion comprises over 70 per cent of all expenditure on promotion activity and has achieved a particularly rapid growth since the 1960s. The growth has been attributed to increasing rates of inflation and changes in management thinking. Rising inflation has made the consumer more conscious of special offers, while management have apparently grown sceptical of the effectiveness of advertising and believe there to be a much clearer and direct relationship between expenditure on sales promotion and sales.

Case 11.1 offers two different illustrations of promotion campaigns. In the first, a travel offer by Hoover, the promotion was far more popular than envisaged by the company, resulting in significant financial losses and generating bad publicity. In the second, a use of cultural stereotypes by McDonald's in Singapore proved to be an outstanding financial success for the company.

| Case 11.1 | **Two sales promotions** |

11.1a Hoover

Hoover, until recently part of the US Maytag group, operates in the highly competitive domestic products market. Hoover has been under pressure for some time and sought a plan to boost sales in the recession. This was particularly important since most people only purchase a new domestic appliance, such as a vacuum cleaner or a washing machine, when the old one breaks down.

In the summer of 1992, Hoover executives launched a sales promotion in association with a travel firm, JSI. The offer was of two free airline tickets to one of six European destinations with the purchase of a Hoover product for £119 or more, the price of a vacuum cleaner. Hoover estimated that the offer would attract 50 000 new customers and in November and December of the same year, when sales usually fall, the offer was enlarged to offer free flights to a number of USA destinations as well.

The process involved in obtaining the offer was complex. Purchasers had to make an application within 14 days and were then promised a registration form within 28 days. Provided the registration form was returned within a further 14 days, customers had up to 30 days to nominate their destinations and flight dates. Should these be unavailable, the company could nominate alternatives. Clearly, Hoover believed that the complexity of the application process would restrict the number of takers.

The promotion was successful in a spectacular fashion and sales were boosted far beyond the company's estimates. Rather than 50 000 as predicted, the offer was taken up by 200 000 with half requesting transatlantic flights. The majority of customers bought the cheapest vacuum cleaner under the terms of the offer.

Shops could not get enough stock and the Hoover production plants were placed on seven days a week operation, with the necessity of overtime payments and the hiring of extra staff to cope with the increased demand. The company was unable to cope with the applications for flights and, in any case, insufficient flights were available. There were innumerable complaints of delay and of forms that did not arrive. Cases were brought before the Trading Standards Office and Hoover received a particularly bad press. Many who received offers of flights found them wholly unacceptable, in terms of either destination and/or date of travel. Maytag, the parent company were forced to send in an investigation team and the three executives responsible for the promotion were dismissed. Hoover had to spend an extra £20 million pounds acquiring flights, and some put the additional cost at nearer £40 million. Several thousand vacuum cleaners were being sold on the second-hand markets, with a corresponding impact on the sale of new cleaners. Since the cheapest available transatlantic flight at the time of the offer was around £200 per person, the offer was viewed by most in terms of two flights for £119, with a free vacuum cleaner thrown in.

Following the bad publicity associated with the promotion, Hoover invested £7 million in a European-wide press campaign to restore its image. However, by the middle of 1995 Hoover's market share had fallen from around 50 per cent to less than 20 per cent by volume and value. This was attributed to an adverse reaction to the free flights promotion and to the introduction, by a new company, of a cleaner using innovative technology. The problems caused by the flights offer brought a particularly hostile reaction in the UK, traditionally the strongest market, where an estimated 200 000 people felt they were out of pocket on the promotion. A pressure group was formed and had little trouble enlisting 10 000 angry consumers. The new competition was likely to provide a much longer-term problem. Just after the free flights promotion, James Dyson launched a new type of vacuum cleaner without a bag, an idea that initially had been turned down by Hoover. The Dyson vacuum cleaner was an instant success and became the market leader by a long way.

Maytag, who had purchased Hoover Europe for US$300 million, sold the company to the Italian-based firm Candy for US$170 million.

Sources: *Financial Times, Marketing*, 1 June, 1995; *Marketing Week*, 23 June, 1995; *Management Today*, December 1996

Questions

1 What do you think was the rationale for Hoover's special promotion?

2 What were the implications for the company?

3 What alternative promotions might Hoover have used?

11.1b McDonald's Kiasu Burger and the fourth flavour

The global fast-food restaurant chain McDonald's has built its reputation on a well-known range of products that it offers around the world. The similarity in its global product range is matched by a similarity in its approach to marketing. The restaurants are easily recognizable by a common approach to design and layout. In almost every location the restaurant can be spotted underneath the sign of the 'golden arch', representing the 'M' in McDonald's. Promotional campaigns everywhere tend to emphasize family values, low cost, good-value nourishing meals and use a 'Ronald McDonald' character to appeal to children.

In reality there have always been variations in the taste and appearance owing to variations in local suppliers around the world, but the core product range remained sacrosanct. In the 1990s the product policy was relaxed to allow the introduction of local products appealing specifically to local tastes, usually accompanied by a fierce promotional campaign. Since 1993 such a policy has operated in Singapore. The first of such products was the Kiasu Burger. Kiasu is a local Chinese dialect word in Singapore which roughly translates as a 'fear of losing out'. The positive connotation of this word is generally associated with healthy competition and the need to be first. The negative attributes are associated with aversion to risk and even selfishness and cowardice. Kiasuism is a well-known concept in Singapore and, since 1990, has been popularized through a comic strip character, Mr Kiasu. The character was developed by four young Singaporeans and his adventures usually depict the worst elements of Kiasuism, such as gluttony and pushing to the front of queues. The comic strip developed cult status, but soon gained wider appeal and became a local craze. The comic strip character was augmented by a range of Mr Kiasu merchandise, such as T-shirts.

A decision was made to launch a new product in May 1993 using the concept of Mr Kiasu. The company developed a local product, the Kiasu Burger, described as 'an extra large chicken patty seasoned with extra spices, marinated in extra sauce, topped with fresh lettuce, all sandwiched in an extra-large sesame seed bun'. The product was sold at 2.90 Singapore dollars and was cheaper than the rest of the McDonald's hamburger range. The product was also introduced as part of a range of value-for-money meal combinations and purchasers of the Kiasu Burger were entitled to buy a Mr Kiasu figurine for 90 cents. Four types of figurine were offered, each bearing a typical Mr Kiasu slogan, such as 'Everything also I want!' and 'Everything also must grab!'. Such slogans poked fun, not only at Singaporean attitudes, but also at 'Singlish', a local dialect version of English. The campaign was supported by television advertising, featuring Mr Kiasu as a cartoon character for the first time.

Within 2 months of the launch, a million were sold and the Kiasu Burger itself had become a craze. Demand for the figurines was also high. At the end of July 1993, McDonald's launched a further promotion celebrating their success and congratulating their Singaporean customers for being able to laugh at themselves. For a limited period the company offered its Kiasu Burgers and figurines at half price.

The Kiasu Burger was developed as part of a series of promotions under the banner of the 'fourth flavour'. The aim of the promotion was to increase turnover by catering specifically to local taste and the use of novelty items. Any specific 'fourth flavour' was never destined to become a permanent feature of the McDonald's product range. Instead it was planned that interest would be maintained by the introduction of a new product at regular intervals, with the subsequent phasing out of the previous 'fourth flavour'. A year after the launch of the Kiasu Burger, McDonald's Singapore introduced the chicken-based Kampung Burger. This too was based on a popular cartoon character, Kampung Boy, and the cartoon characters were seen in animation for the first time as the product was launched by a television commercial. McDonald's saw the product as representing traditional community values associated with village life. The promotion was accompanied by a caption contest.

In 1995, McDonald's introduced another chicken product in the form of the Love Burger. They linked the product with the importance of love within the family and ran a competition to find Singapore's longest-married couple – the prize being an anniversary party at McDonald's. Another competition was launched for newly weds and prizes of McDonald's wedding receptions were offered for the most creative love messages between couples. The Love Burger was followed the following year by the McPepper Burger, a beef hamburger in a thick spicy black pepper sauce. This was the most successful promotional item to date and the company sold over half a million in the first 2 weeks of the launch.

Promotional items also included desserts such as McDonaldland, ice cream exclusively for the Singapore market. The ice cream container was designed as the head of one of four McDonald's characters, 'Ronald McDonald', 'Hamburglar', 'Birdie' and 'Grimace'. Earlier desserts to appeal to local taste had included mango and durian milkshakes.

While the promotions varied in their popularity, the cumulative effect was an increase in turnover for McDonald's, with a knock-on effect to its main product range. During the period of these launches from 1993–7, McDonald's presence in Singapore grew from 50 to over 80 outlets on a small island of around 3 million people.

Sources: McDonald's press releases; *Straits Times*

Questions

1 What risks were McDonald's taking with their launch of the Kiasu Burger?

2 What other forms of promotion does the company use?

3 How could a similar campaign be launched in the UK or in another European country?

Direct marketing   This is both a form of promotion and a channel of distribution. In **direct marketing**, organizations deal directly with the customer without using intermediaries such as retail outlets. There are many forms, which include direct mail shots, inserts in magazines, mail order catalogues, telephone sales, faxes, coupon response forms, door-to-door leaflets and the current growth of electronic commerce. (E-commerce is dealt with in more detail in Chapter 3 and later in this chapter.)

The kind of products and services promoted and sold in this way vary greatly as the following examples reveal. A specialist holiday company will generally advertise its brochure in a magazine and consumers may obtain a copy by sending in a request form attached to the advertisement or by giving details to a telephone-answering service. Customers wishing to buy a holiday usually do so by completing a booking form or after a telephone discussion with a company representative. Clothes offered by mail order were once considered more down- than up-market. This is no longer the case as clothes firms catering for up-market niche market products now offer goods by mail order and some firms, such as Lands End, have built up a considerable reputation solely on the basis of a mail order business. Theatres and restaurants use faxes to send out details of special offers. In addition, many restaurants will fax their menu details to potential customers. Direct marketing is used to sell to organizations as well as to individual consumers. Most firms obtain their most frequently purchased office supplies from mail order catalogues, making orders by telephone or fax.

> ### Key concept 11.4 Direct marketing
>
> Direct marketing involves setting up a direct channel between the organization and its customers. It is thus a channel for both promotion and distribution, targeting specific groups and enabling them to respond without the use of an intermediary. There are a number of methods ranging from mail shots to the use of the Internet.

The advantage claimed for direct marketing over other forms of promotion is that it can be targeted at specific groups. Unlike television or other forms of advertising, the target audience is reached with minimum wastage. Critics of direct marketing attribute to it the growth of 'junk mail' and accuse it of adding to the problems of litter as consumers discard unwanted inserts from newspapers and magazines. Despite its critics, direct marketing has grown in popularity in recent years and some firms, such as Dell, have used it to significantly increase their market share in the computer industry. The popularity of direct marketing is associated with increasing market segmentation and developments in information technology and telecommunications. A key factor has been the growth of name and address lists of all types, which form the basis of databases used by firms in direct marketing. Effective direct marketing depends on accurate data and the ability to refine the target market in response to feedback information.

Personal selling   This is a specialized form of direct marketing favoured by the sellers of industrial goods, recognizing the importance of building good personal relations between seller and buyer. However, the cost of employing a sales force to maintain regular contact with customers means that this can be a most expensive form of promotion. In recent years a much cheaper form of **personal selling** has developed, especially among the manufacturers of double-glazing and fitted kitchens, by employing part-time workers to contact potential consumers by telephone. Such unsolicited selling has attracted much criticism from irritated consumers.

Publicity   This can be an important form of promotion in that the credibility of products or services may be enhanced by linking them with news stories. Many newspapers now have specialist business features or even supplements and such stories can be an effective way of keeping a firm and its products in the public eye. Some of the larger firms institutionalize this function by employing a specialist public relations department.

An examination of promotion raises many important issues. Advertising, in particular, has been challenged for developing an overly materialistic society, and the ethics of advertising goods such as cigarettes and alcohol has been questioned by a number of interest groups. The high cost of promotion campaigns using television advertising sets up considerable barriers to the entry of new firms and may operate in favour of big business. This is another reason for the growth of direct marketing.

Place

Place refers to the processes by which products and services reach the consumer and involves consideration of marketing channels and physical distribution. A marketing channel represents the flow of goods and services and may comprise several stages, involving intermediaries, such as transporters, agents, wholesalers and retailers.

Intermediaries play a number of different roles. They are usually able to distribute goods to customers in a more cost-effective way than the manufacturer, particularly where goods are mass-produced and items are fast moving. The most popular daily newspapers sell millions of papers between them. This would be impossible without a complex and well-organized network of transport, wholesalers and retailers to ensure that newspapers are available for readers each morning. In this case, the intermediaries break down the number of newspapers into more easily managed batches and are geographically dispersed to ensure an effective delivery. Such wholesalers and retailers handle a range of daily newspapers and so facilitate the buying process by offering consumers choice. Manufacturers and consumers are therefore linked in a cost-effective network. The cost of a single newspaper establishing its own network would push up prices to many times their current value.

An intermediary is also an important source of market research and sales promotion since it stands in closer proximity to customers than the manufacturer. For the same reason intermediaries are often better placed to offer a comprehensive after-sales service. Some intermediaries may offer limited processing facilities, such as cutting glass or mixing paint to order. For the manufacturer the intermediary shares some of the risk by buying goods in bulk to sell on (some of which may not sell) and, in so doing, helps finance the manufacturer's operations. The case of Sleek in Chapter 2 demonstrates how a successful business has grown as an intermediary.

Those manufacturers seeking greater control over the distribution process have tried to integrate vertically the **marketing channel** network. Perhaps the clearest example of this is franchising. However, we have already noted in this chapter the power that can be wielded by big supermarket chains over some manufacturers; a case of the marketing channel controlling the manufacturer.

In charting the growth of direct marketing, we noted that not all marketing channels involve intermediaries. In the case of industrial goods it is more common for the manufacturer to deal directly with the purchaser, often by building up a relationship between the sales and purchasing departments in the respective organizations. As we saw in the discussion of supply chain management in Chapter 10, there is a growing tendency for very close relationships to be built up between components suppliers and manufacturers, particularly with the introduction of JIT production methods. This is illustrated by Case 10.1, which examines the relationship between Mercedes-Benz and Eberspächer, a supplier of exhaust systems.

In all cases it is important that the marketing channel makes the goods and services accessible to those who seek them. The importance of accessibility varies with the nature of the product on offer and the needs and wants of consumers. It is important for a fast-food restaurant to be located near centres of population and to be sited so as to encourage casual callers. Accessibility becomes less important for the prestigious restaurant rated by food guides, since customers will often be willing to travel several miles. Hospitals, especially those offering casualty services, also need to be located close to and be easily reached by the populations they serve. The increase in the sale of flowers worldwide is a direct result of the widened access that telephone sales and, more recently, the use of the Internet have produced (see Case 11.3).

The concept of the marketing channel has been revolutionized by the growth of e-commerce and Internet marketing. This was featured in Chapter 3 and will be raised later in this chapter in our discussion of the relationship between technology and marketing. It is also a central feature of Case 11.3.

Buyer behaviour

An understanding of the needs, wants and behaviour of consumers is a vital element in designing a marketing strategy. Buyer behaviour involves considerations of why people buy and how they arrive at the decision to buy. Several writers have attempted to formulate theories of consumer behaviour so that marketers can predict the outcomes of various strategies (e.g., Rogers, 1962; Nicosia, 1966; Howard and Sheth, 1969). As yet the predictive validity of such theories and models leaves much to be desired.

The weakness of such theories lies in the very complexity of buyer behaviour. We have seen how changes in the economy can affect consumer perceptions of their own purchasing power. This is well illustrated by consumer reaction to prices in Disneyland Paris, in Case 11.4. In addition we can identify a number of psychological and sociological influences including: perception, attitudes, patterns of learning, motivation, personality, social class, peer groups and culture. A knowledge of such factors is an important contribution to marketing strategy and may be used in the development of the marketing mix. Advertisers use these influences in a number of ways: by linking products to certain social groups with whom the consumer identifies; by using 'experts' to extol the virtues of particular brands in an attempt to influence the perceptions and attitudes of the consumer.

Predicting buyer behaviour becomes particularly important with innovations and is an important ingredient in decisions concerning new product development. Rogers (1962) attempted to differentiate people according to their response to innovative products and identified five types:

- innovators
- early adopters
- the early majority
- the late majority
- laggards.

The innovators and early majority comprise an estimated 15 per cent of the population and are important as opinion leaders in the diffusion of innovations. The implications for the marketing specialist is to establish the characteristics of these groups and focus the marketing communication accordingly. The diffusion of new products is seen as a chain reaction of influence between pioneering consumers and the mass market. While Rogers found that early adopters tended to be younger, more affluent and more cosmopolitan than later adopters, such generalizations, like so many models, have foundered at the sheer complexity of buyer behaviour. For example, a consumer may be an early adopter of the latest in camera technology but particularly conservative where furniture, clothes or holidays are concerned. In this case we would need to identify the opinion leaders for each product group.

Consideration of buyer behaviour often focuses attention on specific target groups. These are referred to as market segments and we deal with the concept of segmentation in the next section. Not all product markets are highly differentiated. A product such as Coca Cola is bought by the widest possible range of consumers.

Whatever the product or the target market, considerable attention is paid by many managers to the attainment of customer loyalty, based on the assumption that the costs of retaining existing customers are less than those associated with gaining new customers and that loyal customers mean repeat purchases. In the late 1990s, the concept of customer care achieved fashionable status. While for many consumers there is rather more rhetoric than reality, in many organizations customer care has become the focus of training and culture-change programmes, as in BA (see Case 12.2). In the UK, supermarkets and retail chains such as Boots and W. H. Smith have attempted to increase customer loyalty through the introduction of 'loyalty cards', in which purchases attract points which can then be converted into cash refunds or, in some cases, air miles.

Piercy (1997) questions several of the assumptions that underpin traditional approaches to customer loyalty. In particular he challenges the assumption that there is an automatic link between customer satisfaction and loyalty, as illustrated in Figure 11.1.

The classic model of customer loyalty is illustrated by the 'happy stayer'. However, there are customers who gain satisfaction yet enjoy switching brands. These Piercy describes as 'happy wanderers'. 'Hostages' are customers who have no choice either because they are tied in by contract or they are dealing with a monopoly supplier who can exploit market power by charging a high price. 'Dealers' are customers who forever seek the best deal irrespective of brand or supplier. Because the link between loyalty and satisfaction is complex, Piercy questions the value of loyalty programmes for all but the 'happy stayers' and says that in some cases loyalty cards develop 'hostages' rather than truly

Figure 11.1

Customer satisfaction and customer loyalty

Source: Piercy (1997)

satisfied customers. He challenges the notion of loyalty cards as an effective strategy in that they are easy for competitors to copy and sees them as little else but a gimmick that does little to create real customer value.

The complexities of buyer behaviour have led some to conclude that consumer marketing is inherently more complex than is the case with industrial or organizational marketing. Such a perspective ignores the complexities in organizational marketing, which may be different from those in consumer marketing but are just as real. These complexities include the nature of management values and organizational politics, and those involved in the relationship between the buyers and sellers of industrial and organizational goods and services.

Branding, segmentation and the product life-cycle

These concepts deal with issues raised under the various headings of the marketing mix. We deal with them separately because of their importance.

Branding

Branding is the process through which the product is given a name, logo or symbol to distinguish it from the range of other products on offer.

Branding has become big business. It has been used most profitably in fashion-conscious market segments where major producers, such as Calvin Klein, offer a range of clothes, fashion accessories, perfumes and toiletries, each portraying the same fashionable image under a single brand.

Branding has grown significantly in the entertainment industry. Three leading opera singers appear together as 'The Three Tenors'. This has become the brand and is registered as a trademark. The brand is used not only to sell concerts but also tapes, CDs and a range of souvenirs. Would-be copyists have been pursued vigorously through the courts. Branding is an important component of soccer, with major clubs earning a considerable proportion of their revenue through the sale of branded merchandise associated with the club. Chelsea invested £2.5 million on a new mega-store, built as part of a new ground development, which also included apartments, restaurants and a hotel. The Chelsea-branded goods sold in the shop include, as well as football equipment, mountain bikes, home furnishings and clothes. In 1996 Manchester United sold 850 000 official team shirts worldwide and earned over £20 million from the sale of their own branded goods, which

> **Key concept 11.5** Branding
>
> Branding involves giving the product a name, logo or symbol to distinguish it from the range of products offered by competitors or even by the same organization. Branding is an important source of product differentiation in a highly competitive and dynamic environment and can apply to a single product, a range of products or an entire organization. It is used to create awareness and build up customer loyalty to ensure repeat purchases. A well-known brand is seen as a financial asset that can provide firms with considerable competitive advantage.

included their own-brand champagne, wine and beer! By 2001 Manchester United had doubled their income from merchandising.

Brands as a means of differentiation and attraction have become especially important in recent years for a number of reasons:

- The speed of technology transfer has meant that less time is available to capitalize on competitive advantage through technological change. The brand takes over from technology as the source of differentiation.

- The markets for most consumer goods in Europe, the USA and Japan have become stagnant. Brands are an attempt to give a product more prominence in the market place.

- Among certain market segments, such as fashion-conscious young people, particular brands have gained considerable popularity. Firms owning such brands have capitalized on their success by extending both the product range and the product mix under the same brand.

Brand names can be given to a single product or a whole range of products. The latter tends to identify the products with a high profile, as with the aforementioned Calvin Klein or, indeed, Kelloggs. In other cases it may be important to differentiate individual products even though they originate from the same stable. For example, the washing powder market is dominated by two producers, Lever and Proctor and Gamble, yet each markets a range of washing powders under different brand names. In this way the brands assume an identity of their own, so much so that many believe them to be the products of a range of different companies. There may be several reasons why a firm is keen to differentiate a number of brands within the same product range:

- to appeal to different market segments;
- to capture those consumers who like to switch brands;
- to gain more exposure and shelf space in retail outlets;
- as a means of structuring the organization around brands to create healthy internal competition, as in the case of Proctor and Gamble.

Apart from the brand name, a particular logo or mark may be used. Calvin Klein and Ralph Lauren clothes, as well as other goods, are instantly recognizable by their distinctive logo. Some manufacturers feel it is important to create a brand style so that any one of their products from a given range is instantly recognizable. Alfred Sloan insisted to his design teams that all GM cars in the USA possessed the definitive 'GM look' (Sloan, 1986). Alfa Romeo cars are differentiated from rival brands by the use of very distinctive styling.

An important development in branding has been the growth of 'generic' or 'own'-brands. These can be found especially in the major retail stores such as Sainsbury, Safeway and Tesco. A generic is a product that is sold under the brand name of the retailer and applies to all kinds of products. It may, in fact, be identical to a nationally known brand on the same shelf, but is generally sold at a cheaper price to appeal more to the price-conscious shopper. In some cases generics have acquired a brand image that goes beyond price and value for money to indicate real product quality. Historically, Marks & Spencer have deliberately promoted this image with their own generic name 'St Michael'. However, significant falls in profits for 1998 and 1999 may indicate that consumer perceptions of 'St Michael' have changed. The company has responded by sourcing yet more goods from cheaper overseas suppliers.

Aaker (1996) identifies the following potential attributes of a brand, which offer meaning to the consumer. These are not mutually exclusive:

- The brand can represent a product as in the case of Cadbury's chocolate, Kodak films and Michelin tyres.

- The brand can represent the organization. In this case the company has as much if not more meaning to the consumer than the product. There are certain types of consumer who, for example, will only buy their food from Harrods or their shoes from Russell and Bromley. The brand as organization is especially important in Japan, to the extent where employment with a major corporation, such as Sony, is an important source of social status. This is an important source of competitive advantage for such as the Disney Corporation (Case 11.4).

- The brand can acquire a personality that is carefully nurtured by advertising and promotional campaigns. Thus the Marlboro cowboy associates cigarette smoking with the rugged outdoor life and Bacardi forever reinforce the association between the drink and a carefree lifestyle on a tropical island location. Piercy (1997) argues that, in some firms, a person becomes the brand, usually in the form of the founder or leading character. To a greater or lesser extent this can be seen with the likes of Richard Branson at Virgin or Bill Gates at Microsoft.

- Finally, the brand is a symbol. That symbol can represent exclusivity and quality at a high price, as in the case of Harrods, Rolls Royce or Rolex. It can also represent good value for money, as in the case of Boots, or even cheap goods, as in the case of Superdrug and Walmart.

The link between a person and a brand was an issue of much debate during 2003. Martha Stewart, a famous USA television presenter of cookery and lifestyle programmes built up a massive following in the USA with considerable sales of Martha Stewart branded products. She was accused of insider trading and financial improprieties. This led immediately to a drop in television ratings, a fall in her company shares and was the reason given for a 42 per cent fall in profits on branded goods. Stewart was well-known as a television personality and was synoymous with the brand.

Calvin Klein attracted equally bad publicity as a result of his misbehaviour at a basketball game, allegedly due to drink and drugs. However, this had little or no effect on sales of the brand, which is now considered to be bigger than its originator. In any case, the brand had been sold to Phillips-Van Heusen and it was argued that most people outside the USA bought the label and did not know the person behind it (Young, 2003).

The importance of branding lies in the process of creating brand awareness, brand image and, ultimately, **brand loyalty**, thereby ensuring the repetition of purchases of the product, calls on the service, or visits to a particular store. The creation of a popular brand can also mean market leadership, which means increased revenue through volume sales and/or price leadership. However, the market leadership and, in particular, the price leadership of several individual brands has been challenged by the growth of own-brand goods. Branding is also useful in helping the consumer search for goods. The hope is that over time the consumer will develop value judgements about certain brands and use these as a basis for discriminating between products. In this way the brand becomes representative of a whole bundle of product attributes, such as quality or value for money, and can be a vital element in the selling of products as symbols, as in the above example of Bacardi or

Harrods. In this way certain brands, such as Martini, have always been promoted as offering the potential consumer a lifestyle as well as a product.

A successful brand image can be a great attribute to a company when launching new products and entering new product markets. The new products acquire the favourable attributes of other products belonging to the same brand. Ralph Lauren has used the presence of a strong brand in clothing to extend the product range into bed linen, home furnishings and even furniture. Such brands are sometimes referred to as banner brands. The presence of a strong brand enabled Virgin and Sainsbury to successfully enter a highly competitive financial services sector. In this way, some companies use a single brand for a whole range of products. Branding is, however, valuable for all products, new or otherwise, in that it can add value to the product. It is for this reason that many firms protect their brand names by registering them as trademarks. The registration of a trademark enables its owner to use the law to prevent competitors from using the same or similar brand name or mark for the same type of product or service. This also protects the consumer from being deceived and confused about the origin of the goods.

The added value provided by a brand and the use of the brand as a primary source of competitive advantage is referred to as **brand equity**.

> Brand equity is a set of assets (or liabilities) linked to a brand's name and symbol that adds to (or subtracts from) the value provided by the product or service to a firm and/or that firm's customers. (*Aaker, 1996, p. 7*)

Various attempts have been made to measure brand equity both in financial terms and in terms of the strength of attraction to customers. Apart from being highly subjective, the methods are usually fairly complex. It is also debatable whether a brand in isolation can maintain its value if separated from the organization. Nonetheless, the acquisition of Rowntree by Nestlé is often cited as an example of the power of brand equity. In 1988 Nestlé bought Rowntree for £2.5 billion when the tangible assets were valued at around £1 billion (although the actual sums vary widely depending on the source). The difference between purchase price and asset value is the value to Nestlé of brands such as Kit Kat, Polo Mints and After Eight Mints.

Much attention has been given to the growth of global brands such as Mercedes-Benz, McDonald's, Sony and Häagen Dazs. However, as we see from Case 11.1, even a so-called global brand, such as McDonald's, offers local variations in different parts of the world. Moreover, the same brand can represent different images to different groups. In the 1980s the Audi 100 was launched in Britain under the Audi–Volkswagen brand, doubtless stressing the Volkswagen image of reliability. In the USA the same car, with a few minor adjustments to the trim, became the Audi 5000 and was sold as an Audi–Porsche, capitalizing on the latter's reputation for expensive, fashionable, high-performance cars, and appealing to the large American demand for sports cars. In South Africa the same car was sold mainly as a taxi! (Coleman, 1988).

Branding also has its critics:

- They claim that it misleads consumers by drawing false distinctions between products and directing investment away from product development and into packaging and promotion to maintain the myth of product differentiation.

- Branding is further attacked for its encouragement of status consciousness. For many teenagers a simple pair of training shoes will not suffice; they must be the brand favoured by their peer group at that particular time. It is not just the teenage market that is pursued by firms promoting a particular brand image. Increasingly markets have become highly differentiated and branding can assist in the process of market segmentation. It is to this aspect that we now turn.

Case 11.2

Arsenal Football Club – protecting the brand

Arsenal Football Club (FC) is one of England's leading clubs in the Premier League. They have never been outside the top division in their history, have won several championships, including 2002, play regularly in European competitions and most games attract sell-out audiences of just under 40 000. On match days, as with most leading clubs around the world, the streets near the stadium attract a large number of vendors. These set up stalls selling food and drink and a wide range of merchandise connected to the club. In 2001, a case involving Arsenal FC attracted the attention of the national press. The club had taken legal action against one of the vendors, Matthew Reed, and the case reached the European Court of Justice. Reed, an Arsenal supporter, had been selling merchandise such as shirts, scarves, rosettes and other tokens since 1970. There had been other cases taken by other clubs against such vendors, notably by Manchester United and Tottenham Hotspur. Arsenal had been particularly vigilant since 1993 and this was not the first case brought against Reed.

The case was heard in the English High Court by Justice Laddie in April, 2001. In essence, Arsenal argued that Reed was selling merchandise that was being 'passed off' as Arsenal's own and that Reed was infringing two trademarks registered by Arsenal. The two trademarks were a crest containing the word 'Arsenal', a picture of a cannon (the nickname of Arsenal is the 'Gunners') and a coat of arms and a further trademark of the cannon alone. These marks both appeared on the official Arsenal merchandise and were replicated exactly by Reed on the merchandise that he sold.

Justice Laddie dismissed Arsenal's claim that Reed was 'passing off' on the basis that they were unable to prove that consumers actually believed that the goods came from Arsenal. This was reinforced by a disclaimer placed by Reed on his stalls stating that the goods on sale were not official Arsenal merchandise. Laddie also dismissed the trademark claim. Although Reed had identical marks on identical goods, the court ruled that these were not trademarks, the meaning of which was interpreted as a guarantee to the consumer of the real origin of the goods. Instead, Reed's marks were seen as 'badges of allegiance'. However, the case was referred to the European Court of Justice (ECJ) by Laddie on a point of trademark law.

The ECJ sat in November, 2002. They ruled that it was immaterial that the trademark was used as a 'badge of allegiance' or that a disclaimer was posted. The impression given was that there was a link between Reed's merchandise and Arsenal FC. Furthermore they ruled that the holder of a trademark was entitled to protection. Laddie rejected the conclusion of the ECJ, claiming that they had exceeded their brief by reviewing the facts of the case rather than a point of law. Justice Laddie upheld his original decision against Arsenal and the case may go to appeal.

Reed had been running his business successfully since 1970 and at one stage employed 40 people and covered most London grounds. In recent years he has focused on Arsenal, which accounts for some 90 per cent of his sales. He runs three stalls in the vicinity of the ground with collected takings of around £1500 on Premier League match days and around £3000 on European match nights. Sales exceed £50 000 a year and at one stage Reed actually operated his business inside the stadium.

Arsenal FC registered their trademarks for the crest and the cannon in 1989. Merchandising has been a particular focus of Arsenal FC since 1992. They have a large store, 'Arsenal World of Sport', next to a major tube station in North London and two further stores inside the ground. In addition, there is a substantial mail order business. The range of products is broad, with shirts being the best-selling item. Clothing of all kinds is sold, including baby and children's garments and all kinds of memorabilia. The club has issued licences to other sellers and allows them to display a notice, 'Only official Arsenal merchandise sold here'. They have made several attempts to inform the fans only to buy official merchandise through posted notices and statements in the match-day programme. The merchandising business was worth around £5 million to Arsenal in 2001, compared to £40 million to Manchester United and £15 million to Liverpool.

The case has significant repercussions for other football clubs as well as others, such as pop groups, who derive revenue from the sale of merchandise. The case also raises the legal issue over court jurisdiction and responsibilities and the relationship between European courts and those in member countries.

Source: Royal Courts of Justice, 6 April, 2001; *Daily Telegraph*, 14 June and 13 November, 2002

Questions

1 What arguments can you put forward to support the respective cases of Arsenal FC and Matthew Reed?

2 Why was Arsenal FC so intent on pursuing this case?

Segmentation

Segmentation occurs when the market is broken down along a number of different dimensions. Commonly used segments include geographical location, age groups, gender groups, income groups, occupation groups, social classes, and those groups that may be differentiated according to their lifestyle. An increasing feature of cosmopolitan urban areas is segmentation based on different ethnic groups. Kotler defines a market segment as:

> . . . consumers who respond in a similar way to a given set of marketing stimuli.
> (*Kotler, 1983, p. 40*)

The concept of segmentation is the essence of the marketing concept as identified at the beginning of the chapter: the production of goods and services to meet the specific needs of consumers.

Market segmentation and product differentiation go hand in hand, in that products are designed, developed, promoted, and even priced and distributed with a particular market segment in mind. True segmentation occurs when genuinely different products are made

> ### Key concept 11.6 Segmentation
>
> Segmentation is the process through which the total market is broken down to create distinctive consumer groups. The criteria used to form such groups varies and may include geographical location, social class, occupation, sex, lifestyle, and so on. Once market segments have been identified, products can be developed which focus upon a particular group in an attempt to maximize both the marketing effort and the needs of consumers. Some firms specialize in catering for the needs of a particular segment only, while others produce a range of products each aimed at different segments of the same market. In this case, the branding of each product becomes especially important to distinguish it from the others. The process of broadening the segments to which a product might appeal, or changing the market segment altogether, is known as repositioning.

for the different market segments. However, segmentation is not just a feature of products, it also encompasses all aspects of the marketing mix. In 1971, Coca Cola offered a global product using a global promotion campaign, emphasizing a unified world with the slogan, 'I'd like to teach the world to sing in perfect harmony'. Here was a case of an undifferentiated product promoted in an undifferentiated way. In 1993 Coca Cola, in the face of increasing competition especially from own brands, changed its approach. The company launched a promotional campaign, which varied its approach and techniques to appeal to different segments, differentiated by age, culture, social class and lifestyle. From 1993–7, world sales of Coca Cola rose by 21 per cent (*Financial Times*, 5 May, 1997).

Segmentation is an increasing feature of marketing, as the following illustration of the holiday industry will show. Many package tour holiday companies originally promoted all their holidays in a single brochure, leaving the consumer to select the most appropriate holiday from the entire range offered. In 1999, Thomson Holidays offered holidays under 15 different Thomson-labelled brands, each aimed at a different market. The main brochure 'Thomson Summer Sun' caters for the mass market, but the 'À la Carte' holidays aim to capture those groups with a higher disposable income and a different lifestyle. Lifestyle is also an important consideration in the 'Ski', 'Small and Friendly', 'Sports Resorts' and 'All Inclusive' brochures. Income differentiation is a feature of 'Faraway Shores' and 'Platinum Collection', while age and family size are reflected in 'Young at Heart' for the older market and 'Superfamily' for budget-conscious families seeking activities for children. Thomson also owns other brands which are sold under different banners to attract different markets. 'Club Freestyle' is aimed at the 18–30 market and a whole range of 'Simply' holidays, based on different country locations, offer largely self-catering accommodation in more select locations to a mainly middle-class market.

While few holiday companies aim to match Thomson for product differentiation, others do target specific markets. Saga has always designed its holidays and cruises for the older age groups and marketed them accordingly. While its products are aimed at a growing market, the company recognized that an increasing proportion of that market were fitter and more active than the previous generation and did not wish to be associated with 'an older generation'. In 1999 the company attempted to change its image and broaden its market position by offering products to over-50s, emphasizing attractive lifestyle holidays.

Not all such product differentiation is motivated solely by the desire to cater for consumer needs. The growth of the winter holiday market is undoubtedly related to affluence and changing lifestyles. It is also related to the hotel owner and tour operator's desire to utilize capacity all the year round. In some cases, winter holidays are aggressively promoted and attractively priced to push up market demand. In this case some segments, such as the retired population, are especially singled out.

So far we have focused upon consumer goods and services, but segmentation is a feature of industrial goods as well. Many engineering companies in the components industry have successfully targeted specific groups and tailored their products accordingly. As we saw in Chapter 4, Japanese companies often forge very close relationships with their suppliers, although this is more a case of the segment defining the product rather than the manufacturer targeting a segment.

An important strategic decision in marketing is the determination of the most appropriate segments for the marketing effort. There would appear to be three broad options:

- a single or a small range of products or services is offered for a single segment or limited range of segments;
- many products and services are offered to many different market segments;
- a single product or service is offered for an undifferentiated mass market.

The choice will depend on a range of factors, including whether the segment can be accurately identified; if it is large enough to be profitable, can it be served within certain cost constraints and, of course, management goals.

A truly undifferentiated product is a rarity. A fairly ordinary product, such as a can of baked beans, is offered in a number of variations, with various added ingredients, such as sausages or with less salt and sugar (a variation aimed at health conscious consumers). As we saw in the case of Coca Cola, an undifferentiated product can still be offered in different ways to different market segments. In addition, the same product can be offered at different prices to different segments in different places. A bottle of Scotch whisky can be bought at one price in a neighbourhood wine store, yet the same bottle can cost four times as much when bought via room service in an up-market hotel. The premium charged is a function of the added service element but it is also based on the knowledge that the type of clientele at such a hotel will probably perceive price as a less important factor than convenience. All these examples show how different aspects of the marketing mix can be manipulated for different segments of the market.

Aiming for a limited market segment can be a highly successful strategy. This is shown by such holiday companies as Abercrombie and Kent, who operate at the high-price end of the market, or specialist tour operators such as Safari Consultants, who put together tailor-made packages in more remote parts of Africa. Such a strategy can be restricting, and once a certain market size and share have been reached the company may need new products and markets to continue growing. Mothercare recognized this by extending its market to cater for older children as well as its original market of baby and maternity wear. Kuoni, in an attempt to capture a younger market, launched a group of holidays using cheaper accommodation and has made other attempts to widen its appeal. A deliberate attempt to change its market segment was adopted as a survival strategy by the British motorcycle industry in the mid-1970s. Faced with overwhelming competition from Japanese bikes, the British industry continually retreated up-market, ultimately to be defeated in that segment as well by the Japanese. The British manufacturers went for an inappropriate segmentation strategy and might have been more successful had they invested in the process technology to manufacture reliable, low-cost, mass-produced bikes. This interrelationship of marketing, product development and process technology recurs in our discussion of the product life-cycle and marketing strategy.

A differentiated product range serving different markets has long since been the strategy followed by major car producers. As we saw in the car industry case in Chapter 1, the product development and acquisition strategy of the major players is often informed by a desire to extend their range and reach new segments. Thus Ford acquires Jaguar and Volvo, while Mercedes launches a small town car and new sports model. Such strategies are pursued also by firms operating in the service industry. Building societies, for instance, offer a range of investment plans to suit the needs of different groups, often at different stages in their lives and careers.

However, excessive segmentation can pose problems and it has been referred to as 'marketing mania' (Levitt, 1975). The development, production, promotion and administrative costs associated with product differentiation can render excessive segmentation an expensive strategy, particularly where minor product changes result in major process adjustments. Differentiation may be a strategy for survival in a declining market, as shown by Orlake Records in the 1980s (Case 10.3), but the strategy may not always work. The willingness of the British textile and steel industries to take on any order, whatever its size, led to dramatic cost increases and merely hastened the decline of those industries, when product concentration might have been a more appropriate strategy.

Overall, segmentation would appear to offer more benefits than costs. The following can be listed as the advantages of segmentation:

- It can assist in market penetration by catering more precisely to the needs of a particular group than competitors.
- Knowledge of the most appropriate segments for targeting products and services can lead to competitive gains.
- Knowledge gained of a particular sector of the market can assist a company in the development of new products for that sector.
- Products developed for one segment can be adapted to be attractive to other groups.
- Targeting can make more efficient use of a firm's resources.

The issue of resources in segmentation is a theme taken up by Piercy (1997). He believes that a successful segmentation strategy is based on its facilitation by the organizational structure and culture. He argues that effective segmentation depends partly on the ability of the firm to organize itself so that different segments are 'owned' by different groups. He argues further that segments need to be compatible with the values of members of the organization, and that the movement into new market segments can threaten the *status quo* and existing power relations within the organization.

An important element of segmentation is **positioning**. This refers not only to choosing the correct market segment for your product but also to finding the appropriate niche in that market, to differentiate it from its competitors on such matters as price and quality. **Repositioning** occurs when the same product is offered to a different group, either to combat falling sales or as a general growth strategy. This was successfully achieved by Guinness who, in the 1970s, aimed their promotion at the younger drinker with highly successful results. Manikin cigars attempted the same ploy but were less than successful.

The new target market found the cigar too strong for their taste, while the original market disliked the new style of promotion.

The product life-cycle

The **product life-cycle** assumes that all products have limited lives during which they pass through a series of stages, all of which have implications for sales and profitability. The classic life-cycle is depicted by four phases as presented in Figure 11.2. The concept can apply equally to services as well as manufactured goods. Shaving was once a popular service offered by barber shops. With the introduction of safety razors and easy-to-apply shaving cream the need for the service declined. The growth of the unisex hairdresser salon led to a further decline in the number of traditional barber shops. However, by the mid- to late-1990s male grooming had become a highly profitable business and there emerged a small number of male-only hairdressing salons, offering shaving as one of the services. In this way the product life-cycle is revived through the repositioning of the product.

- During the introduction phase sales are slow as both consumers and distributors become aware of the product and decide whether to adopt it. The costs of development and promotion are high and firms may suffer initial losses.
- During the growth phase there is a rapid acceptance of the product and a dramatic increase in sales. This is generally sustained by improved distribution, product improvements and even price reductions. There are normally high profits for pioneering firms but a growing market attracts competitors, leading to brand differentiation. While the production learning curve may lead to a reduction in costs, the need to satisfy an expanding market can involve costly investment in new production processes. The end of this phase is marked by a high level of competition, recognized by Wasson (1978) as a separate phase, which he termed 'competitive turbulence'.

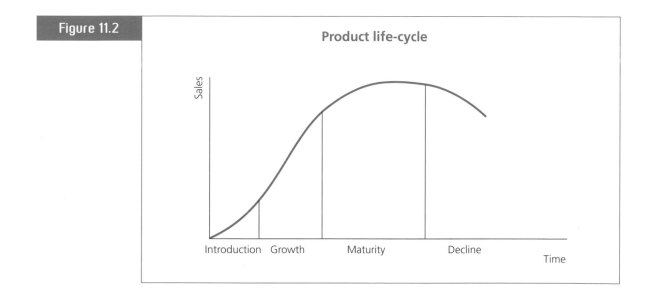

Figure 11.2   Product life-cycle

- As it becomes saturated the market reaches maturity. Sales and profits are still high but there tends to be considerable investment in maintaining sales. This is achieved through product changes, increased promotional activity and price cutting. Products are sometimes re-launched at this stage, usually with new features, different packaging and often an attempt to create a new image. Firms seek to maintain brand loyalty at the same time as attempting to broaden the market by repositioning. At this stage, the less competitive firms drop from the product market.

- The decline phase is marked by a falling off in sales and, while some firms do well as others leave the market, survival is often dependent upon successful product diversification.

The product life-cycle can be useful as a framework for planning a marketing campaign over time and as an indication that marketing strategies need to be adjusted to match changes in the cycle. There is an implicit assumption that careful marketing policies can do much to slow down the cycle of decline, i.e. the cycle may be manipulated by the marketing mix. An understanding of the life-cycles of a range of products may be an important factor in determining the introduction of new products and ensuring that the product mix is well represented at the introductory, growth and maturity stages. A company has significant problems if its entire product range is in the decline phase at the same time.

The utility of the product life-cycle has been questioned on several counts.

- First, it is a gross simplification of the behaviour of markets and seems to ignore changes in the economy, the actions of competitors and governments, and even dramatic swings in consumer fashion.

- Second, the cycle is highly variable for different products, in both the length of time it takes to reach the decline stage and the amount of time spent in each phase. The path for any product is extremely difficult to plot and the model is therefore a poor guide to marketing strategy.

- Third, even if we accept that the model is descriptive of a general process, it may be difficult to assess when a product has reached a particular stage. A temporary rise or fall in sales may be mistaken for a fundamental shift in the cycle, so that action taken is inappropriate at that time.

- Fourth, the model is criticized for ignoring the production implications of a changing market position.

Each stage of the product life-cycle has implications for the design of the product, the volume and variety of production, and the nature of the process of manufacture or delivery of the service to the customer. In manufacturing, the product life-cycle is closely related to a process life-cycle. The introductory stage of the product life-cycle is marked by a highly flexible production process. As markets reach their maximum potential the capacity can only be met by relatively inflexible mass production systems. The cost of such systems necessitates a high market demand and long production runs. There is a similarity here with the 'revised sequence' (Galbraith, 1972), discussed earlier in this chapter. In this situation, marketing becomes production led rather than demand led. However, in the case of manufactured goods, the relationship between the product and process life-cycles has been complicated by the introduction of flexible manufacturing systems (see the discussion in Chapter 10).

The environmental aspects of marketing

Marketing, probably more than any other of the business functions we have dealt with, operates at the interface between the firm and its environment. We will see in this section how marketing activities are not only influenced by environmental factors but that the management manipulation of the 4 Ps represents a deliberate attempt to shape consumer behaviour and hence the market environment within which the firm operates. Marketing strategy is, therefore, a key element in the corporate strategy of any organization. We will view the relationship of marketing with the environment of the firm by looking in turn at the economy, the role of the state and consumer interest groups, technology and, finally, cultural and social factors.

Marketing and the economy

For some, marketing as a subject has emerged as a branch of applied economics, and economic theory is used as the basis for the development of marketing strategies. Marketing activity is influenced by economic factors in a number of different ways, as the following illustrations reveal:

- Major economic shifts, as in the case of manufacturing to service industry, have brought about new directions in marketing.
- The entry of new firms into the market place, especially in the form of overseas competition, may necessitate a change in marketing strategy for existing firms to retain their market share. In general terms, the greater the degree of competition, the greater the use of a wide range of marketing tools.
- In more monopolistic markets, individual firms wield considerable power in terms of the product offering, price and distribution. This is why, in some cases, as with public utilities like gas, water and electricity, regulatory bodies are established to protect consumer interest.
- A feature of oligopolistic competition is a tendency towards similarity of product design and price, as illustrated by car manufacturers and petrol companies.

Most societies are marked by an **uneven distribution of wealth and income**. Companies may, therefore, offer a range of goods and services reflecting such segmentation in the market place.

The **general level of economic activity** has an impact upon marketing activity in a number of different ways.

- In times of prosperity, when demand is high, price becomes less of a factor, particularly in the purchase of luxury goods and services.
- In a recession, when demand falls, the emphasis usually shifts to issues of product utility and value for money. Falling demand may call for price reductions, attempts to broaden the market by appealing to new segments or diversifying into new areas of activity.
- In economically depressed areas, attempts by the unemployed to set up shops are often doomed to failure owing to the low levels of demand in that area. Where demand is so low, little in the way of marketing strategy can change the basic position.

- Changing rates of inflation together with the level of economic activity will affect savings and the availability of credit. Where price inflation rises at a faster rate than wage inflation the demand for certain luxury goods may fall. Some firms combat this by offering favourable credit terms to customers in an attempt to boost sales.

- Expenditure on advertising is often seen as an indicator of the economic health of a nation. A recession in the UK during 2001 and 2002 affected advertising revenues. Overall expenditure on advertising fell by 11 per cent in 2001, with television most affected. Most televison companies reduced their slot prices by 13 per cent. The situation became even worse in 2002 with the advertising industry taking its worst cuts for 50 years.

These illustrations show how marketing strategy has often reacted to changes in the economy. However, many firms will attempt to **manipulate the economy through its marketing activities**. In Chapter 9 we examined the link between levels of investment in new product development and economic growth at both the level of the firm and nationally. We have seen that one of the functions of promotional activities is to persuade consumers and hence attempt to manipulate demand. We have noted several times in this book how very large companies, especially those operating globally, are able to manipulate markets to their advantage through product development, pricing and promotional strategies in such a way as to affect national economies.

While the relationship between marketing and the economy is significant, we saw in our discussion of price elasticity that economic theory has its limitations in our understanding of marketing behaviour, ignoring as it does a range of important cultural, social and psychological influences. Political and pressure group influences also play a part and it is to these we now turn.

Marketing and the role of the state

The state represents a powerful presence in the market place as a dominant employer, supplier and purchaser. We have already noted the increases in government advertising expenditure. Since the 1980s both privatization and deregulation in the UK have changed the marketing environment. The state is involved in marketing in a number of different ways:

- The state provides information on government policy.

- Advertising is often used to direct the behaviour of individuals, as in the case of health education, or to encourage the unemployed to take advantage of training schemes.

- The pricing and promotional policies of state-controlled industries can be used to direct public expenditure and consumption, as was the case with energy. The potential for the government direction of markets in this way is considerable. In reality, particularly in the example of the energy industry, the actual control was often diluted through the absence of an effective coordinating policy. In terms of the present energy industry in the UK, the emphasis has shifted to the establishment of controls for non-private organizations.

- The state attempts to regulate the marketing activity of private firms in a number of different ways. Most of these measures are aimed at regulating free competition and protecting individual consumers and the environment. The majority of the examples are taken from the UK.

- In terms of product development in the UK, the British Standards Institute (BSI) has devised technical standards to which products should comply to ensure minimum standards of quality, and to protect both the consumer and the environment against the potentially dangerous product.
- We have seen in Chapter 9 that the granting of patents gives inventors a monopoly to market their products in return for making their invention public. The aim of such legislation is both to reward and stimulate innovation.
- Through its law relating to monopolies and mergers the state attempts to define and prevent unfair competition. In the UK this is controlled by the Competition Commission (formerly the Monopolies and Mergers Commission). In the USA it comes under the legal framework of the Sherman Anti-Trust Laws.
- The abolition of resale price maintenance under The Resale Prices Act 1977 has loosened the control of major manufacturers over the market place and so protected the consumer from unfair business practices.
- The Trade Descriptions Act 1968–72 tackled the problems of deception in advertising and sales promotion.
- The Sale of Goods Act 1893 and The Supply of Goods (Implied Terms) Act 1972 set out the contractual rights of consumers on such issues as the return of goods and warranty.
- Many governments attempt to limit the advertising of certain types of products such as cigarettes and alcohol.
- Britain's membership of the EU means that firms are subject to a range of further regulations affecting firms and consumers alike, as with the pricing of agricultural produce or the description of products when promoting them for the European market. The Consumer Protection Act of 1987 was, in part, an implementation of EU policy on product liability and price information.

Government intervention in the marketing activity of private firms is a very complex issue, no better illustrated than in the case of cigarette advertising. In 1997 the British government attempted to place a ban on all cigarette advertising. The proposals were met with intense lobbying by a number of interested parties. For a number of years there has been a ban on the television advertising of tobacco products. This had led to the tobacco companies seeking alternative forms of promotion, notably the use of billboard advertising and sports sponsorship. Firms controlling advertising sites and billboards naturally objected to a complete ban. In any case, the billboard advertising of tobacco was already restricted by the government to 30 per cent of the 1980 total. The biggest opposition came from sports bodies, especially those with an interest in Formula One motor racing. This is a very expensive sport that derives significant revenue from cigarette companies, with brands such as Marlboro sponsoring a successful racing team. In 2004 Grand Prix events have been withdrawn from countries, like Canada, that have imposed a ban on cigarette advertising. Successful lobbying earned the ban a reprieve in the UK.

Consumerism

The concept of **consumerism** has developed in the past 30 years around four tenets:

- the right of the consumer to be informed
- the right to choose

- the right of redress
- the right of safety.

If we accept that marketing is nothing more than the effective satisfaction of consumer needs and wants, then consumerism would, in fact, be synonymous with marketing and the presence of organized consumer groups would be no more than an important source of information and market research. The consumer movement has, however, developed as a political interest group to represent the rights of consumers, largely because those rights are seen to be threatened by the marketing activity of many firms. It is interesting to see Baker (1991) deal with consumerism as 'marketing under attack'.

The crusades against dangerous products, by people such as the American Ralph Nader, and the growth and success in Britain of organizations, such as The Consumers' Association and The Campaign For Real Ale, have raised the public awareness of consumer issues. At the same time, magazines such as *What Car?* and the popularity of consumer programmes on television and radio have fed the public need for information. Consumer information exists to satisfy a need but, like marketing promotion itself, it has created an even greater need. The number of consumer magazines has proliferated. Most national newspapers now give significant editorial space to consumer matters and concern themselves with a range of consumer issues, from testing new cars and bottles of wine, to offering advice on financial matters, to highlighting sharp practice in the business world.

Key concept 11.7 Consumerism

Consumerism has developed as a social movement to inform and assist consumer choice and to act as a pressure group to represent the interests of consumers. These interests are represented to organizations in an attempt to influence product design, price and distribution. Consumer interest groups also act as watchdogs to guard against unsafe products and dishonest producers. That consumers are now more aware and better informed is due largely to the activities of consumer groups and the publicity given to consumer matters over the past 30 or so years.

As well as feeding off its own publicity and success, the growth of consumerism is often related to the factors identified below:

- The public needs protection against the effects of dangerous products. A series of articles in the USA trade press and newspapers during the 1970s, focused the public's attention on the large number of fatal accidents involving Ford Pinto cars: all a direct result of the location of the petrol tank. The pressure was such that Ford withdrew the model.
- The public needs protection against the dishonest behaviour of some producers. In the UK, the growth of fierce competition in the home improvements market has resulted in the Office of Fair Trading receiving a number of complaints about such firms misleading the public about the true cost of credit. The Financial Services Act 1987 emerged partly to protect consumers by regulating those firms dealing with such matters as investment, insurance and pensions; several complaints had been received that investment returns were less than promised and costs were much

higher than expected. Strict rules now operate for the promotion of investment and pension plans.

- The growth of pressure groups, like The Campaign For Real Ale, is a reaction to the monopoly power wielded by the main producers in a particular industry. The brewing industry was moving towards a market dominance by a handful of producers and the gradual elimination of beer brewed by traditional methods in favour of a product that was more easily stored and transported. The campaign not only brought pressure against the major producers to produce more 'real' ale but was successful, with the aid of considerable media coverage, in creating a much greater public demand for that product.

- Consumers themselves are better educated, more affluent and, largely because of the growth of the consumer press, more informed. The result has been increased expectations and demand for products of a higher quality. While this is probably true for all consumers, the growth of consumerism is undoubtedly a middle-class phenomenon closely related to the degree of affluence of particular consumer groups.

In some cases consumer pressure has been spectacularly successful. Environmental groups in Europe enlisted considerable public support to oppose Shell's dumping of its oil platform, Brent Spar, in deep water in the North Sea. The lobby caused Shell to rethink its actions. In more general terms, the consumer movement has been influential in broadening public awareness of consumer matters and bringing about a range of protective legislation. In many cases this has led to improved goods and services and more effective marketing. There are still those who feel that the consumer lobby needs to go much further to protect the rights of consumers, while others, particularly in business, may resent the influence of consumer groups on governments, fearing that excessive regulation may stifle innovation.

Marketing and technology

Marketing and technology interact in a number of different ways:

- We have seen in Chapter 9 the process of product design and development and its protection through the patent system. We also noted that marketing was an essential vehicle for the information and promotion of new products and processes.

- In our discussion of the product life-cycle we identified the clear relationship between process technology and levels of demand. It is no good management using product development, pricing and promotional strategies to increase demand if that demand cannot be met by the existing production system. The development of computerized stock systems provides greater information and access for both buyer and seller.

- Developments in technology have had significant impact upon the marketing process itself. Among the most obvious aids to marketing have been the developments that have taken place in mass distribution. A range of developments has taken place in retailing to simplify the process of purchase. The system of 'electronic funds transfer at the point of sale' (EFTPOS) may well, together with the credit card, obviate the need for cash. A wide range of goods may now be bought over the telephone using credit cards for payment, and some firms have set up computer databases of suppliers willing to offer such goods to consumers at highly competitive prices. The fax machine is used by theatres and restaurants to target potential customers. In the late 1990s we witnessed a trading revolution through the use of the Internet (a fuller discussion of e-commerce can be found in Chapter 3 and an illustration of its use in Case 11.3).

- Developments in transport have not only improved distribution systems but enabled consumers to access a wider range of goods. The transnational or even transcontinental shopping trip is commonplace. Cross-channel routes are full in the weeks leading up to Christmas, as UK residents travel to France to access cheaper beer, wine and spirits and other goods. Large stores in many cities around the world attempt to attract the foreign shopper. The tourist authorities in Dubai have designated a shopping month to attract even more visitors to its shops, hotels and restaurants.

| Case 11.3 | **The growth of telemarketing in flower sales** |

At first glance the market for cut flowers would seem to be the province of a large number of small outlets. The reality is a highly competitive market, dominated by a small number of organizations such as Interflora in the UK and 1–800-Flowers in the USA. The business of selling and distributing cut flowers has been one of high growth and profitability. A major reason for that growth lies in the choice they offer the customer in terms of marketing channel and the widening of that choice through the increased use of telephone sales and the Internet.

The four main customer requirements would appear to be easy access, the ability of the business to meet a variety of target prices, fast delivery and the availability of expert advice. These requirements are met by three main channels. The flower shop provides expert advice and offers the customer the opportunity to choose a particular arrangement first hand. This channel is important when customers are concerned to pick the flowers themselves or when they wish to take the flowers as a gift, as in the case of hospital visits or as a token when invited to someone's home. The flower shop may be preferred when buying flowers for oneself. Telesales, either through a call centre or a shop, still offer the opportunity to obtain expert advice, but this method may simply be more convenient, as when sending flowers as a thankyou gift or to commemorate someone's birthday or anniversary. Such a method, while saving a visit to a flower shop, does carry a handling and delivery charge. A more recent development has been the opportunity to buy and organize the delivery of flowers through the Internet. The advantage of this channel lies in its speed, easy accessibility of product and price information, and convenience. The Internet is also used by some organizations, such as Interflora, as a means of making more sales. Such organizations offer an e-mail service to remind people of key dates such as birthdays and anniversaries. The service is usually free and inevitably accompanied by an easy means of ordering flowers for immediate delivery.

In the UK, the largest operator is Interflora. This is an international organization trading as FTD in the USA, Canada and Japan and as Fleurop in parts of Europe. Interflora is a non-profit trade association owned by its members. These comprise over 58 000 florist shops across 146 countries. The members elect the company board from among their constituents and the board members serve for a fixed period before they are replaced. Interflora trades not only in flowers, but also chocolates and other similar gifts. The company aims to provide a seamless service to customers and prides itself on its responsiveness and innovation. The company has grown largely on the basis of telephone sales made by customers to individual shops. In the case of a delivery outside the area the florist will check the nearest Interflora member to the delivery address and pass on the order. This process used to be carried out exclusively by telephone, but the company has introduced a computerized system linking many of the member shops. There has been a recent growth in Internet business but the telephone is still the main source of orders by far.

Teleflorist is the second largest UK organization behind Interflora and operates in much the same way. However, Flowers Direct, another growing firm in the UK market, operates in a different fashion. This is a privately owned company that uses few intermediaries. Flowers Direct claims an advantage over Interflora through the operation of a 24-hour call centre. It sells and delivers not through shops but via a central warehouse and the use of couriers to deliver the flowers. Like Interflora and Teleflorist, it offers an international delivery service.

1–800-Flowers is a USA company and, at a consistent annual growth rate of 25 per cent maintained over the past few years, is claimed by many as one of the fastest-growing companies in any market. Initially a private company specializing in flowers, 1–800-Flowers made a private equity placement in May 1999 and began share trading on Nasdaq in August, 1999. Its product range has widened to include a large range of garden products, including furniture, home décor items, speciality foods and, most recently, a range of gourmet foods. The company has its own headquarters and central staff, some of which specialize in market research to develop new product ranges and also to monitor quality and service standards. The company operates its own call centres and has its own shops branded as Bloomnet. Despite having its own shops, the majority of trading is carried out through partner florists, which number over 1500. The company started with telephone sales and direct sales through its own outlets. Internet sales, while only 15 per cent of the total for 1998–9, increased 85 per cent on the previous year and are viewed by the company as its major focus for the future. The company launched its website in 1995, which is not only used to promote and sell its products, but is also used to announce job vacancies and invite applications.

Sources: Company information from Interflora and 1–800-Flowers; Friedman and Furey, 1999

Questions

1 What advantages do telephone sales and Internet sales offer in the flowers and associated products market?
2 What are the disadvantages of telephone and Internet sales in this market?
3 Why are telephone sales more popular than Internet sales? Is this likely to change in the future and what would be the advantages and obstacles for both the sellers and buyers?

The role of cultural and social influences in marketing

In our discussion of segmentation we suggested that markets were increasingly segmented and the marketing effort was correspondingly targeted at specific groups. Invariably the basis for such segmentation is social and cultural. Differences within societies and between culturally distinctive groups have resulted in different patterns of product adoption. The popularity of a product among one cultural or social group is no guarantee that it will appeal to another, totally different group. Despite the expansion of international travel, the food preferences of different cultural groups can vary widely. For example, the durian is one of the most popular fruits in South-East Asia, yet its taste and smell are unpleasant to many Westerners. However, marketing does not simply react to social and cultural differences, it is actively used to promote products. Using the aspiration of one group in society to acquire the lifestyle of another group is a common theme in advertising. The growth of the teenage market is both a reflection of changing social values and a deliberate creation by producers actively seeking new business opportunities. As with other aspects of our model, the influences are invariably two-way with marketing acting as both a product and a cause of social change. Several social and cultural factors illustrate our point.

Changing demographic patterns relating to age, sex, location and, naturally, incomes may have a profound effect upon marketing. An ageing population in many Western industrial societies has opened up new marketing opportunities in such industries as tourism and in general focused the attention of marketers towards a sector they had previously seldom considered. Geographical shifts in population may have a considerable impact upon consumer demand and property prices. Rising property prices in London and the south east of England has had a knock-on effect on the property market of surrounding areas. This has manifested itself in changes in the types of new property being built, house prices and the way that property is promoted by estate agents. Small terraced housing in areas within commuting distance of London become desirable cottage residences, tempting the buyer with dreams of country living. Such changes also have an impact on the marketing of public transport systems.

Values and attitudes are important influences on the marketing process. Core cultural values, such as family life and concern for children, are constantly used in advertising, and marketing specialists take care not to transgress such social mores. An interesting variation to this is shown in Case 11.1. In 1993, McDonald's in Singapore launched a new product, the Kiasu Burger. Both the naming of the product and the accompanying promotion poked fun at a particular cultural characteristic of Singaporeans. However, the ensuing success of the product would indicate that this was taken in good part by the local population.

Reference groups, such as experts, peers, social classes, and those groups portraying a desired lifestyle, are frequently used in marketing communication as mechanisms of attitude change. This would seem to operate across all cultures. In many countries in South-East Asia a highly visible rich elite, who often favour Western and Japanese goods, are used as important trendsetters for the aspiring middle-classes and play their part in cultural change. In countries such as Singapore and Malaysia, the shopping mall has not only replaced small, traditional local shops; a visit to the city-centre shopping malls has become an important leisure activity for the local population.

Advertising, in particular, uses and builds upon social attitudes, as the following examples show. Ford in the USA sold the German-built Lincoln-Mercury Scorpio as 'imported from Germany for select dealers', while for many years in the UK Rover have promoted their cars as a product of British technology being driven by German businessmen. Both promotions used the widely-held belief that the Germans develop superior technical products. The Americans use this value directly in their advertising. Rover, on the other hand, appear to be promoting the superiority of British technology, yet the promotion is based on the credibility of German technical know-how and the use of Germans as 'expert witnesses'.

Lasserre and Schütte (1999) cite the case of Club Med's attempts to sell holidays to the Japanese. The company had traditionally sold its holidays on the image of easy-going resorts and the emphasis on simple pleasure seeking. They found little interest in the Japanese market until they stressed the opportunity for holidaymakers to learn and participate in organized sporting activities. In Case 11.4 we examine several dimensions of cultural difference and the associated problems in the early days of Disneyland Paris.

Such cultural stereotyping has benefited the Germans considerably as exporters of manufactured goods, and they have been especially successful with more technical products such as machine tools. Japan, on the other hand, had to overcome damaging negative stereotyping, which saw its exported goods in the 1920s and 1930s as cheap, imitative products (Wilkinson, 1983). The cultural stereotyping extends to the role of marketing itself and the emphasis placed on different elements of the marketing mix. The Germans are noted for their emphasis on product development and careful targeting, while the Americans are noted for their emphasis on promotional activities and selling. In Japan, spending on advertising is almost four times that in the UK (Czinkota and Ronkainen, 1995). This is undoubtedly driven by the focus in Japan, not on consumer research but on market growth and incremental product development. In Japanese consumer markets, competition is rarely based on price but on product differentiation and service.

However, as with all stereotyping we should always remember that the differences which exist within a country are often greater than those between countries. Equally the situation can change, not just culturally but economically as well. In Japan the recession of the 1990s has led to increased price competition and in many cities there has been the growth of discount stores. The younger buyer in Japan is more attracted to Western products that reflect individualism than the more traditional older population and is more likely to buy on credit.

The organizational aspects of marketing

We have already dealt with several organizational issues elsewhere in this chapter. In examining the different orientations to marketing we saw how marketing goals have developed over time and how much they vary between organizations. Several references have been made to the impact of organizational size on marketing. We have noted that increasing size has led to increasing specialization within the marketing function and how the costs associated with the various marketing activities have acted as barriers to entry, favouring big business in the achievement of market dominance. As was noted in Chapter 5, there is increasing recognition that so-called 'excellent' companies are built around clearly defined cultures. An important element of such organizational cultures is a close identification with the needs of the customer.

In this section we will focus on structural issues pertaining to marketing, dealing first with the way the function is organized and second with the relationships between the marketing and other functional areas.

The organization of marketing

Marketing was initially viewed as being synonymous with sales. With the growth of the firm and the development of its markets came the problems of organizing the sales force, often achieved by creating sales territories operating under a hierarchy of district and regional managers. The need for improved market research and sales promotion created research and advertising units as sub-divisions of the sales department.

The growth of increasingly complex markets, the emergence of large organizations and changing attitudes by management towards consumers all called for corresponding developments in the functional organization of business activities. Marketing emerged as a function in its own right, with the previously dominant sales department as a subsidiary activity. The marketing effort now spawned further specialisms in advertising, sales promotion and market research, and some marketing departments also assumed responsibility for new product development. In the larger organizations, marketing management became the coordination of a range of specialist marketing activities.

This functional organization of marketing mirrored functional developments occurring elsewhere in the firm, but some companies were experimenting with other forms of organizational structure. As we saw in Chapter 5, in our discussion of structure, divisionalization occurred because some firms such as GM found it most appropriate to organize around products or markets. The marketing efforts in many organizations went down the same route. Piercy and Morgan (1993) take up this theme of structure following strategy and see product market segmentation as the basis of organization structure that, if it is in harmony with the needs of the market, is a source of competitive advantage.

Forms of structural arrangement in marketing

Product management   In the 1920s Proctor and Gamble developed the concept of **product management**. Under this arrangement the firm is organized around its products and each brand or group of brands has its own manager. Such a structural arrangement may be necessary where product knowledge is highly technical, or where the firm is dealing in totally different product markets. The benefits that may be gained by management from such an arrangement include an increased knowledge of the product market and an ability to respond quickly to changing market demands. A healthy internal competition can be built up, leading to increased sales. Furthermore, product management has often been a good training ground for aspiring senior managers, as it interfaces with most aspects of the firm's operation. The customer gains by dealing with people who have real product knowledge. Product and brand management can be costly ways of organizing the marketing effort. Specialist activities, such as advertising, may be unnecessarily duplicated, or product managers may lack expertise in the more specialized areas of marketing. In firms where every brand has its own manager there may be over-staffing of management at the lower and middle levels, with the ensuing problems of career progression.

Organize around markets   An alternative structural arrangement would be to specialize around different markets. The markets may be differentiated geographically, by industry, or even by customer. In consumer marketing some form of geographical specialization is a fairly traditional approach. Sales forces have tended towards regional organization for ease of administration and control, and television advertising is invariably regional. The

USA firm Colgate-Palmolive derives the larger part of its sales revenue and profits from overseas activities and traditionally has based its organization on individual country operations linked through a regional structure. Staff mobility within this structure has been viewed as an essential part of career development within the company. More recently, Colgate-Palmolive, in its expansion into the emerging markets of Indonesia, China and Eastern Europe, has established a centralized division to deal specifically with emerging markets issues alongside its traditional structures (Rosenzweig, 1995).

Industry or customer focus   It is in the marketing to organizations, with the prospect of high-volume, high-value orders, that specialization by industry or by customer is regarded as a factor in increasing sales. The Xerox Information Systems Group switched from selling by product to selling by industry, and organized its marketing efforts accordingly. The advantages of this approach lie in building up a close relationship with individual customers and gaining insights into their operations. Some firms operating in the computer market, like IBM and Digital, offer a consulting service to potential customers. This has led to improvements in the customer's own operating systems and potentially more sales for the computer company. Gaining experience of the customers' operating problems and their marketing environment is often invaluable to the process of developing new products. Such a structure would seem most appropriate where the market is becoming increasingly competitive and there are long-term advantages to be gained from building up such close relationships with customers.

Outsourcing to agencies   The past 40 years have seen the growth of advertising agencies. Some, like Saatchi and Saatchi, have achieved a very high public profile as the creators of the Conservative Party's early successful election campaigns. Specialist agencies also operate in market research and sales promotion. The advantages of **outsourcing** to an agency lie in its ability to stand back and offer an independent assessment of the firm's marketing activities, to offer specialist expertise, which the company may not possess, and to act as a source of fresh ideas.

Dealing with outside agencies can be a costly exercise and may be a potential source of conflict. In fact, any structural differentiation within the marketing function itself may set up internal conflicts. Brand differentiation and management may create competition but that same competition has the potential for unhealthy conflict. Tensions can exist between marketing management who direct operations and the sales force who must carry them out. Much wider tensions can exist in the relationship between marketing and the other functional areas as we see in the next section.

As seen in Chapter 5, organization structures rarely conform to ideal models. Many firms have marketing departments that display elements of all the structural variations identified above. A system of brand management can be backed up by a centralized research or advertising function. The marketing effort can be organized according to different industrial markets but may be further differentiated according to product. The system is further complicated in that marketing departments frequently use agencies external to the firm.

Marketing and other functions

The stereotype view of the relationship between marketing and operations is one of conflict. Operations staff view marketing staff as people who make their life difficult through promises to customers that are difficult to meet. For its part, the marketing department sees operations staff as inflexible and more concerned with the efficiency of their own systems rather than satisfying customer needs. Such myths have some basis in fact. Historically, the two functions have been evaluated according to different criteria. Marketing personnel have tended to be rewarded for achieving a high sales turnover and a high market share, while the primary orientation of operations has been towards the achievement of minimum cost and a smooth operation flow. The marketing staff have been encouraged to create change by developing new opportunities, while the operations staff have tended to resist any change that increases costs. Moreover, the cultures of the two groups have traditionally differed. Marketing specialists tend to deal with vague concepts like image and customer preference and have their focus outside the organization, while operations staff tend to be internally focused and more comfortable dealing with the quantifiable.

Such conflict is not necessarily dysfunctional. Persuading customers to adopt standardized goods and services may enable the firm to offer a better service as well as reducing costs. Where conflict is disruptive it may be tackled in a number of different ways. Management might consider different reward criteria. Marketing staff could be rewarded for accurate forecasts rather than meeting some artificially contrived quota and operations staff rewarded for meeting delivery times. Conflict may also be avoided by encouraging more interaction through joint project teams and mixed career paths.

Similar tensions may occur between other functions, as with R&D over product design or with accounting over methods of payment. Nor are such conflicts the sole property of the marketing department. We have already identified the type of conflict that can emerge between the R&D and operations functions and in the next chapter we see the traditional antagonisms that occur between the HR department and line management. Such conflicts are the inevitable consequence of organizational size and managerial specialization. They may, however, be minimized by strategies focusing on coordination.

The strategic aspects of marketing

The process of developing a marketing strategy bears a striking resemblance to the process of developing a firm's corporate strategy, underlining the centrality of marketing to the firm's planning process. Opportunities are analyzed, target markets are defined, market share objectives are set, segmentation strategy determined and the particular marketing mix is developed. The marketing mix, including issues of positioning, branding and competitive differentiation, is central to the whole process since it identifies and guides the strategic options. Strategic considerations in marketing therefore embrace all of the factors we have discussed in this chapter. We will use the four elements of the mix to examine the various strands of marketing strategy. Finally, we examine how these various elements may be combined and stress the integrated nature of marketing and the other functional strategies.

Product strategy

> The historic fate of one growth industry after another has been its suicidal product provincialism. (*Levitt, 1960, p. 34*)

References have been made to product strategy in our discussion of innovation and operations in the previous two chapters, as well as earlier in this chapter. Levitt's quote from his highly influential article 'Marketing myopia' is a plea to management for a marketing-led product development strategy. Most industries, he feels, restrict themselves by defining their businesses too narrowly, largely because they are product oriented rather than customer oriented. He cites the case of the decline of the USA railway business which identified itself too rigidly with railways rather than the transport needs of its customers and lost ground to the airline and car industries.

Following the market in this way may be desirable but depends upon the firm possessing the appropriate financial resources and skills. A firm's competitive edge may lie in the production of highly specialized goods and skills and resources may not be easily transferred. In such cases survival may depend upon acquisition or merger.

In general terms, a product strategy needs to consider the type and range of products on offer, the style and quality of those products, the use of brand names and packaging, and the nature of the services that are offered with the product, such as warranty and after-sales care. We saw in our discussion of the product life-cycle that product market planning needs careful consideration of the operations process.

Pricing strategy

We have already discussed the various constituents that determine the price of goods and services, and, singly or together, these form the basis of pricing strategy.

- **Cost-plus.** Cost-plus pricing consists of a standard mark-up after all costs have been taken into consideration.
- **Target-profit.** Target-profit pricing involves establishing the price in accordance with projected demand using some form of break-even analysis. In this way a book can be priced according to two criteria: the minimum sales required to cover production costs and the required profit margins based on estimated sales figures.

Both the cost-plus and target-profit methods are based on the assumption that prices are related solely to cost and demand. As we saw earlier, this is too simplistic a view. The pricing strategy needs to take account of factors external to the firm, in particular prices charged by the competition and the perceived value of the product by the consumer. In the former case there is a tendency for firms operating in the same product market to adopt a going rate, although, as we shall see later, more aggressive tactics can be pursued by firms breaking into new markets. By contrast to the going rate, pricing goods according to their perceived value can lead to considerable variation. Such a strategy is based on the customers' assumption that 'they are getting what they pay for' and they relate price to quality and hence to the cost of producing the goods or services.

However, a high price can be used to denote exclusivity and so attract a particular market segment. New Zealand wine is invariably more expensive than many Australian wines of the same grape variety. This is a deliberate strategy on the part of New Zealand growers to maintain high quality, and the mass market is shunned. New Zealanders, in their own country, will purchase Australian wine for everyday drinking and New Zealand wine for the special occasion. Brands can be used in this way and premium prices demanded for fashionable ones. In this case the manufacturer is keen to maintain a premium price for the brand wherever it is sold. In the UK certain supermarkets have attempted to break free from such price control. In 1997, Tesco offered Levi 501 denim jeans at almost half the price of the usual retail outlets. Such a strategy was seen as damaging to Levi's exclusive advertising campaign and to its relationship with its existing retailers. As a result, Levi refused to supply Tesco. Undeterred, the supermarket chain obtained the jeans direct from factories in Mexico. The demand was so high that Tesco had to set up a helpline to direct customers to stores with availability.

All these factors come together in the pricing strategies relating to new products. The simplest method may well be to price goods by comparison to the nearest equivalents, roughly in accordance with the going-rate method. Traditionally, two general strategies have been used, **skimming** and **penetration**, although skimming has become somewhat dated as a pricing strategy.

- **Skimming** operates when the initial price is high and requires a number of factors to be present.
  - Where the price elasticity of demand is low and the barriers to entry are high.
  - The product must appeal to a market segment where price is not an important consideration. The target market is generally a high-income group of market leaders but it may comprise, for products such as cameras and hi-fi equipment, the lower-income 'enthusiast'.
  - The price will offset the high development cost for this type of product and so ease the firm's cash flow.
  - A skimming strategy is usually accompanied by extensive promotional activity, particularly in up-market and specialist magazines. Once a reputation and a market have been established there may be a reduction in price to broaden the market, using the original purchasers as important opinion leaders. Price reductions may also be necessary to maintain a market share as competitors arrive on the scene.

Several products have been priced in this way. Both the VCR and the CD player entered the market at high prices, with considerable price reductions as the market expanded and the competition increased.

The theory behind skimming is that the initial high price at the product launch would attract lead users, who would establish the brand. The price would then be reduced as successive generations of the product were developed for a larger market. Cooper and Chew (1996) believe that globalization has eroded such price advantages of those first to the market. Imitators are now bringing in their products at a faster rate than ever before, giving those that are first to the market no time to establish brand loyalty or to recover development costs. They advocate a pricing policy, which determines the price before product development on the basis of target costing. Under this system, management and those responsible for the development of the product or service must determine the level of functionality and quality that is needed in a particular market segment, given a set price and sales volume. The method ensures that design and development costs do not exceed planned levels and that the company offers products and services at acceptable prices but remains in profit.

- A **penetration** strategy involves setting a low price to attract a mass market at the outset. Such a strategy is used where demand is price sensitive and where economies of scale can be gained by mass production. Penetration is usually associated with competitive markets. However, the strategy can be used to discourage competition by raising the barriers of entry, since those entering the market must be certain of high sales to offset development costs. Such a strategy has been used by many firms. Texas Instruments dominated the American hand-held calculator market in this way and in 1988 Amstrad attempted to dominate the business market for personal computers by selling at 50 per cent less than its rival, Apricot. This strategy is also illustrated by the price wars among certain UK national newspapers in the 1990s, led by News International (see the postscript to the News International case in Chapter 1).

An alternative method to both skimming and penetration is to establish **what the market will bear**. This usually involves getting a sample of consumers to rate products according to attribute and price and make comparisons of rival products.

We can see that the pricing decision needs to take account of a range of interconnected factors. Additional complexities can and do exist:

- The same product may be differentially priced for a number of reasons. It may be discounted for bulk purchase or to specific groups such as senior citizens and students. The same cinema seat may be differentially priced for different performances to even out demand and particularly to attract customers to less popular showings earlier in the week.

- The price may be a function of the number and type of distribution channels. Imported goods may be more expensive because they pass through more intermediaries, and products are generally more expensive in a prestigious store.

- Pricing strategy generally changes over the life of a product as a function of demand, market share, and changes in the economy. Price cuts may be introduced to regenerate a product nearing the end of its life-cycle or to beat off competition, and price rises may be needed to keep pace with inflation.

- Price can be used as a promotion strategy on market entry. The budget airline easyJet entered the car rental market with easyCar offering a standard car for all rentals, the Mercedes A Class. This was offered at £9 per day, £14 cheaper than its nearest rival and significantly cheaper than many. However, there was a small additional preparation charge and the price rose steeply with travel over 75 miles. Once this was reached the car soon became more expensive than its rivals.

Such variations can be confusing and lead to customer complaints, as some airline companies have found. The price of the same seat on the same flight may vary considerably depending upon when and where the ticket has been bought. Tickets bought well in advance and those bought on a stand-by basis are much cheaper, as are those obtained from discount agencies and 'bucket shops'.

Promotion strategy

Earlier we identified the three main functions of a promotion strategy: to inform, persuade and remind. We also suggested that an effective strategy was dependent upon selecting the most appropriate message and media for the product and target market. Two important decisions remain: how much to spend and how to gauge whether a campaign has been effective or not.

It is clear to management that a promotion strategy must be affordable, yet setting an appropriate budget is far from easy. Three common methods are identified:

- **Percentage-of-sales.** The percentage-of-sales method sets the budget according to the previous year's sales figures or is based on sales forecasts. The inherent flaw in such a strategy is that promotion is a function of sales rather than vice versa. Nevertheless, such a method is simple and may appeal to the cautious decision-maker.

- **Competitive-parity.** The competitive-parity method pegs promotional expenditure to that of the major competitors in proportion to the market share.

- **Objective-and-task.** The objective-and-task method has probably the most rational appeal in that specific targets are set and the budget apportioned accordingly. Such a method enables the results of the expenditure to be assessed against the objectives.

In most organizations the marketing manager has to operate from a budget allocated as the result of some complex decision-making process involving all managers in all functional areas. Dhalla (1978) accuses many managers of short-sightedness in setting the promotional budget. He feels that promotion should be treated as a capital investment and not, as in most cases, as an operating cost. A similar approach is often taken with research and development and training.

Promotion may be evaluated on three levels:

- The first consideration is that the particular advertisement or sales promotion has been seen and by how many and what type of people.

- The second consideration is that the public and, in particular, the target market are aware of the product and its attributes.

- The final and most important consideration is that the promotion results in the desired action on the part of the target market. In the case of consumer products, the ultimate test lies in the number of sales; whereas a government campaign to reduce drinking and driving will have to be measured by the number of convictions.

The evaluation of a promotion campaign is especially difficult for two main reasons:

- First, a decision has to be made about the time scale for such an evaluation. Is the impact of an advertisement to be measured over a week, a month, several months or longer?

- Second, it may not be possible to isolate the impact of a promotional campaign from the influence of other variables such as changes in the economy, the behaviour of competitors, changes in social behaviour and so on. Accurate evaluation under such conditions may require extensive econometric models or a level of experimentation not feasible in most organizations. Few firms have done as DuPont and tested advertising expenditure in their paint market by varying the amounts in different parts of the same territory to assess the impact on sales. They discovered that the effect of the heaviest expenditure was weakest in areas where they had a high market share. Perhaps this is a pointer to the diminishing returns of advertising expenditure.

Not all promotion activity has the strategic intention of increasing demand for products, as the following case illustrates. In 1987 Burroughs Wellcome had developed a drug that had been successful in trials in slowing down the effect of the AIDS virus for some people. The company was concerned that the launch would be accompanied by media exaggeration and many would be misled into thinking that a cure had been found. The product was launched simultaneously in open forums at major hotels in several American cities. In each case the launch was linked by television to a panel of medical experts and questions were encouraged. Such a promotion served to limit demand for the drug specifically to those cases who could benefit the most.

Distribution strategy

Distribution strategy is concerned with such issues as the type and number of channels, the location of those channels and how they might be controlled. A number of different channels are available, including a traditional sales force, using a partner firm to handle distribution aspects of the business, distributors, wholesalers and retailers, and more recently **telemarketing** and the Internet. The choice of channel depends very much on the nature of the product or service. Traditionally many organizations used sales representatives. However, the maintenance of a full-time sales force is expensive and may only be justified where transactions are complex, require face-to-face interaction, involve an element of customer training, and where there is clear value added by using this form of distribution. Many organizations no longer have the need for this kind of service. Costs can be reduced significantly through the use of telephone sales, call centres and the Internet. Such forms of telemarketing and the **Internet** often have the advantage of operating 24 hours a day all week. The use of a single channel may limit access to customers and a mix of channels may be required, or the use of different channels for different products.

Traditionally in the manufacturing industry, distribution strategy has focused around stock policy. Incentives in the form of discounts were often given to persuade intermediaries such as warehouses to hold stock. Such strategies became less important with the increased use of JIT strategies. Current emphases in distribution strategy are on the range of distribution channels and the use of new technology. In this way distribution has become the key to success for many organizations. The emergence of Dell Computers from a small firm to a leading player in the PC market in less than 5 years is attributed both to its customer care approach and to its use of direct marketing. Dell was the first computer company to focus on **telesales** and the Internet and its methods have been copied by competitors such as NEC. First Direct has emerged as a success in banking largely through its accessibility to customers by telephone on a 24-hour basis and a call centre is a much cheaper way of operating a bank than a high street branch. Case 11.3 examines the growth of flower sales through telemarketing and the Internet and demonstrates how an industry has widened its customer base by focusing on specific distribution channels.

The advantages of using technology-based distribution strategies lie in lower costs, access to an expanding market and being able to focus investment and staff where they can be most effective, as in after-sales service or customer training (Friedman and Furey, 1999).

However, personal contact can still be important in some industries. Fites (1996) cites the case of Caterpillar Tractors who were successful in maintaining market share despite strong competition from the Japanese in the form of Komatsu. He argues that their success is based on their close working relationship with 186 independent dealers across the world and the support they give to customers. This is central given that the product is expensive, long-lasting and has to operate in a number of difficult environments across the globe. The company feels that the local knowledge of dealers and their close links with customers is a major feature in repeat purchases.

An integrated marketing strategy

Integration can occur along a number of different dimensions: within each component of the mix; between the various elements of the mix; between marketing and the other functional strategies; and integration of the whole company around marketing strategies focusing on enhanced customer loyalty and satisfaction. We will deal with each in turn:

- The various activities and strategies associated with each component of the mix should work together. For example, effective promotion is generally achieved through a campaign in which press and television advertising and sales promotion are carefully coordinated to achieve the maximum impact upon the consumer.

- The elements of the mix should work together. Price reductions are often accompanied by a promotion campaign and both need the reinforcement of sufficient stocks and effective distribution in anticipation of increased demand. Improvements in product quality necessitating increases in price need to be sensitively handled in promotion.

- The effective integration of marketing with the other functional strategies, especially those of innovation and production, is considered essential to the firm acquiring a competitive advantage. An effective product portfolio should be built around the skills and other resources of the organization. A business school that attempts to offer courses in international business but lacks staff with the necessary expertise may attract a poor reputation and see support for all its courses suffer as a result. Some see this integration of functional strategies as an iterative process, requiring the constant monitoring of markets, products, processes and technology, and the firm working these elements around its chosen field of distinctive competence.

- As far as marketing itself is concerned, many suggest that the strategic focus should be towards customer satisfaction and customer loyalty. To be effective this should ideally permeate across the entire organization and therefore is in itself an integrative strategy. Integrated strategies aim to enhance the reputation of the company and secure repeat purchases, but also act as an opportunity to sell additional products. Mercedes-Benz at their Sindelfingen plant and headquarters on the outskirts of Stuttgart have established a visitor centre. This is linked to visits around the plant and embraces a cafeteria and luxury-style restaurant, a shop selling both souvenirs and more expensive extras for the car, model displays, a film theatre and a financial services department. Buyers of a new Mercedes have the option of collecting it themselves from the factory. Those who exercise this option are met by a personal courier and given a personalized factory tour, at the end of which they pick up their car. Not only does this generate enhanced customer satisfaction, it is often treated as a family outing, which includes a meal at the restaurant, the inevitable purchase of souvenirs and, perhaps, signing up for a special Mercedes credit card at the financial services desk.

  Many supermarkets have attempted to enhance the customer experience by introducing a range of extra services. These include ample car parking, petrol stations and car-wash facilities, cash points, cafeterias, loyalty cards and staff employed solely to give customer information. There are dangers with such multifaceted approaches to marketing in that dissatisfaction with a peripheral element of the service can cause the customer to go elsewhere and the main sale is lost.

Disneyland Paris

Disneyland Paris opened its doors for business as Euro Disney in April 1992. It was the fourth of the Disney theme parks and followed the successes of Disneyland in Los Angeles (opened in 1955), Disney World in Orlando, Florida (opened in 1971) and Disneyland Tokyo (opened in 1983).

The idea of opening a Disney theme park in Europe had been around for some time. The corporation had noted that while only 5 per cent of the visitors to its USA parks came from Europe, that figure represented over 2 million visitors a year. The company felt that there was a large potential European market waiting to be tapped and it had been encouraged by the considerable success of its Tokyo operation. This was a faithful copy of Disneyland in California and convinced the Disney executives that if the Disney experience could work in Japan, the concept could be transplanted to a European location with ease.

The proposals for the development began in the early 1980s. Several countries were interested, among them France, Italy, Germany, Spain and, for a short time, the UK. Although Spain was a strong candidate (mainly for its weather), the eventual location was the area around Marne-la Vallée, some 30 km outside Paris. The choice of location was due to a number of factors:

- France had a stable economy and low rates of inflation.
- The location was within easy reach of a large proportion of the French population and near a major road route from Germany. The Eurotunnel project, linking France and the UK, was due for completion in the mid-1990s. In all, over 300 million people were less than 2 hours away by air and the park would be near the major airports of Orly and Charles de Gaulle.
- Market surveys had shown that tourism in Europe was predicted to expand significantly.
- Paris was already a highly popular vacation destination and the proximity of the park meant a large number of visitors would have an extra attraction.
- The French government were highly supportive. Finance was made available for extending existing road and rail links to the park. Low interest loans with delayed repayment terms were made available to Disney and tax concessions were granted through the reduction of VAT on goods sold in the park. The enthusiasm of the French politicians was, in part, a product of rising unemployment in the 1980s and the promise that the park would create at least 15 000 new jobs.
- Market research was carried out among the French and the general feedback was that the park would be welcomed.

Euro Disney was launched by a share issue in 1989, at a share price of £7.07. The Walt Disney Corporation took a 49 per cent share and 51 per cent was offered, in the first instance, to European investors. The flotation was popular and at the time of opening the shares were worth £16.00.

All the Disney theme parks are based around well-known Disney characters. These have proven universal appeal and are reinforced in the public's imagination by

▶

the regular re-release of Disney films such as *Snow White*, *Pinocchio* and *Fantasia*, and the more recent policy of releasing some of the films on video. Disneyland Paris is no exception and a key feature of the experience and creation of fantasy is the interaction between staff dressed up as famous Disney characters and the customers. While the Disney characters create the main theme, each of the parks is divided into a number of imaginary worlds, each stressing a particular theme. In Disneyland Paris the imaginary worlds comprise Main St USA, Frontierland, Adventureland, Fantasyland and Discoveryland. A key element of all these 'worlds' is a number of experiences and rides with an emphasis on creativity and state-of the-art technology. The Disney Corporation has a policy of continuous technological updating. Another key goal is quality of service, which extends beyond the theme park to hotels, catering establishments and souvenir shops. To that end, staff are carefully selected and trained. Stringent selection criteria embrace appearance codes, including rules on dress, hairstyle, weight and so on. The Disney Corporation has created a distinctive corporate culture for its theme park employees. For example, employees are known as 'cast members' and their uniforms as 'costumes' to reinforce the concept of fantasy. In support of this, all events are meticulously planned. At any one time there may be several employees dressed up as the same character, but only one may be seen at any one time in the park. The characters emerge from underground tunnels responding to a centralized control using two-way radio. The fantasy is everything and two Mickey Mouses in the park at the same time would never do.

When it opened, Euro Disney had 29 rides, six hotels, a campsite, golf course and assorted restaurants, food outlets and souvenir shops. At the outset an additional 3000 acres were acquired for future expansion. By 1996 it was expected that the theme park itself would be much bigger and be joined by a conference centre to capture off-season trade. The Disney Corporation was proud of its new European park and claimed it as technologically superior to any that had gone before it.

Despite the overwhelming support of the national government, the Disney Corporation did encounter significant initial problems in dealing with the local bureaucracy and its planning regulations. In the first few weeks of opening, the company encountered demonstrations by local villagers objecting that the park would damage the quality of their lives. However, many locals gained substantially from the sale of land and used the money to build motels, shops and restaurants in the area.

Initial reactions of the paying public were mixed. There were many complaints of high prices, long queues, poor service and technical teething problems with many of the rides. In 1993, an accident on one of the new rides attracted criticism about the safety of the park. The French were especially critical of the apparent lack of intellectual content in the park's attractions and the quote by arts commentator Ariane Mnouchkine that Euro Disney was a 'cultural Chernobyl' was widely reported in the world's press. The initial problems caused another commentator to refer to it as 'corporate America's Vietnam' (*Observer*, 14 November, 1993). The target attendance of 11 million for the first year was almost reached but, thereafter, attendance figures fell to 9.8 million in the second year and 8.9 million in the third but rising to 10.7 million in 1995. Despite the significant criticism of the world's press, in its first year of operation Euro Disney was easily France's top attraction, with several million visitors more than the Pompidou Centre, the Eiffel Tower and the Louvre.

Perspectives on the success or otherwise of the attraction were mixed. Disney CEO Michael Reisner was quick to point out that attendance patterns at other Disney theme parks were similar in the early years. The financial failings of the European operation were, however, inescapable. In the first two tears of operation the park had lost 20 billion French francs and, from its buoyant position at opening, the share price fell from £16 to £3.55. In 1994 trading was suspended on the French stock exchange when the share price fell to less than £2. In 1993, over 10 per cent of staff were made redundant. The park was becoming a drain on the highly profitable Disney Corporation and to protect USA shareholders, Disney executives put pressure on French banks and the French government to support the financial restructuring of Euro Disney. The eventual restructuring of 1994 included a relaxation of loan repayments, the leasing of some attractions and a rights issue, with a Saudi Arabian prince accumulating a large number of new shares. Despite the problems in France, the Disney empire was extended in 1995 through the purchase of ABC Television in the USA to make Disney the world's largest entertainment network.

The relative failure of Euro Disney in its early years has been attributed to economic/financial and cultural causes. In the early 1990s, the French franc was stronger than some other European currencies, notably those of the UK, Italy and Spain. French interest rates had risen, placing an additional burden on loan repayments. The effective devaluation of sterling meant a fall in UK visitors to the park of around 50 per cent. It was only marginally more expensive for a UK family of four to visit Disney World in Florida, given the relatively cheap rate of the USA dollar. Even for those who did visit, spending was down on accommodation, food and souvenirs. Most commentators agreed that both entrance and hotel prices were too high. Price cuts were made during the first year of operation but this meant that, for the hotels, occupancy rates had to rise to levels beyond the most optimistic estimates. While park attendance targets were almost reached, levels of operating profit were well down on targets. Market research discovered that families who stayed overnight preferred cheaper accommodation in Paris where a visit to the park could be combined with other attractions. A vicious circle was created whereby a lack of revenue meant that expansion plans for Phase 2 were shelved. The park needed more attractions so that people would need to stay overnight and push up occupancy rates. As it was, the park's attractions could all be visited in a single day. The postponement of Phase 2 also delayed the construction of a conference centre, which was planned to take up hotel space in off-season periods. Not only were the hotels contributing some 30 per cent to the overall deficit, but their lack of success meant that the company was thwarted in its plans to sell them off at a handsome profit after the first few years of operation.

Many critics claim that the early disappointments were rooted in cultural differences. The Disney experience is very American and particularly alien to elements of the French market. The French claimed that the attractions were lacking in intellectual content and failed to build in any way upon French cultural heritage. While the

American theme parks favour fast-food and have a ban on the sale of alcohol and cigarettes, the French visitors have a preference for table service and alcohol with their meals. The Japanese park made little concession to Japanese culture and had proven a great success. Disney executives believed that if the concept could work in Japan it could work anywhere. However, the Japanese were attracted to the family orientation, uniforms and regimentation and the opportunity to buy souvenirs at every turn, all of which fitted Japanese culture. The French were less enthusiastic and early concessions were made, including: the sale of cigarettes, the availability of alcohol at table-service restaurants, the choice of non-USA-style food, the incorporation of European themes into the attractions and the widespread use of the French language. This became even more important as the recession in Europe made the park even more dependent on the French paying public. There were early problems with some of the cast members who had difficulty embracing their roles with the dedication required by the Disney Corporation and labour turnover rates were around 25 per cent in the first 2 years. Staff morale was further undermined by redundancies. Disney was also criticized for its lack of cultural awareness in its promotion activity. The same style of promotion was used across Europe and no account was taken of cultural differences.

The financial problems of Euro Disney resulted in the company rethinking other aspects of the park's operation. In 1995 the name was changed to Disneyland Paris to give the park a stronger sense of geographical identity and associate it with the image of Paris. At the same time, the name change was an attempt to disassociate the park from its earlier failures and from the link some commentators had made with other failed 'euro' projects. Further price cuts were made in 1995 of up to 20 per cent from entrance fees, hotels, food and souvenirs. The company ran its own promotional packages, including special winter deals and free entry and hotel accommodation for up to two children under 12 years old when accompanied by two paying adults. Strict codes covering working practices and dress were relaxed in an attempt to reduce labour turnover and improve morale. New attractions and rides were added, including a convention centre and the Space Mountain – heralded as the most technically advanced ride in the world.

From 1995 to 1999 the recovery was steady. Attendance improved and settled at around 12.5 million a year. The company moved into operating profit and there was a steady growth of revenue year on year. Guest spending in the park had also risen, and by 1998 hotel occupancy rates exceeded 80 per cent. Recovery was aided by a weaker French franc in the latter part of the 1990s. In 1999 there were plans to open a new themed restaurant in association with McDonald's and approval was given by the French government for a second theme park, based on the concept of the Disney MGM Studios in Florida, to open in 2002. The Disney Corporation also announced plans to open a new theme park in either Hong Kong or Shanghai.

Gilles Pélisson, the chief executive of Euro Disney SA (controlling company of Disneyland, Paris), stated in his 1998 report:

In a tourism environment largely affected by the Football World Cup, Disneyland Paris has confirmed its position as the leading European leisure destination. Nineteen ninety-eight was characterized by a strong improvement in operating performance and the start of important developments aimed at diversifying our product offering. All these elements strengthen our confidence in the future of the Company and we look forward to the major event of 1999, the opening of our new attraction 'Honey, I Shrunk the Audience!'.

The attraction, whose name would have matched ideally the attendance trends of the early years, represented a growing confidence in the future of the park. In 2002 the park expanded with an investment of £370 million in a new theme based on Hollywood films. However, another crisis hit Disneyland Paris in the summer of 2003. Debts had mounted to £1.5 billion. Despite the Disney Corporation waiving its management and royalty fees, there was insufficient revenue from tourists to service the debt. Once again, the company faced bankruptcy. The key problem was the shortfall in tourists to France and, in particular, the dramatic fall in American tourists, due in part to the French lack of support for the USA in the Iraq war and the subsequent USA boycott of French goods.

Sources: *Financial Times*, February–July, 1992, November, 1993, March, June 1994; *Observer*, November, 1993, August, 1995, August, 2003; Euro Disney SA, Annual Reports, 1995–8; Mills *et al.*, 1994

Questions

1 What are the key marketing issues displayed by this case?

2 What were the reasons for Disney opening in the Paris area? Were these reasons justified?

3 What initial problems faced Disneyland Paris and how were they tackled?

4 What marketing strategies could the company use to move out of the 2003 financial crisis? Are there any non-marketing strategies that would help?

Summary

- Marketing involves the understanding of customer needs and behaviour and the researching of markets for the effective development, pricing, promotion and distribution of goods and services. These activities operate in a number of different consumer and organizational contexts and can incorporate the marketing of people, places, company image and ideas as well as goods and services.

- The product, price, promotion and distribution elements of marketing are known as the marketing mix and form the key elements of marketing strategy. There is a growing trend for firms to segment the markets in which they operate, calling for variations in the marketing mix for each target market. Another important element of the mix is the branding of products and services.

- Marketing operates at the interface between the organization and its environment, and changes in the economy, state regulation, technology and social trends all call for changes in marketing strategy. Marketing managers use their knowledge of the environment, especially of those social and cultural influences that shape behaviour, in an attempt to manipulate demand for their product. In recent years marketing activities have been significantly affected by globalization, consumerism and technology-based developments such as telemarketing and Internet marketing.

● The development of an effective marketing strategy depends upon an understanding of the workings of the market place, of customer needs and the appropriate mix for the market segment and prevailing environmental conditions. The implementation of that strategy depends upon the integration of marketing with the other functional specialisms, with a focus on the customer.

Discussion questions

1   Assess Drucker's claim that marketing is not a specialized activity since it encompasses all the activities of the firm.

2   How far and in what industries do the five orientations to marketing operate today?

3   For what reasons do governments engage in marketing? Does this raise any ethical problems?

4   What type of market research information would you need in the following situations: a holiday company offering a new resort location; a manufacturer developing a new vacuum cleaner; a restaurant owner planning a more expensive menu?

5   What factors would you consider to determine the price of the following: a new high-performance sports car; a new breakfast cereal; an MBA at an internationally known business school?

6   Why does market segmentation occur and what are its advantages and disadvantages for management and the consumer?

7   Assess the key contributions of branding to the marketing process and to the success of the business.

8   Assess the contribution of the selection of appropriate distribution channels to effective marketing strategy.

9   To what extent can marketing activities change the environment in which the firm operates?

10   What are the essential ingredients of an effective marketing strategy for fast-moving consumer goods (e.g. toothpaste), a luxury yacht and a firm of professional accountants?

11   Assess the problems and opportunities presented by developments in Internet marketing.

Further reading

There are a number of good general texts on marketing. Two of the best-selling texts are Kotler, P., Armstrong, G., Saunders, J. and Wong, V. (2001) *Principles of Marketing*, 3rd European edn, FT Prentice Hall, Harlow and Kotler, P. (2002) *Marketing Management*, 11th edn, Prentice Hall, Upper Saddle River, NJ. The initial USA influence and the dominance of Kotler have been challenged by a number of texts focusing on UK and European examples. Good examples of these include Dibb, S., Simpkin, L., Pride, W. M. and Ferrell, O. C. (2001) *Marketing: Concepts and Strategies,* 4th European edn, Houghton Mifflin, Boston, MA and Jobber, D. (2001) *Principles and Practice of Marketing*, 3rd edn, McGraw Hill, Maidenhead. A good source of more academic work in marketing can be found in Frain, J. (1999) *Introduction to Marketing*, 4th edn, International Thomson Business Press, London. A different approach offering a highly readable account packed with interesting examples is offered by Piercy, N. (1997) *Market-led Strategic Change: Transforming the Process of Going To Market*, 2nd edn, Butterworth Heinemann, Oxford.

Human resource management

- Define personnel management and HRM and distinguish between the two.
- Critically assess the developments associated with HRM.
- Identify and explain the key activities associated with HRM and how they are carried out.
- Assess the key external changes and their impact upon HRM policies and practice.
- Explain the role of the state and the role of the economy in relation to HRM.
- Identify variations in HR practice due to cultural differences.
- Critically assess the effectiveness of HRM in an organizational context and explain the barriers to effective performance.
- Identify and assess a range of HRM strategies.

Introduction

To use a marketing analogy, attempts were made in the 1980s to relaunch personnel management as human resource management or, as it is more commonly referred to, HRM. The process has been taking place over the past two decades to the accompaniment of 'corporate culture', 'flexibility', 'commitment', 'employee involvement' and 'TQM', all to a greater or lesser extent considered to be part of the HRM family.

HRM initially came to prominence in a course at the Harvard Business School, and in a seminal text is defined as:

> Human resource management (HRM) involves all management decisions and actions that affect the nature of the relationship between the organization and its employees – its human resources. (*Beer* et al., *1984, p. 1*)

Most traditionally minded personnel managers would see nothing in that definition to imply that HRM has emerged as a radically different form of personnel management. Indeed, in the literature, the two terms, HRM and personnel, are used interchangeably. In this book we shall refer to personnel and personnel managers when dealing with the historical development of the function. Otherwise the term HR will be used to describe the function and HR managers or HR practitioners will be used to describe those primarily engaged in the function. The term HRM will be reserved generally for that specific movement and related strategies that emerged in the 1980s. There is no disputing that the transition from personnel to HRM has generated a substantial debate. As David Guest explains:

> To managers it seemed to offer an attractive alternative to the jaded image of personnel management and the dated rhetoric of traditional industrial relations . . . among academics, it offered new hope for those who had begun to despair of the long term potential of industrial relations and personnel management as important academic subjects. (*Guest, 1990, p. 377*)

In this chapter we will examine the extent to which HRM has supplanted traditional personnel management by comparing more traditional approaches to the new-style HRM. The development of both personnel and HRM illustrates well the workings of the Business in Context model. The growth of personnel management as a specialist activity has been influenced by a number of key environmental variables. These include the intervention of the state through an increasingly complex system of employment law, the workings of the labour market, the strength of trade unions, the state of the economy and changes in the competitive environment. In addition to these environmental factors, the role and status of personnel/HR managers themselves have had a significant influence on the scope and effectiveness of personnel/HR strategies. These same factors are associated with the development of HRM.

We will deal with the environmental, organizational and strategic issues after we have examined the comparison between traditional approaches to personnel and HRM.

Identifying personnel/HRM

Traditional approaches to personnel

In this section we will attempt to define more traditional approaches to personnel and the activities most commonly associated with it. This will serve as a useful comparison with the supposedly different approach taken by HRM.

Key concept 12.1 Human resource management

In many organizations, human resource management or, as it is often referred to, HRM or even HR, performs the roles and duties formerly ascribed to personnel management. Many would argue that there is more than a name change and that the function has undergone an ideological shift. Traditional personnel management was concerned with recruitment, selection, training, pay, welfare and industrial relations. HRM deals with all of these, but integrates them within the overall strategy of the enterprise and sees business values as an over-riding consideration. An important element of HRM is the development of a culture that stresses commitment to organizational goals, quality and flexibility. The extent to which the values of HRM have superseded those of traditional personnel management in many organizations is open to question.

There would appear to be as many definitions of personnel management as there are books on the subject. This is hardly surprising for, as we have already noted, the activities are highly dependent upon the context in which they operate. For example, a discussion of personnel management in Britain would place greater emphasis upon industrial relations than it would in the USA, where trade unions play much less of a role and collective action is rarer. Despite these variations, a useful starting point is the definition offered by the Institute of Personnel Management (IPM) now the Chartered Institute of Personnel and Development (CIPD).

> Personnel management is a responsibility of all those who manage people as well as being a description of the work of those who are employed as specialists. It is that part of management which is concerned with people at work and with their relationships within an enterprise. It applies not only to industry and commerce, but to all fields of employment. Personnel management aims to achieve both efficiency and justice, neither of which can be pursued successfully without the other. It seems to bring together and develop into an effective organization the men and women who make up the enterprise, enabling each to make his own best contribution to its success, both as an individual and as a member of a working group. It seeks to provide fair terms and conditions of employment and satisfying work for those employed. (*IPM, 1963*)

If we ignore the somewhat idealistic stance and the absence of precisely defined tasks and duties, the definition stresses the dual goals of serving the needs of employees and the organization. It also serves the useful purpose of distinguishing between a business function and a departmental presence within an organization. Many students of business mistakenly conclude that all businesses conform to textbook models relating, as they do, to fairly large-scale organizations differentiated into specialist departments.

Daniel and Millward (1983) estimated that if all firms, including small businesses, were considered then 75 per cent of companies would have no specialist personnel manager, the function being performed by a manager who deals with personnel matters alongside other duties. The position is little changed. For example, in many professional partnerships, such as solicitors or accountants, one of the senior partners is usually given responsibility for personnel but would view their main role as that of a solicitor or an accountant. Some smaller firms may operate the personnel function through a one-person-secretary-cum-records department. The absence of a personnel specialist may even be deliberate policy. HP, the American multinational, did not introduce a personnel department until staffing levels had reached 1200, its founders preferring personnel matters to be the responsibility of all managers (Beer *et al.*, 1985).

In Table 12.1 we present a detailed list of the various activities traditionally associated with personnel management. These activities may be categorized as people processing and industrial relations (see Key concepts 12.2 and 12.3). The division of the personnel function along these lines was especially prevalent in large unionized firms, such as Ford, where industrial relations plays a particularly prominent role. In the 1990s, many such firms changed their structures to reflect the more integrated approach of HRM and the fact that industrial relations was no longer viewed as a problem. Nonetheless, many of the activities are still relevant to HRM.

All firms will have a need for some of these activities, as identified in Table 12.1, in that management, for example, must conform to the prevailing employment laws and operate a system for paying employees. At some stage all firms will have need for the recruitment

Key concept 12.2   People processing

People processing relates to those activities of HRM that involve the acquisition, development, motivation and control of individuals at work. It includes the various activities associated with recruitment, selection, training, appraisal, pay administration and welfare.

Key concept 12.3   Industrial relations

Industrial relations is concerned with the relations between employers and employees and their respective representatives. These relations focus on such matters as pay, conditions, job security and forthcoming changes. The relationship involves elements of negotiation and bargaining, which in practice are usually dealt with by management on one hand and trade union representatives on the other. The importance of industrial relations is acknowledged by the state, in many countries, with the development of legal frameworks for its conduct. In the UK, political and economic changes and the associated ideologies and practices of HRM have, in many organizations, changed the nature of industrial relations. Such changes include a focus more on the individuals rather than groups of employees represented by unions, although trade union activity and membership levels are still high in the traditional manufacturing industry.

and selection of new staff or the reallocation of existing staff. The extent and formalization of these activities depends very much on the size of the labour force, the extent of trade union membership, and whether or not the firm has a specialist personnel department, as well as other influences, as raised in the next two sections.

Such activities may be performed in a variety of ways:

- They may be performed by a personnel specialist or a general manager with responsibility for personnel matters, or by individual managers themselves acting alone.

- In some cases, personnel specialists operate only in an advisory capacity to other managers. Members of the personnel department will advise on the setting up of personnel systems, which will be operated by other managers. Examples of this could include the establishment of job evaluation and grading systems of criteria for promotion.

- In many cases, the personnel specialists act in conjunction with other managers as, for example, in interviewing candidates for a vacancy, or designing and implementing a training programme for a sales department.

- In all kinds of organizations there is increasing use made of personnel consultants, particularly in the fields of recruitment and training. In this case the personnel specialist operates as a hirer, coordinator and manager of the consultant's activities.

- An increasing trend is the use of outsourcing. The prime activities that are outsourced are payroll, pensions, recruitment, training and relocation. In some cases,

Table 12.1	The traditional activities of personnel management	
	Activity	What it involves
	Manpower planning and control	The analysis of a company's manpower needs in light of its current manpower resources and the nature of the labour market. Such planning lays the foundation for policies related to recruitment, selection, training, pay and so on
	Recruitment	The first stage usually involves a detailed job analysis followed by the selection of the most appropriate method of recruitment, be it the use of government job centres, using specialist recruitment consultants or placing advertisements in newspapers. Decisions made aim to attract a field of suitable candidates
	Selection	The use of one or more of a variety of techniques including application forms, interviewing and tests to select the most appropriate person from a field of candidates. The interview tends to be the most favoured method of selection. Decisions are usually made against some general or specific criteria relating to the type of candidate required
	Training and development	This involves the analysis of the type of training required and the people to be trained, followed by the selection of the most appropriate method. This can range from simple on-the-job instruction to sending people on specific courses. In many firms the training and development of managers is seen as a special case involving long-term planning and consideration for individual career development
	Appraisal	This is a contentious issue in personnel and sometimes resisted by trade unions. It involves the setting up of formal systems to assess the contribution of individuals to the organization. The system is often designed by personnel specialists but administered by all managers

▶

Pay administration	This is a complex area involving decisions about the rate of pay (often involving negotiation with trade unions), about the way pay is differentially distributed (using some form of job evaluation or individual merit rating), and about the viability of one of a variety of payment schemes such as flat-rate payment, payment by results, profit sharing and so on. Decisions made in this area have broadened to include the number and range of fringe benefits such as pensions, company cars, cheap mortgages and the like
Job and organizational design	In some cases, personnel managers contribute to decisions about how jobs are to be carried out and how the organization is to be structured. This may involve the design and administration of programmes, such as job enrichment, organizational development or the quality of working life
Collective bargaining	Personnel management is invariably involved in the preparation of the employer's case and usually in the negotiations with employee representatives. Once collective agreements have been made, it is usually the job of the personnel manager to apply such agreements and deal with the outcomes
Grievance and disputes handling	Related to the above, the personnel manager is usually in the front line in dealing with situations arising from individual or collective grievances. In larger firms specific procedures are laid down, but in all cases there is an expectation of the personnel to solve disputes as and when they arise
Legal advice	With developments in employment law (outlined in the next section) many personnel managers are seen as the resident expert in legal matters pertaining to employment and act as a guide to other managers

Employee communications and counselling	The personnel specialist is often given responsibility for communicating general information to the workforce as well as administering specific programmes for employee participation, such as suggestion schemes. Some firms go further and involve the personnel manager in employee advice and counselling
Personnel information and records	The need for personnel records has increased as firms have grown in size. Such records, kept by the personnel department, are often an important source of information upon which personnel decisions are based

especially with global companies, such outsourcing is carried out in other countries. This is sometimes referred to as 'offshoring'.

As we have seen, in smaller firms the activities tend to be carried out by all managers and no specialist is employed. In larger firms, with formalized procedures, a mixture of all four methods occurs. A personnel manager may advise the sales manager on the type of person he or she is seeking to fill a vacancy and may assist in the drafting of the job advertisement. The personnel manager may interview a number of candidates and then draw up a short-list for a second interview at which time the sales manager will take a leading role. The use of consultants and outsourcing is appropriate for small firms where specialist personnel inputs are an intermittent requirement. In larger firms, consultants are seen as a more cost-effective method of delivering certain personnel services than bearing the cost of maintaining a large internal personnel department. This is particularly the case in training and some recruitment and payroll activities.

Identifying human resource management

The broad definition of HRM offered at the beginning of this chapter gives little hint of what activities comprise and what makes it particularly different from our traditional view of personnel management. Over the past 15 or so years, the HRM concept has spawned a vast literature offering a range of varying perspectives. However, there is some measure of agreement that HRM involves a focus on:

● treating employees as individuals but, at the same time, developing mechanisms to integrate individuals into teams;

● the careful selection, training and development of core staff;

● reward systems that stress individual performance and commitment and which are linked to employee appraisal and development;

- communication networks and the involvement of employees, preferably as individuals, but allowing for trade union involvement as well;

- emphasizing a culture which stresses commitment to organizational goals, quality and flexibility; in many cases it is recognized that this will involve a culture change, more especially in those organizations typified by confrontational industrial relations;

- the integration of not only all personnel-related policies as a meaningful whole but also of these policies within the overall strategy of the enterprise;

- business values as an over-riding consideration.

The analysis of such core characteristics of HRM has led some writers, notably Storey (1989), to see two strands emerging. One is defined as 'hard' HRM with a focus on business values and management strategy. The other is defined as 'soft' HRM, focusing as it does upon the selection, development and reward of people.

Many of the core characteristics of HRM are incorporated in Figure 12.1.

We have commented already on the relevance of the strategic, organizational and environmental contexts in shaping personnel/HRM activities. It is to a convergence of recent changes in those contexts that we must look to explain the emergence of HRM as a concept in its own right. The changes include the following:

- Significant changes in the competitive environment of most companies have placed greater emphasis on the need to innovate, improve the quality of their goods and services and, above all, be more cost-effective in their use of labour. This, in turn,

---

Key concept 12.4 Hard and soft HRM

The distinction between **hard and soft HRM** is attributed to Storey (1989). Hard HRM focuses on business values and management strategy, whereas soft HRM focuses upon the selection, development, involvement and the reward of people.

Figure 12.1

The human resource management process

Application of core ideas of HRM	Changed culture	Improved performancce
• Management communication • Employee involvement • 'Scientific' selection • Individual rewards • Training and development • Integrated strategies	• Business awareness • Commitment • Goal congruence • Quality • Flexibilty • Skills development	• Productivity • Lower costs • High-quality goods and services • Profitability • Job satisfaction

has resulted in many of those companies re-examining the way they select, train, use and reward employees.

- A significant aspect of this new competition was its global nature. Some managers looked at global competitors for alternative models. Management practices in Japan, as we saw in Chapter 4, were used as an explanation of economic success. Some of the features of HRM can be likened to Japanese employment relations practices in larger firms. In addition to these influences, changes in technology have added to the demand to use employees more flexibly than hitherto. However, Guest (1990, 1998) consistently maintains that HRM is a distinctively American (as opposed to Japanese) phenomenon. In Chapter 5 we examined the influential movement that emerged from the USA built around the concept of corporate culture and the notion that 'excellent' companies serve as models for others to follow. Many of the companies, defined by Peters and Waterman (1982) as 'excellent', operate HRM policies. IBM is such a company and aspects of its HRM policy may be found in Case 12.1.

- In Britain and the USA the industrial relations climate had also altered as a result of economic and political changes. A series of recessions had weakened the bargaining power of trade unions, and unemployment in those industrial sectors that were former union strongholds had led to a decline in trade union membership. (Further analysis of these changes is offered elsewhere in this chapter and in Chapter 3.) In both countries, but more especially Britain, the politics of government shifted to the right. The rhetoric included concepts such as the free market, the freedom of the individual, and the enterprise culture. The climate was therefore suitable for those managements seeking alternative models of employment relations.

- Another reason for the growth of interest in HRM lies in the relationship between personnel specialists and other managers in the organization. This is a theme that re-emerges when we examine the organizational environment of HRM later in the chapter. The lack of access to strategic decision-making and low status felt by many personnel practitioners may well have created a receptive environment for HRM to flourish, with its promise of a high-level strategic approach. To other managers who saw the policies of traditional personnel management as inadequate and inappropriate for entry into the 1990s, HRM may have offered a favourable alternative.

A recent study by Guest et al. (2000) into the effectiveness of HR uses as part of its investigation 18 key HR practices associated with high performance HR. These are listed in Table 12.2. It is interesting to compare the list presented here with that in Table 12.1. While many of the core functions remain – such as recruitment, selection, training and so on – the emphasis has shifted towards business and individual performance. There is also no reference to the traditional tasks of industrial relations, except that they may be implied in policies on redundancy.

We will now examine the extent to which these changes have resulted in HRM emerging as something distinctively different from personnel management and the extent to which the practice of HRM matches its rhetoric.

The differences between HRM and traditional personnel management

In examining whether there has been a shift away from traditional personnel practices to a more strategically oriented HRM, the following three positions emerge:

Table 12.2	Eighteen key practices in HRM	
Item	*Key practice*	
1	Realistic job previews	
2	Use of psychometric tests for selection	
3	Well-developed induction training	
4	Provision of extensive training for experienced employees	
5	Regular appraisals	
6	Regular feedback on performance from many sources	
7	Individual performance-related pay	
8	Profit-related bonuses	
9	Flexible job descriptions	
10	Multi-skilling	
11	Presence of work-improvement teams	
12	Presence of problem-solving groups	
13	Information provided on the firm's business plan	
14	Information provided on the firm's performance targets	
15	No compulsory redundancies	
16	Avoidance of voluntary redundancies	
17	Commitment to single status	
18	Harmonized holiday entitlement	

Source: Guest *et al.*, 2000

- There are those who see HRM as a radical departure, offering personnel managers a new strategic role and de-emphasizing industrial relations as a major activity.
- Others see little more than a title change and feel that HRM is really personnel management in a new guise, embodying, as it does, what is viewed as 'good' personnel practice.
- Those subscribing to a middle if somewhat cautious position recognize that changes have taken place in such areas as labour flexibility, employee involvement, appraisal and training. Furthermore, they see some attempts by British firms to blend HRM with traditional industrial relations. However, they view the changes as neither significant nor widespread (Storey, 1992).

Case 12.1   IBM's HR Policies

IBM is the world's largest and most successful computer manufacturer. It has been established in Britain since 1951 and is a market leader in most of its product ranges. There are no unions at IBM, the company has never experienced a strike and, until 1991, had not had to lay people off. Paradoxically, many of its current employment and personnel practices were developed during the depression in the USA and many were ahead of their time. The company scrapped payment-by-results methods for its manufacturing employees in 1936, treating all employees as salaried staff, and in effect, offering them lifetime employment. Around the same time the company introduced job enlargement and flexible working and embarked on a programme involving all employees in the design of new products. Employee training has always been a major feature of the company. IBM is often cited as a model for HRM practice and one that others would do well to emulate.

In Britain, the company expanded rapidly in the 1960s and continued to expand until the early 1990s. Only 27 per cent of employees work in manufacturing, the majority operating in marketing and technical services. Pay has always been high compared with other firms and labour turnover has traditionally been exceptionally low, operating for many years at around 2 per cent. The company is non-unionized; management have always claimed that the employees have no need for a union, nor do they want one. This was supported by an ACAS survey in 1977, which discovered that only 4.9 per cent of employees wanted a union, and 91 per cent claimed they would refuse to join if one were introduced.

The lack of interest in trade union membership is almost certainly a function of IBM's corporate commitment to individualism and of terms and conditions in excess of those usually demanded by trade unions. The key features of the traditional employment practices at IBM may be summed up as follows:

- A fairly sophisticated system of manpower planning, employee recruitment and training.

- Lifetime employment for all employees with the expectation that employees will change jobs as and when required.

- Single status for all employees in terms of canteens, facilities, and fringe benefits. The only exceptions are overtime payment for manufacturing workers and company cars for some senior management and some sales staff.

- Salaries are determined centrally, usually by making a favourable comparison with other firms. The exercise is carried out annually to ensure pay rates keep ahead of those in other companies. Once established, increases are always based on merit and determined through a management-by-objectives type of appraisal scheme.

- Training is emphasized, with management receiving an average of 40 days training a year (40 times the national average). Much of the training focuses upon HRM.

- An opinion survey of all staff is held every 2 years, to ascertain attitudes towards such factors as working practices, pay and conditions, and personnel practices. The response rates are very high.

- Emphasis is placed upon managers sorting out their own problems. A centralized personnel function operates a 'hands-off' policy. The company prefers to leave personnel matters to individual managers, especially grievance handling.

- The company operates two formalized communication procedures. A 'speak up' system encourages employees to raise business-related problems, while an 'open door' system allows employees to appeal against decisions taken by their own managers.

For many years such policies have been well liked by employees. The company has always expected a great deal of its employees but offers them secure jobs at relatively high rates of pay. While the firm operates a philosophy that stresses individuality as part of its commitment to entrepreneurship, individuals are nevertheless expected to conform to IBM norms of behaviour, even to participating in out-of-work company social events and activities. The company has also been accused of operating a recruitment policy that ensures only those committed to the IBM way will be selected. In general, sceptics have attempted to label IBM as running an oppressive system, which is only possible in the rarefied environment of a successful hi-tech company. However, any firm that has developed such a strong corporate culture leaves itself open to attack by those who see it as too good to be true.

By 1991 IBM faced a different kind of attack. The computer market had become even more competitive, both in terms of the number of firms competing and in terms of customers expecting much more for their money. Faced with an unprecedented fall in profits IBM confronted its own lifetime employment policies by embarking on a strategy of cutting labour costs. This needed to be done quickly as the impact of the recession accelerated, not only IBM in the UK but also worldwide. Given the low labour turnover and the absence of opportunity to transfer employees to other IBM operations, the company introduced a programme of voluntary redundancy. It offered an attractive package, amounting to an average 2 years' salary per employee with support mechanisms such as advice on job seeking and personal finance, as well as general counselling. In addition, time off was freely given for job interviews and those employees with company cars were allowed to buy them at favourable terms.

From the company's point of view, it was important to ensure that they did not lose key employees and management constructed manpower planning models to determine target groups and target areas of operation. IBM's internal communication system was used to explain the need for the strategy, to encourage volunteers and to prepare those who may have wanted to leave but who IBM were not prepared to release. Use was made of briefing groups, information releases, information packs and 1-day briefing sessions. In addition employees had access to individual advice. The result of the exercise was a reduction in headcount of 15 per cent of which only 2.3 per cent represented 'normal' turnover. The reduction exceeded the company's expectations. A positive outcome was that some employees used the opportunity to establish their own business out of their IBM activities. The company actively encouraged this and gave assistance reflected in a reduced redundancy package. The companies that were established in this way initially sold back their services to IBM. However, there were cases of dissatisfaction where some employees were prevented from taking advantage of the offer.

In 1993, a further 25 000 jobs were shed globally and altogether IBM had reduced its global workforce by 110 000 in a 6-year period. Most of the redundancies continued to be voluntary. Although non-unionized, in countries like Germany and Sweden IBM was forced to consult with works councils: bodies that can and do wield considerable power. The high trust built up over the years ensured a smooth execution of policy.

Some would advocate that the IBM HR policies made it possible to carry out a relatively trouble-free programme of voluntary redundancy, not just in the UK but across the globe. However, the extent to which it offers other companies a model to follow may well be limited by the ability of their management to carry such policies through effectively in non-IBM settings. For IBM itself, the redundancy programme struck at the heart of one of its key human resource policies. The resilience of those policies lay in the continued commitment of retained employees in an increasingly competitive environment and, in particular, the management of those employees aggrieved by the redundancy policy itself. In 1998, as part of its continued commitment to both globalization and HRM, IBM set up a multi-country HR centre to address global strategic issues.

Sources: Drucker, 1968; Bassett, 1986; Peach, 1992; *Business Europe*, 1993; *Financial Times*, 1998–9

Questions

1 To what extent has IBM adopted classic HRM policies and practices?

2 What has facilitated IBM's IIR policies and practices?

3 To what extent can the policies and practices survive successive job cuts?

Legge (1989), while arguing considerable similarity between what personnel management and HRM both set out to achieve, sees in HRM some important differences:

- First, she views HRM as being much more about management. Personnel is no longer about the treatment of the shop floor but there has been a switch of emphasis to focus on issues of management development and management teambuilding. Furthermore, HRM is the prerogative of senior management whereas personnel management was viewed as an activity to be carried out by more junior managers.

- Second, she argues that IIRM has elevated human resource issues to a position of key strategic importance.

- Third, she sees that HRM is about organizational culture and culture change in a way that traditional personnel management never was.

- Finally, she and others sense a major difference in the language of HRM, which borrows heavily from the rhetoric of the 'New Right'.

Storey (1992) identifies 27 points of difference between HRM and traditional personnel, in terms of beliefs and assumptions, strategic aspects, relationships with line managers and key leavers. For example, in personnel conflict was institutionalized, whereas in HRM it is de-emphasized. In personnel pay was based on job evaluation, but under HRM it moves to a system of individual performance-related pay.

Clearly there are companies that conform to the classic characteristics of HRM. In this league are firms such as IBM, HP and British firms, such as Marks & Spencer and BA. For example, we see in Case 12.3 how BA invested heavily in a massive training programme to change the culture of its organization towards a greater emphasis on customer care. However, most of these classic companies were known for their sophisticated approaches to personnel long before HRM emerged. Furthermore, there is some evidence to suggest that, in firms such as IBM, commitment of employees has waned in the face of successive job cuts (Guest, 1998).

Many of the techniques associated with HRM such as employee involvement, quality circles, increased flexibility, psychological selection testing, appraisal, new forms of individualized payment systems and various methods of culture change have been introduced in a number of companies. However, there is little evidence of any grand design and in many instances the techniques have been introduced in a piecemeal fashion or even in isolation. This position may have emerged as a result of the lack of consensus about what HRM entails; for many practitioners it remains a woolly concept.

For the UK, at least, the research is sanguine about there being a significant shift from personnel to HRM. The focus has been on the extent to which HRM practices occur and has hardly begun to explore the extent to which such practices result in the kinds of favourable outcomes envisaged for the firm and its employees. The evidence does point to differences in application and this will be discussed in the next section when we explore environmental influences. A major obstacle to a strategic approach to HRM in the UK is the traditional short-termism of much management thinking, often the result of shareholder pressure. In addition to this is the traditional low status of HR managers and their inability to influence strategy. The position is not always so negative. Fenwick and Murton (2000) cite Bosch, AEG, Honda, Nestlé and the Virgin Group as examples of firms where effective HRM policies have been possible:

> However, where pressures for short-term results are less immediate, skilled workers at a premium and employee development a key factor in competitveness, HRM policies may be more in evidence. (*Fenwick and Murton, 2000, p. 138*)

Despite the lack of hard evidence, the language of HRM has clearly infiltrated personnel practice, as shown in Table 12.3. The table relates to a survey of job advertisements in the then *IPM Journal* for March 1993 and the renamed *CIPD Journal* for May 1999 and May 2003. Three types of job advertisement were identified:

- Those specifying the need for a **human resource manager** or similar, such as human resource professional.

- Those specifying **personnel manager** or similar.

- Those seeking a specialist role, such as training officer or benefits manager.

Table 12.3

Job titles advertised in *IPM/CIPD* Journal as % of total jobs

Job title	March 1993	May 1999	May 2003
Human resource manager or similar	26	44	61
Personnel manager or similar	36	20	11
Specialist job title	38	36	28

In March 1993, the title HRM tended to be reserved for the higher-status and more highly paid positions. By 2003, HRM featured in the large majority of jobs, even those of a fairly junior nature. The number of positions titled personnel manager had declined markedly and were found mostly in the public sector.

There are those who see the need for coherent HRM strategies as greater than ever (Beardwell and Holden, 1997; Sparrow and Marchington, 1998). Such analyses cite the radical changes that have taken place in work and organizations over the past 15 years, especially volatile labour markets, the simultaneous strengthening of senior and weakening of junior management roles and job losses in the face of almost continual restructuring. They argue that HR systems in most firms remain dated and are based around jobs and cost minimization.

Most, however, remain sceptical of the ability of HRM to deliver. As we have seen above, there is little evidence to suggest its application by practitioners. There is little evidence of increased commitment, culture change and links between HRM and improved performance. It is difficult to persuade employees of the benefits of a 'soft' HRM when they are more concerned with keeping their jobs. Paradoxically, this threat of unemployment makes employee compliance easier and, for many managers, removes the need for complex HRM strategies.

In fact much of the literature focuses on the language and rhetoric of HRM almost as much as its application. To some, it is language that legitimizes management action, while to others the language can actually shape ideas and hence initiate change. However, Fenwick and Murton (2000) conclude that ultimately the whole HRM debate is manufactured by academics. This echoes sentiments expressed by Guest at the beginning of this chapter and probably explains why many students find the personnel/HRM debate so baffling. In the section on HRM strategy, at the end of this chapter, we return to the theme of HRM as strategic innovation or the product of management opportunism in the light of environmental changes. We now turn our attention to the examination of the environmental context of HRM.

Environmental aspects of HRM

In the previous section we examined the emergence of HRM and associated this with certain environmental changes, such as increasing competition and the weakened position of trade unions. In fact, the development of personnel management as a specialist function in organizations owes much to the influence of external events.

- The growth of markets and the creation of the joint stock company led to increases in the size of the firm with a corresponding demand for recruitment, training and some centralized payment administration system.
- The growth of trade unions, especially in Britain, created the need for industrial relations specialists among management.
- The impact of two world wars created problems for the labour supply and a corresponding attention being paid to training methods and employee consultation.
- Full employment in the 1960s once again focused the attention on labour shortages and methods used to tackle them, such as the retraining of existing staff and active recruitment from other companies.

- In the 1970s the focus turned to state intervention and the problems created by new technology.
- The 1980s brought us HRM, legislation to change the nature of industrial relations and the transplantation of practices from other countries.

We can see that all five environmental aspects of our model interact in some significant way with the HR function. We deal with each one in turn.

The role of the state

The state, operating through government policies and the legal system, has had considerable influence on the HR function in three major areas: legislation, manpower policies concerned with the supply of labour and education/training, and **third-party intervention**.

Employment legislation   Employment legislation is concerned with the rights and obligations of employers and employees and the conduct of industrial relations. The growth in employment law in the UK in the 1960–70s and the 1980s laws governing the conduct of industrial relations have had a significant impact on the work of the HR specialist. The following list of a sample of the major Acts of Parliament shows the growth of employment legislation since 1960:

Factories Act 1961

Contract of Employment Act 1963, 1972

Industrial Training Act 1964

Race Relations Act 1968, 1976

Equal Pay Act 1970

Industrial Relations Act 1971

Employment and Training Act 1973

Health and Safety at Work Act 1974

Trade Union and Labour Relations Act 1974, 1976

Sex Discrimination Act 1975, 1986

Employment Protection Act 1975

Employment Protection (Consolidation) Act 1978

Employment Act 1980, 1982, 1988, 1989, 1990

Trade Union Act 1984

Wages Act 1986

Trade Union and Labour Relations (Consolidation) Act 1992

Trade Union Reform and Employment Rights Act 1993

Employment Rights Act 1996

Employment Rights (Disputes Resolution) Act 1998

National Minimum Wage Regulations 1999

Many of the laws have had a direct impact upon the day-to-day work of HR managers. The Industrial Training Act 1964, with its introduction of the levy-grant system for approved training, resulted in the expansion of training programmes and, correspondingly, training departments and training managers. Recruitment advertisements must be carefully drafted so as not to contravene race and sex discrimination legislation. The **Arbitration, Conciliation and Advisory Service (ACAS)** set up by the Employment Protection Act 1975 had, for a time, a significant impact on the conduct of industrial relations. Several of the laws have set up a judicial system of Employment Tribunals, as in the case of redundancy and unfair dismissal cases. Such cases are often prepared by the HR specialist. Despite the growth in the tribunal and the number of cases petitioned, only a small percentage reach the final stages, although there were signs in the late 1990s that more cases are being heard. Most cases are dealt with through a variety of conciliation procedures, sometimes involving ACAS (described later in this section) but almost inevitably involving the HR specialist. The expansion of employment law has been an important causal factor in the increased number of HR specialists.

Some commentators see the expansion of labour law as a vehicle for the increased status of the HR function. This has been reinforced by studies of the role of the HR manager following the introduction of industrial relations legislation of the 1980s (Millward and Stevens, 1986; Millward *et al.*, 1992). Managers, faced with a complex array of new legal provisions, seek expert advice and often turn to the HR specialist as their source. However, not all such legislation had the impact predicted. The Industrial Relations Act 1971 attracted much media attention and was elevated to the status of a political *cause célèbre*. In reality its provisions were dismissed by some managers as much as they were by the trade union movement, its measures were largely ignored and its impact lessened long before its repeal in 1974.

In the 1980s industrial relations entered a new phase and legislation came to the forefront. There is clear indication that this aspect of HRM has been politicized as never before. Historically, the Labour Party, with its traditional allegiances to the trade union movement, has introduced legislation which tended to establish and further the rights of individual workers. The Conservative Party, on the other hand, has been more concerned with establishing laws that control the internal affairs of trade unions and attempt to regulate collective bargaining. As new laws have been introduced and repealed by successive governments, HR managers have had to respond and amend policies accordingly. The politicization of personnel management is seen most clearly in the public sector. In the 1980s and the 1990s, trade unions in coal mining and the health service took stands against government policy on such issues as pit and hospital closures, on pay restraints and attempts to reduce public spending in general. This has clearly placed HR management in those industries in a political arena where consultation and collective bargaining with trade unions have considerable political implications.

The legislation of the 1980s was based on the assumption that trade union power needed to be curbed, that individuals should be free to choose whether they join a union and that the general public needed protection against the damaging affects of strikes and other forms of industrial action. A collection of laws was built up that changed the nature of industrial relations in the UK. The major changes included the following:

- Trade unions as organizations became legally responsible for the actions of their members.
- The occasions when strikes could be called were limited and had to be subject to a ballot.

- Senior trade union officials had to re-present themselves for re-election every 5 years by secret ballot.
- The closed shop (where everyone must join a union) was effectively outlawed.
- Union members had to check-off and effectively renew their membership at regular intervals.
- Contribution to political funds became subject to a ballot.

The 1980s' and 1990s' legislation represented a major shift in the government's attitude towards industrial relations. The resultant changing nature of industrial relations had an impact on the priorities of HR itself. Compare the activities of Table 12.1 and 12.2. Effective HR in 2000 (Guest *et al.*, 2000), Table 12.2, makes little overt reference to industrial relations.

Many court actions involving industrial relations tend to involve smaller firms who have probably most to lose from a dispute. Many larger companies are still reluctant to use the courts for fear of alienating their workforce. Contrary to the image of industrial relations portrayed in the popular press, management and workforce, indeed management and unions, in most firms have reasonably good relations, which recourse to law may damage. Nonetheless, the legislation of the 1980s has changed significantly the nature of collective bargaining and consequently the work of HR specialists. There has been a marked reduction in the number of recorded disputes in British industry. This could be related to changes in the law. It could also be related to economic conditions, which we will discuss later. In some cases it is clear that changes in legislation have been accompanied by deliberate attempts on the part of management to change the employment relations culture of the enterprise. In part this is an attempt to replace traditional adversarial bargaining with a more cooperative approach. This theme recurs in our discussion of labour matters later in this section and when we discuss personnel strategies, at the end of the chapter.

While there has always been a reluctance for UK employers to use the courts, there is evidence of a greater willingness on the part of individuals to use the legislative process. ACAS has reported that in 1998 there were record numbers of cases brought by individuals against employers in Employment Tribunals. During 1998 all cases increased by 6 per cent, the majority relating to unfair dismissal. Cases relating to discrimination on grounds of disability doubled (reported in *People Management*, May, 1999).

With hindsight, the legislation of the 1980s and 1990s has been part of a range of influences that have altered the map of industrial relations in the UK. Other factors have also been significant. These include economic recession, particularly affecting the manufacturing industry, privatization and restructuring in the face of global competition. The combination of these factors has led to a reduction in the workforce and a reduction in union membership to its lowest level for 60 years. The nature of collective bargaining has changed and management has been able to push through changes unopposed. Chapter 3 offers a further analysis.

The election of a Labour government in the UK in 1997 was viewed by some, not least trade unions themselves, as the start of a new legislative era in which individual and collective rights of employees were to be strengthened. The early signs are that the government has accepted the existing legislative framework of its Conservative predecessors. However, the 1999 White Paper, 'Fairness at Work', and the subsequent Employment Relations Bill promise some reform. The Bill aims at providing 'fair treatment' for employees, by such proposals as reducing the qualifying time for unfair dismissal cases and raising the award limit. It proposes giving employees the legal right to be recognized to conduct collective bargaining and, generally, easing provisions for union recognition. Its proposals have also been dubbed 'family friendly' through the extension of maternity rights and the enabling of time off for family emergencies. The proposals are seen as being based on the 'culture of partnership'. While for some this is an attempt to rebalance the legislation more in favour of employees, it is done within the rhetoric of HRM. Both the White Paper and the Bill speak of 'building on the commitment of the work force'; measures for the fair treatment of employees are motivated by the need to underpin more flexible practices; and new proposals for collective bargaining are to achieve 'business objectives'.

Manpower policies   Most governments try to achieve a stable balance between supply and demand in the labour market through a series of manpower policies. The following examples are drawn from the UK. For 20 years after the end of the Second World War unemployment remained below 2 per cent and the major concern was the development of mechanisms to improve the supply of skilled labour. Certainly, since 1852 governments have been consistent in their criticism of the quantity and quality of training in British industry. A government White Paper in 1962 linked the inadequacy of training in British industry to the nation's economic problems and the result was the Industrial Training Act 1964 referred to earlier. Its impact was immediate, with a dramatic increase in levels of training. Training Boards were set up for each industry and several innovations were introduced. The Engineering Industry Training Board radically restructured its apprenticeship scheme to produce trainees with more flexible skills in a shorter time. Skills shortages, however, have persisted to dog British industry. A fuller analysis of training and the role of the state can be found in Chapter 3.

Despite the continuing skills shortages in some areas the focus shifted to introducing measures to combat the problem of rising unemployment. Such measures have tended to fall into two categories: those aimed at increasing the demand for labour and those aimed at reducing the total supply. Schemes to increase the demand for labour have included wage subsidies, job creation and the youth training scheme. Measures to reduce the labour supply have included early retirement, job release, temporary short-time working and job splitting. None of these were especially successful. In more recent times the emphasis has shifted, yet again, to encourage the unemployed actively to seek jobs and there are benefit penalties imposed on those not doing so.

The extent to which government training initiatives have been successful in raising levels of training is debatable. Some firms use such schemes as sources of cheap labour and relatively few trainees obtain permanent employment. If the government saw the Youth Training Scheme as an attempt to introduce to Britain a German-style apprenticeship training programme then it has largely failed. A big obstacle to the government's attempts to raise the profile of training lies with business itself. Many firms tend to see training as a cost rather than an investment, and a cost that can easily be cut in the pursuit of short-term goals.

Third-party intervention   Governments have always been willing to intervene in those industrial disputes they see as damaging to the nation's economy. The UK government currently funds ACAS, set up in 1974, and it was given statutory rights under the Employment Protection Act 1975. ACAS consists of a full-time chairman and nine part-time members made up of equal parts of trade union nominees, employer nominees and academics. It is staffed by civil servants. ACAS is, therefore, a state mechanism, which attempts to influence the conduct of industrial relations without either party having recourse to the use of law.

Given the reduction in the number of disputes, the role of ACAS as a mediator is less significant today. Indeed, the 1993 legislation removed its responsibility for the promotion of collective bargaining. In the new millennium, ACAS retains its role of advising on policy and practice, dealing with such current issues as flexibility. A major change, however, has been an increased involvement with employees as individuals. ACAS figures in 1999 show that requests for individual advice and individual conciliation are rising at around 15 per cent a year.

The role of the economy

As we can see from Table 12.4, in the 1960s and 1970s there was an unprecedented increase in those involved in personnel/HR work. Membership of the Institute doubled between 1969 and 1979. As a rough guide, it is estimated that members of the Institute represent half those involved in personnel HR.

While we have attributed part of the growth to developments in legislation, there is a clear correlation between personnel management and the state of the economy. In the UK, in the two decades of full employment prior to the early 1970s, considerable emphasis was placed on recruitment, selection, training and payment systems, to overcome labour shortages and to assist in the substitution and retention of skilled labour. Traditional activities of HR, such as recruitment and training, are clearly related to full employment economies. During the same period, the increased bargaining power of the trade union movement, especially at workplace level, resulted in increases in shopfloor collective bargaining and hence an increased workload for the personnel manager.

Given the hypothesis that economic growth and full employment lead to a thriving and active personnel function, then the reverse hypothesis might also be true: that an economic recession will not only reduce the need for recruitment selection and training, but that the negotiating power of trade unions will be impaired, resulting in a reduction of the extent and frequency of collective bargaining negotiations.

The evidence, however, paints a different picture. A study of personnel during a particularly severe recession 1980–2 reported that personnel managers had survived better

Table 12.4	Membership of the Institute of Personnel Management/Chartered Institute of Personnel and Development 1959–99	
	Year	*No.*
	1959	4 308
	1969	10 000
	1979	20 194
	1993	30 000
	1999	86 000

Source: Guest, 1982; CIPD

than most other management groups. New opportunities to demonstrate competence had been created in redundancy management and in achieving lower wage settlements in a generally peaceful industrial relations climate (Guest, 1982). While the economy picked up in the latter part of the 1980s, a further recession occurred at the beginning of the 1990s. Despite these fluctuations, HR, as a function of Institute membership, appeared to flourish (see Table 12.4). Much of the large increase in membership in the 1990s is associated with a merger in 1994 between the Institute of Personnel Management and the Institute of Training and Development to form the Institute of Personnel and Development.

There could be several explanations for the durability of personnel/HR.

● As we saw in Chapter 3, structural changes in the economy were especially severe upon traditional manufacturing. HR managers clearly suffered job losses in manufacturing, but there has been a growth of opportunities in other sectors, notably the service sector and newer high-tech industries.

● There has also been an influx of foreign multinationals, many of whom display more sophisticated human resource strategies than their British counterparts.

● In addition to such changes, new types of employment have emerged with an emphasis on flexibility, bringing with it a demand for training and the management of part-time and contract workers.

In one area, industrial relations, there has been reduction in the traditional activities of collective bargaining and dispute management. Unions are weaker, disputes fewer and settlements tend to be speedier. Nevertheless, where bargaining is still the norm, there has been a decentralization of activities placing more and not less emphasis on the role of workplace industrial relations managers.

We have already seen how HRM offers the personnel function new strategic directions and that the British experience is one where HRM is not incompatible with trade union negotiation. This is amply illustrated at Perkins Diesels (Case 12.2) with the negotiation of new work practices. The Perkins case is also a good example of the work of HR during a recession.

An illustration of HR policies changing over time may also be found in a longitudinal study over a decade in a retail bank (Holden and Wilkinson, 1999). The researchers found that with the 1980s banking boom, a number of 'soft' HRM measures were introduced. These were linked to the introduction of TQM and 'customer care' initiatives and included an emphasis on commitment, teambuilding and involvement. The bank unions were incorporated in this process. A watershed was reached in 1991 when the bank experienced operating losses. The following years saw the introduction of a number of 'hard' HRM policies, such as direct communication with the workforce rather than involving the union, and a series of downsizing and restructuring measures. The union resisted initially but were eventually sidelined. Management became much more directive as survival became the major issue.

Economic factors have clearly shaped HR strategies and these will be examined in the final section in this chapter. In all cases, however, economic influences must be seen in conjunction with the role of the state, the power of trade unions, management ideology and the organization structure. This reinforces the idea that the elements of our model cannot be viewed in isolation.

HRM and the labour force

From our brief review of traditional personnel activities in Table 12.1 we can see that the personnel function interacts with the labour force in two ways. It deals with individuals in the labour market through the activities of manpower planning, recruitment, selection, training and by administering payment and other reward and control systems. Second, it deals with the organized labour force through the mechanisms of joint consultation, collective bargaining and conflict management. We have already referred to these two activities in terms of people processing and industrial relations management. Even with the coming of HRM we may still regard these as the core work of the HRM function. As we noted in the first section of this chapter, the difference between traditional personnel and HRM is largely one of emphasis. We examine the interaction between the HRM function and the labour force by examining these two aspects of HR work.

People processing   Operating within a given labour market, the HR manager will attempt to fulfil the organization's demand for labour. This will be achieved mainly through the processes of recruitment, selection and training, often within the framework of a manpower plan.

In some cases the labour market will act as a total constraint to the extent that severe labour shortages in a given area may cause management to rethink its plans. In other cases the labour market operates as a partial constraint, and attempts will be made to entice workers away from existing jobs by offering them attractive pay packages and opportunities for career development. This can cause high levels of mobility among certain groups with scarce skills in an otherwise depressed labour market. A good example of this in the late 1990s can be found in the IT consulting industry, where scarce skills and an abundance of work have resulted in high levels of mobility and spiralling salaries. In other cases the firm attempts to change the composition of the labour market, meeting labour shortages by training substitute labour or by attracting certain groups back to work, such as married women with children by providing working conditions compatible with school hours. The increased use of flexible employment practices has been one of the reasons for the proportion of women in the workforce rising from 33 per cent in 1951 to 48 per cent in 1990 (Edwards *et al.*, 1992).

The student relying on textbooks may be forgiven for the assumption that HRM is an exercise in scientific management. This exercise is a matching process between the labour market and the needs of the organization employing a variety of scientifically based techniques of selection, training and employee motivation and retention. The student is confronted by a vast literature expounding such theories and offering a variety of techniques. However, part of this literature has concentrated upon a critique of these same theories, analyses and techniques, often labelling them as intuitive and subjective. A good illustration of this is to be found in the process of **employee selection**.

HRM textbooks see **selection** in terms of a matching process between the candidate and the job description. The decision to employ or reject a candidate is ultimately the prerogative of line management, but the administration of the process tends to be carried out by HR specialists applying scientific principles of structured interviewing and psychological testing as the following process shows:

● In most cases there will be a job description resulting from a job analysis. The process of creating a job description will generate criteria against which job candidates will be judged. Managers will use such information to build up stereotypes of 'ideal' candidates. However, the job description could well be dated and, in any case, the manager is just as likely to establish criteria based upon his or her own prejudices.

- The most popular form of selection method is the interview. Management literature abounds with advice for the would-be interviewer, but such advice owes more to general experience and deductive reasoning than it does to empirical research. There is considerable evidence that the interview is a relatively poor selection device and is particularly poor in terms of cost-effectiveness to the company. However, it is retained because no better method has yet been devised and it allows management to exercise judgement in the selection process.

If we view other areas of personnel processing we will find much the same story. Attempts by HR managers to use 'scientific techniques' often adapted from the behaviourial sciences have met with mixed results. This is true of a range of techniques incorporating the use of psychological tests in selection and placement, appraisal schemes, approaches to training and devising methods of payment to increase worker motivation.

The major problems with using such techniques in people processing are **reliability** and **validity**. Reliability refers to the extent to which a measure of consistency can be achieved, as, for example, in getting interviewers to behave in a similar fashion and ask candidates similar questions. Validity refers to the extent to which a technique used in personnel has some practical value for the organization. Does a selection interview actually discriminate between suitable and unsuitable candidates? Will a training programme lead to improved worker performance?

Because of such problems, HR managers have difficulty in proving that the work they do contributes in a measurable way to the effectiveness of the organization. For example, the results of a management development programme may not be apparent for a number of years, if at all, and many of the managers may have left the organization by that time. The difficulty of HRM proving its worth is a theme developed when we examine the relationship between HRM and an organization's goals later in this chapter. It is not surprising that many HR managers feel safer dealing with the day-to-day firefighting of employee and other problems than devising policies and procedures where the outcome is uncertain.

Industrial relations management   We can identify four major activities associated with industrial relations management.

- **Recognition of trade unions.** This involves both the recognition of the employee right to organize and the recognition of the union right to represent employees in such matters as wage negotiation. In a number of industries recognition has been slow. In some cases management will positively encourage their employees to join a trade union since they view a healthy union membership as contributing to the stability of workplace relations. This acceptance and encouragement has been a major factor in trade union growth and consequently the development of the personnel function. In recent years there have been new variations on the theme of recognition.

A key approach in companies such as IBM (as illustrated in Case 12.1), HP and Marks & Spencer is the development of employment relations strategies that do not involve trade unions. The growth of Japanese firms in Britain and their preference for company unions has led to the establishment of single union agreements being made in companies such as Nissan and Sanyo. Under such agreements management will allow only one trade union to represent all employees in the workforce. The News International case (see Case 1.1) is an interesting one. A single union deal was originally agreed between the management and the EETPU (the electricians' union). Subsequently the union has been de-recognized for bargaining purposes. Such de-recognition has been widely predicted in the face of weakened unions and alternative HRM strategies. This is largely supported by recent evidence. Over 50 per cent of workplaces in the UK have no recognized trade union and the workplaces with no union members at all rose from 36 per cent in 1990 to 47 per cent in 1998. Furthermore, there is evidence that firms set up in the 1980s are less likely to accept unions (Cully *et al.*, 1998).

Key concept 12.5 Trade union recognition

This involves the recognition by employers of the rights of employees to join and be represented by a trade union. Until the late 1990s such recognition had always been voluntary and the subject of intense conflict where such recognition was denied. However, recognition is now a legal right provided it is supported by the majority of employees. Nonetheless, the weakening of trade unions in the 1980s and 1990s in the UK, as a result of changing politics, economics and workplace cultures, has led to de-recognition becoming a more significant activity.

- **Collective bargaining.** We can see in Table 12.1 that **collective bargaining** involves management and unions in the negotiation of wages and conditions. The growth of localized bargaining in the 1950s and 1960s widened the role of both personnel managers and shop stewards as actual negotiators. The 1980s and 1990s were noted, initially, for a move to increased decentralization of bargaining and more recently to an absence of bargaining altogether as management de-recognize trade unions and favour alternative schemes of pay negotiation and employee involvement. There is clear evidence of an increase in the use of performance-related pay (PRP), usually on an individual basis (Millward *et al.*, 1992).

Key concept 12.6 Collective bargaining

Collective bargaining is a process in which the representatives of employers and the representatives of employees negotiate wages, conditions and other related aspects.

- **Disputes and grievance procedure.** In most organizations conflict is inevitable, either as part of the collective bargaining process or between staff in the operation of their roles. Many firms operate a disputes and grievance procedure to resolve such conflicts. HR managers are normally involved in the development and operation of such procedures. In most cases the formalization and complexity of the procedure is directly related to the size of the firm. In the 1990s there has been a clear growth in the number of *individual* disputes and grievances taken against employing organizations and the willingness of individuals to take civil action in the courts on issues of perceived unfair dismissal and discrimination.

● **Administering procedures relating to employee participation.** These can involve a sophisticated arrangement of works councils and employee committees, as employed by the John Lewis partnership. For many firms, however, it involves no more than the administration of an employee suggestion scheme. As we saw in the first section of this chapter, HRM favours employee involvement over collective bargaining. This has led to a renewed interest in forms of participation such as works councils and briefing groups.

A changing scene   In 1980 a survey of personnel management in manufacturing industry and the health service found that those working in personnel regarded industrial relations as their most important activity (Guest and Horwood, 1980). Since then of course, as we have noted, industrial relations management has undergone considerable shifts in emphasis, although we should be cautious about the speed and extent of that change. There may be a number of possible models of operating industrial relations at the level of the firm. We will view these when we discuss IIR strategies at the end of this chapter.

'New Industrial Relations' appeared as a term in the 1980s. Then it was associated with practices brought in with Japanese transplants in firms such as Nissan. Such 'new' approaches usually embraced a legally binding contract between the firm and the unions and a peace clause where employees agree not to strike while the contract is in force. Around the same time, the term 'employee relations' came to be used in many firms instead of 'industrial relations'. Supposedly, the latter term is associated with trade unions, adversarial negotiations and conflict, while the former conjures images of a more co-operative approach involving the entire workforce. Currently the main features of 'New Industrial Relations' (IR) would appear to have much in common with 'soft' HRM. Union involvement is accepted, but pay rises are linked to productivity and the acceptance of more flexible working practices. Exemplars of this 'New IR' include Rover, Shell, ICI and Mobil. Such changes have even been accepted by the TUC, labelled as the 'partnership'. For John Monks, its General Secretary, 'partnership' means for the employee, job security, an extension of involvement, fair financial rewards and an investment in training. In return the organization gets increased flexibility, commitment, an acceptance of the need to change and cooperation with management (Monks, 1998). This may, of course, be the only pragmatic approach available in the face of a weakened trade union movement and, in some cases, management use this to increase pressure on the workforce.

However, a review of Table 12.2 reveals a number of new priorities. In terms of people processing the emphasis has shifted to job previews, psychometric testing, performance appraisal and feedback and pay related to individual and organization performance. Employees are expected to be flexible, multi-skilled and participate in work improvement and problem-solving groups. The emphasis is clearly upon meeting business goals but employees are rewarded for their commitment with job security and a focus on their welfare. Later in this chapter we will explore the extent to which this matches the reality of organizational life.

HRM and technology

In Chapter 3 we examined the impact of technology and, in particular, technical change on jobs. We deal with two areas of significance to HRM: training and industrial relations, although the type of technology and changes in technology have implications for recruitment, selection and payment systems as well.

Technical change invariably results in a mismatch between the needs of the firm and the skills of the workforce. For example, there are more jobs in Scotland in micro-electronics than in coal and iron and steel, its more traditional industrial base. Some firms tackle the mismatch by the use of outside contractors, but longer-term cost-effectiveness will probably lie in developing training programmes. Such training focuses not only on the development of 'high-tech' skills but upon general workforce orientation towards using new technology, as in using computer terminals to input data, and upon more general management training. The creation of a more flexible workforce has been identified as a training priority for many organizations.

The commonly accepted view of the impact of technical change on industrial relations, doubtless fuelled by media coverage of events at places such as Wapping (Chapter 1), is that it creates problems, largely because trade unions resist change. This resistance is inevitably linked to fears over job losses, deskilling and increased management control. It was such issues that concerned the Fleet Street print workers for several years in their opposition to photocomposition.

However, certain factors may temper this perspective. Trade unions generally attempt to influence the direction of new technology to maximize its benefits and minimize its costs. A survey by Daniel (1987) concluded that the reaction of most workers to technical change has been favourable. He found that technical change was equated with investment and optimism, and was often seen as a route to better jobs and higher wages. There is, however, general agreement that in many companies the level of consultation over technical change issues is low.

The nature of the technology offers some groups of workers more bargaining power than others because they operate and control key technologies. This power has an impact on the negotiating process. In manufacturing industry, those who manufacture special in-house tools are central to the entire operation. UK mineworkers have traditionally used their position as the providers of an essential fuel supply as a strong bargaining weapon. In their disputes of 1972 and 1974 the National Union of Mineworkers used an overtime ban as a tactical weapon to reduce coal stocks in the power stations before calling for an 'all out' strike. The resulting power cuts and their impact on the rest of industry was a significant influence in the collective bargaining process. Not all workers enjoy bargaining power as a result of controlling key technologies. The UK postal workers, in their dispute of 1971, had their case weakened by firms using alternative courier services for mail and by making greater use of alternative technology in the form of the telephone service.

With the decline in the coverage and frequency of collective bargaining the incidences of strategic groups using their collective power is rare. Instead we see groups with scarce skills, such as IT consultants and plumbers, using their labour market position to gain high rewards.

Changes in technology have had an impact on HRM itself. Computerized record-keeping has long been a feature of many HR departments. More recently those same departments have taken advantage of specialist software packages. These not only offer a framework for HR records and planning, but they also provide links with the firm's accounting systems as well.

Cultural influences

We have noted the considerable influences exerted by the state, the level of economic activity and the labour market upon HRM activities. It is, therefore, not surprising that differences in practice can also be traced to cultural variations. In this section we will observe differences between the operation of HRM in various countries and then examine the impact of globalization on HRM.

In Chapter 3 we introduced broad differences in economic systems that we identified as Anglo-Saxon, social market and Asian. Many of the differences between these models have their roots in cultural diversity.

In **Anglo-Saxon** systems, such as in the USA and the UK, there is an emphasis on the free market, job mobility, managerial autonomy and the weakening of trade unions. As a consequence, management are generally given a greater freedom to respond to a dynamic competitive environment and there is less emphasis on job security. In other words, there tends to be an emphasis on 'hard HRM'.

However, there are differences between the UK and USA. In the UK the HR function has reflected the significance of trade unions and industrial relations. In the USA the activities of HR are shaped by prevailing social attitudes which favour the use of law and which tend to be distrustful of trade unions. As a consequence much greater use is made of the law in such matters as the employment contract and equal opportunities. In addition, there is much lower trade union membership than in Britain and therefore much less evidence of traditional industrial relations activity by HR managers. Some companies in the USA have developed HR strategies which actively discourage trade union organizations and focus on keeping the unions out by offering attractive welfare provisions and pay packages. There are, of course, wide variations in practice ranging from fairly sophisticated approaches incorporating both 'hard' and 'soft' elements of HR in some multinational companies to an apparent lack of concern for HR issues in other companies.

The **social market** model is typified by a concern for employee welfare and representation, codified in law.

In Germany, there is highly legalized approach to employee and employer rights and duties. Collective bargaining is highly centralized at an industrial level and industrial relations is not a major concern of the HR manager. Specialist management functions such as HR play a much smaller role in Germany than elsewhere, a correspondingly higher status being accorded to line management. In Scandanavia, management autonomy is challenged by the presence of strong trade unions and employee rights reflect their disposition towards social equality.

The **Asian** model has an emphasis on welfare provision in the form of housing and sports facilities and upon other mechanisms to cement commitment between the employee and the firm as with the emphasis placed on corporate values and lengthy induction processes in many Japanese and Korean firms. However, there are differences both between and within countries. In major companies in Japan, HR policies reflect the operation of a dual-labour market bestowing considerable advantages on a privileged group of employees, including lifetime employment, seniority payments and a whole range of company welfare provisions that are not available to temporary or non-contract workers (the section on Japanese management in Chapter 4 has a fuller account). In South Korea, with a strong trade union presence, there is more emphasis placed on industrial relations.

Despite the differences between these three models, there is some evidence of practices converging. We have already noted the influence of Japanese companies in Britain and the interest in single union, 'no-strike' agreements. Many American companies operating in Britain tend to be non-unionized and the type of strategies employed by firms, like HP and IBM, have gained currency amongst personnel practitioners in Britain. There is an increased use of law in employment in the UK, and in Japan lifetime employment and seniority principles are exchanged for more 'Western' practices.

Developments in HRM are central to this theme of convergence. The assumption that economic and structural change will push firms towards a common HRM model was investigated as part of a study of HRM practices across Europe (Brewster and Bournois, 1991; Brewster *et al.*, 1991). The study found considerable variation in HRM practice, particularly between Britain and the rest of Europe, despite a growth of regional policies and legislation in the EU. The idea of a common model was challenged by different national institutional and legal frameworks. Guest (1990) goes further and puts forward a case that HRM is probably culturally specific to the USA. He likens the core characteristics of HRM to those of the 'American Dream' with its emphasis on individualism, hard work, reward, and fighting the frontier, which in this case is represented both by inefficient practices and by Japanese competition.

In most national settings management practices are derived from a number of influences, some of which will be cultural, while others relate to more common themes of technology, markets and organizational size.

Globalization and HRM   The theme of convergence in HR practices is highlighted by developments associated with **globalization** (Chapter 2 has a full account). The growth of multinational and transnational operations and an increase in the numbers of joint ventures has focused attention on the development of global HR practices. The attention is due to a number of related factors:

- The growth of global business through multinationals and networks of cooperation.
- The difficulties encountered by global firms and joint ventures as a direct result of 'weak' HR policies or significant cultural differences.
- A shortage of skilled international managers.

As a consequence, **global HRM** deals with:

- managing staff in cross-border situations;
- developing international managers;
- the relationships between the multinational and its operations in host countries;
- an understanding of comparative issues: the why and the how practices may vary across different international locations.

There are three approaches to global HRM:

- The **universalist approach** is linked to convergence. The assumption is that there is a model of HRM that can be applied in all countries. Such approaches tend to be found in those multinationals with a strong, centralized corporate culture, as with

HP and IBM. The reality is that even in such firms there tends to be a modification of policy and practice to meet local legal and cultural requirements.

- The **contextualist approach** deems that the most effective HR policies and practices are those that work best in specific situations. This is a culture-specific approach and echoes the work of Geert Hofstede, described in Chapter 4. He believed that HR practices needed to vary as core values differed between cultures. His main study was IBM, thereby refuting the universalist perspective. An example he gave was that of individual performance-related pay. He argued that this worked best in Anglo-Saxon cultures displaying individualism, risk taking and masculine characteristics (Hofstede, 1980b).

- The **globalist approach** argues for a mix of global and local practices, and that the universalist and contextualist approaches can be mixed to good effect. For example, there can exist a global policy about rewarding staff or about employee welfare. However, the application of such a policy will vary depending on local laws and customs. Brewster *et al*. (2002) found that the most global activities in common were communication, recruitment and selection, benefits, training and development and performance management, while the most localized ones were employment law, equality and diversity and industrial relations.

Organizational aspects of HRM

In this section we will view the relationship between organization size and HR activities and focus on the relationship between HRM and other management activities in the organization structure. A major theme to emerge in the dealings with management from other functional areas is that of goal conflict. Attempts to resolve such conflict are currently focused upon organizational culture and strategic HRM. We will deal with this aspect at the end of the section.

HRM and organization size

The relationship between the growth of the firm and the development of formalization, differentiation and specialization has already been discussed in Chapter 5. The development of personnel management departments in UK and USA firms during the early part of the 20th century can be clearly attributed to the increasing size of the organization. A control mechanism was needed, particularly in the areas of recruitment and payment systems, giving rise to specialist positions of 'wages officer' and 'labour officer'. Such positions concerned themselves with recruitment, discipline, timekeeping and general administration of the payment system, including the control of bonus payments. This growth of the size of firms in the UK was also a major factor in the changes in collective bargaining, placing more emphasis on bargaining within individual firms rather than at industry level. We have already noted how this resulted in the creation of industrial relations specialists.

A comprehensive survey of UK practices noted that whereas only 7 per cent of firms employing fewer than 50 people had personnel/HR specialists, the proportion rose to 93 per cent for firms employing over 2000 people (Daniel and Millward, 1983). Furthermore, we can see that the increasing size of the firm has led to increasing specialization within HR itself, although current practice may be reversing that trend.

HRM, organization structure and goals

There is growing evidence, not only in Britain but also throughout Europe, that HRM has become decentralized. This relates in part to the increasing adoption of new approaches with an emphasis on a greater involvement of line managers. However, in Britain, decentralization has also occurred in those firms that retain traditional collective bargaining. A major reason offered for this change is the decreasing role that is played by employers' associations. They play much less of a role in all aspects of business in Britain than elsewhere. For example, major car companies, such as Ford, Vauxhall and Peugeot-Talbot have opted out of membership of their employers' association in Britain, but they have retained membership of associations in other European countries where they operate (Edwards *et al.*, 1992). Despite the trend towards decentralization, several large organizations, such as Marks & Spencer, retain a large centralized presence.

The spread of HRM practices has been cited for the increase in **power and influence** among HR practitioners. Torrington (1989) tends to support that view, but remains somewhat sceptical.

> Most of those in the personnel function who espouse Human Resource Management are doing so in search of enhanced status and power. With the obsession about innovation that currently pervades management thinking, a change of label is a useful indication of innovation, even if you are not too sure there is anything different in the package. (*Torrington, 1989, p. 64*)

While there is considerable disagreement as to whether power and influence have increased, there is no disagreement that traditionally the personnel function did not enjoy high status within many organizations. The same is also claimed for HRM. We can identify three problem areas:

- conflict between HR and other functional managers (these are sometimes referred to generically as line managers);
- difficulties encountered by HR managers in proving their worth to the organization either because of the suspicion of line management towards new techniques or because of the way HR managers organize their work;
- conflict within HRM itself between professional and organizational goals.

Goal conflict within the organization   In general the research has focused on case studies where problems have been identified in the relationship between HRM and other departments. Little is known about how successful HR departments operate and how they successfully integrate with other functional areas. This may well give a somewhat stereotyped view of the HRM function and ignore a wide range of situations where HR managers are happy with their role and are seen to be effective. The various cases should be viewed within the limitation.

Much of what follows in this section is derived from earlier work by Karen Legge, in which she refers exclusively to the personnel function and personnel managers. So as not to cause confusion, these terms are retained. Although now over 25 years old, her perspectives offer considerable insights into intra-organizational conflict and status issues, and, more significantly, the problems and issues are recognizable by today's HR practitioners.

Much of Legge's analysis is based on the line and staff model. This has often been used to analyse the personnel function, depicting personnel operating in an advisory capacity only.

> The personnel department here is as it should be, as service to the line. For example, if we want more labour they get it, train it, and arrange for it to be paid. They provide information for negotiating too, but I do the real negotiating. (*General Works Manager quoted in Legge, 1978, p. 51*)

Legge sees this relationship between personnel and line management as a basis for conflict in that the latter have a 'confused, hazy and/or stereotyped perception of the potential nature and scope of a personnel department's activities' and 'tend to consider that personnel departments are "out of touch" with the kind of problems and constraints which face them' (Legge, 1978, p. 52). In particular, other managers feel that personnel do not identify as closely as they do with the profit goals of the organization.

In her case studies, Legge saw a vicious circle operating, as illustrated in Figure 12.2. Personnel are not involved in planning and decision-making, resulting in human resource problems that are left for personnel to sort out; pressure of time and lack of resources lead to crisis management resulting in line management having a poor perception of the personnel function and hence its non-involvement in decision-making. The circle is reinforced by the failure on the part of some line managers to recognize the need for a specialist role for personnel since many personnel activities are carried out by all managers, as in the case of selection and training. Attempts to break free of the circle by personnel specialists adopting specialized techniques based on the behaviourial sciences are often rebuffed by a suspicious line management. In this way, carefully constructed appraisal schemes flounder in the face of line management opposition. As a result, Legge sees many personnel managers 'opt for an easy life' and concentrate on a more acceptable welfare role.

| Figure 12.2 | A vicious circle depicting the relationship between personnel and line management |

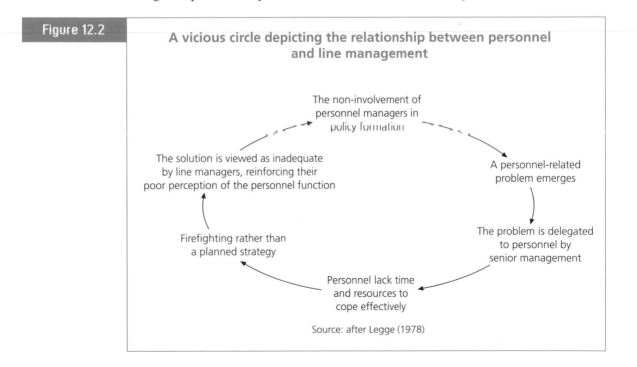

Source: after Legge (1978)

`The effectiveness of HR`   In a study of personnel management in manufacturing and the health service, personnel themselves contributed to the kind of problems Karen Legge outlined. Personnel managers enjoyed crisis management and took on a variety of different activities to boost their credibility in the eyes of the rest of management. This resulted in a too broad and heavy workload with the consequence of ineffectiveness and incompetence. Personnel management were thus unable to contribute effectively to the goals of the organization as identified by line management and reinforced the vicious circle (Guest and Horwood, 1980).

The question of effectiveness and personnel proving their worth was also raised by Legge.

> Personnel management by definition, is chiefly concerned with the acquisition, maintenance and development of one of the resources (i.e., the human resource) through which the organisational ends are achieved rather than with the ends themselves. They are concerned with means rather than ends and inputs rather than outputs, and in situations where there is difficulty in determining the relationship between the two. (*Legge, 1978, p. 60*)

The two consequences of this are first that the credit for a successful personnel policy is taken to line management who actually perform the policy, but personnel carry the blame for an ineffective policy. Second, it is extremely difficult to quantify the outcome of personnel activity or even isolate its effect. As we have already mentioned, the success of a management development programme may be so diffuse and long-term that any financial assessment is impossible.

The following example illustrates the difficulty personnel/HR managers have in proving their value to the organization. A bus company in the north of England was concerned about the growing labour turnover among its bus drivers and used exit interviews conducted by the HR manager in an attempt to reduce the number who actually left. The interviews, which were conducted whenever a bus driver gave notice of terminating his contract, appeared to have very little impact for the first 6 months, but then the numbers leaving began to fall. Closer examination of this particular situation revealed that during the period when turnover was highest, a bus company in a neighbouring area was recruiting at a higher basic wage, while the time of falling turnover coincided with a downturn in the economy when all job opportunities were much scarcer. In other words, HR practitioners often deal with external forces outside their control.

We can now see that the first two problem areas are linked. The conflict between HR managers and other managers is a function of HR managers' seeming inability to prove their worth.

The notion of effectiveness of HR has been the focus of considerable research from the late 1990s to the present day. Richardson and Thompson (1999) have noted more than 30 UK and USA studies since 1990. The overwhelming conclusion from these studies is that people have a considerable impact on performance and productivity and that HR has much to contribute towards organizational success.

Patterson *et al.* (1998) carried out a 10-year study of 100 manufacturing firms, examining a number of variables and their impact on performance. They concluded that HR interventions, such as concern for welfare, training and supervisory support had the greatest impact on both profitability and productivity, being responsible for a 10 per cent variation in the former and 29 per cent in the latter. By comparison, strategy issues accounted for only 2 per cent variation in profitability and concern for quality only 1 per cent.

Guest *et al.* (2000) confirmed much of these UK and USA studies but offered a more sanguine approach in keeping with the earlier work of Karen Legge. They carried out a major study across a large and varied number of UK firms. They interviewed 462 chief executives and 610 HR managers. Their conclusions were as follows:

- Most chief executives recognized the link between HR practices and performance but still failed to prioritize HR issues.
- The study saw effectiveness, not only in terms of the practices themselves but in terms of how they were applied. Such HR processes relied heavily on the capabilities of the HR department.
- There was disagreement between the chief executives and HR people as to which practices were the most significant.
- Both chief executives and HR managers rated the performance of the typical HR department as low.
- The study identified effective practices from a number of other studies and these are shown in Table 12.2 earlier in this chapter. Most organizations failed to make use of these modern practices and the study found that less than 1 per cent of firms used more than 75 per cent of them and only 25 per cent used 50 per cent of them.

Organizational versus professional goals   Our third problem area concerns the potential conflict between organizational and professional goals. HR managers are popularly portrayed as a group in the middle, owing allegiance to both the needs of the workforce and the needs of the organization they serve. As we saw from the IPM's definition of personnel management at the beginning of this chapter, there is no conflict in that the good professional is concerned 'to achieve efficiency and justice, neither of which can be achieved without the other'. This is also the line taken in classic definitions of HRM.

However, it is clear that professional high ideals can conflict with the daily pressures of getting the job done. In practice, however, practitioners rarely feel such conflict. They generally see themselves as part of the management group and, as such, subscribe to management goals, even though they do not always operate as line management would like.

The kind of problems identified above can be tackled through the creation of an organization culture that stresses cooperation and consensus. It is to this we now turn.

The role of organizational culture

We have seen how HR managers reflect the culture of a particular enterprise. In general terms, the activities of HRM, especially those concerned with recruitment, selection and training, ensure that employees fit the prevailing culture of the firm. This takes on a more fundamental aspect in those firms that have identified a mission and build their organization culture around that mission. We dealt with such aspects more fully when we discussed organizational cultures in Chapter 5. In such firms, HRM assumes a role of major importance.

In the 1980s it was common for many UK local authorities to attempt to change the culture of their organizations in accordance with (usually) a guiding political ideology. The focus is usually on the criteria used in the recruitment and selection of new staff, with a special concern for equal opportunities, as the following job advertisement reveals:

> As part of Lambeth's Equal Opportunities Policy, applications are welcome from people regardless of race, creed, nationality, age, sex, sexual orientation or responsibility for children or dependents. (*Guardian, 20 November, 1985*)

In the late 1990s such affirmative action tended to be replaced by more general and less positive statements, such as 'striving to achieve equal opportunities'.

We can see from Case 12.1 that IBM lays great store in selecting the right type of individual, investigating heavily in management training and establishing excellent conditions of employment. In the cases in Chapters 4 and 5 – Nissan and HP respectively – the importance of selection again emerges. In HP the culture is sustained by paying attention to management styles, as in their technique of 'management by wandering around'. In all these cases, the senior management see employment relations as a major route to establishing the kind of company they want.

We have already seen that the development of organizational culture, which stresses commitment, quality and flexibility, is a central device of HRM. For many organizations this implies a strategic change. It is to the notion of HRM strategy that we now turn.

Human resource management strategies

We have already noted that HRM not only places great emphasis upon a strategic approach to human resource issues, but also that such strategies aim for total integration within the corporate objectives of the enterprise. Such a strategic approach is a relatively recent phenomenon. Just over two decades ago, an examination of a variety of companies revealed that specific personnel and industrial relations policies were notable by their absence. From her case studies Legge concluded:

> In company decision-making, the personnel management considerations involved in production, marketing and finance decisions were not so much overruled (although this also occurred . . .) as went by default. (*Legge, 1978, p. 37*)

She noted that where policy did exist it was fragmented, short-term and largely reactive. Traditionally, where HR strategies have existed they have been based around manpower planning. We shall examine this first before attempting to map out some alternative models.

Manpower planning

This process is concerned with matching future manpower requirements with future manpower availability and involves consideration of both the quantity and the quality of the labour force, including the analysis of such factors as the age profile of the staff. A variety of techniques have been used, from simple demand–supply models to more sophisticated statistical models of the type traditionally used by the Civil Service to plan its own manpower requirements. The output of a **manpower planning** exercise should set the guidelines for HR strategies in recruitment, selection, training, retirement and so on. The resulting strategies will vary depending on the relationship of the predicted future demand to predicted future supply.

For example, a firm whose demand for labour exceeds the predicted supply may have to consider changes in its payment strategies with a view to attracting more recruits or investigate the possibilities of introducing new technology to replace labour. Where the existing labour supply exceeds the predicted future demands then plans may have to be formulated for early retirement, redundancy or perhaps looking to marketing strategies to increase the demand for the firm's goods and services. Even where demand and supply are evenly matched, a manpower planning exercise may give management useful insights into the nature of labour utilization and suggest where improvements can be made.

The reality, of course, is much more complex than the kind of model illustrated above. Such complexities are often the result of long lead-times and the impact of other variables over which management have little control. The planning of the supply of future medical doctors is an exercise that must incorporate projected birth and death rates, take account of the age profile of the nation and examine trends in disease and illness. Given that the training time of future doctors is at least 7 years, allowance must be made for drop-out rates along the way. Even if these complexities are overcome, the exercise can be jeopardized by national cut-backs in healthcare spending or changes in EU law which extend the pool of available labour.

In the late 1980s management were fed considerable information about 'the demographic time-bomb', a forecast of a declining birth rate and its likely impact on the recruitment of school leavers in the 1990s. Some firms such as Ford Motor Company set up programmes to counteract a shortfall in the future supply of labour by building closer relationships with local schools and by projecting an improved image to the local community. In practice, any likely impact of a declining birth rate was mitigated by a recession and an increasing trend towards smaller workforces. Rather than scratching around for new recruits, most companies were more active in making employees redundant.

Links to corporate strategy

As a result of interest in HRM, there has been renewed discussion of the relationship between HR strategy and the corporate objectives of the enterprise. There are obvious examples where a change in business strategy leads to a corresponding change in the HR strategy. Survival in a recession may depend on either cutting back on operations or developing new areas of operation. In a recession clear policies may need to emerge on redundancy, as we saw with IBM in Case 12.1, or more flexible ways of working are introduced to cut costs. The development of new products and markets calls for new skills, which may necessitate recruiting new staff or retraining existing employees. Whenever the 'rules' of the business change there is generally an implication for HR policy. In higher education, new arrangements for funding have placed emphasis upon the research and publications record of the academic staff. Many of the newer universities, created from the old polytechnic sector, are attempting to build up their research and publications record through the recruitment of staff who can offer them those skills and who can bring with them a healthy publications record. The emphasis is therefore shifting away from teaching to research. This has implications not only for recruitment and selection but also the promotion and development policies for existing staff.

Different product markets call for variations in HR strategy. A simple way of illustrating this is to use the BCG matrix that we introduced in Chapter 5. This seems to have found renewed favour among HR academics (see, for example, Purcell, 1989).

In a **cash cow** product market the emphasis is upon stable, low-cost production to 'milk' the profits. HR policies associated with cash cows are those that ensure stability and continuity and include formalized procedures for job evaluation, a focus on welfare provision to retain staff, and, where unions are involved, highly structured collective bargaining. Cash cows may be associated with a need to keep costs to a minimum and with the use of a flexible labour force and high numbers of part-timers. However, as Purcell points out, the very profitability of cash cows may lead to complacency, such as over-staffing.

Where **stars** and **question marks** are concerned the emphasis shifts to operating a more flexible approach. HR priorities become the selection and development of innovative staff and the creation of teams across different functional specialisms. The long-term uncertainty associated with both stars and question marks places emphasis upon the management of change.

For **dogs** the focus turns to cutting losses. This may mean redundancy programmes and it could involve retraining, transfer and even relocation.

| Case 12.2 | ## The Perkins Engine Group |

In the 1990s, the Perkins Engine Group was owned by the Canadian firm Varity, a company that also controlled Massey Ferguson. Perkins makes diesel engines of all types ranging from seven to 1500 brake horsepower. Its main manufacturing operation, Peterborough Engines, is based in the town of the same name and currently employs nearly three-quarters of the total workforce. Despite the acquisition of Rolls Royce Diesel Engines in 1984 and Lesley Gardner Diesels in 1986, the overall size of the company was reduced from over 10 000 in the 1970s to 4900 in 1989. Such a change was not possible without a significant change in HR strategies and in the work of the HR function.

In the late 1970s the company appeared to be in a healthy position. The demand for its products was high and the concern was to operate at full capacity. The plant was working 7 days a week and the 10 000 employees were working an average of 10 per cent overtime per person. The company was turning out 1000 diesel engines a day with 86 per cent of these destined for the export market. The company adopted fairly typical personnel and industrial relations strategies for the engineering industry. Payment-by-results was the norm, training tended to focus on an engineering apprenticeship programme, and industrial relations negotiation was highly centralized. The main trade union at Perkins (the AUEW) was strong, with a high membership among shop-floor employees. There was a high number of short unofficial disputes that were highly localized. The high demand for the company's product meant that stoppages had to be avoided at all costs. The strategy adopted by the company was for a central personnel department to handle all industrial relations matters, including the negotiation for local disputes, in a bid to formalize procedures and take grievances away from their immediate location. As a consequence, local line management was seldom involved in industrial relations and related personnel issues.

In 1980 the demand for diesel engines fell sharply. In response, the management opted for a strict control of all overtime working, introduced short-time working, changed working practices to enhance the competitiveness of the firm and embarked on a series of voluntary and compulsory redundancies.

The urgency of change was all the greater because of the company's heavy reliance on export markets and hence competition from diesel engine manufacturers all over the world, competing for a declining market share. The management recognized that such changes could not be made without consultation with the trade unions and the workforce, so that communication became the key to the implementation of the strategic changes. The changes were brought about through a variety of methods:

- All changes were negotiated with the trade union and the AUEW participated fully in the exercise. The union recognized that survival of the firm was the issue, but found the dilemma of protecting jobs for some, while sanctioning the redundancy of others, difficult to reconcile with traditional trade union practices. The redundancy issue was particularly difficult in that management could not afford to let go all those who wanted to under a generous voluntary scheme. The financial burden would be too high and such programmes might leave the company under-staffed in certain key areas. Compulsory redundancy was therefore inevitable with the subsequent difficult negotiations and disputes.

- The union also had to agree to new work practices. These generally involved the broadening of jobs and the introduction of more flexible work methods through the ending of demarcation agreements. Discussion and negotiation on this issue was specific to individual departments and sections, effectively decentralizing industrial relations. Line management became much more involved in personnel matters as the emphasis on the introduction of new work practices was shifted to man-management at the local level.

- There was a concern that all employees received a clear picture of the threats facing the company and fear that information could easily be distorted. The director took it upon himself to brief personally all senior management and trade union leaders. Team briefings were held throughout the organization. A company video was produced which examined the current position and explained the need for change. A training-school programme was set up which gave sessions on the firm's position and encouraged feedback.

- A 'Fair Days Work Charter' was produced which stressed the need for all employees, both staff and hourly paid, to work for the whole day; to achieve output and quality targets set by management; to suggest ways of improving work methods and equipment; and to work cooperatively.

By 1982 employment levels had been reduced to 6000, but it was decided that the strategy had to continue throughout the 1980s despite the acquisition of new plants such as Rolls Royce. Redundancy became an annual exercise with the usual mix of voluntary and compulsory to preserve key skills. Three new strategies emerged:

- First, a major reorganization took place. The company was restructured around autonomous strategic business units operating as independent profit centres. Senior management were given considerable responsibility and scope to enhance the competitiveness of their business unit. Entrepreneurship was encouraged and a fair proportion of senior management salary was tied to performance. There were plans to extend this scheme to all employees at some future date.

- Second, considerable emphasis was placed on the training of employees to widen their range of skills to enhance flexibility and to increase the general level of skill throughout the organization. The company's programme was considered successful enough for them to win a National Training Award in 1987.

- Third, new investments were made in automation to improve quality and reduce staffing costs. Assistance with modernization was obtained by the company participating in an EU-funded project for the furtherance of technology transfer by the dissemination of operating experience and best practice.

As a result of the various changes the company has become much leaner, focusing on the employment of skilled, flexible employees. Consequently the company's workforce remained stable for a number of years.

In 1996, Perkins became part of the LucasVarity automotive and aerospace consortium. In 1997 Perkins was sold to the Caterpillar Engineering Group. A proposed alliance with VW for the provision of electronic diesel injection engines fell through, as this would have required too much investment to move into what would have been a new type of business for Perkins. By 1999 Perkins still employed over 4000 workers and had played a major part in making up, in part, for falling profits elsewhere in the Caterpillar Group.

Sources: Jackson, 1983; Company information, 1988; *Financial Times*, 1995–9

Questions

1 What were the key contextual factors that led to change at Perkins?
2 How did HR strategy change over the period covered by the case?
3 To what extent has Perkins embraced 'new style' HRM?

New approaches to strategy?

> The pressure on human resource managers to be strategic is almost as intense now as the campaign to persuade us to eat healthily. We all believe it is a good thing to be strategic – career progressive for ourselves, prestigious for our profession and it might even do our organizations good as well. (*Herriot and Pinder, 1992, p. 36*)

The emergence of HRM was viewed by some as a strategic lifeline to a group of practitioners without a clear strategy. However, we have seen that the classic HRM approach is perhaps more talked about than practised and that there are significant variations. We will attempt to identify some of those variations by constructing a model of HRM practice in a British context. Many of the models will also be familiar to practitioners in other countries.

We present a model in Figure 12.3, which is based upon the work of Fox (1974), Purcell and Sisson (1983) and Guest (1989, 1990).

The model identifies two broad categories, **unitarist and pluralist frames of reference**. The unitarist approach emphasizes shared goals while the pluralist approach acknowledges that different groups within the organization may have different goals. We have identified several variations.

Figure 12.3	**Strategic approaches to HRM**

Unitarist
       Traditional unitarist
       Sophisticated unitarist

Pluralist
       New industrial relations pluralist
       Opportunistic pluralist
       Sophisticated pluralist
       Traditional pluralist

Key concept 12.7 Unitary and pluralist frames of reference

The unitarist frame of reference emphasizes shared goals among all members of the organization. Those managers who hold such a perspective find it difficult to acknowledge that trade unions have a legitimate role in their organization. A pluralist frame of reference acknowledges that different groups within the organization may have different goals. Within such a perspective, trade unions are seen as legitimate representatives of the wishes of employees.

Traditional unitarists   These represent a management whose predominant view is the opposition to all kinds of trade union groups. Such a strategy can result in direct confrontation, as was seen in the much-publicized Grunwick dispute of 1976 when the managing director of a film-processing plant in Southall denied union recognition to a group of Asian workers. The ensuing dispute had racial as well as industrial relations implications. The 1980s and 1990s has seen traditional unitarists engage more readily in redundancy programmes and be more willing to use contract labour (Millward *et al.*, 1992). It was predicted that the political and economic changes of the 1980s would encourage the traditional unitarists to emerge from their closets embodied in 'macho-management' stereotypes, with Michael Edwardes (ex of British Leyland) and Ian McGregor (ex of British Steel and the Coal Board) as the hero figures. However, such stereotypes perhaps owe more to media distortion than accurate analysis.

Sophisticated unitarists   These are found in companies like IBM and HP that are the role models for HRM practice. In such companies considerable time and effort is taken to ensure workforce commitment to overall company objectives. Such companies are typified by fairly sophisticated personnel policies in selection, training, reward systems and employee involvement. The majority also happen to be non-union.

New industrial relations pluralists   These are to be found in firms that espouse the 'single union, no strike philosophy'. The models for such companies are the Japanese transplants such as Nissan and Toyota. Many such companies attempt to involve their employees through a works council or similar institution. Probably many managers in this category are aspiring unitarists.

Opportunistic pluralists These represent managers in unionized firms who have used the economic and political climate as an opportunity to roll back the influence of the trade unions. They have found no need to adopt the aggressive anti-union stance of the traditional unitarists and are still prepared to work within a **pluralist frame of reference**. As Kessler and Bayliss write:

> most managers took the line that since they could get what they wanted through negotiations or by acting unilaterally, there was no need to attack the unions. (Kessler and Bayliss, 1998, p. 35)

The idea of opportunism occurs frequently in any discussion of HRM in a UK context, particularly with reference to the application of 'hard' HRM and its association with job cuts. Such opportunism is also associated with an absence of long-term strategy.

Sophisticated pluralists On the other hand these see consultation and negotiation with trade unions as the keystone of their HR policies. Such firms have well-established procedures for determining pay and conditions and often have mechanisms for employee participation. Managers in this category see that change is necessary but prefer it to be agreed with employees rather than imposed upon them. Ferner and Hyman (1992) found such an approach more common in European countries other than Britain, but it can be found here as well. Most of the major oil companies, BA and some local governments exhibit such strategies. Perkins Diesels (Case 12.2) also see negotiation as an important part of organization change. The sophisticated pluralist approach suggests that HRM is not incompatible with trade unionism.

Traditional pluralists These tend not to be strategically oriented, preferring instead to adopt the standard reactive response to problems. They manage by 'firefighting', and as such fit in well with our illustrations of personnel management when we discussed the influence of organizational structure and goals upon the HR function.

As we have mentioned throughout this chapter, there is much discussion of firms shifting towards an HRM approach. The above classification implies that managers have not one but several models from which to choose. However, as we saw in our discussion of organizational culture in Chapter 5, culture change is particularly difficult. The adoption of HRM policies is not only costly, but may well meet with resistance from all employees including management. It is not by chance that HRM strategies are often associated with greenfield sites. Nonetheless there is enough evidence to suggest that HR practitioners are reacting to changing circumstances. The relative weakness of trade unions in countries like the UK has reduced the need for extensive exercises in collective bargaining and conflict management. We have seen how some managers have used this as an opportunity to reduce staffing levels and increase labour flexibility. In declining industries there is a reduction in recruitment and training and a focus on redundancy and early retirement. In growth areas there is an increased concern for the selection, development and retention of a core group of employees.

We can see from these models that there is considerable variation in HR strategy and that the explanation for the variation is a function of a number of key variables. These form the basis of the Business in Context model, namely the state, the economy, culture, technology, the labour force, organization size, structure, goals and ownership.

| Case 12.3 | **British Airways** |

British Airways was formed in 1972 through a merger between BEA and BOAC. It possessed a very extensive route network, an exceptionally good safety record, and, in Heathrow, an enviable operating base within easy reach of London.

Its first decade of operation was typified by a number of problems and in 1982 the company reported losses of £100 million. The problems were over-staffing, a lack of operating efficiency compared to its major competitors, a series of industrial disputes and a particularly bad image with the travelling public. Part of the problem was attributed to a highly bureaucratic organization structure and decision-making process, typical of many nationalized industries. In BA's case the problem was compounded by a hierarchical structure that reflected the armed forces rather than a business operating in a fast-changing environment. By the 1980s the airline business was more competitive than ever and new entrants such as Virgin had quickly developed favourable reputations based upon low price and quality service. By 1983 the government had announced its intentions to de-nationalize the airline and the recently appointed chairman and chief executive were given a clear message that the company had to be made commercially viable.

The workforce was cut by some 20 000 and certain routes were withdrawn. A much greater attention was paid to marketing and organizational changes, including a reduction in hierarchical levels and a de-emphasis of status differences and job titles. In 1983 the company launched its major culture change initiative which used as its focus customer care. This was based upon research carried out on effective behaviour in the caring professions and the experience of SAS (Scandinavian Airlines) in implementing a similar programme. British Airways enlisted the help of the same consultants as those involved in the SAS project.

Two major training initiatives were launched. The 'Putting People First' campaign was aimed, initially, at those employees in direct contact with the general public, such as check-in staff and cabin crew, although it was extended to other groups as well. The 'Managing People First' campaign was aimed primarily at middle and senior management. Both campaigns were based on customer perceptions that portrayed BA as bureaucratic and saw its staff, while competent, as aloof and uncaring. The campaigns were launched on the assumptions that people perform best when given the maximum support by their peers and, most importantly, by their supervisors, and also when given maximum discretion in solving problems. Human resources staff were given training in organization change by the consultants and much of the responsibility for personnel issues was passed to line management.

'Putting People First' training confronted staff in groups with the negative image of BA held by its customers and encouraged employees to suggest ways of changing it. Role playing was also used through which staff were encouraged to use their own initiatives to resolve customer problems, such as flight delays and lost luggage. Presentations were given of what various people and groups in the organization did on a daily basis in an attempt to break down barriers and build a greater sense of identity. An important part of the process was the involvement of the chief executive, Colin Marshall, who was present for at least part of the training sessions. An

▶

important outcome of the sessions was the creation of 'Customer First Teams', a variation of the quality circle concept.

'Managing People First' was a 5-day residential programme for managers. The programme comprised three elements: the encouragement of managers to adopt a more visible, open and dynamic style; the coaching, training and supporting of subordinates; and an attempt to get managers to link the goals of their part of the operations with overall corporate objectives. As part of the latter process, managers were encouraged to develop their ideal of the company's mission. At the same time, a management appraisal scheme was launched and tied in to an individual reward system with both performance-related pay and share options.

In 1988 profits of £320 million were reported by BA. Customer feedback was favourable and the airline received several awards for its customer service in the business press. The feedback from employees on their perception of the company was equally encouraging. Measured in terms of profitability and customer and employee satisfaction the change appears to have worked. As with all major changes there were conflicts, notably between maintaining customer care and cutting costs at the same time, a clear case of 'soft' versus 'hard' HRM. Some commentators see that problems still exist in the form of an insecure middle management, too much functional specialization and an overemphasis at the top on acquisitions and takeovers. Others believe these to be relatively understandable but minor issues in a major culture change, successfully tested by a further series of job losses as a result of the recession and the Gulf War in the 1990s.

However, the airline hit financial problems by the mid-1990s and embarked on a series of cost-cutting exercises in the light of falling demand, especially for business-class seats. The exercises also incorporated the use of the lower-cost 777 aircraft on long-haul flights instead of the traditional 747 and the launch of 'Go' – a cut-price airline – as a wholly-owned subsidiary.

Further problems befell BA from 1997 to 1999. In 1997 there was a damaging 3-day strike by cabin crew, largely as a protest over cost cuts. In 1998 the company faced considerable criticism when it replaced its traditional Union Jack tailfin with ethnic designs from across the globe, a policy that it reversed in 1999. In the same year, attempts to form the world's largest airline alliance with American Airlines and other carriers were contested by competitors such as Virgin and questioned by USA regulatory bodies and consumer groups. The following year a much looser alliance was formed with Quantas, Cathay Pacific, Canadian Airlines, Iberia and Finn Air. In 1999 the company was fined £4.4 million by the European Commission for abusing its dominant market position, which included offering travel agents financial incentives for favouring BA.

The net result of such problems was a dramatic fall in share price and a worsening of relations with staff. Although a new agreement was reached with pilots in 1999, the company decided to re-strengthen its message of earlier years in an attempt to win the hearts and minds, not only of its employees, but of its customers as well. The new initiative was called, not surprisingly, 'Putting People First Again'.

This was not the end of BA's problems. By 2003 the company, as with many in the industry, faced increased competition in an industry that had too many carriers. Short-haul routes were under attack from budget carriers such as easyJet and Buzz.

Furthermore, all airlines were reeling from the combined effects of the terrorist attack on New York on 11 September, 2001 and the war with Iraq in 2003. Further job cuts put a strain on staffing and management–staff relations, leading to a series of threatened strikes involving key workers.

Sources: Bruce, 1987; Hampden-Turner, 1990; Höpfl *et al.*, 1992; Kay, 1993; *Financial Times*, 1998–9

Questions

1 What were the major factors which led BA to introduce 'Putting People First' and related programmes?

2 How do we know that such initiatives were successful? What other factors might we need to consider?

3 How does the company sustain interest in such programmes in the face of further problems in the late 1990s and beyond?

4 What other HR strategies might the company consider in the light of current influences on the business?

5 Using the model in Figure 12.3, how would you define BA in terms of its HR approach?

Summary

- The role and activities of human resource management would appear to be reactive, particularly to some problem or crisis. The development of the function is clearly related to economic growth, the increasing size of organizations, government legislation and policy, the growth of the labour movement and developments in collective bargaining. Expectations of the decline of the function in the face of an economy in recession, and reduction in numbers and influence of the trade union movement are, as yet, premature.

- A new role has emerged which gives the former personnel management a new name, HRM, and a new focus which stresses strategic management. At present, evidence as to the widespread existence and influence of the new role is mixed.

- Focus on the activity of HRM in the UK reveals an historic preoccupation with industrial relations, while an analysis of other types of activity reveals a largely intuitive and subjective approach behind a scientific facade. The weakening of the trade union movement throughout the 1980s and 1990s has tended to play down the significance of industrial relations. However, such issues are still at the forefront in more traditional manufacturing, as in the car industry.

- There are variations in HR policy and practice with cultural differences. This makes the application of global HRM difficult.

- Traditionally personnel managers have had low status as a result of their historic association with a welfare role and the fact that most of their activities can be carried out by all managers.
- There are difficulties with HR managers demonstrating the effective contribution of the function towards the success of the organization.
- Such analyses at the level of the firm may well explain a lack of personnel strategy beyond the basic manpower planning, although initiatives in the direction of HRM may alter this state of affairs. However, perhaps too much emphasis has been placed upon the problems of the role and more evidence is needed of effective operation and, in particular, the effectiveness of newly styled HRM policies. Indeed, many firms are displaying a greater concern for productivity and cost-effectiveness and are de-emphasizing traditional industrial relations. Traditional approaches can still be found, however, in many firms.

Discussion questions

1   Is there a case for the elimination of HR specialists, so that the function can be performed by all managers?

2   Assess the role of the state in the development of the personnel and HRM function. How has that role changed and what has been the impact since 1980?

3   Compare the activities listed in Table 12.1 with those in Table 12.2. What conclusions do you draw?

4   In what way have economic changes affected the role of HRM managers and the way they go about their activities?

5   How significant is industrial relations today in the UK? What changes do you foresee in the main activities?

6   What are the main sources of tension between HRM and other management groups? What strategies are available to reduce such tensions?

7   To what extent is HRM a separate activity from personnel management?

8   What are the key factors in an HR strategy for (a) a small, expanding computer software firm, (b) a medium-sized firm manufacturing electrical components for the car industry, and (c) a new university? What key issues emerge in each case?

9   Examine the key environmental, organizational and strategic issues in each of the three cases offered in this chapter. What lessons can be learned by other firms from the situations faced by these three companies?

10   Do HRM policies need to vary for the public as opposed to the private sector?

Further reading

A number of textbooks offer a good coverage of HRM. These include Torrington, D., Hall, L. and Taylor, S. (2001) *Human Resource Management,* 5th edn, FT Prentice Hall, Harlow and Armstrong, M. (2001) *A Handbook of Human Resource Management Practice*, 8th edn, Kogan Page, London. Comparative illustrations are a feature of Price, A. (1997) *Human Resource Management in a Business Context,* International Thomson, London. McKenna, E. and Beech, N. (2002) *Human Resource Analysis: A Concise Analysis*, FT Prentice Hall, Harlow offer a particularly succinct account. A more philosophical and research-based appraoch is taken by Storey, J. (ed.) (2000) *Human Resource Management: A Critical Text*, Thomson Learning, London. An interesting analysis of the role of the personnel specialist that is still relevant today is offered by Legge, K. (1978) *Power, Innovation and Problem-solving in Personnel Management*, McGraw-Hill, London. Two readable approaches to employee relations, including all the more recent developments, are offered by Hollinshead, G. Tailby, S. and Nicholls, P. (2002) *Employee Relations*, 2nd edn, FT Prentice Hall, Harlow and Gennard, J. and Judge, G. (2002) *Employee Relations (People and Organizations)*, 3rd edn, CIPD, London.

13 Finance and accounting

- Outline the contribution of finance and accounting to business decisions.
- Distinguish between different types of funding for business activities and assess their relevance.
- Identify and explain the contribution of management accounting to business decisions.
- Identify the different types of financial report and explain their value to business decisions.
- Identify the various stakeholders who can make use of published financial reports.
- Identify differences in accounting practice around the world and offer a limited explanation.
- Assess the impact of organization size and structure on accounting practices.
- Describe the limitations of accounting information in its contribution to strategy.

Introduction

In this chapter we examine the role played by the finance and accounting function in the operation of a business. We identify the following three main functions:

- The raising of funds or **financial management**.
- The contribution of accounting to management control and decision-making, often referred to as **management accounting**.
- The function of **financial reporting**.

We show these three elements in Figure 13.1, and deliberately portray them as overlapping activities. For example, a manager who decides on a strategy of business expansion into new markets and new process technologies (a decision based on management accounting calculations) will need to present accounting information to a bank or another potential investor (financial reporting) to persuade them to back the expansion with the necessary capital (financial management).

575

Figure 13.1

Finance and accounting activities

Accounting procedures and processes are very much a product of the organization and wider environments in the way that they operate. We will examine the various economic, legal and social influences on the finance and accounting function, and look at variations resulting from the size of the organization, ownership patterns and organization structure. We shall also look at the accounting practices of large multi-divisional companies by examining the procedures for cost allocation and transfer pricing. We end the chapter by giving a broad overview on the contribution of finance and accounting strategies to overall management strategy.

Throughout this chapter it is the intention to present accounting not as a series of technical calculations but as a management function that is influenced significantly by those who prepare and use accounting information. For example, the determination and disclosure of profit levels will be guided by regulations governing accounting practice. It may also be influenced by the wish to minimize liability for tax and the relationship with a variety of stakeholders, including employees and shareholders. It may also be influenced by a desire for merger or by the forthcoming wage negotiations with trade unions. Budgets are determined by management to guide future activities in accordance with plans. The process of budget setting and resource allocation is, in many organizations, a product of organizational politics, power and influence.

It is not our intention to give an introduction to bookkeeping and various accounting techniques. There are a range of suitable introductory books that students may consult and we recommend some at the end of this chapter. Those seeking a much broader coverage of the finance and accounting issues in organizations should refer to the accompanying accounting text in this series by Berry and Jarvis (1997). Many of the issues are also dealt with in more depth in the series economics text by Haslam *et al.* (2000).

Finance and accounting in business

Accountants form the largest professional group in Britain and, numerically at least, are much more significant in the UK than elsewhere. A survey carried out in the 1980s established the presence of 120 000 qualified accountants in Britain, compared with 20 000 in

France, and only 6000 in Japan and 4000 in the former West Germany (Handy, 1987). Many of the accountants in Britain operate in business either as finance and accounting specialists or as general managers, where professional accountancy is often regarded as a training route for senior management.

As we shall see later, such statistics reflect a difference in the nature of businesses in the various countries and may even be misleading. For example, the management accounting function exists in many German firms but is performed by business economists. The variations in the number of accountants in different countries are, however, thought by some to reflect significant cultural differences in the way businesses operate. It has often been claimed that the traditional accountant's attitude to risk aversion can hold back entrepreneurial decision-making and, as we have seen elsewhere in this book, a preoccupation with short-term accounting calculations and financial returns may have damaged the long-term competitiveness of the manufacturing industry. This is a theme that has been explored in the USA by Hayes and Wheelwright (1984) and in Chapters 9 and 10 of this book.

As stated in our introduction, we shall examine the function in terms of the three activities of financial management, management accounting and financial reporting, depicted in Figure 13.1.

Key concept 13.1 Financial management

Financial management is a part of the finance and accounting function that is concerned with the financing of an organization's activities. Finance is normally raised through share capital, loan capital, state finance or through internally generated funds.

Financial management

Financial management is concerned with the raising of capital to finance the organization's operations and with ensuring that the company can generate sufficient revenue to cover the cost of raising this finance. That cost may be in the form of interest rates payable to banks or dividend paid out to shareholders. There is a clear overlap with management accounting in that the funds must be managed by putting them to the most effective use. For example, investments must be carefully appraised. We may identify four sources of finance: **share capital**, **loan capital**, internal funding, and the state. We return to some of the themes outlined in this section in our discussion of cultural differences in finance and accounting later in the chapter.

Share capital   The issue of shares is a means whereby capital can be raised by devolving ownership of a company to a number of shareholders. In return for their investment, shareholders become part-owners of the company and are entitled to a payment each year in proportion to the number of shares held, and, usually, in proportion to the firm's profit levels. Such payments are known as dividend. We have already noted in Chapter 5 that this process, resulting from legal changes in most industrial countries in the 19th century, enabled firms to grow dramatically in size. The creation of the limited liability company not only raised finance in this way but reduced the risk for individuals, who could not be held personally responsible for financial losses incurred by the firm.

> ### Key concept 13.2 Share capital
>
> Share capital is funding raised through the issue of shares offering shareholders part ownership in the firm and an annual payment in the form of dividend. Dividend is usually paid in direct proportion to the amount of profit after tax. Shares are mostly a source of finance for the firm only at the time of the initial share issue. Thereafter, shares may be bought and sold on the stock market with no capital accruing to the organization. The two main types of share are preference shares and ordinary shares.

There are different types of share capital:

- **Preference shares**. Preference shares attract a fixed rate of dividend, usually payable twice yearly. Such agreed dividend must be paid irrespective of the financial performance of the company but, in times of hardship, payment may be deferred until such time as it can be afforded by the company. In this case the shares are known as cumulative preference shares, since the dividend accumulates until it is paid. Preference shareholders have a preference over other shareholders when assets are sold in cases of liquidation.

- **Ordinary shares.** Ordinary shares form the majority of all share capital. Owners of ordinary shares do not receive a guaranteed dividend, but they are normally entitled to a share of the profits after deductions for tax and payment to preference shareholders. Traditionally there are two types of ordinary share, those with voting rights and those without. However, non-voting shares are becoming increasingly rare and several companies have changed the status of their non-voting shares to give the owners voting rights. Ordinary shareholders can vote to elect the directors of the company.

- **Deferred shares** are fairly rare, but the owners of such shares only receive a dividend payment when the dividend for ordinary shareholders reaches an agreed level.

- **Golden shares.** Golden shares refer to those shares retained by governments in the case of privatization issue. The retention is to prevent hostile takeover. In some cases the government may limit the size of shareholding as a condition of the share issue. For example, no one individual may own more than 15 per cent of the British Airports Authority (BAA).

The major source of finance from shares comes in the form of new share issues. Despite the publicity given to this through the popular share issues when companies such as British Telecom and British Gas were privatized, probably less than 10 per cent of all finance comes from share issue (Wilson, 1980). In recent years the emergence of venture capital has had significant impact on the financing of small firms. Overall, however, shares still play a minor role in the raising of funds and evidence suggests that where new share issues do play a part, the money is spent not on investing in current activities, but to fund acquisitions (Mayer, 1988).

The stock market was created to encourage potential investors to finance businesses over which they had no direct control, yet for the majority it is simply a secondary market in which shares are bought and sold by investors, with no funding activity involved. A great deal of stock market activity revolves around the dealings of financial intermediaries. We have discussed their role alongside more general issues relating to the separation of ownership and control in Chapter 5. While funding and share trading are two separate activities, those holding large numbers of shares can influence management decision-making in that, if sufficient numbers of shares are traded, the company itself is traded. Managements tend to be aware that new owners may have different agendas from those of their predecessors.

Loan capital   This represents a riskier form of financing than share capital. With share capital, dividend payment can be deferred and the capital itself does not have to be paid back except when the company is liquidated. With nearly all forms of loan capital, interest must be paid on due dates and some interest charges can be high. The usefulness of loan capital depends on the rate of interest, the time required for repayment and the security that needs to be offered. There are many types of loan financing and we examine a selection below.

> ### Key concept 13.3 Loan capital
>
> Loan capital is raised by borrowing money from a third party and can take many forms. The major forms of loan capital are loans from banks or other financial institutions, debentures, overdrafts, factoring, leasing and trade credit. Loan capital carries more risks than other forms of financing in that interest must be paid and, with most types of loan credit, the capital must be paid back within a stated period of time.

- **Debentures.** Debentures are negotiable instruments that can be bought and sold on the stock market. They are issued in return for loans secured on the fixed assets of a company. The main advantage of debentures over shares is that interest paid can be offset against tax, whereas this is not the case for share dividend.
- **Bank borrowing.** Borrowing from a bank is more common than raising finance through share issues, but, on the whole, UK banks are less willing to lend and less willing to take an active role in the management of business activities than their counterparts in other countries. Banks play a much more significant and much more integrated role in France, Japan and Germany. In countries such as Germany, lending terms are more favourable to industrial borrowers as far as both interest rates and the length of the pay-back period are concerned. Not only are UK banks somewhat conservative in their lending policies, they are also, when acting as institutional investors, quite likely to sell their shares when things go wrong. Inadvertently, through their activities on the stock market, banks may weaken the financial position of a company which can encourage a takeover bid.

   The reluctance of UK banks to finance business was argued, by the Wilson Report, to be a function of the poor performance of UK industrial firms which did not merit investment (Wilson, 1980). There is more recent evidence that the banks are conscious of their poor image as far as investment is concerned and all the major high street banks have engaged in costly advertising and publicity campaigns to attract the business borrower. Managers will always view high interest rates as the major obstacle to bank borrowing. The high interest rates operating in the UK for much of the 1980s and early 1990s as part of the government's attack on inflation acted as such an obstacle. Loans may also be obtained from other types of financial institution, although in the UK banks predominate.

- **Overdrafts** are used by many businesses as a source of loan capital and many firms have permanent or semi-permanent overdraft arrangements with the bank. While this is perceived as usual by many managers, many banks feel less comfortable with such arrangements.

- **Leasing** is a form of loan capital in that the firm will acquire assets that it has not bought, but leased from another firm. Many company cars, security systems and photocopiers are acquired in this way. Leasing agreements usually provide other benefits such as service agreements or replacement after so many years or in the case of a breakdown. Leasing has become very popular for many items over the past 25 years, although the tax advantages associated with leasing have recently been reduced.

- **Factoring** is a means of raising capital. A factoring company will buy debts owing to a firm at some 70–80 per cent of their real invoice value. While money is lost on the value of the invoice, this can be a useful way of improving cash flow quickly.

- **Trade credit** is a form of loan capital in that payment is delayed for an agreed period, thus assisting cash flow.

`Other forms of financing`   **Internal funding** has been shown by many studies to be a major source of funding for most private companies in Britain. Studies in the 1980s suggested that many firms obtain as much as 70 per cent of funds this way (Wilson, 1980; Mayer, 1988). The position would appear to be little different at the end of the 1990s. The finance will come mainly from the redistribution of profits, although funding can be raised through the sale of assets. There are several reasons why management prefer to finance their businesses internally. The major factor is the fear that the involvement of banks and shareholders will weaken their control of the company. This is certainly the case as far as bank borrowing is concerned, but less so for shareholders. However, as we saw in Chapter 5, institutional investors can have considerable influence on management decisions. The shareholding route may be especially resisted by small business owners fearing a diminution of their control over the business. As we suggested above, there is a major reluctance on the part of UK managers to borrow from banks when interest rates are high and when the banks impose short pay-back periods.

State funding plays a relatively minor role in the funding of UK business. Apart from the investment in prestige projects such as Concorde and microchips, the activities of the state in Britain have generally been restricted to supporting declining industries and firms and preventing mass unemployment in economically deprived regions. This would seem to be the logic behind the government's regional policy and its investment in British Steel and British Leyland. Since 1979, the UK governments have generally espoused a free market economy and such funding activity has been limited. We refer you to Chapters 3 and 9 for a further discussion of such issues. Although many governments like the UK have reduced or even stopped the direct funding of business, indirect funding still plays a significant role. Japanese firms, such as Nissan, have benefited from government assistance in their establishment of UK bases. In Singapore, the government has pursued a deliberate policy of providing certain infrastructures and offering tax advantages to attract leading high-tech companies to the country.

There are a number of other factors which influence the source of finance. The attitude of management to risk may be an important factor. A cautious manager may wish to limit the extent of bank borrowing at all costs. The extent to which internal funds can be made available depends on the ability of management to satisfy its shareholders through dividend pay-out. There are also significant differences in the funding of activities between large and small firms, a point we shall return to later in the chapter.

Management accounting

Management accounting is the application of accounting techniques to provide management with the information to assist in the processes of planning and control. There is a clear overlap with financial management in that management accounting is concerned with the use of funds, and with financial reporting in that management accounting uses the data collected as a basis for its calculations.

Key concept 13.4 Management accounting

Management accounting is concerned with the planning, coordination and control of funds. It involves such activities as budgeting, costing, investment appraisal and the management of cash flows. Through such activities, management is provided with necessary information to assist in decision-making.

In terms of planning, management accounting assists in the formulation of plans for other functional areas. For example, an assessment of future labour costs will assist the process of manpower planning. Predictions of the future cost of raw materials will help in devising appropriate purchasing strategies and, where predicted costs are high, may even stimulate the development of new products using alternative materials. An important contribution to the planning process is the assistance offered by management accounting techniques of investment appraisal in selecting the most appropriate course of action from a range of alternatives. Such techniques are more valuable as environments become increasingly complex.

Management accounting plays a very important role in the wider process of management control. It enables clear parameters to be set in the form of budgets and represents a method by which many problems can be sensed and measured. It is especially useful as a control tool for three reasons. First, the data produced offer management one of the few methods of quantifying the effect of their decisions and of the organization's operations. Second, management accounting integrates the information from all the activities of the business and enables management to view operations as a whole. Third, it deals with the control of funds that are essential to an organization's survival.

We deal with five aspects of management accounting. These are budgeting, cost accounting, investment appraisal, the management of cash flows, and the contribution of the management accountant to management decisions. There is considerable overlap between these categories. For example, the control of assets would inevitably involve budgetary control, and the contribution to general management decisions would include all the other four categories. Management accounting is central to strategic planning and many of the issues reappear when we discuss strategy at the end of this chapter. For the moment we examine each of the categories in turn.

Budgeting and budgetary control   A budget is a quantitative statement of expectations concerning the allocation of resources and performance. The two aspects of **budgeting** are the establishment of standards and the setting up of mechanisms to measure and control performance. As a result, budgeting has a central position in the design of most management and accounting information systems.

> ### Key concept 13.5 Budgeting
>
> Budgets are devices for planning and control. They establish standards to be attained, including those for income and expenditure and mechanisms through which activities can be measured against the standards. Budgeting is a means of allocating funds and resources, of delegating authority and of motivating employees and is above all a vital control of all activities.

Budgets are used in many different ways: to allocate funds and supplies, as a means of delegating management authority, as targets to motivate employees, and as a means of control of both spending and performance. For example, a university allocates funds to each department designated as a cost centre. The allocation varies according to the size of the department and the nature of its work, so that science and engineering may get a large capital expenditure budget to purchase essential equipment. Budgets are allocated under a number of headings, including equipment, office supplies, library purchases, the funding of conferences for staff and so on. Such a mechanism serves two main purposes. First, it attempts to ensure that expenditure keeps within clearly defined limits. Second, it spreads the complex task of managing this expenditure by delegating to department heads.

Budgets are normally based on historic information, usually last year's budget. In a highly bureaucratic organization, resistant to change, this can cause difficulties when the needs of organization members change, or in highly dynamic environments. In such cases changes may not be represented in budget allocation, which is based on out-of-date information.

In all organizations there are often significant difficulties in changing the budget allocations. This is because budgeting is a bargaining process dealing with the allocation of scarce resources and those with most to lose have a vested interest in maintaining the *status quo*. It is for this reason that increasing attention has been given to the behavioural aspects of budgeting. The bargaining process can be useful in that it can force management to confront long-held assumptions and face up to underlying tensions which affect decision-making. However, there is a danger that conflict will be dysfunctional. This is especially true where budgeting in the form of targets is used as a control device, and more so where it forms the basis of the organization's reward system. In this case, and also where scarce resources are at stake, there may be a temptation for managers to distort information to place both them and their departments in the most favourable light.

Budgeting is therefore inseparable from the process of organizational politics and the way the organization is structured. In some cases this process has been acknowledged and attempts have been made to introduce some form of participation in the budget planning process.

Cost accounting   Cost accounting involves the analysis and allocation of costs. In large organizations this can be a complex process involving paper transactions between different units, especially in multi-divisional firms. We return to this aspect when we discuss the influence of organization structure on accounting procedures. The nature of costs varies considerably. Some costs, such as rents, are relatively fixed, while others, such as the amount of raw materials used by a manufacturing firm, will vary with the intensity of production. Some costs, such as wages, are highly detailed, while others, such as expenditure on hospitality, can be relatively vague. A variety of terms are used to describe various types of costing. Direct costs are those that can be directly ascribed to a specific product, while indirect costs relate to more general overheads such as labour, heating, lighting and so on and are more difficult to trace to a particular product. The traditional method for sharing out indirect costs across the organization is known as absorption costing. In some organizations, absorption costing has been replaced by activity-based costing. This method focuses on those activities that drive the costs in a particular product and is reckoned to be a more realistic method for apportioning costs, especially in more advanced technological systems where indirect costs are much more significant than direct costs.

Activity-based costing is one of a range of relatively new costing techniques which challenge traditional cost accounting methods. In many manufacturing organizations, technological and competitive changes are taking place, which are challenging the basis of historical costs, and management is having to devise new methods. These changes include the introduction of new manufacturing technology to reduce the cost of production, and a renewed emphasis is placed upon improving quality, increasing operating efficiency and reducing the uncertainty of materials and components supply. We have referred to these changes elsewhere in this book, as with our discussion of target costing under marketing in Chapter 11.

Key concept 13.6   Costing

Costing is the means by which the costs of producing goods and services are calculated. It is therefore an important ingredient of pricing. Some costs, such as those associated with bought-in raw materials and components, are relatively easy to ascribe to particular goods and services. Others, such as rent, labour or the costs of providing a prestigious corporate HQ, are more difficult to relate to specific items. A range of costing techniques such as absorption costing and activity-based costing have been developed to apportion such indirect costs.

Investment appraisal   Capital investment involves the commitment of funds now with the expectation of acceptable earnings in the future. Such decisions are made about the purchase or renting of new or additional premises, investment in new equipment, the development of a new product, or even the acquisition of another business. A careful appraisal of such investments is necessary owing to the usually large amounts involved and the key impact such investments might have on the future viability of the company. A variety of

investment appraisal methods have been devised, including pay-back, rate of return, **net present value (NPV)** and yield.

Key concept 13.7 Investment appraisal

Investment appraisal is the process of calculating whether an investment is cost-effective in the short, medium or long term. Such appraisals can relate to the acquisition of another firm, the development of a new product or the purchase of a new piece of equipment. A commonly used technique is net present value (NPV).

NPV is a popular method since it estimates future returns on investment, but assesses them on current values. Management is therefore able to make more informed judgements. Despite the popularity and frequency of their use, NPV calculations are not without problems. They are difficult to use for long-term investments without management making some rather big assumptions about the future behaviour of markets, the future costs of raw materials and the such. The more assumptions that have to be made, the less accurate the forecasts are likely to be. A problem associated with this is that strong management commitment to a particular investment project may result in a self-fulfilling NPV calculation. The figures are simply made to work to justify the decision. A study of the coal, steel and car industry in Britain in the 1970s concluded that large investments were justified on the basis of highly dubious input data; investment decisions that were subsequently proved unwise (Williams *et al.*, 1986).

The management of cash flow   The management of cash flow is concerned with the movement of cash into and out of the organization. This is an important activity since the firm needs to ensure that it has sufficient cash to cover its current expenditure. Many small firms find their severest problems occur with the management of cash flows. A business start-up has a considerable cash outflow to begin with and it may be some time before sufficient revenue is established to cover these initial costs. Several businesses have ceased trading with full order books, simply because they have insufficient incoming cash to pay bank interest charges and so are unable to stay in business and capitalize on their orders.

Key concept 13.8 Cash flows

Cash which flows in and out of a firm is vital to its survival. Without adequate cash flows a firm may have insufficient funds to pay its bills and may cease to trade, even though it may possess a high-quality product and a healthy order book.

Cash-flow management can be particularly difficult in times of high inflation, when there is a danger that profits become absorbed by escalating costs. Some firms also experience cash-flow difficulties in expanding economies. In such situations there is a temptation to turn profit not into cash but into new investments, by budgeting against future profits. Such a situation led the now defunct Laker Airways to over-reach itself by investing in expensive new passenger aircraft at a time when its markets were limited by the restrictive practices of other airlines. The company was forced into liquidation as a result.

A current concern of cash-flow management is the management of stocks. Many manufacturing firms are attempting to reduce their outgoings through a better control of inventory. Strategies employed include the development of close links with a limited number of suppliers and operating such production control methods as JIT (Chapter 10 has a fuller discussion of such strategies).

General contribution to management decision-making   Any discussion of the various elements of management activity can give the misleading impression that such activities are discrete. In reality the work of the management accountant does not focus on any one of these activities singly but uses them all in conjunction to assist in the general process of management decision-making on an ongoing basis. The accountant would be expected to contribute to most types of management decision, and certainly would have an input in major decisions such as plant closure and decisions to make or buy.

Financial reporting

Financial reporting involves the collection and presentation of data for use in financial management and management accounting. In most countries there are minimum legal requirements governing the kind of statement that must be produced. In the UK, the requirement is for a profit and loss account, a balance sheet, a director's report and an auditor's report. For those firms listed on the stock exchange there is an additional requirement of an interim, usually half-yearly, report. Within the legal requirements, some variation is allowed. For example, some companies, such as BA, now report in euros. Others, such as the NatWest Group, produce an annual review and a summary statement as an alternative to the full annual report and accounts, believing the former to be more accessible than the latter. In recent years the Internet has become significant as a reporting channel, and it is a requirement in the USA for some companies to post results on the Internet. Most large companies and many small ones publish their annual report and accounts on the Internet.

The two major forms of financial statement for companies are the balance sheet and the profit and loss account. Examples of these two statements from the the Premier League football club, Leeds United plc are presented in Tables 13.1 and 13.2, together with a summary statement in 13.3. These statements and the accompanying information are available on the Internet.

Key concept 13.9 Financial reporting

Financial reporting is the presentation of financial information in a form that is useful to interested parties. In most countries the form of such information is prescribed by law. In addition, in the UK firms are expected to conform to the requirements of the Statements of Standard Accounting Practice (SSAPs), which are being superseded by Financial Reporting Standards (FRSs). Such information is useful in management decision-making, for potential investors and for a firm's competitors. Since the financial information is available to such a wide audience, management must decide on the extent of disclosure beyond the minimum required by law.

The **profit and loss account** provides detail of a firm's income and expenditure throughout a stated period of time, known as the accounting period. The profit and loss account

Table 13.1	Leeds United plc consolidated profit and loss account			
	Operations excluding player trading £000	Player trading £000	**Year ended 30 June 2002 £000**	Year ended 30 June 2001 £000
Turnover	81 503	–	**81 503**	86 252
Cost of sales	(17 689)	–	**(17 689)**	(18 680)
Gross profit	63 814	–	**63 814**	67 572
Administrative expenses	(71 744)	(20 576)	**(92 320)**	(73 257)
Operating loss	(7 930)	(20 576)	**(28 506)**	(5 685)
Profit on disposal of player registrations	–	296	**296**	1 657
Loss on ordinary activities before interest	(7 930)	(20 280)	**(28 210)**	(4 028)
Other interest receivable and similar income	306	–	**306**	48
Interest payable and similar charges	(5 971)	–	**(5 971)**	(3 609)
Loss on ordinary activities before tax	(13 595)	(20 280)	**(33 875)**	(7 589)
Tax on loss on ordinary activities	–	–	**–**	547
Loss on ordinary activities after tax retained and transferred to reserves	(13 595)	(20 280)	**(33 875)**	(7 042)
Loss per share			**(9.75p)**	(203p)

The results for both years relate to continuing operations.

There are no recognized gains and losses for either year other than as stated in the profit and loss account.

Source: Leeds United Annual Report and Accounts 2002

Key concept 13.10 Types of financial reporting

There are two main types of financial report. The profit and loss account is a statement of profit and loss in a defined accounting period. The report presents a summary of revenues and shows the expenses incurred in earning the revenues. The difference between the two is the profit or loss. The balance sheet is a statement of assets and liabilities at the close of business on the last day of the accounting year. In addition to these two reports, some firms prepare a statement of cash flows, which is a measure of the solvency of an enterprise.

Table 13.2	Leeds United plc balance sheets			
	Group		Company	
	2002 £000	*2001* £000	*2002* £000	*2001* £000
Fixed assets				
Intangible assets	66 469	63 490	–	–
Tangible assets	42 537	39 583	10 759	35 214
Investments	–	–	29 452	29 452
	109 006	103 073	40 211	64 666
Current assets				
Stocks	2 301	1 324	–	–
Debtors: due within one year	14 120	15 584	34 561	4 148
Cash at bank and in hand	15 354	4 460	–	–
	31 775	21 368	34 561	4 148
Creditors: amounts falling due within one year	(57 042)	(46 052)	(17 031)	(8 508)
Net current (liabilities)/assets	(25 267)	(24 684)	17 530	(4 360)
Total assets less current liabilities	83 739	78 389	57 741	60 306
Creditors: amounts falling due after more than one year	(82 345)	(43 120)	–	(2 948)
Net assets	1 394	35 269	57 741	57 358
Capital and reserves				
Called up share capital	3 476	3 476	3 476	3 476
Share premium account	47 557	47 557	47 557	47 557
Merger reserve	–	–	38	38
Profit and loss account	(58 959)	(25 349)	2 801	(7 167)
Revaluation reserve	9 320	9 585	–	9 585
Capital reserve	–	–	3 869	3 869
Equity shareholders' funds	1 394	35 269	57 741	57 358

Source: Leeds United Annual Report and Accounts 2002

must include the figures from two accounting periods. In almost all cases this involves presenting a comparison of the current figures with those from the previous year. The **balance sheet** represents the summary of a firm's financial position at a fixed point in time. The balance sheet is a statement of a firm's assets and liabilities at the end of the last day of the accounting period. A balance sheet will differentiate between **fixed assets**, such as land, buildings and machinery, and **current assets**, such as cash and stock. Assets can also include such intangible aspects such as goodwill.

Table 13.3	Leeds United plc summary results		
Summary results		2002 £000	2001 £000
Turnover*		81 503	86 252
Cost of sales		(17 689)	(18 680)
Gross profit		63 814	67 572
Administrative expenses before player trading**		(71 744)	(58 922)
Operating (loss)/profit before player trading		(7 930)	8 650
Net player trading		(20 280)	(12 678)
Loss before interest and tax		(28 210)	(4 028)
Loss per share		(9.75p)	(2.03p)
Shareholders' funds		1 394	35 269

* Turnover in 2002 includes revenue of £3.5 million further to the company's existing media rights partnership with British Sky Broadcasting Group plc
** Administrative expenses before player trading in 2001 includes costs of £1.4 million associated with the Leeds Arena development project

Turnover 2002   £81.5m

16%	42%	10%	10%	22%
gate receipts	television and broadcasting	merchandising	travel	other commercial income

Turnover 2001   £86.3m

18%	43%	7%	12%	20%
gate receipts	television and broadcasting	merchandising	travel	other commercial income

Source: Leeds United Annual Report and Accounts 2002

A third form of statement is produced by some companies. This is the **cash-flow statement**. This details the movement of cash during an accounting period and is very useful for planning and control purposes. The cash-flow statement has replaced the statement of source and application of funds. While the profit and loss account and the balance sheet are measures of the profitability of a firm, the balance sheet is a measure of its solvency.

The form and content of such statements in the UK are determined partly by law and partly by requirements of professional bodies and other interested parties, such as the government and the Bank of England. The legal framework for financial statements was drawn up in various Companies Acts 1948–85, with the 1985 Companies Act providing the current requirements. A further set of regulations was provided by the **Accounting Standards Committee (ASC)**, made up of representatives from the various accounting professions, which issued **SSAPs**. Criticisms of the SSAPs from both the professions and managers led to a rethink and, from 1990, SSAPs are being gradually replaced by **Financial Reporting Standards (FRS)**, which were the recommendations of the Dearing Report. Fifteen such

FRSs have been issued to 1999. The Dearing Report also set up a new structure as outlined in Figure 13.2.

The Financial Reporting Council is appointed by the government and the Bank of England. The Financial Reporting Review Panel examines those statements that are in potential breach of the requirements of the 1985 Companies Act, specifically those that may contravene the requirement for a 'true and fair view'. As well as issuing the FRSs, the ASB has also established an 'urgent issues task force' to make recommendations, which reflect the highly dynamic state of modern global business.

The legislation, the SSAPs and the FRSs combine to form **generally accepted accounting practice (GAAP)**. There is a UK GAAP and a USA GAAP, which are sets of practically based accounting rules. There are, of course, significant differences between the UK and the USA regulations, although some companies, notably Shell and BT, report under both systems. There is a divergence of accounting practices across the world. For example, whereas the UK and USA operate to more practically based rules such as FRSs in the case of the UK, Germany and France are more strictly controlled by legislation. Such divergence has led to the creation of a supranational body, the International Accounting Standards Committee, which has a goal of harmonization.

The various financial reports are particularly useful to management in the planning, organizing and controlling of resources. It is not only management who are interested in the financial information of individual businesses; the following also have need of such information:

- **The state** requires public companies to be accountable and present their accounting information in a standardized form according to the requirements of the various Companies Acts 1948–85. All public companies must present to Companies House a balance sheet, a profit and loss account, a directors' report, an auditor's report and notes on the accounts where necessary. As we shall see later, there is some relaxation of these requirements for smaller businesses but only relating to the extent of information provided. However, these relaxations have had little real impact since small firms must still produce detailed information for the tax authorities and usually banks. As well as stipulating the various accounts to be

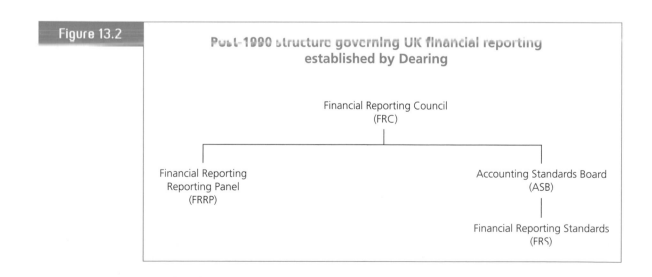

Figure 13.2

Post-1990 structure governing UK financial reporting established by Dearing

Financial Reporting Council
(FRC)

Financial Reporting
Reporting Panel
(FRRP)

Accounting Standards Board
(ASB)

Financial Reporting Standards
(FRS)

presented the law also determines what must be disclosed. The broad content of a profit and loss account and a balance sheet is presented in Tables 13.1 and 13.2 respectively. Apart from the law, the state in the UK now plays a more interventionist role in the development of FRSs through the involvement of the government and the Bank of England. The state also requires financial information to levy appropriate taxes on businesses. The nature of the tax laws certainly affects how firms report, and most use reporting conventions that minimize their liability for tax. The accounting information provided by firms under the requirements of the Companies Acts and tax law is used by the state for the purposes of economic planning and forecasting.

- **Investors** need the information to make informed judgements about future investments, as well as needing to protect their existing investments. The accountability of public companies to their investors was the major factor in the development of rules governing disclosure.

- **Employees** may need the information, especially if they are involved in a profit-sharing or share ownership scheme. There is evidence of the increasing use of various forms of profit sharing. Published accounts are, of course, particularly useful to trade unions in planning wage negotiations. In more general terms, a company concerned with involving its employees in the running of the enterprise may see the disclosure of financial information as an important element of the participation process.

- **Creditors** such as banks and suppliers are naturally concerned with the firm's liquidity and need to assess the risk involved in offering credit and, of course, to safeguard against fraud.

- **Competitors** usually find the financial information particularly useful as a yardstick against which their own performance may be measured, and may derive useful insights into what other firms are doing.

- **Customers** will use the information to ascertain the risk of placing expensive or long-term contracts and perhaps to assess the fairness of a company's pricing policy.

The major issue in financial reporting is the extent of disclosure. The wide availability of the accounts of public companies certainly influence their content and the way information is presented. Managements have a fair amount of discretion since much of the content of accounts is subject to interpretation, such as allowances for depreciation and the valuation of assets. As a result, firms are often accused of manipulating their financial information to minimize tax liability or to present a strong position to shareholders. In addition, firms are also conscious that financial information will be available to competitors and may wish to hide certain facts from them. We have already seen, in our discussion of management accounting, that financial information can be presented in such a way as to legitimize certain courses of action in preference to others.

All this reinforces the notion that accounting is a behavioural and political rather than a technical exercise. Clarke *et al.* (1999) go further in an Australian study of the corporate collapse of certain Australian firms, such as the Bond Corporation, the Adelaide Steamship Company and the Parry Corporation. They show how accounts for such companies were not only produced under existing regulations, but were subject to the legal requirements of external audit. Despite this, the firms concerned managed to keep hidden their real financial positions and eventually collapsed. Similar cases can be found in the UK, notably Polly Peck, BCCI and Maxwell Communications. Cases like these have focused attention of both the professions and academics on both the content and format of financial reports and the role of the auditor.

A classic case is that of Enron, presented at the end of Chapter 8. In this case there were issues of hidden accounts that should have been picked up by the auditors and communicated to shareholders and other stakeholders. The involvement of the auditors, Arthur Andersen, in the proceedings brought down one of the world's largest firm of accountants.

The environmental aspects of finance and accounting

In the last section we saw that financial reporting was greatly influenced by state regulations concerning the disclosure of information for public accountability and for reasons of collecting taxes. In this section we focus on two further environmental influences on the accounting and finance function: the economy and cultural differences.

In keeping with our Business in Context model, influences are two-way. The finance and accounting practices of firms have an impact upon the environment in which they operate. Economic resources in society are often allocated on the basis of accounting information. We have noted elsewhere in this book the growing tendency for firms to engage in the buying and selling of other companies. Financial information is vital to this activity. The closure of the Cortonwood colliery in South Yorkshire was based on accounting information provided for the management of the National Coal Board. The impact of such closures on the local community is considerable. In this case, the impact precipitated a bitter coal-mining strike, which lasted over a year (A discussion of the kind of accounting procedures which resulted in the closure of Cortonwood can be found in Berry *et al.*, 1985. We return to this case at the end of the chapter.)

The role of the economy

In general, accounting practices will vary according to the nature of the economy in which they operate. For example, in many Third World countries there is little need for sophisticated accounting techniques and systems of basic cash accounting predominate. The raising of finance that we discussed in the previous section is a function of the state of the market and the way this influences profit levels, share prices and bank interest rates. Two specific economic features have held particular interest for accountants: inflation and currency exchange.

The relatively high rates of inflation experienced by the British economy in the 1970s led accountants to rethink the basis for their calculations, made popular the concept of inflation accounting and resulted in a government report (The Sandilands Committee on Inflation Accounting). A major problem in times of high inflation is that profits can be overstated by basing costs on historic data made largely irrelevant by inflation. In such situations systems of adjusting balance sheets to account for fluctuating prices were developed. While these have less relevance today, inflation accounting techniques are widely used in such countries as Brazil.

Like inflation, fluctuations in currency exchange rates make historic cost accounting difficult. The effect is particularly significant for those firms reliant on export markets, as with Swiss firms Nestlé and Ciba Geigy with over 90 per cent of their business outside Switzerland.

Cultural differences

Two main issues are discussed here. We look first at differences in financial systems and then at variations in financial reporting.

Differences in financing business   There are some fundamental differences between major countries in the way businesses are financed. Prevezer (1994) has looked at comparisons between the UK, Germany and Japan and Owen (1996) has focused on differences between the UK and Germany. What follows in the first part of this section is largely a summary of their work. Many of the findings reflect differences between the Anglo-Saxon, social market and Asian systems outlined in Chapter 3.

In the UK shareholders play a key role. Seventy-five per cent of all shares are owned by institutional shareholders, who tend to possess diversified share portfolios and have little if any connection with the firm. The share market in the UK is highly volatile with a much higher proportion of shares being traded than in any other country. As a result of such share trading activity, the UK experiences a higher proportion of takeovers, many of them hostile. Banks own shares in UK companies but tend to operate like other institutional shareholders. Under such a system, the primary objective of institutional investors is to make money for their own shareholders. They, therefore, have a preference for selling shares when events are not going to their liking, rather than attempting to influence policy. In response, managers tend to be very aware of the need to maintain share price and to keep such investors happy with high rates of dividend. Indeed, the average amounts of dividend paid by UK companies is 1.5 to 2 times higher than in the USA, 2.5 to 3 times higher than in Germany and 3 to 4 times higher than in Japan.

In Germany the ownership patterns are much more stable. There are fewer stock market quoted firms. Those with shareholders tend to be dominated by one or two major shareholders owning around 25 per cent of the company and having a seat on the Supervisory Board. Takeovers are strictly controlled by law and hostile takeovers are very rare. Banks tend to have a much closer relationship with firms and bank representatives regularly take a place on the board. Employees in Germany also play a role as board members, enshrined in the laws relating to co-determination.

In Japan, as in the UK, 75 per cent of shares are owned by institutions. However, unlike the UK, the trading of such shares occurs very little. Most of the share trading is among those householders owning shares. This is a complete reversal of the situation in the UK. The institutional shareholders have a close relationship with the firms and takeovers are rare. Banks play a major role and, in some cases, are members of large corporate groupings or have a substantial ownership interest in companies. In manufacturing, suppliers also play a major role in that they are often part-owned by the major firms they supply. The Japanese system is one where there is a very close relationship between firms, banks and suppliers.

Such differences as those existing between the UK, Germany and Japan have led many to hold the UK financial system as being responsible for the spread of short-termism, lack of investment and long-term strategy and, hence, the comparative industrial decline of the UK. While Owen (1996) agrees in part with such an analysis he raises a number of questions. He argues that in the period 1950–80 the UK was indeed outperformed by Germany, but it was also outperformed by France and Italy. All three countries possessed different financial systems, thereby making links between industrial performance and specific financial systems difficult. He further that argues that if long-termism was such an advantage to Germany then it would show up most in those industries where long-term investment would be an advantage. He examines pharmaceuticals and electronics. In the former, both the UK and Germany have performed well, whereas in the latter, both lag some way behind the Japanese. He suggests that there are other more significant factors at work in these cases. While he acknowledges that the instability of the UK system creates damaging takeovers, citing the British Motor Corporation and its merger with Leyland, he believes it gives the UK economy a certain flexibility and dynamism. Nonetheless, there are advantages associated with the more stable patterns of ownership and control of German firms. However, by the end of the 1990s there are signs that the systems of Britain and Germany are slowly moving towards one another.

Differences in financial reporting   Many differences can be observed in the accounting practices of different countries. These reflect a variety of factors such as the nature of the legal system, the pattern of ownership and control, the system of taxation, the strength of the accountancy profession, and the general social climate. We have already noted such variations in our section on financial reporting.

In our discussion of the Beijing Jeep case in Chapter 2 we noted that AMC/Chrysler found it difficult working with the Chinese system of accounting. This was different to the one used in the USA and was based on a Russian system and designed for state-controlled enterprises. It offered little information on costs, for example.

In France and Germany, financial reporting systems are highly prescribed by law, yet there tends to be less emphasis on financial reporting in France largely because of the dominance of family ownership and, hence, the private nature of many companies. In the UK and USA reporting requirements are less prescriptive but the information needs of shareholders are much greater, especially in the USA where share ownership is more diffuse. Patterns of ownership are themselves related to the influence of the accounting profession. Public ownership requires accountability and hence accountants play a major role in the auditing of company accounts. Much less auditing is required in France, which may account for their relatively low numbers of accountants. In general, a social climate that encourages openness, social responsibility and consumerism, as in the USA, results in significantly different patterns in the disclosure of financial information than those found in a much more closed society such as Switzerland.

There has been considerable pressure for the standardization of accounting practices across countries. This is partly a function of increased international business via globalization and joint ventures. Harmonization is one of the tasks of the International Accounting Standards Committee. Some harmonization has taken place within the EU and this was reflected by certain changes in the financial reporting requirements of British firms. The pressure for standardization comes from a variety of quarters. Financial reports prepared in one country are used by financial analysts and investors in another, as part of the growing internationalization of capital. In manufacturing, global operations and sourcing of components have hastened the need for internationally usable financial information. Standardization would greatly assist multinational companies to consolidate their accounts, assess potential acquisitions more effectively and even enable them to transfer accounting staff from one country to another more easily. This is just part of the vast changes that have accompanied the globalization of the economy. It should not be forgotten that many of the major accounting firms operate multinationally too and harmonization would greatly assist their operations.

The organizational aspects of finance and accounting

The nature of any organization impinges significantly upon accounting procedures. This is inevitably shown when changes occur in ownership or in the goals of the enterprise, bringing about changes in the organizational culture. For example, the takeover of one firm by another may well result in the consolidation of accounts and perhaps a change in the accounting practices. The privatization of a number of companies in Britain since the 1980s has changed the nature of many of those organizations from a service centre to a profit centre with a corresponding impact upon accounting practices. In the public sector significant changes are taking place as well. In Chapter 5 we presented the changes that were occurring in the new universities as a result of incorporation in 1989. One major change has been the withdrawal of local authority accounting controls and the subsequent elevation of the management accounting function within universities themselves. Another change, affecting all public sector organizations, has been the greater emphasis placed on income generation beyond that normally provided. This places an extra burden upon public bodies but may also give them greater flexibility to pursue their own goals. We may conclude that the nature of the accounting practices is a function of the goals of the organization.

For the remainder of this section we focus on two organizational issues: the accounting implications of the size of the firm, and the influence of structure on accounting procedures. The two issues are linked, as we shall see when we examine the problems of cost allocation and transfer pricing in large multi-divisional firms.

The accounting requirements of large and small firms   Differences in the size of businesses affects their ability to raise capital, the complexity of their accounting procedures and controls, and the extent of their financial reporting. Differences are therefore to be found in all the three functions of finance and accounting that we identified in Figure 13.1.

Larger firms, not surprisingly, have much more complex accounting procedures and generally employ a number of professional accountants in a specialized functional department. In smaller firms the accounting function is often external to the firm with a subsequent reliance on the advice of an outsider, who may not have the detailed knowledge of an internal management accountant. Larger firms may have the problems of satisfying large numbers of shareholders, but their very size often gives them an advantage in raising funds from external sources. In any event, large and complex organizations can often finance themselves internally through their ability to switch funds from one unit to another. Small firms have much more problem raising finance and tend to be more concerned with the management of cash flows.

As with the proposals to harmonize accounting procedures between nation states, there is a lobby to standardize practices across all types of firms irrespective of their size. However, the cost of preparing complex financial statements can be daunting for a small business and the benefits of such information much less than for larger firms. Paradoxically in the light of its general views on harmonization, the EU champions different accounting practices for large and small firms. This was reflected in Britain in the 1981 Companies Act which removed the requirement of smaller firms to produce profit and loss accounts and directors' reports and introduced less onerous requirements for balance sheet information. In reality, however, this does not appear to meet the information needs of banks on which small companies are so heavily dependent for finance. To satisfy their lending requirements, banks are insisting on stringent financial control mechanisms in small firms and much more detailed financial reporting than is required by law (Berry *et al.*, 1987). As a result, the pressure for standardization may well come from the banking community.

Organization structure, cost allocation and transfer pricing   We have already seen how organization structure and accounting procedures tend to reinforce one another, in that a large organization may delegate responsibility and control costs through the creation of individual budget centres. In very large organizations, the structure generally matches the finance and accounting responsibilities of the firm. A centralized headquarters will act as an investment centre determining new initiatives, as well as allocating profit targets for each division. In turn the divisions will determine targets for each operating unit and designate each one as a cost centre in control of a budget. There are occasions when mismatches can occur, as in the case of a department manager who has no effective budget and, hence, limited powers of operation.

The operation of budgetary control can produce a more efficient and effective management control system. It also carries the potential problem of encouraging functional insularity to the detriment of the firm as a whole. Units can become so preoccupied with achieving their own targets and keeping within their own budgets that they may refuse calls for assistance from other units through the fear that this will erode their own performance levels. In some manufacturing firms this has resulted in a total lack of continuity between departments and between production shifts. This has led some firms to examine team-building techniques developed by social psychologists to enhance greater cooperation.

Such problems increase with the size of the firm and with the necessity for funds to flow across many different units of the same organization. The problems come to a head in large multi-divisional firms where each unit operates as a profit centre and is accountable to top management for the achievement of predetermined profit targets. We examine two aspects of this problem: cost allocation and transfer pricing.

The problems of **cost allocation** occur when central services, such as headquarters administration, research and development, and perhaps maintenance, must be paid for by those units in the organization with the responsibility for generating income and profit. A decision needs to be made on the basis of the apportionment of such costs (see the reference to absorption costing in the section on management accounting). Some firms vary cost allocation according to the size of the profit centre, as a proportion of their costs, or the extent to which use is made of the central services. The final criteria is often difficult to measure accurately, but any method is open to challenge by those managers who see their profits eroded by costs which lie outside their control. Some managers are resentful that their efforts are diluted by sections of the firm that do not generate income but merely incur costs. In some cases this has resulted in the marginality of service departments such as HRM and R&D. Once again accounting becomes the focus for political debate at the level of the firm. While accounting is itself a largely advisory function, the importance to decision-making of financial information, which is largely controlled by accountants, often enables the accountant in the organization to wield considerable power and influence.

Transfer pricing is the process through which goods and services produced in one section of the organization are sold internally for use by another. The need for transfer pricing mechanisms is a function of the development of the multi-divisional firm and associated profit centres. An effectively operated transfer pricing mechanism can contribute to the optimum allocation of a firm's resources and to the motivation of division managers towards efficient operation and hence to the overall prosperity of the organization.

Such mechanisms occur wherever there is a need in one unit of the organization for the services of another. A form of transfer pricing occurs in higher education, as the following illustration reveals. Universities and other colleges tend to be organized around specialist subject departments. A department that offers a business studies course may have the need for specialist law inputs which reside outside that department. In many colleges a transfer pricing system has been devised whereby those departments servicing another are allocated points based on the number of hours and students they service. These points, with those generated from their own departments, form the basis for staffing allocations. A major problem with such a mechanism is that it may encourage departments only to service those areas where they can ensure high rates of return.

This is a similar problem to the one we outlined when we discussed organization structure in Chapter 5. A foundry operating as a profit centre in a manufacturing firm may find that the pressure to meet targets conflicts with the demands placed upon it for goods from other units in the same organization. Management may be faced with the dilemma of having to meet internal demand when higher returns may be obtained through meeting the requirements of customers external to the firm. The issue of transfer pricing is particularly pertinent to the operation of global firms and it is to this aspect we now turn.

Transfer pricing and the global firm   A great deal of transfer pricing activity occurs between member organizations of large multinational corporations. Such activity has increased dramatically in recent years with developments in the global economy. While this can cause the kind of organizational political problems outlined above, there are three main reasons for the extensiveness of such activity. These relate to issues of taxation, competition and issues relating to the need of the multinational to protect itself against social, economic and political changes occurring in the host country. These issues should be viewed in conjunction with the discussion on globalization and multinationals in Chapter 2.

- **Tax reasons.** Through its activities worldwide, a multinational company can move profits from high to low tax areas using the transfer pricing mechanism. Firms operating in high tax areas are charged inflated prices for goods and services produced in low tax areas. While this represents only a paper exchange of funds within the same organization it can result in some firms showing a much greater profit than others. In normal circumstances pressure is brought to bear on poorly performing profit centres. Such problems may be avoided by the use of dual reporting systems, one for external consumption and the other for internal use only.

- **Competition reasons.** Some multinationals subsidize member firms through the transfer price mechanism. In order that a new company may develop itself in an established market the other firms could supply goods and services at low prices, buying back the finished products at a high price.

- **Protection against change.** A multinational will wish to protect itself against those economic and political changes that threaten its prosperity and ultimate existence. Problems caused by high inflation, currency exchange and devaluation in a particular country can be tackled by charging high prices for goods supplied to the subsidiary in that country, and buying goods back at low prices. By operating in this way the multinational keeps finance in the family and prevents it being siphoned off by individual nation states.

In Chapter 1 we introduced the case of News International, now part of News Corporation, a global company controlled by Rupert Murdoch. The company makes very good use of its global presence by accessing the various advantages accorded by the tax laws and accounting regulations in the many countries in which it operates. Indeed the attractiveness of some of those countries is their status as a tax haven. News Corporation has a highly complex financial structure with a large number of subsidiary companies. In 1996, 49 of those subsidiaries were registered in the British Virgin Islands where corporation tax is 1 per cent per annum and 29 were in the Cayman Islands under a similar tax regime. As a general rule the company will pay loans in countries with high levels of corporation tax and collect profits in countries where tax levels are low. As a result News Corporation in 1995 declared profits of £793 million, yet paid less than 10 per cent in taxes, when the usual rate for a UK, USA or Australian company is between 20 and 40 per cent. News Corporation also makes large capital investments and is renowned for setting up new businesses. This it does with maximum tax benefit, particularly where it can obtain tax relief in high-tax countries. All this has been achieved within the laws and accounting regulations of the various countries within which News Corporation operates.

Some multinationals do come into direct conflict with the governments of those countries in which they operate. Such a conflict was between the Swiss pharmaceutical firm Roche and the UK Monopolies and Mergers Committee in 1971. The company stood accused of operating an unfair monopoly on its tranquilizer products, Librium and Valium, and thus making excessive profits. The UK representatives were unable to present a fully detailed case, since, as a company operating under Swiss law, there was certain financial information it did not have to disclose.

Strategic aspects of finance and accounting

The three functions of finance and accounting represent strategies of financing and controlling operations, of distributing resources and power through budget allocation, and of information disclosure. Additionally, financial tools and information are invariably used in the making of strategic decisions in other functional areas, such as the decision to invest in new products or equipment, or to take on extra staff. Financial analyses form the basis of most acquisition attempts.

We can therefore see that the finance and accounting function assists management decision-making on a number of key issues that are central to the viability of the firm. These issues include the sources of funds, investment decisions, acceptable levels of debt, the minimization of tax liability and the extent of the pay-out to shareholders.

As with all the functional areas we have discussed in this book there is a growing recognition that the strategies associated with the different activities are linked in some kind of synergistic way. In the manufacturing industry evidence is emerging that cost and quality are not necessarily trade-offs but essential ingredients of the same strategy. Focusing greater attention on improving product quality can also be successful in lowering costs.

This can become a virtuous circle in that extra funds are released for further investment in quality improvement.

Throughout this chapter we have been careful to point out the inexact nature of accounting methods. We can summarize the various limitations on the use of accounting information in strategy formulation:

- Because of the problems of measuring many aspects of business activities, accounting information can be highly subjective.

- Financial statements are summaries. Information is therefore selected and interpreted according to the needs of the compiler and user of financial statements.

- As a result of the above, financial information is often used deliberately to achieve political ends such as the justification of an investment decision or a pay offer.

- There is an added danger in all this in that many assume the data to be scientific and objective, and use it accordingly.

- Because of the bias in accounting to what can effectively be measured, management may place undue emphasis on short-term results and neglect the longer-term implications of strategic decisions, or base too many decisions on historic data which is made redundant by changing circumstances.

A good illustration of the interpretative problems associated with accounting information is offered by the NCB decision to close Cortonwood colliery as part of its rationalization strategy. A Monopoly and Mergers Commission Report calculated the revenue of the colliery at £44.30 per tonne, while its costs were calculated at £50.50 per tonne. On these figures the mine was clearly unprofitable and losing the Coal Board in excess of £1.7 million a year. A study of the accounting methods used by the NCB questioned the basis for many of the costs used, but more significantly suggested that many of the costs, such as surface damage and essential services, would not be avoided by closing the colliery. If these unavoidable costs are eliminated from the equation as constants, then Cortonwood could be shown to be making a net contribution of £5.45 per tonne of coal mined (Berry *et al.*, 1985).

Case 13.1   ## Football – a case of finances out of control?

Football is the UK's most popular spectator sport. Attendances at games surpass those of any other European country and the game has a huge following on television. The game in England is organized in four divisions. There is the elite Premier League of 20 clubs and then three further leagues, Divisions 1, 2 and 3 each with 24 clubs. There is movement between the leagues as a result of promotion and relegation and the most successful clubs in the Premier League are rewarded by being selected to play in European competitions in addition to their normal league programme.

There are fears that the game's finances have spiralled out of control as a result of rising wages and player transfer costs and a stable, if falling, revenue from television, the main source of income for leading clubs. In 2001–2 season, Arsenal, one of the biggest clubs lost £22 million, eclipsed only by Fulham with losses of £40 million and Leeds with £34 million. The problem was not confined to England. In the same season, teams in Italy's Serie A, the top division, had a collective loss of over £500 million and one of the more famous clubs, Fiorentina has since gone out of business. Several English clubs formed public limited companies and floated themselves on the stock market. After an initial enthusiasm, share prices fell dramatically and the sector suffered the biggest fall of any sector outside technology. For example, the share price at Leeds went from a high of £0.24 to a low of £0.04. Aston Villa's price fell from £11 to £1.50. Even a rich club like Manchester United were not immune from falls in share price.

A review of Table 13.3 reveals how much football is dependent upon television income. Leeds United derives 42 per cent of its income from television compared to only 16 per cent from paying customers. Other sources of revenue, including merchandizing and travel, collectively eclipse gate receipts. Television revenue is not guaranteed. ITV Digital established a deal with the non-Premier leagues to televise live matches. The company collapsed and with it the deal. A similar case happened in Germany with the collapse of the Bavarian media company, Kirch. The current TV company with rights to broadcast live Premiership matches is BSkyB. They have re-negotiated the deal and for 3 years, from the 2004–5 season, the income to the Premiership is £1.024 billion. However, this represents a shortfall of £100 million on the current deal and similar cuts have been made by RAI in Italy.

Each year the accountants Deloitte and Touche publish a report on the finances of the English game. Their report on the 2001–2 season makes interesting reading. Only 32 of the 92 clubs recorded a profit and 15 of these were in the Premier League. Table 13.4 shows the average income for clubs in each of the four divisions.

Table 13.4   Average income of English Football League Clubs 2001–2

Division	£ million
Premier	56.6
Division 1	12.4
Division 2	4.3
Division 3	2.7

Source: Deloitte and Touche, 2003

Table 13.4 does not tell the whole story. Only seven clubs in the Premier League exceeded the average income and the figure is skewed by the revenue of the more successful clubs like Manchester United. The cost of relegation to Division 1 is estimated to be in excess of £12 million.

Table 13.5 reveals how wage costs have risen for all clubs. In addition, while £92 million circulated between Premier League clubs in transfer fees only £12 million was paid by Premier League teams for players from lower divisions in 2001–2. By comparison, in the same season £190 million was spent on overseas players, representing money leaving the English game.

Table 13.5	Average wages of players 1992–2002	

	Average annual wage	
Division	1992–3 £000s	2001–2 £000s
Premier	75	600
Division 1	50	200
Division 2	20	70
Division 3	15	42

Source: Deloitte and Touche, 2003

The financial plight of the English game is highlighted by Leeds United (see the accounts in Tables 13.1–3). As a consequence of their poor performance during the season 2002–3, the manager, ex-England coach Terry Venables, lost his job and the high-profile chairman, Peter Risdale resigned. They paid the price for a lack of control over finances and the board faced increasing pressure from institutional shareholders holding increasingly worthless stock. Ex-Asda chief, Alan Leighton, was brought in to assist the club with its financial restructuring. The club had gambled on heavy investments, including £100 million on players to achieve domestic and European success. As a result debts rose to £77 million (an increase in 3 years of 838 per cent). All salaries had increased by 290 per cent over 3 years from 1999 and the numbers employed on the non-playing side rose during the same period from 91 to 246. The team and the board were used to staying at the very best hotels and travelling by private jet.

However, the rewards for success in the Premier League are great. Those finishing at or near the top of the league are selected to play in the European Champions League. This is estimated to bring in an additional annual revenue of £50 million in television deals, increased number of matches, merchandizing and even travel. Many top clubs have established their own travel agencies to arrange travel for fans going to both domestic as well as European matches. Leeds derived 10 per cent of its revenue from travel agency work (see Table 13.3).

For Leeds United, the first step in restructuring has been to sell the club's major assets: its players. Many of the players brought in to fulfil the dream have now left. The most high-profile transfer involved the purchase of Rio Ferdinand from West Ham for £18 million and his sale less than 2 years later to Manchester United for £30 million.

Manchester United offers a stark contrast. In the 10 years since the Premier League was formed they have been its most successful club and in those 10 years had a cumulative profit of £229 million. At the end of the 2001 financial year turnover had increased by 12 per cent to £129.6 million, a figure matched by no other club in the world. In the same year pre-tax profit went from £5 million to £22 million. From August 2002 the club entered into a merchandizing deal with Nike worth £303 million over 13 years. The club had become a global brand, strengthened by pre-season tours to Asia and the USA.

The success of clubs such as Manchester United threatens to destabilize the finances of the game still further. Television rights for live games are sold on a collective basis by the league to the television companies. More money goes to those clubs who appear more on television, so that for the season 2002–3, Manchester United earned £31 million and Arsenal £29 million, but a less successful club, like West Bromwich Albion, with fewer appearances earned only £13 million. However, the successful clubs believe they can earn yet more television income by negotiating their own deals. This has already happened in Italy and has the support of the EU through its policy on competition. The argument is that selling collective rights is anti-competitive and clubs want to achieve their market potential.

There are some signs that English football is attempting to put its house in order to deal with the culture of overspending. Division 3 clubs have agreed to trial a scheme whereby player salary costs do not exceed 60 per cent and all salary costs do not exceed 75 per cent of turnover. Elsewhere there is the introduction of salary caps, performance-related pay, shorter contracts and loan deals to reduce wage bills. Alongside this is the 2003 takeover of Chelsea by the Russian industrialist, Roman Abramovich, who, within weeks of taking over the club, supervised a spending spree of £110 million on new players to achieve the dream of success.

Sources: Deloitte and Touche, 2003; *Guardian* and *Observer* newspapers, July and August, 2003

Questions

1 What are the main financial problems facing English football and how did they arise? Do the problems face all clubs equally?

2 Why does football seem to operate on a different basis to other types of business?

3 What steps would you take to restructure the finances of the game?

4 Assess the accounts of Leeds United in Tables 13.1–3. What conclusions do you draw?

Summary

- The finance and accounting function in business comprises financial management, management accounting, and financial reporting.

- Financial management is concerned with the funding of the business and ensuring such funds can be met by the organization. The major sources of finance are share capital, various forms of loan capital, state finance and internally generated funds, usually through the reinvestment of profit. It is this last source that would appear to be most significant for firms in Britain.

- Management accounting is concerned with assisting management in planning and control. It involves the preparation and control of budgets, the analysis and allocation of costs, the appraisal of capital investments, the management of cash flows and general contribution to strategic decision-making.

- Financial reporting involves the preparation of financial statements such as the balance sheet, profit and loss account and cash-flow statements. Financial reporting must conform to a legal and regulatory framework and take account of the needs of the various groups who are to use this information. Major issues are whether the accounts represent a true and fair picture and the extent of disclosure.

- The finance and accounting function is greatly influenced by the environment in which it operates. Financial reporting is subject to strict state controls and accounting practices have developed to cope with economic changes such as inflation and fluctuations in the value of currency. Despite pressures to harmonize accounting practices there are considerable differences between countries, reflecting a number of cultural influences.

- Accounting practices vary also with the size of the organization, with large and small companies having their own special problems. As organizations increase in size and develop appropriate structures, decisions will have to be made on the allocation of costs and transfer pricing. The latter becomes a particularly useful mechanism in the hands of the multinational corporation.

- Accounting information forms the basis for most strategic decisions within the organization. Its value should be placed alongside a number of limitations, not least of which are the subjective nature of accounts and the role played by accounting information to justify organizational political decisions.

Discussion questions

1 What is the value of the professional accountant to business? Why do professional accountants proliferate in the UK?

2 Why is the internal funding of business so popular in the UK?

3 What would be the most appropriate methods the following organizations could use to raise revenue to fund new activities: a very small firm just making a mark in the office supplies market; a university; a multinational car manufacturer?

4 What specific contributions can the management accountant make to strategic decision-making? What limitations can be placed on the value of this contribution?

5 Identify the different needs of the users of accounting information. To what extent can current methods of financial reporting hope to satisfy them all?

6 What are the specific finance and accounting problems and priorities for small as opposed to large companies?

7 What are the advantages and disadvantages to various interested parties associated with cost allocation and transfer pricing activities in global firms?

8 Identify the behavioural and political nature of management accounting. What problems does this cause and how might they be minimized?

9   What changes do you predict for finance and accounting as a result of developments in IT and the Internet?

Further reading

A good start is Berry, A. and Jarvis, R. (1997) *Accounting in a Business Context*, 3rd edn, International Thomson Business Press, London. As well as covering the fundamentals of finance and accounting it offers a discussion on the key organizational and environmental influences. An excellent basic text is offered by Atrill, P. and McLaney, E. (2003), *Accounting and Finance for Non-specialists*, 4th edn, FT Prentice Hall, Harlow. A good source of information on management accounting is Drury, C. (2001) *Management Accounting for Business Decisions*, Thomson Learning, London. An excellent guide to financial reporting and the interpretation of company reports and accounts is Holmes, G., Sugden, A. and Gee, P. (2002) *Interpreting Company Reports and Accounts,* 8th edn, FT Prentice Hall.

Glossary

3M Minnesota Mining and Manufacturing Company.

4 Ps See *Marketing mix.*

Absorption costing A traditional method of allocating overhead or indirect costs in which, usually, the total cost is divided according to the volume of activity in each cost centre.

ACAS (Arbitration, Conciliation and Advisory Service) This comprises members representing employers, trade unions and the academic community and is funded by the UK government to influence the conduct of industrial relations and assist employers and employees to achieve speedy, mutually satisfying agreements and resolutions of conflict.

Accepted sequence Coined by Galbraith (1972) it refers to the consumer oriented view of marketing. See also *Revised sequence.*

Accounting Standards Committee (ASC) A UK body made up of representatives from the various accounting professions, which issued Statements of Standard Accounting Practice (SSAPs), which govern financial reporting. From 1990, the SSAPs are being gradually replaced by Financial Reporting Standards (FRS).

Accumulation A key aspect of a capitalist system in which profit is *accumulated* by more efficient production methods or through new products and markets. Accumulation is generally linked to expansion. See also *Commodification.*

Acquisitions See *Mergers and acquisitions.*

Activity-based costing A system of allocating costs that focuses on the activity that drives the cost rather than simply apportioning overhead costs on a pro-rata basis.

Advertising A form of promotion that involves four major considerations: the design of the message, the selection of the media, the cost of both production and exposure and the evaluation of its effectiveness.

AMC American Motor Corporation, acquired in the 1980s by Chrysler.

Anglo-Saxon capitalism A belief in the workings of the free market, individualism and private property. A system in which shareholders play a major role. Found in the USA and UK.

Appraisal A formal system of employee evaluation to assess the contribution of individuals to the organization.

Asian capitalism Free market capitalism but with strong state intervention. Based around Asian values of hard work, duty, the role of the family and the importance of savings. A bureaucratic state but weak social welfare provision. Found across Asia but especially in Japan.

Asian tigers A group of countries with, since the 1970s, rapidly developing economies. The initial tigers were Hong Kong, Singapore, Taiwan and South Korea. They have been joined by a second wave of tigers including Malaysia, China and Vietnam. A 'tiger' economy is now a name given to any rapid growth economy.

AUEW Amalgamated Union of Engineering Workers.

Autonomous work groups The creation of a group of staff, who are given responsibility for the completion of a part of the operation.

Backward integration Obtaining control over the source of raw materials or the supply of components to the firm either by acquisition or establishing close ties with suppliers. See also *Forward integration* and *Vertical integration.*

BAIC Beijing Automotive Industry Company.

Balance of payments The difference over a given time between the income and expenditure of the economy in its dealings with other nations, involving exports, imports and other transactions.

Balance sheet The summary of a firm's financial position at a fixed point in time. The balance sheet is a statement of a firm's assets and liabilities at the end of the last day of the accounting period.

Barrier to entry This prevents new firms from entering a particular market. In most cases, cost and experience are the main factors although in some countries, notably China, there are legal and political barriers to entry.

Basic research Fundamental research directed at advancing the state of knowledge in a particular applied field with the very real hope that it will prove useful. See also *Pure research*.

BCG matrix A method of portfolio analysis developed by the Boston Consulting Group. Products and/or markets are classified as cash cows, stars, question marks or dogs. See also *Portfolio analysis*.

Below-the-line See *Sales promotion*.

Benchmarking The comparison of performance in one organization or part of an organization against that in another with a view to finding ways of improving performance.

BJC Beijing Jeep Corporation.

Bolton Report The influential report of the UK Committee of Inquiry on Small Firms, published in 1971, that noted both the decline and economic importance of the small firms sector.

Bounded rationality A concept developed by Cyert and March (1963) linked to decision-making. Information and the choice of strategic direction are taken from a limited range of options due to both complexity and time.

Brand See *Branding*.

Brand equity The value of the brand, which may add substantially to a firm's assets and acts as a major consideration in the price of acquisitions.

Brand loyalty The desired aim of branding, occurring when consumers make repeat purchases of the same branded product.

Branding The process through which the product is given a name, logo or symbol to distinguish it from the range of other products on offer. It is used to create awareness and build up customer loyalty to ensure repeat purchases.

Bretton Woods A conference held in the USA in 1944 by the Second World War Allied Nations, which agreed to set international exchange rates to achieve a measure of regulation and stability. The agreement also established the International Monetary Fund (IMF) and the World Bank. See also *International Monetary Fund* and *World Bank*.

British Standards Institute (BSI) An association that sets standards for units of measurement and technical terminology. It has been particularly influential in setting standards pertaining to functionality, safety and quality. The international equivalent is the International Standards Office (ISO).

'Bubble' economy The term given to an economy built on speculation as was the case in Japan in the 1980s.

Budgeting The setting of standards for income and expenditure and establishing mechanisms through which activities can be measured against the standards. Budgeting is a means of allocating funds and resources, of delegating authority and of motivating employees and is, above all, a vital control of activities.

Bureaucracy A system of organization for large complex organizations that operates through hierarchies of control and a detailed series of rules for all activities.

Business ethics Business ethics is the concern for moral standards and individual choices of right and wrong in the conduct of business affairs. It is a function of individual values, corporate culture, prevailing social norms and the laws of the land. See also *Corporate social responsibility*.

Business Link An organization set up and partly funded by the UK government to assist in the development of small and medium sized enterprises.

Business process re-engineering (BPR) A radical approach to adding value for the customer at each stage of the value chain. The aim is for dramatic improvements, which inevitably involves a fundamental rethinking of the organization and its operations.

Business strategy The strategy of a firm in a single business. See also *Corporate strategy*.

CAD (computer aided design) A computer-based system that enables the designer, through the use of computer graphics and memory, to evaluate the consequences of various design alternatives. This has assisted in both the speed and accuracy of the design stage.

CADCAM systems A linked system of computer aided design and computer aided manufacture. The system has a memory bank of standard designs, and the appropriate machines and tools required for manufacture.

Call centre A centralized facility for dealing with customers by phone or email to handle purchases and/or enquiries. In a global economy the call centre may be located to take advantage of low-cost labour or accommodation and calls are re-routed accordingly.

Capacity planning A process to determine the capacity required to fulfil market demand. The capacity could be measured in terms of space, people, machinery and so on.

Cash flow The movement of cash into and out of an organization. A healthy cash flow is essential for survival.

Cash-flow statement A requirement of UK financial reporting that details the movement of cash during an accounting period and is very useful for planning and control purposes.

CBI (Confederation of British Industry) An employers group that addresses a range of economic and general business and labour issues.

Centrally planned (state controlled) economy State control of the supply and demand of goods and services and targets given to individual enterprises. Control of prices, wages and levels of employment. See also *Transitional economy*.

Chapter 11 bankruptcy A USA form in which a firm, although bankrupt, can retain its assets if it can develop a payment plan to satisfy creditors. It is a means of offsetting debts against future cash flows.

CIM (Computer integrated manufacturing) Links flexible manufacturing systems to CADCAM and computer-controlled order and distribution systems. See also *Flexible manufacturing systems, CADCAM* and *CNC*.

Classical organization theory This is associated with the work of Weber and Fayol and offers a rational (and some would say prescriptive) approach to management and organizations. See also *Bureaucracy*.

Closed shop A situation where all employees must belong to a trade union as a condition of employment. A compulsory closed shop is not allowed under current UK employment law.

CNC (Computerized numerical control) Comprising machines with the capability of performing a number of different machine-tool operations.

Collective bargaining A process in which the representatives of employers and the representatives of employees (usually trade unions) negotiate wages, conditions and other related aspects.

Command economy See *Centrally planned state controlled economy*.

Commodification The development of new goods and services to broaden the nature of consumption and to accumulate profit in a capitalist system. See also *Accumulation*.

Company limited by guarantee A type of UK company owned by a group of members, whose liability is limited to their financial contribution. Such a company is often found in the voluntary sector.

Company unions Trade unions operated by the company, as is the case with unions in Japan.

Competitor–push The pressure to produce goods and services similar to those offered by competitors.

Confucian dynamism A term coined by Hofstede and Bond (1988) to define core Asian values, which include future orientation, perseverance and an importance attached to savings. It is sometimes referred to as long-term orientation.

Consumerism A social movement to inform and assist consumer choice and to act as a pressure group to represent the interests of consumers. These interests are presented to organizations in an attempt to influence product design, price and distribution. Significant concerns are unsafe products and dishonest producers.

Contingency approach An approach to organization theory that sees organization behaviour and practices as a function of a number of influencing variables. In particular, the contingency approach sees successful organizations operating in harmony with their environment.

Convergence A process in which countries become more like one another. Causal factors include technology transfer and the use of similar productive technologies and the expansion of global products, global markets and multinational firms. See also *Globalization* and *Culture free*.

Core competences Core competences refer to those activities of an organization that give it an advantage over its competitors. Such advantages could derive from such as an effective R&D department, an efficient operating system, good internal and external communications, the presence of key individuals or reputation and a loyal customer base.

Corporate accountability Where firms are accountable for their actions to the general public. Firms that transgress socially acceptable standards can expect to be punished, usually by the imposition of fines. In some cases, board members can be held responsible and prosecuted as individuals.

Corporate culture Sometimes referred to as organization culture, although we see *corporate* culture as the product of management as part of a change and control strategy. See also *Organization culture*.

Corporate social responsibility Corporate social responsibility (CSR) involves the application of business ethics. CSR is concerned predominantly with the firm and its relationship to its various stakeholders, such as shareholders, customers, employees, supplier and the community, and its relationship to the environment. The assumption is that in all these relationships business decisions are influenced by moral and ethical considerations. See also *Business ethics* and *Stakeholder theory*.

Corporate strategy The overall strategy of a firm operating in a number of different businesses.

Cost accounting The analysis and allocation of costs. See also *Direct* and *Indirect costs*.

Cost control The collection and analysis of accounting information about all aspects of the business and the use of comparisons, which are either historical and/or based on benchmarking against another organization.

Cost leadership The aim of being the lowest cost producer.

Cost-plus pricing A standard mark-up after all costs have been taken into consideration.

Creditors Those to whom the firm owes money.

Culture All human activity that is socially rather than genetically transmitted. It comprises values, norms and beliefs that are displayed in business behaviour and can result in different approaches and business practices in different parts of the world.

Culture free A situation in which culture is less significant than other factors, particularly technology. In a culture-free situation, business ideas and practices can be transferred between nations. See also *Convergence*.

Culture specific Each culture is differentiated by its own core values and business ideas. Practices can only be successfully transferred between nations with similar core values.

Current assets Assets that are short term and transitory, such as cash and stock.

Cyclical markets Such markets display alternating periods of high and low demand or periods of varying demand. Many product markets, e.g. automobiles, in mature industrialized economies are cyclical.

Debentures Negotiable instruments that can be bought and sold on the stock market. They are issued in return for loans secured on the fixed assets of a company.

Debtors Those who owe money to the firm.

De-industrialization The decline of the manufacturing sector of the economy.

Delayering The flattening of the organization by removing levels of supervision and management. It is usually accompanied by restructuring and redundancies among the management groups. See also *Restructuring*.

Demand–pull The development of new products and processes as a direct result of market demand. See also *Technology–push*.

Deregulation The lifting of government restrictions and controls usually aimed at increasing levels of competition.

Derivatives Financial instruments that are derived from an asset or a product. Their purpose is to allow companies to offset financial risk. The two main types of derivative are futures and options. A future is a contract that places an obligation to buy or sell at a set price on a given future date. An option is similar to a future except that the contract offers the right but not the obligation.

Design The final stage in the R&D process that translates the development into the final product for the consumer. See also *Design mix* and *Product design*.

Design mix Part of the design process incorporating elements such as effective operation, safety, easy maintenance, value for money and aesthetic considerations. These are all focused on satisfying customer needs.

Deskilling The process of reducing the skill content of work, usually through the introduction of new forms of technology.

Development Takes research a stage further by translating the outcome of research into something more tangible. At this stage in the design of a new product, a prototype or a sample would be produced.

Differentiation A strategy that aims to produce goods and services with certain unique dimensions that make them attractive to customers.

Direct and indirect costs Costs that can be directly ascribed to a specific product. See also *Indirect costs*.

Direct marketing Dealing directly with the customer, without using intermediaries such as retail outlets, as with mail shots, mail-order catalogues, telephone sales, and electronic commerce. See also *Personal selling*.

Distribution The process through which goods and services reach the customer. It involves the use of distribution channels and networks.

Diversification Adding new products or markets to the existing portfolio. Diversification can be *related* to the existing business or *unrelated*.

Dividend The payment made to shareholders of a proportion of profit after tax. See also *Ordinary shares* and *Preference shares*.

Divisionalization A form of organization structure that breaks the organization down according to product groups or market territory to form a series of profit centres. A form of organization often found in large complex multinational companies. See also *Profit centre*.

Dominant coalition The interest group(s) that have the most power and influence in an organization.

Down-sizing Reducing the number of people employed in an organization.

Dual apprenticeship system Developed in Germany for the training of young people and involving a combination of time spent in work and time spent in apprentice school each week.

Economic Order Quantity Model (EOQ) A decision model which establishes a trade-off between the cost of acquisition and the cost of holding stock.

Economies of scale The achievement of cost reduction through the volume of operation. In manufacturing the higher the volume produced of a single product then generally the costs of producing that item are reduced. The concept is sometimes linked to that of *Experience curve*.

Economies of scope A form of horizontal integration when the product range is extended to incorporate similar items. The economies of scope include shared central functions such as finance, marketing and R&D. See also *Horizontal integration*.

EDB (Economic Development Board) An arm of the Singapore government concerned with economic development and the attraction of inward investment.

EETPU The Electrical, Electronic, Telecommunications and Plumbing Union.

Electronic business (e-business) Similar to *e-commerce below*, e-business involves a much broader range of activities, incorporating all business activities. It enables the various elements of global firms to work more closely together and can form the basis of much business to business activity.

Electronic commerce (e-commerce) This involves the connection of suppliers and buyers directly through computer-based systems. E-commerce generally relates to trading activity involving information, goods and services. The initial point of contact is electronic although, in the case of goods and services, delivery is made using more conventional systems. The growth of e-commerce and e-business is directly associated with the development of the Internet and company-wide intranet systems.

Emerging markets These are markets where it is believed there is considerable potential for growth. Such markets can include newly industrialized nations, such as Malaysia, less developed nations with large populations, such as China and India, and those nations changing from a centrally controlled economy, as in East Europe.

Employee relations See *Industrial relations*.

Enterprise culture A movement that developed in the UK in the 1980s that emphasized individualism, entrepreneurship, innovation and self-help through self-employment. It was associated with the politics of the Thatcher era. See also *Thatcherism*.

Entrepreneurship The activity of entrepreneurs, who are responsible for the creation of new products, processes, services and markets. They develop new ways of doing business and managing people and create new forms of organization.

Environmental scanning A process of strategic analysis involving the search for opportunities and threats. See also *SWOT analysis*.

Ethical audit An audit of all the firm's activities and relationships, including products and services, processes, terms of employment and conditions for employees and the firm's relationships with its suppliers, local community and the environment. The audit checks that ethical practices are being pursued and establishes action plans where they are not.

Ethical investors There are investors who seek out companies in which to invest, that pursue demonstrably ethical strategies and practices.

Ethics A branch of moral philosophy; the study of morals and principles governing the rights and wrongs of human conduct. See also *Business ethics*.

EU The European Union, currently made up of 15 nation states, many operating with a single currency: the euro. Over the next few years the EU will expand to 25 member states.

European Exchange Rate Mechanism (ERM) An agreement among member states of the EU to keep exchange rates within fixed limits as a precursor to monetary union.

European Monetary Union (EMU) The creation of a single European currency, now the major currency used in 12 of the 15 EU member states.

Excellent company A term derived from the influential work of Peters and Waterman (1982). They define 'excellent companies' in terms of eight characteristics including closeness to the customer, hands on, value driven, autonomy and entrepreneurship and simple form, lean staff. Such companies usually have strong, well-defined corporate cultures. See also *Corporate culture*.

Experience curve An advantage gained over time from producing goods or services or operating in particular markets. Cost advantages associated with economies of scale can often be attributed to the experience curve. See also *Economies of scale*.

Explicit knowledge Knowledge that is available within a firm that is usually obtained through rational processes of data collection and is often contained in documentation. Such knowledge is often available to all and, as a consequence, is rarely a source of competitive advantage. See also *implicit knowledge.*

Factoring A means of raising capital by selling debts owed at some 70–80 per cent of their real invoice value. While money is lost on the value of the invoice, this can be a useful way of improving cash flow.

Family firm A firm owned and managed by family members. Although there are examples of large family firms, most tend to be very small businesses.

Financial management Part of the finance and accounting function that is concerned with the financing of an organization's activities.

Financial reporting The collection and presentation of data for use in financial management and management accounting. In most countries there are minimum legal requirements governing the kind of statement that must be produced.

Financial services A sector of the economy that includes banking, insurance, pensions and investment activities.

Five Forces model Developed by Porter (1990) to assess the bargaining power of suppliers and buyers, the threat of entry from competitors, substitute products and, ultimately, the competitive rivalry of the firm.

Fixed assets Assets that remain on the books for a significant period of time, such as land, buildings and machinery.

Flag of convenience A term used in shipping when a ship owner registers a ship in another country for cheaper insurance or to avoid restrictive laws.

Flexible firm A response to the demands of globalization, competition and cost reduction. Flexibility within organizations occurs in a number of different ways including the employment of part-time and contract workers, out-sourcing, multiskilling and introducing variations in pay and times of attendance.

Flexible manufacturing system (FMS) An integrated system comprising the various elements of advanced manufacturing engineering to solve the problem of offering consumer choice and a quick response to market changes using a minimum of working capital. FMSs enable a range of different models to be built using the same assembly line and pieces of equipment. See also *CADCAM*, *CNC* and *CIM.*

Foreign direct investment (FDI) The full or partial ownership and control of a firm located in one country by investors in another country. See also *Multinational corporation.*

Forward integration This occurs when producers diversify to control the onward processes of delivering their goods to the consumer, as in the case of a manufacturer setting up a transport or retail operation. See also *Backward integration* and *Vertical integration.*

Free market A market in which firms compete on the same basis with little or no government interference. In reality such a system tends to favour large firms and leads to the creation of monopolies or oligopolies. See also *Monopoly* and *Oligopoly.*

FRS Financial Reporting Standard. See *Accounting Standards Committee.*

Futures See *Derivatives.*

G7 (Group of Seven) An economic alliance of the world's major economic nations; Canada, France, Germany, Italy, Japan, UK and USA.

GAAP (Generally Accepted Accounting Practice) An amalgam of legislation, SSAPs and the FRSs, to form sets of practically based accounting rules. There is a UK GAAP and a USA GAAP. See also *Accounting Standards Committee.*

Gap analysis A strategic assessment of the difference between what managers want to achieve and what they can achieve with the resources available.

Gastarbeiter A name given, originally in Germany, to foreign migrant workers. The meaning is literally, 'guest worker'.

GATT The General Agreement on Tariffs and Trade set up by the Bretton Woods' Agreement to facilitate global trade as a means to peace and prosperity. See also *Bretton Woods* and *WTO.*

GDP (Gross Domestic Product) The sum total of the net outputs of each sector of the economy, including those of foreign firms but excluding earnings from overseas. GDP is often expressed *per capita* (per head of population).

GMB   General, Municipal and Boilermakers' trade union.

GNP (Gross National Product)   The sum total of the net outputs of each sector of the economy together with the earnings by its residents from overseas investments. Like GDP, GNP is often expressed *per capita*.

Global market   The sale of a product or service in most countries in the world. Coca Cola and McDonald's can be said to have a global market.

Global production system   See *globally organized production*.

Globalization   A process of economic, political and cultural convergence in which national borders become less significant. The process has been speeded up greatly by developments in information and communications technology.

Globally organized production   The coordination of activities in various locations across the world to produce goods or services. Most manufactured goods are now assembled from parts made in different areas of the world to achieve maximum cost effectiveness.

Goals   Organization goals give direction to the activities of organization members both as broad statements of intent and detailed objectives. Goal formulation can be a highly political process and source of conflict.

Golden shares   Shares retained by governments after privatization issue, usually to prevent a hostile takeover.

Greenfield site   This relates to the siting of a business operation in a completely new location. It usually implies a new building with all modern facilities and new infrastructure.

Hard and soft HRM   Hard HRM focuses on business values and management strategy, whereas soft HRM focuses upon the selection, development, involvement and the reward of people.

Hawthorne Studies   A series of highly influential studies carried out in the 1920s at the Hawthorne plant in Chicago of the Western Electric Co. The studies are associated with human relations and Elton Mayo, although he was not one of the primary researchers. The studies focused on communications, group behaviour and participation. See also *Human relations management*.

Hierarchy of needs   A theory of motivation attributed to Abraham Maslow. The theory states that we are motivated by unsatisfied needs and these are arranged in a hierarchy. We must first satisfy our basic physical needs, but our ultimate goal is self-actualization.

Holding company   An organization whose main purpose is the ownership and overall control of a group of semi-autonomous companies.

Horizontal integration   This occurs most commonly when a firm adds to its portfolio of products by acquisition of companies operating in similar markets. See also *Economies of scope*.

Hostile takeover   See *Mergers and acquisitions*.

Human relations management   A set of theories and approaches originating from the early part of the 20th century and, in particular, the work of Elton Mayo. The approach emphasizes group approaches to work, employee involvement, democratic leadership and effective communication. The approach developed throughout the 20th century and is still influential in some forms of management training.

Human resource management   Management decisions and actions that affect the nature of the relationship between the organization and its employees. A strategic approach to ensuring that people in the organization achieve its goals. It involves recruitment, selection, training, reward systems, industrial relations and employee involvement as an integrated strategy. Also known as HRM and HR. It is considered to be a more business oriented and strategic approach to personnel management. See also *Personnel management* and *Hard and soft HRM*.

Implicit knowledge   The sum total of knowledge acquired by organization members throughout the lifetime of the organization and passed on to subsequent generations of employees. It is rarely documented and is difficult for outsiders to penetrate. It is often a source of competitive advantage. See also *explicit knowledge*.

Indirect costs Costs that relate to general overheads such as labour, heating, lighting and so on. See also *Direct costs*.

Individualism–collectivism An accepted measure of cultural difference used in major studies by Hofstede and Trompenaars. Individualistic societies focus on self and the immediate family, while collectivistic societies are more group oriented and focus on the extended family. Industrialization and globalization are usually accompanied by a shift towards greater individualism.

Industrial relations The relations between employers and employees and their respective representatives with a focus on pay, conditions, job security and participation. They involve negotiation and bargaining. Also known as employee relations. See also *New industrial relations*.

Inflation An increase in the general level of prices and usually accompanied by rises in wages.

Information and communication technology The use of developments in computers and telecommunications to enhance the quantity, quality and speed of information transfer. See also *Internet*.

Innovation The discovery or creation of something new, such as a product, process, strategy or structure, and turning it into economic reality. An innovation is an invention that is economically relevant. See also *R&D*.

Interaction–influence model This sees all business activities as a complex series of interactions that are mutually influencing, hence business activities influence the national economy, that also influences business activities. The *Business in Context* model is an example of an interaction–influence model.

Interest group A grouping within an organization of people with similar goals. Management, the marketing department, a

trade union, a work group, etc. are all examples of interest groups. Interest groups can combine to form coalitions.

International Monetary Fund (IMF) Part of the United Nations established by Bretton Woods to control the international financial system. The IMF can intervene when changes in a nation's economy threaten to destabilize the economies of other countries. Interventions in the 1990s included those in Mexico and South Korea. See also *Bretton Woods*.

Internet A global web of computer networks providing information and a means of communicating via email.

Invention See *Innovation*.

Investment appraisal A process of calculating whether an investment is cost effective in the short, medium or long term. See also *NPV*.

Investors in People A standard introduced by the UK government for the development of staff.

ISO The International Standards Office. See *British Standards Institute*.

Japanese management A set of practices and techniques associated with businesses in Japan, such as just-in-time, quality circles, single-status firms and company unions. Such practices have been associated with the success of Japanese firms and have been copied in other countries.

Japanese transplants These are Japanese manufacturing or service organizations operating in an overseas location and using predominantly Japanese business methods

Japanization This involves both the process of Japanese foreign direct investment and the adoption or adaptation of Japanese business practices by non-Japanese firms.

Job enrichment The application of the theories of Herzberg to create more challenging and meaningful work. See also *Motivation–hygiene theory*.

Joint ventures Two or more firms working together to achieve mutually beneficial objectives. These can include sharing resources, establishing a joint R&D project or setting up a third company with shared ownership. A joint venture is similar to a *strategic alliance*, except that in a joint venture there is usually an element of shared ownership.

Just-in-time (JIT) This is a method of manufacture developed initially in Japan. Starting with customer demand, goods and services are produced at each stage of the operation only as required. It is a pull-through system that eliminates the need for large stocks but requires close cooperation with suppliers.

Kaizen A Japanese system of continuous quality improvement.

Kanban An integral part of a just-in-time system. A *Kanban* is a card or signal, which informs how much is to be produced by each process and the precise quantity each process should withdraw from the previous stage, which may be either another process, a materials store, or even a supplier.

Keiretsu A business group in Japan, typified by a number of cross-holdings. This is typical of all major Japanese firms and *Keiretsu* dominate the Japanese economy. *Keiretsu* are very similar to the *Zaibatsu*, similar business groups, which dominated the Japanese economy prior to the Second World War and had considerable political influence.

Keynesian policy A economic policy involving state investment in the economy to create employment.

Kigyo Shudan A business group in Japan organized around a bank. See also *Keiretsu*.

Labour markets These provide labour for organizations and vary in terms of size and prevailing skills.

Laissez-faire A model of capitalism emphasizing the free market. See also *Anglo-Saxon capitalism*.

Late development effect The advantage enjoyed by newly industrialized countries, whereby they can learn from the mistakes of others, benefit from greenfield sites and catch up economically. See also *Newly industrialized countries (NICs)* and *Greenfield site*.

Leadership Influencing the direction of the organization through a focus on change and inspiring the group to improved performance.

Lean production (or manufacture) A totally integrated system of manufacture, developed initially by Toyota in Japan. The emphasis is on the integration of state-of-the-art techniques, a flexible approach and teamwork. Advocates claim dramatic improvements in efficiency and effectiveness.

Leasing A process through which a firm can acquire assets that it has not bought, but leased from another firm. Many company cars, security systems and photocopiers are acquired in this way.

Liberal pluralism A belief in the free market and the recognition that society is made up of different interest groups. The state helps to smooth out difficulties in the operation of a free market and regulates the cooperation and exchange between different interest groups.

Liberalization This process is part of an economic transition to a free market. It involves the removal of state control on wages and prices: changes that can result in inflation and increasing levels of unemployment. For this reason, some countries favour the retention of a number of state-owned enterprises in each sector to preserve jobs and keep a control of prices.

Licensing A process whereby the owner of a patent on a product allows another firm to produce that product upon payment of an agreed royalty fee.

Lifetime employment A system under which individuals commit their working life to one firm and whereby the firm guarantees them a job for life. Although associated with Japan, lifetime employment is common in other countries, notably Germany. It is threatened by economic recession.

Limited company See *Public limited company (plc)* and *Private company (Ltd)*.

Loading A technique in operations management to determine the amount of work that can be allocated to a particular work centre, be it a department, unit or person.

Loan capital Finance raised by borrowing money from a third party such as a bank or other financial institution.

Long-term versus short-term orientation
See *Confucian dynamism*.

Long-wave economic cycles Cycles of economic growth and decline spanning over 40 years. Upswings are related to the development of particular industries over time and downswings are the result of saturated and contested markets.

Machine tools Tools used in manufacturing and seen by some as a means of developing innovative processes and products.

Management The shaping of activities, strategy and organization, coping with the external environment and organizing people to ensure the long-term survival of the firm.

Management accounting The application of accounting techniques to provide management with the information to assist in the processes of planning and control. It involves budgeting, costing, investment appraisal and the management of cash flows.

Management by objectives (MBO) A system of management whereby individual managers are set targets and their performance is judged against target achievement.

Managerial grid An approach to leadership developed by Blake and Mouton, which enables managers to plot their leadership style in terms of their concern for people and their concern for completing the task.

Manpower planning The analysis of a company's manpower needs in light of its current manpower resources and the nature of the labour market.

Market research The collection and analysis of information about present and future products, markets, competitor strategies and tactics and consumer preferences.

Market segmentation The process through which the total market is broken down to create distinctive consumer groups. The criteria used to form such groups varies and may include geographical location, social class, occupation, gender, lifestyle, and so on. Products can be developed which focus upon the needs of a particular group.

Marketing The design, pricing, promotion and delivery of goods and services to meet or exceed customer needs.

Marketing channel A flow of goods and services, which may comprise several stages, involving intermediaries such as transporters, agents, wholesalers and retailers.

Marketing mix This is the development of a marketing strategy on the basis of product, price, promotion and place (distribution). These are sometimes referred to as the *4 Ps*.

Marque A brand name usually applied to cars.

Masculinity–femininity An accepted measure of cultural difference used in major studies such as that by Hofstede. Masculine societies tend to be assertive and have clearly defined gender roles. Feminine societies have less well-defined gender roles and are more concerned for the welfare of people.

Matrix organization This is a structural device to manage two or more elements of the organization: be they size, products, markets or customers. In a typical matrix an employee is a member of a functional group and of a product or market grouping. The system works best when two or more elements need to be emphasized but it can cause confusion and dissatisfaction.

Mechanistic organization An organization best suited to stable conditions and similar to classical bureaucracies. High degrees of specialization and operations governed by rules. Clear hierarchies of authority and emphasis on vertical communication. See also *Bureaucracy*.

Mergers and acquisitions These occur when two or more firms come together to form a single firm. A merger implies a coming together of equals while an acquisition implies a dominant partner. An acquisition of one firm by another, when the firm that is being acquired does not welcome it, is referred to as a *hostile takeover*.

Method study A set of techniques which focus on improving how the job is carried out and includes not just the methods involved in the tasks themselves, but also equipment design.

Mission A statement of core values which define the purpose of the organization.

MITI The Ministry of International Trade and Industry, an influential branch of the Japanese civil service.

MOF The Ministry of Finance in Japan, which controls the Bank of Japan and investment strategy.

Monetarism The control of the economy by the control of the amount of money in the economy.

Monetary Union See *European Monetary Union*.

Monopoly The control or dominance of a market by a single producer or provider.

Motivation–hygiene theory An approach to motivation developed by Frederick Herzberg. Hygiene factors such as pay, conditions and style of supervision will either result in an acceptable performance or lead to sub-standard performance. Real motivation is the product of interesting work and the opportunity for achievement, involvement and recognition. See also *Job enrichment*.

MRP1 (Materials requirement planning) A computerized planning system that enables managers to determine the requirements for the quantity of materials needed and the timing of that need, particularly where there is a high degree of complexity.

MRP2 (Manufacturing resource planning) A computerized planning system offers dealing with materials requirements, capacity planning and scheduling. See also *MRP1, Capacity planning* and *Scheduling*.

Multinational corporation (MNC) A multinational firm is one that operates and is managed from bases in a number of different countries. While small firms can and do operate multinationally, most multinationals are large corporations with diverse interests coordinated by a centrally planned global strategy.

Multinational enterprise (MNE) Same as the *Multinational corporation (MNC)* (see above).

New industrial relations A term that appeared in the 1980s, associated with practices brought in by Japanese transplants. Such 'new' approaches embraced a legally binding contract between the firm and the unions and a peace clause where employees agree not to strike while the contract is in force.

New Labour A name used by the UK Labour Party to rebrand itself and gain political support as a 'modern', business-friendly party.

New public management The increasing use of private sector firms by managers in the public sector to provide essential services. This is also referred to as *Public private partnership (PPP)*.

New technology The use of computers and electronic circuits to process information for greater control, speed, flexibility and quality in work operations.

Newly industrialized countries (NICs) These are countries, like the Asian tigers, that have developed industrial economies later than the advanced nations of the USA, Europe and Japan. They are able to learn from the advanced nations. See also *Late development effect*.

NGA The National Graphical Association, a trade union representing print workers.

Non-executive directors Directors with no direct involvement in the management of the enterprise who are able to provide experience from elsewhere and can operate as an impartial voice in influencing strategic direction.

No-strike deal This is an agreement by a group of employees, usually as members of a trade union, not to withdraw their labour at any time for the duration of an agreed contract period. See also *New industrial relations*.

NPV (net present value) A popular method of investment appraisal since it estimates future returns on investment, but assesses them on current values.

OECD The Organization for Economic Cooperation and Development, a grouping of 21 industrial nations for the furtherance of trade.

Oil shocks These refer to two periods in the 1970s (1973 and 1979) when the oil producing nations made major price increases with a significant impact on the costs of most businesses around the world.

Oligopoly The control or dominance of the market by a small number of firms. Several global markets, such as those for automobiles, oil and pharmaceuticals, can be called oligopolies.

OPEC Organization of Petroleum Exporting Countries established in 1961.

Open systems A view of the organization using the systems approach in which the inputs and the outputs interact with the environment in which the organization operates. See also *Systems approach*.

Operations A central role in most organizations, transforming materials, finance, information and the like into goods and services wanted by customers.

Operations planning A process to ensure that sufficient goods or services are produced to meet demand in terms of quantity, quality, timing and the degree of flexibility.

Operations research (OR) The application of mathematical models to solve complex organizational problems.

Options See *Derivatives*.

Ordinary shares These represent the majority of all share capital. Dividend is not guaranteed but holders are normally entitled to a share of the profits after deductions for tax and payment to preference shareholders. See also *Preference shares* and *Dividend*.

Organic organization An organization suited to dynamic changing conditions. Emphasis on flexibility and a loose definition of roles and responsibilities. Typified by delegated authority and free flows of communication both horizontal and vertical.

Organization culture Sometimes referred to as corporate culture, although we see *organization* culture as the product of a large number of variables, including history, the economy, technology, product market, strategy, management style, nature of employees and so on. See *Corporate culture*.

Organizational development (OD) A change strategy popular in the 1970s that used an external or internal consultant to achieve planned change through the development of individuals and groups.

Organizational marketing Business to business marketing.

Organization structure The grouping of activities and people to achieve the goals of the organization.

Outsourcing An increasing trend involving the use of another organization to provide essential goods and services. Many manufacturers outsource a proportion of their operations, usually to lower cost operators. Firms often outsource functions such as catering, cleaning and even payroll to other firms.

Over-capacity Having more factory or office space, machines and people than required to satisfy market demand for goods and services. Over-capacity is expensive in that resources are wasted.

Oversupply When the supply of goods and services is greater than the demand. Over-supply usually results in price falls that can be dramatic, as in the case of microchips in the 1990s.

Partnership A legal form of ownership found especially in the professions. Partners have unlimited personal liability, which may be reduced by forming a *limited liability partnership*.

Patent A form of intellectual property granted for an innovative product and giving the inventor a monopoly of production over a stated period (usually around 20 years). See also *Licensing*.

Paternalism A system of management popular in the UK among Quaker employers, such as Cadbury and Lever, which focused on employee welfare. Essentially paternalism takes responsibility for the individual and is sometimes associated with a loss of freedom.

Payment by results Payment tied to increased output subject to quality, wastage and machine utilization.

Pendulum arbitration A system of arbitration in which the arbitrator must favour one side or the other.

Penetration A pricing strategy that involves setting a low price to attract a mass market at the outset.

Personal selling A specialized form of direct marketing, favoured by the sellers of industrial goods, recognizing the importance of building up good personal relations between seller and buyer. See also *Direct marketing*.

Personnel management A traditional approach to the management of human resources which focuses on selection, training, payment and industrial relations. It has been largely superseded by a more strategically focused HRM. See also *Human resource management*.

Picketing An act of protest and persuasion during times of strike, where (usually) trade union members gather at the entrances to workplaces to persuade others to join them. The activity in the UK is regulated by law.

PIMS (Profit Impact of Market Strategies) Established by the Strategic Planning Institute in Britain and the USA offers assistance in strategic choice by identifying those strategies most likely to result in increased profit levels. A record is kept of strategic options and their links to profit levels.

Pluralist frame of reference See *Unitarist and Pluralist frames of reference*.

Portfolio analysis This is used in firms operating within a number of different businesses and markets or in the same market with a number of different products. The technique enables management to assess the relative attractiveness of their businesses and products in their current markets and assist decisions on the direction of future investment. See also *BCG Matrix*.

Positioning Choosing the right market segment for the product and finding the appropriate niche in that market to differentiate it from its competitors, on such matters as price and quality.

Power distance An accepted measure of cultural difference developed by Hofstede. High-power-distance societies accept status differences exist and build upon them. Low-power-distance societies introduce measures to reduce such differences in power and status.

Preference shares Shares which attract a fixed rate of dividend irrespective of the financial performance of the company.

Private company Different from a plc in that shares are not openly available and the company does not have a stock market listing. Shares are owned by the founders, family members or by management. Denoted by *Ltd* after the company name. The equivalent type of company in Germany is a *Gesellschaft mit beshränkter Haftung* (GmbH). See also *Public limited company*.

Privatization The selling of state-owned businesses.

Process innovation The development of a new way of making products or delivering them to the customer.

Procurement The activities engaged in the acquisition of the various resource inputs to the primary activities of the organization.

Product differentiation A means of gaining competitive advantage through the development of a product that is different from those produced by competitors.

Product design This involves consideration of styling and function and the range of products and the degree of standardization. See also *Design* and *Design mix*.

Product innovation The development of a product such as a new model of car or a new form of insurance policy.

Product life-cycle This assumes that all products have limited lives during which they pass through a series of stages, all of which have implications for sales and profitability.

Product line The total number of variations of the same basic product, differentiated by quality, cost or extra features.

Product management The organization of the firm around its products: each brand or group of brands has its own manager.

Product mix The total number of different products offered by the firm, sometimes referred to as the product portfolio.

Profit and loss account This provides detail of a firm's income and expenditure throughout a stated period of time, known as the accounting period.

Profit centre A sub-set of an organization that operates as an independent business with profit targets. These are common in divisionalized structures. See also *Divisionalization*.

Pseudo-innovation No real change in the product or process has occurred but claims are made to revitalize a stagnant market. Pseudo-innovations are often the product of marketing campaigns to change the fortunes of a flagging product.

Public limited company (PLC) A UK company that is a legal entity separate from the owners in which liability is restricted. Unlike a private (limited) company, shares are traded and the company is listed on the stock market. An *Aktiengesellschaft* (AG) is the German equivalent of the UK plc.

Public private partnership (PPP) See *New public management*.

Public sector A very broad area that includes central and local government, hospitals, universities, schools and nationalized industries.

Public-sector borrowing requirement (PSBR) The extent to which borrowing exceeds income in the public sector.

Pure research The advancement of the state of knowledge in a particular field with little immediate concern for its commercial application. See also *Basic research*.

Quality circles A method of quality improvement that involves all employees in discussions to solve problems and implement solutions to improve quality.

Quality control A process that ensures the quality of the finished product or service meets the standards set in the design stage and also meets with the approval of the customer.

Quantity control A process that ensures the throughput of goods and services goes according to the planned schedule. This is sometimes known as production control and sometimes as progress chasing.

R&D See *Research and development*.

R&D intensity Expenditure on R&D as a proportion of sales revenue.

R&D Scoreboard An annual publication of the UK Department of Trade and Industry showing UK and world annual expenditure on R&D by firm and sector.

Rational knowledge Knowledge that is derived from scientific and objective methods.

Recession A period of time when the economy stops growing and goes into reverse. A prolonged recession turns into a depression.

Research and development (R&D) This is the organization function that is the focus for innovation within a firm. R&D refers both to the activity and the name of a department.

Restructuring This refers to a number of measures generally associated with cost-cutting. Such measures include plant or office closure and reducing the number of employees.

Reverse engineering A process whereby products, usually those of competitor firms, are systematically taken apart to see how they were made.

Revised sequence Coined by Galbraith (1972) it refers to a system of innovation and marketing in which product development is led by technology and associated costs and not consumer preferences. See also *Accepted sequence*.

Sales promotion This incorporates a wide variety of different techniques, including free samples, money-back coupons, special offers on loyalty points, contests and so on. Sales promotion is sometimes referred to as *below-the-line* advertising.

Scenario planning A flexible approach to strategy formulation which looks at a number of possible changes in the environment and asks the question 'what if?'.

Scheduling The balancing of the costs of production against demands for goods and services; ensures that demand is met in the most efficient way possible.

Scientific management A highly influential approach to management developed by F. W. Taylor at the beginning of the 20th century. Scientific management is sometimes called *Taylorism*. The key elements are the separation of planning and doing, the scientific analysis and design of work, the application of work study and work measurement and the scientific selection of staff.

Segmentation See *Market segmentation*.

Seniority payment A system favoured in Japan whereby pay increases occur with age and length of service.

Share capital Funding raised through the issue of shares offering shareholders part ownership in the firm and an annual payment in the form of dividend.

Skimming A pricing strategy of setting a high initial price. It is used with products that appeal to a market segment where price is not an important consideration.

Small business See *SME*.

SME (Small- and medium-size enterprise) The EU classifies SMEs as any enterprise employing fewer than 250 people. SMEs play a key role in the development of the business enterprise and in their contribution to the economy.

Social ethics The belief that ethical standards will vary between societies reflecting different histories and influences.

Social market capitalism Free market operation but carefully regulated by the state. A mix of public and private ownership with emphasis on social welfare and employee involvement with legal regulation. Found in Germany and Scandanavia.

Societal marketing The satisfaction of consumer needs through the provision of goods and services that are socially acceptable, non-harmful and non-polluting.

Socio-technical systems The interaction of technology and the social system at the workplace. An underlying assumption is that work is most effective when the social system and the prevailing technology operate in harmony.

SOGAT Society of Graphical and Allied Trades, a trade union representing workers in the print industry.

Sole trader An individual running a company with unlimited personal liability. A common form of business ownership and typical of many small firms.

SSAPs (Statements of Standard Accounting Practice) See *Accounting Standards Committee*.

Stakeholder theory The recognition that the organization is responsible to various groups in society. These may include shareholders, employers, suppliers, government, the community and so on. Stakeholder theory usually includes the responsibility of the firm for the natural environment. See also *Corporate social responsibility*.

State Comprises a number of institutions including government, Parliament, judiciary, the civil service, police and armed forces.

Strategic alliance See *Joint ventures*.

Strategic fit A consideration in the choice of strategy or in the choice of a partner. Does the strategy fit with the prevailing organizational and environmental context of the firm? Do prospective partners in a strategic alliance or joint venture offer complementary rather than conflicting or duplicating products and markets? See also *Contingency approach* and *Joint ventures*.

Strategy A set of objectives and methods of achieving them. Usually formulated by senior management involving a mix of analysis and negotiation.

Sub-contracting A system in which part of the job is done by another firm.

Supply chain This is comprised of suppliers, producers and distributors. In modern business there has been increased emphasis on the management of the supply chain as a route to more cost-effective business and improved customer service.

Supply chain management An integrated set of activities including purchasing and supply, materials handling, stock control and distribution.

Supply-side economics The stimulation of economic growth by cutting taxes and encouraging people to work by cutting social welfare benefits.

Supranational organization These are political or trade organizations that comprise nation states as their members and therefore cross national boundaries. Examples include the *European Union (EU)*, North American Free Trade Association (NAFTA) and the World Trade Association (WTO).

Supraterritoriality A phrase coined by Scholte (2000) to define globalization. The idea is that thoughts, behaviour and practices in the modern world extend beyond national borders and that former constraints imposed by geography become irrelevant.

Sustainability The extent to which an organization's strategy is difficult to copy and is therefore the source of competitive advantage over time.

SWOT analysis An acronym for strengths, weaknesses, opportunities and threats. A simple method of strategic analysis.

Synergy The collective influence of the various activities of the company producing an overall effect that is greater than the sum of the parts.

Systems approach A view of the organization as a set of interrelated parts. Also, a view of organizational activities as a series of inputs, processes and outputs. See also *Open Systems*.

Tacit knowledge See *Implicit knowledge*.

Tactical ethics The assumption that people pursue ethical standards only because it suits them to do so in particular situations.

Taguchi method A procedure which tests the robustness of the design of a product in extreme conditions.

Target-profit pricing involves establishing the price in accordance with projected demand using some form of break-even analysis. Price is a function of both the minimum sales required to cover production costs and the required profit margins based on estimated sales figures.

Taylorism See *Scientific management*.

Technology A broad concept referring to the application of available knowledge and skills to create and use materials, processes and products.

Technology control The maintenance of plant or equipment.

Technology–push The utilization of known technologies to develop innovative products and processes. Many innovations, for example the CD player, are developed as a result of both demand–pull and technology–push. See also *Demand–pull*.

Technology transfer The process of obtaining technology from another firm or country. A number of methods can be used such as *Joint ventures*, *FDI* or *Licensing*.

Telemarketing The offering and selling of products and services over the phone or via the Internet.

Telesales See *Telemarketing*.

TGWU The Transport and General Workers' Union, one of the largest UK trade unions.

Thatcherism A political and economic philosophy that emerged under the UK Prime Minister Margaret Thatcher (1979–91). It espoused the free market, privatization, individualism, self-help and entrepreneurialism. A series of laws were passed to curb the power of trade unions.

Third-party intervention A phrase usually applied to the intervention of the government in disputes between management and labour.

Total quality management (TQM) A strategic approach to quality that permeates the entire organization. It goes beyond control and assurance in that it incorporates a number of different techniques and approaches, and is linked to culture change in the organization that focuses on the needs of the customer by building quality into every aspect of the operation.

Trade barriers These are mechanisms erected by national governments to prevent or restrict imports or to place a high tax on imports to protect home producers.

Trademark A name or symbol used to differentiate goods and services of a particular producer.

Trade union A group of employees who formally come together to achieve mutual goals of job protection, improvements in pay and conditions or a widening of industrial democracy.

Transcendental ethics The belief that there are absolute concepts of right and wrong that apply across all societies.

Transfer pricing The process through which goods and services produced in one section of the organization are sold internally for use by another.

Transitional economy An economy that is changing from one where there is central control by the state towards a free-market model.

Transnational corporation A transnational corporation integrates global resources to achieve economies of scale while still having the capability of responding to local markets. Flexibility, responsiveness and innovation replace control and cost as primary strategic objectives. Such firms generally have weakened ties with their country of origin.

TUC The Trades Union Congress, a national UK organization representing all affiliated trade unions.

Uncertainty avoidance An accepted measure of cultural difference developed by Hofstede. High uncertainty avoidance denotes a reluctance to take risks.

UNISON Trade union representing public sector workers in the UK.

Unitarist and pluralist frames of reference The unitarist perspective emphasizes shared goals among all members of the organization and managers find it difficult to acknowledge that trade unions have a legitimate role in their organization. A pluralist frame of reference acknowledges that different groups within the organization may have different goals. Within such a perspective, trade unions are seen as legitimate representatives of the wishes of employees.

Universalism versus particularism A measure of cultural difference used by Trompenaars. A universalistic culture favours rules over relationships. A particularistic culture favours relationships over rules.

Unlisted securities market Part of the UK stock exchange through which small firms can raise investment capital.

Value added The difference between the value of sales and the cost of the inputs to achieve those sales.

Value chain The value chain offers a view of the organization as a cumulative build-up of added value for the customer through the interaction between key operations activities. The end result is greater than the sum of its parts and, for profit-seeking organizations, means increased margins. The value chain was developed as a model by Porter (1985).

Value engineering The rigorous analysis of the product to investigate where cost savings can be made in the design or manufacture or perhaps where the element can be substituted by one of lower cost.

Vertical integration An integrated system of backward and forward integration. See also *Backward integration* and *Forward integration*.

Virtual organization This refers to a modern organizational form in which members of a team remotely work together using electronic communication devices such as email, video conferencing, web-cam, etc. Such a structure enables people in the same organization in different locations or even countries to work together in real time.

Whistleblowing A process whereby employees report any practice or incident where members of the company have been behaving unethically.

World Bank An organization set up by the 1944 Bretton Woods conference to initiate and fund development projects around the world. See also *Bretton Woods*.

Work measurement The formulation of standard times needed for an average worker to complete the various tasks involved in a single job and is thus a vital component in planning.

Work study An analysis of work. See also *Method study* and *Work measurement*.

Works council A forum for employee representation in organizations that often exist independently from trade unions. A works council represents all employees and can be involved in strategic discussions. It is an important feature of the German system.

WTO (World Trade Organization) An organization set up by the *General Agreement on Tariffs and Trade (GATT)* in the 1980s to promote free trade, to establish rules for international trade and to persuade member countries to remove trade barriers.

Zaibatsu See *Keiretsu*.

References

Aaker, D. A. (1996) *Building Strong Brands*, Free Press: New York.

Abernathy, W. J. and Utterback, J. M. (1978) 'Patterns of industrial innovation', in R. R. Rothberg (ed.) *Corporate Strategy and Product Innovation*, 2nd edn, Free Press: New York.

Adair, J. (1983) *Effective Leadership: A Self-development Manual*, Gower: Aldershot.

Adair, J. (1989) *Great Leaders*, Talbot Adair Press: Guildford.

Adcroft, A., Cutler, T., Haslam, C., Williams, K. and Williams, J. (1991) 'Hanson and ICI: the consequences of financial engineering', University of East London, Occasional Papers in Business, Economy and Society, 2.

Adler, N. (1997) *International Dimensions of Organizational Behaviour*, 3rd edn, South Western College Publishing: Cincinnati, OH.

Aiello, P. (1991) 'Building a joint venture in China: the case of Chrysler and the Beijing Jeep Corporation', *Journal of General Management*, 17, 2: 47–64.

Albrow, M. (1996) *The Global Age: State and Society beyond Modernity*, Polity Press: Cambridge.

Ansoff, H. I. (1968) *Corporate Strategy*, Penguin: Harmondsworth.

Ansoff, H. I. and Stewart, J. M. (1967) 'Strategies for a technology-based business', *Harvard Business Review*, 45, November–December, 71–83.

Armstrong, M. (2001) *A Handbook of Human Resource Management Practice*, 8th edn, Kogan Page: London.

Armstrong, P., Glyn, A. and Harrison, J. (1991) *Capitalism Since 1945*, Basil Blackwell: Oxford.

Ashkenas, R., Ulrich, D., Jick, T. and Kerr, S. (1995) *The Boundaryless Organization: Breaking the Chains of Organization Structure*, Jossey-Bass: San Fransisco, CA.

Atkinson, J. (1984) 'Manpower strategies for flexible organizations', *Personnel Management*, August, 28–31.

Atrill, P. and McLaney, E. (2003) *Accounting and Finance for Non-specialists*, 4th edn, FT Prentice Hall: Harlow.

Baker, M. J. (1991) *Marketing*, 5th edn, Macmillan: London.

Bannock, G. (1981) *The Economics of Small Firms: Return from the Wilderness*, Basil Blackwell: Oxford.

Barclays Bank (2002) *Barclays Bank Survey on Family Business*, www.smallbusiness.barclays.co.uk

Barry, J., Chandler, J., Clark, H., Johnston, R. and Needle, D. (eds) (2000) *Organization and Management: A Critical Text*, Thomson Learning: London.

Bart, C. K. and Baetz, M. C. (1999) 'The relationship between mission statements and firm performance: an exploratory study', *Journal of Management Studies*, 35, 6: 823–53.

Bartlett, C. A. and Ghoshal, S. (1995) *Transnational Management; Text, Cases and Readings in Cross-border Management*, 2nd edn, Irwin: Chicago, IL.

Bassett, P. (1986) *Strike Free*, Macmillan: London.

Beardwell, I. (1997) 'Human resource management and Japan', in I. Beardwell and L. Holden (eds) *Human Resource Management: A Contemporary Perspective*, 2nd edn, Pitman Publishing: London.

Beardwell, I. and Holden, L. (eds) (1997) *Human Resource Management: A Contemporary Perspective*, 2nd edn, Pitman Publishing: London.

Beasley, J. E. (1985) 'Strategies for corporate and business success – a survey', *OMEGA*, 13, 1: 51–8.

Beatson, M. (1995) *Labour Market Flexibility*, Employment Department Research Series No. 44, DfEE, Sheffield.

Beer, M., Spector, B., Lawrence, P., Quinn

Mills, D. and Walton, R.E. (1984) *Managing Human Assets*, Free Press: New York.

Beer, M., Spector, B., Lawrence, P., Quinn Mills, D. and Walton, R.E. (1985) *Human Resource Management, The General Manager's Perspective: Text and Cases*, Free Press: New York.

Berle, A. A. (1954) *The Twentieth Century Capitalist Revolution*, Harcourt Brace: New York.

Berle, A. A. and Means, G. C. (1932) *The Modern Corporation and Private Property*, Macmillan: New York.

Berggren, C. and Nomura, M. (1997) *The Resilience of Corporate Japan: New Competitive Strategies and Personnel Policies*, Paul Chapman Publishing: London.

Berry, A., Citron, D. and Jarvis, R. (1987) *The Information Needs of Bankers Dealing with Large and Small Companies: With Particular Reference to Proposed Changes in Legislation*, Certified Research Report 7, Certified Accountant Publications: London.

Berry, A. and Jarvis, R. (1997) *Accounting in a Business Context*, 3rd edn, International Thomson Business Press: London.

Berry, T., Capps, T., Cooper, D., Hooper, T. and Lowe, T. (1985) 'NCB accounts – a mine of misinformation', *Accountancy*, January: 10–12.

Bhaskar, K. (1980) *The Future of the World Motor Industry*, Kogan Page: London.

Binks, M. and Jennings, A. (1986) 'New firms as a source of industrial regeneration', in M. Scott, *Small Firms Growth and Development*, Gower: Aldershot.

Bird, D., Beatson, M. and Butcher, S. (1993) 'Membership of trade unions', *Employment Gazette*, May: 189–96.

Blake, R. R. and Mouton, J. S. (1964) *The Managerial Grid,* Gulf: Houston, TX.

Blauner, R. (1964) *Alienation and Freedom*, University of Chicago Press: Chicago, IL.

Boddy, D (2002) *Management: an Introduction*, Financial Times Prentice Hall: Harlow.

Bolton, J. (1971) *Small Firms: The Report of the Committee of Inquiry into Small Firms*, HMSO, Cmd 4811, London.

Bowen, A., Buxton, T. and Ricketts, M. (1992)

'The economics of innovation: setting the scene', in A. Bowen and M. Ricketts (eds) *Stimulating Innovation in Industry: The Challenge for the United Kingdom*, Kogan Page/NEDO: London.

Bowen, D (1992) 'Bigger is better in Britain's battered industry', *Independent on Sunday*, 26 July.

Braverman, H. (1974) *Labour and Monopoly Capital,* Monthly Review Press: New York.

Brewster, C. and Bournois, F. (1991) 'Human resource management: a European perspective', *Personnel Review*, 20, 6: 4–13.

Brewster, C., Hegewisch, A. and Lockhart, J. T. (1991) 'Researching human resource management: methodology of the Price Waterhouse Cranfield Project on European Trends', P*ersonnel Review*, 20, 6: 36–40.

Brewster, C., Sparrow, P. and Harris, H. (2002) *Globalizing HR*, CIPD: London.

Bridge, S., O'Neill, K. and Cromie, S. (1998) *Understanding Enterprise, Entrepreneurship and Small Business*, Macmillan: London.

Bright, G., Colvin, M., Loveridge, J., Page, R. and Thompson, C. (1983) *Moving Forward: Small Businesses and the Economy*, Conservative Political Centre: London.

Brittan, S. (1983) 'The myth of the Kondratieff', *Financial Times*, 7 April.

Brook, K. (2002) 'Trade union membership: an analysis of data from the autumn 2001 LFS', *Labour Market Trends*, July: 343–54.

Brossard, M. and Maurice, M. (1976) 'Is there a universal model of organizational structure?', *International Studies of Management and Organization*, 6: 11–45.

Brouthers, K. D., Brouthers, L. E. and Harris, P. C. (1997) 'The five stages of the co-operative venture strategy process', *Journal of General Management*, 23: 39–52.

Brown, A. (1998) *Organizational Culture*, 2nd edn, Financial Times Pitman: London.

Bruce, M. (1987) 'Managing people first – bringing the service concept into British Airways', I*ndependent and Commercial Training*, March–April.

Bryce, R. (2002) *Pipe Dreams: Greed, Ego and the Death of Enron*, Public Affairs: London.

Buchan, J. (1993) 'Withdrawal symptoms', *Independent on Sunday Review*, 23 April, pp. 2–5.

Burnham, J. (1941) *The Management Revolution,* Day: New York.

Burns, P. (2001) *Entrepreneurship and Small Business*, Palgrave: London.

Burns, T. and Stalker, G. M. (1966) *The Management of Innovation*, 2nd edn, Tavistock: London.

Burrell, G. and Morgan, G. (1979) *Sociological Paradigms and Organizational Analysis*, Heinemann: London.

Burrows, G. (1986) *No Strike Agreements and Pendulum Arbitration*, Institute of Personnel Management: London.

Callon, S. (1995) *Divided Sun: MITI and the Breakdown of Japanese High-Tech Policy 1975–1993*, Stanford University Press: Stanford, CA.

Cannon, T. (1986) *Basic Marketing*, 2nd edn, Holt Rinehart & Winston; Eastbourne.

Carlson, S. (1951) *Executive Behaviour: A Study of the Workload and Behaviour of Managing Directors*, Strombergs: Stockholm.

Carr, A. Z. (1968) 'Is business bluffing ethical?', *Harvard Business Review*, 46, January–February: 143–53.

Carroll, D. T. (1983) 'A disappointing search for excellence', *Harvard Business Review*, 63, November–December: 78–88.

Casey, B. (1986) 'The dual apprenticeship system', *British Journal of Industrial Relations*, 14, 1, 63–82.

Cassidy, J. and Holmes, D. (1988) 'IBM spreads workload for quicker pace', *Sunday Times*, 14 February.

Castells, M. (1996) *The Rise of the Network Society*, Blackwell Publishers: Oxford.

Caulkin, S. (2003) 'The bosses we love to hate', *Observer*, 6 July.

Chaharbaghi, K. and Newman, V. (1996) 'Innovating: Towards an integrated learning model', *Management Decision*, 34: 4.

Chandler, A. D. (1962) *Strategy and Structure: Chapters in the History of American Capitalism*, MIT Press: Cambridge, MA.

Chandler, A. D. (1977) *The Visible Hand: The Managerial Revolution in American Business,* Harvard University Press: Cambridge, MA.

Channon, D. F. (1973) *The Strategy and Structure of British Enterprise*, Macmillan: London.

Chase, R. and Hayes, R. H. (1991) 'Beefing up operations in service firms', *Sloan Management Review*, Fall: 15–26.

Chell, E. (2001) *Entrepreneurship: Globalization, Innovation and Development*, Thomson Learning: London.

Child, J. (1969) *The Business Enterprise in Modern Industrial Society*, Collier-Macmillan: London.

Child, J., Fores, M., Glover, I. and Lawrence, P. (1983) 'A price to pay? Professionalism and work organization in Britain and West Germany', *Sociology*, 17, 1: 63–77.

Chong Li Choy (1990) 'Business in the development of Singapore', in Chong Li Choy et al (eds) *Business, Society and Development in Singapore*, Times Academic Press: Singapore.

Chryssides, G. D. and Kaler, J. H. (2002) *An Introduction to Business Ethics*, Thomson Learning: London.

Clark, G. and Johnston, R. (2000) *Service Operations Management*, FT Prentice Hall: London.

Clarke, F. I., Dean, G. W. and Oliver, K. G. (1999) *Corporate Collapse: Regulatory Accounting and Ethical Failure*, Cambridge University Press: Cambridge.

Coleman, T. (1988) 'Travels with a Rover', *Guardian*, 13 August.

Connon, H. (1992) 'Glaxo invests £1bn. Hot-house to foster discovery', *Independent*, 9 June.

Considine, M. and Lewis, J. (2003) 'Bureaucracy, network or enterprise? Comparing models of governance in Australia, Britain, the Netherlands, and New Zealand', *Public Administration Review (USA)*, 63, 2: 131–42.

Cooper, R. and Chew, W. B. (1996) 'Control tomorrow's costs through today's designs', *Harvard Business Review*, January–February: 88–97.

Council for Excellence in Management and Leadership (2002) *Managers and Leaders: Raising Our Game*, Council for Excellence in Management and Leadership: London.

Covey, S. R. (1989) *Seven Habits of Highly Effective People: Powerful Lessons in Personal Change*, Simon & Schuster: New York.

Cully, M., Woodland, S., O'Reilly, A., Dix, G., Millward, N., Bryson, A. and Forth, J. (1998) *The 1998 Workplace Industrial Relations Survey: First Findings*, DTI: London.

Cyert, R. M. and March, J. G. (1963) *A Behavioural Theory of the Firm*, Prentice Hall: Englewood Cliffs, NJ.

Czinkota, M. R. and Ronkainen, I. A. (1995) *International Marketing*, Dryden Press: New York.

Daft, R. L. (1982) 'Bureaucratic v. non-bureaucratic structures and the process of innovation and change', in S. B. Bachovach (ed.) *Research in the Sociology of Organizations*, JAI Press: Greenwich.

Daimler Benz (1996) *Environmental Report*, Daimler Benz.

Daly, M. (1991) 'VAT registrations and de-registrations in 1990', *Employment Gazette*, November: 579–88.

Damanpour, F., Szabat, K. A. and Evan, W. M. (1989) 'The relationship between types of innovation and organization performance', *Journal of Management Studies*, 26, 6: 587–601.

Daniel, W. W. (1987) *Workplace Industrial Relations and Technical Change*, Policy Studies Institute: London.

Daniel, W. W. and Millward, N. (1983) *Workplace Industrial Relations in Britain*, Heinemann: London.

Daniel, E. and Wilson H. (2002) 'Adoption intention and benefits realized: a study of e-commerce in UK SMEs', *Journal of Small Business Enterprise Development*, 9, 4: 331–48.

Daniels, C. (1991) *The Management Challenge of Information Technology*, Economist Intelligence Unit and Business International: London.

Datta, D. K. (1988) 'International joint ventures: a framework for analysis', *Journal of General Management*, 14, 2: 78–91.

Davies, P. W. F. (1997) 'Business philosophy: searching for an authentic role', in P. W. F. Davies (ed.) *Current Issues in Business Ethics*, Routledge: London.

Davis, C. (1999) 'Smoother operators', *People Management*, 5, 9: 56–7.

Davis, S. M. and Lawrence, P. R. (eds) (1977) *Matrix*, Addison-Wesley: Reading, MA.

Dawson, S. (1986) *Analysing Organizations*, Macmillan: London.

de Wit, B. and Meyer, R. (1998) *Strategy: Process, Content, Context: An International Perspective*, 2nd edn, International Thomson Business Press: London.

Deal, T. E. and Kennedy, A. A. (1982) *Corporate Cultures*, Penguin: Harmondsworth.

Deloitte and Touche (2003) *Annual Review of Football Finance*, Deloitte and Touche: London.

Deming, W. E. (1986) *Out of Crisis: Quality, Productivity and Competitive Position*, Cambridge University Press: Cambridge.

Dhalla, N. K. (1978) 'Assessing the long-term value of advertising', *Harvard Business Review*, January–February: 87–95.

Dibb, S., Simpkin, L., Pride, W. M. and Ferrell, O. C. (1997) *Marketing: Concepts and Strategies*, 3rd European edn, Houghton Miflin, Boston, MA.

Dibb, S., Simpkin, L., Pride, W. M. and Ferrell, O. C. (2001) *Marketing: Concepts and Strategies*, 4th European edn, Houghton Miflin, Boston, MA.

Dore, R. (1973) *British Factory – Japanese Factory*, University of California Press: Berkeley, CA.

Dore, R. (1997) 'Good jobs, no jobs and bad jobs', *Industrial Relations Journal*, 28, 4: 262–8.

Dore, R. (2000) *Stock Market Capitalism: Welfare Capitalism: Japan and Germany Versus the Anglo-Saxons*, Oxford University Press: Oxford.

Drucker, P. E. (1964) *Managing for Results*, Harper & Row: New York.

Drucker, P. E. (1968) *The Practice of Management*, Pan Books: London.

Drucker, P. E. (1985) *Innovation and Entrepreneurship*, Heinemann: London.

Drury, C. (2001) *Management Accounting for Business Decisions*, Thomson Learning: London.

DTI (1998) 'Entrepreneurial Activity and Entrepreneurship within Higher Education', Durham University Business School, DTI Conference, DTI: London.

DTI (2002a) *The 2002 R&D Scoreboard: Company Data*, DTI: London.

DTI (2002b) *The 2002 R&D Scoreboard: Commentary and Analysis*, DTI: London.

Edwards, P., Hall, M., Hyman, R., Marginson, P., Sisson, K., Waddington, J. and Winchester, D. (1992) 'Great Britain: still muddling through', in A. Ferner and R. Hyman (eds) *Industrial Relations in the New Europe*, Basil Blackwell: Oxford.

Eilon, S. (1985) 'Recasting the die', *OMEGA*, 13, 3: 135–42.

Ekvall, G. (1991) 'The organizational culture of idea-management: a creative climate for the management of ideas', in J. Henry and D. Walker (eds) *Managing Innovation*, Sage/OU: London.

El-Namiki, M. (1993) *Contemporary Dynamics of Entrepreneurship*, Netherlands International Institute for Management: Netherlands.

Elger, T. and Smith, C. (1994) *Global Japanization? The Transnational Transformation of the Labour Process*, Routledge: London.

Emery, F. and Thorsrud, E. (1976) *Democracy at Work*, Nijhoff: Leiden, Netherlands.

Evans, H. (1983) *Good Times, Bad Times*, Weidenfeld and Nicholson: London.

Fagan, M. (1991) 'Is it right that the scientists should take the decisions?', *Independent*, 10 June.

Fayol, H. (1949) *General and Industrial Management*, Pitman: London.

Feigenbaum, A. V. (1961) *Total Quality Control*, McGraw Hill: London.

Fenwick, P. and Murton, A. (2000) 'Human resource management and industrial relations', in J. Barry *et al.* (eds) *Organization and Management: A Critical Text*, International Thomson Business Press: London.

Ferner, A. and Hyman, R. (1992) *Industrial Relations in the New Europe*, Basil Blackwell: Oxford.

Feurer, R., Chaharbaghi, K. and Wargin, J. (1995) 'Analysis of strategy formulation and implementation at Hewlett-Packard', *Management Decision*, 33, 10: 4–16.

Fiedler, F. E. (1967) *A Theory of Leadership Effectiveness*, McGraw Hill: New York.

Fincham, R. and Rhodes, P. (1999) *Principles of Organizational Behaviour*, 3rd edn, Oxford University Press: Oxford.

Fites, D. V. (1996) 'Make your dealers your partners', *Harvard Business Review*, March–April: 84–95.

Fox, A. (1974) *Man Mismanagement*, Faber & Faber: London.

Foy, N. (1983) 'The public productivity poser', *Management Today*, July: 67–71.

Frain, J. (1999) *Introduction to Marketing*, 4th edn, International Thomson Business Press: London.

Freeman, C. (1989) 'R&D, technical change and investment in the UK', in F. Green (ed) *Restructuring the UK Economy*, Harvester Wheatsheaf: London.

Friedman, L. G. and Furey, T. R. (1999) *The Channel Advantage*, Butterworth-Heinemann: Oxford.

Friedman, M. (1970)' The social responsibility of business is to increase profits', *New York Times Magazine*, 13 September.

Friedman, T. L. (2000) *The Lexus and the Olive Tree*, Anchor Books, New York.

Galbraith, J. K. (1972) *The New Industrial State*, 2nd edn, Penguin: Harmondsworth.

Galbraith, J. R. (1971) 'Matrix organization designs', *Business Horizons*, 14: 29–40.

Galbraith, J. R. and Nathanson, D. A. (1978) *Strategy Implementation: The Role of Structure and Process*, West Publishing Co.: St Paul, MN.

Gamble, A. (1985) *Britain in Decline*, Macmillan: London.

Garratt, B. (2003) 'Board game', *People Management*, 10 July: 26–9.

Garvin, D. A. (1988) *Managing Quality*, The Free Press: New York.

Gennard, J. and Judge, G. (2002) *Employee Relations (People and Organizations)*, 3rd edn, CIPD: London.

Giddens, A. (1991) *Modernity and Self-identity: Self and Society in the Late Modern Age*, Polity Press: Cambridge.

Gill, C., Krieger, H. and Froelich, D. (1992) 'The employment impact of new technology: recent European evidence', *Journal of General Management*, 18, 2: 1–13.

Goldthorpe, J. (1977) 'Industrial relations in Great Britain: a critique of reformism', in T. Clarke and L. Clements (eds) *Trade Unions under Capitalism*, Fontana: Glasgow.

Goodstein, L.D. and Burke, W. W. (1991) 'Creating successful organization change', *Organizational Dynamics*, 19: 5–19.

Gordan, G. G. and Ditomaso, N. (1992) 'Predicting corporate performance from organizational culture', *Journal of Management Studies*, 29, 6: 783–98.

Gould, A. and Keeble, D. (1984) 'New firms and rural industrialization in East Anglia', *Regional Studies*, 18, 3: 189–201.

Greater London Council (GLC) (1983) *Small Firms and the London Industrial Strategy*, Economic Policy Group Strategy Document, No. 4, GLC: London.

Greenley, G. E. (1990) 'Does strategic planning improve company performance?', in D. Asch and C. Bowman (eds) *Readings in Strategic Management*, Macmillan: London.

Greenly, D. (1999) 'Journey of joint discovery', paper presented at the Ford Global Dean's Conference, Cologne, Germany, May.

Guest, D. E. (1982) 'Has the recession really hit personnel management?', *Personnel Management*, October: 36–9.

Guest, D.E. (1989) 'Human resource management: its implications for industrial relations and trade unions', in J. Storey (ed.) *New Perspectives in Human Resource Management*, Routledge: London.

Guest, D. E. (1990) 'Human resource management and the American dream', *Journal of Management Studies*, 27, 4: 377–97.

Guest, D. E. (1998) 'Beyond HRM: commitment and the contract culture', in P. R. Sparrow and M. Marchington (eds) *Human Resource Management: The New Agenda*, Financial Times/Pitman Publishing: London.

Guest D. E. and Horwood, R. (1980) *The Role and Effectiveness of Personnel Managers: A Preliminary Report*, The Nancy Seear Fellowship Personnel Management Research Programme, Research Report No. 1, LSE: London.

Guest, D., Michie, J., Sheehan, M., Conway, N., and Metochi, M. (2000) *Effective People Management*, CIPD: London.

Hahn, C. (1993) 'The importance of manufacturing in a robust economy', *RSA Journal*, June: 540–9.

Hakim, C. (1996) *Key Issues in Women's Work*, Athlone Press: London.

Hales, C. P. (1986) 'What do managers do? A critical review of the evidence', *Journal of Management Studies*, 23: 88–115.

Hall, S. (1998) 'The great moving nowhere show', *Marxism Today*, November–December: 9–14.

Hamel, G. and Prahalad, C. K. (1990) 'The core competence of the corporation', *Harvard Business Review*, 68, 3: 79–91.

Hamel, G. and Prahalad, C. K. (1994) *Competing for the Future*, Harvard Business School Press: Boston, MA.

Hammer, M. and Champy, J. C. (1993) *Re-engineering the Corporation: A Manifesto for Business Revolution*, Nicholas Brealey: London.

Hampden-Turner, C. (1990) *Corporate Culture Management: From Vicious to Virtuous Circles*, Economist Books, Hutchinson: London.

Hampden-Turner, C. and Trompenaars, A. (1993) *The Seven Cultures of Capitalism*, Currency Doubleday: New York.

Hampden-Turner, C. and Trompenaars, A. (1997) *Mastering the Infinite Game: How East Asian Values are Transforming Business Practices*, Capstone: Oxford.

Handy, C. (1987) *The Making of Managers; A Report on Management Education, Training and Development in the USA, West Germany, France, Japan and the United Kingdom*, MSC, NEDC and BIM: London.

Handy, C. (1993) *Understanding Organizations*, 4th edn, Penguin: Harmondsworth.

Harbison, F. and Myers, C. A. (1959) *Management in the Industrial World: An International Analysis*, McGraw Hill: New York.

Harrison, A., Harland, C., Johnston, R., Chambers, N. and Slack, N. (2003) *Cases in Operations Management*, 3rd edn, FT Prentice Hall: London.

Harrison, B. (1994) *Lean and Mean: The Changing Landscape of Corporate Power in the Age of Flexibility*, Basic Books: New York.

Harrison, C. R. (1972) 'Understanding your organization's character', *Harvard Business Review*, 50, 3: 119–28,

Harrison, P. (1981) *Inside the Third World*, 2nd edn, Penguin: Harmondsworth.

Haslam, C., Neale, A. and Johal, S. (2000) *Economics in a Business Context*, 3rd edn, Thomson Learning: London.

Hawkins, K. (1978) *The Management of Industrial Relations*, Penguin: Harmondsworth.

Hayes, R. H. and Wheelwright, S. C. (1984) *Restoring Our Competitive Edge: Competing Through Manufacturing*, John Wiley: New York.

Held, D. (1998) 'The timid tendency', *Marxism Today*, November–December: 24–7.

Held, D., McGrew, A., Goldblatt, D. and Perraton, J. (1999) *Global Transformations: Politics, Economics and Culture*, Polity Press: Cambridge.

Henderson, C. (1998) *Asia Falling*, McGraw Hill: Singapore.

Herriot, P. and Pinder, B. (1992) 'Human resource strategy in a changing world', *Personnel Management*, August, 24, 8: 36–9.

Herzberg, F. (1968) 'One more time: how do you motivate employees?', *Harvard Business Review*, 46: 53–62.

Hetherington, P. (1986) 'Perfection in the land of rising productivity', *Guardian*, 5 March, p. 23.

Hickson, D. J., Pugh, D. S. and Pheysey, D. (1969) 'Operation technology and organization structure: an empirical appraisal', *Administrative Science Quarterly*, 14: 378–97.

Hill, T. (1991) *Production and Operations Management: Text and Cases*, Prentice Hall: London.

Hirst, P. and Thompson, G. (1999) *Globalization in Question*, 2nd edn, Polity Press: Cambridge.

Hitt, M. and Ireland, D. (1987) 'Peters and Waterman revisited: The unending quest for excellence', *Academy of Management Executive*, 1, 2: 91–8.

Hobsbawm, E. J. (1968) *Industry and Empire*, Weidenfeld and Nicholson: London.

Hofer, C. W. and Schendel, D. (1978) *Strategy Formulation: Analytical Concepts*, West Publishing: St Paul, MN.

Hofstede, G. H. (1980a) *Culture's Consequences: International Differences in Work-related Values*, Sage: London.

Hofstede, G. H. (1980b) 'Motivation, leadership and organization: do American theories apply abroad?', *Organizational Dynamics*, Summer: 42–63.

Hofstede, G. H. (1994) *Cultures and Organizations: Intercultural Cooperation and its Importance for Survival*, McGraw Hill: London.

Hofstede, G. H. (1999) 'Problems remain, but theories will change: the universal and the specific in 21st century global management', *Organizational Dynamics*, 28, 1: 34–44.

Hofstede, G. H. and Bond, M. H. (1988) 'The Confucius connection: from cultural roots to economic growth', *Organizational Dynamics*, 16, 4: 4–21.

Holden, L. and Wilkinson, A. (1999) 'Long-term patterns in strategic HRM: case study evidence', *Occasional Paper 51*, Leicester Business School: Leicester.

Holden, N. J. (2002) *Cross-cultural Management: A Knowledge Management Perspective*, FT Prentice Hall: Harlow.

Hollinshead, G., Tailby, S. and Nicholls, P. (2002) *Employee Relations*, 2nd edn, FT Prentice Hall: Harlow.

Holmes, G., Sugden, A. and Gee, P. (2002) *Interpreting Company Reports and Accounts*, 8th edn, FT Prentice Hall: Harlow.

Höpfl, H., Smith, S. and Spencer, S. (1992) 'Values and Valuations: The Conflict Between Culture Change and Job Cuts', *Personnel Review*, 21 1: 24–37.

Horne, M. and Stedman-Jones, D. (2001) *Leadership: The Challenge for all?*, The Institute of Management: London.

House, R. J. and Mitchell, T. R. (1974) 'Path–goal theory of leadership', *Journal of Contemporary Business*, Autumn: 81–97.

Howard, J. A. and Sheth, J. N. (1969) *The Theory of Buyer Behaviour*, John Wiley: New York.

Hu, Y. S. (1996) 'Globalization and corporate nationality', in M. Warner (ed.) *International Encyclopaedia of Business and Management*, Routledge: London pp. 1664–72.

Hyman, R. (1972) *Disputes Procedure in Action*, Heinemann: London.

IMF (2003) *The Impact of Globalization on Workers and their Trade Unions*, www.imf.org

Institute of Personnel Management (1963) Statement on personnel management and personnel policies, *Personnel Management*, March.

International Labour Organization (2003) *Labour Market Trends and Globalization's Impact on them*, ILO.

Jackson, P. (1983) 'How Perkins positively tackled the recession', *Personnel Management*, November: 24–7.

Jewkes, J., Sawers, D. and Stillerman, R. (1970) *The Sources of Innovation*, W. W. Norton: New York.

Jobber, D. (1995) *Principles and Practice of Marketing*, 3rd edn, McGraw Hill: Maidenhead.

Johnson, G. and Scholes, K. (2002) *Exploring Corporate Strategy: Text and Cases*, 6th edn, Prentice Hall: London.

Johnson, R. (2002) 'Trust funding', P*eople Management*, 26 September: 36–9.

Jomo, K. S. (1998) *Tigers in Trouble: Financial Governance, Liberalisation and Crises in East Asia*, Zed Books: London.

Jones, G. (1996) *The Evolution of International Business: An Introduction*, Routledge: London.

Juran, J. M. (1988) *Quality Control Handbook*, McGraw Hill: New York.

Kaplinsky, R. (1983) 'Firm size and technical change in a dynamic context', *The Journal of Industrial Economics*, 32, 1: 39–59.

Kay, J. (1992) 'Innovations in corporate strategy', in A. Bowen and M. Ricketts (eds) *Stimulating Innovation in Industry: The Challenge for the United Kingdom*, Kogan Page/NEDO: London.

Kay, J. (1993) *Foundations of Corporate Success: How Business Strategies Add Value*, Oxford University Press: Oxford.

Kennedy, C. (1988) 'Global strategies for 3M', *Long Range Planning*, 21, 1: 9–17.

Kerr, C., Dunlop, J. T., Harbison, F. and Myers, C. A. (1973) *Industrialism and Industrial Man*, Penguin: Harmondsworth.

Kessler, S. and Bayliss, F. (1998) *Contemporary British Industrial Relations*, 3rd edn, Macmillan: London.

Kets de Vries, M. (1996) *Family Business: Human Dilemmas in the Family Firm*, International Thomson Business Press: London.

Kirkbride, P., Pinnington, P. and Ward, K. (2001) 'The state of globalization today', in P. Kirkbride (ed.) *Globalization: The External Pressures*, John Wiley and Sons: Chichester.

Kirkpatrick, S. A. and Locke, E. A. (1991) 'Leadership: do traits matter?', *Academy of Management Executive*, May: 48–60.

Koh, H. C. and Boo, E. H. Y. (2001) 'The link between organizational ethics and job satisfaction: a study of managers in Singapore', *Journal of Business Ethics*, 29, 4: 309–24.

Kondratieff, N. D. (1935) 'The long waves in economic life', *Review of Economic Statistics,* 17, 105–15.

Kotler, P. (1983) *Principles of Marketing*, 2nd edn, Prentice Hall: Englewood Cliffs, NJ.

Kotler, P. (2002) *Marketing Management*, 11th edn, Prentice Hall, Upper Saddle River, NJ.

Kotler, P., Armstrong, G., Saunders, J. and Wong, V. (2001) *Principles of Marketing*, 3rd European edn, FT Prentice Hall: Harlow.

Kotter, J. P. (1990) 'What leaders really do', *Harvard Business Review*, May–June: 103–11.

Kuhnert, K. W. and Lewis, P. (1987) 'Transactional and transformational leadership: a constructive/developmental analysis', *Academy of Management Review,* October: 648–57.

Kumar, K. (1978) *Prophecy and Progress,* Penguin: Harmondsworth.

Lane, K. A. (1985) 'The UK machine tool industry', *OMEGA*, 13, 4: 247–9.

Lasserre, P. and Schütte, H. (1999) *Strategy and Management in Asia Pacific*, McGraw Hill: London.

Lawrence, P. (1980) *Managers and Management in West Germany*, Croom Helm: London.

Lawrence, P. R. and Lorsch, J. (1967) *Organization and Environment*, Harvard University Press: Cambridge, MA.

Leach, P. and Bogon, T. (1999) *Guide to the Family Business*, 3rd edn, Kogan Page: London.

Legge, K. (1978) *Power, Innovation and Problem-solving in Personnel Management*, McGraw Hill: London.

Legge, K. (1989) 'Human resource management: a critical analysis', in J. Storey (ed.) *New Perspectives in Human Resource Management*, Routledge: London.

Legge, K. (1998) 'Flexibility: the gift wrapping of employment degradation?', in P. R. Sparrow and M. Marchington, *Human Resource Management: The New Agenda*, Financial Times/Pitman Publishing: London.

Legrain, P. (2002) *Open World: The Truth about Globalization*, Abacus: London.

Lei, D. (1989) 'Strategies for global competition', *Long Range Planning*, 22, 1: 102–9.

Levitt, T. (1960) 'Marketing myopia', *Harvard Business Review*, 38, July–August: 24–47.

Levitt, T. (1975) 'Marketing myopia: retrospective commentary', *Harvard Business Review*, 53, September–October: 177–81.

Levitt, T. (1983) 'The globalization of markets', *Harvard Business Review*, 61, May–June: 92–102.

Likert, R. (1961) *New Patterns in Management*, McGraw Hill: New York.

Lindblom, C. E. (1959) 'The science of muddling through', *Public Administration Review*, 19, 2: 79–88.

Littler, C. R., Wiesner, R. and Dunford, R. (2003) 'The dynamics of delayering:

changing management structures in three countries', *Journal of Management Studies*, 40, 2: 225–56.

Lorenz, C. (1994) 'Ford's global matrix gamble', *Financial Times*, 16 December.

Luthans, F. (1988) 'Successful v. effective real managers', *Academy of Management Executive*, 2, 2: 127–32.

Lynch, R. (2003) *Corporate Strategy*, 3rd edn, FT Prentice Hall: Harlow.

Lyons, M. P. (1991) 'Joint ventures as strategic choice – a literature review', *Long Range Planning*, 24, 4: 130–44.

McClean, M. and Rowlands, T. (1985) *The Inmos Saga: A Triumph of National Enterprise*, Frances Pinter: London.

McClelland, D. (1961) *The Achieving Society*, Van Nostrand: Princeton, NJ.

McIntosh, M. (1998) 'Introduction, in Financial Times Management', *Visions of Ethical Business*, Financial Times Management: London.

McKenna, E. and Beech, N. (2002) *Human Resource Analysis: A Concise Analysis*, FT Prentice Hall: Harlow.

Mahoney, J (2002) 'Business ethics', in M. Warner (ed.) *International Encyclopaedia of Business and Management*, Thomson Learning: London.

Mansfield, E. (1963) 'Size of firm, market structure and innovation', *Journal of Political Economy*, 71, 6: 556–76.

Marjoribanks, T. (2000) *News Corporation, Technology and the Workplace: Global Strategies, Local Change*, Cambridge University Press: Cambridge.

Marris, R. L. (1964) *The Economic Theory of Managerial Capitalism*, Macmillan: London.

Marshall, E. (1993) *Business and Society*, Routledge: London.

Martin, J. (2001) *Organizational Behaviour*, 2nd edn, Thomson Learning: London.

Mayer, C. (1988) 'New Issues in Corporate Finance', *European Economic Review*, June.

Mead, M. (ed.) (1951) *Cultural Patterns and Technology*, UNESCO: Paris.

Medcof, J. W. (1997) 'Why too many alliances end in divorce', *Long Range Planning*, 30, 5: 718–32.

Mensch, G. (1979) *Stalemate in Technology*, Ballinger: Cambridge, MA.

Mercado, S., Welford, R. and Prescott, K. (2001) *European Business*, 4th edn, FT Prentice Hall: Harlow.

Miles, R. E. and Snow, C. C. (1978) *Organizational Strategy, Structure and Process*, McGraw Hill: London.

Miliband, R. (1969) *The State in Capitalist Society*, Quartet, London.

Miller, A. and Dess, G. G. (1996) *Strategic Management*, 2nd edn, McGraw Hill: New York.

Mills, R., Dimech Debeno, J. and Dimech Debeno, V. (1994) 'Euro Disney: A Mickey Mouse Project?', *The European Management Journal*, 12, 3: 306–14.

Millward, N. and Stevens, S. (1986) *British Workplace Industrial Relations 1980–84*, Gower: Aldershot.

Millward, N., Stevens, S., Smart, D. and Hawes, W. R. (1992) *Workplace Industrial Relations in Transition: the ED/ESRC/PSI/ACAS Surveys*, Dartmouth: Aldershot.

Min Chen (1995) *Asian Management Systems: Chinese, Japanese and Korean Styles of Business,* Routledge: London.

Mintel (1994) *The Green Consumer, Vols 1 and 2*, Mintel: London.

Mintzberg, H. (1973) *The Nature of Managerial Work*, Harper Row: New York.

Mintzberg, H. (1973) 'Strategy making in 3 modes', *California Management Review*, 16, Winter: 44–53.

Mintzberg, H. (1990) 'The Design School: reconsidering the basic premises of strategic management', *Strategic Management Journal*, 11, 176–95.

Mintzberg, H., Lampel, J. B., Quinn, J. B. and Ghoshal, S. (2003) *The Strategy Process: Concepts, Contexts and Cases*, 4th edn, Prentice Hall: London.

Mintzberg, H. and Quinn, J. B. (1991) *The Strategy Process*, 2nd edn, Prentice Hall: London.

Monks, J. (1998) 'Trade unions: enterprise and the future', in P. R. Sparrow and M. Marchington, *Human Resource Management: The New Agenda*, Financial Times/Pitman Publishing: London.

Morrison, J. (2002) *International Business*, Palgrave: Basingstoke.

Mowery, D. C. and Rosenberg N. (1989) *Technology and the Pursuit of Economic Growth*, Cambridge University Press: Cambridge.

Murton, A. (2000) 'Labour markets and flexibility: current debates and the European dimension, in J. Barry *et al.* (eds) *Organization and Management: A Critical Text*, International Thomson Business Press: London.

Naisbitt, J. (1996) *Mega-trends Asia*, Nicholas Brealey Publishing: London.

Narin, F. (1993) 'Patent citation analysis: the strategic application of technology indicators', *Patent World*, 51, April: 25–30.

National Economic Development Office (1985) *Advanced Manufacturing Technology*, NEDO: London.

Needle, D. J. (1984) 'The selection process in Britain and West Germany: a cross-national study', unpublished MSc thesis, London School of Economics.

Needle, D. J. and Needle, J. (1991) 'The value of patents', *Patent World*, 35, September: 20–36.

Needle, D. J. (2000) 'Culture at the level of the firm: organizational and corporate perspectives', in J. Barry *et al.* (eds) *Organization and Management: A Critical Text*, International Thomson Business Press: London.

Nicholls, T (1969) *Ownership, Control and Ideology*, Routledge: London.

Nicosia, F. M. (1966) *Consumer Decision Processes: Marketing and Advertising Implications*, Prentice Hall: Englewood Cliffs, NJ.

OECD (1993) *Education at a Glance*, OECD Publications: Paris.

Ohno, T. (1988) *Toyota Production System: Beyond Large Scale Production*, Productivity Press: Cambridge, MA.

Owen, G (1996) 'The impact of financial systems on British and German industrial performance', presented at *PERC Conference on Stakeholder Capitalism*, 29 March.

Parker, D. (1995) 'Privatization and the internal environment: developing our knowledge of the adjustment process', *International Journal of Public Sector Management*, 8, 2: 44–62.

Parker, R. C. (1982) *The Management of Innovation*, John Wiley & Sons: Chichester.

Partnoy, F. (2003) 'When greed is fact and control is fiction', *Guardian*, 14 February.

Pascale, R. and Rohlen, T. P. (1983) 'The Mazda turnaround', *Journal of Japanese Studies*, 9, 2: 219–63.

Patterson, M., West, M., Lawthom, R. and Nickell, S. (1998) *Impact of People Management Practices on Business Performance*, IPD: London.

Paul, W. and Robertson, K. (1970) *Job Enrichment and Employee Motivation*, Gower Press: London.

Pavitt, K. (1983) 'Characteristics of innovative activity in British industry', *OMEGA*, 11, 2: 113–30.

Peach, L. (1992) 'Parting by mutual agreement. IBM's transition to manpower cuts', *Personnel Management*, 24, 3: 40–3.

Peck, M. J. and Goto, A. (1982) 'Technology and economic growth: the case of Japan', in M. L. Tushman and W. L. Moore (eds) *Readings in the Management of Innovation*, Pitman Books: London.

Peltu, M. and Land, F. (1987) *Thomson Travel: TOP Travel Agents' Reservation System*, London Business School: London.

Perrow, C. (1961) 'The analysis of goals in complex organizations', *American Sociological Review*, 26: 854–66.

Peters, T. J. (1987) *Thriving on Chaos*, Macmillan: London.

Peters, T. J. (1992) *Liberation Management: Necessary Disorganization for the Nanosecond Nineties*, Macmillan: London.

Peters, T. J. and Waterman, R. H. (1982) *In Search of Excellence: Lessons from America's Best Run Companies*, Harper & Row: London.

Pettigrew, A. M. (1973) *The Politics of Organizational Decision-making*, Tavistock: London.

Piercy, N. E. (1997) *Market-led Strategic Change: Transforming the Process of Going To Market*, 2nd edn, Butterworth Heinemann: Oxford.

Piercy, N. E. and Morgan N. A. (1993) 'Strategic and operational market segmentation: a management analysis', *Journal of Strategic Marketing*, 1: 123–40.

Pirie, I. (2000) 'The social politics of business ethics', in J. Barry *et al.* (eds) *Organization and Management: A Critical Text*, International Thomson Business Press: London.

Pollert, A. (1987) 'The flexible firm: a model in search of reality (or a policy in search of a practice)?', *Warwick Papers in Industrial Relations*, No. 19.

Porter, M. E. (1980) *Competitive Strategy: Techniques for Analyzing Industries and Competitors*, Free Press: New York.

Porter, M. E. (1985) *Competitive Advantage: Creating and Sustaining Superior Performance*, Free Press: New York.

Porter, M. E. (1990) *The Competitive Advantage of Nations*, Macmillan: London.

Porter, M. E., Takeuchi, H. and Sakakibara, M. (2000) *Can Japan Compete?*, Macmillan: London.

Prevezer, M. (1994) 'Overview: capital and control', in T. Buxton, P. Chapman and P. Temple (eds) *Britain's Economic Performance*, Routledge: London.

Price, A. (1997) *Human Resource Management in a Business Context*, International Thomson: London.

Price, R. and Bain, G. S. (1983) 'Union growth in Britain: retrospect and prospect', *British Journal of Industrial Relations*, 21: 339–55.

PricewaterhouseCoopers (1999) *Privacy . . . a Weak Link in the Cyber-chain: Privacy Risk Management in the Information Economy*, PricewaterhouseCoopers: London.

Pugh, D. S. (1969) 'The context of organization structures', *Administrative Science Quarterly*, 14: 570–81.

Purcell, J. (1989) 'The impact of corporate strategy on human resource management', in J. Storey (ed.) *New Perspectives in Human Resource Management*, Routledge: London.

Purcell, J. and Sisson, K. (1983) 'Strategies and practice in the management of industrial relations', in G. S. Bain (ed.)

Industrial Relations in Britain, Blackwell: Oxford.

Quayle, M (2002) 'E-commerce: the challenge for UK SMEs in the twenty-first century', *International Journal of Operations and Production Management*, 22, 10: 1148–61.

Rainnie, A. (1985) 'Small firms, big problems: the political economy of small business', *Capital and Class*, 25, Spring: 140–68.

Ray, C. A. (1986) 'Corporate culture: the last frontier of control', *Journal of Management Studies*, 23, 3: 287–97.

Reich, R. (1993) *The Work of Nations: Preparing Ourselves for 21st Century Capitalism,* Vintage Books: New York.

Rice, A. K. (1958) *Productivity and Social Organization*, Tavistock: London.

Richards, M. D. (1978) *Organizational Goal Structures*, West Publishing: St Paul, MN.

Richardson, R. and Thompson, M. (1999) *The Impact of People Management Practices: A Review of the Literature*, IPD: London.

Rifkin, J. (1995) 'The end of work', *New Statesman and Society*, 9 June: 18–25.

Roberts, E. B. (ed.) (2002) *Innovation: Driving Product, Process and Market Change*, Jossey Bass: New York.

Robbins, S. P. (2003) *Organizational Behaviour*, 10th edn, Prentice Hall: Upper Saddle River, NJ.

Rogers, E. M. (1962) *Diffusion of Innovations*, Free Press: New York.

Rohwer, J. (1995) *Asia Rising*, Butterworth Heinemann Asia: Singapore.

Rondinelli, D. A. and Black, S. S. (2000) 'Multinational strategic alliances and acquisitions in Central and Eastern Europe: partnerships in privatization', *The Academy of Management Executive*, 14, 4: 85–98.

Rosenzweig, P. M. (1995) 'Colgate Palmolive: managing international careers', in C. A. Bartlett and S. Ghoshal (eds) *Transnational Management: Texts, Cases and Readings in Cross-border Management*, 2nd edn, Irwin: Chicago, IL.

Rothwell, R. and Zegveld, W. (1981) *Industrial Innovation and Public Policy*, Frances Pinter: London.

Royal Dutch/Shell (1998) *Profits and Principles – Does there have to be a Choice?*, Royal Dutch/Shell.

Rumelt, R. (1974) *Strategy, Structure and Economic Performance*, Harvard University Press: Cambridge, MA.

Scase, R. and Goffee, R. (1980) *The Real World of the Small Business Owner*, Croom Helm: London.

Schein, E. H. (1990) 'Organizational culture', *American Psychologist*, 45, 2: 109–19.

Schein, E. H. (1996) *Strategic Pragmatism: The Culture of Singapore's Economic Development Board*, Toppan: Singapore.

Schmookler, J. (1966) *Invention and Economic Growth*, Harvard University Press, Cambridge, MA.

Scholz, C. (1987) 'Corporate culture', *Long Range Planning*, 20, 4: 78–87.

Scholte, J. A. (2000) *Globalization: A Critical Introduction,* Macmillan: Basingstoke.

Schumpeter, J. A. (1939) *Business Cycles*, McGraw Hill: London.

Schumpeter, J. A. (1961) *The Theory of Economic Development*, Oxford University Press: Oxford.

Scott, J. P. (1979) *Corporations, Classes and Capitalism*, Hutchinson: London.

Seaton, M. (2002) 'Here comes the chopper', *Guardian*, 5 May.

Selznick, P. (1949) *TVA and the Grass Roots*, University of California Press: Berkeley, CA.

Senge, P. M. (1990) *The Fifth Discipline: The Art and Practice of the Learning Organization*, Doubleday: New York.

Sheldrake, J. (2003) *Management Theory*, 2nd edn, Thomson Learning: London.

Silver, J. (1987) 'The ideology of excellence: Management and neo-conservatism', *Studies in Political Economy*, 24: 5–29.

Skinner, W. (1974) 'The focused factory', *Harvard Business Review,* May–June: 113–21.

Slack, N., Chambers, L. and Johnston, R. (2000) *Operations Management*, 3rd edn, FT Prentice Hall: London.

Sloan, A. P. (1986) *My Years with General Motors*, Harmondsworth: Penguin.

Smircich, L. (1983) 'Concepts of culture and organizational analysis', *Administrative Science Quarterly*, 28: 339–58.

Solow, R. W. (1957) 'Technical change and the aggregate production function', *Review of Economics and Statistics*, 1, 3: 312–20.

Souder, W. and Sherman, J. (1994) *Managing New Technology Development*, McGraw Hill: New York.

Sparrow, P. and Marchington, M. (1998) 'Introduction: is HRM in crisis?', in P. R. Sparrow and M. Marchington (eds) *Human Resource Management: The New Agenda*, Financial Times/Pitman Publishing: London.

Stanworth, C. (1998) 'Telework and the information age', *New Technology, Work and Employment*, 13, 1: 51–62.

Starr, M. K. (1972) *Production Management: Systems and Synthesis*, Prentice Hall Inc.: Englewood Cliffs, NJ.

Steedman, H. and Wagner, K. (1987) 'A second look at productivity, machinery and skills in Britain and Germany', *National Institute Economic Review*, November: 84–94.

Stewart, R. (1967) *Managers and their Jobs*, McGraw Hill: Maidenhead.

Stogdill, R. M. and Coons, A. E. (eds) (1957) *Leader Behaviour: Its Description and Measurement*, Research Monograph No. 88, Ohio State University: Columbus, OH.

Storey, J. (ed.) (1989) *New Perspectives in Human Resource Management*, Routledge: London.

Storey, J. (1992) *Developments in the Management of Human Resources: An Analytical Review*, Basil Blackwell: Oxford

Storey, J. (1994) *Understanding the Small Business Sector*, Routledge: London.

Storey, J. (ed.) (2000) *Human Resource Management: A Critical Text*, Thomson Learning: London.

Storey, J., Okasaki-Ward, L., Edwards, P. K., Gow, I. and Sisson, K. (1991) 'Managerial careers and management development: a comparative analysis of Britain and Japan', *HRM Journal*, 1, 3: 33–58.

Tannenbaum, R. and Schmidt, W. H. (1973) 'How to choose a leadership pattern', *Harvard Business Review*, May–June: 178–80.

Tayles, M. and Woods, M. (1993) 'Total quality management at Akzo', *Research Update*, 3, 1, CIMA Research Foundation.

Taylor, F. W. (1947) *Scientific Management*, Harper & Row: New York.

Thomas, A. B. (2003) *Controversies in Management: Issues, Debates, Answers*, 2nd edn, Routledge: London.

Thomas, T. and Eyres, B. (1998) 'Why an ethical business is not an altruistic business, in Financial Times Management', *Visions of Ethical Business*, Financial Times Management: London.

Thompson, P. and McHugh, D. (2003) *Work Organizations: A Critical Perspective*, 3rd edn, Palgrave Macmillan: London.

Tidd, J., Bessant, J. and Pavitt, K. (2001) *Managing Innovation: Integrating Technological, Market and Organizational Change*, 2nd edn, John Wiley: London.

Tighe, C. (1986) 'Behind the lines at Nissan', *Sunday Times*, 13 April, p. 67.

Torres, L. and Pina, V. (2002) 'Changes in public service delivery in the EU countries', *Public Money and Management*, 22, 4: 41–8.

Torrington, D. (1989) 'Human resource management and the personnel function', in J. Storey (ed.) *New Perspectives in Human Resource Management*, Routledge: London.

Torrington, D., Hall, L. and Taylor, S. (2001) *Human Resource Management*, 5th edn, FT Prentice Hall: Harlow.

Trist, E. L. and Bamforth, K. W. (1951) 'Some social and psychological consequences of the Long-wall method of coal getting', *Human Relations*, 4: 3–38.

Trompenaars, F. (1993) *Riding the Waves of Culture: Understanding Cultural Diversity in Business*, Economist Books: London.

van der Merwe, R., Pitt, L. and Berthon, P. (2003) 'Are excellent companies ethical? Evidence from an industrial setting', *Corporate Reputation Review*, 5, 4: 343–55.

Verschoor, C. C. (1998) 'A study of the link between a corporation's financial performance and its commitment to ethics', *Journal of Business Ethics*, 17, 13: 1509–16.

Walton, R. E. (1987) *Innovating to Compete*, Jossey Bass: San Francisco, CA.

Wasson, C. R. (1978) *Dynamic Competitive Strategy and Product Life Cycles*, Austin Press: Austin, TX.

Waters, M. (1995) *Globalization*, Routledge: London.

Watson, T. J. (1986) *Management, Organization and Employment Strategy*, Routledge: London.

Watson, T. J. (1994) *In Search of Management: Culture, Chaos and Control in Management Work*, Routledge: London.

Wells, J. (1989) 'Uneven development and deindustrialization in the UK since 1979', in F. Green (ed.) *The Restructuring of the UK Economy*, Harvester Wheatsheaf: London.

Whipp, R., Rosenfeld, R. and Pettigrew, A. (1989) 'Culture and competitiveness: evidence from two mature UK industries', *Journal of Management Studies*, 26, 6: 561–85.

White, M. and Trevor, M. (1983) *Under Japanese Management – The Experience of British Workers*, Heinemann: London.

Whittington, R. (1993) *What Is Strategy – And Does It Matter?*, Routledge: London.

Wickens, P. D. (1993) 'Lean production and beyond: the system, its critics and the future', *Human Resource Management Journal*, 3, 4: 75–90.

Wiener, M. J. (1981) *English Culture and the Decline of the Industrial Spirit 1850–1980*, Cambridge University Press: Cambridge.

Wild, A. (2003) 'Pressure point', *People Management*, 10 July, 34–5.

Wild, R. (1985) *The Essentials of Production and Operations Management*, Holt Rinehart & Winston: London.

Wilkinson, A., Marchington, M., Goodman, J. and Ackers, P. (1992) 'Total quality management and employee involvement', *Human Resource Management Journal*, 2, 4: 1–20.

Wilkinson, B. (1986) *The Shopfloor Politics of New Technology*, Gower: Aldershot.

Wilkinson, E. (1983) *Japan Versus Europe*, Penguin: Harmondsworth.

Williams, A., Dobson, P. and Walters, M. (1989) *Changing Culture: New Organizational Approaches*, Institute of Personnel Management: London.

Williams, K., Haslam, C., Wardlow, A. and Williams, J. (1986) 'Accounting for the failure in nationalized industries – coal, steel and cars since 1970', *Economy and Society*, 15, 2: 167–219.

Williams, K., Cutler, T., Wardlow, A. and Williams, J. (1987) 'The end of mass production?', *Economy and Society*, 16, 3: 405–39.

Williams, K., Haslam, C., Williams, J. and Cutler, T. (1992a) 'Against lean production', *Economy and Society*, 21, 3: 321–54.

Williams, K., Haslam, C., Williams, J., Adcroft, A. and Johal, S. (1992b) 'Factories or warehouses: Japanese manufacturing foreign direct investment in Britain and the United States', *University of East London Occasional Papers in Business, Economy and Society*, No. 6.

Williams, K., Haslam, C., Johal, S., Williams, J. and Adcroft, A. (1994) *Cars: Analysis, History, Cases*, Bergbahn: London.

Williamson, O. E. (1991) 'Strategizing, economizing and economic organization', *Strategic Management Journal*, 12: 75–94.

Willmott, H. (1993) 'Strength is ignorance; slavery is freedom: managing culture in modern organizations', *Journal of Management Studies*, 30, 4: 515–52.

Wilson H. (1980) *Report of the Committee to Review the Functioning of Financial Institutions*, HMSO, London.

Wilson, A. (1997) 'Business and its social responsibility', in P. W. F. Davies (ed.) *Current Issues in Business Ethics*, Routledge: London.

Womack, J., Jones, D. T. and Roos, D. (1990) *The Machine that Changed the World: The Story of Lean Production*, Rawson Associates, New York.

Wong Kwei Chong (1991) 'The style of managing in a multicultural society' in J. M. Putti (ed.) *Management: Asian Context*, McGraw Hill, Singapore.

Woodall, P. (1996) 'The end of work?', *The Economist*, 28 September: S19–23.

Woodward, J. (1965) *Industrial Organization: Theory and Practice*, Oxford University Press: Oxford.

World Bank (1993) *The East Asian Miracle*, Oxford University Press: New York.

World Bank (1997) *The State in a Changing World*, World Development Report, Oxford University Press: Oxford.

Yip, G. (1995) *Total Global Strategy: Managing for Worldwide Competitive Advantage*, Prentice Hall: Englewood Cliffs, NJ.

Young, G. (2003) 'Klein and fall', *Guardian*, 16 April.

Subject index

Author index